Political Power in America

Political Power in America

Class Conflict and the Subversion of Democracy

Anthony R. DiMaggio

Cover image: Wikipedia.org / Women's March on Washington on January 21, 2017

Published by State University of New York Press, Albany

© 2019 State University of New York Press

For information, contact State University of New York Press, Albany, NY
www.sunypress.edu

Library of Congress Cataloging-in-Publication Data

Names: DiMaggio, Anthony R., 1980– author.
Title: Political power in America : class conflict and the subversion of democracy / Anthony R. DiMaggio.
Description: Albany : State University of New York, [2019] | Includes bibliographical references and index.
Identifiers: LCCN 2018059960 | ISBN 9781438476933 (hardcover : alk. paper) | ISBN 9781438476940 (pbk. : alk. paper) | ISBN 9781438476957 (ebook)
Subjects: LCSH: Power (Social sciences)—Political aspects—United States. | Political participation—Social aspects—United States. | Social conflict—Political aspects—United States. | Elite (Social sciences)—Political activity—United States. | Protest movements—Political aspects—United States. | Democracy—Economic aspects—United States. | Neoliberalism—United States.
Classification: LCC JK275 .D55 2019 | DDC 320.473—dc23
LC record available at https://lccn.loc.gov/2018059960

10 9 8 7 6 5 4 3 2 1

Contents

Illustrations

Tables

Images

Figures

Acknowledgments

This book—in various forms—has been in the works for nearly a decade. I began using chapters of it in my American Government introductory course in the early 2010s and used it continuously throughout the decade. During that time, the work was read by hundreds of undergraduate students, many of which provided valuable feedback on earlier drafts and on how to improve them. I want to thank these students for their insights, which have undoubtedly made this a better book. From my experiences, I have learned that students are hungry for a critical introduction to American politics. Unfortunately, the vast majority of American government texts have little to offer by way of critical analysis. This book is meant to address this deficiency in the discipline, and I hope it is as valuable to students in the future as it has been to those in the past.

I also want to thank my family for their support and patience during my countless hours working on this project. Most of all I am grateful to my wife, Mary, and sons Frankie and Tommy, for their unconditional support and love during the trying months in which I was completing this book. I also want to extend thanks to my parents and siblings for their support over the years during the development of my academic career.

Special thanks are also due to my peers and friends at Lehigh University. The university and my department provided valuable resources in helping with the preparation of the manuscript. I particularly want to thank Rick Matthews for taking the time to read and provide constructive feedback as related to my historical analysis of the founding era. His comments were significant in terms of improving the book.

Finally, I would like to thank a variety of fellow scholars, whose works have been instrumental to my own intellectual development as a radical scholar. Thanks go to many people, including Henry Giroux, Amentahru Wahlrab, Noam Chomsky, Michael Parenti, Robert McChesney, Andy McFarland, Andy Rojecki, Mark Major, Carlos Parodi, Ali Riaz, Jamal Nassar, Chris McDonald, John Vinzant, Colin Suchland, David Reynolds, and my editor at SUNY Press, Michael Rinella, for his patience in working with me over the last few years on this book.

Introduction

A Class Analysis of the American Political System

We live in a time when political officials manipulate information with minimal consequences. Many Americans' political opinions are formed independently of evidence-based reasoning. Political officials regularly misrepresent reality, as seen in the 2016 presidential election. The non-partisan fact-checking group *Politifact* analyzed statements made by presidential candidates, finding that only a third of them were true. For the Democrats, 53 percent of Hillary Clinton's statements were true, compared to 51 percent for Bernie Sanders.[1] Republican candidates were even worse. Just 9 percent of Donald Trump's statements were true, while 78 percent were false.[2] Only 22 percent of Ted Cruz's statements were true, 53 percent for John Kasich, 7 percent for Ben Carson, 48 percent for Jeb Bush, 37 percent for Marco Rubio, and 28 percent for Carly Fiorina.[3] In a troubling sign for democracy, the second most deceptive candidate of all—Donald Trump—won the election, with 78 percent of his statements deemed "mostly false," "false," or "pants on fire."[4] Trump's rampant deceptions and falsehoods continued throughout his presidency, much to the chagrin of fact-checkers and reporters.[5]

The public's tolerance of manipulative official rhetoric represents a fundamental threat, in that democracy is premised upon citizens making informed political decisions. The prevalence of deception in American politics suggests that the political system no longer serves the interests of the many. Instead, our system increasingly serves the interests of the American upper class—as represented by large corporations, business leaders, and the professional class that is attached to corporate America. In this vein, I echo the claims of previous critical scholars, such as political scientist Michael Parenti, who documents "upper-class dominance of public life," including politics, by business interests.[6] In the words of sociologist C. Wright Mills, there is a "power elite" that is comprised of business officials, political leaders, and military officials, all working in service of the "the corporate rich."[7] G. William Domhoff similarly forwards a "class theory" of societal power, examining the working relationship between major corporations, members of the upper class, and policy-oriented advocacy organizations.[8]

A Marxist analysis of American politics places economics—and particularly the corporate class and business elites—at the center of political power. Through a "historical materialist" analysis, the Marxist framework envisions upper-class and business interests as dominant over other realms of public life, including political institutions, the media, individual identities, and social interactions. Power in society has an economic foundation, which determines how various social institutions function. One need not be a Marxist, however, to believe that business and upper-class interests play a dominant role in influencing the political process, as most Americans see government as controlled by the wealthy. I adopt a broader framework in this book than simply talking about the "business class." The American upper-class includes business interests, but also trade associations that are tightly linked to corporate interests, and professional associations.[9] These professional groups include doctors, lawyers, engineers, and other service-based professionals, who operate within the capitalist system working for major corporations, although others may be employed by public institutions or be self-employed. It is this upper class, and particularly its core corporate component, with which I am interested.

It is common today to hear Americans complain about the role of money in elections. But this is only one part of upper-class power in politics. The link between interest groups giving campaign donations and favorable votes on policies from legislators is inconsistent at best. Rather, a more expansive view of American political power is needed. This expanded view recognizes that politics is heavily dominated by corporate interests, with the political system itself being captured by the wealthy. This domination occurs in numerous ways, with wealthy Americans increasingly comprising the political elite who run Washington, with bureaucratic officials being courted and captured by business lobbies, with corporate media reinforcing a pro-business ideology via news and entertainment media, and with political officials and media directing public attention away from political discussions in an age of mass political demobilization. The demobilization of the public makes it increasingly difficult to challenge upper-class political power. The masses are relegated to the sidelines due to the growth in anti-government rhetoric from political leaders, which turns the public off from politics. Simultaneously, the rising prominence of non-political, diversionary mass-media entertainment programming also diverts Americans from political matters.

The Italian Marxist Antonio Gramsci spoke of the power of "hegemony," which referred to the process through which business and political leadership indoctrinate the mass public in favor of political rhetoric and policies that favor upper-class interests. Hegemony, which means to guide or lead, essentially refers to the brainwashing of Americans in favor of developing an ideology that favors corporate capitalist prerogatives—and with Americans embracing policies that run contrary to their own economic interests.

While there has always been an upper-class of Americans that dominates politics, this pattern of governance was not static throughout history. The American society of 1787 was far more dominated by the upper class than today. Most Americans were politically disenfranchised, since state laws required that they own property to vote. Membership in the upper class, unlike today, was not based predominantly on being a part of the corporate class, since the United States was a pre-capitalist, agriculturally-based society. Rather, societal elites hailed from various backgrounds and occupations; they were slave and land owners, lawyers, creditors, shippers, traders, and merchants, among other professionals. Within this system, women, African Americans, Native Americans, and non-property-owning males—the vast majority of the population—were explicitly prohibited from participating in politics. Due to a series of popular struggles throughout the nineteenth and twentieth centuries, however, the United States moved in a radically more democratic direction in which the masses of Americans eventually gained the power to participate in the political process. Still, political dominance by the upper class goes through cycles. In the 1930s and in response to growing public anger over the Great Depression, President Franklin Roosevelt undertook a series of "New Deal" reforms that introduced significant regulations on corporations, while establishing basic protections for American workers and basic welfare programs for the poor. A tax system based on heavy redistribution of wealth from rich to the middle class and poor emerged by the end of World War II, and the welfare state was dramatically expanded during the 1960s under President Lyndon Johnson's "War on Poverty." From the 1930s through the 1960s, mass social movements emerged to challenge upper-class domination of American politics and society, and demanded democratic reforms that enhanced the representation and living conditions of the masses.

Despite the rollback of business power during this period, in the last four decades, we have seen the rise of a "neoliberal" era, marked by the growing power of a corporate capitalist upper class which exercises power over politics, and in which the mass public's impact on the political system has significantly declined. In these pages, I define neoliberalism as including many policy proposals, all of which seek to enhance corporate and upper-class power, at the expense of most Americans. These include: support for deregulation of businesses and corporations; demands for personal responsibility and sacrifice, in an effort to gut the social welfare state; failure to prioritize infrastructure spending on public education, roads, bridges, and other necessary public goods; constant demands for tax cuts on wealthy Americans and corporations, under the promise that the benefits will one day "trickle down" to workers; efforts to privatize vital social welfare programs such as Social Security, Medicare, and Medicaid, to funnel increased profits to Wall Street; militant resistance to raising the minimum wage to match inflation-based increases in consumer prices, or to increase wages past the inflation rate to keep pace with increased worker productivity rates; assaults on public and private sector unions that bargain for pay raises and benefits for workers, which are seen as a burden on government budgets and corporate profits; opposition to free college tuition and universal health care, to be paid for through an increasingly progressive tax system in which the wealthy pay higher tax rates than poorer Americans; and opposition to government efforts to combat global warming, through regulations on fossil-fuel-burning corporations and large increases in taxpayer funding for renewable energy research and development. These policies, while greatly enriching upper-class and corporate interests, have resulted in serious insecurity for working Americans, and produced record inequality.[10] Only recently, in the post-2008 era, have citizens begun to rise up in mass to protest the emergence of record inequality in society, and in an effort to rollback growing upper-class and corporate power over politics.

Defining American Politics

American politics is a contested terrain. Politics, defined by political scientist Harold Lasswell as the process of deciding who gets what, when, and how, is filled with conflict.[11] Politics is contentious because it represents a process whereby individuals, interest groups, and political officials decide who will benefit from government via the allocation of taxpayer funded benefits and other protections.

Government is vital to the people. Regardless of whether one is ignorant to politics or not, government will continue to tax people to pay for programs, and set policies that regulate the behavior of the masses. Government is expected to provide public services and goods, providing security against foreign and domestic threats, collecting taxes for public services, and preserving law and order. But in an era when many Americans are tuning out politics and the news, civic competence is endangered.[12] Despite such ignorance, politics will not become irrelevant. Rather, if mass apathy continues, it is the public that will lose its ability to critically engage in important political matters. Sadly, in a media system that diverts public attention away from politics and toward entertainment, Americans are losing their ability to think critically about enduring issues in the world around them.[13]

To understand the importance of government, one must recognize the point of government. Government refers to a system of institutions that creates rules to regulate the behavior of, and provide services for individuals. U.S. governing institutions exist at the state, local, and national levels. All governments rely on top-down authority, with officials setting rules and regulations impacting how people live and interact. Democratic governments rely on public consent, while dictatorships have little interest in the people's will, instead relying on violence to suppress the people.

The U.S. is a representative, republican political system. It relies on Americans to participate in choosing their political leaders. But direct participation in government by the public is limited by political officials, who dominate policy deliberation, lawmaking, and policy implementation. In a republican system, government-public relations are based on a social contract, which is an agreement between people and political leaders in which the latter represents the common interests of the former. But the rise of upper-class and business dominance of politics inhibits democracy, with the wealthy disproportionately impacting politics over the many.

Americans are educated by schools and the media to believe they live in a democracy, and that government empowers the masses. A constitutional system supposedly ensures that no government branch dominates over others, while voting guarantees that political officials represent the people. These beliefs provide comfort to many people. But little of this narrative is an accurate reflection of reality. In the neoliberal era, political leaders have done little to promote the interests and preferences of the average American.[14] Government has done little to stem the rising tide of income and wealth inequality at a time when officials adopt a "hands off" mentality toward business, which has allowed for record profits and a declining sense of corporate responsibility to workers. The commitment to a form of politics that favors the upper class has grown with the election of Donald Trump, whose administration the *Washington Post* reports is "the richest in modern American history."[15]

Many Americans have disassociated themselves from politics. They view the political system as irrelevant or harmful to the masses, or both. Government distrust is at record levels. A crisis of confidence has emerged, with most feeling political officials are failing to democratically represent the public. In line with an upper-class bias, most Americans see government as run by the few, and for the few.[16] Critics have long complained that corporations and the wealthy control American politics, and public concern about this control of politics is growing.[17] None of this is meant to suggest that the U.S. has abandoned all democratic aspects of government. The system is still able to represent the masses in various ways. But if current trends continue, there will be little left of the democratic system in coming years and decades.

The State of Politics Today: Engagement or Apathy?

If American politics is dominated by upper-class and business interests, it would take a massive uprising from the citizenry to combat this encroachment on democracy. Are most Americans up to the challenge? Many scholars are pessimistic about the masses and their knowledge of politics. Numerous political scientists view the public as generally ignorant, incapable, or unwilling to take the necessary steps to develop informed political opinions.[18] Only a third of Americans can name all the branches of the federal government, and a third cannot name a single branch. Most Americans do not know which party controls the House and Senate.[19] Seventy-seven percent of young Americans cannot name one of their two U.S. Senators.[20] If most Americans are uninformed on political issues, how can they present a unified front to fight against growing corporate power?

Public ignorance to politics is not new. By the turn of the twenty-first century, polls demonstrated that political knowledge levels were comparable to mid-twentieth century levels, despite the percent of high school graduates nationwide growing from about 50 percent in the 1940s to about 90 percent by 2011, and Americans with a bachelor's degree increasing from about 5 percent to a third of the public.[21] The growth in formal education over time should have produced greater political knowledge, not stagnation. But mass political ignorance was prevalent in the 2010s, with 77 percent of young Americans unable to recall the name of one of their Senators, with only one-in-four Americans correctly identifying all three branches of government, with less than one-in-three able to identify the Chief Justice of the Supreme Court, and with less than four-in-ten recalling the name of their member of the House of Representatives.[22]

Recent evidence suggests that public ignorance is intensifying. While about a third of young Americans (18–29) voted in the 1978 Congressional elections, it fell to about 20 percent by 2014.[23] And while about half of young Americans (18–24) voted in the 1964 and 1968 presidential elections, it had fallen to 38 percent by 2012.[24] The young's attention to politics via newspapers also fell during this time period, as did traditional political activities such as writing to public officials, giving money to political campaigns, and working for a political campaign.[25] Overall attention to the news was significantly lower for younger Americans in the 2010s compared to the 1990s, with 57 percent of those 18–29 saying they paid attention to political news, compared to 79 percent of those 30–39, 73 percent of those 40–59, and 79 percent of those 60 and older, and with only a quarter of Americans 18–29 saying they pay close attention to the news, compared to a third of those aged 30–39, over 40 percent of those 40–59, and more than half of those over 60.[26] These numbers suggest that declining political attentiveness is a significant concern across the board.

Why do so many fail to pay attention to politics? A number of reasons may explain this trend. For one, Americans are working harder and longer hours for stagnating to declining pay over the last four decades. As the American middle class is squeezed by increased workplace demands, deteriorating pay, and spiraling credit card, health care, and educational debt, these impositions limit the time many have to pay attention to politics. Government failure to address these concerns is troubling at a time when officials are lambasted for siding with business interests over the mass public.

Another reason for declining attention is the fragmentation of the media. In the era of *Netflix*, cable, satellite television, *YouTube*, *Facebook*, and other social media, Americans have more media choices than ever. In the mid-twentieth century choices were radically constricted, and it was more difficult to avoid the news with so few options. With growing fragmentation of the media, Americans are subject to an endless barrage of entertainment programs, making it easier to avoid politics and the world around them. Many who are not forced to pay attention to the news will not pay attention, and media providers are happy to cater to their alternative preferences. In this case, corporate pursuit of profits trumps interest in informing the masses. This process is another example of the elevation of corporate interests over the political empowerment of the people.

A final reason for declining political attention is the transformation of American culture. Many Americans are socialized to assume that politics is bad, and not worthy of their time. Distrust of government has risen dramatically in recent decades, first during the Vietnam War, and later after the 2008 economic crash. During the Vietnam War, Americans discovered that the Johnson administration lied to the public about the reasons for war. This deception was apparent with the release of the "Pentagon Papers," a declassified record of government documents chronicling government lies about war. Trust continued to fall greatly through the mid-to-late 1970s. In addition to the Pentagon Papers, the public also experienced the Watergate scandal, which involved Republican President Richard Nixon illegally ordering a break-in at the Democratic National Headquarters in Washington DC. The twin blows of the Pentagon Papers and Watergate shook public confidence in government, radically changing American political culture. And public disgust with government began to grow again in the early twenty-first century. Many white Americans were angry about their own economic stagnation and their growing work obligations (as represented by their increased work hours), which translated into increased voter support for Donald Trump, who had promised to "Make America Great Again" by helping the working- and middle-classes.[27]

The 2010s were years of intense displeasure with government. In 2015, just 38 percent of Americans—the lowest number since 1972—trusted the national government to handle domestic problems "a great deal" or "a fair amount."[28] Only 20 percent trusted government "to do what is right" "just about always" or "most of the time," a record low since this question was first tracked in 1958.[29] Only 20 percent of Americans felt in 2015 that government was "run for the benefit of all," rather than the few. These numbers suggest a massive crisis of confidence.[30] Much of the public's anger is related to the perception that American politics unfairly favors the upper class and wealthy. Most Americans feel the rich are not being taxed enough.[31] They think elections are dominated by elites and money, rather than controlled by the people.[32] As the *Washington Post* reports: "by nearly a 2-to-1 margin (64 percent to 36 percent), Americans believe their 'vote does not matter because of the influence wealthy individuals and big corporations have on the electoral process.'"[33] Most feel government should do more to reduce the gap between rich and poor, but with a political system that fails to prioritize aiding the needy and poor, inequality continues to grow.[34]

Despite the evidence of declining political involvement, other evidence suggests fears about public ignorance may be exaggerated. Americans—particularly the young—are more directly engaged in politics than previously believed. While the young are less likely to follow the news, vote, or be a member of a political party, they are more likely to participate politically in unconventional ways. Engaged citizens are less trustful of government, but *more* likely to sign petitions and participate in boycotts of consumer products in pursuit of social justice causes, and more likely to participate in political demonstrations and rallies.[35] Young Americans have become more likely in recent decades to be involved in community-based political activities, and to converse with others on election-related matters.[36] Young Americans are more likely to be "active member[s]" of a group outside of political parties "that tries to influence public policy or government."[37] Relevant to the upper-class business bias in politics, young Americans are also more likely to oppose capitalism entirely and to support socialism. Counter-cultural values within this group are pronounced, with American youth less likely than older Americans to prioritize consumerism, and more likely to base their identities on shared communal experiences.[38] These findings reveal a profound youth alienation from a political-economic system that many feel does not represent their political or economic interests.

Other evidence suggests that Americans as a whole are more attentive to politics than previously thought. Drawing on the data from table I.1, a review of *Pew Research Center* surveys from 2011 through 2016 finds that across 16 different political issues, 52 percent of Americans report paying attention to the news, either "somewhat" or "very closely." These findings suggest that large numbers of Americans are paying attention to what is happening around them.

An overall assessment of available evidence suggests that public ignorance is a serious problem, but that Americans—especially the young—are beginning to mobilize against the political-economic status quo. Those bemoaning the inadequacies of the public are correct that many Americans are politically ignorant and fail to pay attention to politics and the news. These problems are real threats to democracy and are a serious impediment to any mass rebellion against a political system favoring upper-class and wealthy business interests.

American elections have *not* succeeded in shaking much of the public of their ignorance. And despite Americans being better educated than ever before, a shocking number of people are blissfully ignorant to politics, and many are poorly informed.

Massive numbers of Americans fail to participate electorally in selecting their leaders. Over 40 percent of voting-eligible Americans did not vote in 2016, and 63 percent did not turn out in the 2014 midterm elections.[39] The United States has among the lowest voter turnout rates in the world, contradicting

Table I.1. Public Attention to the News (2011–2016)

Event	Date	% Paying Very or Somewhat Close Attention	% Paying Very Close Attention
Presidential Election	10/2016	78%	41%
Presidential Election	4/2016	69%	38%
Violence in Syria	9/2015	52%	24%
Wildfires	9/2015	41%	15%
Presidential Election	5/2015	41%	16%
Same-Sex Marriage Ruling	5/2015	40%	18%
Protests Police Violence	12/2014	66%	35%
Midterm Congressional Elections	10/2014	42%	16%
Safety Defects GM Cars	4/2014	44%	19%
Obamacare Exchanges Opening	11/2013	65%	37%
Federal Government Shutdown	10/2013	73%	43%
Senate Immigration Reform Bill	6/2013	50%	21%
Violence in Syria	3/2013	35%	13%
Shooting Portland, Oregon	12/2012	47%	19%
Egyptian Presidential Election	6/2012	33%	13%
Occupy Wall Street Protests	11/2011	50%	20%
Congress Budget Talks	9/2011	57%	31%

Source: Pew Research Center, Monthly Polls, 2011–2016

notions that other countries should look to America as a model of democratic empowerment.[40]

On the other hand, many Americans pay attention to politics and engage in the political process in various ways. Most Americans pay attention to what is happening in the news, and young Americans are increasingly participating in politics in unconventional ways, while challenging the entire foundation of a political system dominated by corporate and upper-class values. We live in the era of mass protest, be it the Tea Party, Occupy Wall Street, Black Lives Matter, anti-Trump protests, or MeToo—a period of protest unrivalled since the 1960s. Much of the public expresses a fundamental distrust of the American political system, feeling it is dominated by the corporate rich. These developments have fueled protests, and suggest that corporate and upper-class power in American politics and society is in an increasingly precarious position in the early twenty-first century.

Book Outline

This book covers many issues related to the U.S. political system. The focus overlaps with the sections typically taught in American government introductory courses. The chapter layout is as follows: chapter 1: Theories of Government and a History of the Founding Era; chapter 2: The U.S. Constitution; chapter 3: Federalism; chapter 4: Interest Groups; chapter 5: Congress; chapter 6: The Presidency; chapter 7: The Bureaucracy; chapter 8: the Courts; chapter 9: Political Parties; chapter 10: Elections and Voting; chapter 11: The Media; chapter 12: Public Opinion; chapter 13: Civil Liberties; chapter 14: Civil Rights; chapter 15: Economic Policy; chapter 16: Foreign Policy; and the conclusion: Where Do We Go from Here?

Chapter 1

Theories of Government, Early American History, and the Politics of Class Conflict

Framer of the U.S. Constitution and first Chief Justice of the Supreme Court John Jay was hardly democratic in his politics. He famously sided with members of the upper class when he wrote that "the people that own the country ought to govern it."[1] Although respected today by many in the scholarly legal community, Jay was no savior of the working man or woman. Born to a wealthy New York merchant family, Jay was opposed to slavery, but his politics in the run-up to the Revolutionary War were far from radical. His interests were with the upper class; his own background was one of decadent wealth, as his family was one of the richest in New York City. He owned multiple homes at a time when most Americans owned no land. His wealth was drawn from numerous sources, including his salary as a lawyer, banking assets, and the large amounts of land inherited from his father.[2] If any framer of the Constitution was a strong supporter of propertied elites, it was John Jay.

Jay was just one of 55 framers of the Constitution, but his background is symbolic of a broader phenomenon in which those who founded the United States disproportionately held personal economic interests in creating a Constitution that served the wealthy. One historical researcher argues that the framers actively sought to foster "a conservative counterrevolution against what leading American statesmen regarded as the irresponsible economic measures enacted by a majority of state legislatures in the mid-1780s," which demonstrated an "excess of democracy" via prioritizing aid to the masses and poor by promoting tax and debt relief during a time of economic depression.[3]

This chapter is devoted to laying out an "economic interpretation" of U.S. Constitutional history, to borrow a phrase from historian Charles Beard. As Beard argued, the Constitution's framers were strongly motivated by their own personal economic interests. Their economic backgrounds as lawyers, land owners, debt holders, slave owners, and businessmen with mercantile, shipping, and manufacturing interests meant they were part of an upper class, which was more likely to

1

Image 1.1. John Jay, Framer to the U.S. Constitution.

side with the priorities of their fellow class members, rather than with those of small land owners, non-propertied males, and other socially disadvantaged groups.[4]

Most Americans are ignorant to the historical details of the country's founding. We are taught we live in the "land of the free" and the "home of the brave." We are told that the Founding Fathers created American democracy. They are practically deified in classrooms, and celebrated as central to our cultural heritage. But this whitewashing of history obscures the class tensions characterizing American society during the founding. The myth of the benevolent Founding Fathers obscures the ways in which they distrusted and opposed democracy. In this chapter I reject many of the myths associated with the founding, while also discussing positive values of the Enlightenment period that contributed to the eventual democratization of U.S. politics. Western history is characterized by a conflict between democratic and elitist values, and the American people have seen many successes in democratizing American society over the last two centuries, contrary to upper-class efforts to limit democratization.

Liberalism in Context

When we talk about modern government, we are really talking about liberal government. Modern history is defined by the ascendancy of liberalism. This means the prevalence of representative government over dictatorship. When I speak of liberalism, I am not talking about modern day Republicans and Democrats. Historically, liberal theory refers to a governing framework based on respect for human rights, representation, and limited government. The rise of liberalism was a serious challenge to monarchies. Under monarchical systems, the kings, queens, and aristocrats who controlled the state saw themselves as society's rightful rulers. Liberal government—in which political officials are restrained by the public—did not for the most part exist during the era of monarchies.

John Locke (1632–1704) is widely credited with developing the intellectual rationale that *eventually* led to modern, liberal representative government. Locke was more concerned with what government could do to protect the public during times of turmoil. He helped establish a system of thought that was more representative of public wishes than anything imagined by previous Western philosophers.

Locke's liberalism was based in the *Enlightenment*. The Enlightenment was a historical period of intellectual thought in Western Europe during the eighteenth century, which continued into colonial America, with the thinking and writings of the Founding Fathers and framers of the Constitution. As one scholar explains, the Enlightenment produced "people [who] started to question all forms of authority" existing prior to the emergence of representative government. It was "a movement against religious intolerance and arbitrary rule" and was responsible for "threatening courts, princes, and lay and clerical oligarchies" that ruled contrary to the interests of the masses.[5] The Enlightenment popularized the idea of representative government. It embraced the notion that people were endowed with rationality and reason, and that monarchies were illegitimate, because individuals can be trusted to govern based upon their own self-interest and capacity to hold political leaders accountable. The Enlightenment forwarded the radical notion that kings were not divinely ordained to rule, and that individuals have natural rights guaranteed by their creator. For government to be legitimate, it must establish a social contract with individuals—with public demands represented by political leaders elected by the people.

In his *Second Treatise of Government,* Locke wrote of the need for government by consent, with all men being born equal and holding "a right to freedom." He wrote of the "public good"—understood today as the greatest good for the largest number of people. The public good was tied to the idea that men are born with God-given rights. Locke wrote of the "equality of men by nature." Individuals enjoyed a human right to security, and are not to harm others' "life, health, liberty, or possessions." "The preservation of property" was the primary "end of government" and the main "reason why men enter into society."[6]

Locke felt government was needed to protect individuals from each other. He felt government should do more for men than "keeping them safe" from fellow citizens and foreign dangers, as the philosopher Thomas Hobbes had previously argued. Public consent is based on political systems in which people unite, authorizing government "to make laws for [them] as the public good of the society shall require."[7] Locke did not lay out a step-by-step plan of what constituted a violation of the public good. But this is the point. Determining government violations of the public trust and human rights falls on the public.

Still, Locke had in mind some grievances when he spoke of government violations of the rights of man. He wrote that "whenever the legislative acts against the trust reposed in them, when they endeavor to invade the property of the subject . . . whenever the legislators endeavor to take away and destroy the property of the people, or reduce them to slavery under arbitrary power, they put themselves into a state of war with the people." Locke referenced the problem of taxation without representation. He wrote of the problems of "absolute obedience and submission" which officials expect under "absolute monarchy." These expectations are "indeed inconsistent with civil society." Locke also sup-

Image 1.2. John Locke, 1632–1704.

ported limited government in his call for "restraining any exorbitances of those [government] to whom they [the public] had given the authority over them, and of balancing the power of government, by placing several parts of it in different hands."[8] Attempts to ensure "checks and balances" later appeared in the U.S. Constitution, seeking to prevent arbitrary authority by a president, congress, or the courts.

Locke's liberal ideas served as a foundation for the principles embraced in the American Revolution of 1776. Locke's influence is apparent in the Declaration of Independence, which overlaps heavily with his *Second Treatise of Government*. The Declaration borrowed directly from Locke's notion of God-given rights, stating: "We hold these truths to be self-evident, that all men are created equal, that they are endowed by their Creator with certain unalienable rights, that among these are Life, Liberty, and the pursuit of Happiness." The Declaration's reference to rights to life, liberty, and happiness corresponds with Locke's discussion of the rights of man, which include life and liberty, and property. This overlap is not coincidental, as Thomas Jefferson was strongly influenced by Locke's writings.[9]

The Declaration of Independence addresses the need for government via representation: "Governments are instituted among men, deriving their just powers from the consent of the governed." And the Declaration incorporated Locke's social contract. With a social contract, citizens vote for officials, and confer power upon them to govern; in return, government is to promote the common good of the people. The social contract is violated, however, if government fails to fulfill its duties to the public. The Declaration states: "whenever any Form of Government becomes destructive . . . it is the Right of the People to alter or to abolish it, and to institute new Government, laying its foundation on such principles and organizing its powers in such form, as to them shall seem most likely to affect their Safety and Happiness." Spotlighting violations of the social contract, the Declaration listed a "long train of abuses and usurpations" committed by the British, including:

- "Suspending our own Legislatures, and declaring themselves invested with power to legislate for us in all cases whatsoever."

- "Imposing Taxes on us without our Consent," with rebels angered over their lack of voting power in the British Parliament, despite being taxed by the British.

- Keeping "among us, in times of peace, Standing Armies without the Consent of our legislatures," and the "quartering large bodies of armed troops among us."

Class Conflict, the Constitutional Framers, and the Threat of Democracy

To say the Declaration set the stage for government based on representation is not to say that it fostered democracy. To the contrary, most of the Constitution's framers had contempt for democratic representation, instead favoring a political-economic system that favored various segments of the upper class. This preference contradicts popular depictions in American government textbooks of the framers as heroic and benevolent supporters of democracy. This is not to say that democratic impulses were entirely lacking in the founding era. As one historical account argues, many of the framers were opposed to the centralization of political authority in a national government, and instead favored more democratic state-based policies that appealed to popular demands.[10] But this group was a minority, considering the Constitution received the support of nearly three-quarters of the framers.

Much of what is written about the Founding Fathers in textbooks is mythic, fashionable nonsense, or outright distortion. In *Interpreting the Founding*, Gibson reminds readers that "nineteenth century studies often celebrated the framers as disinterested patriots and maintained that the Constitution embodied objective principles of justice and was a reflection of the will of the whole people, not the product of a single interest or class."[11] These depictions appear in textbooks too. *American Government: Roots and Reform* claims "the Framers charted new territory when writing the Constitution in 1789. Their achievement has survived for more than 200 years, and constitutional democracy has spread to many other countries. How did they do it? What issues did they face? What logic did they use? How can we understand their results?" The book discusses the "miracle at Philadelphia," referring to the Constitutional Convention, seemingly deifying the framers in an aura of selfless sacrifice and benevolent concern with the public good and democracy.[12] *American Government and Politics Today* discusses the Constitutional Convention of 1787 as populated by a "group of nationalists . . . of a more democratic stripe," which was "led by James Madison" and other "democratic nationalists [who] wanted a central government founded on popular support."[13] *Government by the People* claims Americans are ignorant of the framers' alleged sacrifices, in giving the gift of democracy to future generations, and in creating a system that "enables the ruled to check the rulers": "We Americans take democracy for granted. We somehow consider it inevitable. We take pride in our ability to make it work, yet we have essentially inherited a functioning system. Its establishment was the work of others, ten or more generations ago. The challenge for us is not just to keep it going but to improve it."[14]

The main problem with the narrative of the framers' commitment to democracy is that it is largely inaccurate. American society, prior to and following the American Revolution, was not a democracy, since only property-owning males participated in politics. Economic wealth was concentrated in the hands of the few. The vast majority of people were legally disenfranchised and denied basic rights. At the country's founding, society was dominated by five major groups who constituted the upper class: merchants in the New England area, planters and large landholders in the South, royalists loyal to the British crown, artisans, laborers and shopkeepers, and small farmers. The early colonies were marked by extreme economic inequality. One historical account draws attention to the founding period as "stratified among a group of elites composed of merchants, planters, and officeholders, and a deferential and disenfranchised populace."[15] Political participation was limited, with most-all states (except Pennsylvania) prohibiting voting for non-property owners. Colonial America was not marked by as much inequality as Western Europe, since there was wider availability of land for white males in the former. But power in the colonies was stratified among those who owned property and held political power on the one hand, and the disempowered masses on the other.[16]

Statistics during the colonial era were rudimentary compared to modern standards, but they do allow us to speak with some confidence about inequality. As one historical account finds, by 1760, less than 500 men in five major cities "owned most of the commerce, shipping, banking, mining, and manufacturing on the eastern seaboard . . . in twelve of the thirteen states, only property owning white males could vote, probably not more than 10 percent of the total adult population . . . excluded were all indigenous people, persons of African descent, women, indentured servants, and white males lacking property. Property qualifications for holding office were so steep as to exclude even most of the white males." Other historical accounts identify pronounced inequality, although it was less severe in America than Europe.[17] In New York, Philadelphia, and Boston from the 1760s through the 1790s, about 10 percent of the population held half to three-quarters of all wealth.[18] In the 1770s, the richest five percent of Boston residents owned half of all taxable assets.[19] Inequality also grew during the hundred-year run-up to the founding. In Boston, from the late 1680s through 1770, the percent of males who were poor increased from 14 percent to 29 percent.[20] One-third of the population in the revolutionary period were small farmers; only three percent were wealthy large land holders.[21]

Colonial America was defined by political disenfranchisement and repression. Involuntary servitude was common—with poor migrants pushed into signing service agreements with wealthy persons for years—ensuring that those without property toiled in slave-like arrangements. One historical account suggests that indentured servants were "bound by contract to serve a master for four to seven years in order to repay the expense of their passage" from another country. "In the early days of the Virginia colony, most workers were white indentured servants. In fact, 75 percent of the colonists came as servants during the seventeenth century."[22] As one historical account put it, in colonial America 80 percent [of indentured servants] were "shiftless, hopeless, ruined individuals" who "died during their servitude, returned to England after it was over, or became 'poor whites.'"[23]

Indentured servants were prohibited from marrying without permission, could be forcibly separated from their families, and suffered corporal punishment for various offenses.[24] Colonial laws aimed at preventing such repressive punishments were inconsistently enforced.[25] Servants seeking to escape were subject to extradition, and this legal protection for owners was later codified in a U.S. Constitutional provision guaranteeing "No person held to Service or Labor in one State, under the Laws thereof, escaping into another, shall in Consequence of any Law or Regulation therein, be discharged from such Service or Labor, But shall be delivered up on Claim of the Party to whom such Service or Labor may be due."

The political system heavily favored upper-class property holding whites, while repressing people of color. From the late-1600s onward "free" blacks were denied the right to vote, hold office, and testify in courtrooms.[26] Popular thinking dictated "blacks and whites could never coexist in America because of the 'real distinctions' which 'nature' had made between the two races."[27] At the time of the founding, black Americans were either slaves and denied basic human rights, or "free" and discriminated against by the legal system. Freed African Americans could only vote in four states, assuming they owned property. In most states, free blacks were still not allowed to sit on juries or sue in court. Most blacks were not free men, but slaves. By 1775, for example, just five percent of Delaware's blacks were not slaves.[28] By the 1790s, about 60,000 free blacks lived in the U.S., representing eight percent of the entire black population. In the north, just 40 percent of blacks were "free," and in the south it was less than five percent.[29] The Constitution's three-fifths compromise ensured slaves only counted as a fraction of a person for the representation purposes of southern slave owners, while preventing slaves any citizenship rights. Legal contempt continued for more than a century, for example with the Supreme Court's 1857 *Dred Scott v. Sanford* decision, ruling that slaves could never be considered U.S. citizens. Even "free" blacks were denied citizenship rights. While the number of states prohibiting African Americans from voting was fairly small in the late-1700s, it rose dramatically from 1790 through the mid-1800s. States such as New Jersey, Connecticut, and Maryland permitted blacks the right to vote following independence, but later limited that right to whites by 1820. Blacks were refused the right to vote throughout the South until the 1960s, when the Civil Rights movement forced states to grant equal voting rights and protections against racial discrimination. Since the vast majority of states in the late-1700s to the early-1800s granted the right to vote only to property owners, most "free" blacks could not participate in electoral politics even if they were not legally prohibited from voting due to their skin color.

Women were also denied rights during the founding. Women's "rights" were historically determined by their husbands. As one historian writes: "for women, the marriage contract superseded the social contract. A woman's relationship to the larger society was mediated through her relationship with her husband. In both law and social reality, women lacked the essential qualification of political participation—the opportunity for autonomy based on ownership of property or control of one's own person."[30] Laws in the early American states failed to protect women's property rights after marriage, as their assets were transferred to their husbands. The first law allowing women independent control over their property after marriage was passed in New York in 1848 as a result of pressure from women's rights activists such as Elizabeth Cady Stanton and Paulina Davis, among others. Other states followed, and most had such a law within the few decades following New York's actions.

The vast majority of states prohibited women from voting in early American history. The New Jersey state constitution, passed in 1776, did grant this right, but it was limited by a state law forcing a transfer of a wife's property to her husband after marriage. With the state's property requirements to vote, only propertied women who were unmarried or widows were able to cast a ballot. New Jersey rescinded the right of women to vote in 1807. The next law recognizing women's voting right was not passed until 1869, in Wyoming. Other territories and states followed, including Utah (1870) and Colorado (1893). It was not until 1920—nearly a century and a half after the country's founding—that the Nineteenth Amendment was passed, guaranteeing all women the right to vote. These historical legal actions—particularly the confiscation of female's property upon marriage—suggested a strong bias in the law in favor of affluent white males.

Like indentured servants, African Americans, women, and Native Americans were repressed throughout history. They were depicted as savages to be "civilized." President Andrew Jackson referred to these "savage bloodhounds" and "blood thirsty barbarians" as needing to be suppressed by the government and military.[31] He wondered: "what good man would prefer a country covered with forests and ranged by a few thousand savages to our extensive Republic?"[32] Dehumanization was used to rationalize forced "negotiations" with the Chickasaw native peoples to steal their land and transfer it to whites. As a general during the "Creek Wars" of 1813–1814, Jackson forced negotiations with the Chickasaw at the barrel of a gun. The failure to "negotiate," he promised, meant Congress would pass a law forcing the purchase of their land, supposedly providing legitimacy to the forced expulsion. As president, Jackson also supported efforts by Mississippi and Georgia to eliminate sovereignty for the Choctaw and Cherokee tribes over their lands, and to enact state jurisdiction over Native American territories, which were later handed to white settlers. This aggression was a violation of U.S.–Native treaties and a violation of the Supreme Court's judgment that Congress, rather than the states, was to decide on U.S. Native American relations. U.S. treaties were broken in pursuit of westward expansion, and in the name of white's "God-given" "manifest destiny." Natives who opposed these attacks were subject to removal, fines, imprisonment, or death.

Native Americans under the federal government's jurisdiction were routinely denied citizenship rights. As one historian recounts: "the ability of Native Americans to participate in politics was narrowed between 1790 and the 1850s. In some states, they were finally judged not to be legally white, and only whites were eligible to vote. More distinctively, Native Americans were kept from the polls through a series of court decisions and legal circumstances that circumscribed their ability to become citizens."[33] Members of "Indian tribes were domestic, dependent nations and thus, individual Indians, living in their tribes, were aliens, even if born in the United States."[34] By the 1850s, the U.S. Attorney General established that Native Americans could never become citizens via naturalization because that process applied only to whites and those of foreign origin.

In addition to the above groups, non-property-owning white males were prohibited from voting throughout much of early U.S. history. As of the 1790s, fewer than half of the original thirteen states allowed voting based on paying taxes, rather than relying on property ownership.[35] It was not until the 1820s through the 1850s that most property requirements for voting were abolished.[36] By 1830, taxpaying as a criterion for voting existed in just 8 of 24 states.[37] Other financial restrictions, however, continued to haunt blacks, as Jim Crow policies following the Civil War such as the poll tax prohibited them from voting. Taking into account all the restrictions above, estimates suggest that perhaps only one-third of white males, and just one-sixth of the entire population, was eligible to vote at the time of the founding.[38] White upper-class males disproportionately benefitted from this system, with little by way of democratic representation for the many.

Class Conflict and the Articles of Confederation

From 1781 to 1789, Americans were governed by the Articles of Confederation. The articles empowered states to determine their political affairs independent from a national government. There was no "united" states, but instead thirteen sovereign states with minimal obligations to each other. States maintained their own armed forces, while the national government could request funds and forces, but not compel them, to suppress domestic insurrections and foreign attacks. The national government had little power. It had no army. It could not print money. There was no national court. It had no power to regulate commerce between states, and its taxation powers were severely limited. It could request, but not demand, funds from states. States held power over issues related to land, natural resources, labor, and regulation of capital.

States struggled to conduct relations under the Articles of Confederation. Votes from 7 of the 13 states were required to decide on policy matters and disputes between states. Nine votes were needed to pass treaties and decide on economic policy matters. State officials were afraid of replicating the kind of centralized power they experienced under British rule, fearing a strong central government would produce a leader similar to a king. And weak state militias failed to provide the people with much protection from foreign colonial powers.

Preservation of inequality, and of the upper class itself, was a challenge under the Articles of Confederation. In the 1780s, Americans suffered under a crippling depression and credit crisis. Consumer spending rose in the early 1780s because of widely available credit from British firms. But by mid-decade, increased state taxes hurt the nation's purchasing power, and made it more difficult for Americans to help service the national debt.[39] After six years of war, the nation's debts were massive.[40] Congress was responsible for paying back the debt, although the states controlled the means of taxation for raising revenues. Congress recommended yearly state contributions to decrease debt over time, to be paid for over a period of 25 years.[41] Collecting on the debt, however, was increasingly difficult when Congress could not compel states to contribute funds. The economic situation became more severe as the British and French sealed off their colonies to U.S. exports, and as cheap British goods flooded the American market, competing with domestic ones.[42] The Revolutionary War virtually ended the trans-Atlantic trade, and British and French postwar actions produced an economic crisis in the American states.

The 1780s depression, coupled with high national debt, placed Americans in a difficult position. The money supply was based on the gold and silver standards, which were established in the early 1780s. Gold and silver were the desired form of payment for war debts, but both were in short supply.[43] Some state legislatures' unwillingness to print more paper money made it difficult for debtors to pay their taxes or pay back creditors. The situation was dire: a decline in the money supply during the mid-to-late 1780s was accompanied by depreciating livestock prices, which fell by half, while land values fell by two-thirds.[44]

In this market, a farmer who purchased a horse on credit had to sell off three horses to pay back the debt.[45]

Aggressive advocacy of debt collection on war bonds by officials such as James Madison ensured that bond holders, who represented the wealthiest Americans, saw their financial interests protected while poor farmers faced imprisonment for failure to pay back their debts.[46] Farmers who were unable to meet their debt obligations saw their livestock, land, and other possessions auctioned, while the money raised was used to pay bondholders. Auctions often brought far less revenue than consumer and other goods were worth.[47] The shortage of paper money meant that few buyers attended these auctions, so commodities put up for sale were severely undervalued. When a debtor failed to raise enough money in the auction to pay off his creditors, the rest of his belongings were often auctioned to serve his debts.[48]

In serving the interests of bondholders and creditors, officials blamed the poor for their lot in life. Class war was a central feature of this historical period. Poor farmers were demonized for refusing to "live within" their own "bounds."[49] The upper class condemned the poor's "sumptuous clothing and other frivolities," which "not only drove consumers into debt but ruined their morals." The poor were addicted, they argued, to spending more than they earned, and to luxurious living and dangerous habits such as overconsumption of alcohol.[50] Modern characterizations of poverty echo these early attacks, with the poor depicted as lazy, over-indulgent, on drugs, and abusive of the welfare system.

Much of what was written about the poor was propagandistic. These attacks ignored structural problems such as the shortage of gold and silver, and the reluctance of various state legislatures to print paper money for debtors to pay their bills. Bond holders' questionable motives were also ignored, particularly the self-serving rhetorical attacks by members of the upper class against the poor. State officials leveled crushing taxes on farmers, while bond holders were paid off with the increased revenues. Government overestimated the value of bonds when translating their value from the paper money speculators initially paid for them to the hard currency gold or silver in which they were redeemed.[51] This upward redistribution from the poor to the upper class occurred largely because of inflationary pressures, which contributed to the devaluation of paper money compared to gold and silver. Over-valuation insured that bond holders were repaid more than three times the value of their initial investment.[52] Attacks on the poor served to rationalize the redistribution of wealth from the poor to the wealthy.

The shortage of currency during the 1780s led indebted farmers to pressure states for relief against the speculative and corrosive effects of the investor class. They pressured state legislatures to close courts to avoid property foreclosures and imprisonment. They effectively pushed most states to print more paper money, to make repayments to creditors easier.[53] The national Congress in 1781 requested that states pay back war debts with gold and silver, rather than paper money, but most Americans had no access to either. States were pressured to grant relief via demands for tax abatement and legal reduction or elimination of personal debts.[54]

No effort at debt relief was blunter than Shays' Rebellion. Led by farmer and Revolutionary War veteran Daniel Shays, the uprising occurred in western and central Massachusetts from 1786–1787, and was a stark example of the escalating dangers of class war between the upper class and poor. The rebellion participants were angry with state officials for siding with creditors and instituting high taxes that hurt the poor and small land holders, while benefitting the investor class. The Massachusetts legislature refused to print paper money to allow debtors to pay their taxes and loans for fear of inflation, instead demanding repayment of war debts in gold and silver. The state refused to consider debt restructuring or debt abolition; such efforts were a threat to wealthy creditors. Debtors, who often paid their bills in goods and services, were increasingly pressured by wholesalers to pay for items in hard currency.[55]

While early America was divided by class conflict, enough Americans held property in land that the depression of the 1780s directly threatened them. While just three percent of the public held large amounts of land so as to be classified as wealthy, a third of white men were small farmers, holding some amount of property.[56] Farmers in Massachusetts faced major challenges. Many expanded their land holdings and debt to meet rising needs during the Revolutionary War, but when the conflict ended were left with reduced demand, increased debt, and struggled to pay their bills. Those unable to pay their debts were thrown into debtor prisons. In the Massachusetts town of Worcester, 80 percent of prisoners were those who were unable to pay their debts.[57] Farmers also feared being forced by creditors into long-term tenant agreements on their land.[58]

By mid-1786, angry and increasingly desperate small farmers—led by Daniel Shays, Luke Day, and Charles Harding—took action against the state and against the creditors based in Boston.[59] By late 1786, rebels protested against and shut down courts in Springfield, Northampton, Worcester, and Concord. Wealthy creditors quickly recognized the threat.[60] One historian writes that investors saw debt relief "as the breakdown of laws that protected contractual obligations between rich and poor." Such efforts made property "insecure" and could produce "a general economic leveling" between the upper class and poor.[61] Such worries were at first overblown, since the rebels initially sought only reform of state debt and tax laws, which had already happened in other states. It was only later on, when investors and state officials organized a militia to suppress the rebellion, that Shays and his followers' goals became more radical. In 1787, Shays and his supporters attempted to seize the federal arsenal in Springfield, seeking to overthrow the Massachusetts government. Shays announced the goal of his rebellion: "march directly to Boston, plunder it . . . destroy the nest of devils, who by their influence, make the court enact what they please, burn it and lay the town of Boston to ashes."[62]

Shays' Rebellion was suppressed by the state militia in 1787, but creditors across the nation understood the danger it represented. Shays and his supporters exposed American states as vulnerable to internal rebellion. Massachusetts was unable to afford its share of the 1786 Congressional request to raise forces to put down Shays' Rebellion, revealing how weak it was in protecting upper-class creditors' interests against the poor.[63] Debtors in other states threatened to take matters into their own hands. Following the Rebellion, Virginian protesters assaulted public facilities, including courthouses and jails, seeking to destroy public records for personal debts.[64] The punishments for those involved in Shays' Rebellion were swift, as more than thirty-three rebels were charged with crimes and six were sentenced to death.[65] Samuel Adams intended the crackdown to be a warning for others: "in monarchy the crime of treason may admit of being pardoned . . . but the man who dares rebel against the laws of a republic ought to suffer death."[66]

Shays' Rebellion strengthened the commitment of those supporting the creation of a federal system, unifying what otherwise would have been disparate economic and political interests across the country.[67] Shays' efforts at debt relief were met with alarm. Madison opposed "the evil effects of legislative majorities within some of the states" in their efforts to seek debt relief, at the expense of upper-class creditors' interests.[68] Henry Knox, a military commander in the Revolutionary War and the first Secretary of War, complained that Shays and his rebels were "determined to annihilate all debts, public and private," a goal "easily affected by the means of unfunded paper money."[69] Virginia politician George Mason warned of state assemblies that had become "too democratic" in catering to the indebted.[70]

Debtors' interests were not seen as central to the common good by members of the upper class. Alexander Hamilton, the first Secretary of the Treasury and an author of *The Federalist Papers*, spoke of debt relief as working "against every well-wisher to the Constitution, laws, and the peace of their country."[71] Hamilton argued that rebellion represented a "temptuous situation from which Massachusetts has scarcely emerged."[72] He advocated for "a certain portion of military force" as "absolutely necessary in large communities" such as Massachusetts, which "is now feeling the necessity" of protection against the masses.[73] Madison agreed: "the states neglect their militia now . . . the discipline of the militia is evidently a national concern, and ought to be provided in the national constitution . . . without such a power to suppress insurrections, our liberties might be destroyed by a domestic faction" such as indebted farmers.[74] George Washington acknowledged the "commotions among the Eastern people [which] have sunk our national character much below par," bringing American "credit to the brink of precipice."[75]

The Constitutional framers recognized the class divide in society and sought for government to protect the interests of the wealthy. Many of them held the masses in contempt, viewing democracy as undesirable. Hamilton stated: "all communities divide themselves into the few and the many. The first are the rich and well-born, the other the mass of people. The voice of the people has been said to be the voice of God; and however generally the maxim has been quoted and believed, it is not true in fact. The people are turbulent and changing; they seldom judge or determine right."[76] He advocated for a "permanent body" to "check the imprudence of democracy" and "repress domestic faction and insurrection."[77]

The Founding and the Constitution:
The "Miraculous" Victory for the Upper Class

We celebrate the Constitution as a victory for democracy, but it was the upper class that benefitted most from the document. The Articles of Confederation could well have crumbled under the anger of the masses, if the political status quo of the 1780s continued. The Constitution's framers were aware of the shortcomings of the Articles of Confederation and advocated for a stronger national government. Much of the contempt for the public among the framers was openly articulated.

Image 1.3. George Washington, the Signing of the U.S. Constitution, September 17, 1787.

As Robert Dahl explains in *How Democratic is the American Constitution?*: "a substantial number of the framers believed that they must erect constitutional barriers to popular rule because the people would prove to be an unruly mob, a standing danger to law, to orderly government, and property rights."[78] A review of the writings of the framers reveals contempt for democracy and concern for upper-class property rights. When making the case for the creation of a new federal government in *The Federalist Papers*—a series of essays written in favor of the Constitution—Madison conceded that conflicts among "factions" within society were driven by class interests: "the most common and durable source of factions has been the various and unequal distribution of property. Those who hold and those who are without property have ever formed distinct interests in society."[79]

A primary goal of government at the time of the founding was to protect interests of the wealthy against the masses. As indicated in Federalist #10, Madison was concerned with the class conflict between the upper and lower classes, as seen in debtors' "rage for paper money, for an abolition of debts, for an equal division of property, or for any other improper or wicked project." Some states' indulgence of debtors' demands led Hamilton to attack what he felt was the "excess of democracy."[80] Rather than allowing debtors to dominate public policy against the interests of investors, John Jay, the first Chief Justice of the Supreme Court, famously prescribed that "the people who own the country ought to govern it," while Madison sought a government "to protect the minority of the opulent against the majority."[81] As respected historian Gordon Wood notes, the framers were quite "aristocratic" in their view that states had fallen victim to "democratic excesses."[82] Reflecting this aristocratic view, Madison wrote in Federalist #51 that a nation "must first enable the government to control the governed," and argued in Federalist #10 that "the only policy by which a republic can be administered on just principles" is via a "divide and conquer" strategy in which different groups in society are pitted against each other.

Madison also wrote in Federalist #10 that "the first object of government" was "the protection of different and unequal faculties of acquiring property," so as to ensure that "the possession of different degrees and kinds of property immediately results." The problem with government under the Articles of Confederation was that "the United States, as now composed, have no powers to exact obedience, or punish disobedience to their resolutions" via Constitutional or other methods. Without such methods of discipline, the poor majority could threaten upper-class interests, as they did during Shays' Rebellion. As Madison wrote in Federalist #51: "different interests necessarily exist in different classes of citizens. If a majority be united by a common interest, the rights of the minority will be insecure." An "unjust combination of a majority of the whole" was dangerous, whereas the limiting of democracy ensured "the rights of individuals, or of the minority, will be in little danger from interested combinations of the majority."

The above passages reveal Madison's distrust of majority and democratic rule. Contrary to claims that the framers were relatively democratic for the time period in which they lived, the most important figures in the creation of the Constitution had little interest in even representative government.[83] Hamilton preferred presidents with lifetime terms and senators who were appointed, not elected—neither of which would be accountable to the public.[84] Similarly, Madison was skeptical of the entire practice of voting. He worried that extension of voting to the masses of non-property owners "may throw too much power into hands which will either abuse it themselves or sell it to the rich who will abuse it."[85] Madison spoke with anxiety about the "vices" of "popular government," warning: "In popular Governments the danger lies in an undue sympathy among individuals composing a majority, and a want of responsibility in the majority to the minority."[86] In other words, the flaw of democracy was that the masses believed they, rather than the wealthy few, should rule.

A Victory for Divide and Conquer

Class interests were a central motivator for the writers of the Constitution. Of the 55 men who met in Philadelphia in 1787 for the Constitutional Convention, most were from wealthy financial backgrounds, owning land, or holding manufacturing, shipping, or slaveholding interests. About half were creditors. Forty held government bonds, and had a financial stake in opposing debtors seeking government relief from high taxes imposed to pay back bondholders.[87] Three were physicians; half were college graduates; seven were former governors; six were plantation owners; eight were businessmen.[88] Absent from the convention were representatives of five groups: indentured servants, property-less men, women, Native Americans, and slaves. Simply put, their interests were not represented.

A number of studies highlight the elite economic interests of the Founding generation. Beards' *An Economic Interpretation of the Constitution* suggests the Founding Fathers' motives were not benevolent or democratic, but self-interested. He wrote about the elite groups discussed above, whose "property rights were adversely affected by the government under the Articles of Confederation." These groups' "economic interests" were well represented at the Constitutional Convention, and they held significant wealth in public securities (debt), among other assets.[89] Beard summarized: "a majority of the [convention] members were lawyers by profession . . . Not one member represented in his immediate personal economic interests the small farming or mechanic class. The overwhelming majority of convention members, at least five-sixths were immediately, directly, and personally interested in the outcome of their labors at Philadelphia, and were to a greater or lesser extent economic beneficiaries from the adoption of the Constitution."[90]

Some historians rejected Beards' analysis, and downplayed the significance of the economic interests at stake during the founding. Historians have focused on the Founding Fathers as concerned with issues such as personal rights or security from foreign powers.[91] While popular in the early twentieth century, Beard's economic interpretation of the Constitution became the subject of many challenges. Recent research, however, suggests it remains a powerful explanation of the concerns driving the Founding Fathers. In *To Form a More Perfect Union*, historian Robert McGuire presents evidence that the individual economic backgrounds of the Founding Fathers influenced how they looked at the Constitution. He finds that the federalists—who favored strong central government power—were "mainly merchants, shippers, bankers, speculators, and private and public securities [debt] holders."[92] Delegates who were creditors were more likely to vote against a convention initiative to prohibit states' ability to issue paper money for farmers and other debtors to pay their debts and taxes. Delegates hailing from geographic areas with significant commercial activities, living near trade routes off of navigable water, were more likely to support the Constitution than delegates from states without important trade routes. Trade interests were likely seen as more effectively protected by a stronger federal government. Finally, holders of public securities (debt) were also more likely to support the Constitution, presumably understanding that agrarian revolt against high taxes invoked to pay back debt holders represented a threat to their ability to collect on past investments.

How *does* one deter or limit alliances of the poor masses, while protecting the affluent few? The framers established an effective system for suppressing the will of the masses, in line with Madison's goal in Federalist #10 to "secure the public good and private rights against the danger of such a [majority] faction." The goal of the government, Madison explained, was "to break and deny the violence of faction," as seen in events like Shays' Rebellion. A faction representing the majority of Americans would be limited by "controlling its effects"—by removing popular ability to influence government, and by empowering the wealthy, privileged few to control political discourse and politics. As Madison promised, democracy and the passions and transgressions of man would be limited by taking "auxiliary precautions."[93] As described in Federalist #51, these precautions included empowering different branches of government to limit the ambition and powers of other branches. These branches were separated from mass influence, since only white, property-owning males could vote.[94]

In Madison's view, public beliefs could be "refine[d]" by "passing them through the medium of a chosen body of citizens, whose wisdom may best discern the true interest of their country, and whose patriotism and love of justice will be least likely to sacrifice it to temporary or partial consideration." To provide "security against a gradual concentration of the several powers in the same department," those who "administer each [government] department" would be granted "the necessary constitutional means and personal motives to resist encroachments of the others."[95] As is written in Federalist #51, the Constitution would "arrange the several offices in government in such a manner as that each may be a check on the other." "In a republican government," since "the legislative authority necessarily predominates . . . the remedy for this inconvenience is to divide the legislature into different branches."[96] Through a fragmentation of the parts of government, the framers deterred mass democratic empowerment.

The framers created a government that was largely immune from popular pressures. Hamilton wanted a Senate, in addition to a president, to be chosen for life, rather than be elected. In Federalist #63, he wrote about a "well-constructed Senate" as "sometimes necessary as a defense to the people against their own temporary errors and delusions." Gouverneur Morris, the Pennsylvania representative at the Constitutional Convention, supported a Senate limited to men of "great personal property" and of "aristocratic spirit." The Senate created under the Constitution was elitist. Its members were not elected by the public, but chosen by state legislatures to serve six-year terms. No more than one-third of its members were up for reelection in any given election year, ensuring that a full turnover of the body would take three election cycles, or six years. The selection of Senators by state legislatures was not replaced with direct election until the Seventeenth Amendment (1913).

Other elements of government were also insulated from popular pressure. The president is *selected* by an institution called the Electoral College, consisting of electors from each state that filter the public vote. Federal judges are appointed by the president and confirmed by the Senate. Of all the "democratic" branches of government, only the House of Representatives was originally subject to popular vote. Even the House, however, was accountable to only a small minority of citizens because of property restrictions for voting. Few Americans voted in early American elections. Only a fifth to a quarter of the population was eligible to vote, and even among eligible voters, turnout was anemic, at just 11.6 percent in 1788–89, 6 percent in 1792, and 20 percent in 1796.[97]

Changing the Constitution was difficult, as the document was designed to be independent of popular pressures. As Madison wrote of the amendment process: "frequent appeal to the people would carry an implication of some defect in the government [and] deprive that government of the veneration which time bestows on everything, and without which perhaps the wisest and freest governments would not possess the requisite stability." Amendments need a two-thirds vote in both chambers of Congress, the president's signature, and support from three-fourths of state legislatures. With this high threshold, the Constitution has been amended just 17 times since the passage of the Bill of Rights. Basic rights have also been blocked because of the Constitution's resilience to change. For example, the Equal Rights Amendment—prohibiting gender and racial discrimination—has never been passed despite being introduced regularly in Congress for decades. Although the public commonly expects government to protect seniors and the poor in terms of providing health care and income security for the elderly, these protections are not guaranteed in the Constitution.

Other aspects of the Constitution also catered to wealthy interests, while demonstrating little interest in the needy or poor. The Constitution gave the federal government the powers to "lay and collect taxes, to regulate interstate and foreign commerce." The commerce power was used by Hamilton, as U.S. Treasury Secretary, to establish a national bank, in order to promote investor interests and to aid in the emergence of a capitalist economic system. The Constitution's taxation powers also enabled the federal government to claim fiscal power when it came to paying off the national debt. The Constitution states: "no state shall enter into any treaty, alliance, or confederation; grant letters of marquee and reprisal; coin money; emit bills of credit; make anything but gold and silver coin a tender in payment of debts; pass any bill of attainder, ex post facto law, or law impairing the obligation of contracts or grant any title of nobility." Of note here is the prohibition on state challenges to legal contracts, which prohibited efforts at debt relief through the reduction of money owed by debtors to creditors. This gift to an upper class heavily comprised of creditors spoke to Madison's concern with stifling debtors' "rage for paper money, for an abolition of debts, for an equal division of property, or for any other improper or wicked project." With a Constitution fragmenting power between state and national government, and within national government itself, the framers ensured poor Americans' push for debt relief would "be less apt to pervade the whole body of the union than a particular member of it."[98]

Democratic Elements of the Constitution

Relative to the time it was created, the Constitution was a fairly progressive document. It protected voting rights, even if only for the few. It prohibited monarchy, and recognized basic rights of citizens. A more charitable interpretation of early U.S. history might suggest that, even if the framers of the Constitution were opposed to democracy, they still created a political system containing *elements* of democracy, or at least ideas that were eventually interpreted to be compatible with democracy. Among these democratic elements is the commitment to individual rights, representation through voting, and limited government via the rule of law. Voting was hardly democratic in that only a small number of Americans could participate, but this changed over time as property restrictions on voting were abolished, and as slavery and indentured servitude were outlawed. The Bill of Rights established citizen protections that are necessary in any democracy, and one should credit state legislatures at the time of the founding with pressuring for these protections to be added to the Constitution via amendment. In the process of demanding a Bill of Rights, these legislatures provided a significant democratic service.

Slavery and the Constitution

The protection of slavery under the Constitution, and the document's siding with upper-class slave owners over people of color, were additional signs of the repressive, anti-democratic nature of the document. The Constitution stated at the founding: "the migration or importation of such persons [slaves] as any of the states now existing shall think proper to admit, shall not be prohibited by the Congress prior to the year 1808, but a tax or duty may be imposed on such importation, not exceeding ten dollars for each person." This clause allowed for the expansion of slavery for twenty years. Madison opposed protecting the slave trade, concluding that "twenty years will produce all the mischief that can be apprehended from the liberty of importing slaves . . . so long a term will be dishonorable to the national character than to say nothing about it in the Constitution."[99] Madison's concern with a Constitution that enabled slavery was validated by the fact that slavery had been banned during the Revolutionary War, and was not reinstated until *after* the Constitution authorized it, when South Carolina, Georgia, and Louisiana began importing slaves again.[100]

Despite Madison's objections, the fugitive slave clause, coupled with the "Full Faith and Credit" clause both reinforced the institution of slavery. Article 4, Section 1 of the Constitution stated, "no persons held to service or labor in one state, under the laws thereof, escaping into another, shall in consequences of any law or regulation therein, be discharged from service or labor, but shall be delivered up on claim of the party to whom such service or labor may be due." As the Supreme Court ruled in *Dred Scott v. Sandford* (1857), non-slave states were bound to return escaped slaves to their owners, because the Constitution stated that "full faith and credit shall be given in each state to the public acts, records, and judicial proceedings of every other state." The fugitive slave clause complemented the Full Faith and Credit Clause, demanding that free states respect slavery.

Slave states knew the value of the Fugitive Slave Clause. As one historical account explains: "The slave states would have been reluctant, perhaps even unwilling, to agree to the Constitution without obtaining what they deemed adequate federal legal protection against fugitive slave flight. Inclusion of the clause meant that the slave states could avoid the future creation of any significant northern free jurisdiction magnets for fugitive slaves . . . the clause added legitimacy to their control of slave property by establishing direct constitutional legal protection for it . . . it prevented an influx of runaway slaves whose presence white taxpayer majorities [in non-slave states] often either objected to on racist grounds or believed would result in unwanted social costs such as increased poor-relief taxes and discouragement of white immigration."[101]

The Philadelphia Constitutional Convention was characterized by a favorable climate toward expanding slavery. Northern states did little to oppose the expansion of slavery to western territories. And southern states opposed any use of the Commerce Clause that would empower the government to outlaw slavery. Representatives from Georgia and South Carolina argued that without "security for their slave property . . . the union would never have been completed."[102] Both free and slave states retained interests in perpetuating slavery—the former of which saw the return of escaped slaves as a way of limiting slave flight to their own states.

Finally, the Three-Fifths Compromise helped strengthen slavery. In Article 1, Section 2, the Constitution stated: "representatives and direct taxes shall be apportioned among the several states which may be included within this union, according to their respective numbers, which shall be determined by adding to the whole number of free persons, including those bound to service for a term of years." The Constitution granted extra representation to southern slaveholders to block legislative attempts to eliminate slavery.[103] The Three-Fifths Compromise was a concession granted by free states that protected upper-class slaveholding interests.[104]

The Constitution *facilitated* the growth of slavery, greatly enhancing the profits of wealthy slave owners. Because of the document, slaveholder wealth grew significantly over time. Slaves in the U.S. numbered nearly 700,000 in 1790, but grew to 1.2 million by 1810, a 70 percent increase. By 1860, the slave population had increased to about 4 million, as slavery expanded west when new states were admitted into the union.[105] From the late-eighteenth through the mid-nineteenth century, the number of slaves grew by nearly 500 percent. This would not have been possible without significant legal protections for upper-class slave owners.

Early Challenges to Inequality and Corporate Power

While the framers were generally opposed to democratic government, it is inaccurate to depict them as pro-"free-market" capitalists, or as dismissive of concerns about inequality and rising business power. The framers operated in an environment that was pre-capitalist, and many were skeptical of the rise of a political system dominated by upper-class corporate interests. Distrust for business power and displeasure with extreme inequality permeated many early discussions of American politics, as seen in the writings of Thomas Jefferson, Thomas Paine, John Adams, and James Madison. Adams articulated a concern with the rise of an American oligarchy, even if aristocracy and nobility was formally banned under the Constitution.[106] He was concerned about "a natural and unchangeable inconvenience in all popular elections . . . that he who has the deepest purse, or the fewest scruples about using it, will generally prevail."[107]

It was possible for society to become too unequal, and elite groups too powerful, thereby threatening the established political order and raising the specter of a revolution led by the poor masses. This fear was manifested in Madison's concern with the growing power of individual elite factions, which was to be limited by a system of Constitutional checks and balances.[108] With the rise of modern corporations, capitalism, and industry, a serious concern among the founders and later generations was that the value of goods was no longer determined by labor and access to land, as it had been in early America, but rather through a top-down system of corporate ownership of industry in which the fruits of labor were confiscated by upper-class business elites. The labor theory of value—which placed individual work at the center of any valuation of societal wealth—ran through the classic works of earlier thinkers such as John Locke and Adam Smith, and figures such as Thomas Jefferson, Thomas Paine, and Benjamin Franklin, and later politicians, activists, and thinkers such as Abraham Lincoln, Henry Carey, Karl Marx, and Eugene Debs.[109] The labor theory of value fell under assault by labor contracts between capitalist owners and workers, in which the latter signed away ownership of their labor under a wage system in which corporations and a corporate upper-class sought to maximize profits by minimizing workers' share of all wealth created.

Uncontrolled growth in inequality and poverty was viewed as a threat to the republic. To address this problem, Paine supported government policies that would assist the poor and needy. He recognized that "fortunate opportunities, or the opposite" helped account for inequality—suggesting a degree of inequality was inevitable.[110] Still, he expressed disdain for the economic stratification of society into separate classes, and advocated for programs such as social security for the elderly, and higher pay for public servants, to address the needs of common people. He railed against wealth built on the exploitation of others' labor, and denounced slavery as the starkest example of labor coercion.[111]

Madison worried about excessive power in the hands of early American corporations and the emerging corporate class. He envisioned a government controlled by "enlightened statesmen," who would limit the power of business factions—and in that process help avoid extreme inequality.[112] As one recent historical account claims, conflicts between creditors and debtors, between the rich and poor, were seen as contributing "to economic stagnation," and "led to rising inflation, produced revenue shortfalls, undermined national credit, and ultimately threatened the right to private property."[113]

Concerning the rise of a corporate class, Madison wrote in 1827 that "incorporated companies, without proper limitations and guards, may in particular cases, be useful, but they are at best a necessary evil only. Monopolies and perpetuities are objects of just abhorrence."[114] He held it "as a truth that commercial shackles are generally unjust" and "oppressive," referring to the growing power of the second national bank—favored by Hamilton—as a way of promoting capitalist growth and business power throughout the country.[115] Madison's suspicion of banks was not unique among the founders, as the feeling that banks played a parasitic role, profiting off of the labor of others, was commonplace.[116] In addition to distrusting banking interests, Madison warned of the dangers flowing from extreme inequality: "there is an evil that ought to be guarded against in the indefinite accumulation of property from the capacity of holding it in perpetuity by ecclesiastical corporations. The power of all corporations, ought to be limited in this respect. The growing wealth acquired by them never fails to be a source of abuses." This concern was reflected, Madison wrote, in the "misuse" of corporate wealth "in many Countries of Europe," which "has long been a topic of complaint."[117]

Jefferson also worried about corporate power. He wrote in 1816: "I hope we shall take warning . . . and crush in its birth the aristocracy of our moneyed corporations, which dare already to challenge our government to a trial of strength and bid defiance to the laws of our country."[118] The comparison of corporations with aristocracy is noteworthy, as Jefferson viewed them as a continuation of monarchical politics by other means. Jefferson's concerns about business power run throughout American history. In the early-nineteenth century, President Andrew Jackson wrote about the rise of upper-class business interests: "the question is distinctly presented whether the people of the United States are to govern through representatives chosen by their unbiased suffrages or whether the money and power of a great corporation are to be secretly exerted to influence their judgment and control their decisions."[119]

Warnings continued into the early-twentieth century. President Theodore Roosevelt commented in 1906: "behind the ostensible government sits enthroned an invisible government owing no allegiance and acknowledging no responsibility to the people. To destroy this government, to befoul the unholy alliance between corrupt business and corrupt politics is the first task of the statesmanship of the day."[120] President Franklin Roosevelt echoed this concern:

> We had to struggle with the old enemies of peace-business and financial monopoly, speculation, reckless banking, class antagonism, sectionism, war profiteering. They had begun to consider the Government of the United States as a mere appendage to their own affairs. We know that Government by organized money is just as dangerous as Government by organized mob. Never before in history have these forces been so united against one candidate as they stand today. They are unanimous in their hatred for me—and I welcome their hatred. I should like to have it said of my first administration that in it the forces of selfishness and of lust for power met their match. I should like to have it said of my second administration that in it these forces met their master.[121]

The concerns during the founding era with corporate power and inequality remain prominent themes in American politics. Income and wealth inequality were higher in the 2010s than at any other point in a century. As Americans found themselves working longer hours for stagnating pay, concerns with inequality remained in the public mind. As businesses benefit from reduced government regulation, corporations become far more profitable, and share little of this wealth with the people. Growing inequality, amidst increased corporate power, is an increasingly salient issue in national politics. Democratic Presidential candidates Bernie Sanders, and to a lesser extent Hillary Clinton, articulated support for progressive policies aimed at reducing inequality, such as raising the minimum wage, providing for taxpayer-funded college tuition, and increasing taxes on the wealthy. Republican Presidential victor Donald Trump also promised to aid the sagging middle class by focusing on creating well-paying jobs. In short, the issue of inequality is as relevant to American politics today as ever.

Chapter 2

A Constitution in Question

How Democratic is the Founding Document?

In the case of *Sebelius v. the National Federation of Independent Businesses* (2012), the U.S. Supreme Court ruled in favor of the Affordable Care Act, commonly referred to as "Obamacare." For many liberals, this was a time to rejoice, since the law had survived one of what was to be many attacks on a cornerstone of the Obama administration's legacy. The Supreme Court validated Obamacare by a 5 to 4 vote, deeming the law's fine of $695 annually against those who do not purchase health insurance as falling under the federal government's taxation power within the U.S. Constitution. The mandate that all Americans purchase health insurance, and that they be provided a taxpayer subsidy to do it (this subsidy was funded in part by the fine), was central to the law. Without the mandate and fine, it would be difficult to guarantee that the private insurance pools created in each state by the law would be large enough for insurance companies to cover the significant cost of providing care for the sick.

Although Democrats celebrated Obamacare as a tool for helping the poor, the law could also be viewed as an example of how the Constitution enhances the power and profits of the corporate class, and at the expense of the taxpayer. Millions of Americans did receive insurance under Obamacare via the law's expansion of Medicaid eligibility for the poor and due to the federal insurance subsidies, which helped families earning between more than 133 percent, but less than 400 percent of the federal-poverty level, to purchase insurance at a more affordable rate. This program was justified under the Obama administration as a legitimate Constitutional power, in that the federal government holds the power under Article 1, Section 8 to tax Americans and to provide services in the name of serving the "general welfare."

But was this program the most effective way to provide for the common good? The law itself contained no provisions for regulating the growth in insurance premiums, out-of-pocket costs, or deductibles. The mandate, coupled with carte blanche authority granted to insurers to charge whatever rate increases they wanted from year-to-year, meant that Obamacare threatened to become a massive expense for taxpayers. Other options were available, such as a nonprofit "public option" in which the federal government paid for the cost of health insurance to the uninsured, in much the same way that it does for the poor with Medicaid and the elderly with Medicare. One of these options would have cut out the "middle-man" of corporate insurers, and removed profit-motive from health care, which drives up costs beyond those of all other wealthy countries (all of which rely instead on nonprofit universal health care systems).

As predicted, the cost of U.S. care under Obamacare continued to skyrocket in the years after its passage. As the *Kaiser Family Foundation* estimated, health insurance premium costs in the U.S. grew by more than 10 percent in about two-thirds of American states from 2016 to 2017 alone, and the typical cost for a 40-year-old purchasing a "silver" health insurance plan on an American health insurance exchange increased by 24 percent within this same period.[1] Growing costs on the exchanges mirrored overall growth in cost of health care. As *Forbes* estimated, from 2005 to 2016, health insurance costs for a family of four increased by 67 percent after accounting for inflation. This translated into a 6 percent growth per year past the inflation rate, despite average household income declining by 3 percent during this period, after accounting for inflation.[2] *Forbes* estimated that health care costs grew significantly beyond the inflation rate after Obamacare was passed in 2010, by 28 percent from 2010 to 2016.[3]

Obamacare provides a useful lesson regarding the Constitution and corporate power in America. Although the law helped millions of Americans secure health care, it also strengthened the private health care system, while gouging taxpayers for a cost of care that significantly exceeds that paid by any other wealthy country. In this case, the Constitution was central to expanding corporate power in that the taxation and "General Welfare" clause was used to justify granting the insurance industry greater control over American health care. Contrary to claims that the law was "socialist," the law was a significant boon to various corporate health care interests. It expanded market-based insurance, equating the "general welfare" and the common good with tightened corporate control over health care in America.

Health care reform is merely one issue of many regarding Constitutional law. But the broader question remains: to what extent, across many issues, does the U.S. Constitution empower the wealthy and upper-class corporate interests? And to what extent does it democratically empower the masses? I address these questions in detail in this chapter, arguing that, despite the many democratic elements of the Constitution, it is also a vital tool in the fight to enhance corporate power in American politics and society.

Ratified in 1789, the U.S. Constitution has remained in place for more than 225 years. But does it serve the political interests and needs of Americans today? Despite numerous strengths, the Constitution is also limited in its democratic potential. There is little in the document that explicitly commits government to enhancing the power of corporate interests, but there is also little in the document that commits it to protecting the masses, the poor, and the disadvantaged in the face of growing corporate power and record inequality. On the issue of who holds power, the Constitution is noteworthy, not so much in the specific provisions within the document that reinforce rule by the corporate class, but in the document's *lack* of provisions encouraging a progressive approach to regulating corporations, the lack of any serious effort to combat poverty and inequality, and the lack of provisions for preventing the ascendance of upper-class dominance in politics.

Strengths of the Constitution

The Constitution has served as the central component of U.S. law for more than two centuries. Advocates maintain that this is because of its many strengths. The Constitution has many positives aspects and strengths, and these elements speak to the document's importance in providing democratic representation and protecting individual citizens from political repression. But as I argue in this chapter, if the goal of government is limiting upper-class and business power and providing for the poor and the disadvantaged, the Constitution is severely limited.

The Bill of Rights

The Bill of Rights was a progressive initiative in the late 1700s, protecting fundamental liberties. These include protections for free speech and expression, religious freedom, and freedom of the press under the First Amendment; the right to bear arms under the Second Amendment; the right to privacy and protection against unreasonable search and seizure under the Fourth Amendment; the right to due process and protection against double jeopardy (being tried twice for the same crime) under the Fifth Amendment; the right to a grand jury under the Sixth Amendment; the right to a jury by a trial of one's peers under the Seventh Amendment; and protection against "excessive bail," "excessive fines," and "cruel and unusual punishment" under the Eighth Amendment.

Table 2.1. The Language of the Bill of Rights (Ratified 1789–1791)

Amendment	Language
1st Amendment	Congress shall make no law respecting an establishment of religion, or prohibiting the free exercise thereof; or abridging the freedom of speech, or of the press; or the right of the people peaceably to assemble, and to petition the Government for a redress of grievances.
2nd Amendment	A well regulated Militia, being necessary to the security of a free State, the right of the people to keep and bear Arms, shall not be infringed.
3rd Amendment	No Soldier shall, in time of peace be quartered in any house, without the consent of the Owner, nor in time of war, but in a manner to be prescribed by law.
4th Amendment	The right of the people to be secure in their persons, houses, papers, and effects, against unreasonable searches and seizures, shall not be violated, and no Warrants shall issue, but upon probable cause, supported by Oath or affirmation, and particularly describing the place to be searched, and the persons or things to be seized.
5th Amendment	No person shall be held to answer for a capital, or otherwise infamous crime, unless on a presentment or indictment of a Grand Jury, except in cases arising in the land or naval forces, or in the Militia, when in actual service in time of War or public danger; nor shall any person be subject for the same offence to be twice put in jeopardy of life or limb; nor shall be compelled in any criminal case to be a witness against himself, nor be deprived of life, liberty, or property, without due process of law; nor shall private property be taken for public use, without just compensation.
6th Amendment	In all criminal prosecutions, the accused shall enjoy the right to a speedy and public trial, by an impartial jury of the State and district wherein the crime shall have been committed, which district shall have been previously ascertained by law, and to be informed of the nature and cause of the accusation; to be confronted with the witnesses against him; to have compulsory process for obtaining witnesses in his favor, and to have the Assistance of Counsel for his defence.
7th Amendment	In suits at common law, where the value in controversy shall exceed twenty dollars, the right of trial by jury shall be preserved, and no fact tried by a jury, shall be otherwise re-examined in any court of the United States, than according to the rules of the common law.
8th Amendment	Excessive bail shall not be required, nor excessive fines imposed, nor cruel and unusual punishments inflicted.
9th Amendment	The enumeration in the Constitution, of certain rights, shall not be construed to deny or disparage others retained by the people.
10th Amendment	The powers not delegated to the United States by the Constitution, nor prohibited by it to the States, are reserved to the States respectively, or to the people.

The Bill of Rights, although vital to democracy, does not protect economic rights. These are "negative" political rights that government cannot take away. But they are irrelevant to the broader question of what economic rights, if any, the population holds, as related to taxpayer revenues used to provide for necessities such as food, clothing, shelter, or health care. While political rights are a vital part of any democracy, they are not the end of the story when we speak of human needs. In a time of growing inequality, and as Americans increasingly struggle to provide for basic needs such as health care, the Constitution's preoccupation with political rights means it is of limited value in addressing Americans' growing financial insecurity in the neoliberal era of upper-class dominance of politics. Corporations deemed "too big to fail" are virtually guaranteed government subsidies, as happened in the 2008 bank bailout, but there are no Constitutional economic guarantees for the masses and needy during times of crisis.

Equal Protection under Law

Equal protection under law is vital to ensuring freedom from discrimination. Equal protection was established in the Fourteenth Amendment, passed after the Civil War to provide basic rights for former slaves. It states: "No State shall make or enforce any law which shall abridge the privileges or immunities of citizens of the United States; nor shall any State deprive any person of life, liberty, or property, without due process of law; nor deny to any person within its jurisdiction the equal protection of the laws." In modern times, the Equal Protection Clause serves as a significant tool for protecting minority rights, and for prohibiting discrimination based on race, gender, or sexual orientation and identity.

While the Equal Rights Clause is now a cornerstone of guaranteeing rights to citizens, it is also a double-edged sword in that it was used in the post-Civil War period, from the late nineteenth to early twentieth century, to usher in an era of corporate ascendance and power that is still with us today. The Supreme Court ruled in the late 1800s that corporations were legal persons, guaranteed the same rights of other persons under the Equal Protection Clause of the Fourteenth Amendment.[4] Corporations regularly used the courts to pursue their "rights" as corporate persons in the decades after the Civil War, despite the Fourteenth Amendment equal protection rights being intended to empower former slaves.[5] This "right" to personhood was used during the twentieth and twenty-first centuries to solidify corporate power in politics, guaranteeing businesses free speech rights, religious expression rights, and a right to privacy.[6]

Interpretative Language and the "Living Constitution"

The Constitution has remained relevant for centuries due to its ability to change over time. While it is difficult to amend, the document changes via new interpretations of already-existing provisions. Numerous phrases in the Constitution allow for expansive interpretations of federal power, granting government authority to promote the "general welfare," engage in actions deemed "necessary and proper" for executing the enumerated powers (those listed in the document), for regulating "commerce" among the states, and for introducing new laws via the "Supremacy Clause," which states that national laws are "supreme" over state and local laws.

The effort to interpret old Constitutional provisions in new ways, in order to better serve the citizens of today, is referred to as "living Constitution" theory. Consider, for example, the Supreme Court case *Helvering v. Davis* (1937), which ruled that Social Security, although not referenced in the Constitution, is legal since it falls under the government's powers to tax and promote the general welfare. Our common-law system establishes that courts interpret the Constitutionality of laws via legal decisions, which serve as *precedents* guiding future government actions. In summary, the Constitution is continually reinterpreted in ways that accommodate newly emerging needs of the public, as should be expected in a democratic society. The taxation and "General Welfare Clause" could also be used to introduce new programs, such as universal health care, in which all Americans are provided with health insurance by the government and taxpayers, independent of their ability to pay. This potentially progressive Constitutional tool, however, is only useful insofar as citizens pressure government to enact democratic social welfare reforms benefitting the masses, while taxing wealthier Americans and the corporate class to pay for these redistributionist programs. Such reforms are sure to face significant legal challenges in the courts, although the General Welfare Clause provides a potentially powerful tool to counter an upper-class backlash.

Separation of Powers

A claimed strength of the Constitution is that it divides power between the executive, legislative, and judicial branches. The courts interpret the Constitutionality of laws and executive actions. The president nominates judges and bureaucratic officials, while the Senate confirms or rejects those nominees. Congress passes laws, and can override presidential vetoes, while the president can veto Congressional laws. Through checks and balances, the monopolization of power by one branch of the federal government becomes less likely, thereby limiting government power. In dictatorships, checks between branches of government generally do not exist, as presidents, kings, and generals exercise power over other parts of government.

While the separation of powers provides for a potential check against concentration of political power, these Constitutional provisions can do little to ensure democracy for the masses when government positions across the board are increasingly dominated by the upper class. At a time when most members of Congress, presidential candidates, and judicial appointees are millionaires, the "separation of powers" mantra rings hollow, at least as a check against the dominance of government by members of the upper class.[7] Such a separation of powers may help protect against elite rule if there is greater economic diversity in public office, but the growing dominance of money in the election process makes it increasingly difficult for working-class voices set on challenging corporate power to win political offices.

State and National Competition for Power

Federalist countries divide political authority between different levels of government. Madison believed this system makes it easier to protect against the abuse of power. Unitary governments, in contrast, include one level of government (national) that controls local governments. A federal republic like the U.S. is set up by the Constitution to share power between national and state governments. Federal powers are "enumerated" under various provisions of the document, while states' "reserved" powers are discussed in the Tenth Amendment.

Unitary governments are not automatically repressive. Democratic unitary governments exist—for example the United Kingdom, France, Italy, and Japan. However, unitary governments are on average less democratic. The simple reason for this may be that dictators do not share power with state governments, legislatures, or courts. Dictatorships suppress dissent. The U.S. Constitution establishes separation of powers between different parts of the national government and between national and state government, to prevent small elite groups from seizing power. Dictatorship is supposed to be less likely—and democracy more probable—in a country characterized by power sharing between different parts of government.

Despite the democratic potential for federal systems of government, there is little chance of this system combating business or upper-class political power when both national political offices and state offices are dominated by the wealthy. Most major party candidates who run for president are millionaires or wealthier, and the average net worth of members of Congress is more than $1 million, while most judicial appointees under Presidents Bush and Obama were also millionaires.[8] At the state level, legislative research finds that lobbying organizations tend to play a "dominant" role in impacting political outcomes across most states, while it is only in a minority of states that they play merely "complimentary" or "subordinate" roles.[9] Most of these lobbying groups—nearly two-thirds—represent well-paid professionals and business groups.[10] In other words, these lobbies largely represent the upper-class in American society. With the dominance of both national and state politics by upper-class political and lobbying actors, it is difficult to speak of federalist division of state and federal powers as enabling the democratic empowerment of the masses.

The Constitution's Democracy Deficit

In early American history, the Constitution impeded democracy by blocking rights for repressed groups. It was impossible, for example, to outlaw slavery via amendment, to the satisfaction of the southern slave-owning class, because of the supermajorities needed in Congress to act. Despite a growing number of Americans who supported abolishing slavery, it took nearly 80 years after the founding to eliminate the practice. Women did not gain the right to vote until 1920, and even now there is no equal rights amendment. Furthermore, state property rights restrictions for voting were never challenged by the Constitution at its founding, although these laws meant that participation in government would be dominated by the white propertied class. In short, in numerous ways, the Constitution was an impediment to democratic empowerment throughout history.

The Constitution is no longer viewed as a model for many other countries drafting their constitutions. A 1987 study reported on by the *The New York Times*—coinciding with the 200 year "bi-centennial" anniversary of the Constitution—found that more than 160 countries had "written charters modeled directly or indirectly on the U.S. version."[11] Twenty-five years later, researchers found that, while "democratic constitutions as a whole became more similar to the U.S. Constitution" during the 1960s and 1970s, that pattern "reverse[d] course in the 1980s and 1990s." By the beginning of the twenty-first century, a "steep plunge" had begun in which the U.S. Constitution became less popular as a model for other countries.[12]

Journalistic accounts of the Constitution's declining relevance claimed that "it guarantees relatively few rights," and the "commitment of some members of the Supreme Court to interpreting the Constitution according to its original meaning in the eighteenth century may send the signal that it is of little current use."[13] The Constitution's failure to recognize individual rights to food, health care, education, and other necessities was also cited as a reason for the unpopularity of the founding document. The Constitution's perceived rigidity in resisting change and the difficulty of the amendment process likely contribute to the perception worldwide that it is an outdated document. There are numerous criticisms of the Constitution, explored below, and in one way or another, they all relate to the problem of upper-class dominance of politics.

Staggered, Infinite Elections

The Constitution established staggered elections, making it difficult to turn over government quickly. Senators serve six-year terms, and only one-third of the Senate is elected any election year, so it takes six years to turn over the body. In contrast, House members serve just two years, making it difficult to govern without worrying about constant campaigning. The constant cycling between presidential and midterm elections, not to mention primaries, ensures that elections are never-ending. This permanent "campaign mode" can lead to election fatigue among the public.

Infinite elections relate to the problem of upper-class power in politics in two ways. First, with voting fatigue comes a declining willingness of Americans to participate in politics—particularly in Congressional midterm elections. With such low voter turnout, it makes it increasingly difficult, if not impossible, for the public to work toward turning over a legislative body that increasingly represents upper-class interests via its very demographic composition. Second, decreased public attention to and participation in legislative elections means that any effort to pressure Congress to pass reforms limiting the role of corporate money in politics is also difficult. With business groups in such a dominant position regarding campaign finance, it makes it increasingly difficult for candidates who are independent of corporate donations and support to win political office.

No Congressional Term Limits

Both the House and Senate lack term limits. In modern politics, congressional incumbents win reelection close to 90 percent of the time.[14] The advantage likely has to do with their ability to raise large campaign contributions. At a time when disapproval of Congress is at record highs, the entrenchment of legislators is difficult to justify. The lack of constitutional term limits means that turning over Congress is incredibly challenging. Term limits could provide an incentive for larger numbers of Americans to vote, especially if new candidates have a better chance of winning elections. But the Constitution provides no way to rein in the power of incumbents. As with the problem of infinite elections, the lack of term limits poses a serious challenge to citizens who wish to reverse the growing upper-class dominance of Congress as it is currently constituted.

The Bicameral Congress

Bicameralism refers to a legislature with two chambers. This constitutional feature makes legislation more difficult to pass than in a unicameral system. Bicameralism lends itself to obstruction, which is common in the Senate. The use of the filibuster to block legislation reached a record high in the 2010s, with hundreds of pieces of legislation held hostage by the Republican Party.[15] In an era when legislative productivity has reached record lows, constitutionally-enabled Congressional obstruction is increasingly common. Recent evidence suggests that upper-class Americans—those in the top 20 percent of the income distribution—are significantly more likely to see their policy preferences turned into law than the bottom 80 percent.[16] With a Congress that routinely prioritizes the wants and needs of the top 20 percent at the expense of the many, having two chambers of Congress makes it twice as difficult to pass legislation aimed at assisting the masses, needy, and poor.

Weak Limits on Federal Judges

Judges are nominated by the president and confirmed by Senators. But judges are formally immune from public pressure. The Constitution does not allow the election of judges, although judicial elections are common in states. Without elections, the public has no direct role in choosing judges. Rather than lifetime appointments, the Constitution could be amended to establish term limits for judges. For those concerned that elections subject judges to the corrupting influence of money, term limits would ensure that judges who lose public faith do not serve indefinitely.

The issue of the lack of judicial accountability to the public is also relevant to class rule. Most judicial appointees in the modern era hail from wealthy, upper-class backgrounds, and in the neoliberal era of politics, the increasingly conservative Supreme Court has sided with business interests in many cases, as related to granting corporate personhood rights. Most Americans oppose the Supreme Court's efforts to enhance the "rights" and powers of corporate "persons"—especially as related to their role in elections.[17] But without the ability to remove judges who have lost the public's confidence due to siding with wealthy interests over the public, the prospect of democratic accountability in the courts is greatly reduced.

No Economic Bill of Rights

Although President Franklin Roosevelt supported an economic Bill of Rights, it was never added to the Constitution. The Bill of Rights includes only negative political rights—those which government must not take away. Positive rights—those government actively provides—are not in the document. These include the right to a job, shelter, food, health care, clothing, secure retirement, public education, a living wage, access to public roads and other infrastructure, and access to information (libraries). Popular programs like Social Security and Medicare are not constitutionally protected. They are not deemed inalienable rights, despite being overwhelmingly popular throughout most wealthy countries. State constitutions guarantee access to public transportation and public education,

Image 2.1. Franklin D. Roosevelt, 32nd U.S. President.

but the U.S. Constitution has done nothing to guarantee economic rights. The guarantee of basic economic rights would likely do much to reduce inequality and poverty in the U.S., and will require the introduction of a more progressive taxation system to redistribute resources from the upper-class to the middle- and lower-classes. The commitment to a strong welfare state throughout most of the first world means that inequality levels between the upper class and the masses are significantly lower in most countries than in the U.S.[18]

Poor Representation of the Young and Foreign Born

The Constitution prohibits anyone under 35 years old from being president. Individuals 25 and over can serve in the House, but one must be 35 to serve in the Senate. Presidential requirements ensure that government cannot demographically represent adults between 18–34 years old. This stipulation is puzzling considering that the right to vote begins at age 18. Also, foreign-born citizens cannot run for president. Foreign-born citizens can serve in the Senate, but must be citizens for nine years before serving. For the House, foreign-born citizens must live in the country for seven years prior to serving. By granting citizenship to foreign-born Americans, these individuals are supposedly guaranteed the same legal rights as other Americans. These practices could be seen as violating equal rights protections under the Fourteenth Amendment.

The young and foreign born are generally two disadvantaged groups, economically speaking. Many immigrate to the U.S. looking for improved job and earning opportunities. And young Americans have suffered most under an economy with dwindling prospects for middle-class sustaining jobs for new college graduates. So long as the Constitution under-represents these groups in the political process, the document makes it more difficult for the young and foreign-born to assert themselves politically, or to support progressive economic policies that are vital to reducing economic inequality between the upper-class and poorer Americans.

Limits on Direct Citizen Participation

Many American states allow citizens to propose legislation via "initiative," which can become law with a majority vote in support. There is no initiative in the U.S. Constitution, however. Other limits on public participation hinder public empowerment, for example the lack of a "recall" option for officials who lose public faith. The Constitution allows Congress to impeach the president or members of Congress, but this power falls only on legislators, not on the public.

This makes it more difficult to hold leaders accountable. While many American states recognize the power of citizens to recall governors, this power does not exist in national politics.

The lack of an initiative or recall in the Constitution or in national politics is not, by itself, a sign that the document serves corporate or upper-class interests. But with record mass distrust of government, with three-quarters of Americans saying they have "too little" influence on Washington politics, and with most agreeing that "lobbyists, big business, and the rich" have too much power in politics, the lack of mechanisms to directly empower the masses remains a serious concern.[19] Without those tools, it is increasingly difficult for the "average" American to challenge corporate and upper-class dominance of the political system.

A Difficult Amendment Process

The amendment process is fraught with difficulties. One way to change the Constitution is by both the House and Senate voting with two-thirds majorities for an amendment, which also requires three-quarters of states to approve. Another method is by two-thirds of state legislatures holding a convention to pass an amendment. But constitutional amendments are difficult to pass. Since the passage of the Bill of Rights, the Constitution has been amended 17 times. Seventeen amendments over more than 230 years means just one amendment every 13.5 years. This figure, however, overestimates the frequency of constitutional change in recent times. From 1970 to 2016—the Constitution was amended just twice (or once every 23 years)—once related to Congressional pay rules, and the other time for lowering the voting national age from 21 to 18. In sum, the Constitution is extremely resistant to change. As one study found, it is one of the most difficult Constitutions in the world to amend.[20]

On the one hand, the difficulty of the amendment process does not appear to be a significant problem, since the Constitution is able to change via Supreme Court precedents and reinterpretation over time. This allows the document to potentially remain relevant to the interests and needs of the many. On the other hand, the near impossibility of changing the Constitution also means that progressive protections for the masses and poor remain in a precarious position. Social welfare programs in the neoliberal era are always within one federal budget of being reduced or eliminated. And without a fundamental guarantee of a right to health care or other basic human needs, government is able to avoid providing these necessities to much of the population, and to continue prioritizing policies that are more likely to benefit corporations and the upper class.

The Electoral College

As a system comprised of electors who are chosen by states or elected to cast their votes according to the preferences of the public, the Electoral College is a filtering mechanism between the public and president. There are 538 electoral votes, with one per member of the House and Senate, and three for the District of Columbia. As a presidential candidate wins a state, he or she receives all the electoral votes for that state. Under this "winner-take-all" system, a candidate's number of electoral votes gained per state is not equal to the percent of the popular vote they received. Such discrepancies can, and have, played havoc on election outcomes, particularly in the 2000 and 2016 elections. Americans recognize the problems associated with the Electoral College. A 2001 *Gallup* poll found "a majority of Americans have continually expressed support for an official amendment of the U.S. Constitution that would allow for direct election of the president."[21] Over the next decade and a half, majority support was continually voiced for eliminating the Electoral College.[22] The Electoral College may be constitutionally mandated, but it has long been opposed by most Americans.

The Electoral College occupies a special place in reinforcing the politics of elitism today. In the last two decades, it has been used twice to overrule the majority vote, and put in place a reactionary political official that blatantly prioritized public policies that benefitted the wealthy and the corporate class, while marginalizing the interests of the many and the disadvantaged. The Bush administration significantly increased economic inequality between the upper class and the rest of the population with trillions in tax cuts, while the Trump administration sought to strip millions of Americans of health care benefits in favor of tax cuts for the wealthy.[23] Both of these presidencies, and their commitment to enhancing the wealth of the rich, would not have existed without the assistance of the Electoral College.

Constitutional Strengths versus Weaknesses

The Constitution has numerous strengths, but also suffers from many weaknesses when it comes to democratic representation. The document has persisted for centuries, largely because of the efforts of the courts to reinterpret Constitutional language as new issues arise in American politics. To say the Constitution is compatible with a republican system, however, does not mean it excels in promoting democracy, or that it provides strong tools for combating growing inequality or corporate upper-class power over politics. Despite the mass celebration of the Constitution by most Americans, the document does not appear to be up to the task of limiting the power of corporations and the wealthy. While mass public efforts to limit corporate power have existed alongside the U.S. Constitution in various periods throughout American history, the document provides few explicit tools, outside of its reference to promoting the "general welfare," for combating upper-class dominance of politics.

Revising the Constitution

Some scholars would like to revise the Constitution to improve its democratic representation of the public and to bring it up to date with current societal needs. Some have called for a second Constitutional Convention to rewrite the document and to eliminate antiquated provisions, while introducing democratic ones.[24] The strengths of the Constitution could be retained, while improving upon our system of representation. Convening a second convention, however, is unrealistic short of some major societal turmoil or mass uprising in which the country's very stability is threatened. Far greater public pressure must be applied before one can begin to talk about constitutional reforms that guarantee basic economic rights to the public, or that limit the political power of the corporate class and the wealthy.

Chapter 3

Federalism and the Struggle for Democracy

Federalism refers to a hybrid system of government. It is defined by the sharing of, and conflict over, power between two or more levels of government. U.S. federalism is defined by a Constitution, which establishes political powers for both the national and state governments. The Constitution establishes "enumerated" and "reserved" powers for the national government and states, while state constitutions establish rules for how local governments are regulated, and for addressing political, social, economic, and election issues within states' borders.

Federalism is contested political terrain. For example, health care reform has been the subject of great dispute between the national and state governments. In the fall of 2017, Independent Senator Bernie Sanders introduced a universal health care proposal intended to replace the United States' for-profit health care system. The *Washington Post* reported that the bill "would revolutionize America's health-care system, replacing it with a public system that would be paid for by higher taxes. Everything from emergency surgery to prescription drugs, from mental health to eye care, would be covered, with no co-payments . . . Employer-provided health care would be replaced, with the employers paying higher taxes but no longer on the hook for insurance . . . But the market-based changes of the Affordable Care Act [Obamacare] would be replaced as Medicare becomes the country's universal insurer."[1]

In contrast to Sanders' bill, Congressional Republicans offered their own health care bill that would empower states over the federal government. Republican Senators Lindsey Graham and Bill Cassidy proposed to provide a large "lump sum" of federal funding to each state in the form of a block grant, in which each state could spend it as it saw fit with regard to health care services. The Republican plan would also have repealed Obamacare, which mandated that individual states create health insurance exchanges in which individuals could purchase health plans with a federal subsidy.[2]

On the issue of federalism, Graham and Cassidy's plan could not have been more different from Bernie Sanders' bill. Sanders' plan represented a massive growth in federal authority and responsibility for providing for the health needs of the mass public. In contrast, Graham and Cassidy's plan largely absolved the federal government of direct responsibility for determining rules regarding individual health care spending in insurance marketplaces. Sanders's plan, however, was only supported by 15 Senate Democrats, although universal health care was reportedly supported by more than 100 Democrats in the House of Representatives. Neither the Democratic "Medicare for All" plan, nor the Republican "throw health care back to the states" plan received support from a majority in both chambers of Congress, meaning that Obamacare would remain the law of the land moving forward.

The ongoing debate over health care reform spoke to the federalist conflict over state versus national responsibility for this essential service. But regardless of whether the approach was primarily national or state-based, the similarity between both parties' plans was the reliance on the private marketplace, rather than socialized medicine. Sanders's proposal for universal health care was significant in that it suggested a divide in the Democratic Party between more progressive Democrats who wanted Medicare for all Americans, and the more corporate-centered Democrats who were content with market-based care. Sanders lamented that "we remain the only major country on earth that allows chief executives and stockholders in the health care industry to get incredibly rich, while tens of millions of people suffer because they can't get the health care they need. That is not what the United States should be about."[3] But in a federalist system committed to the enhancement of corporate power and business profits, market-based health care continued to dominate health care policy.

The U.S. federalist system has changed greatly over the last century. On the issue of upper-class influence in politics, a number of counter-currents are evident. On the one hand, the federal government has instituted a great many regulations on corporations and the business class that have greatly enhanced American democracy, including environmental regulations for corporate polluters, labor laws, workplace safety standards, and progressive federal taxation on income in order to pay for social welfare programs, among other reforms. The modern welfare state, although significantly less generous than other wealthy countries, does provide a basic safety net for the needy and poor, especially during times of economic instability and crisis. On the other hand, corporate power and upper-class dominance of American national and state politics has grown significantly over the last three to four decades. With the rise of neoliberalism, government itself is increasingly populated by political officials from upper-class backgrounds. Federal taxes have become steadily less progressive over time with the fixation on tax cuts for the wealthy and for businesses. Labor laws protecting the right to unionize are not enforced, as employers fire employees seeking to organize with impunity. Popular welfare programs are routinely under assault from the federal government and states. And political officials are significantly more likely to take seriously the wishes and agendas of the upper-class, compared to middle- and lower-class Americans. In short, the U.S. federal system, while far more progressive today than it was a century ago, has increasingly become the playground of upper-class business elites.

Federalism and Public Opinion

Recognizing the value of progressive governance, most Americans strongly support redistributionist welfare programs that aid the masses and poor. Although many Americans claim to distrust national political institutions, the federal government has grown in authority and power in modern times because Americans support government, if not in principle then in practice, because of the benefits it confers to the people. And growing government responsibilities reflect increased public demand for goods and services. Previous political science scholarship situates federalism within a "benefits coalition" framework, in which governments provide services because groups form to demand representation from political officials. These groups pressure the national, state, and local governments to provide various social programs and other benefits. These benefits may be economic, juridical, or symbolic. Examples of economic benefits include food stamps, Social Security, and Medicare. Juridical benefits include legal services provided to citizens, such as police protection, enforcement of contract law, and civil rights protections. Symbolic benefits include patriotic expressions from officials.[4]

In modern times, growing federal efforts to provide social programs to the needy began with the Great Depression. This was a time of desperation for many Americans, following the stock market crash of 1929. A "free market" approach to politics meant that government allowed Wall Street speculators to engage in risky investments without oversight, while the masses of Americans were forced to endure the consequences in the wake of the 1929 economic crash. With massive growth in unemployment, approximately one in four Americans was without a job, and more than half of those employed in non-farm jobs were under-employed, working part time.[5] State and local governments were overwhelmed by the needs of an increasingly desperate public.[6] The national problem of the Great Depression necessitated a national plan for dealing with unemployment, poverty, and a weak economy. But this need was largely neglected by the Hoover administration. Rather than introducing a strongly progressive taxation system aimed at redistributing resources via welfare programs from the upper class and wealthy to the masses and poor, Hoover believed individuals were ultimately responsible for their economic success or failure.[7] His embrace of the rhetoric of personal responsibility, however, was belied by the fact that the U.S. economy was fundamentally broken and was unable to provide even basic employment opportunities for much of the population.

Despite Hoover's intransigence, a plan emerged under the next president—Franklin Roosevelt—to deal with the economic crisis. Roosevelt introduced his "New Deal," which included government regulation of business, expanded worker protections and rights, and social welfare spending for the needy. During a time of growing poverty and instability, charity alone could not provide for the growing number of needy Americans. This New Deal, as I argue later in this chapter, was instrumental in fostering a shift away from the "free market" politics of personal responsibility, and toward the rise of the social welfare state, which was based on the redistribution of economic resources from the rich to the middle-class and poor.

Today, Americans complain about wasteful spending, yet expect a lot from government. Polls suggest a tension in public opinion regarding federalism. When asked broad questions most Americans express negative attitudes toward the federal government, which seem to fall within a conservative, "free market" and personal responsibility-based politics that is often embraced by the Republican Party and many members of the American upper class. Americans give better performance ratings to state and local governments than the federal government. They trust the federal government less than state and local government, and say the national government should be more limited.[8] Most Americans believe the federal government "has too much power," and most say they prefer "concentration of power" at the state, rather than national level.[9] The overwhelming majority of Americans agree that the federal government must reduce its spending to reduce the national deficit.[10] And a plurality of Americans believe that poverty is a function of individual laziness and an overly-generous welfare state.[11] These findings suggest that people prefer decentralized, conservative governance, and are sympathetic to a neoliberal pro-business agenda that seeks to minimize government assistance to the poor.

A closer look at public attitudes, however, reveals a contradiction with regard to federalism. When asked what level of government people look to "when it comes to solving many of the problems and issues we face," Americans are most likely to cite the national over state and local governments.[12] And most believe the "national government should do more to solve pressing problems in American society."[13] Furthermore, a majority or plurality of Americans state that the federal government "should take the lead" across most policy issues they are surveyed on, including "assisting the poor," "assisting the elderly," "assisting the disabled," on dealing with "illegal firearms," "controlling narcotics," "reducing unemployment," on responding to "natural disasters," on cleaning up "toxic waste," on "protecting the environment," on promoting "equal opportunity" and "equality for women," and on addressing "illegal immigration" and "health care." On just two issues does the public want local government to lead: "urban development" and "reducing crime." States do a bit better, with the public preferring they take the lead on "public transportation," "assisting the elderly," "public works," "education," "economic development," and "reducing unemployment."[14] But again, most Americans prefer federal responsibility across a majority of the issue areas in question.

Although most Americans distrust government, a majority express "favorable" views of 13 different federal agencies surveyed, in comparison to just 2 in which a majority expresses "unfavorable" views.[15] When asked about the federal government's performance on specific issues, large majorities believe the government is "doing a good job" in the following areas: "keeping the country safe from terror," "responding to natural disasters," "ensuring safe food and medicine," "maintaining infrastructure," "protecting the environment," "strengthening the economy," "ensuring access to high quality education," "setting workplace standards," "ensuring access to health care," and "advancing space exploration." On just three issues—"managing the immigration system," "ensuring basic income for people 65 and over," and "helping people get out of poverty," do a minority believe the federal government is "doing a good job." Most Americans believe there is a "major role for the federal government" for every issue above, with the exception of "advancing space exploration."[16]

Despite most Americans saying they want to cut government spending to reduce the deficit, support for cuts is low when examining specific programs, departments, and services. Most Americans support either keeping spending the "same" or "increasing" spending for every program or service surveyed by the *Pew Research Center*, including "veterans' benefits," "Social Security," "education," "aid to the world's needy," "State Department" spending, "unemployment aid," "military defense," "aid to the needy in the U.S.," "health care," "environmental protection," "energy," "scientific research," "agriculture," "anti-terrorism defenses," "roads and infrastructure," "Medicare," "combating crime," "food and drug inspection," and "natural disaster relief." In none of these areas do most support reducing government spending.[17]

Americans are strong supporters of the federal government when examining specific political issues, programs, and benefits. This likely relates to the feeling of most Americans that the federal government is more effective than state and local governments in providing services. When asked "from which level of government do you feel you get the most for your money," the largest number of respondents claim it is the federal government.[18] This is not surprising, since the federal government is the only political entity that can guarantee benefits and protections to the entire public, whereas state and local governments are limited by their jurisdictions and have fewer resources in comparison to the national government.

The above findings suggest citizens are conflicted about government power. On the one hand, most distrust the national government and want it reduced in size; on the other hand, they expect the most help from the federal government, think fondly of most government programs, services, and agencies, and oppose cuts to specific programs. These findings suggest Americans are really supportive of the federal government, despite their anti-government rhetoric. And most Americans reject the neoliberal political framework, which denigrates welfare programs aimed at the middle- and lower-classes, while being curiously silent about the billions in corporate welfare subsidies for the upper class and affluent that are included in federal budgets each year.[19]

Approaches to Federalism

Under federalism, conflict between states and the federal government is commonplace. State governors and legislators prefer generous grants from the federal government, but with few strings attached, to retain control over spending, while avoiding responsibility for unpopular taxes. Those advocating greater decentralization of power claim states are closer to the people, and can better represent the masses. But this claim is controversial at best, considering that Congressional Senators and Representatives also represent specific geographic localities.

A drawback of freeing states from national regulations is that state empowerment means the federal government is unable to provide common benefits and set uniform standards for behavior. For example, if one leaves regulation of corporate fossil fuel, automotive, and other polluters to states, there will be many different regulatory standards. Some states will choose higher environmental standards, others lower ones. But the standards will not be uniform as they would if regulatory power resided with the federal government. The same issue arises with welfare programs. If Social Security and Medicare, for example, were left to state governments, some states would establish more generous benefits, while others, lacking the financial capacity or political will, would spend less, if anything. If Americans reject a neoliberal system that serves corporate and upper-class interests, while neglecting the masses, then setting federal standards for welfare benefits and corporate regulations are the most effective way to reduce corporate power, while protecting the masses.

Over the last century, the federal government has increasingly asserted itself over states. Despite Americans' attacks on government, growing national power has benefitted from strong public support, at least with regard to the specific programs that benefit the people. An empowered federal government can provide minimum guaranteed benefits to all regarding welfare spending, public health and environmental regulations, worker protections, and other benefits. For example, all lower income Americans benefit from a minimum wage, regardless of the state in which they reside. Low income Americans are eligible for Medicaid benefits, food stamps, housing subsidies, and other benefits, regardless of the part of the country in which they live. Over the last hundred years, the federal government has become dramatically more democratic by providing for these basic interests in which the public relies and expects. The neoliberal turn, in which tax cuts for corporations and the wealthy are a growing priority, and social spending is under assault, represents a threat to representative government.

Federalism's Growth and Transformation

Growing federal power and enhanced representation of the masses often occurs during times of crisis and instability. These periods produce growing public demand for new forms of government protections and services. It is easy for Americans today to forget the government's long history of improving democratic representation considering the rise of anti-government rhetoric, and amid government's escalating commitment to dismantling popular social welfare programs for the middle class and poor. Many Americans suffer from political "amnesia," lacking historical narratives that recognize government's role in helping the people.[20]

Below I trace the historical process by which government power expanded over time, always in the name of empowering the masses, and at times explicitly done in the name of limiting and regulating the power of the upper class. Dramatic changes in our federal system occurred in five different eras: 1. The Civil War period; 2. The New Deal; 3. The Great Society; 4. New Federalism; and 5. Following the 2008 economic crisis.

The Civil War

The Civil War (1861–1865) was a crisis moment in American history. The nation was tearing itself apart over slavery. The Constitution failed to remedy this conflict, and it was unrealistic to expect a legal document to accomplish such a massive feat. Rather, the conflict was solved at the barrel of a gun, resulting in 1.1 million people dead or wounded.[21]

The Civil War centered on slavery and the preservation of the union, and ended with the elimination of states' "right" to protect slavery. As relevant to federalism, southern apologists—those who historically referred to the Civil War as the "war of northern aggression"—argued that this war was not primarily about slavery, but "states' rights." Historians reject this claim; the central conflicts in the Civil War were about whether slavery would be allowed to expand into western territories and news states admitted into the union, and whether slavery would be allowed to exist at all.[22] Abraham Lincoln opposed the extension of slavery into new states admitted into the union.[23] This opposition challenged slave owners' power in Congress, and the ability to ensure slavery's survival. Over time, and without the expansion of slavery, free states would gain enough votes in Congress to abolish slavery. Fear over the future of slavery and the perception that their "way of life" was under threat provided the impetus for southern states to secede.

But the Civil War also contained an economic dimension. The north was transforming into a modernized, industrial economy by the mid-to-late 1800s—one free of slave labor—which put it on a collision course with southern, agricultural slave states. A national abolition movement emerged in the years prior to the Civil War, pressuring the national government to end slavery.[24] On the one hand, the government's elimination of slavery stands as a historical example of growing federal accountability to the people—a majority of which lived in non-slave states and supported abolition.[25] On the other hand, the war also represents the federal government siding with one part of the upper-class industrial business interests in the north against another elite interest—slave owners.

As documented in historical studies, the Civil War and slave owners' opposition to abolition was not simply about racism, but also driven by their economic interest in perpetuating their wealth via the slave system.[26] Slavery's time in America was rapidly coming to a close by the early-1860s, in part because of growing domestic and foreign moral opposition, because of opposition from northern laborers who deplored the aristocratic wealth associated with southern slave owners, and because of the growing societal and economic divide between the north and south due to the rise of the industrial revolution in the north.[27] The foundation of northern wealth—the rise of modern industry—meant that northerners had no personal or selfish economic motive, unlike many southerners, to protect slavery. But the Civil War also had the effect of empowering northern industrial corporate interests. The industrial revolution, although in its early stages in the mid-1800s, quickly came to be dominated by wealthy business interests during the "gilded age" of the late-nineteenth and early-twentieth centuries. While Lincoln himself did not fight the Civil War in the name of enhancing corporate power, the war did have the effect of empowering northern industrial interests, which became the dominant economic force in the U.S. following the war.

The Civil War ended with the defeat of the secessionists and with the abolition of slavery. The Thirteenth Amendment eliminated slavery. The Fourteenth and Fifteenth Amendments guaranteed due process and equal protection to former slaves, and ensured them the right to vote. These basic protections represented serious threats to southern efforts to reinstitute white supremacy following the Civil War. However, the withdrawal of northern troops from southern states, coupled with the emergence of the "Jim Crow" system of segregation and discrimination, allowed southern whites to prevent former slaves from exercising political rights for nearly a century. African Americans were denied equal access to public accommodations by a segregation system applied to lunch counters, schools, bathrooms, and other spaces. They were assaulted, terrorized, and killed when they challenged segregation. Blacks were denied work opportunities and discriminated against in housing. They were prohibited from voting by literacy tests, poll taxes, and Grandfather clauses, the last of which allowed those whose grandfather was white to be exempted from the literacy test and poll tax. As previously discussed, the Fourteenth Amendment became a tool, not primarily for aiding black Americans in achieving equal rights, but for the corporate class to assert "personhood" powers via the courts. As the Supreme Court ruled in the 1896 case of *Plessy v. Ferguson*, segregation between blacks and whites was deemed "separate but equal," and equal rights for black Americans were denied until the rise of the civil rights movement in the 1950s and 1960s.

The New Deal

Many developments occurred between the Civil War and the early twentieth century concerning the growth of federal power. Anti-trust laws were introduced to rein in the power of monopoly corporations. A federal bureaucracy emerged, with agencies devoted to war planning, promoting worker rights, and promoting food and drug safety, among other activities. Congress established the Federal Reserve to limit volatility in investment banking and prevent radical swings in economic growth and decline. But it was not until the 1930s that the next major period of federal transformation occurred—the New Deal. This reform period extended from 1933 to 1938, under the leadership of Democratic President Franklin Roosevelt.

The New Deal was a series of legislative initiatives that regulated Wall Street and business interests, protected workers, and introduced basic welfare protections. The New Deal was a response to the Great Depression, the most severe period of economic hardship in U.S. history. Following the stock market collapse of 1929, unemployment increased from less than five percent to nearly one quarter of the public, creating tremendous strain. Deteriorating economic conditions produced social instability for poor and middle-class Americans, as labor strikes and urban riots for food demonstrated the dangers of government inaction in light of mass poverty and desperation.[28] Roosevelt was elected by promising he would take steps to promote economic recovery. The New Deal is relevant to federalism in that state and local governments were quickly overwhelmed by the growth in poverty during this crisis period. They were unable by themselves to deal with the growing needs of citizens, prompting greater pressure on the federal government. Acting on growing public demands for action, the FDR administration introduced a new regime of regulations on the corporate class, while institutionalizing various protections for working-class Americans.

The name "New Deal" came directly from Roosevelt's pledge to the people in a 1932 campaign speech, in which he promised government would make a concerted effort to address the needs of the people, and citizens in return would restore their faith in government. Roosevelt proclaimed: "Throughout the nation men and women, forgotten in the political philosophy of the government, look to us here for guidance and for more equitable opportunity to share in the distribution of national wealth . . . I pledge myself to a new deal for the American people. This is more than a political campaign. It is a call to arms."[29] Roosevelt

Image 3.1. The Great Depression.

called not only for citizens to vote him into office, "but to win in this crusade to restore America to its own people."[30] His reference to economic inequality was a clear recognition of the push by the federal government to address the growing divide between the upper class and the rest of the country.

The New Deal focused on regulating Wall Street and its destructive, speculative investment practices. New Deal reforms included the creation of the Federal Deposit Insurance Corporation (FDIC), Securities and Exchange Commission (SEC), the National Industrial Recovery Act (NIRA), and the Glass-Steagall Act. The FDIC protects individuals' bank accounts, as much as $250,000 per account, per bank. It was created to help stabilize the banking system during the Great Depression. "Bank runs" were a danger at the time, since individual accounts were not insured by the federal government. A "bank run," refers to the process whereby economic instability prompts account holders to withdraw their funds, seeking to secure their money prior to a potential bank collapse. The problem with bank runs is they virtually guarantee a bank collapse, and that people will *not* get their money when individuals act in mass to withdraw their money during crisis periods. Government stabilization of banking suggested that the concern of the New Deal was not only with aiding the needy. Restoring confidence in capitalism was obviously a huge boon for investors and the corporate class.

The New Deal was also introduced to deal with the problem of speculative investment on Wall Street. With Wall Street banks' extension of credit to the masses, Americans were able to "invest" on a margin, putting down 10 percent of a stock purchase, with another 90 percent on loan from the bank. This system of easy credit led to rapid growth in debt and vastly inflated stock market prices, collapsed by 1929. To restore economic stability, the Securities and Exchange Commission (SEC) was created in 1934 to regulate Wall Street investing, curb investor speculation, and prevent manipulation of stocks. The SEC was needed to curb the worst speculative practices on Wall Street, such as "churning" and "painting the tape." Churning was the practice whereby investment brokers use a client's account to excessively buy and sell stocks in a short period of time, artificially inflating demand and price. "Painting the tape" involved a pool of investors secretly agreeing to repeatedly buy and sell a stock, so it would appear to unsuspecting investors that a stock was in high demand. The rising stock value allowed the original pool of investors to sell off stock at a profit before it collapsed. Both practices were made illegal by the SEC. While Wall Street opposed regulation, it also had a positive effect on the marketplace by cracking down on dangerous speculative investments.[31]

Additionally, the Glass Steagall Act required a legal separation between traditional banks and riskier investment banks to ensure that the latter would not destroy the entire economy if they failed. Glass Steagall was passed to protect Americans from banks that might become "too big to fail," with their collapse threatening macro-economic instability. In monopoly capitalism, a very small number of banks gain tremendous control over national finances, endangering the entire system. Government may be forced to bail these corporations out when they fail, short of risking the collapse of banking services. With Glass Steagall, the separation of different forms of banking protected the economy against a small number of banks becoming too big to fail. This reform was opposed by investors in the corporate class, but served an important function in stabilizing corporate capitalism and preventing future economic crashes due to speculation.

The New Deal also introduced basic social welfare and worker protections. In the housing sector, the Home Owners' Loan Corporation (HOLC) and the Federal Housing Administration (FHA) were created. The HOLC was instituted to purchase mortgages for working and poor families in danger of losing homes, to help them avoid foreclosure, and to refinance at more favorable rates. The FHA regulated interest rates and mortgage terms, thereby expanding the pool of home buyers and stabilizing the housing market. Public works projects greatly aided unemployed Americans, putting to work individuals building schools, playgrounds, hospitals, national parks, dams, roads, and bridges.[32] At their height during the 1930s, organizations like the Public Works Administration, Civil Works Administration, and the Works Progress Administration (WPA) employed millions.[33] For example, at its height in 1938, the WPA employed 3.3 million people, or a third of all unemployed Americans.[34] These programs were vital for providing a modicum of stability to poor and working-class families.

The New Deal was defined by a concern for aiding the needy via social welfare. The Social Security program, created in 1935, guaranteed elderly Americans a retirement check into old age. This safety net ensured those who worked for decades were not left without a means of sustenance when they could no longer work. The program was so popular it was expanded in later years to cover cost-of-living adjustments, to provide for more generous monthly benefits, and to cover disabled citizens. Under the New Deal, the government also created a cash subsidies program for poor families, "Aid to Families with Dependent Children," as part of the Social Security Act. The program was designed to help poor children, who through no fault of their own, were unable to fulfill basic needs. Finally, the New Deal provided food subsidies to the poor as part of the Agricultural Adjustment Act (1933), which was formalized into a temporary food stamps program in 1939. These programs served as a safety net for the lower class during times of desperation and need.

The final pillar of the New Deal was the push to protect American workers, manifested in the National Labor Relations Act (NLRA) of 1935 and the Fair

Labor Standards Act (FLSA) of 1938. The NLRA protected the right of workers to form labor unions, to engage in collective bargaining for benefits and pay, to file unfair labor practice complaints against employers, and to go on strike if collective bargaining efforts failed. The act also made it illegal to fire workers for union activities. Due to increased protections for worker organizing, unionization grew significantly in the following years, as seen in figure 3.1. The middle-class grew significantly too, as working Americans used collective bargaining to push for better wages and benefits. The FLSA also established a national minimum wage. It created the maximum 45-hour work week, as well as guarantees for "time-and-a-half" pay in specific occupational areas, and prohibited child labor. In sum, government was instrumental in limiting oppressive working conditions that had been created and supported by the corporate business class in the early twentieth-century. Many of these protections remained with American workers over the next century.

The New Deal represented a major change in American politics. It addressed the failings of the marketplace, stabilizing and regulating the economy after the 1929 economic crash, and reining in the unchecked power of elites in the corporate class. It provided national welfare guarantees and protections to the elderly, poor, unemployed, and American workers. Its many successes are still with us today, as seen in the continued popularity of the welfare state.

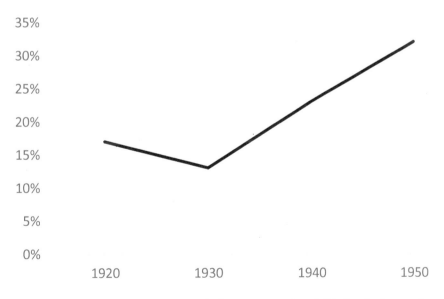

Figure 3.1. Unionization Rate (% of all Non-Agricultural Workers). Source: Leo Troy, "Trade Union Membership: 1897–1962," *National Bureau of Economic Research*, 1965: 1–10.

THE GREAT SOCIETY

While the crisis of the 1930s was a crumbling economy, the cause of social instability in the 1960s was the growing conflict over race relations, fed by the civil rights movement and the racist backlash against it. Denied legal protections since the end of the Civil War, black Americans organized during the 1950s and 1960s to demand their rights. The protests were successful in pressuring the federal government to introduce a series of reforms between 1964 and 1965, aimed at fighting poverty, promoting racial equality, aiding the elderly, and assisting lower-class whites and poor people of color.

Growing federal concern with racial inequality was in large part a response to protests over the denial of economic opportunities for minorities. The Civil Rights Movement pressured government to address the problem of poverty, in addition to tackling segregation in public facilities and accommodations. The movement also succeeded in transforming American culture, by creating a political climate that rejected racial prejudice. These changes speak positively to the growth in government powers in pursuit of democracy and empowerment of the disadvantaged.

Democratic President Lyndon Johnson coined the term "Great Society" in 1964. In his May speech in Ann Arbor, Michigan, Johnson spoke of the need to build a society that was not merely "rich" or "powerful," but a "great society" embracing the principle that prosperity is built "on abundance and liberty for all," and a demand to "an end to poverty and racial injustice." Johnson spoke of the problem of inequality in funding education: "poverty must not be a bar to learning, and learning must offer an escape from poverty." Johnson wanted "to give every citizen an escape from the crushing weight of poverty."[35] His declaration of a "War on Poverty" informed his vision of a Great Society, and spoke to his commitment to enhancing federal powers and responsibilities, to the benefit of the lower class, people of color, and others in need.

The Great Society was a federalist matter for two reasons. First, it produced tremendous conflict between the federal and state governments over equal rights for black Americans. Second, the War on Poverty required coordination between the federal and state governments in the delivery of welfare programs for the needy and poor. The 1960s represented another crisis period in American politics, with the federal government stepping forward to improve democratic representation and fulfill the demands of minorities left behind in the postwar, "golden age" of American capitalism. At a time when middle-class incomes were at their highest in a century and economic growth was far stronger than in later decades, the federal government became increasingly interested in what it could do to aid the disadvantaged in a time of plenty.

Image 3.2. Lyndon B. Johnson, 36th U.S. President.

If the New Deal established bedrock protections for workers and the poor, the Great Society further institutionalized protections for the disadvantaged. Front and center was Johnson's civil rights platform, including the Civil Rights and Voting Rights Acts of 1964 and 1965, which prohibited federal, state, or local governments, businesses, and individuals from discriminating against minorities in public facilities and accommodations, in occupations, and in voting. But the Fourteenth and Fifteenth Amendments already guaranteed equal protection under law and the right to vote, so what made the Great Society legislation different? The main divergence between the post-Civil War amendments and the Great Society was that the latter included a Congressional and executive commitment to promote equal rights by punishing non-compliant states. Minorities denied equal rights had standing under both laws to sue state and local governments in order to achieve their rights, but more importantly, the federal government was willing to monitor state polling facilities for voting violations, and deny states federal grants due to violations of civil rights law.

The Great Society included numerous anti-poverty initiatives. Amending the Social Security Act of 1935, the Social Security Act of 1965 created two national healthcare programs: Medicaid (health insurance for the poor) and

Medicare (health insurance for the elderly). Other welfare initiatives included the Higher Education Act of 1965, which allocated funding for student loans to make attending college more affordable, and the Elementary and Secondary Education Act of 1965, which allotted federal funds to improve elementary and secondary educational performance in poor minority communities. The act also created the Head Start program, providing additional education assistance to poor families via childhood literacy programs, nutrition and health aid, and funds for the popular "Sesame Street" television education program.

Other Great Society programs also aimed to help disadvantaged and lower-class citizens. The food stamps program became permanent with the Food Stamp Act of 1964. Although it is intended merely as supplemental aid for families, the program plays a vital role in aiding poor and working Americans. Another Great Society initiative was the Housing and Urban Development Act of 1965, which created the Department of Housing and Urban Development for providing housing subsidies for the poor. The Economic Opportunity Act of 1964 provided federal funds for adult basic education and vocational job training to assist poorer Americans in developing marketable job skills. The law also created the Community Action Program, which allocated funds to assist the urban poor in providing various community services that were to be determined by individual communities' demands. Great Society programs cut poverty nearly in half by the early 1970s.

New Federalism

New federalism refers to a form of federalism emphasizing the importance of "devolution"—or the reduction of federal authority over states. It is generally associated with the rise of neoliberal governance, as seen in declining notions that the federal government has an ethical or moral responsibility to aid the poor and disadvantaged. The language of New Federalism was originally embraced by the Nixon administration, but Americans did not see cuts in federal aid to states until the 1980s and 1990s with the Reagan and Clinton presidencies. New Federalism represented a step back for the federal government, as it took on fewer powers and responsibilities in providing for social benefits to needy populations. Unsurprisingly, this theory gained traction during a period that was *not* associated with crisis. Without facing mass public demands for greater assistance, the Reagan administration reduced federal funding for grants to state governments. It reduced funding for Medicaid, and cut aid to cities, public housing funding, transportation funds, and food stamp benefits. The loss of federal aid dollars to state and local governments was likely due to two factors: 1. The growth of conservative "free market" ideology in government which celebrated "personal responsibility" for the poor, as reflected in Reagan's support for reducing size of government; and 2. A political calculation, with spending cuts directed toward non-Republican voters—particularly poor urban minorities, which benefitted disproportionately from programs like Medicaid, food stamps, and public housing.

Government's commitment to New Federalism continued under Bill Clinton. One of his most notable actions as president was terminating the welfare program, Aid to Families with Dependent Children (AFDC), in 1996. Through the Personal Responsibility and Work Opportunity Act, Clinton converted AFDC into Temporary Assistance to Needy Families (TANF), a federal block grant program granting maximum power to states to choose benefit and eligibility levels for recipients. The shift to TANF allowed states to significantly cut benefits in subsequent years, as they pushed many poor Americans off the welfare rolls.[36]

Conservatives defended New Federalism because it allowed them to reduce the responsibilities of the federal government toward the needy. Reagan claimed: "government is not the solution to your problems, government is the problem."[37] Similarly, Clinton announced when he terminated AFDC that he was "ending welfare as we know it" and that "the era of big government is over."[38] Such claims, however, were inaccurate. While Clinton promoted a balanced budget, the Reagan administration dramatically increased the government deficit due to a combination of large tax cuts for the wealthy and a massive increase in military spending. Reagan was also not "small government" in his economic policy, as he was one of the most protectionist presidents in history. Reagan strengthened U.S. tariffs (taxes) on foreign goods, against principles of free trade. When one speaks of "small government" and the Reagan administration, that description only reflects his position toward the lower class and poor. His agenda was a boon for wealthy upper-class interests, and represented an active government intervention on their behalf.

The 2008 Economic Crisis

A major period of instability emerged following the 2008 economic crash. This crisis led to another wave of government welfare spending. Government initiatives included: 1. The 2009 economic stimulus; and 2. The 2010 "Affordable Care Act," commonly known as "Obamacare." Both related directly to federalism. The stimulus included federal efforts to supplement state budgets at a time when states faced massive deficits. The health care reform was sold as a means of aiding tens of millions of uninsured Americans in a time of growing economic insecurity.

The stimulus was over $800 billion in spending allocated to jump starting the U.S. economy following the 2008 housing market crash and subsequent recession. With the economy quickly contracting, credit markets frozen, unemployment growing, and states facing major budget shortfalls, the federal government sought to ensure economic stability and recovery. The stimulus included various programs to aid citizens and states: payroll tax cuts, money for public works programs and infrastructure projects, financial aid to states to assist them in funding educational institutions and to fill budget shortfalls, and funding for renewable energy research, among other projects. States were happy to accept federal funds, if the alternative was unpopular spending cuts. States' acceptance of federal aid is an example of "cooperative federalism." When states are not worried about the national government creating coercive rules that truncate their authority, it is easier to cooperate with federally-funded initiatives. The stimulus demonstrated that, during times of crisis, Americans still looked to the national government to provide aid to the masses and the needy.

Obamacare committed the federal government to the most significant health care reform in 45 years. As previously discussed, the law required each state to set up a health insurance exchange where private insurance policies could be bought and sold, and required all 50 states to accept additional federal funds for expanding Medicaid to cover individuals with incomes up to 133 percent of the poverty line, compared to the previous 100 percent threshold.

Coercive federalism refers to the practice whereby the federal government compels states into action through increased regulations and mandates. Federal funds may be removed in the case of state non-compliance with federal mandates. This was a central point of contention in the conflict over Obamacare, since refusal to accept Medicaid expansion funds meant states would see all their Medicaid funds cut. The Supreme Court ruled the federal threat to remove all Medicaid funds was unduly coercive; the Medicaid expansion under Obamacare was legally acceptable, but states had to participate voluntarily. The requirement that states set up health care exchanges was certainly coercive, but many states refused to set up exchanges, forcing the national government to offer insurance to consumers directly through the federal exchange.

Obamacare represented a significant government intervention in aiding lower-, middle-, and upper-class Americans. It expanded Medicaid access for many poor Americans. It provided taxpayer subsidies to middle-class families who purchased insurance on an exchange. And it was a financial boon for health insurance companies, which benefitted from tens of millions of new customers. Gallup polling data summarized in figure 3.2 demonstrates that the uninsured rate among American adults fell dramatically under Obamacare, despite the cost of health continuing to rise during the late 2000s and early-to-mid 2010s.[39] The growing cost was not surprising, however, since the law never introduced regulations to limit the growth in health insurance premium, out-of-pocket, and deductible costs.

Whatever one thought of Obamacare, the law meant the growth in federal authority and responsibility in providing for the health care needs of millions. It

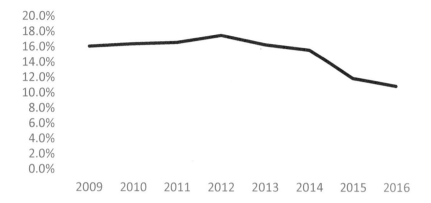

Figure 3.2: Obamacare and Insurance Coverage (% of Adults Uninsured). Sources: Zac Auter, "U.S. Uninsured Rate Holds at Low of 10.9% in Fourth Quarter," *Gallup*, January 9, 2017, http://www.gallup.com/poll/201641/uninsured-rate-holds-low-fourth-quarter.aspx; Jenna Levy, "In U.S., Uninsured Rate Dips to 11.9% in the First Quarter," *Gallup*, April 13, 2015, http://www.gallup.com/poll/182348/uninsured-rate-dips-first-quarter.aspx

was an unprecedented act of corporate welfare for the upper class, guaranteeing millions of new clients to health insurers and doing nothing to regulate what insurers, doctors, and hospitals could charge for care. The political preferences pursued by both parties on health care were symptomatic of a neoliberal turn in American politics. Republicans sought to repeal the law, meaning large tax cuts for upper-class Americans, and declining federal responsibility for aiding the middle class and poor. Democrats sought to work within the confines of a marketplace characterized by skyrocketing health care costs and minimal federal efforts to regulate the cost of care, although Obamacare did grant significant concessions to the mass public by expanding Medicaid and aiding citizens in purchasing health insurance.

Conclusion

This chapter argued that growing federal power is the product of increased public demands for goods, services, and a desire for improved democratic representation. Neoliberal attacks on federal programs that aid the many have grown in recent decades, as both political parties shift toward representing the corporate class and the wealthy. Still, the federal government is far more committed to aiding the middle class, poor, and disadvantaged today than it was a century ago. Popular struggles and pressures were vital in pushing the national government to improve democratic representation by increasing the number of programs that provide economic and legal benefits to working Americans and the poor. With growing public pressure, the federal government could again prioritize such programs in an effort to combat the rise of economic inequality in the United States.

Chapter 4

Interest Groups and the
Upper-Class Perversion of Political Power

In the summer of 2017, the Republican Party controlled both chambers of Congress and the White House, and sought to fulfill a long-standing promise to its voters to repeal Obamacare. The House of Representatives had voted dozens of times to repeal the law in the years prior to 2017, but there was no chance of this happening so long as Barack Obama was president.[1] Perhaps unexpectedly for many Republicans, a strong grassroots resistance to the repeal emerged by early-to-mid year, with many middle-class and poorer Americans angry that the repeal would terminate their insurance plans purchased on the federal or state health care exchanges, or that the proposed repeal of Obama's Medicaid expansion would take away their health care entirely. These concerns were well-founded, considering that the non-partisan Congressional Budget Office estimated that competing Senate and House versions of a repeal, even though they included replacement plans, would result in 22 to 24 million Americans losing their insurance.[2]

Intense grassroots pressure was applied against Congressional Republicans to derail efforts to repeal Obamacare, with "eroding enthusiasm" from constituents suggesting there could be serious electoral repercussions if a repeal was passed. As *The New York Times* reported: "Republican opposition to the repeal bill was led mainly by senators from states that have expanded their Medicaid programs under the Affordable Care Act, providing coverage to millions of people who had been uninsured. Now senators from largely rural states, where hospitals stand to lose millions of dollars under the bill, are expressing concerns."[3] Protests across the nation, coupled with angry constituent calls to members of Congress and visible anger at town hall meetings, meant significant pressure on Republicans not to pass legislation that would eliminate insurance for tens of millions of people.[4]

The Republican repeal effort failed. Although the House of Representatives passed a repeal bill in early 2017, the Senate was more divided. Nine Republicans voted against repeal and replace, and for most of these Senators, public pressure played a significant role in fueling their "nay" votes.[5] Reasons for opposing the bill were numerous. Senators Susan Collins, Dean Heller, and Susan Murkowski cited constituent pressures and concerns that the cuts to Medicaid would adversely affect poor residents of their states.[6] Senators Jerry Moran and Mike Lee cited concerns with the Republican replacement plan, criticizing it for not doing enough to help constituents lower their health care premiums.[7] Senators John McCain and Lindsey Graham felt the repeal plan would introduce more instability to the U.S. health care market, hurting their constituents and the public-at-large.[8] Senator Tom Cotton announced that he opposed a repeal and replacement effort, preferring to wait on a replacement plan until after the election, suggesting he was concerned about an electoral backlash against repeal.[9] Senator Bob Corker criticized the repeal and replacement bill for cutting taxes on wealthier, upper-class Americans earning over $250,000 a year, while cutting Medicaid benefits for his poor constituents. The "nay" votes from these Senators were enough to derail Republican health care reform.[10] Despite the Democratic Party being too weak to mount an effective resistance campaign on its own, citizens were able to impact the health care vote outcome. Seven of the eight Republican Senators who voted against repeal and replace originally voted in favor of repeal in late-2015, under a previous piece of legislation passed in the Senate.[11] This outcome speaks to the independent power of the public, when effectively mobilized, in impacting the political process.

Public opinion was largely split on Obamacare in late 2015, although Obama himself was committed while in office to vetoing any Republican repeal effort. But by 2017, there was no longer any institutional check on the repeal campaign from Democrats. Recognizing the very real threat to Obamacare, Americans began to shift their attitudes in opposition to repeal, and in favor of preserving health care benefits allocated under the law. While public disapproval of Obamacare reached a high of 55 percent in 2014, it had fallen down to 43 percent by 2017. Although public approval of the law reached a low of 35 percent in 2010, 54 percent supported Obamacare by 2017.[12] These numbers, when coupled with mounting public pressure, suggest a serious impact of public opinion on Congress. Republican Senators who philosophically favored repealing Obamacare were forced to support the law due to the fear of negative electoral consequences. Although Republicans eventually repealed the federal mandate that individuals purchase health insurance, taxpayer subsidies for state insurance exchanges continued under President Trump, providing significant aid to Americans in securing health care.[13]

Interest Groups and Political Power

A wide array of citizens' groups joined together to pressure Congressional Republicans to oppose repealing Obamacare.[14] And interest groups have long played a significant role in influencing Americans politics. Interest groups seek to exercise power over government, although there has long been debate about how effective citizens' groups are at doing this, in comparison to interest groups that represent the wealthy and the upper class. Despite the significant victories of citizens and social movements in politics—as the story about Obamacare suggests—the evidence throughout this chapter suggests that corporations and the upper class hold a consistent advantage over the public regarding public policy outcomes.

Lobbying

Interest groups make use of different lobbying strategies. In political science, it is common to refer to three different lobbying strategies: inside lobbying, outside lobbying, and mixed lobbying.[15] Inside lobbying tactics are typically engaged in by the select few, including wealthier Americans, corporate lobbies, and other members of the upper class seeking to influence government policy. These tactics include: campaign donations, election ad spending, meeting face-to-face with officials, corporate litigation against government regulations, and testifying before Congress to influence legislative deliberation. These strategies are "inside" because they are engaged in by small numbers of wealthy individuals *within* the halls of power.

One example of inside lobbying and the prominence of the corporate classes' political power involved Enron. One of the country's largest energy corporations in the 1990s, Enron was the biggest donor to the George W. Bush presidential campaign in 2000.[16] Between the early-1990s and mid-2000s, the company gave nearly $2 million in donations to Bush during his time as Texas governor and president.[17] What sort of influence could a corporation have with such large donations? Critics argued Enron unduly influenced national energy policy with its donations.[18] In the first few months of 2001, numerous fossil fuel companies met with the Bush administration, providing recommendations for how to structure national energy policy. Vice President Dick Cheney set up an Energy Task Force to hear all recommendations, and Enron executives, among other energy companies, played a dominant role in guiding the meetings.[19] The Bush administration kept the meeting details classified for six years. The administration's energy policy, however, was a different matter. It rejected environmentalists' concerns. President Bush killed the Kyoto Protocol, which had committed the U.S. to reducing fossil fuel emissions and to combating global warming. The administration denied global warming was real, although it later announced that humankind needed to adapt to this warming, rather than prevent it.[20]

Wall Street's close ties to President Obama also appeared relevant to inside lobbying. Goldman Sachs investment bank's Political Action Committee

(PAC) was one of the largest donors to Obama's 2008 campaign, giving nearly $1 million in donations, and receiving $10 billion in bailout funds from the federal government in late-2008.[21] Obama sat down with members of Congress and President Bush, negotiating a Wall Street bailout. It was easy for many to conclude that Goldman Sachs exchanged campaign contributions for bailout funds. Political scientists refer to this claim—that public officials are bought and sold like products—as "clientelism."[22]

In contrast to inside lobbying, outside lobbying strategies are often used by those lacking formal contacts within government. These individuals are on the outside looking in at the policy process, and often cannot afford lobbyists, but want government to represent their interests. Their strategies include: demonstrations, rallies, circulating petitions to pressure political officials, contacting one's legislators, and civil disobedience (non-violently opposing laws one sees as immoral). Outside lobbying strategies are engaged in by those who seek public and media attention for their causes in an effort to influence government indirectly via transforming American culture and values. These individuals are often members of the middle- or lower-class, and are frustrated by their apparent lack of direct influence in the halls of power in Washington.

One example of citizens engaged in outside lobbying was Occupy Wall Street. This social movement formed in late-2011 in Zuccotti Park, New York City, and quickly spread to other cities. The protesters were young and angry about many issues, including inequality in the U.S., economic stagnation that had threatened work opportunities for the young, record student loan debt, and Wall Street greed.[23] Occupy Wall Street protesters never developed a formal platform for political change, but they did seek to transform American culture by helping develop a critical class consciousness in which the public would begin to challenge the pro-corporate status quo in American politics. It set up encampments in New York City and elsewhere, organized demonstrations, and engaged in mass outreach in seeking to build public support.

Outside lobbying is not always used by the disadvantaged. It is at times utilized by upper-class interests as a means of molding public opinion. These campaigns, in which business interests lobby public opinion through the media, are at times quite successful. For example, historians have documented how fossil fuel corporations lobbied the public by seeking to undermine scientific research documenting the dangers of climate change, with such efforts tracing back decades. Tobacco companies pursued a similar strategy during the twentieth century, when they sought to obscure the dangers of smoking. These campaigns sowed public doubt and confusion, thereby stifling government regulations of the tobacco and fossil fuel industries.[24]

Whether inside or outside lobbying is more successful in influencing politics depends on one's goals. If one seeks to avoid critical attention, like Enron, inside lobbying allows corporate interests to seek policy change, while avoiding the spotlight. But if one seeks to transform the entire culture of a country, and as a result indirectly influence the political process, outside lobbying is essential. Campaign donations, meeting with legislators, litigation in court, and other inside lobbying strategies do not transform popular values. To accomplish this goal, one must engage in protest, demonstrations, and other forms of media-community outreach.

Mixed lobbying involves inside and outside strategies. Some groups are not completely elitist or mass-based. For example, the Tea Party protests of 2010 contained elements of citizen and elite participation. On the citizen side, conservative Americans attended demonstrations demanding lower taxes, expressing anger over the government's Wall Street bailout, voicing displeasure with welfare programs benefitting the poor, and opposing Obamacare—which was framed as a "government takeover" of health care.[25]

Tea Party activists claimed to be part of a grassroots uprising against oppressive government, and received heavy news coverage. But these protests fed into the 2010 midterm congressional elections, with "Tea Party" Republican candidates claiming a public mandate against government overreach. Many of these candidates were elected to office, providing the Tea Party an insider position to influence government. After all, what could be more inside than being a member of Congress? The Tea Party, through inside and outside lobbying strategies, had a significant impact on politics, pulling the country in a conservative direction. The movement also represented the interests of the upper class, with its citizen supporters and members of Congress supporting an extension of the Bush tax cuts, which largely benefitted the top 20 percent of income earners, while supporting cuts in welfare benefits for the lower class and poor.[26]

Citizen Movements in Rebellion

The rise of contemporary social movements suggests escalating public anger against a political system dominated by the corporate class and the wealthy. Some examples of these movements, explored below, include the "Fight for $15," the environmental movement, and the anti-Trump protests.

The "Fight for $15" movement emerged in the early-2010s, protesting working conditions in the U.S. service sector. Demonstrators focused on Wal-Mart, McDonalds, and other retailers, seeking to combat declining worker pay.[27] The U.S. minimum wage declined from its highest value in 1968 of $11.17 an hour in inflation-adjusted 2017 dollars, compared to the 2017 value of $7.25—a 35 percent reduction over 40 years. "Fight for $15" sought to reverse this decline via the establishment of a living wage that allows workers to pay for their basic needs.

Service worker protests received national attention. USA *Today* reported: "thousands of low-paid workers and their supporters marched in 190 cities across the nation" in December 2014, "calling for [a] $15 an hour [minimum wage] . . . the protests have focused on fast-food and retail chains, but workers in other low-paying jobs joined the action in 35 states."[28] Protests included worker walkouts and silent strikes during work hours, demonstrations demanding higher wages, and lobbying of state and local governments for a higher service worker pay. In November 2016, the U.S. saw the largest protests yet in the "Fight for $15," with demonstrations across "hundreds of cities" including, New York, Chicago, Los Angeles, and others.[29] Such protests continued in later years as well.[30]

Worker protests came at a time when employers such as Wal-Mart and McDonalds were paying such poor wages that their workers qualified for billions a year in welfare benefits.[31] The plight of workers is known to employers like McDonalds. As a 2013 *Bloomberg* report found, the company was running a "McResource" hotline providing advice to employees that they enroll in state and local welfare programs to supplement their low salaries.[32] McDonalds also provided a "monthly budget," suggesting employees earn another $955 through a "second job," since the company did not pay the income necessary for workers to pay their bills.[33]

The service worker movement challenges the alleged inevitability of low wages, in which corporate interests seek higher profits at the expense of paying a living wage. It demonstrates that a growing number of Americans have joined together to fight the increasingly upper-class bias in U.S. politics, which did not raise the minimum wage at all during the 2010s. Public patience is waning with a political system that shows little concern with the well-being of those at the bottom of the income distribution. In the mid-2010s, most Americans—73 percent—supported increasing the minimum wage to more than $10.10 an hour, and 59 percent support a $12 an hour minimum wage.[34] And nearly six-in-ten supported a $15 minimum wage when asked in 2016, during Democratic candidate Bernie Sanders's presidential primary run (Sanders himself supported a $15 minimum wage).[35]

The growth of inequality and the decline of workers' wages contradicts everything Americans are told about how "working hard" leads to prosperity.[36] Labor productivity among American service workers grew significantly in recent decades, as did the wealth of the upper class via increased corporate profits and executive pay.[37] But working families put in a greater number of work hours in the post-2000 era compared to in earlier decades, despite stagnating family incomes.[38] Now service workers are placing greater pressure on government to improve the wages of the working poor.

Protester pressure helped create a political environment increasingly receptive to raising low-wage workers' pay. Both New York and California announced they would raise their minimum wages to $15 an hour by 2018 and 2022, respectively. Arizona, Colorado, and Maine also passed initiatives in 2016 to raise their minimum wage to $12 by 2020, while Washington passed legislation to raise their wage to $13 by 2020.[39] In 2015, 20 states raised their minimum wage, compared to 13 states in 2016, and 19 states in 2017.[40] This represents a dramatic increase since the early 2000s, when five to six states raised their minimum wage, on average, per year. "The Fight for $15" demonstrates the impact that citizen's movements can have—especially in more liberal states—on raising the living standards for the working poor, and it speaks to the power of the people to challenge the privileges of the corporate class in politics.[41]

Environmentalists have also risen up against business power in politics—in this case by corporate polluter-fossil fuel interests. The environmental movement has existed for decades, although environmentalists are more active today than at any other time on the issue of global warming. Groups such as "350.org" demand dramatic reductions in CO_2 emissions. The group's name is in reference to the maximum level of carbon dioxide in the atmosphere—350 parts per mission—that scientists warned could build up, beyond which the globe would suffer significant ecological consequences. The level of global CO_2 reached over 400 parts per million as of mid-2015, making "350.org's" mission even more pressing.[42]

During the 2010s, environmental activism grew significantly. In September 2014, activists across the world from Melbourne to Manhattan came together to draw attention to climate change. The *Guardian* reported: "more than 300,000 marchers flooded the streets of New York," in "the largest climate change march in history, vaulting the environmental threat to the top of the global agenda."[43] Activists demand the U.S. and other countries take swift action to avert the worst effects of global warming, including increased droughts, flooding, famine, mass starvation, rising temperatures, intensified heat waves, and expansive forest fires.

The Intergovernmental Panel on Climate Change (IPCC)—comprised of climatologists across the planet—warns that bold steps are needed to reduce the growth in greenhouse gases. Scientific estimates predict global temperatures could increase by three to four degrees Celsius by 2100 if developing and developed countries do not take further action.[44] To keep from crossing a two-degree Celsius threshold, greenhouse gas emissions must fall by 70 percent by 2050, and to zero by 2100.[45] Despite the U.S. under Obama introducing regulations to increase automobile fuel efficiency and to reduce greenhouse gas emissions by 30 percent for coal burning power plants by 2030, the U.S. and other countries are nowhere near reaching the prescribed 70 percent cut in emissions. President Trump's insistence that climate change is not real, and that no action need be taken at all, means the U.S. took no action at all on the climate.[46] To the delight of fossil-fuel business interests, the president provoked an international outcry following his announcement that the U.S. was pulling out of the Paris Accord, which set international standards for limiting further growth in global CO_2 emissions. But the refusal to address the mounting problem of warming temperatures went beyond simply serving the interests of fossil fuel corporations. National survey data also show that fighting climate change is an extremely low priority for the top one percent of wealth-holders, not just for fossil fuel interests. The wealthy would prefer government focus on other issues such as budget deficits, unemployment, education reform, terrorism, and energy politics, not on climate change.[47]

American scientists and their counterparts in other countries are among the leaders of the environmental movement, directing government resources and public attention to the growing menace of climate change. They criticize U.S. officials for their willful ignorance regarding the dangers of mounting global CO_2 emissions. Their efforts to address global warming are based on the overwhelming scientific consensus that it is occurring and due primarily to human activities.[48] Throughout American history, government catered to fossil fuel interests, endangering public safety in the face of a steadily warming planet. And the corporate class has worked to benefit the automobile, coal, and oil industries, with political leaders empowering them to externalize the effects of their pollution on the rest of the population and world. By directing public attention toward climate change, environmentalists are taking a stand against the business interests that for so long have dominated American politics.

Finally, the anti-Trump protests occurred in a pivotal moment in American politics. Never in history had so many protested a president so soon into his office.[49] Multiple waves of protests occurred against Trump within his first year in office. One immediately followed his electoral victory, with protests in major cities such as New York, Los Angeles, San Francisco, and Philadelphia, among others.[50] A subsequent wave of protests occurred during Trump's inauguration weekend, across many cities, with millions challenging the legitimacy of the new president.[51] The January inauguration protests suggested the opposition to Trump had grown into a mass national movement. Other protests throughout the year centered on Trump's travel ban against Muslim-majority countries, protests of his refusal to release his tax returns, protests against his administration's contempt for science, and opposition to Trump and the Republican Party's efforts to repeal Obamacare.[52]

Trump's immigration ban against Muslim-majority nations represented a milestone moment in his presidency. Although he claimed the ban was not directed against Muslims, this assertion was belied by his long-standing calls to ban Muslims, and the admission from Trump's advisor Rudy Giuliani that the intent of the ban was to discriminate against Muslims, while simultaneously claiming that the ban had nothing to do with religion.[53]

Image 4.1. The Women's March on Washington D.C., January 22, 2017.

Image 4.2. The Women's March on Washington D.C., January 22, 2017.

Trump's Muslim ban was quickly challenged in the federal courts, which initially ruled that it violated basic constitutional freedoms such as due process and equal protection under law, while failing to present any compelling evidence of a terror threat from the countries banned.[54] However, by mid-2018, the Supreme Court had overruled lower court rulings, allowing the ban to move forward.[55]

Protests of Trump did little to faze the president or deter him from his reactionary social policies. But the mounting protests did overlap with a significant decline in public support for the president. Trump entered office with the lowest approval rating for a president—46 percent—in the history of polling, and his numbers quickly fell. Within eight months of taking office, and amidst mass protests of his policies, Trump's job approval rating had fallen by nearly 10 percentage points.[56] No president had ever been reelected with a less than 40 percent approval rating, and Trump's rapid fall in popularity—with a 40 percent approval rating in February 2017, raised questions about his political future. Not all of the protests against Trump related to the issue of class or class conflict. The travel ban related more to concerns about racism and prejudice against immigrants, and the marches for science were primarily motivated by concern over the quality of American education. But protests about Trump's taxes and Obamacare clearly had a class dimension driving them. The opposition to repealing Obamacare was strongly driven by opposition to taking health care benefits away from the lower- and middle-classes, while providing an additional tax cut for the upper class. And protests of Trump's refusal to release his tax returns were driven by a suspicion of the billionaire, and raised the question of whether he was paying his fair share of taxes compared to working Americans.

Theories of Power: Elite Theory and Pluralism

Intellectuals and academics have disagreed for decades about who holds power in American politics. Traditionally, many political scientists claimed the government democratically represented the people. This theory is referred to as "pluralism" and overlaps with the belief that we live in a democracy that empowers the masses through citizen participation in and impact on politics. In contrast, "elite theory" claims politics is controlled by wealthy and upper-class interests, with the political system representing the "shadow cast on society by big business."[57] Pluralism is based on the notion that many citizens and public interest groups are able to influence political outcomes via the electoral process, which provides an incentive for officials to listen to the concerns of constituents and citizens groups.[58] The past successes of labor unions, environmentalists, and consumer-rights advocates are highlighted as examples of citizens influencing government.[59]

Interest groups compete to impact government policy; no group of citizens will fully dominate politics if large numbers of people pressure their political leaders to represent them. Social movements also help Americans to overcome individual apathy and to influence politics.

Pluralism claims that citizens serve as a check on government abuse, limiting corruption and preventing rule by the few. Individuals are thought to form political groups because of the human need to interact with others and form group-based identities. Humans are social creatures, and group relations are vital to individual development.[60] And citizens are said to be more politically active when their interests are at risk. "Disturbance theory" claims that individuals are most vigilant in fighting for their interests when they fear the possibility of losing an essential service, benefit, or protection.[61] For example, Occupy Wall Street and Fight for $15 formed due to public anger over record inequality and amid stagnant to declining wages for the working poor. In sum, citizens are more likely to be active and make demands from government when they are vulnerable or desperate.

Image 4.3. Democracy, Not Plutocracy.

Elite theory depicts the upper-class and corporate interests as dominant in politics. Society is divided and conflicted along economic class lines, between upper, middle, and lower classes. The upper class determines the country's politics, maximizing its own benefits from government at the expense of the other classes. Government does not represent a blank slate upon which people set policy; rather, it is the playground of an upper-class comprised of corporate interests and various professional and trade groups operating within corporate America. Some critics use the word plutocracy—or rule by the rich—to refer to the how power is exercised in the U.S. political system.[62]

While pluralism sees voting as a means of democratic empowerment, elite theory sees elections as dominated by a "one dollar, one vote" principle. The more money an individual or group has, the more effective they are in influencing politics. Corporate lobbies spend massive amounts on campaign ads, thereby exposing the public to some candidates and pushing them away from others. And money means the ability to supply campaign donations to preferred candidates, who rely on those donations to get reelected.

The rise of elite theory was reflected in the growing popularity of sociologist C. Wright Mills's *The Power Elite*.[63] In the book, Mills argued that society is dominated by a small group of elites, including political, military, and business leaders, who exercise control at the expense of democratic representation for the masses. Some political scientists also developed their own versions of elite theory. One school of thought established a "multiple elite" theory, in which various groups of elites with distinct economic interests each dominated specific policy areas.[64] Oil corporations focus on energy policy, while insurance companies concentrate on federal regulations of the insurance industry, and so on. Government is said to be dominated by "clientelism" and "sub-governments." Clientelism theory envisions public policy as bought and sold by the wealthy. Business lobbies "buy" political leaders via campaign donations and campaign advertising, ensuring candidates are beholden to the financial interests that got them elected. As a result, laws inevitably benefit corporate lobbyists, while inhibiting democracy.

Under "clientelism" public policy is dominated by small groups of economic elites.[65] "Sub-governments" operate in specific policy areas, in which various business groups dominate public policy. In reference to clientelism, textbooks use the metaphor of "iron triangles" to describe the relationship between corporations, lobbyists, and government.[66] Business groups dominate legislative outcomes—and are so strong that their hold over government is cast in "iron." The "triangles" metaphor refers to the three political actors in clientelistic sub-governments: interest groups/lobbyists; Congress; and the federal bureaucracy, all of which are said to work together to strengthen corporate interests and power.

In applying clientelism theory, one could look to the health care industry, which is one of the largest donors to the Democratic Party. Democrats spearheaded a pro-health care industry reform via Obamacare, which was a large financial boon to health care corporations.[67] Obamacare, which passed in 2010, was complicated and convoluted. At more than 1,000 pages, the law was written in a complex "legalese" language that was difficult for your "average" American to understand. The law mandated that individuals buy private insurance, required states to set up health care exchanges to sell the insurance, expanded Medicaid coverage for the poor and the near-poor, and included new taxes to pay for the reforms.

Did Congress need to pass all these reforms to ensure Americans receive health insurance? It would have been simpler to cover all uninsured Americans through a taxpayer-funded, government health care system via expanding an already-existing program like Medicare. A Medicare-for-all system would provide insurance to needy Americans, avoiding the IRS-enforced penalties on those without insurance that were mandated under Obamacare, and would allow citizens to avoid shopping around on health care exchanges for expensive private policies. Administrative costs would be lower since profit-hungry insurance companies would be cut out of the process. Providing inexpensive insurance to all Americans via Medicare-for-all, however, would mean health insurance companies receive no subsidy from government to enhance their profits. Insurance companies would be greatly hurt by Medicare-for-all, losing millions of clients. Avoiding this threat, Obamacare rewarded private insurers, while failing to introduce cost controls for pharmaceutical drugs, health insurance, or medical procedures and care.

Obamacare's supports for the health care industry could be interpreted as an example of the "iron triangles" principle in action. From this perspective, health care industry lobbyists wielded power over candidates via campaign donations and campaign ads, ensuring strong representation of corporate health care interests once these candidates were elected. Figure 4.1 explores the Iron Triangles metaphor as related to health care reform and Obamacare. Health care lobbyists make up one corner of the triangle. Members of Congress, beholden to health care interests, comprise the second corner. Finally, government bureaucracy is the third corner. While Congress sets government policy, mandating individuals purchase private health insurance, the bureaucracy implements it. More specifically, a federal bureaucracy/exchange was created to work alongside state exchanges to create a marketplace for private health insurance plans that were subsidized by the federal government. The IRS bureaucracy enforced the mandate, fining those without insurance. In sum, all three of these interests operate together to ensure the protection of corporate health care interests.

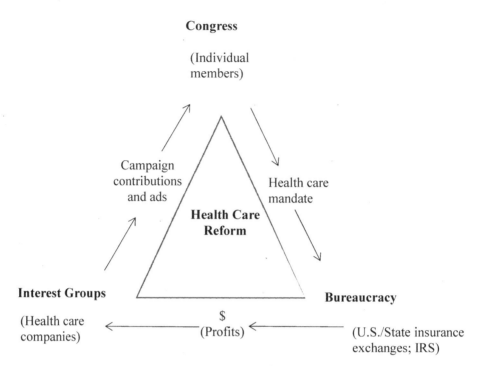

Figure 4.1. Iron Triangles and Political Power.

Elite theorists also frame business interests as holding inherent advantages over citizens and citizen groups. Corporations within individual industries are united by a narrow focus on enhancing each corporation's profits, which makes it easier for them to collectively agree and lobby for policies that will enhance those profits. Large public interest groups, in contrast, suffer from a "free rider" problem, since large numbers of people seek benefits from the group, while directly contributing little to nothing. Corporate lobbies, however, are comprised of far fewer members, and have a greater incentive to act, since the benefits secured from favorable policy outcomes will be greater per person than for large public interest groups. Because of these disadvantages, large public interest groups are thought to be far weaker than smaller business groups in impacting government policies.[68]

GETTING BEYOND THEORY

The state of knowledge in political science has progressed well beyond the theories of power addressed above. In recent decades, various studies have assessed elite theory and pluralism. Because of these works, we now know a lot more about who really holds political power.

Evidence for Pluralism

An abundance of research argues that citizens make a difference in impacting politics. For example, previous investigation finds a significant correlation between the mass public's political attitudes and government policy outcomes.[69] These findings suggest democratic responsiveness to mass preferences, with more liberal states producing more liberal political outcomes, and vice versa with conservative states and outcomes. Many studies emphasize the significance of social movements and citizen's groups in influencing government policy and mass cultural values.[70] These works suggest that political power is about more than campaign contributions and inside lobbying strategies.

Not everyone agrees that large groups are destined to fail because of their large numbers and the "free rider" problem. Many members of interest groups and social movements join together for solidarity reasons.[71] They feel better by associating with others holding similar beliefs because of the social value and camaraderie involved in working with like-minded people. Citizens also organize for moral purposes, and are motivated by "purposive" beliefs—or those relating to ideological goals.[72] For example, anti-war activists protest because they feel war is morally wrong; advocates for equal rights believe it is wrong to deny equal rights to individuals based on race, sex, or sexual orientation. Activists also join groups to secure personal benefits. Civil rights activists oppose racial discrimination in society. Gay and lesbian activists seek equal rights to their own benefit.

Although many members of large public interest groups prefer a free ride, patrons help overcome this problem.[73] A patron is an individual or organization providing financial support to a group. Entrepreneurs donate money to citizen's groups they agree with ideologically. Government also serves as a patron, allocating funds to groups. These resources are vital for sustaining groups' day-to-day functions, such as paying for professional staffers, organizing various campaigns and initiatives, paying lobbyists, and providing benefits to members.

Individual patrons come in various forms. George Soros, the billionaire investor, provides donations to liberal citizens groups, including the American Civil Liberties Union and Amnesty International, which are dedicated to promoting civil rights and liberties. David and Charles Koch are industrialist billionaire patrons who have given millions to right-wing Tea Party groups such as Freedom Works and Americans for Prosperity. Examples of government serving in a patron role include annual federal funds allocated for Planned Parenthood, grants to groups such as the American Legacy and American Cancer Society (which fund anti-smoking initiatives), and funds for community "faith based" education groups promoting abstinence-only campaigns.

Patrons are an important part of citizen organizing, but as the examples below suggest, mass action is also needed to democratically transform politics in favor of the people's interests. Throughout the twentieth century, women organized in mass to secure basic rights. They gained the right to vote in 1920 via the Nineteenth Amendment. From the 1960s and 1970s onward, women's groups challenged cultural stereotypes treating women as second-class citizens and pressuring them to accept bread-winner-homemaker gender roles. Their activism radically changed American culture, stigmatizing sexist beliefs and practices, eventually forcing changes to the law. These legal changes included: prohibitions on discrimination against women in employment and public accommodations (The Civil Rights Act of 1964), the right to an abortion within the first two trimesters of a pregnancy (*Roe v. Wade*, 1973), guaranteed unpaid leave from one's job following a child birth (The Family and Medical Leave Act of 1993), and the right to equal pay for equal work (The Equal Pay Act of 1963 and the Lilly Ledbetter Fair Pay Act of 2009). In the 1930s, a growing labor movement pressured the federal government and the Democratic Party to protect the right to unionize and collectively bargain for wages and benefits, the right to a minimum wage, and prohibition of child labor.[74] In the 1950s and 1960s, civil rights activists protested racial discrimination in politics and society. They transformed American culture and stigmatized racism, and passed political reforms outlawing racial discrimination in employment, public accommodations, and voting.[75]

More recent social movements have also achieved successes. The environmental movement directed public attention to the dangers of nuclear power, pollution, acid rain, and ozone-depletion, and pressured government to take action. More recently, environmentalists and scientists are capturing public attention by speaking out on the dangers of climate change. They stress the need for government to fund renewable energy sources, mandate higher fuel efficiency standards, and limit CO_2 pollution. The gay and lesbian rights movement has ushered in a tidal wave of change, seen in growing public support for equal rights regardless of sexual orientation. Legal successes include the striking down of state anti-sodomy laws, legal protections for same-sex marriage, and prohibitions on discrimination based on sexual orientation in public and private places and employment. These movement successes suggest government can (and does) accommodate citizens' interests and establishes democratic protections for vulnerable social groups.

What of the claim that public policy is bought and sold via campaign donations? Numerous social science studies suggest there is *no* consistent relationship between interest groups giving campaign donations and receiving favorable votes on legislation.[76] Most of the time business lobbies fail to win the benefits they seek from political officials.[77] Usually, the status quo prevails in politics, with no change occurring from one year to the next for most policy issues.[78]

Although clientelistic arguments about government are popular with the public, the notion that policy is bought and sold is too simplistic to explain how the political process really works.

Lobbyists' failure to consistently win legislative victories would not be surprising if many of their demands are unrealistic. For example, fast food businesses and retail corporations would love to avoid minimum wage increases, or eliminate the minimum wage entirely, but this is unlikely to happen because of a mass public outcry that would emerge. Pharmaceutical corporations, meat producers, and agri-business firms would like to reduce regulations on drug production and food quality, but Congress is unlikely to eliminate the Food and Drug Administration or the Department of Agriculture. Many conservative and wealthy Americans may want to eliminate the Internal Revenue Service—as Presidential Candidates Ted Cruz, Ben Carson, Mike Huckabee, and Rand Paul proposed, but they do not have enough political sway to make it happen.[79] Upper-class Americans hold many preferences, but there is no guarantee they will get what they want when a demand is unpopular with the rest of the public.

If lobbyists are not buying political officials via campaign dollars, what are they doing? One possibility is lobbyists merely buy *access* to officials. Political leaders grant lobbyists a hearing, but there is no guarantee they will comply with lobbyists' requests. Some research suggests lobbyists do not even try to buy votes; rather, they support legislators who are already sympathetic to their positions.[80] Rather than trying to buy votes, lobbyists may simply be networking and providing information and other resources to allies in Congress.[81]

Most of the time, there are not large changes to public policy over short periods of time. But sometimes major changes do occur. Scholars refer to this process as "punctuated equilibrium." A general equilibrium endures regarding federal program spending and policies over time, with little change evident from one year to the next. In other words, most of the time lobbyists fail to push through their preferred policy changes. However, policy equilibrium may be "punctuated" when major changes do finally occur. What this means is that, at certain points in history, there are opportunities for citizens and social movements to influence policy. For example, consider the rapid changes in state, local, and national tobacco policy in the late-1990s and 2000s.[82] There were previous regulations of cigarettes before this period. In 1969, Congress prohibited cigarette advertising on T.V. and radio, and in 1966 required cigarette manufacturers to warn consumers about the hazards of smoking. In 1988, Congress banned smoking on airlines.

Despite these restrictions, cigarette companies still marketed their products in movies, periodicals, and elsewhere. Cigarette vending machines were available at businesses frequented by minors. Cigarette smoking was allowed in most private and public venues. Scientists documented the relationship between cigarette smoking and cancer for decades, but not a single individual who smoked and developed cancer successfully sued a tobacco company for poisoning them. The legal justification for dismissing these cases was that individuals chose to smoke of their own free will, so the responsibility for developing cancer was their own. Finally, tobacco producers benefitted from relatively low state taxes on cigarettes compared to today.

By the turn of the century, significant cultural change was occurring. Millions of Americans were killed over the years by lung cancer, and millions more endured the pain associated with friends and loved ones dying. By the late-1990s, a critical mass developed, with a tidal wave of change expressed via growing public opposition to smoking. While less than half of Americans believed smoking was "very harmful" in the early-to-mid 1990s, the number had reached a majority by 2001. In 2007, just 40 percent of Americans said smoking should be banned in public places, although the number jumped to 59 percent by 2011.[83]

Citizen activism appeared to be a main driver of growing public opposition to smoking.[84] In the 1980s, anti-drug groups such as DARE (Drug Abuse Resistance Education) and MADD (Mothers Against Drunk Driving) lobbied in schools and elsewhere, focusing on the dangers of cigarettes and alcohol. In subsequent years, government became increasingly critical of big tobacco. The CEOs of America's largest tobacco companies were called to testify before the House Subcommittee on Health and the Environment in 1994 to uncover what they knew about cigarette addiction. These CEOs lied to Congress, claiming cigarettes were not addictive. A 1996 CBS investigation later showed these executives not only knew cigarettes were addictive, but had manipulated the chemical properties in cigarettes to make them more addictive.[85]

The CBS investigation helped turn the tide against big tobacco. Americans became more supportive of regulating smoking. From the late-1990s through the 2000s, a window of opportunity presented itself, in which government and citizens reined in the power of tobacco companies. Forty-six states filed a joint lawsuit against tobacco companies, suing for billions in damages to recover taxpayer funds used under Medicaid to treat poor smokers with lung cancer. Unlike the individuals who sued tobacco companies, these states succeeded, winning a "master settlement agreement" in 1998 mandating large financial concessions from big tobacco.[86] While individuals consented to smoking, state taxpayers did not, and were not responsible for covering the societal costs of smoking.

The joint Medicaid lawsuit resulted in a court-mandated $250 billion in payouts from tobacco companies to the states over 25 years.[87] It mandated tobacco companies spend millions on anti-smoking initiatives—and fund the prominently-placed "Truth" anti-smoking ads. This outcome was unthinkable in previous decades. After the Medicaid lawsuit, the politics of cigarette smoking shifted rapidly. State and local governments began introducing laws and ordinances to discourage cigarette smoking. Local ordinances banned cigarette smoking in bars, restaurants, other business establishments, and public facilities. State laws banned cigarette vending machines except in 21-and-over locations like casinos. These laws also banned smoking on government property. States imposed large tax increases on cigarettes to discourage new smokers and encourage current smokers to quit.[88] A massive shift in attitudes during the last few decades translated into a significant decline in smoking. According to Gallup, in the mid-1950s, 45 percent of adults regularly smoked; in contrast, the number fell to 29 percent by 1990, and to 20 percent by 2008.[89] As of 2015, the Kaiser Family Foundation estimated just 17 percent of adults smoked cigarettes.[90] By 2012, 67 percent of Americans thought smoking was a "very" or "extremely serious" threat to society, up from 57 percent in 2003.[91] In 2013, 82 percent thought smoking should be prohibited in cars occupied by children under 13; 75 percent supported banning smoking in any homes with asthmatic children.[92]

The tobacco case study suggests that, when citizens unite, they can make a difference in politics, even defeating a big business interest that for decades benefitted from favorable government policies and seemed beyond challenge. The transformation in government tobacco policy suggests that corporate interests may be subjected to meaningful regulation in favor of the common good, *if* citizens pressure government to act.

If citizen groups and social movements are able to influence political outcomes, how does it occur? Recent research suggests media attention is vital. Two major factors are associated with a group gaining attention in the news: financial resources and membership size.[93] The former speaks to elite theory and upper-class dominance of politics, since groups with deep pockets are able to secure greater attention. This finding is not surprising. Money means resources, and resources mean the ability to hire lobbyists who work full time to get out a group's message. Money means the ability to put out reports and studies that get covered in the news and may influence how the public thinks about an issue. However, the latter factor—population size—speaks to pluralism and citizen empowerment. Citizens groups use their power in numbers to gain media attention, seeking to guide public discourse on issues of importance. This finding is reinforced in numerous studies documenting how social movements use the media to cultivate mass public support, and is also relevant to the increasingly salient public campaign against smoking.[94]

Evidence for Elite Theory

Most of the time, business lobbies fail to push through their policy proposals, and campaign donations never guarantee policy victories. But this does not mean that the upper class fails to exercise dominance in politics. It is now common to hear about how the political system is "captured" by corporate interests, without lobbyists needing to "buy" off officials via campaign spending. Capture works in at least two ways: 1. Political leaders are increasingly likely to come from upper-class backgrounds; and 2. Government regulators are co-opted into the ranks of the economic elite, taking jobs in industries they regulate in exchange for reducing regulations.

The lobbying process is increasingly dominated by the upper class. Organizations representing wealthy Americans, including business, trade, and professional associations, comprise nearly three-quarters of all interest groups active in national politics. These groups also comprise 75 percent of all the sides involved in national policy conflicts.[95] If, as pluralism argues, groups participating in politics influence political outcomes, then wealthier Americans will dominate the policy process, since they are responsible for organizing the vast majority of groups lobbying. When changes do occur in public policy, upper-class interests are the most likely to benefit if they are the ones offering most proposals being considered. For example, a 2011 International Monetary Fund study examined 51 pieces of legislation related to Wall Street considered by Congress from 2000 to 2006. In line with previous research, the study concluded that advocates for both increasing and cutting regulations on Wall Street failed most of the time in securing their interests via passage of new legislation. Ninety-five percent of the time, advocates for tightening regulations failed to get what they wanted; similarly, supporters of deregulation failed 84 percent of the time. But advocates for deregulation were more than three times as successful as advocates of greater regulation.[96] These results reinforce the conclusion that, *when* policy changes occur, they more often benefit corporate and upper-class interests.

Even if campaign donations and other spending do not dictate legislative outcomes, they may translate into negative power to block unfavorable outcomes. Campaign donations can be a powerful tool for ensuring that progressive candidates seeking to challenge corporate power are not elected. In congressional elections from 2000 to 2010, an average of 93 percent of candidates who spent more money in House elections won their races, compared to 83 percent of candidates in the Senate.[97] *The Washington Post* reports that for the 2012 congressional elections, 91 percent of the time, the better financed candidate won.[98] These success rates suggest that money matters in determining election outcomes. Candidates with greater resources buy more exposure than their competitors. Greater exposure means an increased likelihood of mobilizing one's base to vote, and potentially influencing undecided voters.[99] And wealthy upper-class interests dominate the campaign donation process, deterring progressive challenges to the status quo.

Much has been made of the decadent wealth of President Donald Trump and his cabinet. *The New York Times* reported in early 2017: "Mr. Trump has selected what would be the wealthiest cabinet in modern American history, filled with millionaires and billionaires with complicated financial portfolios."[100] But Trump is merely the most extreme case of the capture of government by wealthy interests. Most congressional officials are also part of the upper class. As the *Houston Chronicle* reported in 2012, incoming members of Congress received a minimum income of $174,000 a year, placing them in the top six percent of nation's income distribution.[101] From 2014 to 2015, the "typical" Congressperson held net assets worth more than $1 million, while the average Congressperson held assets of $13.4 million.[102] The cumulative net worth of Congress grew by 107 percent from 2004 to 2015, from $3.5 billion to more than $7.2 billion.[103] These statistics suggest Americans from the upper class are in a profound position to directly determine public policy outcomes.

If political leaders are mostly upper class in their backgrounds, this suggests that buying members of Congress with campaign donations and spending is an anachronistic idea. Buying off politicians is unnecessary when officials are already part of the upper class and hold views overlapping with those of other wealthy Americans and corporate donors.[104] Political and business leaders do not merely work together, they are one-and-the-same. Most political leaders earn elite incomes, and are from elite backgrounds. By being part of the capitalist class, political officials are socialized throughout their lives to embrace upper-class values.[105]

The executive branch is a classic example of the business capture of government. President Trump's financial net worth was estimated at between $800 million and $3.7 billion in 2016.[106] Former President Obama held assets of $12.2 million by 2016.[107] Obama's first Secretary of State and 2016 Democratic Presidential candidate Hillary Clinton had a family net worth of $110 million in 2016.[108] John Kerry, Obama's second Secretary of State, and Democratic Presidential candidate in 2004 held a family net worth in 2012 of $238 million.[109] The previous administration was no different. President George W. Bush had a net worth of $9.5 million by the end of his second term.[110] Vice President Dick Cheney's net worth was $48 million in 2005, and Bush's Secretary of Defense Donald Rumsfeld's was $55 million in 2001. Mitt Romney, the 2012 Republican Presidential candidate, had a net worth of $230 million.[111] Other notable Republicans running for president in 2012 such as Jeb Bush, Ted Cruz, and John Kasich, had a net worth of $22 million, $3.5 million, and $10 million, respectively.[112] These officials were not only major political figures, but were also part of the upper class.

Critics of American politics speak of a "revolving door" system, in which those working in government agencies are "captured" by the industries they are supposed to regulate.[113] These bureaucrats may come to believe they will slide into well-paying lobbyist positions for firms they are supposed to regulate, so long as they ease such regulations. To provide two examples from the 2000s, Tom Scully of the Medicare agency and Joann Smith of the Department of Agriculture were bureaucrats who were captured by business interests. Scully served as administrator of the Centers for Medicare and Medicaid Services from 2001 to 2003, at a time when Congress was considering a Medicare prescription drug program. More specifically, Scully served as the Bush administration's "lead negotiator" on a prescription drug bill that provided federal drug benefits to seniors. But the law also failed to regulate the cost of drugs, despite the federal government becoming the largest purchaser of drugs in the country.[114]

Concerns grew in Congress regarding whether the prescription bill was too expensive, a concern that corresponded with chief Medicare actuary Richard Foster's estimate that the reform would cost $530 billion over ten years.[115] But Foster's concerns were suppressed by Scully, who warned Foster he would be fired if he informed Congress about the higher-than-expected costs.[116] Scully's censorship of Foster looked even more suspicious after Scully resigned his position once the bill passed, and became a lobbyist for the drug industry.

As an Assistant Secretary at the Department of Agriculture, Joann Smith signed off on regulatory changes allowing "pink slime," to be used in mass beef production.[117] Pink slime was an insider term coined by USDA scientists to refer to a beef-substitute—including tendons, ligaments, cartilage, and other scraps used as filler for beef sold to schools, in grocery stores, and in fast food. As the *Scientific American* described the production process: "Connective tissue, trimmings, and scraps from industrial butcher plants are mixed in a large steel reactor, where technicians heat the mixture to 100°F, initiating tissue lysis—fats and oils begin to rise up, while thicker bits like protein sink. After a spin on the centrifuge to separate these components, lean, squishy pink goo emerges. Ammonium hydroxide—ammonia dissolved partially in water—sterilizes the resulting mass against microbes such as E. coli or salmonella."[118] Pink slime was approved for inclusion in beef products in 2001; previously, it was used only in pet foods.[119]

Pink slime is a cheap additive created to enhance the profits of meat packing corporations. It is not the nutritional equivalent of ground beef, so there is no health-related reason for including it in meats.[120] Smith's endorsement of pink slime looked suspicious when considering that after leaving the USDA, she went to work for the beef industry as a member of the board of directors for IBP—later known as Tyson Fresh Meats. Smith's capture by the beef industry speaks to the danger of officials associating too closely with the industries they are supposed to regulate.

The stories above are anecdotal, but the concept of the revolving door is not. The Center for Responsive Politics (CRP) estimated more than 430 former government officials in Congress in the early-to-mid 2010s worked as senior advisors or lobbyists after serving in office.[121] The Center for Public Integrity reported that 12 percent of lobbyists in 2005 were former government officials from the executive or legislative branch.[122] CRP reported in 2014 that more than half of former members of Congress who were employed that year worked as lobbyists.[123] Half of retiring Senators and a third of Representatives end up working as lobbyists. This number has climbed dramatically since the 1970s, when less than five percent found lobbyist jobs after retiring from public service.[124] In short, political officials are captured to a far greater extent in modern times than in previous decades.

System capture seeks to explain the ways in which the political system is dominated by corporate and upper-class interests. But to what extent do the wealthy dominate public policy? Numerous empirical studies suggest that wealthy Americans are radically better at influencing politics than the masses. Political officials are much more likely to seriously consider the appeals of affluent professionals and business persons over blue-collar Americans.[125] And in cases when political opinions diverge between the top 10 percent of income earners and the bottom 90 percent, upper-class Americans are much more likely to get what they want from government.[126] In these cases, the mass public is completely unable to assert its interests by pressuring government to produce desired policy outcomes, while—statistically speaking—wealthy Americans are far more likely to get what they want. Furthermore, most legislative officials are millionaires, and pro-business views are more commonly embraced by legislators who are part of the upper class than they are among legislators from working-class or blue-collar backgrounds.[127] Finally, the extent to which individual states are committed to social welfare policies is directly related to the level of inequality within each state. States with high inequality commit less revenues to welfare, while states with lower inequality commit greater resources to welfare benefits.[128] In other words, inequality in society becomes a self-fulfilling prophecy, with high inequality states producing less pressure on government to rectify historic inequalities between the rich and poor.

Marxian elite theory is premised on the notion that the upper-class exercises power in a "free" society through the "manufacture" of public "consent."[129] Antonio Gramsci argued that under modern capitalism, political and business elites seek to control what people think, rather than coerce or intimidate them through violence. The upper class exercises leadership of the masses through the corporate media and one-sided pro-business political rhetoric. Government officials and corporate media rely on propaganda to cultivate support from the masses. Gramsci used the term "hegemony" to refer to the process by which business interests led the mass public. For Gramsci, "consent is 'historically' achieved through the prestige, and consequent confidence that dominant groups enjoy because of their prominent position and function in the world of [economic] production."[130] In other words, political and business leaders socialize the public to support pro-consumerist, pro-capitalist, pro-upper-class worldviews through messages disseminated in the media, in campaign ads, and even within educational institutions.

In line with Gramsci's hegemonic framework, one can look to the 2001 Bush tax cuts as an example of manipulation by the upper class. The Bush administration—itself populated by millionaires—dominated national news on the proposed tax cuts, which removed $2.5 trillion in federal revenues over a decade, most of it going to the top 20 percent of income earners.[131] Rarely did reporting emphasize that these earners would receive three-quarters of all tax cuts.[132] Instead, Americans consistently heard the President speaking of how Americans would receive significant "tax relief." They were told the government was running a revenue surplus, and these revenues should be returned to the public.[133] Most Americans supported the Bush tax cuts, which was unsurprising considering that news coverage was so dominated by Republicans. Those paying attention to the news were significantly more likely than those not paying attention to support tax cuts.[134] Public opinion changed significantly in later years, once it became clear that the cuts primarily benefitted the upper class. By the early 2010s, most Americans opposed further extending the Bush tax cuts.[135] Still, Republican success in selling the tax cuts suggests political officials and the corporate media hold significant power in selling pro-business policies to the public.

Numerous studies suggest that political elites often succeed in molding the minds of the masses. For example, the Bush and Obama administrations dominated foreign news coverage during the 2000s and 2010s, and succeeded twice as often as they failed in building public support for their foreign policy positions.[136] As I argue in the foreign policy chapter, these policies are supportive of U.S. domestic capitalist interests, and hostile to non-capitalist countries. For domestic issues, there is also evidence that political and business officials manufacture public support and consent. For example, the media seldom cover issues such as income and wealth inequality, class conflict, or the class divide in modern America. As a result, the media suppress class consciousness, despite the emergence of record inequality and the persistence of a political-economic system that serves the upper class.[137]

Some research finds that both political parties have become more conservative and pro-business in their politics in recent decades.[138] Simultaneously, news reporting limits discussion of political issues to the narrow range of pro-business views expressed by Democrats and Republicans, while neglecting the views of the masses.[139] This does not mean the public always accepts what they are told by the media and by political leaders. On issues with which the public is already familiar and in which public opinion runs counter to that of political officials, it is much harder for government officials to manipulate public beliefs in favor of policies that benefit the wealthy.[140] On the other hand, there are many issues in which the public is less familiar with, in which political officials effectively use the media to manufacture consent.[141] In short, manipulation by the upper class is integral to reinforcing the American power structure, even if it is not always successful.

The Final Verdict

Evidence exists to support both pluralism and elite theory. But what broader lessons can one draw from the evidence above? The findings suggest citizens really can make a difference in influencing what government does. Social movement successes demonstrate the protesters are able to gain attention in the news, transform cultural values, and pressure the political system to change. They even force regulations into place that limit the power of businesses, as the successes of organized labor, environmentalists, and the anti-smoking movement have shown. But citizen's groups face an uphill battle in promoting change. Government consistently favors the wealthy and the upper class over the middle-class and poor. Recent empirical work finds that the preferences of citizen's groups, business groups, and wealthy citizens all exercise an independent impact on policy outcomes. But business groups and the upper class are far more effective than citizen's groups. This suggests that a form of pluralism exists, although it is best described as a "biased pluralism" (sometimes called "neopluralism") that privileges the interests of the corporate upper class.[142]

Politics increasingly favors the wealthy, as demonstrated by the rapid increase in economic inequality in recent decades and the reluctance of political leaders—who have benefitted from growing inequality—to do much about it. The political system's capture by the upper class means that government is more likely to view the world the same way the corporate class does, because government officials are part of that class. Upper-class dominance of politics does not mean democracy is impossible; but empowering the masses is difficult when government consistently privileges the wealthy few over the many.

Chapter 5

Congress

The Dysfunctional Branch

In April of 2017, just 34 percent of Americans said they held a favorable view of the U.S. Congress.[1] Most Americans felt the Republican majority was doing "too little" to "work with Democrats in Congress" to solve America's problems, and a majority also disapproved of the job Republican Representative Paul Ryan was "doing as Speaker of the House."[2] A majority of Americans opposed the effort by House and Senate Republicans to repeal Obamacare, with millions becoming increasingly anxious about how the law's repeal would hurt them, as they would lose access to Medicaid, or lose taxpayer aid for purchasing their health insurance. By February 2017, a majority of the public said they supported Obamacare, and just 17 percent were on board with repealing the bill in its entirety.[3] This opposition was a stinging rebuke for the Republican health care repeal agenda, which prioritized eliminating insurance for tens of millions of Americans, and cutting taxes on wealthy citizens earning more than $250,000 a year.

Congress is sometimes referred to as "the people's branch" of government because citizens from individual districts and states retain their own representatives and senators, and these officials are supposed to democratically represent their constituents. But as the findings above suggest, few Americans were happy in 2017 with the job Congress was doing, especially with regard to health care. Congress is widely perceived to be broken, failing to represent the people, and putting petty rivalries for power, personal enrichment, and protection of the wealthy before the general welfare. Much of this dysfunction stems from the disintegration of the Republicans as a normal parliamentary party. The party used to promote conservative, pro-business agendas, while being committed to compromise. But it is no longer a normal party in the traditional sense, in that its main goal is not aiding the masses, but supporting the upper class. The same can be said of the Democrats, although programs like Obamacare benefit millions of people, in addition to enriching health care business interests.

Historically, parties pursued liberal and conservative agendas, but recognized they needed to compromise with the opposition to get things done. But in recent years, the Republican Party has committed itself to an unflinching, staunchly pro-business policy agenda, with little interest in compromising with Democrats or promoting legislation that benefits the masses of Americans who struggle in a time of record inequality. During this period of economic uncertainty, most people want Congress to pursue policies that promote economic growth, restore wage growth for American families, and reduce inequality between the rich and poor. But Congress has done little to make this happen.

How Does Congress Work? Four Explanations

Legislative scholars emphasize competing explanations for how Congress works. These include: 1. The party-based explanation; 2. The committee-based, informational approach; 3. Distributive politics; and 4. Congress as an upper-class institution. Although there is evidence to support each explanation, the class-based approach provides the best over-arching framework for understanding how Congress works amidst growing upper-class dominance of government.

I. THE POWER OF POLITICAL PARTIES

Parties are generally seen as central to influencing how Congress operates. Congress is run by parties. Party leaders guide the legislators within their party, influencing how they vote.[4] Some legislative scholars speak of a "cartel theory," arguing that each party acts as a coalition of individuals holding similar beliefs.[5] Party leaders use committee assignments to influence party members. They withhold assignments from defiant party members, and reward those who are compliant by granting preferred assignments.[6] The power to appoint and remove committee members is important, since Senators and Representatives seek committee appointments to influence the legislative process. Committee appointments allow them to influence legislation for topics of personal interest. Party leaders use the "Rules" committee to "set the agenda" for how political issues are deliberated upon. These leaders control the Rules committee via their ability to appoint its members, and as a result, influence how, when, and whether pieces of legislation are introduced to committees and to the floor of each chamber for a vote.[7]

To provide an example of party leaders setting the legislative agenda, consider the government shutdown in 2013, driven by Republican opposition to Obamacare. House Republicans knew they did not have enough votes in the Senate to repeal the health care law, so they proposed a budget attached to health care repeal legislation. Republican House Speaker John Boehner and other Republicans thought they could coerce Senate Democrats (who were in the majority) to abandon the law by threatening a government shutdown. But when the Senate refused to pass a budget attached to a health care repeal, the House and Senate were deadlocked on reaching a budget agreement. This deadlock resulted in a government shutdown that lasted for weeks. In a sign of their power, House Republican leadership rebuked Democratic Representative Chris Van Hollen's effort to pursue a vote on a budget independent from the repeal of the health care law.[8] Only the House Speaker (or a representative filling in for the speaker in his absence) has the power to allow a floor vote on legislation. Without Boehner's approval, Democrats were unable to force a vote on their preferred budget legislation.

Party leaders also exercise power through party whips, who are highly successful in influencing how rank and file members vote. In the 2010s, polarization in Congress reached a record high for the last century. Congressional polarization between the parties is measured by examining how often members of each party vote with each other, and against the other party, on legislation. Greater polarization suggests party leaders are effective in pressuring party members to vote with party leaders. Party whips are instrumental in the process, pressuring party members according to party leaders' wishes. To provide a recent example, consider Congressional votes on health care reform. In the vote over Obamacare, not a single Republican in the Senate or House voted for the bill. In a sign of party unity on the other side of the aisle, 219 Democrats (87 percent of all Democrats) voted in favor of the law; only 34 voted against (13 percent of all Democrats) in the House of Representatives. In the Senate, party unity was even greater, as all 58 Democrats voted in favor of the law.[9]

Scholars discussing the importance of parties to Congress are not primarily concerned with an upper-class bias among legislators. They implicitly assume that Congress functions adequately for the public, in that their emphasis is on understanding how parties impact the legislative process. But with the rise of partisan gridlock, there is a growing public concern that Congress no longer effectively functions as a governing institution. By choosing gridlock over dealing with important issues such as rapidly rising health care costs and declining wages among the working poor, the major political parties have quietly sided with corporate and upper-class interests over those of the needy.

2. COMMITTEES AND THE POWER OF INFORMATION

A second approach to understanding Congress stresses the importance of committees and how they control information in the legislative process. Numerous scholars focus on committees' role in deliberating on and influencing legislation.

There is much uncertainty in the legislative process.[10] Since legislators are not experts on the topics they vote on, they rely on committee members who are perceived to have expertise on an issue. Committee members retain more knowledge of policy issues in their area than other members of Congress.

Congressmen and women have legislative goals. But policy outcomes are uncertain, since no one has a crystal ball to see what laws will actually accomplish, compared to what one wishes they will accomplish. How can legislators minimize the differences between what they *prefer* a law to do and what it *actually* does? To address this problem, legislators rely on committee members, their researchers, and staffers.

One example of uncertainty in the legislative process is seen in the passage of Obamacare. Democratic legislators wanted to pass legislation to make health care affordable, and to provide better quality of care to the public. The hope was that whatever law was passed would accomplish these goals. But individual members of Congress—the vast majority of which were not experts on health care—were unable to produce the desired outcomes on their own. To achieve their goals, they looked to individuals on health care committees in the House and Senate, while the committee members relied on academic experts, staffers, and Congressional researchers to craft legislation. Even relying on these experts, it was not clear that the law passed would guarantee affordable care. Since the law did nothing to regulate private health insurers and their ability to increase health costs, Obamacare—to a large extent—was a gift to the corporate class, specifically to the health care industry. That health care costs continued to grow by leaps and bounds demonstrates that, even with so-called health care experts, laws do not always achieve what they promise.

A major goal for lawmakers is to be confident of what a law will accomplish before its passage. As one legislative scholar writes about the importance of committees: "a well-designed legislature is a producer, consumer, and repository for policy expertise, where 'expertise' is the reduction of uncertainty associated with legislative policies."[11] Those who control information hold power; they can influence legislative deliberation, and even votes. Information is provided by committees through various mediums, including: 1. committee reports produced for legislators; 2. Expert witness testimony in committee hearings, which can influence whether legislators recognize a problem; 3. The specialized knowledge of committee members, their staffers, and other experts, which is necessary for writing laws; and 4. Committee deliberations and amendments, which influence the content of legislation.

Committee members influence how members of Congress deliberate and vote on policy issues. For example, one can look to Republican House Representative Paul Ryan's influence on budget-related voting. For the fiscal year 2012 and 2013 budgets, Ryan released his proposed "Path to Prosperity" plan, which called for the privatization of Medicare, requiring seniors to purchase insurance from private insurance companies. His proposals called for large budget cuts for social welfare programs, and for large tax cuts for wealthier Americans.[12] The proposals were blueprints for how to achieve upper-class control of government policy. They were roundly rejected by Congressional Democrats, but embraced by Republicans—98 percent of which voted for the 2012 proposal in the House.[13] Reasons provided by legislators for supporting the plan included the claim that Ryan offered a competent plan for how to return the U.S. to fiscal responsibility and promote economic growth.[14] Republicans' embrace of Ryan's proposals is indicative of the House budget committee's influence on the legislative process. Ryan's "Path to Prosperity," however, suggests that perceived expertise is also in the eye of the beholder, with Republicans embracing the plan and Democrats rejecting it. Perceived expertise cannot be divorced from the partisan games played in Washington DC, meaning that party-based and committee-informational explanations for how Congress works share a significant overlap.

3. DISTRIBUTIVE POLITICS

Distributive politics refers to the claim that members of Congress are motivated to "distribute" benefits to constituents in return for campaign contributions and votes, both of which are central to reelection. Critics of distributive politics refer to it as "pork barrel politics," in that legislators "bring home the bacon" to their home state and district constituents.[15] This happens in various ways, including special projects, jobs, and program spending written into legislation. As the thinking goes, if monetary benefits are brought back to one's home state or district, these tax dollars will provide a significant boost to the local economy, helping build a positive self-image for members of Congress seeking reelection. These officials will claim credit, reminding constituents of the ways they aided citizens in the run-up to election day.

Research on Congress suggests distributive politics accounts for much of how Congress works. On low visibility issues that are not heavily reported or in the public's mind, campaign contributions are linked to favorable legislative policy outcomes for those giving campaign donations.[16] Pork barrel politics is used to build majority coalitions for spending in specific areas, such as highway and infrastructure spending.[17] For example, in the 2005 transportation spending bill, Congress included $286 billion in spending across 6,376 projects, in more than 1,000 pages of legislation. The bill was so large it took two years to write.[18] Examples of projects included were $3 million for a documentary about the infrastructure of Alaska, $5.9 million for a snowmobile trail in Vermont, $2.3

million for beautifying the Ronald Reagan expressway in California, $6 million for removing graffiti in New York, $2.4 million for the Henry Ford Museum in Dearborn, Michigan, and $2.4 million on a national wildlife center in Louisiana. Because there were so many projects included for individual legislators, the bill was extraordinarily popular. The Senate voted 91 to 4 in favor, while the House voted 412 to 8.[19]

Transportation and infrastructure spending are not the only areas where distributive politics persists. Military projects also operate according to the principles of distributive politics. For example, consider the B-2 bomber. It cost taxpayers $46 billion to develop.[20] Each bomber costs approximately $2.2 billion to build, and employs a "stealth" technology that is supposed to make it invisible to radar.[21] The plane is manufactured across most American states, but why disperse production across such a wide area?[22] The answer: if Representatives have a financial incentive to keep the program going, it will be more likely to continue, regardless of criticisms. Military spending is a particularly acute example of corporate power in politics. Military contracting is a big business, and the ability of these companies to impact public policy is significant in light of the hundreds of billions annually going to military spending.

The B-2 bomber's story is not unique. Legislators serving on military-related committees are very different from other legislators. They are more likely to come from rural districts of the country that are heavily reliant on military spending.[23] They are significantly more likely than non-defense-related committee members to receive campaign contributions from military contractors.[24] Finally, defense committee members allocate greater military spending to their districts than to other districts in Congress.[25] Clearly distributive politics plays a significant role in driving military spending.

Do the trends documented above apply to other areas of legislation? Recent evidence suggests they do. Interviews with members of Congress reveal they are influenced by both campaign contributions and by talking with constituents. Both forms of interaction produce greater efforts on the part of legislators to represent their constituents in committee meetings and in legislative floor debates.[26] Personal contacts and campaign contributions do not guarantee a specific legislative outcome; they do suggest legislators will *attempt* to represent the groups with which they have contact.

In 2011, Republicans in Congress technically banned "earmarked projects" that were used to direct government spending to specific Congressional constituencies.[27] But this did not stop distributive politics, which continues due to the subtle efforts of legislators to direct money to specific projects, without formally designating money to their state or district. As *Politico* reported in 2015, "lawmakers pepper bills with provisions that mention no companies or programs by name but are written in specific ways to nudge agencies toward the intended recipients or shut out potential competitors." Regarding military spending, "the ban has changed the ways lawmakers get projects to their home districts. Because it is more difficult for Congress to start new, small projects for specific contractors, lawmakers and federal contractors have shifted to pressing the Pentagon to include those projects in its initial budget request."[28]

4. Congress as Servant of the Upper Class

It is difficult to deny the importance of parties, committees, or distributive politics when analyzing Congress. But these frameworks provide an incomplete understanding of the institution, since they omit discussion of Congress's upper-class bias. It is certainly the case that political parties, committees, and concern with campaign contributions and votes all matter to influencing Congress, and it would be foolish to argue otherwise. But these frameworks for understanding Congress are also incredibly pedestrian, in that they fail to recognize an overarching bias in favor of corporate and upper-class interests that drives legislators' partisan, committee-based, and distributive activities. Without understanding how class impacts Congress, we will understand little about why Congress operates the way it does.

The upper-class bias in Congress was documented in detail in chapter 4, as numerous studies suggest that government policy is more likely to reflect the interests of wealthier Americans. Just six percent of legislators during the 1990s and 2000s came from working-class backgrounds.[29] The rest were from the upper class, with most legislators coming into office from professional or business-related occupations. The average member of Congress is a millionaire, and, as discussed in chapter 4, more affluent legislators are significantly more likely to adopt elitist, pro-business, anti-worker policies than legislators originally from working-class or blue-collar backgrounds. Considering these findings, it is difficult to take any understanding of Congress seriously that does not address this branch's blatant upper-class bias.

Aside from looking at policy outcomes, a simple examination of the composition of Congress demonstrates the fact that the wealthy dominate legislative decision making. In 2014, the Center for Responsive Politics (CRP) reported that the median wealth of members of Congress was $1.1 million, with every member of Congress being guaranteed an annual salary of $174,000, placing them in the top 6 percent of all income earners. As figure 5.1 below documents, the wealthiest one percent of Congress owned an incredible $1.4 billion in assets, while the next 4 percent owned about as much—$1.38 billion. The next 15 percent of Congress owned $1.1 billion in assets, while the next 40 percent of Congress

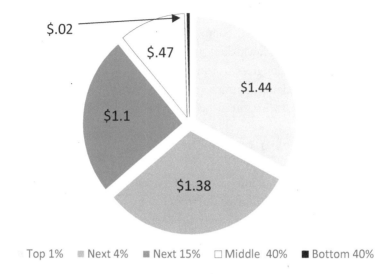

Top 1%   ■ Next 4%   ■ Next 15%   □ Middle 40%   ■ Bottom 40%

Figure 5.1. Wealth of Congress, in $ Billions (2014). Source: Will Tucker, "Personal Wealth: A Nation of Extremes, and a Congress Too," *Opensecrets.org*, November 17, 2015, https://www.opensecrets.org/news/2015/11/personal-wealth-a-nation-of-extremes-and-a-congress-too/

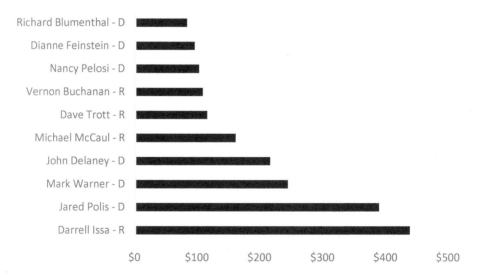

Figure 5.2. Ten Wealthiest Members of Congress, in $ Millions (2014). Will Tucker, "Personal Wealth: A Nation of Extremes, and a Congress Too," *Opensecrets.org*, November 17, 2015, https://www.opensecrets.org/news/2015/11/personal-wealth-a-nation-of-extremes-and-a-congress-too/

owned nearly $500 million in assets. The "poorest" 40 percent of Congress held $20 million in assets. In total, this meant that the members of Congress owned nearly $4.4 billion in assets.[30] To put this into perspective, this level of wealth is greater than that held by the poorest quarter of Americans combined.[31]

Consistent with my claim that the perversion of Congress by wealth is a bi-partisan affair, one can see that the wealthiest members of the chambers were both Democrats and Republicans. As figure 5.2 documents, four of the wealthiest members of Congress were Republicans, while six were Democrats.[32] The most common assets held by these executives were from large corporations across various sectors of the economy, including General Electric, Wells Fargo, Proctor and Gamble, Bank of America, Walt Disney Co., AT&T, Exxon-Mobil, Pfizer, Coca-Cola, Qualcomm, Cisco, and Schumpberger Ltd.[33]

As CRP reported, the top four industries in which members of Congress held wealth included the real estate sector, security and investment, commercial banking, and the finance industry. These figures suggest that Congress holds a serious vested interest in the major post-industrial, service sector corporations of the twenty-first century. If many Americans feel like Congress does not represent the interests of the "common person," it is likely because it does not. These officials do not come from the middle-class or working-poor segments of this country. Even those who hold little to no assets—the bottom 40 percent in Congress—earn yearly incomes that outpace the bottom 94 percent of American income earners.

The above statistics speak volumes about the upper-class bias of legislative governance in the U.S. The Congressional governing structure is one of extreme privilege. Eighty-one percent of its members are white, compared to 61 percent of the general population. Eighty-one percent of Congress is male, compared to half of the public.[34] Nearly every member of Congress holds a college degree, compared to a third of Americans older than 25.[35] The average member of Congress is 58 years old, compared to the general public, while the average American is 38 years old.[36] Finally, all members of Congress are in the top 6 percent of income earners, and their average net worth of more than $1 million far exceeds the average American's net worth, which is approximately $56,000.[37] In short, by the mid-to-late 2010s, Congress was overwhelmingly upper class in orientation. It was an institution of privilege and affluence, run largely by old, white, highly-educated, wealthy males. While the institution had become more racially diverse than in the past, the economic elitism of Congress had actually grown compared to previous decades.

Most mainstream political science studies of Congress avoid discussion of class, apparently viewing this approach as controversial, biased, or beyond the pale. Criticisms of Congress's blatant upper-class bias are filtered out of academic discussions, especially textbooks, in favor of research that is often myopic, and focusing on arcane and esoteric aspects of Congressional rules, functions, and procedures. While these aspects of Congress are not unimportant, pursuing research agendas divorced from understanding the upper-class bias of the body, and of lawmaking more generally, greatly limits our knowledge of "the people's branch."

Broken Politics: The Dysfunctional Congress

Another way to examine who Congress really serves is to look at legislative output. Do the House and Senate pass policies that benefit the masses, poor, and needy, or do they favor the wealthy? Increasingly, it appears that Congress is interested in "getting out of the way of business" and taxing members of the upper class less and less, while doing little to aid the middle, working, and lower classes. To take sides in the American class conflict, Congress does not have to actively work to hurt the masses and poor. Rather, through the politics of inaction, it can simply sit by while issues such as rising poverty, record inequality, stagnating to declining wages, and economic insecurity take their toll on the many. Inaction reached record levels under the Obama administration, with most Republicans in Congress defining "success" as opposing Democratic legislative proposals.[38]

Growing Obstructionism

In recent years, obstruction in Congress increased dramatically. Much of this dysfunction was observed via record partisan polarization and declining legislative productivity in the Senate. Growing polarization has made legislation difficult to pass, especially during periods of split party control of government between Congress and the White House. Even during periods of Republican control, such as 2017 onward, Republican policy ideas as related to health care reform were so unpopular that they were effectively resisted by the mass public.

The politics of inaction, while favoring an economy that is already biased in favor of the wealthy, has become increasingly common. Obstruction regularly occurs through growing use of the filibuster in the Senate, which is utilized by both Democrats and Republicans. In previous decades, the filibuster was a tool of obstruction that required Senators to speak for long periods of time to block a legislative vote. Senate rules allow unlimited time for discussion of legislation, unless 60 Senators vote for cloture. Cloture represents a choice on the part of Senators to end debate on legislation and move toward a vote. In the cloture process Senators cast a preliminary vote on whether they want to have a final vote on legislation. By adding this middle step between Senators and a final vote, the chamber's rules lend themselves to obstruction.

Obstruction in the Senate became easier in 1975, when the rules for filibuster usage were changed. Prior to 1975, if a Senator wanted to filibuster legislation, he or she had to talk for an entire session length, thereby preventing a vote. But the rule change allowed for filibusters without having to speak on the Senate floor. More specifically, the Senate rules were changed in 1975 from requiring a two-thirds vote "of Senators present and voting," to requiring a three-fifths vote "of Senators sworn."[39] This allowed for the use of virtual filibusters, in which no actual debate has to take place, but voting on legislation is still blocked so long as the Senate lacks enough votes to invoke cloture. Filibuster use, while seldom prior to 1975, increased significantly once the virtual filibuster was introduced. By the mid-to-late 1970s, the number of filibusters per session of Congress often reached over 40, compared to only a handful of filibusters being used each session in the late 1960s and early 1970s. The filibuster's use continued to rise after that. From 1981 to 2010, the use of the filibuster increased by 4.5 times, or 450 percent.[40] The number of filibusters filed in Congress reached record levels by the early-to-mid-2010s. While there were less than 100 filibusters filed in each session of Congress in the early-to mid-2000s, that number increased to nearly 150 in the 2009 to 2010 session and 250 in the 2013 to 2014 session. Never before had the filibuster been used so often.[41]

Growing use of the filibuster translated into near-government paralysis. If there were 253 cloture motions filed to deal with Republican obstructionism and filibusters during the 113th Congress (2013–2014), and there were 292 work days in this same session, that means a filibuster was occurring, on average, 87 percent of the time.[42] These figures suggest tremendous Senate dysfunction. The 112th and 113th Congresses were the least productive in 70 years.[43]

By the 2010s, the Senate had become far less productive than the House in voting on legislation. On average, the House voted on one piece of legislation per working day in the 1990s, and the average remained constant through the early-2010s. In contrast, the Senate saw a large decline in productivity. In the early 1990s, the Senate averaged .4 votes on legislation per working day, but fell to less than .2 votes per day in the early 2010s.[44] As documented in figure 5.3, with the growth in filibuster use, legislative productivity fell dramatically.[45] There were 498 laws passed during 108th Congress (2003–2004)—when Republicans had unified control of government, and 383 passed during the 111th Congress (2009–2010)—the last time Democrats held unified control. In the 113th Congress—which was marked by divided partisan government—just 296 bills were passed, a decline of 23 percent from 2009 to 2010, and of 41 percent from 2003 to 2004. Divided government was not always associated with gridlock. For example, 713 bills passed in the divided 100th Congress (1987–1989), translating into a 58 percent decline in productivity compared to the 113th Congress.[46] Legislative productivity remained low in the 114th Congress (2015–2016), with only 329 laws passed.

Senate obstruction has occurred not only with legislation, but in the confirmation process. The Senate is tasked with confirming or rejecting presidential nominees for the heads of federal bureaucratic agencies and for judicial nominations. But during the Obama years, the Senate saw record obstruction. About half of all filibusters of presidential nominees in history occurred during the Obama administration.[47] This statistic is astounding; never in history was the Senate so devoted to stifling government by preventing federal agencies and the judiciary from performing their basic functions. Senate obstruction was so abused that Democrats eventually voted in late 2013 to prohibit the use of filibusters for judicial nominations. Since the U.S. Constitution says nothing about, it is up to the Senate to decide how to form its parliamentary rules.

Historically, both parties used the filibuster, when they were in the minority, to obstruct the majority party agenda. While both parties increasingly relied on this tactic from the 1970s onward, Republicans set a new precedent under Obama with their radically increased filibustering. The danger moving forward is that both parties will make regular use of the filibuster whenever they are in the Senate minority, making governing difficult to impossible.

Figure 5.3. Legislative Productivity by Congressional Session, 1973–2016. Source: GovTrack, "Statistics and Historical Comparison: Bills by Final Status," *GovTrack*, 2017, https://www.govtrack.us/congress/bills/statistics

Growing polarization between the two parties during the Obama years—due to Republican filibustering and obstructionism—meant that the Democratic Party had little incentive to work with Trump or Congressional Republicans on serious political reforms. Democrats had little reason to try and develop a bipartisan health care reform bill throughout 2017. Instead, they preferred to sit back and watch Republicans flounder amidst internal party divisions. The cost of their previous obstruction, it appeared, had now come back full circle to sting the Republican Party.

Congressional dysfunction now has two primary components. The first is complete inaction under divided government, with Republicans preferring record filibustering to governance. The second component of broken politics is Congressional inaction in terms of helping the middle and lower class during periods of Republican control of government (2017 onward), coupled with active efforts to aid the wealthy and the upper class, as seen in the attempted repeal of Obamacare and the law's taxes on the wealthy, amidst additional Republican efforts to pass tax cuts for the rich via reforming the federal tax code. Through these dual blows, progressive proposals for tackling corporate abuses and reining in the power of the upper class are cast aside.

Why is Congress Broken? Case Studies in Dysfunction

The fall 2013 government shutdown is one the greatest modern examples of legislative dysfunction. The federal government shut down because of disagreement between the Democratic Senate and Republican House over Obamacare. House Republicans insisted the yearly budget for 2014 be attached to a repeal of the law. They understood that Senate Democrats opposed repeal, so Republicans sought to coerce a repeal by attaching it to must-pass budget legislation. They hoped the negative public backlash of a shutdown would be directed primarily at the president and his party. If Americans pressured the Democrats, then the party might be forced to pass a repeal. Republican Speaker of the House John Boehner refused to consider passing a clean budget bill, unattached to health care repeal. Boehner pushed forward, and the government officially shutdown on October 1, for the first time since the mid-1990s.

The standoff was supported by most Republicans, but Democratic officials refused to be coerced into repealing Obamacare. In the face of Democratic resistance, Republicans insisted they were willing to compromise to achieve a budget.[48] First they called for a defunding of the law, which realistically was equivalent to repeal, since the program could not be enacted without funding. When this failed, Republicans called for a one-year delay in the law's mandate that individuals and employers purchase health insurance.[49] The call for a delay also failed to gain Democratic support. Despite their initial vigilance, within a few weeks Republican House leadership abandoned the shutdown entirely due to the negative public backlash.

During the shutdown, Republicans insisted they were opposed to Obamacare in principle. The law, they argued, would kill jobs.[50] It would impose a great burden on businesses and employers, and the mandate itself was a tyrannical, authoritarian assault on the "liberty" of individuals to decide whether they wanted health insurance or not.[51] For years, Republicans lamented that Obama was a socialist bent on destroying America, and they had no choice but to take a stand against his authoritarian acts.[52] Little in the Republican narrative was accurate. According to the rules of Obamacare, no American was required to purchase health insurance. Individuals could opt-out of purchasing health insurance, but they had to pay a $695 tax per year. While many Americans probably preferred to avoid the tax, to argue that imposition of a modest tax on Americans is tantamount to socialism and dictatorship is propagandistic. Many Americans would prefer to pay fewer taxes if allowed to do so by the government.[53] But whatever one thinks of Obamacare, displeasure with paying taxes is not tantamount to living in a dictatorship.

There was reason to question the purity of Republican motives regarding the shutdown and attempted health care repeal. A major warning sign came when Republican Senator Ted Cruz, who symbolically led the shutdown effort in the Senate, explained his reason for opposing the health care law: "If we don't do it now [repeal the law], in all likelihood we never will . . . in modern times no major entitlement, once it was implemented, has ever been unwound . . . On January first, the [health care] exchanges kick in and the [taxpayer] subsidies [to help Americans buy insurance] kick in . . . once those kick in, it's going to prove almost impossible to undo Obamacare. The administration's plan is very simple: get everyone addicted to the sugar so that Obamacare remains a permanent feature of our society."[54]

Cruz's admission as to why he supported the shutdown centered not on a principled concern that Obamacare would hurt the public, but that it would *help* those seeking affordable insurance. For Cruz, Americans should not embrace the idea that government exists to help them. Relying on government to assist Americans with their health care costs was tantamount to "addicting" them to the "sugar" of government assistance. Better to leave individuals to their own devices, whether or not they can afford health care. At the heart of Cruz's opposition was the ideological assumption that government aid to needy Americans was inherently bad. The belief contradicted Republican claims that they opposed reform because it would harm the public.[55] Instead, they were afraid it would help large numbers of people.

So why are Congress and the Republican Party broken? A mentality of extremism took over within the party with regard to the health care repeal. There were major flaws in Obamacare, as it represented a boon to the health care industry by expanding market-based health care, while doing little to regulate ever-increasing health care costs for the masses. But Republicans were even more extreme in pushing a pro-business agenda that almost exclusively benefitted the upper class. Obamacare was deemed "socialist" because it included modest concessions for the poor such as the expansion of Medicaid, and taxpayer subsidies for individuals to purchase health insurance. During the Obama years, if laws were not deemed overwhelmingly favorable to the Republicans' pro-business, deregulatory, anti-tax agenda, they were dead on arrival in Congress. Republican support for repealing Obamacare meant eliminating aid from tens of millions of needy Americans who had struggled to afford health care, all in favor of a tax cut on wealthier Americans.

The prohibition on health insurance companies from denying care to citizens due to preexisting conditions was widely seen as a major strong point of Obamacare. But Congressional Republicans' silence in the face of President Donald Trump's efforts to allow health care corporations to once again deny medical care to individuals with "preexisting conditions" speaks to the rightward extremism of the party, which prioritized taking away life-saving protections from millions of Americans.[56] Republican efforts to enrich health care corporations ran contrary to the public interest, and threatened to harm large numbers of people. Most Americans want Republicans and Congress to be active in passing laws that aid, rather than hurt, the masses.

A second example of legislative dysfunction is seen in the Republicans' fixation on tax cuts for the wealthy, at the expense of collecting government revenues that are needed for popular social programs. This anti-tax agenda was evident in Republican politicking on the national debt. In the 2011 Republican leaders John Boehner, Mitch McConnell, and Eric Cantor and President Obama entered discussions over cutting government spending in future budgets. Obama called Republican leaders together in search of a "grand bargain," in which the federal government would achieve $4 trillion dollars in savings over a decade.[57] Obama proposed that more than three quarters of deficit reduction should come from spending cuts over that time, including unpopular cuts to Social Security spending, if Republicans agreed that 25 percent of savings would come from tax increases falling primarily on the wealthy.[58] The outcome of the talks was predictable in an age of Republican obstructionism in favor of the wealthy. Republican leaders rejected the compromise on tax revenues, insisting that Obama abandon this demand. Boehner justified his opposition to getting more than 75 percent of what he wanted by arguing that he and the President were "not close" to an agreement because of Obama's proposed tax increase.[59] Under this definition of "compromise," Republicans sent a clear message that "negotiations" had to result in 100 percent victories for their party in favor of no tax increases, and with no concessions for their Democratic opponents. While Boehner claimed during negotiations that he was open to raising some tax revenues via closing various tax loopholes, this "offer" from Republicans was not substantive, since the rest of the party leadership rejected the proposal out of hand and pushed Boehner into backing away from the "offer."[60] Obviously, under such conditions the ability to reach a deal through compromise was impossible. Republican intransigence was again confirmed in the 2012 presidential primary debates. All of the Republican frontrunners for the 2012 race confirmed during that debate that they would not only refuse a 3:1 debt agreement in favor of cutting spending over raising taxes, but that they would reject any agreement on deficits with tax hikes attached. When asked if they would agree to raising $1 in tax revenues for every $10 in tax cuts (a 10:1 ratio, over Obama's 3:1 offer), all Republican candidates were opposed.[61]

The 2011 debt fiasco is an important historical example of the movement of both political parties toward embracing a neoliberal, upper-class bias in politics. By attacking Social Security, the Democratic Party under Obama adopted an elitist approach to governing, threatening a vital welfare program in which tens of millions of Americans relied. Republicans were even more reactionary in their

Image 5.1. Obama and Boehner Meeting to Discuss the Debt, 2011.

political approach, demanding cuts to social welfare spending, while refusing to consider any tax hikes on wealthier Americans.[62] Neither party put Main Street America first, as the fight was merely over how much to cut spending benefitting the middle class and poor.

The Republican decision to become the "party of no," by obstructing the Democratic Party intensified following the 2008 election.[63] At a dinner attended by prominent Republican leaders shortly after Obama's electoral victory, party leaders did some "soul searching" regarding how Republicans could recapture Congress and the Presidency.[64] The agreement from the dinner was described by House Republican Majority Leader Kevin McCarthy as follows: "we've gotta challenge them on every single bill and challenge them on every single campaign." Republican congressmen Bob Bennett and Arlen Specter remarked after their interactions with Senate Majority Leader Mitch McConnell that the decision was made: "we can't let you [Democrats] succeed in anything. That's our ticket to coming back."[65]

Recalling his discussions with McConnell, Republican Senator George Voinovich reflected on the marching orders handed down to the Republican rank-and-file that "if he [Obama] was for it, we had to be against it . . . he [McConnell] wanted everyone to hold the fort. All he cared about was making sure Obama could never have a clean victory."[66] However, Republicans still claimed publicly that they were committed to "negotiations" and "compromises" with Democrats. As one McConnell aide reflected: "McConnell realized that it would be much easier to fight Obama if Republicans first made a public show of wanting to work with him."[67] Perhaps the bluntest comment revealing systematic Republican non-cooperation and obstructionism was from Republican Representative Jerry Lewis, who reflected on the position of Republican House leadership on working with Democrats: "It doesn't matter what the hell you [Democrats] do, we ain't going to help you. We're going to stand on the sidelines and bitch."[68] Although Democrats offered market-based reforms such as Obamacare, while calling for cuts in popular welfare programs, these policies were opposed by the Republicans because they weren't friendly enough to corporate and upper-class interests. Obamacare included taxes on the wealthy to pay for health care reform, while the 2011 debt negotiations would have also taxed the wealthy. Instead of compromising with the Democrats' moderate-to-conservative agenda, the party became more radicalized, making governing nearly impossible during the 2010s.

Republicans were rewarded for their obstruction via the 2010 and 2014 midterm elections and the 2016 presidential election. During those midterms, Democratic constituencies did not turn out in large numbers, while Republican voters did, handing control of the House to Republicans. In 2016, many working-class voters flocked away from the Democrats, angry at the party for its years of supporting the outsourcing middle-class jobs.[69] Rather than being punished for obstruction, Republicans were rewarded by a Presidential victory and by taking over the Senate. This sent a message to both parties that, as the minority, it is more lucrative to be obstructionist than to provide solutions to national problems.

The significance of the broken Congress for democracy could not be starker. A radical precedent has been set regarding how national politics is conducted. Active governance in favor of regulating corporate power or aiding the masses through new social spending has become impossible under the new status quo. Citizens can no longer look to the national government to solve national problems. Major issues are left unaddressed, despite most Americans desiring government action on these matters. These failures include: a refusal to raise the minimum wage, even to adjust for inflation during most of the 2010s; opposition to taking action on climate change; refusal to deal with the student loan crisis-debt bubble; and a failure to push for immigration reforms as related to providing a path to citizenship for undocumented immigrants. Congress is no longer willing or able to address serious issues facing the masses of Americans. Such obstruction and inaction are toxic to democracy.

Public Opinion of Congress:
The Fallout from Broken Politics

Americans are not happy with Congress, and the resentment they share for "the people's branch" appears to be related to years of inaction. Political scientists speak of growing congressional disinterest in aiding the masses and the needy, as citizens are allowed to "drift" along on their own, harmed by rising prices for goods such as health care, and stagnating-to-declining wages.[70] And Americans recognize the increasingly upper-class and pro-business bias of congressional politics. One 2015 poll found 74 percent agreed Congress failed to represent "people who have trouble making ends meet." In contrast, 87 percent agreed Congress did "very" or "somewhat well" in representing "wealthy people."[71]

Although Republicans had control of Congress following the 2016 election, this is more of a victory by default, driven by growing disillusionment among the working class and poor against the Democrats.[72] Republican victories did not represent a majority mandate supporting their style of governance, since most Americans do not vote in midterm congressional elections, and more than three-quarters of voting eligible Americans did not vote for Trump. Most Americans express disgust with the status quo in Congress. In a two-party system, characterized by broken politics, it should not be surprising that people distrust government. Support for Congress remains near record lows. Congressional approval stood at just 13 percent in May 2018, while the approval rating for Republicans in Congress ranged from just 12 to 25 percent from 2015 through 2018.[73]

Discontent with Congress is longstanding, with Americans historically seeing it as a "public enemy."[74] In one 2010 *Gallup* poll, reasons cited included the following feelings: 1. That Congress is "not working in the best interests of the country as a whole"; 2. That legislators are "self-serving" and "corrupt"; 3. That they are "too partisan" and not committed to "working together"; 4. That Congress is "not listening to the American people"; 5. That legislators are too focused on "catering to lobbyists" and "special interests"; 6. That they have "been there too long" in office, and that Americans "need new members" and "fresh ideas."[75] Additional survey data from *Public Policy Polling* in 2013 found Congress was less popular than cockroaches, lice, and traffic jams, although it did rate better than the Ebola virus, the Kardashians, and Lindsay Lohan.[76] In 2015, 69 percent of Americans agreed "most members" of Congress "are focused on the needs of special interests" rather than "on the needs of constituents."[77]

With such high disapproval, how are Congressional reelection rates so high? A study by *Politifact* found that Congress in November 2014 had a 14 percent approval rating, but a 95 percent incumbent reelection rate. This discrepancy is astounding since one would expect high disapproval to produce high institutional turnover. This, however, is not the case. The keys to reelection in this hostile environment include: 1. The ability to raise more money than one's competitor, which incumbents are very good at, so they can drown out their competition via ads; 2. Growing partisan polarization, with many states and districts becoming increasingly reliable in cutting consistently in favor of Democrats or Republicans; and 3. Related to point one, successful efforts by legislators to brand themselves and build up perceptions of a "personal" connection with voters.[78] The branding strategy helps members of Congress build support from voters, even as Americans' negative attitudes about Congress as a whole have grown.

The Congressional scholar Richard Fenno spoke of the power of legislators to brand their campaigns as part of their "home style"—or the way they present themselves to their constituents. The goal is to cultivate trust among potential voters, through activities such as campaign speeches, canvassing, ads, speaking events, town hall meetings, emails, letters, phone calls, and granting of distributive "pork" benefits to constituents. Members of Congress increasingly prioritize aiding the upper class and the privileged, but if one can make enough voters *think* their specific members of Congress care, that is usually enough to get reelected. While most Americans distrust Congress, getting elected or reelected has never been about winning support from most constituents. Rather, it is about cultivating *enough* votes to beat one's opponent. In the typical midterm election, around a third of the public votes. A successful candidate needs only a simple majority (and sometimes a plurality), meaning he/she could win with votes from 15 to 20 percent of a state's or district's population. This threshold is easy to reach with incumbents' tremendous monetary resources and their significant media exposure.

In the process of seeking reelection, legislators interact with constituents, thereby creating the perception of personal ties. As a result, although most Americans disapprove of Congress, individual legislators perform much better in polls.[79] One might argue that "home style" branding is a good thing because it suggests meaningful ties are established between legislators and citizens. But this claim is problematic for various reasons. First, one should not simply ignore the historically high levels of Congressional disapproval. It makes little sense to talk about Congress being rotten in its entirety: individual members of Congress represent constituents. This is classic false consciousness on the part of the public. Congress is an aggregation of its members. If Congress as an institution is rotten, that is because its members are rotten.

A second problem is that "home style" branding creates a false sense of connection between legislators and constituents. Fenno found that, over time, direct ties between legislators and the public began to wane. The longer representatives remained in Congress, the less likely they were to spend time in their home districts. Research since Fenno's study finds that legislators spend most of their time in Washington, not with their constituents.[80] And more recent research finds that Congress is far better at representing top income earners than the rest of the population. These findings undermine claims that legislators are strongly connected to the mass public.

Concluding Points

This chapter has not been optimistic about the quality of democratic representation in Congress. Gridlock, extremism, and an upper-class bias increasingly define the legislature. There are reforms, however, that might improve the quality of representation. These include:

- Introducing term limits, to prevent entrenchment in Congress, and to ensure new candidates and ideas get a hearing. Numerous states have term limits for their legislatures. The U.S. Congress could have them too if there was enough public pressure.

- Limiting the harmful reliance on filibustering to obstruct majority voting. In the fall of 2013, Senate Democrats invoked the "nuclear option," eliminating the use of filibusters for judicial and bureaucratic confirmations. Filibuster rules could be rewritten to rescind the changes made in 1975, thereby limiting obstructionism.

- Limiting the role of money in elections. In 2002, a bi-partisan campaign finance reform bill was passed to limit campaign spending in elections. Although the Supreme Court struck down these rules, the public could pressure Congress to reinstate them.

- Increased vigilance on the part of various demographic groups, including the poor, people of color, and millennials. These groups suffer from low voting levels, and their apathy enables legislative elitism. To address this problem, disadvantaged groups need to exert more pressure on the political process through voting for progressive candidates willing to challenge upper-class dominance of the political process.

American legislative politics does not have to be dominated by the wealthy. The key to positive change lies in public pressure on the political system. Creating a more democratic system requires clearing out many of the current legislators from office, particularly those who define their political success through obstructionism and elitist policies that serve the wealthy over the people.

Chapter 6

The Executive Branch

Political Power, the Imperial Presidency, and the Threat to Democracy

The growing elitism of the American Presidency means an intensifying divide between government and citizens. Nowhere was this more apparent than in an interview Republican President Donald Trump did with *The New York Times* on health care reform. Complaining about government efforts to aid those who struggle to afford health insurance, Trump railed against Obamacare and taxpayer health care subsidies for working- and middle-class Americans. "Once you get something, it's awfully tough to take it away. As they get something, it gets tougher. Because politically, you can't give it away. So preexisting conditions are a tough deal. Because you are basically saying from the moment the insurance, you're 21 years old, you start working and you're paying $12 a year for insurance, and by the time you're 70, you get a nice plan. Here's something where you walk up and say, 'I want my insurance.'"[1]

There were numerous things to take away from Trump's rambling response in the above interview. First, he demonstrated a strong contempt for government aid to Americans who rely on federal assistance regarding health care, as seen not only in Trump's efforts to repeal Obamacare, but also in his complaints about government efforts to help millions of people. Second, Trump displayed a complete ignorance to what it was the government was even doing regarding health care benefits and services under Obamacare. He clearly confused life insurance—in which individuals pay relatively small amounts over the year, and their children collect upon their death—and health insurance, which citizens rely on for day-to-day care. But even in his confusion and incompetence, Trump displayed a profound disconnect with the average American, especially those who have struggled to afford their insurance due to runaway premiums, out-of-pocket costs, and deductibles. That Trump conflated low-cost life insurance benefits with health insurance costs, the latter of which in the U.S. are higher than in any other wealthy country, revealed how out-of-touch he was with the financial stresses and needs of the public. Clearly, Trump, like other members of the upper class, does not have to worry about whether he can afford health insurance.

The divide between Trump and the common citizen on health care is not unique to this President. It is a systemic feature of American society in an era of record inequality, one in which upper-class elites and the wealthy dominate public policy, with little interest in, or knowledge of the struggles of the middle class and poor. These individuals can afford to deprioritize health care aid for the many, since they have no trouble affording their own care, and do not need to rely on the government for assistance. In an increasingly narcissistic, highly individualistic political culture, government aid to the masses is seen as a waste of political resources, and that point clearly came through in *The New York Times*' interview with Trump.

The Presidency is the most prominent office in U.S. politics. Presidents are expected to provide leadership to the entire country, rather than merely representing the wealthy few. This office is vital to government's ability to provide for citizens' needs. If presidents do not execute the law to the benefit of the people, government cannot serve the public. But there is a significant democratic deficit with the presidency. Presidents, like Congress, are increasingly elitist, favoring upper-class political interests. This trend manifests itself domestically, with neoliberal policies that seek to discipline the masses and poor, and via economic policies aimed at enhancing the wealth of the rich. One also sees the privileging of business in U.S. foreign policy, which is designed to promote capitalist interests, while assaulting foreign nations that embrace socialist values or challenge U.S. military and economic power. The upper-class bias in politics has intensified over the last few decades, especially with the rise of Donald Trump.

Presidential Power

Should they choose, Presidents have significant power to fight for the common person. The unity of the office—in contrast to Congress, which has 535 members—gives the President an advantage in any negotiation regarding the development and passage of legislation. And Presidents exercise outsized influence when it comes to leading national political debates. Presidents have consistently led the nation on foreign and domestic initiatives. During the 2000s, two of the largest legislative changes passed included the 2001 tax cuts and the 2009 stimulus. President Bush led the effort to pass the tax cuts, receiving significantly more attention in the news than all of Congress combined.[2] Obama led the charge for the stimulus, garnering more attention in the news than all legislative voices put together.[3] On foreign policy post-September 11, 2001, presidents led the nation in initiating foreign conflicts. President Bush stood before the nation after the terror attacks and declared a "War on Terrorism." Bush made the case for why the U.S. was going to war with Afghanistan. Congress responded to the President's push for war by authorizing the use of force. Bush also led in making the case for war with Iraq, while Congress signed off on war. Obama did not even ask Congress's permission when going to war with Libyan President Muammar Gadhafi in 2011. Nor did he ask for Congress's authorization in 2014 when he engaged in airstrikes against the Islamic State in Iraq and Syria (ISIS).

Regarding the lawmaking process, presidents are highly successful in gaining concessions from Congress. Presidents do not sit idly by and wait for Congress to offer them legislation. They actively push Congress to include presidential proposals in legislation being considered by the House and Senate. Presidents use the threat of the veto to achieve concessions from Congress. This amounts to "negative" power, with Presidents impeding legislation that is unfavorable to their agendas.[4] Analyzing more than 400 vetoes from the Truman administration (1945) through Bush (1992), one study finds that, in 80 percent of their terms, Presidents regularly succeeded in extracting concessions, as Congress moved toward second round attempts to pass legislation. Research by *Congressional Quarterly* suggests Presidential influence via veto bargaining is a potent weapon. Examining legislative outcomes from 1953 through 2009, the organization found presidents got on average 64 percent of what they proposed included in House legislative items, and 74 percent of what they proposed in Senate legislation. During those same years, presidents pushed most of their proposals through the House in 69 percent of the years they served. In the Senate, presidents pushed through most of their proposals for 95 percent of the years they served.[5] Another study of presidential rhetoric and foreign policy found that, post-September 11, presidents succeeded twice as often as not in selling their proposals to Congress and the public.[6] The above studies collectively suggest presidents are quite successful in getting what they want. That power is available to them, either to serve the interests of the wealthy and the upper class, or to help the masses of middle-class and poorer Americans.

Presidential power is also significant with regard to the courts. Although the judicial branch reviews presidential acts, judges regularly defer to the executive. Executive influence over the courts can be measured by examining legal cases involving both the Solicitor General (representing the executive branch in legal challenges to national laws and presidential acts) and the courts. If judges routinely tell the executive branch "no" by striking down laws and presidential acts, this would suggest strong judicial independence. If, however, judges defer to the Solicitor General, it suggests a lack of independence from the executive.

Judges defer to the Solicitor General in a large majority of legal cases brought before the courts. Looking at the Obama administration and cases involving the Solicitor General, the executive prevailed in 61 percent of all cases, and in 77 percent of cases when the Solicitor General served as Amicus Curiae (filing a legal argument on behalf of one party as a "friend of the court").[7] The success rates across presidents is high, as documented in figure 6.1.[8]

When petitioning the Supreme Court to hear a case, the Solicitor General succeeds about 70 percent of the time in securing a hearing. This is a dramatic success rate, considering the meager 3 percent success rate of non-presidential litigants. With regard to the merits of cases, the Solicitor General is extraordinarily successful, winning 70 to 80 percent of the time, depending on the historical period examined. The Solicitor General prevails in approximately three-quarters of all cases when it submits an amicus brief, making a legal argument on behalf of an interest it is defending.[9]

The potential reasons why the courts defer to the president are numerous. One is that judges vote based on their ideological values, and judges appointed by a president are less likely to rebuke that president in cases involving the

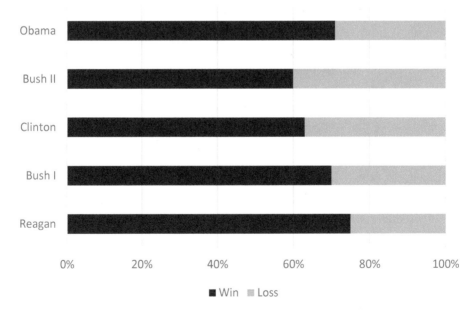

Figure 6.1. Executive Success-Loss Rates at the Supreme Court. Source: Pincus, "The Solicitor General's Report Card," 2014, http://www.scotusblog.com/2014/07/the-solicitor-generals-report-card/; Adam Liptak, "Why Obama Struggled at Court and Trump May Strain to Do Better," *The New York Times*, January 23, 2017, https://www.nytimes.com/2017/01/23/us/politics/obama-supreme-court-win-rate-trump.html

executive. The overlap between the ideologies of the executive and its appointees would be expected to produce judicial deference to the president.[10] A second possible reason is the Solicitor General simply has greater legal expertise, and is more widely respected because of that expertise.[11] A third potential reason is cherry picking. Solicitor Generals, some scholars argue, may choose "to participate in cases" they feel they are "favorably disposed to win."[12] A final reason for judicial deference may be judicial impotence and fear of irrelevance in the face of a powerful executive branch. As judicial scholars have long argued, judges may feel pressure to issue decisions that align with the other branches, out of fear that to challenge those branches is to risk having their decisions ignored.[13]

With deference to the executive, presidents are in a position of significant political power. They are the face of the nation, and command more media attention than members of Congress. The prestige and resources of the office confer upon it serious legitimacy from the courts. And the President's veto over Congress is an impressive power that can be wielded at will. Within this political context, the President is in a strong position to fight for the interests of the people, and to represent the masses, rather than simply prioritizing the wealthy or the corporate class. Unfortunately, the presidency has been defined by growing elitism in recent decades.

A Presidency for the Upper Class

Political scientists speak of the development of the presidency as defined by eras and "regimes" that dominate politics in various periods of "political time."[14] The modern regime is a decidedly neoliberal one, with politics—and the presidency in particular—dominated by corporate and upper-class interests. This neoliberal "regime" may decline one day with the return of a more progressive period of governance, as Americans saw with the New Deal and Great Society/War on Poverty regimes, although such a transformation does not appear to be likely in the near future.

The bias toward wealth and the upper class that persists within the executive branch greatly inhibits democracy. Examining the history of the American presidency, the office has always been defined by its elitism. Thirty-eight out of the 45 presidents who have served—or 84 percent—were millionaires or wealthier.[15] Looking at the 2016 presidential race, 18 of the 22, or 81 percent of the major candidates running under the Democratic and Republican tickets in the primaries were millionaires or wealthier, including from most to least wealthy: Donald Trump, Carly Fiorina, Hillary Clinton, Lincoln Chafee, Ben Carson, Jeb Bush,

George Pataki, John Kasich, Mike Huckabee, Jim Gilmore, Jim Webb, Bobby Jindal, Ted Cruz, Chris Christie, Rand Paul, Rick Santorum, Lindsey Graham, and Rick Perry. Only four candidates were not millionaires—Bernie Sanders, Martin O'Malley, Scott Walker, and Marco Rubio.[16]

Regarding education, most modern Presidents come from elite, Ivy League universities and most have held graduate degrees, unlike most Americans. Presidents George H. W. Bush, George W. Bush, and Bill Clinton attended Yale University for their graduate studies, while Barack Obama went to Harvard University. Historically there is little diversity in presidents by race, gender, and age. No president has ever been elected who was younger than his forties—only Bill Clinton and Barack Obama were younger than 50. George W. Bush was in his fifties, George H. W. Bush in his sixties, and Donald Trump in his seventies. The United States has never had a Hispanic-descent or female president, and has only had one African-American president. In short, the office has historically been incredibly elitist, representing privileged upper-class groups, as seen in the typical profile of a U.S. president as older, white, highly educated, wealthy, and male.

The election of Donald Trump to the Presidency meant an even stronger turn toward an upper-class bias in the executive. The U.S. never had a billionaire president prior to Trump, and the president made no secret about hiding his pro-business politics, including his support for deregulation and tax cuts for the wealthy. Trump's executive branch nominees were also unique, in that never had so many people of such opulence been nominated to key federal positions. *The New York Times* reported in January 2017: "Trump has selected what would be the wealthiest cabinet in modern American history, filled with millionaires and billionaires with complicated financial portfolios. Mr. [Rex] Tillerson [the Secretary of State] is worth at least $300 million, but is hardly the richest among them; Wilbur L. Ross, Jr., the Commerce Secretary; Betsy DeVos, the Education Secretary; and Steven T. Mnuchin, the Treasury Secretary, each hold assets estimated at more than a billion dollars."[17]

Trump's election has accelerated an already-existing trend in tax policy that increasingly favors not the upper class, but the super-rich. President Reagan prioritized tax cuts for wealthier upper-class Americans across the board, cutting the tax rate on American households earning over $260,000 (in 2017 dollars) from 70 percent to 50 percent in 1981, and down to 28 percent in 1986.[18] The tax cuts passed in 2001 and 2003 under the George W. Bush administration also heavily favored the entire upper class, with nearly 40 percent of the cuts going to the top one percent of income earners, and two-thirds going to the top 20 percent of earners.[19] President Bush and members of his administration were millionaires, so it is no surprise that they prioritized aiding affluent Americans.

Donald Trump
$3.1 billion

Ben Carson
$29 million

Elaine Chao
$24 million

Wilbur Ross
$2.5 billion

Betsy DeVos
$1.25 billion

Tom Price
$10 million

Rex Tillerson
$325 million

Steven Mnuchin
$300 million

Jeff Sessions
$6 million

Figure 6.2. Profiles in Elitism—The Trump Administration, 2017. Sources: Chase Peterson-Withorn, "Here's What Each Member of Trump's $4.5 Billion Cabinet is Worth," *Forbes*, December 22, 2016, https://www.forbes.com/sites/chasewithorn/2016/12/22/heres-how-much-trumps-cabinet-is-really-worth/#432cc31d7169; Forbes, "The Definitive Net Worth of DonaldTrump," *Forbes*, February 2017, https://www.forbes.com/donald-trump/#319915d28992

President Trump's economic background is even more decadent than previous presidents, with the commander in chief and various members of his administration each holding billions in financial assets. Trump made the uber-rich within the upper class the target of his tax cuts. In late-2017, Trump put forward a plan to cut taxes that would have reduced federal revenues by $5.8 trillion, with the majority of the cuts going to the top one percent of income earners, while raising taxes on poorer, middle-class, and lower-upper-class citizens.[20] As the *Tax Policy Center* estimated, by 2027, 40 percent of the proposed Trump tax cuts would go to the top .1 percent of income earners, while an additional 40 percent would go to the rest of the top one percent, for a total of 80 percent of the tax cuts benefitting the top one percent of earners, and the other 80 percent receiving just 20 percent of the Trump tax cuts. In contrast, the *Tax Policy Center* estimated that a third of families earning between $10,000 and 20,000 a year, nearly half of those making $20,000 to 30,000, and more than 40 percent of those earning from $30,000 to 40,000 a year would see their taxes increase. Three-quarters of households earning from $200,000 to $500,000 a year would also pay more taxes.[21] These numbers are a stark indication that the presidency now almost exclusively serves the wealthiest one percent of Americans.[22]

At the heart of the right-wing tax cut agenda is an effort to deny the federal government the revenues needed to pay for popular welfare and social spending programs that benefit the middle- and lower-classes. The "starve the beast" mentality was famously articulated by conservative anti-tax advocate Grover Norquist, who once proclaimed that "I don't want to abolish government. I simply want to reduce it to the size where I can drag it into the bathroom and drown it in the bathtub."[23] This mindset was also reflected in Bush's rhetoric during the 2000s, when the president sold the 2001 tax cuts as imposing "a fiscal straightjacket for Congress" which would limit future federal spending.[24] The Trump tax cut agenda is particularly harmful to the principle of democratic governance, in that it represents a brazen money-grab in which taxpayer resources are redistributed upward from the 99 percent to the top one percent.

Trump's elitism extended beyond economics, as one could see in his verbal and policy-based attacks on historically disadvantaged groups. The revelation that Trump joked about sexually accosting women demonstrated his sexist, patriarchal orientation toward gender relations in America.[25] His support for a ban on immigration from Muslim-majority countries, and his plan to build a separation wall between the U.S. and Mexico both demonstrated his support for racist, xenophobic policy positions. Finally, Trump demonstrated that he was blatantly out of touch with black Americans, via his support for "law and order" policing strategies such as "stop and frisk," which the Department of Justice concludes are applied in a racially discriminatory manner, not to mention the Trump administration's disinterest in communicating respectfully with black constituents.[26]

Political officials claim to speak for all Americans. As the argument goes, just because someone is a white, upper-class male, does not mean they cannot represent the poor, women, or other disadvantaged groups. But privilege does impact political officials' views and actions. Officials hailing from disadvantaged groups are more likely to try and help disadvantaged Americans in their policy proposals. Female officials are more likely to prioritize policies that benefit women.[27] And black political officials are more likely to represent the interests of black Americans.[28] Political officials from more affluent, white-collar occupational backgrounds are more likely to represent conservative, pro-business interests, as compared to those with less privileged, blue-collar backgrounds.[29] Higher-income Americans are better represented by political officialdom than middle- and lower-income individuals.[30] These findings should give citizens pause to reflect on the quality of their democracy. Both Congress and the White House are dominated by upper-class economic interests, and it shows in policy outcomes that are biased in favor of the wealthy.

The Imperial Presidency

The concept of the imperial presidency was popularized by historian Arthur Schlesinger, who used the term to refer to the Pentagon Papers—which were a declassified government record demonstrating that the Lyndon Johnson administration lied to the public about U.S. motivations and actions in the Vietnam War, and the Watergate scandal, in which Richard Nixon's administration was responsible for an illegal break-in and spying on the Democratic Party. The imperial presidency is based on the notion that the president has exceeded his authority under the Constitution, particularly on foreign policy. While the first imperial presidency period spanned the late 1960s to the early 1970s, a second period emerged after September 11, 2001.

The imperial presidency is relevant to the study of class bias in politics in that it is defined by increasingly aggressive Presidents who seek to further U.S. economic and military power throughout the world. The modern campaign to further U.S. power is driven by economics, with U.S. leaders seeking to promote capitalism abroad and strengthen capitalist allies, while opposing socialist regimes and other countries not aligned with capitalist interests. In light of these efforts to promote Western corporate interests, it makes sense to speak more broadly of a capitalist bias in U.S. foreign policy, rather than simply an upper-class bias. Of course, members of the upper class—particularly business elites—are directly served by U.S. foreign policy, and by the imperial presidency.

The first imperial presidency began with the infamous "Pentagon Papers," which are a declassified, multi-volume history of U.S. involvement in the Vietnam War. The Pentagon Papers, leaked in 1971 by U.S. military analyst Daniel Ellsberg, and printed in *The New York Times* and other media, were controversial for several reasons. First, they revealed that, although Johnson was elected president in 1964 promising the U.S. would not send ground troops to Vietnam, the administration secretly planned on escalation. Second, U.S. officials deceived the public by promising the U.S. sought no larger war, despite secret planning to expand the war to Laos and Cambodia to disrupt Vietnamese supply routes. Third, U.S. officials held the leaders of South Vietnam with contempt, despite claiming the U.S. was committed to that country's sovereignty and defense.[31] The Pentagon Papers are an important part of American history, in that they chronicle the U.S. commitment to deceiving the public with regard to a war that was openly fought to promote capitalist interests, in opposition to communism.

The first imperial presidency collapsed under the weight of the Nixon administration, which illegally conspired with the Watergate burglars, who were arrested attempting to bug the Democratic Party's national headquarters in 1972. Public confidence in the presidency fell dramatically for decades following the first imperial presidency. But the crisis of September 11, 2001, was accompanied by the emergence of the second imperial presidency, with Americans surrendering massive powers to President Bush that were unthinkable prior to the 9/11 terror attacks. The most contentious battles after September 11 centered on administration deception regarding the Iraq war, illegal NSA spying, suspension of due process, the growth in governance by executive signing statements, and the use of torture and assassination.

The Downing Street Memo represents perhaps the best case of the Bush administration's lies and deceptions on Iraq. Bush spent six months in 2002 and 2003 selling the American public on the need for war, discussing Iraq's alleged ties to Al Qaeda and supposed possession of Weapons of Mass Destruction. But the U.S. never found any WMDs in Iraq, and the claim that Iraq supported al Qaeda was rejected by U.S. intelligence experts and government inquiries.[32] The Downing Street Memo—a declassified record of a deliberation between British Prime Minister Tony Blair and his subordinates—revealed the following: 1. Blair recognized the case for war based on Iraq's alleged WMD threat was "thin," since Iraq was not threatening its neighbors and no WMDs had been found; 2. The Bush administration was set on war in 2002, despite Bush's declarations that the U.S. sought to avoid war if Saddam Hussein would cooperate with weapons inspectors in Iraq; 3. The "facts" regarding Iraq's supposed WMDs were being "fixed around the policy of regime change." In other words, the administration had long wished to remove Saddam Hussein from power, and was using the pretext of WMDs as an excuse; 4. Rather than avoiding war, the administration sought to provoke a conflict. The alleged support for U.N. inspections was disingenuous. U.S. and British officials discussed painting a U.S. spy plane in U.N. colors and flying it over Iraq to provoke the Iraqi government into firing—thereby justifying war.

More recent evidence suggests the Bush administration knowingly deceived the public on WMDs. A Department of Defense report from 2002 gained attention in 2016, as it revealed that U.S. officials had "struggled [before the war] to estimate unknowns in Iraq" regarding "knowledge on various aspects of their [WMD] program." The U.S. had little authoritative evidence of a threat to the West. As the report acknowledged: "our knowledge of the Iraqi (nuclear) weapons program is based largely—perhaps 90 percent—on analysis of imprecise intelligence." The report continued: "We cannot confirm the identity of any Iraqi facilities that produce, test, fill, or store biological weapons." With regard to chemical weapons, the DOD reflected: "we do not know if all the processes required to produce a weapon are in place." Iraq "lack[ed] the precursors for sustained nerve agent production," while the U.S. "cannot confirm the identity of any Iraqi sites that produce chemical agent."[33] These assessments suggest the Bush administration was highly deceptive in its pre-war rhetoric. It publicly projected the notion that U.S. officials were sure Iraq posed a significant threat, when in reality that was not the case.

So if the war in Iraq was not about fighting terrorism or protecting the public against WMDs, what was it about? I document in detail in chapter 16 how U.S. foreign policy after World War II has consistently been driven by an interest in promoting corporate and capitalist interests. In the case of the Middle East, president after president has spoken about the importance of oil as a strategic asset that the U.S. must control, for the benefit of oil corporations and U.S. capitalism and our petroleum-based economy more broadly. While U.S. leaders rarely speak brazenly about U.S. policy as driven by corporate interests, declassified government documents across many decades confirm that petroleum interests are central to U.S. foreign policy in the Middle East, and with regard to Iraq.

The National Security Agency (NSA) wiretapping scandal was one of the most blatant violations of national law by the Bush administration. In early 2006, *The New York Times* reported the administration illegally ordered the NSA to spy on alleged terrorists' phone calls going in and out of the country. The spying was illegal, because the administration was required to first present evidence to a secret national security court, under the rules of the 1978 Foreign Intelligence Surveillance Act, before spying. Rather than impeach the president, Congress endorsed the violations via 2007 legislation that legally authorized warrantless NSA spying.[34]

The Bush administration also gained infamy for its embrace of torture, which it referred to euphemistically as "enhanced interrogation techniques." These methods included waterboarding, or the forced drowning of detainees by placing a cloth over their mouth while pouring water through it; use of hypothermia (forcing naked prisoners to stand in 50 degree Fahrenheit temperatures while being routinely doused with cold water); forced stress positions in which prisoners stood or were tied down for days, causing extreme pain and muscle failure; physical attacks against detainees; and sleep deprivation for days on end, often via the blaring of loud music.[35] Many of these activities are outlawed under the international rules of war established via the Geneva Conventions and the United Nations Convention Against Torture.[36]

The Bush administration also relied on rendition, a practice whereby the U.S. sends prisoners to an allied country to be tortured. Use of rendition was advantageous to the administration in that it allowed the U.S. to conceal its role in brutal forms of torture. An estimated 1,245 prisoners were subject to rendition during the 2000s, via the CIA's secret flights that sent detainees to interrogation facilities in 54 countries.[37] There was a strong backlash against this practice among those condemning the U.S. for violating prisoners' basic human rights.[38]

The use of torture was fraught with danger, considering its potential for mobilizing anti-Americanism. Perhaps half the people detained at the U.S. prison in Guantanamo Bay Cuba did not belong there according to intelligence analysts.[39] Journalists investigated the effects of torture at Guantanamo, which was directed against those whose terrorist ties were questionable to nonexistent.[40] Their torture led to a further intensification of anti-U.S. sentiment, as McClatchy news service concluded in its investigation. U.S. detainees were often kept "on the basis of flimsy or fabricated evidence . . . McClatchy interviewed 66 released detainees, more than a dozen local officials in Afghanistan, and U.S. officials with intimate knowledge of the detention program . . . most of the 66 were low level Taliban grunts, innocent Afghan villagers, or ordinary criminals. At least seven had been working for the U.S. backed Afghan government and had no ties to militants . . . many of the detainees posed no danger to the U.S. or its allies." McClatchy found that "prisoner mistreatment became a regular feature in cellblocks and interrogation rooms at Bagram and Kandahar air bases, the two main way stations in Afghanistan en route to Guantanamo . . . top Bush administration officials knew within months of opening the Guantanamo detention center that many of the prisoners there weren't 'the worst of the worst,'" as "it was that at least a third of the population didn't belong there."[41] American soldiers accepted "false reports passed along by informants and officials looking to settle old grudges in Afghanistan, a nation that had experienced more than two decades of occupation and civil war before U.S. troops arrived." Mistreatment of detainees produced blowback toward the U.S. "U.S. detention policies fueled support for extremist Islamist groups. For some detainees who went home far more militant than when they arrived, Guantanamo became a school for jihad."[42]

Illegal wiretapping, torture, and rendition do not speak directly to the promotion of imperial or capitalist interests abroad. Rather, these tactics were defended as necessary to winning the "War on Terrorism." But members of the Bush administration never tried to divorce the "War on Terror" from broader principles of power politics, militarism, and empire. The administration's 2002 National Security Strategy spoke explicitly about sustaining American military power, fighting terrorism, and pursuing strategic interests as related to access to global oil and energy markets. These declarations revealed that the global anti-terrorism agenda was subsumed under a broader global imperial project.

One of the most blatant violations of Constitutional law was the Bush administration's designation of detainees as "enemy combatants." According to the Third and Fourth Geneva Conventions, those detained during conflicts fall into one of two designations: civilians or prisoners of war.[43] There is no inter-mediate status. The classification of detainees as "enemy combatants" was an attempt by Bush to circumvent Constitutional protections for the detained. The Fifth Amendment states: "no person shall be deprived of life, liberty, or property, without due process of law." All persons have the right to try and prove their innocence in a court of law. They cannot sit in jail indefinitely, as this prac-tice violates the legal principle of innocent until proven guilty, in addition to violating basic habeas corpus rights. By holding detainees in Guantanamo Bay prison without charge, the Bush administration violated the Fifth Amendment and international law.

When the Bush administration finally decided to try "enemy combatants," they pushed them through military tribunals, rather than civilian courts. This practice is also illegal, the Supreme Court ruled in 2006, because international and national legal obligations require that the accused be provided civilian legal protections in a court of law.[44] Detainees are not representatives of foreign countries with which the U.S. is at war, hence they are civilians to be guaranteed civilian legal protections. International protections under the Geneva Conventions require detainees under U.S. jurisdiction to be provided access to regularly constituted civilian proceedings. A regular court proceeding is missing from military tribunals, which deny basic protections for the accused in numerous ways:

- Tribunals allow for the introduction of hearsay against defendants.[45]

- They allow for secret evidence, if military lawyers introduce clas-sified evidence, meaning defendants are not allowed to challenge the evidence against them.[46]

- They allow for government monitoring of attorney-client communications. This monitoring means prosecutors already know the legal defenses to be used in court.[47]

- They allow for a majority vote to convict—a lower threshold than the unanimous conviction requirement in civilian courts.[48]

While the Supreme Court ruled the Bush administration had to try detainees in civilian courts, Congress and the president circumvented these protections by passing the 2006 "Military Commissions Act" authorizing use of military tribunals.

Obama continued the consolidation of executive power under the imperial presidency. This occurred in various ways: 1. The continuation of unlawful detainment at Guantanamo Bay prison, despite Obama's promise to close the facility and guarantee due process to detainees. As *The New York Times*, reported, Obama claimed authority under the 2012 National Defense Authorization Act, "authorizing the government to detain without trial, suspected members of al Qaeda or its allies—or those who 'substantially supported' them."[49] This justification echoed the Bush administration's assumption that trials were unnecessary, since the U.S. government could determine guilt or innocence independent of the legal process; 2. The continued use of rendition against terror suspects, despite Obama's promise that allied countries undertaking interrogations would no longer engage in torture.[50] This promise was bizarre, considering the entire point of rendition is to allow interrogators to "take the gloves off," and provide actionable intelligence to fight terror, while leaving Americans' hands "clean" when it came to engaging in the most deplorable forms of physical torture; 3. The continued use of drone strikes to assassinate alleged terrorists, in violation of international law. While President Bush ordered 50 strikes during his time in office, Obama undertook ten times as many[51]; 4. The intensification of NSA spying on Americans, going beyond the spying on foreign phone calls, and including domestic surveillance.[52]

One of Obama's highest profile acts in reinforcing the imperial presidency was his attack on the Libyan regime of Muammar Gaddafi. Although the War Powers act prohibits presidents from using force for more than 90 days without Congressional authorization, and the U.S. had exceeded this threshold in its military operations in Libya by July 2011, the Obama administration argued that it could continue military activities, since "U.S. operations do not involve sustained fighting or active exchanges of fire with hostile forces, nor do they involve U.S. ground troops."[53] This legal "argument"—if one could call it that, was belied by a plain reading of the War Powers act, which states that the president has 60 days to engage in "any use of United States Armed Forces," and another 30 days to end such activities, so long as the executive lacks official Congressional authorization.[54] The reference to "any" activities involving the "armed forces" left little room for interpretation on the use of force, meaning the Obama administration's dismissal of the law represented a blatant violation of the rules of war.

The Trump administration continued the imperial presidency in many ways. One way was through its illegal strikes on sovereign nations. In early 2017, Trump ordered a Navy SEAL raid against an al Qaeda target, which resulted in the death of one U.S. serviceman, several alleged militants, and up to 15 women and children.[55] The highly publicized incident was illegal under international law, which prohibits unauthorized military attacks on other nations. But Trump, like presidents before him, demonstrated no concern for international law, national sovereignty, or civilian deaths. A second use-of-force action that was illegal under the war powers act was the sustained use of special forces and other troops in Syria against militant Islamic fundamentalist groups, starting in late 2015, and continuing through 2018 onward.[56] Although these activities began under Obama, they continued under Trump, with the latter claiming that "the United States will not hesitate to use necessary and proportionate force to defend U.S. coalition, or partner forces engaged in operations to defeat ISIS and degrade al Qaeda."[57] Again, these actions were in violation of the war powers act.

As with assassinations and drone strikes, use of torture via rendition and expanded NSA spying were also illegal. The U.N. Convention Against Torture (1987) forbids the use of torture, as does the Torture Victim Protection Act of 1991. NSA spying, while legalized following revelations of Bush's illegal spying program, was deemed illegal by a federal appeals court in 2015. The court ruled the mass collection of citizens' phone and other communication records violated the right to privacy under the Fourth Amendment, since the federal government was collecting data on communications between millions of citizens, and independent of specific terror suspect investigations.[58]

The many powers seized by presidents after September 11 were pursued in the name of keeping Americans safe from terrorism. But as previously mentioned, these acts are also part of a broader imperial strategy in which the U.S. ignores international law, while relying on military force to assert itself politically across the world in pursuit of capitalist economic interests. The "War on Terror" is inextricably linked to this political and economic power game, since Western capitalist interests stand to lose out with the rise of radical Islamic fundamentalist and terrorist groups. This point was conceded by President Bush when he argued that the U.S. could not withdrawal from Iraq during the mid-2000s, since the takeover of the country by radical terror groups would allow them to use oil as a weapon against the United States.[59] The public, fearful of terror threats, acquiesced to the rise of the imperial presidency.

Most recently, the Trump administration has pioneered the use of executive orders and decisions in pursuit of enriching corporate interests. Most notable was Trump's announcement that he was rescinding the U.S. commitment to the Paris Agreement, which committed the U.S. to cutting down on corporate polluters and CO_2 emissions, as related to climate change.[60] The repeal was a gift to the fossil fuel industry by an administration known for its blatant contempt for environmental conservationism. Another Trump order rolled back regulations on large banks passed during the Obama Presidency, which were created to prevent predatory lending practices.[61] A third executive order committed U.S. federal agencies to eliminating regulations on businesses and in other policy areas, requiring the removal of two regulations for every new regulation introduced. Those regulations must also be cost-free, essentially making any new government regulatory effort toward corporate America impossible to implement.[62] Finally, one of Trump's orders opened up federal land in the Arctic to businesses looking for new opportunities for natural gas and oil exploration. The environmentalist campaign to stop drilling in the artic has been ongoing for more than a decade, but the Trump administration displayed unbridled contempt for such concerns.[63]

Rather than governing through the execution of Congressional laws, the Trump administration mainly preferred to govern through executive orders. As *Newsweek* reported, the Trump administration used executive actions twice as often as the Obama administration, using 50 alone in its first year in office.[64] Trump's reliance on such orders represents a clear danger to limited, democratic governance. It blatantly contradicts any notion of separation of powers or checks and balances within the federal government. It empowers presidents to govern by fiat, with little concern regarding the concentration of power within the executive branch. And such actions also mean a lack of accountability to the American people, considering that most disapprove of Trump's executive orders covering various major political issues.[65]

Finally, Trump also displayed a fundamental contempt for the rule of law that was Nixonian in orientation. He argued that presidents—because of their high status in American politics—cannot have conflicts of interest with regard to the Emoluments Clause, which prohibits accepting gifts or profits from foreign leaders.[66] Trump continued with this authoritarian mindset, offering claims that he was beyond the law, in relation to the federal investigation into Russian meddling in the 2016 election. More specifically, his administration maintained that the president "can't have a conflict of interest" and can never commit obstruction of justice in the investigation (for example, by firing FBI Director James Comey in an effort to shut down the inquiry), since the president "has unfettered authority over all federal investigations."[67] This line of defense is blatantly contradicted by Article 2, Section 4 of the U.S. Constitution, which states that Congress has the power to investigate, impeach, and remove the president for breaches of public faith or violations of the law. Trump's insistence that he was above the law spoke to his authoritarian personality, and called back to a previous era of the imperial presidency when President Richard Nixon insisted that an illegal act (for example his ordering of the break-in of the Democratic National Headquarters) "is not illegal" "when the president does it."[68]

Various dimensions of the modern imperial presidency have been adopted in the pursuit of corporate and upper-class political agendas. Some of these actions are a direct boon to the wealthy, including imperial wars and executive orders aimed at enriching the profitability of American corporations. Other actions are only indirectly relevant to strengthening upper-class and corporate capitalist power, including illegal acts such as torture, rendition, denial of due process, and drone strikes. Either way, the U.S. presidency today has revealed itself increasingly as a tool of corporate capitalist interests, domestically or in relation to foreign policy.

Presidential Rhetoric and Propaganda

Presidents have consistently used militarism throughout the last century to pursue corporate capitalist interests abroad. Manipulative political rhetoric, long engaged in by presidents, is vital to selling corporate-friendly foreign policies. In this section I look to a specific example of propaganda rhetoric, used by the George W. Bush administration, in defense of the 2003 invasion of Iraq. This rhetoric effectively downplayed U.S. interests in securing control of Iraq's oil reserves for U.S. oil corporations, while diverting public attention to "security"-related questions. By utilizing the press, the Bush administration was able to drum up fears of terrorism following the September 11, 2001 attacks, despite the lack of a real threat from Iraq.

Antonio Gramsci believed that rhetoric in pursuit of a dominant capitalist ideology was instrumental in propagandizing the masses. In a country defined by political freedoms that allow individuals to openly disagree with government, rhetoric becomes even more important for impacting and controlling the thoughts and actions of the public. The executive's reliance on propaganda is not surprising, considering previous research documenting presidents' rhetorical effectiveness in selling foreign policy.[69] In *Presidential Power and the Modern Presidents*, political scientist Richard Neustadt argued that presidential power depended on three factors: 1. A President's level of public prestige, or popularity among the public; 2. His professional reputation with Congress, with more respected presidents being more effective; and 3. His formal Constitutional powers, which are necessary to pass legislation and execute the law. Neustadt believed presidential power was based on the "power to persuade" others in favor of an idea or course of action.

A growing social science literature emphasizes the importance of propaganda and spin in building mass support for official agendas.[70] Recent research documents how, following the September 11 terror attacks, the Bush administration heavily stressed the threat of terrorism, pressuring the Department of Homeland Security to exaggerate the threat via the "color coded" terror alert system. As journalists more frequently covered alleged terror threats, citizens became more fearful, less likely to question the president, and more likely to support his agenda.[71]

Presidential efforts to "manufacture consent" through rhetoric and manipulation include use of one-sided rhetoric on important policy matters, and superficial rhetoric designed to satisfy one's party base and those Americans who stand undecided between the two major parties.[72] Presidents use fluffy, vague language to build support during election seasons and beyond. Obama rose to power promising "hope" and "change" against the political status quo in the 2008 election, riding a populist wave of public anger against the banks, business elites, and the political order. But Obama's presidency was weak, in comparison to his election rhetoric, when it came to actually combating corporate political power, mass economic insecurity, and record inequality. Donald Trump won the Republican presidential nomination in 2016 promising to "Make America Great Again," despite pursuing policies that benefitted the super-wealthy once in office.

Presidents also use superficial rhetoric once in office. In George W. Bush's 2003 State of the Union address, he spoke of the importance of "work[ing] for a prosperity that is broadly shared," while emphasizing "lift[ing] the standards of our public schools" through No Child Left Behind, a law he claimed would help "every child in America" to "read and learn and succeed in life."[73] Such rhetoric was quite vague in describing *how* educational improvements benefitting the masses would be achieved.

State of the Union addresses are staged for maximum effect in terms of trafficking in superficial messages. For example, Obama's 2016 State of the Union was about an hour, with 88 rounds of applause, translating into one round of applause every 41 seconds.[74] While Obama was skilled in delivering speeches, I know of no speaker who is so skilled as to dictate applause every 41 seconds without being prompted.

Donald Trump proved capable of manipulating public perceptions after his first State of the Union as well. After more than a year of trafficking in clumsy, easily refutable propaganda claims in his campaign and the early days of his presidency, all it took was one smoothly delivered State of the Union to win numerous converts among media pundits and the public. In that speech, Trump celebrated American men in uniform, spoke of the need to condemn hate against minority groups, and promised again to "drain the swamp" of Washington corruption.[75] These promises blatantly contradicted Trump's own actions, considering his prejudiced rhetoric against minorities, his poor record of respecting military veterans (seen in the case of Humayun Khan), and his empowerment of Wall Street insiders and other business elites, who make up much of his executive cabinet. Despite the superficial elements of his speech, media personalities such as Chris Wallace and Van Jones hailed Trump for finally becoming "presidential."[76] Similarly, a large majority of those who watched the speech—76 percent—said they approved of Trump's performance.[77] Trump's success in the State of the Union suggested that even highly controversial officials trafficking in bigoted rhetoric can use the media to cultivate public support. These findings suggest State of the Union speeches are heavily superficial in nature.

Other presidential rhetoric is more substantive, focusing on specific policy issues. I explore one historical case study below, in which rhetoric was used to push the public into supporting the president's foreign policy goals: the 2003 Iraq war. Strategic oil interests played a major role in driving this conflict, despite President Bush denying this materialist motivation for the intervention. The case study, when added to other recent social science findings, suggests that presidents can be quite effective in manipulating public opinion on vital foreign policy matters.

Propaganda in the 2003 Iraq War

The 2003 U.S. war with Iraq was fought in the wake of the September 11, 2001 attacks. The Bush administration exploited the public's real anxieties and fears about terrorism, in light of al Qaeda's attacks on the World Trade Center and the Pentagon, portraying Iraq as a sponsor of Osama bin Laden and Islamic fundamentalism. Claiming Iraq possessed Weapons of Mass Destruction—including chemical, biological, and possibly nuclear weapons, and ties to terrorism—Bush insisted the U.S. needed to confront these threats. Bush also made comparisons between Saddam Hussein, Iraq's president, and Adolf Hitler. In his March 17, 2003 speech, days before the war began, Bush warned: "in this century, when evil men plot chemical, biological, and nuclear terror, a policy of appeasement could bring destruction of a kind never before seen on this earth."[78] This statement was clearly a reference to criticisms of British Prime Minister Neville Chamberlain, who in 1938 signed a "peace" agreement with Hitler and Mussolini ceding partial-control of Czechoslovakia to the Nazis. This was seen as the first step in the "appeasement" of Hitler, and as a massive strategic mistake. Students of world history no doubt picked up on Bush's "appeasement" line with regard to Hussein. Other language also conjured parallels to World War II. In his 2002

State of the Union, Bush spoke of Iraq, Iran, and North Korea as an "Axis of Evil," referring to the Axis powers: Germany, Italy, and Japan.[79]

Bush focused on Iraq's alleged threat to the west. In late-2002 and early-2003, he embarked on one of the most extensive propaganda campaigns for war in U.S. history. In September 2002, Bush claimed that Iraq "admitted to producing tens of thousands of liters of anthrax and other deadly biological agents for use with Scud warheads, aerial bombs, and aircraft spray tanks." He announced that Hussein "likely maintains stockpiles of VX, mustard, and other chemical agents."[80] In his 2003 State of the Union address, Bush warned:

> The United Nations concluded in 1999 that Saddam Hussein had biological weapons sufficient to produce over 25,000 liters of anthrax— enough doses to kill several million people. He hasn't accounted for that material. He's given no evidence that he has destroyed it. The United Nations concluded that Saddam Hussein had materials sufficient to produce more than 38,000 liters of botulinum toxin—enough to subject millions of people to death by respiratory failure . . . He's given no evidence that he has destroyed it.[81]

The Bush administration also stressed the "threat" of nuclear weapons. Vice President Dick Cheney warned: "many of us are convinced that Saddam will acquire nuclear weapons fairly soon."[82] Bush warned in October 2002:

> We have experienced the horror of September 11. We have seen that those who hate America are willing to crash airplanes into buildings full of innocent people. Our enemies would be no less willing—in fact they would be eager—to use a biological, or chemical, or a nuclear weapon. Knowing these realities, America must not ignore the threat gathering against us. Facing clear evidence of peril, we cannot wait for the final proof—the smoking gun—that could come in the form of a mushroom cloud.[83]

The claim that Iraq was developing nuclear weapons was made with 16 now infamous words from Bush's 2003 State of the Union, which stated that Hussein was secretly attempting to secure "yellowcake" uranium from Niger to produce a nuclear bomb.

The president also sought to link Hussein's regime to terrorism, claiming: "Iraq and al Qaeda have had high-level contacts that go back a decade . . . Iraq has trained al Qaeda members in bomb-making and poisons and deadly gases . . . Before September the 11, many in the world believed that Saddam

Hussein could be contained. But chemical agents, lethal viruses and shadowy terrorist networks are not easily contained. Imagine those 19 hijackers with other weapons and other plans—this time armed by Saddam Hussein."[84]

Human rights were also raised by the administration as a major concern. Bush reminded Americans of Hussein's "extremely grave violations" of Iraqi human rights, such as his "arbitrary arrest and imprisonment, summary execution, and torture by beating, electric shock, starvation, mutilation, and rape."[85] One concern was Hussein's gassing of Iraqi Kurds in Halabja. In the days before the 2003 invasion, Bush used the 15-year anniversary of the Halabja attacks as a justification for war: "The chemical attack on Halabja—just one of 40 targeted at Iraq's own people—provided a glimpse of the crimes Hussein is willing to commit, and the kind of threat he now presents to the entire world . . . He is among history's cruelest dictators, and he is arming himself with the world's most terrible weapons."[86]

Deceiving the Public on Iraq

President Bush exuded certainty about the dangers of Iraq. However, most all of the statements he made were not based on evidence, but instead on innuendo,

Image 6.1. George W. Bush and the Invasion of Iraq, March 2003.

suggestion, and wild speculation. There was never any evidence that Iraq possessed ties to al Qaeda, or that it possessed chemical, biological, or nuclear weapons. Bush's rhetoric was at odds with reality, and as the Department of Defense's pre-war report intelligence made clear, the administration knew there was huge uncertainty regarding claims of an Iraqi threat.[87] The president simply chose to ignore the intelligence that raised questions about the case for war. Recognition that the case against Hussein was weak was also apparent among U.S. allies, as the Downing Street Memo revealed.

Bush's claim about Iraq's attempt to secure uranium from Niger was false. Former U.S. diplomat Joe Wilson was asked by the State Department to review alleged Niger government documents related to Iraq. After analyzing them, Wilson concluded they were forgeries.[88] Despite Wilson's report, Bush continued making extravagant claims about nuclear weapons. Wilson concluded: "Based on my experience with the administration in the months leading up to the war, I have little choice but to conclude that some of the intelligence related to Iraq's nuclear weapons program was twisted to exaggerate the Iraqi threat."[89] Allegations also arose from Mohamed ElBaradei of the International Atomic Energy Agency, who reported that claims about Iraq seeking aluminum tubes for use in enriching uranium to build nuclear weapons were baseless.[90] These findings suggest the administration ignored critical intelligence that questioned the war effort.

Claims about Iraq's alleged chemical and biological weapons were also questioned by international weapons inspectors. Hans Blix, Scott Ritter, and Rolf Ekeus all served as United Nations weapons inspectors, and claimed prior to the U.S. invasion that the case for war was lacking. Ritter concluded that his inspection team dismantled 90 to 95 percent of Iraq's WMDs in the 1990s.[91] Ekeus explained: "there could be old weapons here and there," but no program existed by 2003.[92] Blix, as part of the U.N. inspection team sent to Iraq before the invasion, also raised concerns that Iraqi WMDs might not exist.[93]

U.S. intelligence knew prior to war that Iraq had no ties to al Qaeda. As former National Security Council and counter-terrorism advisor Richard Clarke recounts, the President dismissed his assessment that Iraq had no links to al Qaeda: "I think they wanted to believe that there was a connection, but the CIA was sitting there, the FBI was sitting there, I was sitting there saying we've looked at this issue for years. For years we've looked and there's just no connection."[94]

Outside of intelligence issues, Bush's claims were fraudulent in other ways. The claim that Iraq was as an equivalent threat to the Nazis was outlandish. The "Axis of Evil" claim was a fiction. Iraq and Iran had no operating political, economic, or military alliance. They were bitter enemies during Hussein's reign, as seen in his pursuit of the Iran-Iraq war from 1980–1988. Neither Iran nor Iraq retained a working military alliance with North Korea either. And even if these countries had allied, no working relationship would come close to the threat of the Axis Powers from World War II. In short, the "Axis of Evil" claim was purely propaganda.

Concerns with human rights and the Kurdish victims of Hussein at Halabja were disingenuous. Members of the George W. Bush administration were largely recycled Reaganites and Bushites who had supported Hussein during the 1980s. Secretary of Defense Donald Rumsfeld personally traveled to Baghdad in 1983 and shook hands with Saddam Hussein to establish relations between the U.S. and Iraq, despite the Butcher of Baghdad having recently used chemical weapons against Iranian troops.[95] Secretary of State Colin Powell and Vice President Dick Cheney both served in the George H. W. Bush administration, Powell as Chairman of the Joint Chiefs of Staff and Cheney as Secretary of Defense, when the U.S. was providing chemical weapons agents to Hussein. Deputy Secretary of Defense Paul Wolfowitz also served under the George H. W. Bush administration as Undersecretary of Defense for Policy. None of these officials were remorseful about their role in enabling Hussein's crimes, suggesting their "concern" for his victims was merely opportunistic.

At various points in the 2000s and earlier, members of the Bush administration conceded that oil interests were a paramount concern. During the Iraq war, President Bush publicly warned against withdrawing troops, stating terrorists could use Iraqi oil as a weapon against the U.S. As Bush stated in 2006: "You can imagine a world in which these extremists and radicals got control of energy resources . . . We're going to pull a bunch of oil off the market to run your price of oil up unless you do the following. And the following would be along the lines of, well, 'Retreat and let us continue to expand our dark vision.' "[96]

Bush's concessions about oil interests were echoed by other members of the administration. Wolfowitz, the Deputy Secretary of Defense in 2003, authored a document when he served in 1992 under George H. W. Bush entitled "Defense Planning Guidance," which laid out an aggressive plan for asserting U.S. global dominance. The doctrine stated the United States' "first objective" is "to prevent the reemergence of a new rival" following the collapse of the Soviet Union. Of primary concern was maintaining "access to vital raw materials, primarily Persian Gulf oil." Additional threats to U.S. dominance included the "proliferation of weapons of mass destruction," and "threats to U.S. citizens from terrorism."[97] Concern with U.S. global dominance was reiterated by the Bush administration immediately following the 2003 Iraq invasion. As *The New York Times* reported in a story titled "Bush Aides Envision New Influence in the Region," the invasion was a "first test, but not the last," of U.S. resolve. The war would have a "demonstration effect" conveying to the world that "the U.S. would never allow American military supremacy to be challenged in the way it was during the cold war."[98]

What impact did all of the Bush administration's rhetoric on Iraq have on the public? A number of studies suggest that the role of this pro-war rhetoric was significant in increasing public support for war. American news coverage in the prewar period was heavily biased in favor of administration claims that Iraq was a threat.[99] And those who paid attention to this news coverage were significantly more likely to believe Iraq was a threat, and that the U.S. should go to war. While corporate oil interests were largely driving U.S. policy, Americans bought hook, line, and sinker into administrative propaganda about an Iraqi threat.

The above revelations suggest U.S. actions in the Middle East are driven by concerns with projecting power, and protecting corporate capitalist interests—particularly control over Iraqi oil. Presidents' manipulation of the public during wartime fits within a larger effort to obscure the primary U.S. goal in the region—the projection of power. In elevating power politics above concerns with democracy and human rights, presidents side with domestic plutocratic interests such as the oil industry and other business interests.

Chapter 7

The Bureaucracy and Rising Threats to the Common Good

Consumer safety and the quality of consumer goods are sensitive issues for the American public. Most people would prefer to avoid unnecessary health risks whenever possible. And the concern with public health is relevant with regard to the safety of food, particularly when it comes to the meat industry. Public anger at the poor quality of beef products grew in 2012, when a USDA whistle-blower identified a long-standing practice in which beef producers padded meat with a filler, referred to in an internal agency document as "pink slime." "Pink slime," until its production was ended due to public outcry, was included in 70 percent of beef found in supermarkets, and made up as much as 25 percent of beef patties.[1] The product is not actually beef, but rather made up of slaughterhouse trimmings from cattle that were previously used only in pet food and cooking oil. The trimmings—comprised of connective tissue and muscle—were spun through heated centrifuges to separate ligament from fat and sprayed with ammonia gas to eliminate bacteria. The "pink slime" was later added to actual beef and sold to stores across the country. USDA rules do not require that meat labels acknowledge the inclusion of the product.[2]

The controversy was worsened by the stark language used by USDA scientist Gerald Zirnstein, who coined the term "pink slime." Zirnstein labeled the product an "economic fraud . . . it's not fresh ground beef . . . it's a cheap substitute being added in." His description was not the only negative framing of this product. For example, Kit Foshee of Beef Products, Inc. explained pink slime "kind of looks like play dough . . . it's pink and frozen, it's not what the typical person would consider meat." The controversy intensified when *ABC News* reported that Joann Smith, the former federal undersecretary of Agriculture authorized the use of the product, later taking a position with Beef Products, Inc., which was responsible for producing "pink slime." The public outcry over "pink slime" led to the product's discontinuation in 2012 among risk-averse producers seeking to avoid bad PR. It had been quietly incorporated into lunch meals across the country, without the knowledge of the public.

Image 7.1. "Pink Slime" Pellets, FDA Approved.

Calling back to my experiences as a student worker at a major state university in the early-2000s, I remember that the shift to cafeterias using "pink slime" was an open secret among food-service workers. The "Mexican" food venue at the school's food court was infamous among employees for trafficking in low-quality "beef." The joke among workers was that, while the venue's menu offered "beef" tacos, the actual boxes in the back were labeled "taco filler." This deceptive marketing practice speaks to an ugly reality—in the era of deregulation, corporations deceive customers in the quest for profits. By 2013–14, "pink slime" was again being worked into American beef, as Beef Products, Inc. resumed production of the item, shipping out a million pounds per week in partnership with Tyson Foods.[3]

The story of pink slime is relevant to this chapter in that it showcases how the quality of consumer goods may decline when corporations seek to cut corners and raise profits by actively misrepresenting the products they sell to the public. The pink slime scandal is powerful symbolically, because it speaks to the rise of neoliberalism in America. Federal officials, such as Joann Smith, are trusted to represent the public interest by ensuring quality control with regard to American consumer goods and services. But in the case of the meat industry, Smith betrayed that trust by siding with corporate prerogatives over those of consumers. Her actions are an example of how bureaucratic "capture" functions to elevate upper-class and business interests above the notion of a public good—one in which citizen's interests come first.

What is a Bureaucracy? Why Does it Matter?

The federal bureaucracy often flies under the radar of public attention, but it is vital to running the government. In the neoliberal political era, bureaucracies increasingly find themselves under attack from conservative, libertarian, and pro-business interests. Government and the bureaucratic institutions needed to run it are depicted as inefficient and broken. By attacking the bureaucracy, officials play into government by the wealthy, in line with upper-income Americans' embrace of "free-market" values and support for the downsizing of government programs aimed at providing services to the mass public.[4] The neoliberal attack on bureaucracy translates into an assault on public goods and services. Public goods such as social welfare spending for the poor, public education, infrastructure projects, environmental regulations, health care spending, and Social Security, are significantly less valued by wealthy Americans, or even actively opposed by them.[5] Since much of the upper class can already afford to pay for these goods on their own, many would prefer to reduce their tax burdens by exempting themselves from paying for public goods.[6]

Bureaucracy, simply translated, means "government by desk," and refers to the professional federal employees responsible for running the executive branch, implementing national laws, and providing benefits to citizens. While some members of the federal bureaucracy work under the courts and Congress, most are managed under the executive or work in independent government agencies. More practically, a bureaucracy is defined as "a hierarchical authority structure that uses task specialization, operates on the merit principle, and behaves with impersonality."[7] Translated into plain English, hierarchical structure means managerial officials oversee bureaucratic agencies in an effort to ensure that they run efficiently. "Task specialization" and the "merit principle" mean that federal employees are hired because of their professional qualifications. These individuals are supposed to be punished or rewarded based upon the quality of their performance. And they are expected to work, dispassionately, in favor of providing public services and needs.

Bureaucratic Stereotypes

In the neoliberal period, bureaucracies are under attack, and many Americans fall victim to conservative stereotypes and propaganda claims that the federal bureaucracy is broken and rife with "red tape." People joke about how mentally unbalanced persons "go postal"—a negative reference directed at government employees. Stereotypes of bureaucrats as maladjusted, inefficient, incompetent, and lazy are common. While these characterizations may accurately describe *some* federal employees, these stereotypes are more a function of an ideology that is handed down from upper-class and business elites, than a reflection of what bureaucracies actually do. Contrary to popular perception, bureaucracies perform vital services, without which our lives would be far more difficult.

Attacks on the bureaucracy as inefficient stem from a neoliberal political culture embraced by government officials, media pundits, corporate media, and conservative intellectuals. Government bureaucracies are a threat to the ascendancy of neoliberal market values which seek to eliminate public goods and replace them with privatized services propped up by taxpayers. Wealthy, upper-class Americans have little need for socialized programs such as libraries, public schools, and government-guaranteed income security in retirement. Many would rather eliminate these programs, or privatize them to enhance the profit of Wall Street, and lower their own tax burdens. This opposition reveals a pronounced narcissism on the part of the American upper class, which holds little by way of solidarity with middle-class and poorer citizens.

The attack on the federal bureaucracy is apparent in the privatization of the administration of welfare services for the poor that is occurring in many states, in efforts to cut government regulations of business entities. The conservative right and wealthy Americans see private and for-profit organizations as more effective than government in administering these services. For example, the wealthy are more likely than the rest of the public to favor privatizing Social Security, and investing individuals' retirement resources in the stock market.[8] This is unsurprising, since wealthy citizens benefit disproportionately from stock market growth.

One major misconception about the federal bureaucracy is that it is oversized, representing a threat to individual liberty and freedom. This fallacy is common in neoliberal political rhetoric, but has little bearing on reality. Federal employees are actually the smallest group—size wise—compared to state and local employees. While there were 2 million full-time federal employees between 2015 and 2016, there were 3.75 million state and 10.6 million local government employees.[9] The federal numbers have steadily declined for decades. There were only 2.1 million federal employees in 2014, compared to 1.8 million in the 2000, and 2.2 million in the 1990.[10] The decline in federal employees from 1990 to 2014 is deceptive, however, since one must also take into account population growth. Approximately 319 million people lived in the U.S. in 2014, compared to 281 million in 2000 and 249 million in 1990. After accounting for population change, the number of federal employees was 25 percent lower in 2014 than it would have been if federal employment kept pace with population growth. So federal employment has shrunk dramatically in recent decades. This reality is captured in figure 7.1.

Federal employment fell by more than half from 1960 to 2016, when measured as a percent of the total civilian workforce.[11] These findings contradict elite-driven propaganda depicting the federal government as a three-headed monster, growing uncontrollably at the expense of the public.

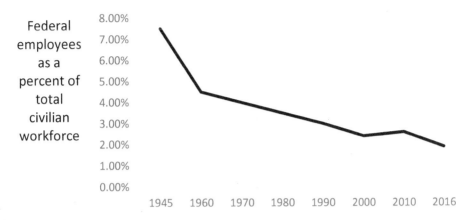

Figure 7.1. Declining Federal Employment, 1945–2016. Source: Max Sier, "Five Myths About Federal Workers," *Washington Post*, December 5, 2010, http://www.washingtonpost.com/wp-dyn/content/article/2010/12/03/AR2010120303160.html; Lauren Carroll, "Sean Spicer's Claim of a 'Dramatic Expansion in the Federal Workforce' is Exaggerated," *Politifact*, January 24, 2017, http://www.politifact.com/truth-o-meter/statements/2017/jan/24/sean-spicer/sean-spicers-claim-federal-workforce-has-expanded-/

Privatizing Public Services?

The growing popularity of the rhetoric of privatization is drawn straight from elite business interests involved in U.S. education reform. Most notable is the Gates Foundation, which advocates for market reforms, including charter schools, merit pay, performance-based funding, and an elimination of tenure and teachers' unions.[12] From the position of upper-class business interests, public schools are seen as superfluous at a time when the wealthy send their children to elite private schools and charter schools. Opposition to public goods is increasingly reflected in the commentary of American reactionaries, who complain that any tax dollar spent that they do not directly benefit from is illegitimate.[13]

Despite growing calls to privatize education, many challenge the position that privatization leads to improved academic performance. There is no consistent evidence suggesting merit pay or charter schools are associated with better academic performance, and recent studies suggest charter schools perform significantly worse.[14] The failure of charter schools as a model for education undermines the conservative notion that non-unionized, non-tenure schools are the ticket to educational success. The alleged gains of market-based education reforms are anything but certain, but the losses are apparent. The shift to charter schools means the loss of job security for faculty via the elimination of tenure, and the decline of community influence over school curriculum, since charters answer to state officials, not parent-teacher organizations, local school boards, or faculty union membership. The rise of private voucher-funded schools also poses problems. Such schools do not generally allow for tenure or unions. Without tenure or unionization, teachers may struggle to achieve a livable wage, secure health benefits, and maintain job stability. Greater unionization rates are associated with increased citizen happiness, since they provide a means for workers to be democratically empowered in the workplace.[15] The decline of unions means unhappy workers, who will have little ability to influence the conditions under which they work. Furthermore, many poor families simply cannot afford the more expensive tuition costs at elite private schools, meaning this "solution" to the education problem is simply not workable for lower-income groups.[16] In sum, the market-based assault on public education, embraced by much of the upper-class and corporate "reformers," has not only been a failure in terms of educational outcomes, it is also a major threat to the common good.

Public vs. Private Goods

Those lambasting public education fail to recognize the importance of government bureaucracy and public goods. But what is a public good? And what is a private good? How are they different? Why does society need public goods in the first place, and why is it dangerous to embrace an elitist approach to governing that seeks to eliminate public goods in favor of private ones? I address all of these questions below.

Public goods are vital to a functioning democratic society, and they are provided by government and bureaucracies through taxpayer dollars. Public goods are any benefits or services, provided on a non-profit basis, and regardless of the ability or inability of beneficiaries to pay. Homeless persons can use a public library, even if they do not pay property taxes. City police are expected to "protect and serve" all individuals, regardless of whether a person who is assaulted pays taxes to the city. A town's public roads are for all to use, whether one contributes taxes to their construction or not. Public goods include various popular services, such as police protection, public roads, bridges, highways, firefighting services, public schools, community centers, public libraries, and regulations of the private sector vital to protecting the public.

Private goods are different. A private good is a service or benefit that is provided by a for-profit corporation or a nonprofit private association for the good only of those who can pay for it. Individuals are denied private goods based on their inability to pay. Private schools, gated communities, private security services, private pools, golf clubs, and consumer goods are examples of private goods.

One problem with neoliberal rhetoric is that it fails to distinguish between the value of government—in providing public goods—and the strength of corporations and private associations—in providing private goods. Corporations, by mandate, are required to profit from selling goods and services, and they discriminate in offering these benefits based on the ability of individuals to pay. Corporations are accountable to their owners and stockholders, and must post a profit. Corporations and private nonprofit associations are not designed to provide public goods. Rather, corporations merely profit from private goods. For example, Apple Inc. makes sizable profits innovating in the fields of technology, communication, and music. Private nonprofits are often quite effective at providing quality services based upon the ability of beneficiaries to pay—whether these benefits are private education, security, or community services. Private universities like Harvard, Princeton, and Yale are widely recognized for their research and for high-prestige degrees, despite most Americans not being able to afford these schools. In short, private corporations and associations often excel at providing private goods, but they are not designed to provide public goods.

Private corporations and associations cannot hand out services and goods for free. But public bureaucracies and institutions intentionally run at a loss—paying out to cover benefits and services, and failing to make profits—because of their mandate to provide low-cost public goods to the masses. Public libraries provide services to patrons for "free" (people do pay taxes) because they are not out to make a profit. If an individual wanted to build up a large library comparable in size to a community library, without the help of public tax dollars, the cost would be so large that only members of the upper class could afford to do so. Because of the public nature of libraries, they can pool community resources together, and with the help of inter-library loan networks, guarantee virtually any book or article to patrons. The same cannot be said of private book providers such as Barnes and Noble or Amazon.com, which only sell books on a book-by-book, for-profit basis.

Governmental entities and public goods draw support from the philosophical notion that some services are so important, such as public roads, access to information, fire and police protection, and education, that all individuals must benefit from them, regardless of how wealthy or poor they are. Society risks losing these vital public services in the rush to embrace neoliberal ideals that push for privatization of the commons, to the benefit of wealthy, upper-class interests. Most Americans strongly support public goods. They recognize the importance of these services to a modern society. Most Americans reject the elitist notion that goods such as education, police protection, and roads should only exist for those who can afford to pay for them.

Public Goods, Private Goods, and Externalities

Corporations' activities are at times associated with negative "externalities" imposed on individuals and communities. An externality is the negative impact of a private party transaction between two or more individuals or entities that is imposed on the public at large and on those not party to the original trans- action. One example of an externality is pollution. Say you purchase a large, gas-guzzling sport utility vehicle over a more fuel efficient, smaller hybrid car. You have always wanted an SUV, and you travel to a nearby dealer to make this dream a reality. In the process of buying your SUV, numerous parties are involved in the transaction. First, there is the buyer (you). Next are the dealership and the corporation that manufactured the SUV.

But there are more parties to this transaction. To drive your SUV, you must pay for fuel. Oil corporations and gas stations are inevitably parties to your many transactions, as they profit by refining petroleum into gasoline and selling it. Finally, auto repair services are needed to maintain your SUV. All the above actors are parties to your purchase. But other individuals are involved as well, and must pay the negative costs associated with your vehicle choice. I am speaking of the public, who are inevitably affected by problems such as smog, air pollution, and climate change due to the lack of serious regulations on fossil fuel emissions. While any single SUV does not create enough pollution to harm a community, the government's reluctance to protect the environment against automobile and coal-burning power-plant emissions greatly escalates climate change.

The challenge of global warming is not theoretical; it is real. Fossil fuel burning corporations impose the negative externality of a warming planet on the public at large. And the Trump administration ensured by its jettisoning of the Paris Agreement that the U.S. would continue its failure to address the threat. The externality of pollution manifests itself in rising temperatures, more frequent droughts and famines, melting of the polar ice caps and flooding coast lines, more intense wildfires, and species extinction on a potentially massive scale. Human sustainability is very much in danger if current pollution trends continue indefinitely into the future.

The private marketplace has refused to consider the externality of pollution in its business dealings. Oil corporations go to great lengths to deny that global warming is even real, despite privately conceding that it has been occurring for decades.[17] Returning to the SUV anecdote, one can see how multiple parties to a transaction refuse to take into account negative externalities. If an SUV driver were really concerned with pollution, he or she would not have bought an SUV. That person might have looked for a more fuel-efficient vehicle, used public transportation, or even biked or walked instead of using a polluting vehicle. Will an SUV dealer refuse to sell you a heavily polluting vehicle because of a fear of global warming and the effects of such warming humanity? Will an oil or gas company encourage you to buy less gasoline because of the crisis of climate change? Will auto repair companies refuse profits because they are anxious about global warming? The obvious answer to all of these questions is "no." In fact, many corporations—such as auto manufacturers, coal burning power plants, and oil companies—actively work against government regulations for auto emissions and power plants.[18] In the case of fossil fuels, the private marketplace refuses to address the issue of climate change.

Governmental agencies such as the Environmental Protection Agency and Department of Transportation are empowered to regulate auto fuel efficiency. These organizations are tasked with setting auto fuel efficiency standards ("CAFE standards"). The EPA is tasked with implementing new limits on CO_2 pollution at coal burning power plants, although the implementation of these regulations was endangered by the election of Republican President Donald Trump, who denied that climate change was even real. This *public* good—government efforts to limit climate change—is opposed by "free market" libertarians who prefer no regulations on fossil fuel corporations or automobile manufacturers.

While scientists worry that the U.S. and other countries are not doing enough to limit emissions to avoid the worst ecological effects of climate change, "free market" fundamentalists deny that global warming is even real. Meanwhile, the concentration of CO_2 in the atmosphere continues to grow to dangerous levels, as documented in figure 7.2.[19]

For years scientists warned that we should not let the CO_2 concentration exceed 350 parts per million in the atmosphere in order to avoid serious con-

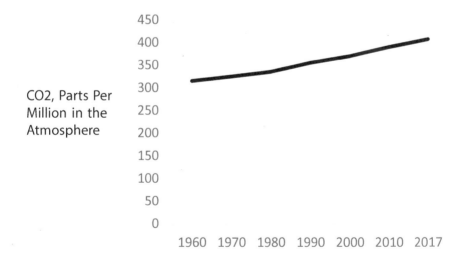

Figure 7.2. Runaway CO_2 Emissions and the Threat of Climate Change. Source: Nicola Jones, "How the World Passed a Carbon Threshold and Why it Matters," *Yale Environment 360*, January 26, 2017, https://e360.yale.edu/features/how-the-world-passed-a-carbon-threshold-400ppm-and-why-it-matters

sequences associated with climate change, although that milestone had been reached by 1990. The concentration reached over 400 parts per million by the 2000s, prompting renewed calls from climate scientists warning that temperatures could grow by 2 to 6 degrees Celsius or more over the twenty-first century if sufficient action was not taken.[20] Environmental activists still seek to take dramatic action, although free-market fundamentalists have stifled government regulation of emissions and still seek to foster doubt in the public mind over climate change.[21] While the threat of climate change is almost universally recognized by climatologists, those embracing "free-market" philosophies demonstrate willful disregard for environmental regulation.[22]

The Limits of Private Goods: Health Care in America

Few sectors of the economy demonstrate the problem of private goods better than for-profit health care. This health care system is notoriously dysfunctional, in terms of its runaway costs and poor health outcomes. It is the worst system in all first-world countries in terms of quality care. But this should be expected in a system in which there is little governmental effort to regulate cost, and for-profit corporations are allowed to charge what they see fit without limit. As a result, the health care industry is empowered to gouge consumers via ever-growing prices in the pursuit of greater profits. I document the numerous problems with U.S. health care in this section, arguing that a public, nonprofit system of care would function far more efficiently, *if* society's goal is to provide the best quality outcomes at the lowest cost. If, on the other hand, the goal is to make as much money as possible for health care corporations, regardless of whether many Americans can afford care, then a for-profit system is superior.

A somewhat recent anecdote (from the late 2000s) personalizes the dysfunctional nature U.S. health care. In this story, my wife stepped awkwardly off a train, after traveling back from the city of Chicago to the suburbs, and fractured her foot. The experience remains imprinted in my memory, because of what it suggests about the U.S. health care system. Since she was insured, my wife went to the Emergency Room to get fitted for a walking boot. Working for an employer who relied on a for-profit HMO (Health Maintenance Organization), however, she did not realize how difficult securing care would be. Upon visiting the ER, the doctor informed her that her insurer did not cover an in-patient procedure at the hospital. Rather, she had to leave, with crutches, and make a separate appointment for a doctor within her insurance "network." The next day, she called her "primary caregiver"—what HMOs call your general doctor. The doctor issued her a referral to visit a specialist orthopedic doctor dealing with foot injuries. But she was also expected to travel into the primary care-giver's office and *pick up* the referral. The problem obviously was that with a fractured foot, this was very difficult. Lucky for her, I took off of work and picked it up.

Upon making an appointment and visiting the orthopedic doctor, we thought her problems would be solved. But we were naïve. The orthopedic doctor showed us the walking boot in his office after the examination, but told her she could not have it. If we wanted to pay him out of pocket, he would give her a boot immediately. We declined, based on the logic that there was no point in having insurance if we have to pay entirely out of pocket for a medical service. The doctor said that HMO rules mandated that the notes from that day's meeting had to be approved by the primary caregiver and the insurer prior to receiving medical treatment, which meant we had to leave the office—still with no boot. An additional problem was that the notes from the meeting would not go directly to the primary caregiver. First, they would be sent to an independent-contracting for-profit medical transcription service, to translate the notes and send them back to the primary caregiver. After the primary caregiver received the notes and signed off, however, my wife was *still* not eligible for the boot. The recommendation from the orthopedic doctor and primary caregiver still had to be sent back to the insurer for approval.

After insurance approval, we were still not done. The next step in the process was for me to travel back to the primary caregiver *a second time* to pick up the new referral for the walking boot. Then, we needed to make a second appointment with the orthopedic doctor to get sized up for the boot. My wife was lucky enough to have an employer that let her off work for an entire week in order to resolve her health problem.

The HMO story above is relevant to the question of whether private goods are efficient. Is the above process "efficient," if the goal of a health care system is to provide care as quickly as possible, and as easily as possible? Obviously not. This process was highly inefficient for someone with a fractured foot. If the goal of health care, however, is to provide as many bureaucratic hurdles as possible, many of which empower insurance providers to veto expensive health care services, thereby increasing profits for the HMO, then this process is highly "efficient." This is precisely the point when it comes to for-profit health insurers. They are very efficient at taking in insurance premiums from clients, and not so efficient, at least compared to universal health care systems, at providing quality service at a lower cost.

The many hurdles discussed in my anecdote are important because they suggest insurers (at least prior to the government outlawing it) retained maximum leverage to deny costly health care services if they viewed them as a threat to profits. While an HMO is unlikely to block payment for something as inexpensive as a walking boot, they are more likely to do so (if allowed to) for those with serious, life-threatening illnesses requiring costly treatments. The threat of being denied care due to "preexisting conditions" was longstanding prior to Obamacare, and would reemerge with a repeal of the law. The *Kaiser* foundation estimated 52 million people had a preexisting condition that would interfere with their ability to get private health care in 2016 if Obamacare was repealed.[23]

There is no profit in insurance companies covering very sick individuals, and the denial of care to millions is what one would expect when health care is treated as a private good, existing to benefit corporations. Obamacare required individuals to buy private insurance via a mandate, rather than providing government-funded insurance to all uninsured citizens. Although more Americans were insured under Obama's mandate, the number of uninsured Americans still stood at 8.6 percent of adults in late-2016.[24] Health care costs continued to rise considerably after Obamacare passed, because the law did not regulate private-sector health care costs.[25]

My wife's story is not unique. The for-profit health care system is dysfunctional. The World Health Organization ranks the U.S. 37th, behind almost all other wealthy countries, in health care quality.[26] In terms of cost, the U.S. is the worst in the first world, and it is the only country with a for-profit health care system. Prior to Obamacare, approximately 50 million Americans were uninsured, with millions of working-class and poorer Americans unable to afford coverage.[27] The Commonwealth Fund estimated that, in 2013, the U.S. spent 17.1 percent of GDP on health care. Comparatively, France spent 11.6 percent, Sweden 11.5 percent, Germany 11.2 percent, and the Netherlands, Switzerland, and Denmark 11.1 percent. Other countries spent even less, including New Zealand, Canada, Japan, Norway, Australia, and the U.K.[28] Contrary to libertarian rhetoric, the Commonwealth Fund found that "inefficient" socialized medicine systems provided cheaper and superior health care outcomes compared to the U.S. for-profit system.[29] Significant differences also exist in U.S. public and for-profit health care organizations. Regarding HMOs, a study published by the *Journal of the American Medical Association* found "investor owned" HMOs performed more poorly than nonprofit HMOs in 14 different areas of service. Private HMOs funded eye exams at a rate 27 percent lower than nonprofit HMOs, at 16 percent less for drug treatment and for heart attack survivors, and at 9 percent less for mental patients.[30]

Costs in the U.S. for-profit health system increased since the above studies were conducted. Family health care costs increased by 120 percent from 1999 to 2008 according to the Kaiser Family Foundation.[31] Despite Obamacare, Forbes estimates health care costs for a family of four reached $25,826 in 2016, up from $18,074 in 2010, and $12,214 in 2005.[32]

Image 7.2. Health Care for Profit is Sick.

This represents a 43 percent increase in the six years after Obamacare was passed. Inequality in access to care was also pronounced by income. In 2011, the top one-fifth of income earners spent on average 43 percent more per year on health care than the bottom one-fifth of earners.[33]

In a for-profit system, those who can afford better care receive it, while the less fortunate often fend for themselves. One 2009 survey found that 35 percent of all respondents chose to rely on "home remedies or over-the-counter drugs instead of going to see a doctor" within the last year. Thirty-four percent skipped dental checkups; 23 percent put off "recommended medical tests and treatment"; 21 percent could not afford medical prescriptions; 27 percent could not get basic health care they needed.[34] The lack of health care was deadly for many citizens. A 2009 study by the *American Journal of Public Health* found that an estimated 45,000 Americans died each year because they lacked health insurance, while a 2012 report found an estimated 26,000 died annually due to a lack of coverage.[35] In a privatized health care system, corporate profits supersede the needs of the uninsured. Government does not seek to rein in health costs charged by corporations that rake in massive profits at the expense of the public.

The Politics of Privatization in American Education

As a symbol of growing societal attacks on public goods, David Harmer gained notoriety as a conservative Tea Party candidate who was running for Congress. While he lost his bid to serve in the House of Representatives, his campaign received significant attention because of his radical ideas about education "reform." Harmer wanted to get rid of public education, privatizing all educational services. The assumption Harmer operated under was that bureaucratic inefficiency ensures government cannot provide for the public's educational needs.

In an op-ed for the *San Francisco Chronicle*, Harmer wrote: "To attain quantum leaps in educational quality and opportunity . . . we need to separate school and state entirely. Government should exit the business of running and funding schools . . . this is no utopian ideal; it's the way things worked through the first century of American nationhood, when literacy levels among all classes, at least outside the South, matched or exceeded those prevailing now, and when public discourse and even tabloid content was pitched at what today would be considered a college-level audience."[36]

Harmer's rhetoric no doubt appealed to libertarians convinced that government can do no good and that only the private sector can provide for the needs of the people. Harmer's message is embraced by other reactionaries—including *Netflix* CEO Reed Hastings, *Fox News* pundits, and various state, local, and national political officials—who call for privatizing public education via greater funding for non-community-controlled charter schools.[37] Donald Trump's Education Secretary, Betsy DeVos, also gained much public attention due to her support for privatizing education via federal vouchers, providing taxpayer funding for private schools. DeVos's support for privatization was based in part on the fallacious notion that charter schools—which are funded by taxpayers but independent of community control or regulation—are more efficient than community public schools in providing a quality education. This finding is blatantly contradicted by numerous studies, which find that charter schools and other private schools perform more poorly, academically speaking, than public school students.[38]

The story of David Harmer is not unique in American politics today. Increasingly, many education "reform" advocates believe that government should be minimized in favor of citizens relying increasingly on private, market-based institutions for their wants and needs. This worship of private goods, private markets, and private institutions is dangerous, however, because it neglects the important functions that government and governmental bureaucracies provide the public. For example, in the case of education, not all Americans can afford to attend expensive private schools, and the charter schools that do perform well academically are often in high demand. These schools often rely on a lottery system due to limited space, thus failing to offer acceptance to all interested students. But we hear little about these failures of the privatized educational marketplace. Rather, the focus of education reform today is largely driven by fanatical, far-right ideological propaganda, rather than a reasoned discussion of the U.S. public education system.

The neoliberal political system also imperils higher education as a public good. Alleviating the burden of higher taxes on wealthy, upper-class Americans, higher education has transitioned from a taxpayer-funded model to a tuition-funded one. This means transitioning from collective to student responsibility for funding schools. Public higher education was long considered a vital public good, but education has also historically been provided as a private good. With private educational institutions, there are two types: nonprofits and for-profits. Private for-profits such as the University of Phoenix charge high tuition rates, much higher per credit hour than public colleges and universities.[39] These exorbitant costs are subsidized by taxpayers and the federal government through student loans, meaning that for-profits do not operate within a "free market."[40] These schools are skilled at profiting from taxpayers and students, but are widely recognized to perform poorly in providing quality education. Education for some for-profits like ITT was so poor that in 2016 the college lost its access to federal loan funds due to allegations of predatory lending practices, excessive tuition rates, and low educational standards, which resulted in ITT credits being turned away by transfer schools, and employers dismissing ITT degrees as of dubious value.[41]

For-profit degrees are widely ridiculed in the academic world. In my experience, graduate degrees at for-profits are derisively referred to as "mail-it-in degrees," in reference to their lack of rigor. Teachers at these schools are typically part-time and paid poorly on a course-by-course basis, usually no more than a few thousand dollars per course. Their meager salaries qualify them for food stamps and other forms of public aid. These teachers receive few to no employee benefits, and for-profits do not provide the security of tenure. Couple poor treatment of teachers with high costs, and one can see why for-profits are so often criticized.

Many nonprofit, private colleges also operate in the U.S. These schools are different from for-profits; they are more likely to pay their employees better salaries than the for-profits, provide employee benefit packages covering health care and retirement, and offer tenure to professors. Generally speaking, nonprofit private schools provide a far superior educational experience compared to for-profit colleges. But a major limitation of nonprofit private schools is that they do not provide education as a public good. They fill a specific niche in higher education, providing quality education—but at a much higher cost than public colleges, and to only a select number of people. Liberal arts colleges and Ivy League schools practice "selective enrollment," to maintain higher levels of prestige than public institutions like community colleges, the latter of which practice open-enrollment. Most young Americans do not attend elite universities and colleges, either because of the selective acceptance standards, which are very high with Ivy League schools, or due to the high cost, which makes them inaccessible to many lower-income and working- and middle-class students. In short, private nonprofit colleges cannot provide for the educational needs of most students. Like private for-profits, they are not generally designed with the needs of the masses in mind.

On the other hand, public community colleges are the only institutions in an era of skyrocketing tuition that still provide quality educational opportunities at a low cost, while offering universal access. Community colleges, unlike selective enrollment private schools, make public education available to all as a public good. Community colleges, by their mandate, include strict price controls to ensure that tuition costs remain affordable. Boards of Trustees have to vote to raise tuition, and they are often reluctant to do so in light of community college's explicitly public and community mission of providing low-cost education.

In community colleges, faculty are generally treated better than in private for-profit colleges. They provide tenure to many of their faculty, unlike for-profits. Professors often benefit from a faculty union, which collectively bargains for pay raises and health and retirement benefits. Needless to say, tenured faculty at community colleges do not qualify for food stamps. While faculty are not expected to engage in research, the larger number of courses taught per faculty member helps ensure lower cost of attendance. In sum, community colleges are a great example of how governmental bureaucracies provide a vital public good. The high quality and low cost of attendance makes these schools attractive to students of modest economic means.

While the example of privatized health care demonstrates the limits of private goods in providing for public needs, the privatization of higher education reveals the dangers of turning public goods into private ones. For years, American "public" universities have slowly been privatized, to the point where state universities today are largely public in name only. State legislators cut large amounts of funding from state universities under the assumption that college degrees should be treated as "private goods," with the costs paid by students, rather than taxpayers. The abandonment of higher education as a public good led to skyrocketing student loan debt, which became unsustainable as millions struggled to pay back these loans. Where previous generations of college graduates secured college degrees with little to no borrowing, by 2016 the average college student held over $30,000 in loan debt.[42]

In 2011, the U.S. Department of Education issued its first annual "shame list" of colleges and universities—which was updated regularly in subsequent years.[43] The list was created to inform students about schools deemed by the government to be exorbitantly expensive. But the DOE's efforts had little impact on college prices. Average student loan debt has grown well beyond the rate of inflation for decades.[44] In 2014, about 12 percent of student loans were "seriously delinquent," and this was not counting many of those loans in forbearance because of graduates' inability to make payments.[45] By 2016, 40 percent of Americans with student loans were not making payments or were delinquent on more than $200 billion in loans, raising questions about mass defaults.[46] By 2017, total U.S. student loan debt reached $1.3 trillion.[47] As captured in figure 7.3, student loan debt had grown by more than 400 percent since 2003.[48]

The federal government made some effort to address rising student loan debt. In 2011, Obama announced via executive order that student borrowers were eligible for an "income-based repayment" plan, originally introduced under the Bush administration, in which college grads would contribute no more than 10 percent of their income (compared to the previous 15 percent under Bush) to student loan payments.[49] This effort eased the student loan crisis, but did not eliminate the education-related financial struggles of millions of Americans.

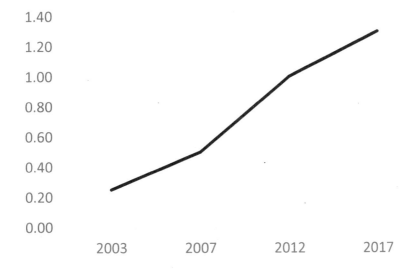

Figure 7.3. Total U.S. Student Loan Debt, in $ Trillions. Source: Maggie Severns, "The Student Loan Debt Crisis in 9 Charts," *Mother Jones*, June 5, 2013, http://www.motherjones.com/politics/2013/06/student-loan-debt-charts/

In 2014, *The Washington Post* reported loan applications for homes fell by 20 percent in late 2013, compared to one year earlier. "First-time buyers, the bedrock of the housing market, are not stepping up to fill the void. They have accounted for nearly a third of home purchases over the past year, well below the historical norm, industry figures show. The trend has alarmed some housing experts, who suspect that student loan debt is partly to blame. That debt has tripled from a decade earlier, to more than $1 trillion, while wages for young college graduates have dropped."[50] By 2016, 40 percent of young Americans lived with their parents, which was a 75-year high. The "failure to launch" phenomenon was due in large part to low wages and high student loan debt among the young.[51]

The radically growing costs of higher education were due in significant part to cuts in state funding. As the Center on Budget and Policy Priorities reported in 2016, state funding (inflation adjusted) for "public" colleges was down almost $10 billion from prior to the 2008 recession. "Years of cuts in state funding for public colleges and universities have driven up tuition and harmed students' educational experiences by forcing faculty reductions, fewer course offerings, and campus closings."[52] The decline of state funding meant higher education was increasingly unaffordable for many students. This transformation of public education into private education—via the outsourcing of college operating revenues from state taxpayers to individual students—speaks to the pernicious effects of neoliberal politics and the culture of privatization.

The Politics of Deregulation

A third issue of interest regarding public bureaucracy is the effort to gut government regulatory powers. Under the neoliberal ideology, many conservatives and libertarians, and even liberal officials, assume the private sector can self-regulate without government oversight. This claim is demonstrably false in the case of consumer products. Concerning prescription drugs and the food industry, the decline of public bureaucratic regulation causes serious consumer health risks. By empowering business interests via deregulation, we have endangered the public health.

The Food and Drug Administration (FDA) is responsible for regulating prescription drugs. But for years the agency failed to regulate foreign ingredients for U.S. drugs. A *New York Times* investigative report from 2007 reflected: the FDA "cannot guarantee the safety of the nation's drug supply because it inspects few foreign drug manufacturers and the inspections it does carry out abroad are less rigorous than those performed in this country."[53] Foreign ingredients were of major concern because they represented 80 percent of all the ingredients that comprised U.S. prescription drugs. The FDA's recordkeeping regarding the safety of foreign manufacturing plants was so weak it could not even account for which factories had been inspected and which had not.[54] While the FDA is required to inspect domestic drug producers every two years, there was no such requirement imposed on the agency regarding foreign plants manufacturing drug ingredients. At the 2007 rate of inspection of foreign plants, it would have taken the FDA 13 years to inspect each foreign factory once. The FDA was so short staffed that it relied on volunteers for inspections, with inspector activity driven not by organizational mandates and needs, but by travel availability of volunteers. Additionally, the FDA provided foreign plants advanced notice of inspection, allowing manufacturers time to cover up hazardous practices.[55] Such toothless investigative powers raised questions about what happens when regulatory agencies are prohibited from regulating consumer products.

The danger of foreign drugs was not idle. The push for increased FDA regulatory powers over foreign drug ingredients was encouraged by the well-publicized case of Heparin, the blood-thinning drug consumed by tens of thousands of Americans. Heparin was linked to the 81 deaths, because Chinese plants were knowingly substituting dangerous ingredients for the required dried pig intestines needed to manufacture the drug.[56] The Chinese plants were never investigated by the FDA in the run-up to the contamination.[57]

Historically the FDA has been unable to unilaterally order recalls for drugs that threatened consumers, thereby increasing the risks to public health.[58] The inability to protect consumers is an outcome of a neoliberal system that empowers corporations by pharmaceutical companies and manufacturers to self-police, rather than relying on government inspections and drug recall powers. Nothing was done about the foreign drug problem until 2011, when Congress granted the FDA additional investigative powers. As *The New York Times* reported, "the federal government and the generic drug industry have reached an agreement . . . that will lead to routine inspections of these overseas plants, potentially transforming the enormous global medicine trade . . . Under the landmark agreement . . . generic drug companies would pay $299 million in annual fees to underwrite inspections of foreign manufacturing plants every two years, the same frequency required of domestic plants."[59] Despite the growth of foreign inspections, the FDA still cited staffing problems in late-2016 estimating that it had yet to inspect a third of foreign manufacturing facilities even a single time.[60]

In addition to problems with drug safety, the issue of meat safety is also a major concern. The failure of government to regulate the meat industry is a consequence of neoliberal ideology, which assumes markets can effectively self-regulate. My first experience with meat deregulation occurred in the year 2000. As a waiter at a major national chain restaurant, our store's General Manager sat all servers down for a staff meeting to talk about changes in company practices. He informed us the restaurant would no longer allow customers to order burgers cooked at medium-rare or rare. When we asked why, he told us that quality standards at meat packing plants had fallen significantly, and that the restaurant would no longer allow meat to be cooked under medium due to concern with bacteria and E. coli poisoning, and resulting lawsuits that could be filed against the corporation. This new standard, which never existed before 2000, is still in practice across major restaurant chains, which only provide patrons a choice between "some pink" or "no pink" burgers.

The experience stayed with me all these years because it demonstrates how quickly companies sweep health dangers under the rug when it is financially advantageous. I returned to that same restaurant years later and asked a waitress if I could order a burger cooked at medium-rare. She told me no, and when I asked why, explained the restaurant went out of its way to "kill all the bacteria" in the beef. It was obvious she had been coached on how to make the threat of E. coli poisoning *sound* like the restaurant was committed to customer safety. I knew the opposite was true, having been a waiter at that very restaurant. The concern with meat quality was nearly nonexistent, superseded by the drive for profits. And many American beef consumers seem unaware that E. coli (from cow's intestines) is mixed with ground beef due to low quality control standards on the manufacturer's killing floor.[61] This ignorance is potentially dangerous, considering an estimated 48 million people are made sick by foodborne pathogens per year, with more than a million sickened by infected meat.[62]

My beef industry anecdote highlights the inadequacy of regulation by the U.S. Department of Agriculture (USDA). Many fast food consumers do not ask: how it is that restaurants offer burgers from a "dollar menu" while maintaining high quality of meat? "Out of sight, out of mind" is the typical approach for many who consume fast food. Such prices are possible due to the high volume of meat that flows through processing plants, amidst minimal regulation. With higher quality control standards, it is likely that prices would increase significantly.

My experiences with the beef industry overlap with the observations of social critics like Eric Schlosser, author of the best-selling *Fast Food Nation*. Schlosser documented how beef packing plants exploited low-wage, immigrant workers, and highlighted the lax standards involved in raising, slaughtering, and processing beef that caused the E. coli beef threat. Since Schlosser's book release, numerous reports have highlighted problems with the USDA's failure in regulating the beef industry. The pressure from *Fast Food Nation* and negative publicity on programs like *Oprah*—which ran a special on E. Coli-contaminated beef—led to greater pressure on government to increase beef packing plant inspections.[63] As *The New York Times* reported in 2002, the USDA announced it would "begin randomly testing for E. coli at all meatpacking plants in the United States." This marked the "reversing [of] a 1998 policy that exempted some plants from such tests for the bacteria." The new policy provided the USDA "greater authority to close plants if inspectors find contamination."[64]

Post-2002, other serious concerns about meat safety emerged. In 2003 there were two significant beef recalls that caused eight deaths and almost 100 illnesses across 16 states.[65] The problem got worse over time, with the USDA participating in the recall of 143 million pounds of beef in 2008 due to concerns with E. coli. This was the largest recall in history.[66] Food pathogen threats continued in subsequent years. Pew Charitable Trust's 2016 report warned: "Meat and poultry are among the leading vehicles for foodborne illnesses in the United States . . . beef, pork, and poultry products are responsible for more than 2 million Americans getting sick each year, with an annual cost exceeding $5.7 billion. The U.S. Centers for Disease Control and Prevention (CDC) has found that meat and poultry commodities account for 40 percent of bacterial foodborne illnesses."[67]

Limits on the USDA's regulatory power add to the dangers of meat consumption. As the Government Accountability Office concludes: "Weaknesses in USDA's and FDA's food recall programs heighten the risk that unsafe food will remain in the food supply. The USDA and FDA do not know how promptly and completely the recalling companies and their distributors are carrying out recalls, and neither agency is using its data systems to effectively track and manage its recall programs. For these and other reasons, most recalled food is not recovered and therefore may be consumed." The USDA and FDA do not have unilateral authority to order recalls of food products. Rather, they can merely participate in the voluntary recalls of food manufacturers.[68] This lack of enforcement power must change in order to force quick recalls and limit public exposure to unsafe meats.

In the 2010s, the USDA continued to struggle in identifying meat contaminations. In 2011, House Republicans pushed for cuts to federal spending on food safety efforts, in the name of reducing government influence over private meat markets. Among other cuts in the proposed 2011 budget was a reduction of $35 million in funds for USDA inspections of packing plants, under the assumption that the U.S. meat supply was already safe enough. The proposed cuts would have led to the furlough of thousands of inspectors, in addition to a decline in the inspections of packing plants.[69] As *Mother Jones* reported, "without sufficient monitoring, the risk of tainted meat in the nation's food supply is likely to increase . . . there's also the economic impact to consider: Slaughterhouses may be forced to close if there are big cutbacks in inspections, since such facilities must be inspected daily to remain open."[70]

While only a small amount of all beef is recalled by manufacturers, the concern with bacterial infections is real. Much of the American meat supply is infected with antibiotic-resistant bacteria. According to a 2013 FDA report, 81 percent of ground turkey, 69 percent of pork chops, 55 percent of ground beef, and 39 percent of chicken were infected with such microbes as of 2012.[71] Furthermore, the problem of lax government regulation worsened over time. The 2013 federal "sequester" (which saw an 8 percent cut in federal spending), imposed cuts on the USDA, which forced a furlough of 8,400 federal meat inspectors for several weeks.[72]

This sequester was accompanied by a USDA proposal for the self-inspection of poultry manufacturing plants, in response to federal budget cuts. The USDA planned to save $85 million over three years by laying off 1,000 federal inspectors and handing over their inspection responsibilities to companies, which were expected to self-monitor.[73] As ABC News reported, this handover of power meant lower inspection standards: "the poultry companies expect to save more than $250 million a year because they, in turn, will be allowed to speed up the processing lines to a dizzying 175 birds per minute with one USDA inspector at the end of the line. Currently, traditional poultry lines move at a maximum of 90 birds per minute, with up to three USDA inspectors on line." This change was met with skepticism by one USDA whistleblower warning that the meat industry "cannot be trusted to watch over themselves" since "companies routinely pressure their employees not to stop the line or slow it down, making thorough inspection for contaminants, tumors, and evidence of disease nearly impossible."[74]

Deregulatory campaigns have not been limited to the above stories. Under the Trump administration, the very idea of regulation is under assault, as is the notion that government should provide cultural, environmental, and social benefits. Trump made clear his intentions upon taking office to muzzle government scientists, prohibiting scientists at the USDA and EPA from even speaking with journalists.[75] He appointed a known climate change-denier—Scott Pruitt—to head the EPA, in a blatant example of industry capture of government regulators.[76] The administration also proposed numerous significant cuts to various government programs and agencies, including the National Endowment for the Arts, the Office of Violence Against Women, the Office of Community Oriented Policing Services, the Minority Business Development Agency, the National Endowment for the Humanities, the Corporation for Public Broadcasting, the Civil Rights Division and the Environmental and Natural Resources divisions of the Justice Department, and the UN Panel on Climate Change.[77] Trump's assault on the federal bureaucracy posed a significant risk to public goods. It revealed that the billionaire saw little value in social, cultural, and political education, environmental protections, or minority rights. Trump's attacks on government were merely an intensification of the neoliberal assault on political programs that are seen as either inessential or as a threat to profits by corporations and the upper class.

This chapter highlighted the dangers inherent in the failure to regulate corporations. As of the late 2010s, the regulatory powers of bureaucratic agencies were still limited, with neither the USDA nor FDA claiming recall authority for meat and drug products. While neoliberals celebrate the benefits of deregulation and depict government regulation as unnecessary, deregulation represents a danger to public health. With the rise of neoliberalism and business power in American politics, public goods are under assault because they do not contribute to the profit interests of corporations and the upper class. The effort to destroy public goods means the decline of vital services—such as education—that are necessary to a democratic society. That many Americans demonize public goods and bureaucratic agencies, with little understanding of the role they play in aiding citizens, is a sign of the deterioration of political and intellectual discourse in the neoliberal era.

Chapter 8

The Courts and Judicial Process

Ideology, Conflict, and Class Elitism

The Supreme Court case of *Citizens United v. FEC* (2010) was a landmark ruling in American history. The ruling freed up political action committees (PACs) to spend unlimited amounts of money on election-related ads. In an effort to get money out of politics, the Bi-Partisan Campaign Reform Act of 2002 prohibited PACs from spending money on issue ads in the 60 days before general elections and the 30 days before primary elections. The court ruled that spending restrictions on campaign ads were an unconstitutional violation of the alleged First Amendment "right" of corporations and the wealthy individuals who run corporate PACs to free speech. This interpretation of the First Amendment drew on a previous Supreme Court case, *Buckley v. Valeo* (1976), which stated campaign spending was a form of free speech. *Citizens United* also drew on *Santa Clara County v. Southern Pacific Railroad* (1886), in which the Supreme Court decided that corporations are legal persons, guaranteed equal protection rights under the Fourteenth Amendment. *Citizens United* extended those "citizen" rights to the First Amendment, and to spending on election advertisements.

While the Supreme Court eliminated restrictions on campaign spending, the public was less enthusiastic. On the one hand, some conservatives will likely agree that, since corporations are comprised of individuals, they should be guaranteed free speech. On the other hand, most Americans, Republicans, independents, and Democrats, did not agree with *Citizens United*. A 2012 Pew poll found that two-thirds of those familiar with *Citizens United* thought it would have a negative effect on elections. A 2015 *Pew* survey showed that 76 percent of Americans felt that "money has [a] greater influence on politics today than before," while 64 percent agreed the "high cost of presidential campaigns discourages good candidates."[1]

Citizens United had negative implications for citizen empowerment. If corporations are legal persons, contributing unlimited amounts of money to elections, then "free speech" will be dominated by the wealthy, businesses, and the upper class. The average American has little money to spend on elections. Corporations spend billions of dollars per presidential election year expressing their views, while hundreds of millions of Americans are unable to disseminate any message via election ads. The top .01 percent of income earners account for 42 percent of all campaign spending, while just 195 wealthy donors account for 60 percent of all donations to Super PACs.[2] In this context, to speak of empowering citizens to influence elections really means empowering the super-wealthy, elite segment of the upper class.

The Courts as an Upper-Class Instrument

Judges typically see themselves as above petty partisan bickering, not as politicians, but as expert, objective practitioners and interpreters of the law. This chapter argues the opposite, that judges, like political officials, have increasingly fallen into endorsing the neoliberal system. This does not mean that class elitism, and an upper-class, pro-business bias is new to the courts. Far from it. They have consistently been elitist in their political-economic orientation over the last century. This bias in favor of the wealthy and privileged was declining, however, by the early to mid-twentieth century, when the court stepped back from challenging progressive New Deal reforms in the 1930s, and then began to fight for the rights of minority groups, including black Americans and women, from the 1950s to 1970s. But more recently, with the rise of neoliberalism, the courts have seen a significant conservative turn, privileging business and upper-class interests, while neglecting the interests of the citizenry.

In theory and practice, the courts have the power to represent disadvantaged groups. This much is clear from looking at the history of the Supreme Court in the mid-twentieth century. In the 1930s, despite initially opposing President Franklin Roosevelt's New Deal reforms, the court relented, allowing for the constitutionality of the minimum wage, unionization, and child labor laws, regulations on Wall Street, and social welfare spending on programs such as Social Security. By the mid-twentieth century, the court was led by liberal Chief Justice Earl Warren. Warren presided over numerous decisions that favored disadvantaged minority groups, including *Brown v. Board of Education of Topeka* (1954), which rolled back government support for segregation, and *Miranda v. Arizona* (1966) and *Gideon v. Wainwright* (1962), which protected Americans' right to remain silent upon arrest, and their right to legal representation, which had previously been denied to many poor and historically disadvantaged groups. Later, the Berger court of the 1970s established a right of women to abortion, which was based in women's right to privacy under the Fourth Amendment. These cases demonstrate that the court has at times played a significant role in fighting for poorer and disadvantaged groups, or at least not standing in their way.

The courts also have the power to provide democratic representation by relying on public opinion and public preferences in their rulings. It has long been known among judicial scholars that public opinion influences Supreme Court rulings.[3] One prominent example is the string of Supreme Court decisions expanding same-sex marriage rights and striking down discriminatory anti-gay and lesbian laws. These rulings echo positions that are increasingly popular with the mass public, since most Americans support same-sex marriage and oppose discrimination based on sexual orientation.[4] But why do judges' rulings overlap with public attitudes? One possible explanation is that, since the public elects its political leaders, it also has an indirect impact on the kinds of judges selected, since Americans choose those making court nominations and appointments. Another possibility is that the courts seek legitimacy from the public, so they often rule in favor of prevailing public expectations to demonstrate that they are not out of touch with dominant cultural norms.

At first glance, the finding that the Supreme Court reflects the public will seems incompatible with the claim that courts serve wealthy and upper-class interests. But it is possible that Americans support Supreme Court rulings that run contrary to their own interests. The notion that Americans are susceptible to hegemonic manipulation from political and business elites is not new.[5] And previous research finds an overlap between public attitudes and official agendas, even though the federal government has pursued policies in recent decades that harm the average American in favor of elites.[6] In short, one need not interpret the overlap between public opinion and Supreme Court rulings as evidence of the public's democratic empowerment.

Competing Characterizations of Judicial Politics

There are competing models that seek to explain how the courts function. One of these models—the legal model—depicts the courts as acting dispassionately in the pursuit of justice. This depiction sees courts as the cornerstone of checks and balances in a vibrant democracy. In contrast, the attitudinal model depicts judges as politicians in robes, acting on behalf of dominant societal political ideologies that drive government more generally. Finally, the class elitism model sees judges as unabashed advocates for wealthy, elitist, and upper-class interests, and as strengthening corporate power in politics. I explore all these models in detail.

The Legal Model

The legal model is sometimes referred to as requiring "judicial restraint," with judges refusing to allow their ideological biases to impact how they decide on court cases. This school of thought claims that judges are neutral or unbiased in how they rule on legal disputes.[7] This model is widely celebrated by political officials, who announce that judges must ensure their personal views and values do not influence their legal reasoning. Judges are supposed to apply the law without prejudice, and simply enforce previous legal precedents (a practice referred to as "stare decisis"), that have been set by the Supreme Court. According to this thinking, applying the law in court cases is almost a robotic affair, with legal statute written in accessible black-and-white language, and applied without controversy to the facts of a case.

The legal model is not taken seriously by most judicial scholars, although it is often invoked during judicial confirmation hearings by Senators demanding that nominees separate their ideology from their judicial decision making. Several problems arise with the legal model. For one, judges often disagree in court cases when interpreting the law, and lower courts often disagree with higher courts on the same case. Split rulings between judges are common, suggesting there is no uncontroversial, black-and-white, or single interpretation of the law as applied to the facts of a case. Furthermore, judges do not simply apply previous precedent to future cases, since there are competing precedents that one can potentially draw on, depending on which one a judge feels is *most* relevant to a case. Choosing the "correct" precedent is a potentially contentious process. Judges cite competing precedents as a justification for ruling in different ways on cases under consideration. In sum, interpreting the law is more complex than the legal model admits.

A second problem with the legal model is that most judges (begrudgingly) admit that biases are at work in the judicial system. On the one hand, survey data finds that judges claim they are objective in their decision making. On the other hand, however, most judges also agree the national courts have become more conservative over time, that presidents appoint judges who agree with them ideologically, and that partisan politics dominates the appointment and confirmation process.[8] None of these things would occur if judges were truly neutral in their decisions, since partisan politics would not play a role in influencing judicial nominations and confirmation votes. And if judges were unbiased, the national courts would not be shifting in a more conservative direction, as they have been doing for decades.

Judges do not always agree when interpreting the law, in part because interpretations of the law shift over time. This is apparent in the case of equal rights. The Supreme Court has taken different stances throughout history on segregation and equal rights. In *Plessy v. Ferguson* (1896), the court declared segregation of rail cars to be legal. Homer Plessy was arrested for sitting in a "whites only" railroad car. Because of his mixed racial background, he was required to travel in the "colored" car. Contrary to Plessy's claim of being denied equal treatment under the Fourteenth Amendment, the court ruled 7 to 2 in favor of segregation. Justice Henry Brown wrote: "a statute which implies merely a legal distinction between the white and colored races—has no tendency to destroy the legal equality of the two races . . . The object of the Fourteenth Amendment was undoubtedly to enforce the absolute equality of the two races before the law, but in the nature of things it could not have been intended to abolish distinctions based upon color, or to enforce social, as distinguished from political equality, or a commingling of the two races upon terms unsatisfactory to either." In other words, "equality" was fine, even if it did not exist, so long as one claimed it did. Under these circumstances, blatant violations of equal rights were sanctioned by the court. The vast majority of Americans today would consider this an appalling interpretation of the Fourteenth Amendment, although the judges at the time were the product of a dominant political culture viewing segregation as not only legal, but moral.

The civil rights movement forced a rethinking of segregation and the legal justifications used to defend it. In the 1954 case, *Brown v. Board of Education of Topeka*, the Supreme Court overruled the decision made in the *Plessy* case. *Brown* was a joint lawsuit including five previous cases that challenged the constitutionality of state-sponsored segregation in public schools. In this case, the Supreme Court unanimously ruled that segregated public schools violated the equal protection clause of the Fourteenth Amendment. *Brown* was in line with the modern understanding of discrimination as repressive of minorities. How can public schools *not* violate equal rights when minorities are discriminated against and not allowed to attend the same schools as whites? This point about discrimination was ignored in *Plessy*, although the threat of discrimination was well understood by judges in the *Brown* case.

The Importance of Ideology and Attitudes

Why were the rulings in *Plessy* and *Brown* so contradictory, considering they were dealing with the same issues: segregation and equal rights? The answer is simple: members of the Supreme Court in 1896 were racist, and like others during their time, they valued the institution of segregation. Much had changed by 1954, however, due to the civil rights movement, which transformed how Americans looked at race and segregation. No longer seen as an acceptable institution, segregation was deemed by the Supreme Court to be unconstitutional and a violation of equal protection under law. This segregation case study is important because it shows court rulings are the product of cultural values and competing interpretations of the law over time.

A second example of judicial interpretation relates to abortion. In *Roe v. Wade* (1973), the Supreme Court ruled 7 to 2 that abortions in the first two trimesters of a pregnancy are constitutionally legal. The court claimed the right to an abortion is guaranteed under the First, Fourth, Ninth, and Fourteenth Amendments to the Constitution. These amendments, the judges claimed, recognize an individual's "zone of privacy," which covers marriage, parenting, and contraception. Women retain the choice within this "zone of privacy" to decide whether or not they want to seek an abortion. *Roe v. Wade* was a classic example of legal interpretation. There is no specific provision in the Constitution discussing a right to abortion. To create this right, judges claimed it was subsumed within the right to privacy. But the Fourth Amendment does not refer to a right to privacy either. It states: "the right of the people to be secure in their persons, houses, and papers, and effects, against unreasonable searches and seizures, shall not be violated."

The notion that individuals retain a right to privacy is implied in the Bill of Rights, per the Supreme Court's *Griswold v. Connecticut* (1965). However, the Bill of Rights is still silent about abortion as part of one's right to privacy. To include it within one's privacy rights required another ruling—*Roe v. Wade*. Why would the Supreme Court interpret the right to privacy as including abortion? The simple answer is that, ideologically speaking, most judges believed access to abortion and the ability to choose *should* both be included as a part of a woman's right to privacy. As *Roe v. Wade* suggests, judges do not divorce their personal values from their rulings. Values influence how judges look at and rule on legal issues before the courts.

The above rulings suggest that, while judges are inherently political in their thinking and rulings, they are also able to fight for disadvantaged groups. Courts do not have to privilege wealthy, upper-class individuals over minorities, women, and the poor. If strongly pressured by progressive social movements, judges will respond by prioritizing the expansion of representation for disadvantaged groups, including black Americans and women.

The legal model cannot account for the realities of judicial decision-making. Judges hold attitudes that influence their legal reasoning. In contrast, judicial scholars have outlined an "attitudinal model," arguing that judges rely on personal beliefs and ideological preferences when ruling on cases. Adopting the attitudinal model, judicial scholars argue that "the Supreme Court decides disputes in light of the facts of the case vis-à-vis the ideological attitudes and values of the justices. Simply put [Chief Justice William] Rehnquist vote[d] the way he [did] because he [was] extremely conservative; [Associate Justice Thurgood] Marshall voted the way he did because he was extremely liberal."[9] It is no secret that judges who serve on the Supreme Court have developed reputations for being more liberal or conservative based on their previous legal decisions. As reflected in figure 8.1 below, by 2013, four judges on the Supreme Court had developed reputations as liberals, while another four were widely known as conservative, and with one serving as a "moderate" or "swing" judge in the middle.[10]

Judicial scholarship finds that the history of a judge—more specifically whether he or she consistently votes in a liberal or conservative direction in cases—helps to predict how judges vote 77 percent of the time.[11] One could easily get the impression from this finding that judges are essentially politicians in robes, in that they pursue their own political and ideological goals through the judicial process. Clearly, Supreme Court judges allow their political ideologies to influence how they interpret the law.

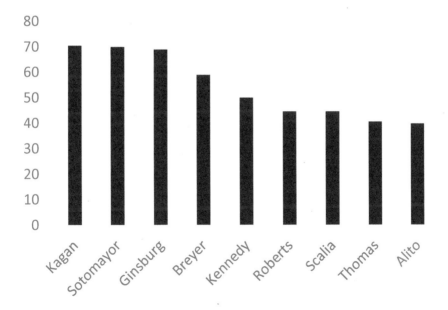

Figure 8.1. Ideology and the Supreme Court: Percent Liberal Rulings (through 2013). Source: Hannah Fairfield and Adam Liptak, "A More Nuanced Breakdown of the Supreme Court," *New York Times*, June 26, 2014, https://www.nytimes.com/2014/06/27/upshot/a-more-nuanced-breakdown-of-the-supreme-court.html

Judicial Ideology and Obamacare

Obamacare was a high-profile example of the attitudinal model in action, as it demonstrated how ideology influenced legal reasoning. In this case, judicial scholars and journalists expected the conservative judges on the court—Samuel Alito, Clarence Thomas, [the late] Antonin Scalia, and John Roberts to declare the law unconstitutional. The court's four liberal judges—Elena Kagan, Sonya Sotomayor, Stephen Breyer, and Ruth Bader Ginsburg—were expected to argue for its constitutionality. The court's "swing judge," with a history of split ideological rulings, but often leaning in a conservative direction on major court rulings—Anthony Kennedy—was expected to vote against the health care law. How did the court actually vote on health care? The predictions were mostly accurate. As a conservative swing judge, Kennedy voted against Obamacare. As liberal judges, Kagan, Sotomayor, Breyer, and Ginsburg voted in favor of the law. As conservatives, [the late] Scalia, Thomas, and Alito voted against the law. Only one judge—the conservative Roberts—voted in favor of the law, contrary to attitudinal model's predictions. For Obamacare, the attitudinal model correctly predicted judges' votes in 8 of 9 cases, a high success rate for any model seeking to explain judicial politics.

Why did Chief Justice John Roberts vote for Obamacare, contrary to common expectations? Roberts provided legal reasoning that suggested he was strategically deferring to the executive. Roberts concluded the law could not be defended under the Commerce Clause, but agreed that the fines central to the mandate constituted a tax, and that the federal government retained the power to tax Americans under the Taxation and General Welfare Clause.[12] But Robert's decision was also based in practical considerations, factoring in the power dynamics between the executive and judicial branches. Roberts expressed in his written decision "a general reticence to invalidate the acts of the Nation's elected leaders. 'Proper respect for a coordinate branch of the government' requires that we strike down an Act of Congress only if the 'lack of constitutional authority to pass [the] act in question is clearly demonstrated.' Members of this Court are vested with the authority to interpret the law; we possess neither the expertise nor the prerogative to make policy judgments. Those decisions are entrusted to our Nation's elected leaders, who can be thrown out of office if the people disagree with them. It is not our job to protect the people from the consequences of their political choices."[13]

Roberts's statement suggested that the court deferred to the executive on health care. The dispute over Obamacare suggests judicial decision making in the U.S. is not simply driven by the ideology of judges or deference to the elected branches. Both factors are simultaneously at work. The attitudinal model predicted the behavior of most judges, but judges are also concerned with not undermining the credibility of an already weak judicial branch by challenging executive power. Roberts was concerned with the legacy of the Supreme Court, and recognized its limited powers over Congress and the president with regard to Obamacare.

A closer examination of the Obamacare ruling demonstrates the merits of the attitudinal model. Liberal judges looked to previous Supreme Court precedents to validate their liberal interpretations of law, while conservative judges looked to other precedents to validate their conservative interpretations. Competing precedents were invoked by the court's judges, some of which validated the law, others challenging it. Judges supporting Obamacare invoked *Wickard v. Filburn* (1942) and *Gonzales v. Raich* (2005), which lent themselves to expansive views of federal power and a liberal interpretation of the Commerce Clause. In *Wickard v. Filburn*, the Supreme Court ruled that federal wheat quotas for limiting farmers' own consumption of wheat were legal under the Commerce Clause. The question was asked in this case: could a grower exceed a quota, even if they used the excess crop for personal consumption, rather than selling it on the open market? The Supreme Court answered "no," concluding that the farmer's consumption indirectly influenced interstate commerce. If the grower did not produce extra wheat for personal consumption, he would have had to buy it in the marketplace, or he would have had to sell less wheat. This case retained positive implications for the Obamacare ruling, supporters argued, because regulating wheat quotas and personal consumption of wheat were similar, practically speaking, to regulating a commodity like health insurance in the market place. Liberal Supreme Court judges, including Kagan, Sotomayor, Ginsburg, and Breyer, invoked *Wickard v. Filburn* in their written opinions on Obamacare, while conservative judges, including Scalia, Kennedy, Thomas, and Alito, rejected this case as an appropriate precedent.[14]

Gonzales v. Raich was also invoked by liberal judges. In that case, the Supreme Court ruled that outlawing marijuana was justified under the Commerce Clause, since selling drugs is an example of commerce and the federal government has the power to regulate it. Supporters of Obamacare also drew on this precedent, arguing that regulating marijuana was substantively similar to regulating health insurance, since both are commodities. The conservative judges, Scalia, Kennedy, Thomas, and Alito rejected the above comparison, while the liberal judges, Kagan, Sotomayor, Ginsburg, and Breyer, embraced *Gonzales v Raich*.[15]

In contrast to the above precedents, two other precedents were relevant to Obamacare: *U.S. v. Morrison* (2000) and *U.S. v. Lopez* (1995). In *U.S. v.*

Morrison, the Supreme Court ruled the Violence Against Women Act (1994) could not be justified under the Commerce Clause. The law allowed women to sue perpetrators in federal court, in cases of violence against women, when state or local courts fail to follow through with the cases. Supporters of the law argued the accumulated effects of violence against women had a negative effect on interstate commerce, but this argument was rejected by the court's majority, since such violence is not *directly* associated with commerce. Conservatives used *U.S. v. Morrison* to argue that the health care law was similar to the Violence Against Women Act, in that both overstepped the legal boundaries of what is permissible under the Commerce Clause. The four conservative Supreme Court judges cited the Morrison case as justifying their opposition to Obamacare.[16]

Finally, *U.S. v. Lopez* (1995) was also invoked by opponents of Obamacare. In this case, the Supreme Court stated that a law prohibiting possession of a gun by a school could not be justified under the Commerce Clause. Supporters of the anti-gun law argued that gun violence near schools creates a toxic environment for learning. If students cannot learn, they will be unable to secure a quality education, and the lack of quality education would have a negative effect on the economy across the 50 states. The Supreme Court rejected this argument, since gun violence is not directly related to commerce. For conservatives, forcing citizens to buy health insurance exceeded government's powers under the Commerce Clause, just as regulating guns near schools exceeded government commerce powers. With Obamacare the court's four conservative judges concurred that *Lopez* was an appropriate precedent guiding their decision.[17]

Judges' reliance on ideology in interpreting the law means they are unable to divorce themselves from personal biases or from broader political conflicts in society. With the rise of neoliberalism, both political parties have embraced an elitist brand of politics that privileges wealthy, upper-class, and corporate interests. If judges restrict themselves to ideological voting that falls within the bipartisan spectrum of opinion, then they also conform to a neoliberal system that prioritizes business and upper-class power in politics. The case of Obamacare demonstrates this point. Conservative judges argued for a return to the old status quo in which health care corporations were empowered to deny individual care via discrimination against those with preexisting medical conditions. In contrast, liberal judges argued for Obama's expansion of market-based care, which granted significant concessions and benefits to the needy, but was primarily a boon for the health care industry, and which failed to introduce even basic price regulations in a time of runaway health care costs. In sum, although judges are political in their rulings, the rise of upper-class and business dominance of politics means the emergence of a judiciary that is increasingly elitist in its political orientation in the ways it shadows Democratic and Republican Party politics.

Upper-Class Elitism

A third account of the judicial process depicts judges as favoring business interests and wealthy elites. Judges do not seek social transformation against the prevailing currents of society. As one judicial scholar argues: "justices are subject to the same economic, social, and intellectual currents as other upper-middle class professional elites"; the court "identifies with and serves ruling political coalitions . . . it is staffed by men (and women) who for the most part are in tune with their times."[18]

Demographically, federal judges have long represented business interests. Parenti notes in *Democracy for the Few* that judges are often drawn from corporate and business law backgrounds, so their rulings will reflect an upper-class bias. Most federal judicial appointees today are millionaires. Under both the Bill Clinton and George W. Bush administrations, 51 percent of appointees were millionaires, and under Obama, two-thirds were millionaires.[19] On numerous indicators, judges appeared to become more elite over time. The percent of federal appointments coming from Ivy League schools, for example, grew significantly from the Reagan to the Obama years, as did the number of judges coming from large law firms.[20]

An elitist bias manifests itself in various ways. First, there is the longstanding pattern of deferring to other political elites—who themselves increasingly represent business and upper-class interests. A second form of bias is seen in pro-business decisions that historically characterize the courts' actions. During the nineteenth and twentieth centuries, the national courts consistently sided with wealthy interests over the people. Courts were instrumental in creating the rights of modern corporations, recognizing the legal principle of "limited liability"—originally established by Congressional law—in which individuals investing in corporations are only liable for the amount they invest in a business. Limited liability is a boon to investors in cases where corporations are responsible for behaviors that impose economic harm on individuals, workers, or communities. Limited liability was recognized by the courts in *Salomon v. A Salomon & Co. Ltd* (1897). Additionally, courts were vital to the recognition of corporations as legal persons with "rights" equal those of actual persons. These rights were recognized in *Trustees of Dartmouth College v. Woodward* (1819) and *Santa Clara County v. Southern Pacific Railroad* (1886). Corporate charters are no longer revoked by government in the modern era of corporate personhood, since the state governments granting them are reluctant to commit the "death penalty" against businesses, regardless of the severity of their legal transgressions. Recognized as persons, corporations can now devote unlimited amounts of funds to electoral "issue ads," since they are guaranteed free speech under the First Amendment.[21]

The courts also favored businesses over workers during the late-1800s and early-1900s. State efforts to establish a minimum wage were struck down by the federal judiciary (*Adkins v. Children's Hospital*, 1923), and deemed a violation of employers' "right" to determine pay rates for workers, without a guaranteed floor income. The Supreme Court also invalidated a legislative effort to outlaw child labor, which the federal government supposedly could not regulate under the Commerce Clause (*Hammer v. Dagenheart*, 1918). Finally, the courts routinely issued injunctions in the late-1800s and early-1900s ordering workers on strike back to work, under threat of physical attack by National Guard forces.[22]

Although the mid-twentieth century saw the courts prioritizing representation for disadvantaged groups, in the twenty-first century, the courts increasingly side with business elites. The most blatant example is *Citizens United* (2010), but there are other cases as well, which suggest an elitist bias as related to sexual discrimination and unions. Regarding women's rights, the Supreme Court dismissed a class action lawsuit (*Wal-Mart v. Dukes*, 2011) alleging sexual discrimination by 1.5 million, largely low-income, female workers. The court justified the dismissal by claiming the experiences of the women were not similar enough to be grouped together as a class action. Justice Antonin Scalia wrote there was not enough of a "commonality needed for a class action" suit to demonstrate the women involved were "disfavored."[23] Stripping out the technical jargon, Scalia's complaint

Image 8.1. Wal-Mart is Anti-Woman.

essentially amounted to a "too many women are complaining" response, which terminated the most important class action suit in a decade. This dismissal was a PR gift to Wal-Mart, which claimed it was cleared of the charges.[24]

A final example of pro-business (and anti-worker) bias involves anti-labor rulings such as *Harris v. Quinn* (2014) and *Janus v. American Federation of State, County, and Municipal Employees* (2018), declaring that public and private sector employees who are not part of a union are no longer required to pay "fair share" dues to keep unions operating, even though unions negotiate pay increases and benefits that apply to these same workers (state laws used to mandate that non-union members pay their "fair share" of union dues so long as unions are negotiating for pay raises and benefits on their behalf). In the *Quinn* and *Janus* cases, the Supreme Court clearly demonstrated that it was sympathetic to the neoliberal anti-union agenda, which has long been embraced by the upper-class in America.

The Supreme Court argued in the 2018 *Janus* case that requiring public sector employees to pay dues to unions was a violation of First Amendment free speech rights for dues-paying members, particularly for those who disagree with the specific types of political advocacy engaged in by unions. This reasoning, however, was contradicted by the fact that the Supreme Court had already ruled in *Abood v. Detroit Board of Education* (1977) that those paying dues to unions can insist that their funds are not used for such political advocacy. With the *Abood* ruling, employees were already protected against forms of union-related political speech that they found objectionable. Furthermore, the court majority failed to recognize that paying dues for a union to engage in collective bargaining is not directly relevant to "First Amendment" "freedom of speech" concerns, which apply against government efforts to limit individual expression. As the First Amendment states, "Congress shall make no law . . . abridging the freedom of speech." This language, even when broadened by the courts to apply to all parts of government, is still irrelevant to unions, which are non-governmental actors.

The rulings in the *Quinn* and *Janus* cases were flagrantly and hypocritically biased against unions. The Supreme Court does not recognize "free speech" rights in the workplace, as applied to public sector and private sector employees.[25] So, to claim that these same workers now have "free speech" rights against unions, suggests a double-standard at work in the logic of the Supreme Court's conservative majority, which is happy to create employee "rights" so long as they assault unions, while exempting public and private sector employees from similar protections related to actual speech in the workplace.

The logic at work in the *Janus* and *Quinn* cases was fundamentally flawed. Collective bargaining is a political act, but it represents an economic transaction between three parties—the employer, the union itself, and those paying dues to the union. This is not a "free speech" issue, legally speaking. Unions are not prohibiting those who pay dues from expressing their political opinions, whatever they may be. Rather, collective bargaining efforts merely seek to enhance workers' economic standing by securing higher pay and benefits for all those employed in a given workplace. The court's majority in the *Janus* ruling disingenuously used the rhetoric of "free speech" in a naked union-busting effort on the part of the court's five conservatives, who made no effort to mask their contempt for the very act of collective bargaining itself, which the court's majority referred to as "coercive" in nature.[26] By allowing workers to withhold fair share union dues, the Supreme Court effectively chopped out the financial foundation of unions—a foundation that was necessary in order to compensate union representatives for the arduous task of collectively bargaining with employers for pay raises, health insurance, and other benefits.

In the neoliberal era, hopes that the courts will play a leadership role in creating rights for society's disadvantaged are misplaced. Some see the Supreme Court as vital to strengthening civil rights and women's rights, but this claim is questioned by the historical record. At the height of the liberal Supreme Court from the 1950s through the 1970s, social movements were primarily responsible for creating the pressure to change U.S. laws in favor of disadvantaged groups.[27] Some may look to cases like *Roe v. Wade* and *Brown v. Board of Education* as examples of the court creating rights for citizens, but the civil rights and women's rights movements were active before these rulings. Still, this period in American history demonstrates that the courts can be forced into supporting progressive legal positions that benefit disadvantaged and poorer groups, if strongly pressured.

This chapter analyzed the judiciary and its various biases, exploring different explanations for why the courts function the way they do. Summarizing main points: judges are not technocratic, unbiased interpreters of the law. They hold ideologies that influence their legal decisions. In a time of growing inequality, the courts have not remained neutral; rather they have favored business and upper-class agendas. Notions that the courts are an ally of progressive social movements are exaggerated. In the modern era, the courts have shown little interest in fighting for marginalized social groups, and have prioritized enhancing corporate "rights" and business power. In the politics of the twenty-first century, the courts are largely a pro-status quo political force.

Chapter 9

Political Parties

A Crisis of Public Confidence

In a late-2016 poll by the Public Religion and Research Institute, nearly two-thirds of Americans agreed that neither political party adequately represented their opinions. The dissatisfaction was bi-partisan, with Democratic Presidential candidate Hillary Clinton and Republican candidate Donald Trump viewed positively by 41 percent and 33 percent of the public, respectively. Disenchantment had grown since the 2012 presidential election, with 74 percent of Americans agreeing the country was headed in the wrong direction in 2016, compared to 57 percent in 2012.[1]

There are many reasons that Americans provide for why they are unhappy with government and the political parties. However, I argue that dissatisfaction with parties is driven to a large extent by anger at the perceived failure of government to address citizens' economic needs and interests in a time of growing inequality and economic insecurity. While upper-class and corporate interests are well-represented in the halls of Washington, "average" Americans feel more disconnected from the parties and government than ever.

A political party is a union of like-minded individuals pursuing common political, economic, and social policies. These parties include citizens, political officials, and political institutions. Scholars lay out many expectations for what political parties are supposed to do in a democracy. These responsibilities include: representing the interests of the people, uniting diverse groups and mobilizing the masses to vote, providing collective goods to the public, and making it easier for voters to choose between candidates by providing "brand names" from which citizens can select.[2]

But political parties are also increasingly elitist in orientation, raising questions about their ability to serve the public. Six of the top eight donors to the Democratic Party during elections represent upper-class interests, including communications firms, the health industry, lawyers associations, finance, insurance and real estate associations, the entertainment industry, and Wall Street investors, while only two represent the mass citizenry—retirees and civil servants.[3] Republican support is even more elitist, with all eight of the top donor groups representing upper-class and corporate interests, including the finance, insurance and real estate associations, agribusiness corporations, the construction industry, energy firms, the transportation industry, lawyers associations, the health care industry, and communications and electronics firms.[4] While campaign contributions do not automatically translate into "control" over political officials, they do stack the deck in favor of candidates who themselves come from the upper class (most members of Congress) and who receive their money from corporate interests. This corporate dominance of elections is important, considering the dominant role of campaign spending in determining electoral outcomes.[5]

The Rightward Drift of the Political Parties under Neoliberalism

The shift to the right in U.S. partisan politics traces back decades. Although American politics and society have become more liberal with regard to social issues, as related to women's rights, black Americans' rights, gay and lesbian rights, and other minority groups, there has been a clear turn rightward on economic issues, via the growth of corporate and upper-class power over politics. The Democratic Party was widely seen as left in its economic policies from the 1930s through the 1960s, championing the needs of the poor and disadvantaged. Roosevelt's New Deal was a massive liberal policy initiative, aimed at expanding government and helping the masses in a time of crisis. The Democrats institutionalized various liberal political changes, including worker protections, such as the minimum wage, child labor laws, and the 40-hour work week, and introduced social welfare programs such as Social Security, food stamps, homeowners' assistance, and Aid to Families with Dependent Children. The liberal economic direction of the party continued through the 1960s. Johnson's "Great Society" was aimed at fighting poverty and reducing economic and racial inequality. Johnson introduced numerous liberal economic initiatives, including a permanent food stamps program, adult education spending, "Head Start" educational aid for needy children, Medicare for the elderly, and Medicaid for the poor.

Economically speaking, the Democratic Party of the last four decades is far less liberal than it used to be. It is increasingly committed to aiding and enriching the power of the wealthy, while the masses are left behind. There was no modern equivalent to the "War on Poverty" or the "New Deal" under Presidents Bill Clinton or Barack Obama. Clinton spearheaded an anti-labor, conservative "free trade" agreement called NAFTA that was pro-business in nature, allowing for the export of American manufacturing jobs to sweatshops in Mexico. He also helped eliminate the Aid to Families with Dependent Children welfare program, tracing back to the 1930s, in favor of a smaller, less generous state-based program—Temporary Assistance to Needy Families. Obama promoted market-friendly, conservative health care reform, rather than a liberal, government-funded plan to cover uninsured Americans. He strongly pushed cuts in Social Security spending in addition to cuts in other welfare programs, in the name of deficit reduction. He will be remembered for promoting the Trans Pacific Partnership "free trade" deal, which was opposed by most Americans for fear it would cost Americans more jobs.[6]

The Democratic Party refused to push for fundamental change in the area of health care reform. Obamacare did aid poor and working Americans by expanding Medicaid and providing taxpayer subsidies to many working- and middle-class individuals and families. But the law did nothing to regulate the ever-escalating costs of health care. It failed to introduce any sort of socialized program similar to Medicaid or Medicare to cover the tens of millions of Americans who were uninsured, many of which earned too much money to qualify for Medicaid, and who were too young to qualify for Medicare. Obamacare was not the equivalent of Medicaid or Medicare, in that those programs were liberal-left, ideologically speaking, and demonstrated a government commitment to socialized care. Obamacare merely required citizens to purchase private health insurance on state marketplaces, providing tax revenues to do it.

Contemporary Democrats are conservative on education. They promote a "market"-based reform agenda championed by wealthy philanthropist groups like the Gates Foundation, which greatly harms teachers, and ignores a prime cause of poor school performance—poverty in minority communities.[7] In various settings, they favor the curtailment of tenure and unionization among teachers, and they promote market-based reforms such as merit pay for teachers, "school choice" vouchers, and performance-based funding, despite little evidence that these reforms improve educational performance.[8] To make matters worse, the quality of charter schools is strongly questioned in recent evidence suggesting these schools perform worse than community public schools on various academic metrics.[9]

Democrats have done little to fight for organized labor, despite Obama promising he would promote legislation to make it easier for workers to form unions. When in control of government, Democrats have refused to index the minimum wage to inflation or to introduce a living wage for all Americans, with the minimum wage's value dropping by 2015 to about a third from its height in purchasing power in 1968.[10] The vast majority of the job creation in the age of Obama was in low-pay, contingent, and temporary labor positions.[11] In sum, the economics of today's Democratic Party have moved far to the right. The party's inaction is a gift to corporate interests, which seek to keep wages low and prevent workers from improving benefits and pay via collective bargaining. By siding with upper-class business interests over the middle class and poor, Democrats ensured that inequality grew significantly over the last four decades.

Republicans have also moved in a rightward direction on economics. The Republican Party of the 1950s through the 1970s was somewhat liberal compared to later decades. Republican President Dwight Eisenhower spoke with condescension against Republicans seeking to dismantle or privatize Social Security, or to attack labor unions.[12] Eisenhower and Congress increased government spending on Social Security by expanding the types of workers covered by the program.[13] Although he wanted less federal responsibility in coordinating war on poverty programs, Republican President Richard Nixon signed into law the creation of the Environmental Protection Agency, which mandated a greater government role in regulating corporations polluting the air. Nixon expanded federal funding for the food stamps program, in addition to increasing Social Security spending by indexing benefits to the inflation rate.[14] In short, the Republican Party, like the Democratic Party, used to be (at least somewhat) committed to aiding the masses, and even the poor.

The modern Republican Party is nothing like the party of Eisenhower. It serves corporate interests, contributing greatly to rising economic inequality. President George W. Bush sought to privatize Social Security and invest its trust fund on Wall Street, which would have greatly enriched the investor class. The risks of an economic crash to retirement savings invested in the stock market would have been paid entirely by senior citizens. Republican House Speaker Paul Ryan called for privatizing Medicare, which would be a boon for health insurance companies, but produce a significant growth in costs for seniors.[15] When in power, Ryan also called for large cuts to programs like food stamps and other programs benefitting the needy.[16]

The Republican Party is notoriously anti-union and holds contempt for organized labor. Its members refuse to vote for even minimal minimum wage increases to keep workers' wages on par with inflation. Republican presidents in previous decades presided over a tax code that was far more progressive, taxing the wealthy and the upper class at a much higher rate than during the Bush years onward.[17] Finally, Republicans today are deeply reactionary on the environment, refusing to recognize global warming even exists, let alone being willing to tackle the problem.[18] In sum, Republicans have transformed from a moderate party to a rightwing, pro-business party. They openly serve the interests of the upper class over the many.

Americans agree that in modern times the two parties reside between the moderate to conservative part of the political spectrum. Perceptions that Republicans are more extreme than Democrats are longstanding, as captured in figure 9.1. In 2004, nearly two-thirds of Republicans saw Republican President George W. Bush as conservative, while just a quarter of Democrats saw Democratic candidate John Kerry as liberal.[19] In 2012, just a third of Democrats saw Barack Obama as a liberal.[20] In 2011, more than half of Americans thought Republicans were the more extreme party in their political positions, while just a third of Americans saw Democrats as the more extreme party.[21] Furthermore, as figure 9.2 makes clear, most Americans believe the Republican Party is further from the "moderate" center than Democrats. In 2014, more than half of Americans thought Democrats were "more willing to work with the other party to compromise"—a hallmark of moderate behavior—while just a quarter felt the same about Republicans.[22] In 2017, more than half of Americans thought the Republican Party was "more extreme in its positions," while only a third felt that way about Democrats.[23]

Taken as a whole, the data suggest that most Americans perceive the political system to be center-right in ideological orientation. This center-right ideology is strongly sympathetic to enhancing corporate and upper-class interests, despite growing anger from middle and lower-class Americans about the elitist bias of the political system.

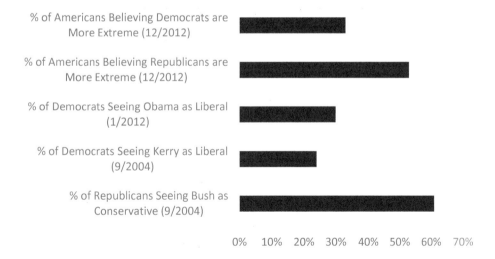

Figure 9.1. Public Perceptions of Extremism and the Parties, 2004–2012. Sources: Pew Research Center, "Section 2: Perception of the Candidates," *Pew Research Center*, September 16, 2004, http://www.people-press.org/2004/09/16/section-2-perception-of-the-candidates/. Pew Research Center, "Section 1: Barack Obama's Performance and Image," *Pew Research Center*, January 19, 2012, http://www.people-press.org/2012/01/19/section-1-barack-obamas-performance-and-image/. Pew Research Center, "As Fiscal Cliff Nears, Democrats Have Public Opinion on Their Side," *Pew Research Center*, December 13, 2012, http://www.people-press.org/2012/12/13/section-1-views-of-obama-congress-the-parties/.

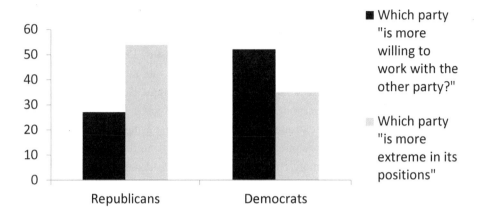

Figure 9.2. Public Opinion on Obstruction in Government, 2014; 2017. Source: Pew Research Center, "October 2014 Monthly Poll," *Pew Research Center*, October 2014; Pew Research Center, "January 2017 Monthly Poll," *Pew Research Center*, January 2017.

Why have both parties become increasingly geared toward serving the wealthy? The potential answers are many, with various changes in society overlapping with the rise of the neoliberal political system. I explore four reasons for growing elitism in politics below.

1. GROWING INEQUALITY

Political science scholars emphasize the threat of growing inequality to democracy. Inequality has grown dramatically in recent decades, especially under Republican presidents.[24] And political-historical scholarship recognizes that U.S. government increasingly favors upper-class and corporate interests.[25] It appears that growing inequality played a role in pushing both parties in a rightward direction. A small number of wealthy Americans retain larger financial resources to influence electoral outcomes via campaign contributions that advantage congressional incumbents, with most of these incumbents being members of the upper class in terms of their incomes and wealth. Both political parties are increasingly reliant on financial contributions from the wealthy, more so than they were in previous decades. These wealthy donors are far more likely to be conservative, and to pressure Congress to enact conservative political reforms.

The electoral process is increasingly captured by wealthy interests. The total cost of presidential elections, for example, increased from $4.3 billion in inflation-adjusted dollars in 2000, to $6.9 billion in 2016, a growth of 60 percent.[26] From 1908 through 2008, the cost of U.S. elections—inflation adjusted—increased by more than 2,000 percent, with the vast majority of the growing cost occurring from the 1960s to today.[27] Furthermore, Congress is increasingly elitist in its composition. The median net worth of members of Congress increased from $280,000 in 1984 to $720,000 in 2009, after adjusting for inflation, a 159 percent increase.[28] As of 2014, the median net worth of a Congressperson reached over $1 million.[29] These individuals were in the top tenth of the American wealth distribution, making them solidly upper class.[30]

Even if campaign contributions are not effective in consistently "buying off" members of Congress, money still matters to influencing political outcomes. In politics today, there are more millionaires in Congress than in previous decades. And members of Congress with white-collar professional backgrounds are significantly more likely to embrace conservative, pro-business positions than the dwindling number of Congress men and women coming from blue-collar backgrounds.[31] In sum, the growth of economic inequality and its impact on empowering wealthy donors in elections means that Congress is increasingly the province of corporate and upper-class interests.

2. Declining Labor Unions

In the 1960s, a third of Americans were in labor unions.[32] Unions were historically a leftist force in politics. Union members are more liberal than non-union members and historically vote Democratic.[33] When unions were strong in America, they played a vital role in galvanizing union members and their families to vote for Democratic candidates, and to pressure Democratic candidates to support liberal, pro-working-class policies. Recent scholarship argues the decline of unions contributed significantly to growing inequality, and that union decline meant the decline of liberal government policies more broadly. The decline of unions meant a decline in voting pressure among working-class Americans, and less pressure on the Democrats to be a progressive party.[34] By 2016, only 10.7 percent of Americans were in a union.[35]

Organized labor's decline meant the deterioration of a major liberal voting bloc in elections. The Democratic Party's loss of its solidly liberal labor constituency, particularly their support from white working-class Americans, occurred in the 1990s onward.[36] Working-class whites became increasingly disenchanted with the Democratic Party under Clinton, as the president embraced "free trade" legislation under NAFTA that punished working-class Americans by allowing the outsourcing of manufacturing jobs. Support for NAFTA signaled a shift in policy away from supporting workers, and in favor of corporate interests.

3. The Growth of Immigration

Immigration policy has changed significantly in the last half-century, and it appears to be indirectly contributing to the rightward shift of the political parties.

Immigration increased after 1965 with the passage of the Immigration and Naturalization Act, which maintained previous per-country limits on immigration, but instated new visa categories for skilled immigrants and for those qualifying for entrance because they had family in the United States. These reforms contributed to a steady growth in immigration in subsequent decades.[37]

According to the Congressional Budget Office, the percent of foreign-born individuals living in the U.S. was about 5 percent of the total population in the early 1970s. Foreign-born individuals increased to 8 percent by the early 1990s, to more than 10 percent by the early 2000s, and to more than 12 percent by the early 2010s.[38] The growth in immigrants significantly impacted politics. Many immigrants do not have citizenship—hence they cannot vote. The process through which immigrants gain citizenship and the right to vote is arduous, requiring at least five years of residency, federal fingerprinting, a formal application process, a formal interview process, passing civics and English literacy tests, providing various documents to confirm one's identity, and fulfilling an oath of allegiance. Many immigrants never complete these steps, especially if they are not eligible to remain in the country for more than five years.

The growth of immigration appears to be relevant to the rise of business and upper-class power in politics. Large numbers of immigrants are unable to participate in the electoral process. As the number of non-citizens increases, an ever-larger number of immigrants, who are historically on the poorer side of the income distribution, are unable to influence the political process by voting. This development matters since poorer people are more likely to be liberal in their political ideology. If immigrants are unable to vote, then an entire group of Americans, who could potentially serve as a leftist force in politics, are unable to pressure the parties to take liberal positions on economic issues. According to the Center for American Progress, the number of authorized and unauthorized non-citizens in the U.S. reached 26.5 million in 2012, or 8.4 percent of the population.[39] The weak political position of immigrants means reduced pressure on the political system to represent liberal interests. This trend indirectly contributes to upper-class dominance in politics since immigrants' ability to compete with business elites and other affluent organized interests for political power is limited.

4. The Rise of Right-Wing Media

Both conservative and liberal partisan media have become increasingly popular in recent years. Liberals are more likely to watch *MSNBC*, while conservatives are more likely to follow *Fox News* and rightwing talk radio.[40] As partisan media became more popular, they exerted a significant impact on the beliefs of viewers and listeners, stoking conservative anger and encouraging incivility in political discourse. The vast majority of partisan media programs are conservative, and their rise has helped mobilize right-wing Americans, who tend to sympathize heavily with the Republican Party and business and upper-class interests.[41]

Talk radio listeners and cable viewers represent a minority of Americans, but their numbers are politically significant. Rush Limbaugh's weekly listeners number 13 million, and 21 percent of American adults claim they "regularly" watch *Fox News* on cable.[42] Many partisan media consumers show a passion for politics and regularly vote in general elections, primaries, and midterm elections. Furthermore, numerous studies suggest conservative media consumption increases voter turnout for the Republican Party, so partisan media appear to have a significant impact on elections.[43] The growing prominence of these outlets means political discourse is pulled to the right, empowering conservatives in the Republican Party, while further solidifying the party's pro-business and upper-class political bias.

The Fallout from Neoliberalism: Declining Public Support for Government

The right-ward, neoliberal drift of the major American parties has been accompanied by mounting public anger at the parties specifically, and the political system more generally. It is difficult to identify an exact year in the modern era in which Americans began to view government as serving the wealthy over the many. But it seems clear that such distrust began to grow significantly by the early-1970s. It is unlikely an accident that the era of neoliberalism began in the 1970s, at precisely the time the American public began to feel the political system was increasingly biased in favor of the wealthy and upper-class interests.[44] These feelings were not apparent in the previous decades, when the Johnson administration and Congressional Democrats prioritized inequality and poverty reduction in its "war on poverty"—which included the introduction of various social welfare programs to help the poor and needy, such as Medicare, Medicaid, and food stamps. In the 1960s, a majority of Americans agreed that "government is run for the benefit of all the people," rather than "by a few big interests looking out for themselves."[45] A majority—73 percent—supported Johnson and the Democratic Party's war on poverty initiatives, and most believed the program was driven by a sincere interest "in helping the poor," rather than a product of administration efforts to "gain political advantages."[46] Confidence in the government was high when it came to implementing the anti-poverty mandate, with 60 percent of Americans agreeing that Johnson was doing an "excellent" or "good" job of implementing the initiative.[47] Inequality and poverty fell significantly in the 1960s as a result of the war on poverty, and only a minority of Americans—45 percent—agreed in 1966 with the statement that "the rich get richer" and "the poor get poorer" in America.[48]

But the neoliberal era was already beginning to emerge by the early-to-mid 1970s. President Richard Nixon, while far less conservative in his policies than modern Republicans, led the charge against the 1960s "Great Society" initiatives, arguing under a "New Federalism" framework that the federal government should step back from actively providing welfare programs for the needy and poor. He led a racial backlash against the Civil Rights Movement, pursuing a "southern strategy" of cultivating votes from disaffected southern whites who were angry about the Civil Rights Movement's successes in the previous decade. Nixon's rhetoric about the need for "law and order" and to fight a "War on Drugs" was a thinly veiled effort to demonize and criminalize people of color, as was later conceded by Nixon's domestic chief John Ehrlichman.[49] Although the war on poverty initiatives of the 1960s resulted in the halving of poverty in the U.S., by the 1970s political leaders had begun to speak of government overreach and the need of the federal government to pull back from aiding the poor.

Unsurprisingly, public support for the federal government on economic issues began to fall under the Nixon and Ford administrations. A large majority of Americans—74 percent—in 1973 agreed that "tax laws are written to help the rich, not the average man."[50] In 1975, 61 percent of Americans agreed that government was "doing too little in providing assistance to those families whose incomes are below the poverty line."[51] A plurality of Americans that same year felt that "rich people" had a "bad influence on politics and government."[52] While 64 percent of Americans believed government was "run for the benefit of all the people" in 1964, that number had fallen to 38 percent by 1972, and 25 percent by 1974.[53] Similarly, while only 36 percent of Americans agreed in 1964 that "public officials" did not "care much what people like me think," that number grew to 51 percent by 1976.[54] While only 45 percent of Americans believed "the rich get richer and the poor get poorer" in 1964, the number had climbed the 76 percent by 1973.[55] The mass public still believed in the anti-poverty agenda, even if the Republican Party had embarked on a neoliberal program designed to undermine it. Seventy-two percent of Americans said it was important that "government in Washington ought to reduce the income differences between the rich and poor, perhaps by raising the taxes of wealthy families or by giving income assistance to the poor."[56] The rise of neoliberalism in American politics in the 1970s overlaps with the rapid decline in public attachment to the two political parties. It is unfair, however, to blame public dealignment from the parties exclusively on the rise of the neoliberal paradigm. Government deception, as seen in the Johnson administration's lies about the Vietnam War (revealed via *The New York Times*' reporting of "The Pentagon Papers"), and in the Nixon administration's criminal surveillance of the Democratic Party via the "Watergate" scandal, obviously were important historical moments that shook public faith in the parties and in government. Still, the political parties' movement away from prioritizing poverty-reduction and aiding the needy also played an important role in shaking public trust in government.

Changing Partisanship in America

Scholars sometimes speak of the decline of partisanship, and it is clear that American partisanship declined significantly from the 1970s onward.[57] According to the National Election Study, more than half of Americans identified as Democrats between the early 1950s and mid-1960s. Less than a third of Americans were Republicans. In total, about 80 percent of Americans were members of one of the two major parties. Just 20 to 25 percent identified as independent during the 1950s and 1960s. But the number of Democrats fell from nearly 60 percent of Americans in the late 1960s to about 40 percent throughout the 1970s. Similarly, while just under a third of Americans were Republicans in the early 1960s, that number fell to under a quarter by the mid-1970s.[58] And alienation from the parties continued from that point forward. The number of individuals describing themselves as "independent" of the parties doubled from the late-1950s to the late-2000s, growing from 20 percent to 40 percent of Americans. By 2014, 42 percent of Americans identified as independents according to Gallup polls.[59] In contrast, the number of Democrats fell from half of Americans to about a third from the 1950s through the 2000s. By 2016, just 30 percent called themselves Democrats.[60] The percent of Republicans fell from a third of Americans in the 1950s to just over 20 percent in the 1970s, but increased to about a third by the 2000s. In 2016, just 27 percent of Americans identified as Republican.[61]

Although 57 percent of Americans considered themselves Republicans or Democrats in 2016, the rise of independents suggests the public is less partisan today compared to previous decades.[62] There are various reasons for why many Americans do not associate with parties. One significant reason is the feeling that the parties fail to represent the mass public, and are biased in favor of corporate and upper-class elites. Recent polling data demonstrates this point. The Republican Party receives particularly poor marks on its economic policies. Nearly two-thirds of Americans felt in 2016 that the party "is too willing to cut government programs, even when they work," while 54 percent felt the Republican Party does not care about "middle-income" individuals. A plurality of Americans agree the Republican Party does "too much to address the concerns and priorities of higher-income people," while a majority feel the party does "too little" to represent the "priorities of lower-income people."

Public distrust does not apply only to the Republican Party, but to Democrats as well. The party, although it has at times passed laws that aided the masses and poor in recent decades, has played an active part in the rise of a neoliberal system that favors upper-class and corporate interests. And much of the public appears to recognize the Democratic Party's failure in aiding middle- and lower-class citizens. A plurality of Americans felt in 2016 that the Democrats do "too much" to "address the concerns and priorities of higher-income people." In contrast, 58 percent believed the Democrats did "too little" to aid "middle-income" Americans, while 62 percent felt the same with regard to "lower-income" Americans. These results suggest a profound distrust of both political parties, and an alienation from a neoliberal political system that is biased in favor of the upper class.

Millennials and Political Parties

Millennials (born between 1981 and 2000) are more alienated from the political parties than older generations. Many young Americans feel the party system does not represent their interests. In 2014, 50 percent of Millennials (ages 18 to 33) claimed to be political independents, compared to 39 percent of Generation X (34 to 49), 37 percent of Baby Boomers (50 to 68), and 32 percent of the Silent Generation (69 to 86). Just 31 percent of Millennials agree that there is a "great deal of" difference between the parties, compared to 43 percent of Generation X, 49 percent of Baby Boomers, and 58 percent of the Silent Generation.[63] Millennials are also less attentive to elections, politics, and the news. In 2011, just 13 percent of Millennials had "given a lot of thought to candidates" running in the 2012 elections, compared to 27 percent of Generation X, 36 percent of Baby Boomers, and 42 percent of the Silent Generation. Similarly, just 17 percent of Millennials were "following election news very closely," compared to 22 percent of Generation X, 28 percent of Baby Boomers, and 36 percent of the Silent Generation.[64]

Millennials' lack of attachment to the major parties appears to be driven by their strongly progressive views, which run contrary to Democratic and Republican policies favoring business interests. Millennials' overwhelming support for Democratic "socialist" Bernie Sanders over the neoliberal Hillary Clinton demonstrated that younger Americans were not in line, ideologically, with the business-oriented wing of the Democratic Party. And many Millennials who were affiliated with the Republican Party—about a quarter in total—fled the party between 2015 and 2017, largely in opposition to Trump's reactionary political agenda.[65] But neither party receives much support from Millennials, with only 43 percent of this age group holding a favorable view of Democrats, and almost half disagreeing that the party cares about young Americans. Distrust is even greater for the Republican Party, with just 26 percent of Millennials having a favorable view of the party, and only 3 in 10 believing it cares about young people.[66]

Is Millennials' distrust of the neoliberal party system based on rational, thoughtful opposition? One could claim that Millennials are simply out of touch with the political process, as complaints about the willful ignorance and apathy of the young are commonplace. *Pew* found just 41 percent of those aged 18–24 voted in 2012, compared to 72 percent of those 65 and older. Compared to those 18–24, more than half of 25–44-year-olds voted in 2012, while nearly 60 percent of those 45–64 voted.[67] In 2014, only 20 percent of Millennials voted in the midterm elections.[68] Less than half of Americans 18–29 voted in 2016, compared to more than half of those aged 30–44, about two-thirds of those aged 45–64, and nearly three-quarters of those aged 65 and older.[69] Millennials are also different from previous youth generations with regard to voting. Census Bureau data finds that 51 percent of 18–24-year-olds voted in the 1964 presidential election, compared to just 38 percent within this age group in 2012.[70]

Millennials are also less attentive to politics and the news. While 80 percent of those aged 18–29 followed politics in a newspaper in 1960, it was just a third by 2008.[71] In 2010, *Pew* found that 18–29-year-olds spent just 45 minutes a day on the news, compared to 81 minutes for those 50–64 years old. Not only were the young paying less attention than older Americans, they also paid less attention than young Americans did decades ago.[72] From 1994 through 2010, the number of minutes 18–29-year-olds spent on the news per day fell by 20 percentage points. By comparison, attention fell among those 40–49 years old by just one percent, and by two percent for those 50–64 years old.[73]

There are at least two possibilities for explaining why young Americans are less attached to parties. One is that parties do not adequately represent the young, since they are preoccupied with representing the wealthy and upper-class interests. Programs like Social Security and Medicare benefit the elderly, consuming 40 percent of the federal budget.[74] Corporate interests benefit from tens of billions in federal welfare subsidies per year, and higher-income Americans have benefitted from trillions in tax cut benefits in the last two decades.[75] But there is no comparable set of programs benefitting the young. Millennials are disproportionately more likely to earn low incomes, often toiling away at the minimum wage. They are asked to borrow tens of thousands of dollars, on average, to attend college for a chance at well-paying jobs that were far more common decades ago, and which people were often able to secure simply with high school degrees. Under these conditions, the political and economic systems in America are increasingly failing to serve the young as they did in previous generations.

If the political system did a better job of representing young Americans, participation in voting would probably be higher. This was the message sent during the "Sanders revolution" of 2016. Young Americans were more than twice as likely to vote for Sanders in the 2016 primaries, than for Trump or Clinton.[76]

The preference for Sanders is no accident. He was calling for a $15 an hour minimum wage, free college tuition, and universal health care, all of which would disproportionately benefit young Americans, and which would have required a redistribution of societal resources from upper-class individuals to less fortunate, younger Americans. And economically insecure young Americans—those expressing concerns about the high costs of education and health care—were significantly more likely to support Sanders than other groups of Americans.[77] The Sanders phenomenon suggests millennials may be refraining from voting, not because they are ignorant, lazy, or stupid, but because the political system as constructed does not represent their interests like it does those of wealthier citizens.

On the other hand, one can take Millennials to task for their lack of vigilance in electoral politics. If Millennials turned out in greater numbers to vote, candidates like Bernie Sanders, who challenge upper-class and corporate dominance of politics, would have a better chance of winning political offices. If young Americans do not follow politics or vote as often as older Americans, what pressure is placed on the political system to introduce or strengthen benefits for Millennials? Millennials may have it backwards: many believe that, because the system represents the wealthy over the young, they should not bother to pay attention to politics or vote. But perhaps the opposite is true: *because* so many young Americans do not pay attention or vote, the political system is not pressured to represent them.

Whatever one concludes about Millennials, there is no question that young Americans are increasingly alienated from a political system they feel benefits wealthy Americans at the expense of the mass public. Some evidence suggests young Americans are *more* active than ever in engaging in protests, boycotts, and volunteer work. Many would celebrate these forms of participation, but one could also ask: of what use is protest if it is not accompanied by concrete demands for political change via electoral participation? This problem emerged with Occupy Wall Street. Young Americans who participated in these protests were angry about growing inequality, but as part of a generation that is alienated from politics, it was difficult for these activists to agree on and pursue concrete proposals for change that challenge upper-class power in politics. In the end, Occupy Wall Street failed to coalesce around any specific political agenda, and dissipated soon after it formed.

Party Failure and the 2016 Presidential Election

It became increasingly difficult to deny the growing dysfunction of the party system during the 2016 election. Most Americans were clearly unhappy with the choices available to them. The top reason provided by Americans for why they planned to vote for Trump, and the second most common reason provided by those preferring Clinton, was that they held a "negative assessment" of the opposing candidate.[78] In other words, voter turnout was motivated by the feeling that the main leaders of the parties failed in representing the interests of the masses of working class, middle class, or poor Americans. Large numbers of Americans voted for the person they thought was the lesser of two evils.

On the Democratic side, the front running candidate hailed from the dominant wing of the Democratic Party, which has long celebrated harmful "free trade" agreements associated with hollowing out the American middle-class workers via outsourcing of manufacturing jobs to other countries. Hilary Clinton's support for the Trans Pacific Partnership mirrored Bill Clinton's support for NAFTA more than two decades earlier. Reflecting on the exit polls, it was clear Clinton lost many votes from traditionally less affluent demographic groups. Crucially, 41 percent of women, 28 percent of Hispanics, 51 percent of those with a high school diploma, 42 percent of union members, and 40 percent of those making under $30,000 a year voted for Trump.[79]

It was *not* the case that Trump won working-class, blue-collar voters, so much as that Clinton and the Democrats lost them. Among those earning less than $50,000 a year, the decline in voting for a Democratic presidential candidate from 2012 to 2016 was 3.5 times greater than the rise in voting for a Republican candidate.[80] The Democratic Party is supposed to represent disadvantaged social groups, but Clinton's poor performance with the less affluent exposed the party's failure to adequately assist the working class, the less fortunate, and the working poor.

Despite the Democratic Party's failings, one should not lionize Trump or Republicans for being heroes of the common man or woman. The party's descent into conspiracy theory propaganda under Trump suggested a fundamental failure of Republican leadership. Trump's open dismissal of global warming as a secret plan hatched by China to hurt the U.S. economy played into the hands of corporate fossil-fuel interests set on derailing efforts to tackle climate change.[81] And Trump's fixation on demonizing minorities, on conspiracy theories about how "illegal" voters "stole" the popular vote from him, and his shameless efforts to fabricate terror attacks that never occurred in Bowling Green, Tennessee, and Sweden, all directed critical attention away from the issue of rising corporate and upper-class power in American politics.[82]

The claim that Republicans—and particularly Trump—were supported by masses of working-class Americans who were tired with the Democratic Party's elitism is exaggerated. The Republicans offered no progressive policy platform that would raise the incomes or living standards of working-poor or working-class voters. And the claim that blue-collar Americans flocked to Trump due to his anti-free trade rhetoric was false, as was the claim that working-class Americans suffering from various forms of economic anxiety were more likely to vote for Trump. Numerous studies demonstrated that most Trump voters were middle, middle-upper, and upper-class in terms of their incomes. They were not more likely to have lost a job due to "free trade" and outsourcing of factory jobs. They were not particularly concerned with issues such as inequality between the upper-class and the lower-class poor, nor were they more likely to support progressive policies such as raising the minimum wage, or to express concerns that there were not enough "good paying jobs" in the U.S.[83]

Much of Trump's support base was derived from white, older males with middle-to-upper-class backgrounds.[84] Support for Trump among this group was heavily driven by their embrace of his reactionary social positions, which attacked Muslims, stoked fear over "Islamic terrorism," lamented that white males were victims of modern feminism, and which demonized Mexican immigrants, calling for a border wall between the U.S. and its southern neighbor.[85] While much of the reporting surrounding the 2016 election framed Trump as representing the interests of frustrated working Americans, the reality was the opposite.[86] Trump, the Republican Party, and far-right media pundits played on the preexisting prejudices of Republican voters, demonizing minorities and people of color in an effort to strengthen white, male, upper-class dominance of American politics via a political agenda pushing government deregulation of business, elimination of social welfare programs such as Obamacare, and greater tax cuts for businesses and the upper-class. Despite record inequality in America and growing economic insecurity among most citizens, Trump and the Republican Party succeeded in mobilizing tens of millions of voters, largely in pursuit of his reactionary social agenda, while offering little by way of concrete proposals for improving the living standards of the lower- and middle-classes.

What about Third Parties?

Third parties have long existed in American politics. Examples include the Constitution Party—a far-right conservative party, the Green Party—a leftist party, the Libertarian Party—another far-right conservative party, and the Reform Party—founded by Ross Perot, and based on a mix of various ideologies. These parties, however, receive virtually no support from the voting public. The Green Party in particular has historically offered a progressive political platform that seeks to limit corporate power in politics and society, expand social welfare spending for the middle- and lower-classes, and prioritize environmentalist polices that would regulate the fossil fuel industry in the name of combating pollution and climate change. But the Greens have made few inroads electorally with the American public. Why have the Greens and other third parties failed to gain mass support in an era of mass distrust of government?

On the surface, it would appear that the stars are aligned for a serious third-party challenge to the Democrats and Republicans. Consider the following:

- Only 19 percent of Americans expressed trust in government in October 2015, while 74 percent said public officials put their needs ahead of the public, and 55 percent said ordinary Americans could "do a better job solving problems" than political officials.[87]

- In 2015, 60 percent of Americans supported a "major" third party in politics, and in 2016, 47 percent of registered voters said they would consider voting for a third-party candidate—up from 38 percent in 2008.[88]

- Voter turnout is low compared to previous decades, and compared to other countries. The U.S. has one of the lowest turnouts in the world. Furthermore, voter turnout was 8 percentage points lower in 2012—at 55 percent of the voting-age public, compared to 63 percent turnout in 1960.[89]

- There has been significant growth in the number of independents in American politics. They are the single largest political group today, more numerous than Republicans or Democrats. Furthermore, 71 percent of independents support having a major third party, compared to 52 percent of Republicans and 49 percent of Democrats.[90]

- Historically, third parties have played an important role, not in replacing major parties, but in gathering votes from those disillusioned with those parties. The Free Soil Party, which ran on an abolition platform, captured 10 percent of the presidential vote in 1848.[91] The Progressive Party, which supported expanding rights for women and promoting labor unions, captured 28 percent of the presidential vote in 1912.[92] These parties placed pressure on the two major parties to adopt, or "co-opt" the increasingly popular proposals of third parties. While these parties died, their legacies endured, suggesting that third-party voting can be meaningful in promoting political change.

- Most Americans believe the two-party dominated system serves the wealthy, rather than the middle- and lower-classes. In 2016, almost two-thirds of Americans said the federal government did not do enough to aid the middle-class, and nearly 60 percent felt the same about federal aid for the poor. Only 28 percent of Americans agreed the Republican Party favored the middle- or lower-class over the upper-class and wealthy.[93]

Despite all these developments, voting for third party candidates was very low in the 2000s and 2010s. Countless independent and third-party candidates run in congressional and presidential elections, and almost none won. In the 114th Congress (2016–2017), there were no independents in the House of Representatives, and just two in the Senate—Bernie Sanders and Angus King. While voting for third-party presidential candidates reached a high in modern history in 1992, with 19 percent of Americans voting for Ross Perot of the Reform Party, the numbers have declined since. Just 8 percent of Americans voted for a third-party candidate in 1996, and less than five percent voted for third party candidates in the 2000, 2004, 2008, 2012, and 2016 presidential elections.[94]

If third parties fail to break into American politics, it is because the system creates numerous barriers to their entry. These barriers, documented in previous

Jill Stein, Green Party
Presidential Candidate

Gary Johnson, Libertarian Party
Presidential Candidate

Image 9.1. 2016 Third Party Candidates.

scholarship, are described below.[95] All of these factors relate to a broader pattern, in which the political system, while serving the interests of the wealthy, deters third-party challenges, especially from the Green Party and the left, that seek progressive political reform.

1. A Cultural Stigma and Third Parties

Corporate media have long been aligned with the neoliberal system, elevating both Republican and Democratic worldviews above those outside the bipartisan status quo. The common "understanding" in mass discourse via the corporate media is that voting for a third-party candidate is a waste of time. Many Americans worry voting for a third-party candidate is "throwing their vote away," since these candidates have "no chance" of winning, and merely "spoil" elections for serious candidates. After the 2000 election, Green Party presidential candidate Ralph Nader was commonly referred to as a "spoiler" who took votes from Al Gore, helping George W. Bush win. Third-party candidates get little attention in the news, and are not seen as serious candidates by reporters and pundits. One study found that "major" presidential candidates from the Democratic and Republican parties received about ten times the news coverage of third-party candidates.[96] Third-party presidential candidates received no feature coverage in major newspapers in the 2016 election cycle.[97]

2. Major Parties' Fundraising Advantage

Most money raised and spent in elections is from wealthy, upper-class Americans and organized interests. And these elite interests prefer Democratic and Republican candidates, who hold a massive fundraising advantage over third-party candidates—especially over progressives running with the Green Party. According to the Center for Responsive Politics, spending is highly correlated with electoral outcomes. Candidates who spend more usually win their respective races. In 2008, for example, the candidate who raised more money won in 93 percent of House races and 94 percent of Senate races.[98] Estimates from other recent elections bare similar outcomes.[99]

Candidates who raise more money are able to buy greater exposure by running more political ads. Candidates with little money struggle to reach the public. For example, in 2008, Barack Obama and John McCain collectively raised $1.6 billion in campaign revenues. In contrast, third-party candidates Cynthia McKinney (Green Party), Ralph Nader (Independent), and Bob Barr (Libertarian Party) collectively raised just $5.3 million. Third partiers were not able to compete on a level playing field with Obama and McCain, and this was no accident. Wealthy patrons to Democratic and Republican campaigns starved third-parties of funds, ensuring that these dissidents were blacklisted from the media, thereby limiting their impact on election outcomes.

3. RIGGING THE PRESIDENTIAL DEBATES

The Commission on Presidential Debates (CPD)—which is responsible for coordinating presidential election debates—operates as an informal arm of the major parties.[100] The CPD operatives are members of the major parties, and explicitly state that their goal is to promote the two-party duopoly.[101] The CPD mandates that third-party candidates cannot participate in debates if they are not polling at 15 percent public support before the debates.[102] This creates a Catch-22 for third parties; they cannot get in the debates if they are not supported by 15 percent of voters, but they cannot get 15 percent of the vote without public exposure and participation in the debates. By limiting third-party access to debates, the CPD ensures that Democrats and Republicans do not face public pressures from more progressive candidates seeking to address problems such as growing corporate power and upper-class dominance of politics.

4. STATE BALLOT ACCESS LAWS

Third-party candidates struggle to gain ballot access, despite major party candidates being granted automatic access.[103] Third-party candidates must receive a certain number of signatures to gain ballot access. As *USA Today* reported during the 2012 elections, "there are probably fewer than half a dozen minor parties that will qualify for the presidential ballot in more than five states." In 17 states, third parties must collect at least 10,000 signatures or more to gain access. Some states like California and Florida are particularly extreme, requiring more than 100,000 signatures. If a candidate cannot get on the ballot, it is nearly impossible to win political office. Voters can write-in a candidate, but these efforts are almost never successful. There is nothing in state ballot access laws that explicitly favors the wealthy or corporate interests. But by creating additional electoral impediments to progressive third-party candidates such as the Greens from running for office, these laws indirectly aid wealthy and upper-class business interests set on continuing the two-party stranglehold on politics.

5. WINNER-TAKE-ALL ELECTIONS

The winner-take-all electoral system hinders third-party candidates. In this system, congressional candidates with the most votes win single political seats in the

House and Senate. These single races are geographically based, with two Senators in each state, and Representative seats contingent upon how many people live in each state. Only one person is able to represent each House district. In contrast, a proportional representation (PR) system allows third parties to build on small victories from one election cycle to the next. Individuals do not vote for single members to represent individual districts. Under PR, voters select between various political parties. Those parties populate lists of candidates, and these lists are used to fill open seats in the legislature. The proportion of legislative seats a party wins is contingent upon the proportion of all national votes it receives. Examples of PR legislative systems include: Australia, Argentina, Belgium, Brazil, Denmark, Finland, Iceland, Israel, Indonesia, the Netherlands, South Africa, and Turkey, among other countries.

PR systems allow for third parties to win small amounts of representation in the legislature, and build on those wins over time. If a party receives five percent of all votes, it receives five percent of all seats in the legislature. The party may receive more votes, and more seats, in the next election. Available evidence suggests that PR systems better represent the average voter compared to winner-take-all systems.[104] In a PR system, each party receiving votes earns seats in the legislature, and different groups of citizens are represented by government, whereas in a winner-take-all system, those voting for third parties receive no representation. Simply put, PR systems are more favorable to non-mainstream parties. Green Party pressure on the Democratic Party to be more progressive in its politics would likely be more successful if the electoral system made it easier for Greens to get elected. But without a PR system, it is much harder for progressive third-partiers to challenge upper-class and bipartisan dominance in elections.

Conclusion

This chapter addressed political parties and their failure to empower the masses. In part due to growing corporate and upper-class dominance of the parties, citizens are more independent of Democratic and Republican politics than they used to be. Most Americans are unhappy with the political status quo, and most want a competitive third party. But this will not happen under the current rules of the game, which rig elections in favor of "mainstream" parties that are biased toward upper-class elites. The party system does not adequately represent the needs of citizens. But this system will not change until Americans demand serious electoral reform.

Chapter 10

Elections and Voting

Electoral Capture by Elites

Primary elections are supposed to democratically empower the masses, providing many choices to voters. In the 2016 Democratic primary, Bernie Sanders represented the progressive wing of the party, while Hillary Clinton represented the moderate contingent. In the Republican Party, John Kasich was considered the moderate, Ted Cruz and Ben Carson represented the religious right, and Donald Trump was a maverick candidate, defying party elites on various issues. But these elections do not count for much in terms of democratic empowerment if the masses fail to participate in them, as has long been the case with primaries. Bernie Sanders's call for a "revolution" to fight corporate political power and reduce inequality had little chance of success without a mass primary turnout among progressively-minded Americans.

There would be no mass, electorally-based challenge to neoliberal capitalism in the 2016 general election. Democratic voter turnout, and support for Sanders, while stronger among young Americans, was not enough to defeat Hillary Clinton, the establishment candidate. This should not be surprising, as low voter turnout has long been a problem in primary elections. As figure 10.1 indicates, voter turnout in primaries is weak, even in presidential election years, averaging perhaps one-quarter of eligible voters.[1] Americans are quite apathetic compared to citizens of most countries. They refrain from voting in mass, claiming they do not "have a choice," and that candidates do not represent their interests. Most prefer to skip primaries, ignoring the dramatic differences between primary candidates like Sanders and Clinton. This trend clearly worked against Sanders, who needed mass support from alienated, disadvantaged, and poorer groups of citizens to defeat Clinton. For the disillusioned American, it was easier to claim apathy or complain about not having choices than to exercise choice when it mattered.[2]

Elections are supposed to be a primary means through which citizens exercise control in a democracy. But increasingly, American elections seem to do the opposite, turning off voters from a system they believe is controlled and run by the affluent few. In fairness to the critics, American elections suffer from a democracy

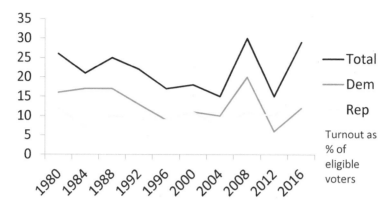

Figure 10.1. Primary Turnout by Election Year, 1980–2016. Source: Drew Desilver, "Turnout was High in the 2016 Primary Season, but Just Short of 2008 Record," *Pew Research Center*, June 10, 2016, http://www.pewresearch.org/fact-tank/2016/06/10/turnout-was-high-in-the-2016-primary-season-but-just-short-of-2008-record/

deficit. Despite a significant attachment of many Americans to political parties, and despite citizens' efforts to cast meaningful ballots in favor of change, the growing superficiality of elections dulls their potential for enabling reform. And the decline of democracy in American elections means that prospects for dramatic changes that reduce corporate and upper-class power in politics are significantly reduced.

Turnout in presidential elections is low. About two-thirds of eligible Americans voted in presidential elections in the 1950s and 1960s, and between 40 to 50 percent voted in midterm elections. The numbers fell to just over half in the presidential election of 1996, and under 40 percent in the 1998 midterms.[3] Turnout has improved some since then, however. In 2012 and 2016, 59 percent and 60 percent of eligible Americans voted in the presidential election, although midterm voting remained low in 2014 at 37 percent.[4] The decision of millions of working-class and blue-collar Americans not to vote in 2016 played a major role in the empowerment of far-right, pro-business forces in the Republican Party.[5] Trump's rise meant the ascendance of political rule by the very wealthiest of the American upper class, with his administration being wealthier than any other administration in modern history, and his economic policies being thoroughly elitist in orientation.[6]

Comparative Voter Turnout

Turnout in the U.S. is low relative to most other countries. In 2016, 45 percent of voting age Americans did not vote.[7] The U.S. ranks thirty-first in voter turnout

out of the thirty-four countries in the Organization for Economic Cooperation and Development (OECD)—a group of largely wealthy countries.[8] According to the Institute for Democracy and Electoral Assistance (IDEA), the United States ranks 138th out of 169 countries in the world in voter turnout—placing it in the bottom fifth.[9] For a country claiming to be the world's leading democracy, this meager turnout is troublesome. How can a country purporting to be the leader of the free world have so many citizens who do not take seriously a central democratic obligation? I argue below that low voting in the U.S. is caused by many factors, although all these factors relate to the broader problem of government failure to represent and empower the masses. Political leaders seem fine with low voter turnout, considering that the masses of un-mobilized Americans are more likely to be poorer or lower class in their background. If mobilized, they would likely vote for progressive-left candidates set on attacking corporate and upper-class power in politics.

There are many reasons why Americans do not vote. I explore those reasons below.

1. NON-COMPETITIVE ELECTIONS AND THE ROLE OF CORPORATE MONEY

Democratic government is premised upon competitive elections. The vast majority of Congressional races, however, are not competitive, with one candidate defeating the other by more than 10 percentage points.[10] For example, 93 percent of House races and 94 percent of Senate races in 2008 were non-competitive.[11] Congressional races remained highly non-competitive in the 2012 and 2014 elections as well.[12] And voter turnout is lower in states defined by non-competitive races between Republican and Democratic candidates.[13]

Lack of competitiveness is likely related to campaign spending, since spending and electoral outcomes are linked.[14] Greater campaign spending is associated with victory in an overwhelming majority of electoral races. Non-competitive elections are driven by large imbalances in media exposure. As one 2016 study found, candidates benefitting from greater amounts of advertising were better able to alter the composition of the electorate, encouraging more of their own partisans to vote. "Political advertising" may not "have a lasting impact on preferences or beliefs," but it does increase a candidate's vote share "by bringing the 'right' set of voters to the polls."[15] Other research finds that campaign donations matter greatly in primary elections, with candidates raising more money being far more effective at winning their respective races than those with fewer financial resources.[16] Furthermore, with campaign spending on ads dominated by the major parties and their corporate and other wealthy donors, third-parties struggle to gain public attention. An electoral system in which money rules is also a system in which upper-class interests rule, since they donate most of the money to political campaigns and are responsible for most issue-ad spending.[17]

2. Mass Apathy, Weak Partisanship, and Government Distrust

One of the most common reasons for non-voting is disinterest in politics.[18] Large numbers of Americans pay little attention to politics and elections. Less than half followed election news "very closely" in September 2012, and the number had reached just 48 percent by mid-October, and 52 percent in the week before the November election.[19] In the 2014 midterms, just 15 percent of Americans said they were following the elections "very closely."[20] A large number of Americans identify as "independent" of the political parties. These independents are unique, politically speaking, because they are less likely to pay attention to the news and less likely to vote. With the rise of independents, American attention to politics and the news has fallen significantly.[21] And previous research suggests that declining partisanship is statistically associated with declining voter turnout.[22]

Apathy in the post-Second World War era appears to be linked to structural factors, such as the rise of television. Putnam finds increased television consumption is associated with declining political participation.[23] Profit concerns in corporate media—manifested in the rise of an increasingly fragmented, entertainment-oriented media landscape—has discouraged political participation and attentiveness.[24] With citizens increasingly preoccupied with fashionable consumption and entertainment, both of which increase the profits of the corporate class, millions of Americans are less interested in paying attention to politics.

One of the most prominent reasons people cite for not voting is "lack of confidence in government."[25] Government distrust became a serious concern in the post-Vietnam, post-Watergate era. From the early-1970s through the mid-2010s—with the exception of a few years after September 11, 2001—only a minority of Americans expressed trust in government.[26] Non-voting is most pronounced among independents—those who express the greatest distrust of government and a majority of which believe that the major parties "care more about special interests than [about] average Americans."[27] *Gallup* survey data from the 2000s and 2010s suggested trust in the federal government increased or decreased among Democrats and Republicans depending on whether their party was in control of government. But independents consistently ranked low in terms of government trust in most surveys.[28] These findings suggest that Americans are increasingly claiming independence from the parties and from voting, which is no surprise when considering that most Americans believe government is dominated by the wealthy and the corporate class.

3. Roadblocks to Voting and Government
Failure to Mobilize Voters

Historically, political parties have done a poor job mobilizing voters. At times they actively try to deter voting. Ex-felon laws prohibit millions of Americans from voting, despite these individuals having supposedly paid their debt to society. Ex-felon laws are highly punitive, designed to create a permanent outcaste status for a select group of Americans, disenfranchising them from their democratic obligation of voting. By the mid-2010s, nine states had ex-felon laws.[29] Two percent of all Americans cite being barred by states from voting due to ex-felon laws, translating into more than 3 million Americans.[30]

Immigration law has also played a role historically in limiting the vote. Following the 1965 Immigration and Nationality Act, immigration quotas were removed in favor of admittance rules based on whether an immigrant has family in the U.S. or a marketable skillset from which the U.S. could benefit. Most Americans think immigration has historically been a positive force.[31] It ensures population growth and is essential to promoting multiculturalism and diversity, in addition to the U.S. benefitting from the importation of various skilled and unskilled laborers. But easing immigration quotas also had a negative effect on democracy. The number of foreign-born persons who are voting-age, but not voting-eligible, changed significantly with the rapid growth in the number of legal permanent residents, which more than tripled between 1965 and 2014.[32] Growing immigration means a growing number of people in the U.S. who are not able to vote. In total, the Census Bureau estimates that there were more than 17 million foreign-born non-citizens aged 18 and older and legally in the U.S. in 2010. This is a large population of non-voters.[33]

The Department of Immigration and Naturalization Services' rules for granting citizenship are often cumbersome, taking many years for immigrants to complete the process, assuming they are even able to apply for citizenship before their visa expires. As a result, millions of immigrants live in this country, follow the laws, pay taxes, and contribute to the health of the economy, but have little ability to influence the political process. An expedited process for granting citizenship to immigrants, however, could help increase voter turnout.

Voter identification laws are another government-imposed impediment to voting. These laws were created amidst claims that voter fraud represents a serious electoral concern.[34] But contrary to President Trump and other Republicans' rhetoric, voter fraud is virtually nonexistent in the U.S., and is scarcely documented in election years.[35] Furthermore, Republican officials in states implementing voter ID laws admit the primary goal of these laws is to disenfranchise Democratic voters, since many poor Americans living in urban areas use public transportation or do not own a car, so they do not possess driver's licenses.[36] Poorer Americans are more likely to be transient, moving from one residence to another, so they are more likely to lose the materials necessary to secure an identification card or driver's license. The practical effect of these laws is to limit the voting power of less affluent, Democratic citizens. Millions of Americans are prohibited from voting due to registration problems in modern elections.[37]

The unifying thread with all these roadblocks to voting is socioeconomic class. Ex-felons, immigrants, and urban residents without licenses, are all more likely to come from working and lower-class backgrounds. Political officials actively seek to disempower these disadvantaged and marginalized groups. This strategy is highly effective in deterring poorer Americans—who are more likely to be progressive in their politics—from challenging the upper-class bias in politics. If one includes those disenfranchised by ex-felon laws, voter ID laws, and those living in America, but barred from voting due to immigration policy, approximately 22 to 23 million voting-age individuals are prohibited from voting, translating into about 10 percent of the adult population. These are far from marginal numbers.

Some forces deter voter turnout, even if political officials do not go out of their way to discourage voting. For example, the U.S. does not allow for weekend elections. Many Americans who work during the week find it difficult to juggle long work hours, multiple jobs, and family responsibilities, in addition to voting. And the busyness of American life is a serious voting deterrent. Of all the reasons cited for why Americans do not vote, being "too busy" is the most common.[38]

Citizens are also not required to vote as a civic duty, as some countries require. Australia and Chile historically required voting, and as a result, saw much higher voter turnout. Australia's voter turnout in its 2013 election was 93 percent, while Chile's 2009 turnout was 88 percent.[39] Chile eliminated required voting in 2009, and saw a precipitous decline in turnout, suggesting that compulsory voting had a significant impact on political participation.[40] Australia fines its citizens the equivalent of U.S. $20 for not voting.[41] Other countries automatically register citizens to vote, like Germany, which saw a 72 percent voter turnout in 2013.[42] The types of policies discussed above, if introduced in the U.S., would likely produce higher voter turnout, especially among poorer and lower-class voters, who are historically less likely to vote.[43]

One last phenomenon that deters voting is the growing prevalence of negative ads.[44] Most political election ads are negative in one way or another.[45] Americans watch endless ads on television during election season, and these ads appear to depress voter turnout. For example, one study finds that negative ads that avoid "mudslinging" against a candidate are associated with declining likelihood of voting.[46] Another study finds negative ads that are deemed "harsh" or "shrill," and focusing on topics directly relevant to public policy also decrease voter turnout.[47] These ads provide reasons to prospective voters to *not* vote for a candidate. Unsurprisingly, many Americans conclude elections are too negative.

4. ORGANIZED LABOR

Nationally, a stronger labor union presence is associated with higher voter turnout, while lower unionization rates are associated with decreased working-class voting.[48] Labor unions exist to represent the needs of working people. Voter turnout among the working-class and the working poor was higher when unions were more prevalent. More than a quarter of Americans were in a union in the mid-1960s, but less than 15 percent were in a union by the mid-2000s. If unionization remained at the mid-1960s level, voting among the poorest third of Americans would have been nearly 4 percentage points higher by the mid-2000s.[49] With the decline of unions, the working poor are less able to pressure the Democratic Party to represent them. De-unionization is also linked to growing inequality, as working Americans without a union find it more difficult to bargain for higher pay and benefits compared to unionized workers.[50] And growing inequality, as I show below, is associated with lower voter turnout.

The decline of unions relates directly to government policy. U.S. corporations have sought to destroy or deter unionization via outsourcing of union manufacturing jobs, and through union-busting threats against those seeking to organize in the workplace.[51] Punishing someone for union organizing is illegal under the National Labor Relations Act, but this practice is common. Government has failed to enforce labor laws against companies seeking to disrupt unionization, and shown little interest in passing laws making it easier to unionize. For example, the Employee Free Choice Act would allow a simple yes-no vote by employees over whether to form a union, although Republicans and Democrats reject this legislation.[52]

5. Growing Inequality

The U.S. has the highest income inequality of all wealthy countries, and the lowest voter turnout.[53] Across countries, and across states in the U.S., as inequality grows, voter participation declines.[54] High inequality is bad for democracy. It leaves less time for citizens to pay attention to politics, contemplate government's relevance to their lives, have discussions with friends and family about the political process, or register to vote. It also reinforces the notion that politics, economics, and society are dominated by the rich, and that there is little that poorer Americans can do to change this. For example, recent research finds that Americans who endure poor and worsening personal finances are more likely to see U.S. society as divided between "haves" and "have-nots," and to agree that "people like me don't have any say" in what government does, that elected officials quickly lose touch with the public, and that elected officials "do not care what I think."[55] In other words, worsening economic circumstances in a time of growing inequality have a toxic, negative effect on one's sense of political efficacy.

There is a well-known affluence divide that influences voting behavior. *Politico* reports that in 2012, 80 percent of those earning more than $150,000 a year voted, compared to just 47 percent of those earning less than $10,000 a year.[56] In that same year, 52 percent of those earning less than $30,000 a year were non-voters, compared to just 14 percent of those making more than $75,000 a year.[57] The affluence divide produces disempowerment among working-class and working-poor Americans. By failing to participate in the political process, poorer people have little power to reward political leaders for taking positions that benefit the masses, or punish those who are out of touch with majority needs. The failure of poorer Americans to vote ensures upper-class voices are exaggerated in the political process.

Why People Vote: Competing Accounts

While 40 percent of voting-eligible Americans did not vote in 2016, 60 percent did. Why did these individuals vote the way they did? Political scientists provide competing explanations for voting. I explore each of these accounts below, before taking a stance on which theory best accounts for voting behavior. Competing theories include: party voting, ideological, issue-based voting, economic voting, and superficial voting. These theories get to the heart of a vital question: just how democratic is American politics?

PARTY VOTING

Since the 1950s, political scientists have argued that parties are central to voting behavior. One classic study, *The American Voter*, offered a "funnel model" for explaining voting outcomes, in which forces such as socialization in adolescence, economic conditions, and parenting were thought to influence one's party attachment. Socialization via parenting has a significant impact on one's partisan affiliation.[58] Economics matters as well. More affluent societal groups are more likely to vote Republican, including higher-income individuals, white-collar, upper-class professionals, men, and whites. In contrast, working-class and poorer Americans are more likely to vote Democratic.[59]

Partisanship influences how people look at candidates, issues, and how they vote. More than 50 years after *The American Voter*, political scientists still believe that parties drive the voting process, with some concluding that most voters hold little interest in issues or ideology, but rather maintain a longstanding emotional tie to a party.[60] As the argument goes, candidates present themselves to voters based on criteria such as alleged competence, leadership, integrity, and charisma, rather than based on policy stances.[61] Party affiliations serve as a "short cut" for helping voters select candidates, without having to worry about policy issues.[62] This model of voting can be seen as compatible with democratic accounts of voting. Citizens choose between parties, which represent various groups in the mass public.

Do parties influence opinion formation and voting, even when Americans claim they are more independent from parties than ever? Available evidence suggests they do. Partisanship is the most consistent predictor of individuals' political attitudes, more reliable than education, sex, race, income, or age.[63] And for the vast majority of those in a political party or leaning toward identifying with a party, partisanship accurately predicts voting outcomes. Between the 1950s and the 2000s, more than 80 percent of self-identified "strong partisans" and "weak partisans" consistently voted for the presidential candidate of the party with which they affiliated.[64] The numbers were similar for independents claiming to lean toward one party or the other. Seventy-five percent of these individuals vote from one election to the next for the presidential candidate of the party they lean toward. In 2012, the numbers were higher, with 88 percent of independent Democratic-leaners voting Obama, and 86 percent of independent Republican-leaners voting Romney.[65] In 2016, 89 percent of Democrats voted Clinton, and 88 percent of Republicans voted Trump.[66]

Parties are so influential that they are able to manipulate the beliefs of supporters in favor of elite business agendas. Most partisans would probably deny this unflattering claim, insisting they think for themselves. But political scientists have documented how parties provide cues that influence the attitudes of party members, and recent case studies leave little doubt that parties mold the minds of their members.[67] For example, Republican Americans' interest in the national debt ebbs and flows, depending on whether Republican political officials are holding political power. During the 2000s, when Congress and the White House were Republican-controlled, party officials made little effort to reduce the national deficit and debt, despite the fact that both were higher than at any other point in decades. The Bush administration did not focus on debt reduction, instead borrowing trillions of dollars to pay for foreign wars and running up deficits to "pay" for tax cuts for the wealthy and the corporate class. Vice President Dick Cheney stated that "no one cares about deficits anymore," with those deficits being used to pursue objectives favored by Republican party elites and by the upper class.[68]

Most Republican Americans were not concerned about the national deficit or debt. *Pew* polling from January 2004 found that just 44 percent of Republicans listed "reducing the budget deficit" as a "top policy priority."[69] By 2014, however, when Republicans no longer controlled the White House and Senate, Republican political leaders regularly warned Americans about the dire consequences of borrowing beyond our means. This message became a main staple of Republican rhetoric.[70] Republican Americans followed the leader, prioritizing the deficit to a level never seen in the Bush years. By January 2014, 80 percent of Republicans listed "reducing the budget deficit" as a "top policy priority," nearly twice as many as a decade earlier.[71] No doubt Republican Americans thought they were sincere in their position. But their preferences were being manipulated by party elites. The national deficit was smaller in 2014 than in 2004, so Republicans should have been at least as concerned about the deficit in 2004 as they were in 2014.[72] This, however, was not the case due to the Republican agenda, which downplayed the deficit in 2004, but amplified its importance in 2014. Deficit manipulation continued into the Trump years. In late-2017, the president and Republicans in Congress pushed a massive tax cut of over a trillion dollars, which would primarily benefit corporations and the upper class, while actually raising taxes for members of the upper-middle class.[73] Without significant cuts in social programs, the bill would significantly expand the deficit. Despite these issues, a majority of Republicans in late-2017 supported Trump's proposal to cut taxes for businesses.[74] There was little uproar from conservative or Republican Americans over Trump's deficit busting, debt-inducing tax cuts for the wealthy.

Manipulation is a bipartisan phenomenon. During the 2000s, Democratic support for free trade fell significantly, from 51 percent of party supporters in 2001—the first year of Bush's presidency, to 36 percent in 2008—the last year of his presidency. And yet, support grew dramatically during the Obama years, by 7 percentage points alone between Bush's last year in office and Obama's first year. Overall, Democratic support for free trade grew to 61 percent by 2015, a massive 30 percentage-point increase since 2008.[75] The reason for the change of heart was likely related to the rhetoric of President Obama, who consistently spoke of the virtues of his Trans-Pacific Partnership (TPP) agreement, and the positive impact it would have on U.S. economic growth and increased exports to other countries.[76] Most Democrats supported free trade and the TPP, despite estimates that the bill would encourage the export of 2 million jobs from the U.S.[77] Democrats' opposition to free trade under Bush, but support for it under Obama, suggests that the party's members were just as susceptible as Republicans to party manipulation in favor of corporate and upper-class interests.

Ideological and Issue-Based Voting

Claims that Americans vote based on their assessments of candidates and issues reside at the heart of the democratic theory of voting. Issue-based voting was first popularized in the 1950s. In *An Economic Theory of Democracy*, political scientist Anthony Downs described a "spatial theory" of voting, arguing that Americans identify with specific points on an ideological spectrum including liberal, conservative, and moderate positions. Most Americans cluster in the moderate part of the spectrum, with Democratic and Republican parties appealing to the "median voter" in the center.[78] According to spatial theory, "citizens make their decisions" on who to vote for "based on their ideological proximity to candidates."[79] Issues matter, as Americans vote for or against candidates after assessing their stances on issues. Citizens' assessments of where candidates stand on issues are said to drive voting behavior, with democracy requiring informed citizens who vote based on policy considerations.

Do most citizens vote by assessing candidates' policy positions? If so, that would represent strong evidence of democratic public empowerment, suggesting that the voting process represents a meaningful way for voters to assert themselves in politics. Numerous studies find that citizens pay attention to, and vote based on the policy positions of candidates. Political scientist V.O. Key argued in *The Responsible Electorate* that interviews with voters suggested they selected between candidates based on the latter's issue stances.[80] Voters recognize major issues that are discussed in the news in each election cycle, while also identifying party positions and differences on these issues.[81] While issues were less important in the 1950s—in the decade when *The American Voter* was published—subsequent research suggested that issues became more central to voter decisions by the 1960s.[82] And in modern times, most Americans are able to accurately recognize numerous policy positions espoused by both parties.[83]

Survey data in the 1990s found citizens' policy preferences still influenced their voting behavior.[84] Later evidence, from the 2012 and 2016 presidential elections, suggested most Americans accurately identified the major issues defining each election cycle, and recognized where Republican and Democratic candidates stood on these issues. The four issues voters claimed were "very important" to them in 2012 were: the economy, jobs, the budget deficit, and health care.[85] Voter priorities closely overlapped with the main issues that defined the election, which included the poor state of the economy and the need for job creation, Republican fixation on government spending and the deficit, and Obamacare. Furthermore, most Americans correctly identified where the parties and presidential candidates stood on numerous major issues, including taxation on the wealthy, immigration reform, same-sex marriage, cuts in military spending, abortion, and drilling in the arctic. Registered voters were much more likely to provide correct answers to where parties and candidates stood on policy issues than non-voters.[86]

In 2016, most voters claimed to be aware of their preferred presidential candidate's positions. Fifty-seven percent of Democratic and Democratic-leaning independents said they knew "a lot" about "where Hillary Clinton stands on the important issues facing the country," while 53 percent of Republican and Republican-leaning independents said the same about Trump.[87] The most cited issues voters said were "very important" included the economy, terrorism, foreign policy, and health care. These answers overlapped with the main issues discussed during the campaign, which included outsourcing and jobs (Trump's concern), ISIS and the Middle East, and Obamacare.[88]

Negative ads typically emphasize how candidates are unqualified or unfit for public office. These ads often speak to specific issues in a campaign, for example, Barack Obama's religious faith in 2008 or Mitt Romney's business record in 2012. They can also influence how voters look at candidates. In 2008, a prominent Republican ad depicted Obama as a radical, anti-American extremist. It took aim at Obama's Reverend, Jeremiah Wright, who had a history of controversial statements, including claims that the U.S. is a racist nation, and that "America's chickens" were "coming home to roost" following the September 11 attacks. His last comment referred to U.S. foreign militarism, which Wright saw as detrimental to human rights and democracy.[89] Conservative critics interpreted Wright's words as support for terrorism, although he was criticizing U.S. policy, and had condemned al Qaeda for committing an "unthinkable act."[90]

Regardless of Wright's intent, the Republican ad influenced how voters assessed Obama. The Wright controversy received a massive amount of news coverage from March to April 2008, and it caused a sizable public backlash against Obama. The percent of Americans who felt Obama was "ready to be president," and "has the judgment needed to be president" fell significantly in March, coinciding with the rising public attention to the controversy, with half of Americans being exposed to Wrights comments.[91] It was not until Obama's March 18th speech that he responded to the ad and to Wright's comments. The speech appeared to turn the tide, defusing the mounting suspicion of Obama, as his polling numbers began to climb again afterwards.

In 2012, negative ads again had a significant impact on a presidential candidate—this time Republican Mitt Romney. In numerous battleground states, Obama endorsed negative ads focusing on Romney's time as the CEO of an investment firm, Bain Capital, which profited from buying companies and pushing spending cutbacks, layoffs, and eliminating pensions. Bain Capital made enemies among those who lost benefits and jobs. These voices appeared in anti-Romney ads, which framed the candidate as an elitist who put profits over people. In a June 2012 NBC-Wall Street Journal poll of various swing states, one-third of citizens said hearing about the Romney-Bain Capital controversy made them look at his candidacy more negatively, compared to just 18 percent who said it made them see him more favorably.[92] Independent voters participating in focus groups reported that the ads "raised questions in their mind about Mr. Romney's experience."[93]

Issues continued to matter in 2016. Various issues in the campaign were associated with fluctuations in the polls for both Trump and Clinton. For Clinton, her controversial attacks on Trump supporters as "deplorables," and news reports about her trafficking in classified materials via a private email server, both produced a significant public backlash immediately prior to election day, the latter incident perhaps costing her the election. Trump's poor performance in the first debate, and his racist attacks on a Mexican-American judge and a Muslim-American family of a veteran killed in action, also led to a significant decline in voter support.[94] These cases provide more evidence that issues matter in U.S. elections.

None of the above evidence proves that the masses of Americans are empowered in producing democratic outcomes that inhibit corporate elites and the upper-class, or that favor the working- and middle-classes. But a knowledgeable public is a basic prerequisite for democracy, in that citizens must be adequately informed on political issues for their votes to be meaningful. Issue voting suggests that Americans are generally well-informed on the political issues, at least enough to effectively vote for candidates who represent their personal interests and desires.

ECONOMIC VOTING (PROSPECTIVE AND RETROSPECTIVE)

Economic theories of voting have been popular for decades. Like the theory of issue voting, these theories assume that Americans are well-informed enough and rational enough in their calculations to effectively hold political leaders accountable for their proposals and actions. Like issue voting, the theory is fundamental to arguments that the public is empowered in its pursuit of democratic governance. Retrospective voting is the notion that citizens look at their past economic experiences, and at the health of the economy, when deciding how to vote. In contrast, prospective voting argues that citizens assess candidates and their promises during campaigns, and judge how well they are likely to perform in delivering on their promises in the future, particularly as related to the economy. Numerous studies in the 1970s and 1980s presented evidence that factors such as the inflation rate, the unemployment rate, and changes in individuals' personal finances and incomes predicted their vote choices.[95] Recent research suggests that voters look back six months in the past when reflecting on the economy and their experiences when choosing a candidate.[96] This is to be expected, since people recall more recent events in greater detail than older events. Other studies also verify that retrospective voting occurs in elections.[97]

Poor economic performance spells trouble for the presidential party's reelection prospects. But when the economy is doing well, the chance of reelection for the president's party improves. "Pocketbook issues" like personal finances influence electoral behavior.[98] But whether voting is more likely to be prospective or retrospective depends on circumstance. When there is a standing president running for reelection, retrospective economic calculations are more likely to impact presidential party members' election chances. If there is no sitting president, the party's candidates are more likely to be assessed based on their [prospective] promises if elected.[99] Furthermore, citizens are more likely to vote retrospectively for Congressional races when an incumbent is running for reelection, and prospectively when the candidate is running for the first time.[100] Some research concludes that prospective and retrospective voting occur hand-in-hand, meaning a candidate's past record matters for expectations of future performance.[101]

Sitting presidents know that a poor economy works against them, and challengers know to use a bad economy to their advantage. During bad economic times, incumbent presidents often succeed electorally by drawing attention away from the economy and toward some perceived weakness of their competitor. Challengers gain advantage by associating the incumbent with a poor economy.[102] This happened in 2012, when Romney emphasized the poor economy's effects on homeowners and workers. As *Gallup* polling suggested, "Americans tend[ed] to see Mitt Romney as better able to handle key issues than Obama [was], particularly relating to the economy," although "Americans [gave] Obama the edge on most character dimensions, especially basic likability."[103]

Sometimes economic forces have a major impact on election outcomes. In the 2008 election, the economy disadvantaged Republicans, since George W. Bush was president during the financial meltdown. Voters could not punish Bush since he would no longer be president in a few months. Instead, voters blamed his party, handing Congressional Republicans some of the worst electoral losses they had seen in decades, and voting against Republican Presidential candidate John McCain. The economic meltdown occurred at an opportune moment for Obama—during October, one month before election day—and the effect on McCain's candidacy was sizable, as seen in figure 10.2. While McCain was polling neck-and-neck with Obama in August, Obama won by more than seven percentage points by election day.[104]

By the 2010 midterm elections, many Americans were unhappy with the Democratic Party's failure to ensure a recovery from the 2008 economic crash. Much of the Democratic constituency stayed home in these elections, and Republicans turned out in mass, resulting in shifting control of the House from Democratic to Republican hands.[105] But Democratic losses were about more than Democratic voters not showing up. Worsening economic conditions worked against the Democrats, as states with the largest declines in citizens' personal finances from 2008 to 2010, and with the weakest recoveries in individuals' finances, were more likely to see Republican victories in Congressional races.[106]

Finally, the 2016 election also saw economic factors influence the vote in retrospective and prospective ways. Democratic presidential candidate Bernie Sanders gained much of his support from young Americans anxious about their economic insecurity. One spring 2016 survey of college students found that Sanders

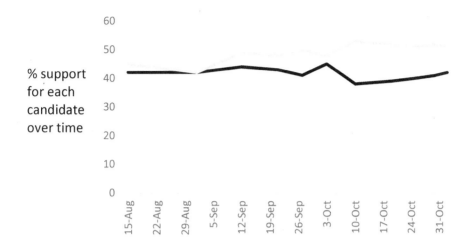

Figure 10.2. Obama-McCain Voter Support, 2008. Source: Mark Blumenthal, "Will Obama's Post-Convention Bounce Fade Like McCain's in 2008?" *Huffington Post*, September 13, 2012, http://www.huffingtonpost.com/2012/09/13/obamas-post-convention-bounce-polls-2012_n_1880520.html

was by far the most popular presidential candidate, with 60 percent of students wanting him to be president. This was predictable considering the Sanders' campaign platform, which emphasized making college more affordable and creating a universal health care system. College students have limited incomes, and often express anxiety over skyrocketing student loan debt and dwindling career prospects. In this context, Sanders' progressive promises of free college tuition and universal health care were cited most often by college students as motivating their support for Sanders.[107] These findings mirror those from national surveys.[108] The evidence here speaks to the importance of prospective economic voting.

Economic voting among Trump supporters was heavily retrospective. Trump voters were not more likely to be financially poorer or insecure, or to have lost jobs to the outsourcing of manufacturing jobs abroad. But occupational strain was a significant predictor of Trump support, with white Americans working a second job or overtime hours being significantly more likely to support his candidacy. Support for Trump was particularly significant for occupationally strained whites who held negative opinions of immigrants and people of color.[109] The mindset of Trump supporters appeared simple enough: in line with Trump's own rhetoric, they saw "lazy" and "deviant" immigrants and minorities as drags on society, and felt that their own sacrifices (working harder to "get ahead") were for naught if minorities were simply going to monopolize tax dollars and welfare programs for their own benefit. Whatever one thinks of Trump supporters' attitudes toward minorities and immigration, the evidence here suggests that retrospective occupational assessments mattered for Trump voters.

As with issue voting, economic voting does not guarantee that policy outcomes favor the masses over the upper class. But again, an informed public is vital to a functioning democracy. And the evidence above does suggest that many Americans make rational, self-interested economic calculations when deciding on which candidates to support or oppose.

SUPERFICIAL VOTING

Contrary to other theories, superficial voting frames the public as largely ignorant to issues, and as making voting decisions based on trivialities. Americans are seen as unable to effectively challenge business and upper-class political power, since elections are artificial and biased in favor of spectacle and entertainment, and lacking in substance. Americans are not seen as sophisticated in their voting decisions, but as easily manipulated. The political scientist Murray Edelman argued in his book *Symbolic Politics* that voting was a largely symbolic affair. Individuals vote as a ritual—because it makes them feel better about themselves—that they have "done their part" in contributing to democracy.[110] But little of substance is produced in these affairs.

According to critics, U.S. electoral campaigns are largely meaningless events with no real messages.[111] Candidates deliver scripted "stump speeches," repeated verbatim from one town to the next. Rallies are chock full of confetti, balloons, and streamers, with citizens reaching out to candidates the same way star-struck fans ogle Hollywood actors and music artists. Clichéd songs abound on the campaign trail—Journey's "Don't Stop Believin'" comes to mind—but little substance is communicated between candidates and audiences. Questioning corporate power is simply not on the agenda in these highly scripted, superficial electoral campaigns.

Sloganeering is common in American elections. Barack Obama promised "hope" and "change" during the 2008 election, despite Americans' continued economic struggles in subsequent years. John McCain called himself a "maverick," refusing to take orders from the Republican establishment. Ted Cruz called on Americans to "TrustTed" as part of his official campaign message, while Donald Trump promised to "Make America Great Again." None of these slogans carried with them specifics for how these candidates would improve the growing economic insecurity of the masses.

Superficiality in campaigns is not new. A notorious example is the 1960 Presidential debate between John Kennedy and Richard Nixon. Their debate was the first-ever to be televised. It was also a natural experiment, in that we were able to observe how radio and television independently affected how audiences assessed the candidates. The visual difference between both candidates could not have been starker. Nixon had recently been hospitalized, chose to forego makeup, and looked sweaty and sickly. He was significantly shorter than Kennedy, older, had thinner hair, was seen as less attractive, and wore a gray suit which was absorbed into a similarly colored background on the black-and-white broadcast. In contrast, Kennedy looked more telegenic, no doubt in part due to the assistance of his health and makeup.

The voting public favored Kennedy following the debate, although opinions varied based on the news medium consumed. Most who listened to the debate on the radio felt Nixon won, whereas television audiences preferred Kennedy. While all Americans heard the same messages from Kennedy and Nixon, impressions of the candidates varied based on whether the public heard or watched the debate.[112] As *Time* Magazine reflected, "Nixon performed much better in the subsequent debates," but "the damage had been done." As one presidential historian recounts, "you couldn't wipe away the image people had seared in their brains from the first debate." Kennedy acknowledged the importance of the event, stating that "It was the TV more than anything else that turned the tide" in the campaign.[113]

The Kennedy-Nixon debate represents anecdotal evidence of superficiality in voting, but is there more systematic evidence? Recent studies suggest the answer is "yes." One common criticism of American elections is that the media make it difficult for the public to become well-informed about candidates' policy stances. Candidates' ads and rhetoric are dominated by glittering generalities, proclaiming America's greatness and promising prosperity, economic growth, and freedom. Campaign ads are characterized by one-sided, negative messages that turn off many voters and make it more difficult for them to develop an informed opinion of competing candidates. Television coverage—where most Americans get their information about elections—is notoriously superficial. For example, in the 2012 presidential primary elections, television coverage emphasized candidates' campaign strategies—which represented 64 percent of all "frames" in the news. Discussion of candidates' personal issues represented 12 percent of frames, while candidates' public records in office counted for another 6 percent. Just 9 percent were devoted to domestic political issues.[114]

General election coverage was not much more substantive in 2008 or 2012. Much of it focused on the horse-race aspect of campaigns, reporting who was ahead or behind each week. Thirty-eight percent of the election "newshole" was devoted to "horse-race" stories in 2012; 53 percent of stories were devoted to the horse-race in 2008. Public records of candidates comprised 6 percent of the newshole in both 2008 and 2012; discussion of candidates' personal issues counted for 5 percent and 4 percent of coverage in 2008 and 2012. Just 20 percent and 22 percent of stories were devoted to policy issues in 2008 and 2012. In sum, approximately 80 percent of stories had little or nothing to do with public policy issues.[115]

Furthermore, 2016 campaign coverage echoed early elections in its superficiality. One study by the *Media Tenor* group found that in the primaries, 56 percent of coverage was comprised of reporting on the "competitive game," including discussions of "poll results," "election returns," "delegate counts," "electoral projections," and "candidates' tactical and strategic maneuvering." One-third of coverage emphasized "campaign process," emphasizing "the election timetable, upcoming debates, the candidates' appearance schedules, and the rules of the nominating process." Just 11 percent of reporting addressed "substantive concerns" such as "candidates' policy positions," "their personal and leadership characteristics," "their private and public histories," and "background information on election issues."[116]

If television coverage is so superficial, one would expect TV viewers to demonstrate limited rationality in their voting. This is what researchers find, with one study concluding that television-reliant citizens make vote choices based heavily on candidates' physical appearances. In U.S. Senate and gubernatorial races, heavy-television-viewing Americans who ranked low in terms of their civic knowledge tend to look at images of candidates running for office and judge between them based on "gut" reactions of which look more "competent" to hold office. Candidates who are more "appealing-looking" do significantly better electorally than those deemed less physically appealing.[117]

Other studies also find evidence of how candidates' physical appearances affect voter choices.[118] Individuals shown pairs of competing House and Senate candidates running for office and asked to rate their competence based on image alone are able to effectively predict winners of races between two-thirds to three-quarters of the time.[119] Local election candidates who are ranked more visually appealing by voters have a 90 percent chance of winning their respective races, whereas less appealing candidates only have a 10 percent chance.[120] This is powerful evidence of across-the-board superficial voting. Many voters think they are exercising meaningful vote choices, selecting between candidates based on perceived "electability," "experience," and "character," but these findings suggest voter rationalizations are a smokescreen to obscure superficial voting that is heavily based on physical appearance and "looks."[121] The implications of these findings are dire. How does the public hold candidates accountable, or limit growing corporate and upper-class power in politics, when voting is so superficial? If citizens merely "follow the leader," basing their opinions on the statements of their own party's officials, it is difficult for the public to hold political leaders in check.[122]

Assessing the Theories

There is evidence for each of the above accounts of voting behavior. It is not a question of whether one approach is entirely "right" and the others "wrong."

Previous research did seek to assess competing theories of voting alongside each other, to determine which theories benefitted from greater evidence. Looking at the 1988 and 1992 elections, one study found that partisanship, policy considerations, candidate qualities, and economic factors all influenced voter choice. However, economic factors were most powerful in accounting for patterns in voting. Partisan considerations and "policy-related predispositions" were nearly as powerful. Evaluations of "personal qualities" of candidates, however, were the least powerful predictor of voting.[123] A major limitation of this research, however, is that it did not represent an adequate test of superficial voting. Citizens' assessments of candidates "personal qualities" may or may not be based on superficial considerations, depending on the specific quality or issue being assessed. Unfortunately, I am not aware of any systematic effort to assess the explanatory power of the superficial voting theory alongside all of the competing theories of voting.

The 2016 Election

The 2016 election represents a timely case in terms of helping assess competing theories of voting. I argue that, with regard to this electoral contest, superficial voting appears to best explain why people voted the way they did. Party voting undeniably occurred, with the vast majority of partisans voting for their party's presidential candidate. The problem with the party theory, however, is that it is not clear how useful it is to state that Republicans vote Republican and Democrats vote Democratic. This claim may have been novel more than a half-century ago when *The American Voter* was first published, but it does little to enhance our understanding of elections today. Even though party pressures do matter, they can hardly be divorced from superficial voting. I presented evidence in this chapter that partisans are manipulated at will by party leaders, and argue throughout the rest of this book that parties increasingly seek to serve upper-class agendas. This manipulation in pursuit of an elite agenda suggests a significant superficiality component in party-based voting.

As discussed earlier in this chapter, economic concerns were a significant motivator for Sanders and Trump voters, and public attention to many political issues in the election influenced the shifting favorability levels of the candidates, as related to Trump's racist comments and Clinton's emails and her attack on Trump supporters as "deplorables." But the fact that Trump won the election spoke volumes about how superficial American elections have become. Trump's entire campaign was centered on a vague promise to "Make America Great Again," but he never offered a realistic political plan for how to bring jobs back to America. His proposed 20 percent tax on imported Mexican goods would do nothing to stop corporations from shifting that cost to consumers and, even if implemented, it would have no effect on the goods manufactured in sweatshops in other countries. Trump's promise to label China a "currency manipulator" was derided by trade analysts, who pointed out that it was "a jaw-boning exercise" with little likelihood of the move resulting in a return of jobs.[124] And Trump's imposition of sanctions on Chinese goods were widely derided as threatening to provoke a trade war. There were tools at Trump's disposal that would create pressure for upward wages in jobs already existing in the U.S., including raising the minimum wage and promoting legislation making it easier for American workers to unionize. But these options were never part of Trump's agenda. Instead, he preferred to demonize immigrants and Muslims, while putting forward a tax reform plan that was heavily biased in favor of the upper class.

Probably the most compelling evidence of superficial voting in 2016 was the admission from Americans—expressed across many surveys—that they were not voting for policy-related reasons. Of the four leading primary candidates—Cruz and Trump on the Republican side, and Clinton and Sanders on the Democratic side—superficial voting was pervasive. According to *Gallup*, in the cases of Cruz, Trump, and Clinton, four of the top five reasons cited by supporters for why they preferred each candidate had little to nothing to do with policies. For Clinton supporters, the order of reasons from most to least important included feelings that: 1. she is a qualified, capable leader; 2. she has political experience related to the White House; 3. she cares about the people and their needs; 4. she is a woman; and 5. she has a good policy platform. Only reason five dealt directly with policy, and this was the *weakest* of all the top reasons cited by voters.[125] For Cruz, the top five reasons included: 1. they "like[d] his decisions/views/outlook"; 2. he would "protect constitutional rights"; 3. he was the "best" candidate; 4. he was a "true conservative"; and 5. he was "experienced." Only the second issue related directly to policy, while the others were personal qualities.[126] For Trump, support sprang from the following feelings: 1. he was not "a career politician"; 2. he was a "good businessman"; 3. he "speak[s] his mind"; 4. his stance on immigration; and 5. he was a "strong leader."[127] Save for immigration, these reasons all centered on the strong persona that is Donald Trump. Even for Sanders, most reasons given by supporters did not directly relate to policy. Support came primarily from these feelings: 1. he "care[d]" about the people; 2. he had a "good [policy] platform"; 3. he was "honest" and "trustworthy"; 4. support for his push for free college tuition; and 5. he was the least disliked candidate of all.[128] Of these reasons, only two were directly policy-relevant.

Superficiality in voter considerations continued into the general election. Most Trump and Clinton supporters viewed their vote more as "against the other candidate" than in favor of the candidate they chose.[129] As depicted in figure 10.3, depending on the survey, no more than 22 percent of Clinton supporters cited

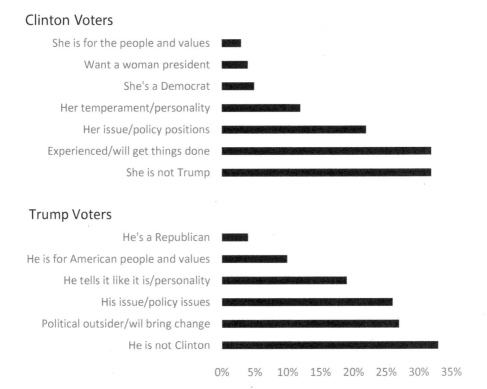

Figure 10.3. Reasons Why Voters Preferred Each Candidate, September 2016. Sources: Lydia Saad, "Aversion to Other Candidate Key Factor in 2016 Vote Choice," *Gallup*, October 6, 2016, http://www.gallup.com/poll/196172/aversion-candidate-key-factor-2016-vote-choice.aspx; Pew Research Center, "In Their Own Words: Why Voters Support and Have Concerns About Clinton and Trump," *Pew Research Center*, September 21, 2016, http://www.people-press.org/2016/09/21/in-their-own-words-why-voters-support-and-have-concerns-about-clinton-and-trump/

policy issues as motivating their vote. Only 26 percent of Trump supporters cited policy reasons as driving their choice.[130] The most common argument provided by Trump supporters was that they preferred him because "he is not Clinton," while the dominant reason provided by Clinton supporters was that "she is not Trump." Under these conditions, it seems fair to conclude most Americans were not voting for policy-related reasons.[131] The data—especially surveys of primary voters—is troublesome considering these voters are *more* politically attentive and involved than general election voters and should have been more sophisticated in their calculations. Few of the reasons provided by voters here had to do with substance; rather, voters preferred amorphous candidate "qualities." Those qualities, however, have little meaning if not linked to policy stances.

Trump's rise took superficial voting to new heights. In many ways, his candidacy was supremely shallow. First, his speeches were light on policy prescriptions, and were saturated with vague references to politicians as clowns, with simple-minded promises to "Make America Great Again," and a narcissistic focus on how much better Trump was polling than his competitors. Focus group studies found backing of Trump was largely visceral, based on emotions and general impressions, not policy details: Trump support was often based on "more of a gut reaction to the person he is and how he comes across and [had] less to do with a list of specific issues." Based on conversations with Trump supporters, one reporter summarized that attraction to the candidate "has nothing to do with policy, with the exception of immigration. It [voter support] is all persona [based]."[132]

In a damning indictment of "informed" voting, Trump won the election, despite evidence that he was one of the most dishonest of all candidates. Nonpartisan fact-checking groups and journalists routinely identified large numbers of false statements from Trump, but the spotlighting of manipulative rhetoric did little good when many voters looked past fact-checking and had little interest in basing their support on real issues. Democracy is based on the notion that voters cast ballots for candidates after being effectively and accurately informed about their policy plans for the future. This is simply not possible when a candidate systematically deceives the public. It is also difficult to hold political officials accountable for pursuing agendas privileging business and upper-class elites when voters are more interested in superficiality than in candidates' voting records and policy proposals.

Why Elections are Superficial

What purpose do superficial elections serve? Political critic Noam Chomsky argues that superficial election rhetoric serves the interests of parties trying "to exclude the population from participation. So they [candidates] don't present issues, policies, agendas, and so on. They project imagery, and people either don't bother [to vote] or they vote for the image."[133] The vaguer campaign rhetoric is, the less bound candidates are to fulfilling policy promises to the masses. For Chomsky, candidates' aversion to issues reveals contempt for democratic accountability. In these superficial electoral extravaganzas, there are winners and losers. The winners are the political officials themselves, who get elected or reelected, wealthy donors hailing from the upper class, who benefit from holding the ear of the candidates they get elected, the media and their corporate owners, which profit from billions in advertising revenues, and public relations firms, which run American elections. The loser in these elections is the American public, which struggles to cast informed ballots, thereby failing to hold their political leaders accountable and struggling to rein in corporate and upper-class power in politics. In short, American elections are superficial because they do not serve the interests of the public, but rather those of political and economic elites who dominate election funding, and enable officials to avoid democratic accountability.

Chomsky writes of the public relations industry's role in dumbing down politics: "elections are run by the same guys who sell toothpaste. [In ads] they show you an image of a sports hero, or a sexy model, or a car going up a sheer cliff or something, which has nothing to do with the commodity, but it's intended to delude you into picking this one rather than another one. [It is the] same when they run elections."[134] Voters are treated like passive subjects, manipulated by a PR industry running ads that are short on substance and heavy on superficiality.

Election campaigns are a big business. According to the Center for Responsive Politics, in 2012 and 2016, candidates running for President and Congress raised $6.2 and $6.9 billion respectively, each one a record. By comparison, the 2008 election saw $5.3 billion raised, the 2004 election $4.1 billion, and the 2000 election $3.1 billion.[135] Over just twelve years, the cost of U.S. elections more than doubled.

A major concern with the growth of big money and business dominance of elections is not that corporate and upper-class donors will automatically "buy" policy outcomes from Congress. This narrative has already been discredited by interest group scholars. Rather, greater spending on campaigns means increased public exposure via ads, so wealthy individuals and their allies are able to dominate what citizens see in elections, while marginalizing progressive-left third-party candidates who challenge upper-class dominance of elections and politics. If well-funded candidates buy elections, who gets left out of this process? Clearly, poorer Americans, and working- and middle-class individuals who lack financial resources, will find it radically more difficult to run for, and win office. Politics is increasingly the playground of the upper class, not the masses. Without a serious change in how elections are run, the decline of American democracy will continue.

Chapter 11

Politics and the Media

Bias in Pursuit of Elite Agendas

Americans' sense of class-consciousness is thoroughly underdeveloped. Most Americans dislike inequality, recognize that it is growing, and wish to see government reduce it.[1] But they significantly underestimate how much inequality exists today. And most Americans do not believe that the U.S. is divided economically between haves and have-nots, despite half of the country owning no financial wealth, and inequality reaching record levels.

The media make it difficult for citizens to understand just how severe inequality has become, or what government can do about it. In the years prior to and following the 2008 economic crash, coverage of economic inequality, as related to discussions of American politics and government, was at a minimum. Looking across a wide variety of terms that speak to economic inequality and an American class divide—via news references to "income inequality," "wealth inequality," "income disparity," "wealth disparity," "economic disparity," "inequality" more generally, or references to "class war," "class warfare," or "class conflict," table 11.1 demonstrates that inequality coverage—at least in stories covering American politics—was sparse across American media.[2] In the pre-2008 period, references to inequality and class conflict appeared at most a couple times a month in individual news outlets examined. Although such discussions grew more frequent in the post-2008 period, this discourse was still quite rare. This trend means that reporting on American politics routinely fails to provide a context to consumers of U.S. media regarding the potential for government to address growing (and record) inequality in the early-twenty-first century.

In addition to downplaying inequality, journalists often avoid stories that are critical of businesses and advertisers. These practices serve the interests of the corporate class and, as a result, these media suppress awareness of the growing class divide. More specifically, Americans who pay close attention to the news are no more likely than those who do not to recognize that the U.S. is divided between haves and have-nots. And public attention to the news is *not*

219

Table 11.1. The Erasure of Inequality and Class Conflict in Political News 2006–2011

Outlet	Inequality References Average # of stories per month 1/1/2006–12/31/2008	Inequality References Average # of stories per month 1/1/2009–12/31/2011
New York Times	4.8	4.3
Washington Post	2.3	2.6
CBS News	.15	.5
NBC News	.4	.8
ABC News	.3	.8
Associated Press	2.6	7.2
CNN	2.4	7.4

Source: Nexis Uni Academic Database

associated with being more likely to feel that corporations make too much profit or that corporations hold too much power in America.[3] These findings should be no surprise considering the mass media are corporations that are devoted to promoting advertiser, consumer, and corporate profit interests.

There is a political relevance to the erasure of inequality in the news. Without being adequately informed about the problems of record inequality and a growing class divide, Americans are not in a position to demand that government take steps to reduce that divide. As a result, government continues serving corporate and upper-class interests, while ignoring mass economic insecurity, with the help of a corporate media system that blunts public consciousness on the issue of inequality.

The rise of the corporate media in modern times is relevant to this book's discussion of growing corporate power in America. By the twenty-first century, much of the mass media were controlled by less than a dozen major corporations, representing the interests of wealthy advertisers, and corporate class interests. Media now exist in modern society, not primarily to educate Americans about politics, but to make money by promoting mass consumerism.

Serving the Public Interest?
The Mass Media and Common Expectations

The media are vital to politics. Reporters are expected to inform the public about what is happening in the world. Americans hold high expectations for the media. These expectations include: 1. representing the public; 2. providing vital information, 3. exploring diverse and competing points of view, and 4. exposing government or corporate corruption via investigative journalism. Reporters are supposed to represent the public as they engage with political officials. Most Americans do not have interactions with political leaders, so journalists are supposed to serve as surrogates for the public, asking relevant and timely questions of government officials.

Because journalists control information, they influence public consciousness on political and economic matters. Journalists have power to "set the agenda" for what political issues Americans think about.[4] Media also influence *how* people think about politics, in addition to influencing political attitudes.[5] In sum, media are important to socializing the public.

The media are also supposed to report diverse and competing points of view so that Americans develop informed political opinions. If people are only exposed to certain points of view over others, it hinders their ability to develop critical thinking skills. Democracy is impossible without an informed citizenry.

Finally, reporters are supposed to engage in investigative journalism. Like other citizens, political and business leaders violate the law, behave unethically, and lie. Reporters can expose these behaviors through relentless investigation of wrongdoing. But if journalists do not expose corruption, who will?

A History of the Media, Mass Consumerism, and the News

To understand what elite interests the media serve, it is first necessary to understand the history of the media. Reporting on politics has changed dramatically throughout U.S. history. There are three distinct phases in the history of political reporting. These include: 1. the partisan press (late-1700s through the late-1800s); 2. mass commercialism and the rise and dominance of journalistic "objectivity" (the late-1800s to late-1900s); and 3. the hybrid era (late-1900s through early-2000s), marked by a combination of "objectivity" and the return of partisan media. Across these periods, the organizational mandates and functions of media transformed. While the media primarily served political elites during the partisan press era, by the turn of the twentieth century media had shifted to primarily serving the corporate class via their fixation on commercialism, mass consumerism, and maximizing profits.

In early American history, newspapers were the primary vehicle through which political officials disseminated party messages to the people. Most newspaper editors and reporters were blatantly partisan, favoring one party or the other. Newspapers were subsidized by the government, which paid to mail out subscriptions through the U.S. Postal Service.[6] By the 1790s, newspaper shipping comprised 70 percent of post office business, and by the 1830s it had risen to over 90 percent. As one media historian notes, "The crucial debate in the 1792 Congress was how much to charge newspapers to be sent through the mails. All parties agreed that Congress should permit newspapers to be mailed at a price well below actual cost—to be subsidized—to encourage their production and distribution."[7]

Why would Americans tolerate partisan propaganda masquerading as news? Simply put, there were many newspaper choices for consumers to pick from in most cities. It was common to have more than a dozen newspapers to choose from in major cities in the late-1800s, although the range of choices was curtailed dramatically by the turn of the twentieth century.[8] The rise of monopoly capitalism by the late-1800s marked the end for many newspapers. Those that were advertiser-funded and profit-oriented came to dominate media markets, while the old partisan papers fell by the wayside.

By the early-twentieth century, a fundamental shift had occurred. The primary function of the media shifted from political to economic, due to the rise of monopoly capitalism and the emergence of mass consumerism. Media outlets changed from primarily serving political parties to being profit-oriented institutions concerned with delivering audiences to advertisers. In *Land of Desire*, historian William Leach documents the rise of mass-mediated consumerism: "in its sheer quest to produce and sell goods cheaply in constantly growing volume and at higher profit levels," American businesses, including the media, "began the transformation of American society into a society preoccupied with consumption, with comfort and bodily well-being, with luxury spending and acquisition, with more goods this year than last." With advertisers leading the way, a "culture of consumer capitalism" emerged in just three to four decades.[9]

The shift from a partisan press to a commercial one saw a transformation in the role of media consumers. Whereas in the partisan era readers were seen as voters serving the ends of political parties; in the commercial era, they were consumers expected to purchase products, contributing to the enrichment of the corporate class via mass consumerism. With the commercialization of the press already occurring by the mid-to-late 1800s, there was a significant decline in the coverage of political content in major newspapers. Such was to be expected in a system that prioritized profits and consumerism over reporting of political matters.[10]

The rise of commercialism coincided with the emergence of "objective" news, and these two trends were interlinked. By the early twentieth century, professional journalism schools were established in major universities, training reporters to no longer be biased in favor of one party, but to be "objective" by reporting the views of "both sides." Objectivity came to be referred to as "non-partisan, strictly factual" reporting by the turn of the twentieth century.[11] But that "objectivity" masked the growing monopolization of the news within a single-paper market, advertiser-funded system of reporting.[12] With the rise of advertising as the dominant form of newspaper funding, advertiser-funded papers held an advantage over partisan papers. The former could afford to run their competitors out of business through monopolistic price cutting tactics, or simply by buying up competing newspapers and dismantling them. These practices resulted in the rapid monopolization of the news by the beginning of the twentieth century.

By the early-1900s, a consumer-commercialist media system dominated America. By that time, most communities only had one or two daily newspapers. And the monopoly power of these media corporations made it almost impossible for smaller upstarts to succeed.[13] Whereas in the partisan era, consumers could compensate for the blatant bias of one newspaper by reading another, the rise of corporate monopolies posed a credibility problem. The partisan model no longer worked with one newspaper in a single market. Many citizens would simply refuse to read the newspaper because of its partisan bias running contrary to their own.

Major changes were necessary by the turn of the twentieth century in a rapidly shifting media landscape. The day of the partisan newspaper was dead, and by pushing one-sided partisan content, monopoly media corporations risked undermining their own journalistic credibility.[14]

With the rise of objectivity, media monopolies operating in single markets captured a full market of readers without appearing biased in favor of one party. Reporters claimed to be neutral, and removed their own personal partisan biases from stories, reporting the news based on the perspectives expressed by both political parties.[15] This monopoly system continues today. Most all media markets are dominated by one daily newspaper, a handful of radio corporations, and a small number of television news outlets.

Significant changes occurred in the media in recent decades. On the one hand, objectivity remains central to political reporting. Journalists report the views of both political parties, without openly expressing their own partisan opinions. Corporations still control the news. There are some developments, however, that distinguish the modern era from the previous one. These include: the rapid concentration of media ownership via mega-conglomerated corporate monopolies; the de-politicization of the public via the rise of entertainment media and the decline of news; and the return of partisan forms of media on cable TV and talk radio. With these three changes, a "hybrid" media system emerged mixing objective and partisan political content.

The rise of partisan media began with the rise of right-wing talk radio, and its most influential personality, Rush Limbaugh. Limbaugh will be remembered for demonstrating that media corporations could profit from partisan content by appealing to audiences already predisposed to accept conservative political beliefs. Limbaugh's success spawned an army of imitators, and the success of talk radio led to the extension of partisan programming to cable. *Fox News* became famous by appealing to conservative Americans. In the mid-to-late 2010s, its nighttime lineup included notable conservatives such as Bill O'Reilly, Tucker Carlson, Megyn Kelly, and Sean Hannity. *MSNBC* also entered the partisan game in the late 2000s, appealing to liberal and Democratic viewers. Their nighttime lineup in 2017 included liberal hosts such as Chris Hayes, Rachel Maddow, and Lawrence O'Donnell.

Partisan talk radio and cable hosts disseminate propaganda rhetoric in favor of Republican and Democratic talking points. These outlets engage in "narrowcasting," appealing to small partisan audiences, which are already likely to agree with the ideological nature of the political content being disseminated. Narrowcasting is different from "broadcasting," with the latter engaged in by the nightly news networks *CBS*, *ABC*, and *NBC*. The newscasters on these channels pursue objective reporting by omitting their own personal partisan biases from newscasts. These programs collectively reach tens of millions of viewers, compared to the partisan cable and radio.

The origins of modern partisan media trace back to the 1970s. Roger Ailes could be described as the grandfather of modern partisan "news." An aide for the Nixon administration, Ailes called for the Republican Party to traffic in partisan media content. He was contemptuous of news viewers, seeing them as a passive vessel for the accepting Republican propaganda, and writing about television's power as a medium for mass manipulation: "Today television is watched more than people read newspapers, than people listen to the radio, than people read or gather any other form of communication. The reason: people are lazy. With television, you just sit—watch—listen. The thinking is done for you."[16] Recognizing the political value of television, Ailes sought a Republican-controlled network to spread the party's talking points. "Pro-administration, videotape, hard news actualities" would be inserted into local television newscasts in major cities.[17] Republicans would "go around the press and go directly to the people" by creating content to disseminate "without it being interpreted for him [the voter] by a middleman."[18]

Ailes's vision for Republican TV was realized two decades later when he became president of *Fox News*. Ailes created a media giant tailoring its "news" stories and commentary to Republican positions, and in the pursuit of corporate profits. Little of the content on *Fox* resembles traditional journalism, but it has succeeded in influencing millions of Americans who are oblivious to the paternalistic contempt which motivated Ailes to create the network.

Partisan political programs reach significant numbers of Americans. Twenty-one percent of Americans "regularly" watched *Fox News* in 2012.[19] Daily viewership is about 5 million primetime and daytime viewers, or just 2 percent of the total U.S. population.[20] But an estimated 60 million Americans are "regularly" exposed to *Fox* programming, perhaps weekly, which is evidence of significant viewership. *Fox News* was an important political actor in the 2016 election as well, with 19 percent of Americans saying they relied on it as a "main source" of information.[21] Other partisan media benefit from significant audiences too. *Pew* estimated that 11 percent of Americans regularly watched MSNBC in 2012.[22] Five percent of Americans relied on MSNBC as a "main source" of information in the 2016 election.[23] And in 2015, an estimated 20 percent of adults listened to radio news or talk radio.[24]

In the hybrid system, partisan news outlets profit off of the political parties' guiding the "news." Advertisers and media executives enrich themselves by trafficking in partisan propaganda consumed by millions of Americans, and driven by billions in advertising revenues. Additionally, political parties' interests are served, since they dominate media content. While the rise of the partisan media benefits officialdom and the corporate class, citizens are denied access to perspectives outside the bipartisan spectrum of opinions. By feeding into a political system biased in favor of official and corporate interests, partisan media are instrumental to exercising social control in favor of the established political-economic order.

The Backlash against Partisan "News"

The hybrid media system is not defined only through partisan media, but by entertainment-oriented political programming. One can look to various programs on Comedy Central, HBO, and elsewhere to observe this phenomenon. These programs are defined by criticisms of partisan media, and have been led by various personalities, including John Stewart (previously on Comedy Central), Trevor Noah (Comedy Central), John Oliver (HBO), Bill Maher (HBO), Samantha Bee (TBS), Stephen Colbert (CBS), and Jimmy Kimmel (ABC). These programs built their reputations on fusing comedy with political content in a late-night entertainment format. This format for disseminating political information is referred as "soft news," in contrast to "hard news" programs which cover news developments without editorializing. While these outlets work within corporate media, they use comedy to undermine a political system that is increasingly dominated by corporate power and upper-class interests.

Operating on the periphery of the corporate mass media, soft news benefits from a significant audience. In 2015, "The Daily Show" with John Stewart reached 1.5 million nightly viewers, while it averaged 820,000 viewers in 2016 under Trevor Noah.[25] Stephen Colbert reached 680,000 viewers a night in 2016, while John Oliver reached 4.1 million viewers per episode and Jimmy Kimmel averaged 2.1 million.[26] In contrast to partisan media like *MSNBC*, *Fox News*, and talk radio, whose demographic audience are older (in their 40s to 50s or older), the typical age for soft news viewers is 18 to 34 years old.[27] Soft news personalities are significantly different from partisan media pundits, in that they subversively seek to undermine the bipartisan dominated political system. Refusing to endorse one party over another, Colbert, Noah, Oliver, and others are left-leaning in their ideology. Still, they have been effective in undermining public confidence in political leaders, and criticizing journalists for failing to provide critical analysis of the U.S. political establishment. These outlets have fueled the skepticism of the millennial generation, whose members express deep reservations about corporate domination of American politics.[28]

A major criticism of the partisan media from Colbert, Stewart, and others is that they are not serious news outfits. Allied closely with the political parties, they are seen as a propaganda arm for government. Stewart and Colbert have hammered partisan media outlets like *Fox News* for being anti-science, anti-poor, manipulative and one-sided in their content, mean-spirited, anti-intellectual, and engaging in "partisan hackery."[29] Although Stewart and Colbert never considered themselves to be reporters, their programs have provided original research on political topics, while exposing the hypocrisy and deceptiveness of political leaders.

As with partisan media content, soft news programs have a significant impact on audiences. Their effects, however, are different from *Fox News* or *MSNBC*. Whereas partisan programs have ideological effects on viewers' attitudes, soft news consumption increases viewers' interest in political issues. Most viewers tune into comedy programs to be entertained after a long day's work. But as a byproduct of watching soft news, they also become more concerned with politics.[30] In a corporate media system that prioritizes a business agenda fixating on entertainment programming and mass consumerism, soft news programs are holding the line by discouraging de-politicization and stoking youth interest in politics.

Positive and Negative Effects of Modern Media

The evidence is somewhat mixed regarding the effects of partisan media. On the one hand, partisan audiences are highly interested in politics and politically active. One *Pew* survey finds that 96 percent of those who get their news primarily from *Fox* are registered to vote, compared to 89 percent of those who receive their news mainly from *MSNBC*.[31] Furthermore, *Fox* and *MSNBC* viewers perform well on surveys measuring knowledge on politics and civics questions.

A 2012 *Pew* poll, for example, measured civic awareness by asking Americans which party controlled the House of Representatives, about the unemployment rate, about which presidential candidate favored raising income taxes, and regarding who was the Chancellor of Germany. The survey found that 71 percent of Rachel Maddow viewers on *MSNBC*, 63 percent of "Hannity" viewers on *Fox*, 61 percent of Rush Limbaugh listeners, and 60 percent of "Hardball" viewers on *MSNBC* answered three or four out of four of the questions correctly.[32] These findings suggest that consumers of these programs retain basic knowledge about politics and government. Such political and informational literacy is a vital component of any democracy.

On the other hand, there is serious concern that partisan media are negatively affecting American politics. Partisan media outlets contribute to significant polarization, via the "echo chamber" phenomenon, in which partisan audiences increasingly look to media with which they already agree, while tuning out media they disagree with ideologically.[33] Furthermore, consumption of partisan media is associated with increased misinformation and blindness to government propaganda. This is to be expected for those consistently trafficking in one-sided information, and considering the original purpose of partisan media was to manipulate audiences. By relying heavily on partisan media content, many consumers are playing into an informational propaganda system that reflexively favors a political system that is biased in favor of corporate and upper-class agendas.

While partisan news consumers are informed on simple civics questions, they are often quite poorly informed on deeper political matters. For example, one study of the 2003 Iraq war found *Fox News* viewers were the most likely of all news viewers examined to hold misperceptions. Eighty percent of *Fox* viewers held one misperception or more regarding claims that Iraq had ties to al Qaeda (it did not), that WMDs in Iraq had been found after the invasion (they had not), and that world public opinion favored the U.S. war (the war was widely unpopular).[34] A 2009 *NBC-Wall Street Journal* poll found 79 percent of *Fox News* viewers inaccurately believed that the Obama health care law would result in a "government takeover" of health care, in line with Republican claims that Obamacare empowered government to "make decisions about when to stop providing care for the elderly."[35] A 2010 Stanford University study found *Fox News* viewers were more likely to accept Republican Party claims that global warming was not real, despite the consensus among 98 percent of climatologists that 1. climate change is in fact real, and that 2. humans are primarily responsible for warming of the planet via growing fossil fuel emissions.[36] Similarly, *MSNBC* viewers' political knowledge is often unimpressive. As documented in table 11.2, misinformation is a common problem among many *MSNBC* viewers, although it is an even bigger problem for *Fox News* viewers.[37]

Rampant public misinformation is toxic to any democracy. It is troublesome when partisan media consumers fall victim to reactionary propaganda that aids the corporate class by confusing the public about climate change, and encouraging conspiracy mongering over fictional "government takeovers" of the health care industry. These propaganda campaigns succeed in blunting critical public consciousness, and in inhibiting progressive agendas aimed at confronting corporate power and upper-class dominance of politics.

Some Americans worry about the effects of soft news consumption on the public. Some concerns include: 1. the claim that young Americans look too much to these programs to be informed, instead of following real news; and 2. the criticisms of government on soft news programs may turn people off from politics. If these two charges are accurate, then soft news programs may be failing in providing young Americans with the tools to empower themselves politically. Available evidence suggests soft news consumption is associated with positive and negative benefits. On the positive side, as previously mentioned, these programs make

Table 11.2. Misinformation and Cable News Viewers, 2010

Viewers	% of daily news viewers who are misinformed on each statement
Most economists agree the stimulus had little to no effect on creating jobs	
Fox News	91%
MSNBC	64%
Obama's health care law will increase the deficit	
Fox News	72%
MSNBC	45%
Obama's stimulus did not include tax cuts	
Fox News	63%
MSNBC	34%
It is unclear Obama was born in the U.S.	
Fox News	63%
MSNBC	39%
The 2008 bank bailout was passed under Obama presidency	
Fox News	47%
MSNBC	38%

Source: Clay Ramsay, Steven Kull, Ethan Lewis, and Stefan Subias, "Misinformation and the 2010 Election," *Worldpublicopinion.org*, December 10, 2010, http://drum.lib.umd.edu/bitstream/handle/1903/11375/Misinformation_Dec10_rpt.pdf

traditionally apathetic audiences more interested in political issues. Furthermore, consumption of soft news is associated with developing critical thinking skills, as viewers of these programs are more likely to be critical of leaders from both political parties and to look critically at U.S. elections and mass media, rather than simply holding blind faith in institutions that are driven by a pro-corporate agenda. Finally, looking at both the Colbert and Stewart programs, one finds that they exercise[d] no demobilizing effect on voting. More specifically, Colbert and Stewart viewers are/were no less likely to vote compared to non-viewers.[38]

What about political knowledge among soft news consumers? Existing surveys speak highly of these viewers. A 2012 *Pew* poll found Colbert and Stewart viewers were highly educated, with a plurality (39–45 percent) holding a four-year college degree or better, and a majority (73–74 percent) having at least some college education.[39] Sixty-one percent of both Stewart and Colbert viewers correctly answered three or four of the civic awareness questions that *Pew* questioned news consumers on, covering knowledge of government, the economy, and foreign leaders.[40] This political knowledge is vital to ensuring that young Americans are able to develop informed opinions—a prerequisite for any democracy.

But what about concerns that soft news viewers are using these programs as an alternative to actual news and walling themselves off in a liberal echo chamber? If soft news viewers are failing to seek out alternative sources of information, they may not be equipped to understand political issues or events or consider different points of view. A 2012 *Pew* survey found that soft news viewers were less likely to watch *Fox News*, and more likely to listen to *NPR*, watch *MSNBC* and *CNN*, and read the *New York Times*.[41] These findings suggest the concern that young Americans are using comedy programs as an alternative to following news is unfounded. There was no evidence, except in the case of *Fox News*, that viewing soft news was associated with being less likely to consume various news outlets. However, these findings also suggest soft news viewers were more likely to gravitate to other liberal content. Clearly, the echo chamber effect is also operating with regard to young, liberal soft news viewers. Simply put, soft news viewers are missing competing political perspectives by tuning out right-wing media sources. Familiarity with competing points of view is necessary if one is to be well-informed about politics.

Who Profits from a Changing Media Landscape?

Old Media, New Media, and Depoliticization

The modern hybrid system has transformed the way Americans engage in media. Media consumption is increasingly fragmented, as the number of channels and consumer choices has proliferated beyond anything seen in previous decades.

With the rise of cable, satellite television, online services such as Netflix, Hulu, YouTube, and On Demand television, consumers are split between more electronic programing than at any time in history. Consumers no doubt appreciate all the new choices, but fragmentation has also contributed to a decline in attention to the news.[42] In past decades, it was difficult for Americans to avoid the news with the limited media channels available. If someone watched television during primetime in the 1950s or 1960s, they were going to be exposed to the news.

The limited-choice media of the past is now gone, due to the proliferation of cable, online media, and streaming services. Those with little interest in politics can now entirely avoid it due to countless media options and services that focus on entertainment programming. The new media system allows consumers to personalize their viewing choices and to avoid programming seen as disagreeable or uninteresting. These developments are advantageous to corporate media from a profit perspective, since fragmentation allows advertisers to more effectively target products to audiences and demographic groups in ways that were previously impossible. Fragmentation serves the corporate class by more effectively selling consumer products and enriching advertising firms and other corporations, but it is harmful to civic political education. Large numbers of people flock away from politics and news, pursuing a narrow entertainment and consumer-oriented agenda. Fragmentation is great for business, but lousy for democracy.

Recent survey data make clear the gravity of the decline in political attentiveness in the era of fragmentation. Many traditional news organizations are in decline. From the early 1990s through the early 2010s, consumption of "old media," including newspapers, news radio, and broadcast news, fell significantly.[43] The percent of Americans watching television news declined from 68 percent to 55 percent.[44] Broadcast programs have not recovered either, with audiences remaining stagnant from the late-2000s through the mid-2010s.[45] Newspaper readership also decreased from 56 percent to 29 percent of Americans from the 1990s onward.[46] In every year but one between 2003 and 2014, total U.S. newspaper readership and circulation decreased.[47] Radio news listeners declined from 54 percent of Americans to 33 percent of the public from the early 1990s through early 2010s. NPR listeners have remained relatively constant from 2005 through 2014, but the demographic for talk radio is overwhelmingly older and male, and will experience significant decline in coming years as many listeners pass away.[48]

While old media are in decline, there is some growth in "new media" outlets such as online and cable news. Online news consumption increased from 24 percent of Americans in the early 2000s to 39 percent by 2012.[49] Cable news consumption grew significantly, with viewership of CNN, Fox News, and MSNBC more than doubling between 2001 and 2010.[50] From the late 2000s through mid-

2010s, cable viewership remained steady, averaging 3 million primetime viewers between *CNN*, *MSNBC*, and *Fox News*.[51]

While old media declined, and new media grew, overall news consumption has fallen.[52] The percent of Americans 65 and over reading a daily newspaper decreased from three-quarters in the early 1960s to 60 percent in 2010; readership declined from three-quarters to 40 percent for those 30 to 44 years old, and from three-quarters to 50 percent for those 45 to 64. For individuals aged 18 to 29, more than 75 percent read a newspaper in the early 1960s, but just one-third did so in the early 2010s.[53] These statistics suggest the largest decline in news attentiveness is among young Americans, who are less likely in modern times to follow the news than young Americans in decades past. This conclusion is undeniable in light of *Pew* data concluding that, while the average 18- to 29-year-old spent 56 minutes per day with the news in 1994, it was just 45 minutes in 2012, a reduction of 20 percentage points in two decades.[54]

Survey data from the National Endowment for the Arts also finds that youth readership has declined, with the number of Americans who read for pleasure falling by ten percentage points from 1984 to 2004.[55] These changes mean a growing number of young Americans are ignorant to literature, popular writings, and politics. Ignorance and apathy have become defining traits of American culture. The problem of being ignorant to ignorance is acute: many citizens are unaware of their ignorance, or of how problematic ignorance is for an informed citizenry and for democracy. If people do not pay attention to what is happening around them, they will struggle to form educated opinions about political issues. Without adequate knowledge of politics, citizens cannot hold political leaders accountable. Although most Americans may share a general sense that politics is the province of the upper-class and business elites, most do not hold a nuanced understanding of the political process or how parties operate, and struggle to cast informed votes in an era of mass-media-induced political illiteracy.

Even if young Americans are increasingly following news online and through social media, the decline of old media consumption endangers Americans' ability to be informed. Broadcast television networks and newspapers historically bear primary responsibility for reporting. Cable primetime programs and talk radio are geared toward commentary, not news. Political blogs are growing in popularity, but much of their content is repackaged from traditional news gathering old media.[56] If Americans struggle to gain access to quality reporting due to declining old media, numerous issues emerge: 1. Who will fund reporting in the future? and, 2. How will Americans become informed? Media corporations are not preoccupied with how to better inform the public, as their focus is on increasing profits. But in pursuing a profit-based agenda, these corporations indirectly contribute to the watering down of American political discourse through their diversion of the mass public toward entertainment and away from the news.

Although the focus on mass entertainment is a successful business strategy, it has contributed to the growing troubles of the corporate model of political reporting. In earlier decades, when many Americans read print newspapers, large numbers of advertisers funded the news. But with the massive decline of newspaper readers, advertisers flocked in mass away from the industry. According to the Newspaper Association of America, while print advertising revenues totaled more than $45 billion in 2003, they decreased to $19.9 billion by 2014, a whopping 56 percent decline.[57] The collapse of newspaper advertising was not accompanied by a significant enough growth in online advertising newspaper revenues to compensate for the loss. Online revenues barely increased from 2003 to 2014, since the volume of online advertising revenues is far lower than that existing in newspapers.[58] The average newspaper runs hundreds of ads, but the average number of ads a reader is exposed to in an online news story is small. With newspapers limiting free access to online stories, this restricts the number of ads to which newsreaders are exposed.

The decline of newspaper readership translates into a massive decline in professional journalism. The number of U.S. reporters declined by 40 percent from 2003 to 2015.[59] The decline in newspaper readership, coupled with newspapers' pursuit of greater profits, meant the mass closure of foreign news bureaus. According to the *American Journalism Review*, 18 newspapers closed their foreign news bureaus from 1998 to 2010. "Many other papers and chains reduced their coterie of foreign correspondents . . . an untold number of regional and local newspapers have dramatically decreased the amount of foreign news they publish. Television networks, meanwhile, slashed the time they devote to foreign news and narrowed their focus largely to war zones . . . The 'big four' national newspapers—the *Wall Street Journal*, *The New York Times*, *The Washington Post*, and the *Los Angeles Times*—all continue to have vibrant foreign reports, though each has closed some foreign bureaus in recent years."[60]

The unfolding crisis of the news means that investigative journalism is increasingly in danger. Fewer dollars for reporting means that investigative reporters and units see significant decline. *Investigative Reporters and Editors* (IRE) reports that membership in their organization declined by a third, from 5,391 in 2003 to 3,695 in 2009. Furthermore, IRE reports, applications for Pulitzer reporting prizes also fell by more than 40 percent for various investigative rewards.[61] Media corporations improve their bottom lines by cutting down on investigative journalism, but this trend is also a threat to an informed citizenry.

Some intellectuals argue that if corporations are more interested in entertainment and profits than in sustaining quality reporting, we should replace a declining corporate media with nonprofit journalism, provided via taxpayer dollars, and as a public service.[62] The idea of taxpayer-funded journalism may raise suspicion that government would try to pervert content to serve official agendas. This concern is warranted, but perhaps exaggerated considering all the examples of taxpayer-funded journalism across the world in which reporters remain independent of formal government censorship. Some examples include: the *Canadian Broadcasting Corporation*, *PBS*, and *NPR* in the *U.S.*, and the *British Broadcasting Corporation*. Furthermore, with strong First Amendment protections, journalists benefit from a powerful weapon to protect themselves against formal government censorship. On the other hand, a vigorous public media system would require constant public vigilance, as government could seek to cut funding for this system to punish reporters for unflattering coverage, without formally censoring journalists.

If an advertiser-funded news system is no longer viable, then Americans need to discuss what kind of system should replace it. Should for-profit newspapers be regularly bailed out by taxpayers? Such a practice seems unsustainable, and would be unpopular with the public. Another alternative is to do nothing and witness the rise of mass ignorance to a level beyond what has already occurred, as media outlets continue to serve the corporate class by diverting public attention away from the news and toward mass advertising and consumerism. This could happen if newspapers collapse, but are not replaced by a viable alternative news option. With diversionary, apolitical entertainment becoming even more prominent than is already the case, American ignorance will grow to unparalleled heights.

A public media system could help reduce public political apathy, if such a system was well-funded and supported by taxpayers. This system will be opposed by media corporations, which seek to maintain their monopoly control over information, despite sharing less and less interest in informing the public about political issues. It will also be opposed by upper-class elites more generally, who view the media, like other societal institutions, as existing primarily for private profit rather than for the public good. And the government is unlikely to establish a viable public media system without mass pressure and strong public support.

Theories of Media Bias

What interests do the media serve? Are they biased against conservatives, brainwashing the public by bombarding us with liberal views? Or do journalists do an admirable job of covering a multitude of viewpoints, providing a "pluralistic" public forum for many different political voices in society? Are journalists biased in favor of government, disseminating official propaganda and fearmongering in an effort to pacify the public? What about a broader pro-business, corporate bias? All of these questions are addressed below.

Americans agree that the media are biased. In 1999, 55 percent of Americans held a "great deal" or "fair amount" of "trust and confidence" in the media "when it comes to reporting the news fully," but the number fell to 32 percent by 2016.[63] Two-thirds of Americans in 2011 felt news stories were "often inaccurate," an increase from a third of the public in 1985.[64] Similarly, 74 percent of Americans felt the media "favor one side" when covering the news, compared to 53 percent in 1985.[65] These numbers suggest significant distrust. The distrust is based on two understandings of bias, one critical of the media for disseminating "one-sided" news content, the other suggesting media distort reality by painting "inaccurate" pictures of the world.

The Liberal Media?

Conservative and Republican officials complain about liberal journalists and their alleged efforts to distort the news in favor of Democratic political elites.[66] Conservatives make numerous claims: 1. Reporters are more likely to identify in surveys with the Democratic Party and vote for Democrats over Republicans; 2. Reporters are more likely to hail from liberal north central and northeastern states; 3. Reporters express liberal attitudes in surveys on issues like abortion.[67] These personal biases are thought to impact how journalists report news.

Little scholarly evidence exists to validate claims of liberal media bias. Four major problems with the theory are identifiable. First, reporters are trained in journalism schools to remove their personal partisan views from stories. In major newspapers, journalists who report the news do not openly express their partisan preferences. One will *never* see a journalist saying "I believe this" or "I believe that" regarding political matters. Instead, reporters are trained to cover the news by incorporating and quoting the views of others. A second problem is that, while surveys suggest reporters are liberal on various social issues, they are conservative on economic issues. One survey of reporters found that, although journalists were 21 percentage points more likely to say they were "left" on social issues, they were eight percentage points more likely to say they were "right" on economic issues. Journalists were to the right of the public on free trade, on reducing regulations on corporations, with regard to privatizing Social Security and Medicare, and on environmental conservation.[68] If one takes liberal bias claims at face value, and we assume that journalists' personal biases *do* influence their reporting, the above findings cannot possibly demonstrate a consistent liberal bias. For social issues, reporters would be more liberal, but they would also be more conservative on economic issues.

A third problem with the liberal media claim is that the majority of scholarly studies fail to find evidence of such a bias. One meta-study from the *Journal of Communication*, which summarized the results of nearly 60 academic studies on reporting of politics and elections, concluded there was scarce evidence of liberal bias in the news.[69] Few academic studies even allege a liberal media bias; most of these complaints come from political officials, media pundits, and the public.[70] The lack of support for the liberal media theory is problematic for those embracing an evidence-based approach to understanding the social world.

A fourth and final problem with the liberal media claim is that we see little evidence of it when looking at segments of the media that *are* openly biased. For example, on talk radio and cable news, pundits openly express their views, and the most dominant personalities are right-wing, and generally quite favorable to corporate and upper-class interests. *Fox News* is far and away the most watched cable channel. More than 90 percent of talk radio hosts are conservative, while just nine percent are liberal. The high-profile hosts are right-wing, including Rush Limbaugh, Sean Hannity, Glenn Beck, Michael Savage, and Mark Levin.[71]

If most scholars reject the liberal media theory, why is it so popular? A 2014 *Pew* survey found that 44 percent of Americans thought the media were "too liberal," while 34 percent said they were "just about right" in their reporting, and 19 percent said they were "too conservative."[72] A simple explanation for this is that many Americans see what they want to see concerning bias, independent of the evidence. Partisan identification is a significant predictor of opinions regarding media bias: Republicans are more likely to think the media are biased in favor of liberals, while Democrats are more likely to reject this claim.[73] This phenomenon is so well-studied that it has a name—the "hostile media effect."[74] Put simply, people interpret news content as biased against their own personal beliefs, preferring to focus mainly on the parts of news coverage that they find objectionable.[75]

Despite lacking evidence, perceptions of liberal media bias are perpetuated by Republican officials and pundits. Rush Limbaugh, Sean Hannity, and others regularly complain to their audiences about liberal media bias.[76] Audiences for these programs are heavily conservative and already open to Limbaugh's and Hannity's claims, so it is not surprising that perceptions of bias are higher among conservatives. Communication research suggests that discussions of bias drive perceptions of bias, meaning individuals are socially conditioned to accept liberal bias claims.[77]

In the era of Trump, critics—including the president—have renewed claims of liberal media bias, charging journalists with pushing "fake news" that undermines the president. The relationship between the president and the media was tense when Trump took office. But journalists were not the only ones to distance themselves from, or criticize Trump. He was widely distrusted by much of the Republican Party establishment, by many right-wing corporate donors, by the Democratic Party, and by much of the public. To single out journalists for criticizing Trump is to ignore a broader, bipartisan political culture, including Republican officials, which denigrated Trump as a deviant who lies outside the bounds of respectable behavior and acceptable politics. It also means ignoring the reality that Trump received far more news coverage than other 2016 election candidates, as media corporations saturated the news with stories on Trump due to the large ratings and profits he brought news outlets.[78] A corporate bias in favor of larger audiences and greater advertising revenues meant that Trump remained a media darling throughout the 2016 election season.[79]

Bad News Bias

Some scholars argue that, rather than exuding a liberal bias, journalists are attracted to negative, sensationalistic, even tabloid-style news, in their pursuit of ratings and profits. Of particular note are crime stories and sex-scandals involving political officials. Journalists are fixated on crime, as the famous saying "if it bleeds, it leads" suggests. And the data reinforces this old adage, with media coverage of crime well outpacing actual crime rates. For example, television and newspaper coverage of crime increased by 473 percent between 1990 and 1998, despite the homicide rate declining by 33 percent in that same period.[80] Media coverage of crime typically intensifies in periods when political officials pay greater attention to crime.[81] Heavy crime coverage continued in the 2000s, and local news across the country made crime stories the most heavily covered, along with traffic and weather. This trend continued in the 2010s, with crime stories one of the most covered issues in local news alongside traffic and weather, and ahead of politics, science, sports, human interest pieces, accidents, business stories, foreign affairs, and health issues.[82]

Scholars also note that journalists fell in line behind political officials who sought to stoke fear of crime in order to justify the "War on Drugs."[83] Public support was "cultivated" for mass arrests that disproportionately targeted minority poor neighborhoods, despite comparable drug use among blacks, Hispanics, and whites. But the journalistic fixation on bad news came with a price. Individuals who paid greater attention to the news were more likely to be fearful of crime, to over-estimate the frequency of crime, and to be less trusting of others.[84] These findings are documented in national surveys measuring public television consumption and opinions of crime, and in experimental studies, which show how exposure to violent television content produces growing fear of others.[85] Journalists have remained in the good graces of officials by fixating on the "War on Drugs," and brought in extra ratings, thereby satisfying the corporate advertiser interests, by over-emphasizing crime stories. But this fixation on violence and drugs has also produced a population that is more paranoid and alienated than in the past.

Bad news also manifests itself through journalists' fixation on tabloid-style sex scandals involving government officials. Stories about extra-marital affairs receive sustained media attention, and draw in news audiences, in the process pleasing advertising interests. These stories were beyond the pale decades ago. For example, reporters did not saturate audiences with information about President John F. Kennedy's affairs, despite knowing they were occurring.[86] Journalistic standards and practices changed dramatically by the 1990s, when President Bill Clinton's affair with Monica Lewinsky received mass attention in the news. Clinton's affair became a generation-defining event, even if many thought it was over-covered. In January 1998, 72 percent of Americans thought that coverage of the Clinton scandal was "too much"; less than a quarter said the coverage was "the right amount" and only 4 percent thought the coverage was "too little."[87] Tabloid-style coverage of sex scandals continued under Trump, as related to allegations that the president had an affair with former porn star "Stormy Daniels." This story received heavy attention in the news during Trump's time in office. The obsession with sex scandals and politics is not surprising considering so many news viewers tune into these stories. So long as advertising revenues grow, advertisers are satisfied, and as long as the corporate class is enriched via sustained mass consumerism, tabloid crime and sex stories will always have a place in the news.

Pro-Government Bias

Much of the scholarship on politics and media concludes that reporters demonstrate a bias in favor of government officials, and in favor of a bipartisan neoliberal system that privileges corporate and business interests. Federal officials are highly effective in driving news narratives, in influencing what kinds of issues the public thinks about, and in framing politics in ways that are favorable to the major parties.[88]

Noam Chomsky and Edward Herman depict the media as lapdogs of government. They offer a "propaganda model," claiming that reporters limit news content by fixating on official views at the expense of non-official perspectives.[89] Propaganda as practiced in the U.S. media is different from that practiced in authoritarian societies. In countries like Iran, Russia, and Saudi Arabia, government formally controls news outlets such as *Press TV*, *Russia Today*, and *Al Arabiya*. Unlike these countries, U.S. journalists have legal freedom under the First Amendment to report political issues without government interference. Despite this freedom, reporters voluntarily surrender their independence to political leaders, allowing the latter to (informally) drive news narratives. Voluntary deference to the state is not the same as formal government censorship, but the outcome of both is the same in terms of officials dominating news content. While indirect, the pro-government bias translates into a pro-corporate bias, since Democrats and Republicans increasingly favor pro-corporate and upper-class viewpoints in the neoliberal era.

Why would journalists allow themselves to be used by government? Part of the answer lies in how they are trained. Journalists pride themselves in being objective, meaning they do not explicitly include their partisan opinions in stories. This approach to reporting has its advantages, in that many Americans prefer not to be preached to by those providing them information. But there are also dangers. If journalism is defined by uncritically transmitting official views, to challenge officials is to risk losing access to governmental sources, which means losing the ability to do one's job.[90] Journalists uncritically disseminate official misinformation, in the process limiting the views expressed in the news to those of political elites, while marginalizing citizens and non-official voices. These practices are problematic considering that most Americans distrust the political system and feel that it serves wealthy, upper-class individuals instead of the masses. When journalists treat the words of these political officials as the final say on political matters, it threatens to create a rift between political and media elites and the general public.

Scholarly studies documenting a pro-government media bias are numerous. Studies from the 1970s through the 2000s showed that government officials comprised three-quarters or more of sources appearing in political news.[91] A case study helps elaborate on the official source bias in the news, specifically news coverage prior to the 2003 U.S. war against Iraq. In late 2002 and early 2003, the Bush administration was preparing to invade Iraq. President George W. Bush embarked on a sustained campaign, traveling across the country and delivering numerous speeches, claiming: 1. Iraq possessed chemical, biological, and possibly even nuclear weapons; 2. Iraq possessed ties to al Qaeda; and 3. This supposed alliance represented an imminent threat, with al Qaeda potentially able to use WMDs on U.S. soil. Democratic officials did little to nothing to challenge any of these talking points.

Most Americans were understandably scared after the September 11 attacks, and willing to believe most anything their president told them if they thought it would keep them safe. Furthermore, reporters did a poor job of questioning Bush's pro-war arguments. There was a strong pro-government bias in the news. Journalists rarely asked whether the president's claims were accurate.[92] The coverage was one-sided and distorted. Iraq never had ties to al Qaeda, and Iraq possessed no WMDs prior to the 2003 invasion, but these points were seldom conveyed in the news.[93] Furthermore, numerous international weapons inspectors, who had disarmed Iraq of its WMDs in the 1990s, raised questions about whether Iraq was really a threat to the U.S., but these figures were rarely consulted by journalists.[94]

If the media fail to explore views outside of those embraced by officialdom, citizens will struggle to gain access to non-elite perspectives. And recent research leaves little doubt that official viewpoints dominate the news. For example, one study concludes that the structure of government influences what kinds of biases appear in the news. Whenever Democrats control the White House and Congress, reporters allow Democrats to dominate news sourcing. When Republicans control the White House and Congress, reporters are biased in favor of Republicans. And when both parties share control of government, coverage is split, favoring neither party. In short, the structure of government determines how reporters cover the news.

A pro-government media bias also serves the interests of the corporate class. Reporters' over-reliance on official sources complements the financial bottom line of news organizations. Routine access to official sources means that journalists can consistently produce news stories around "news beats" located at the White House and on Capitol Hill. The consistent production of news that legitimates the political status quo aids news outlets in maintaining a stable flow of advertising profits.[95] In short, the pro-government bias is good for business.

A second way that the official source bias overlaps with profit interests is the tabloidization of news via the bad news bias. News producers seek to draw in new audiences, thereby expanding their audience size and profits from advertising, by tailoring politics to a carnivalesque presentation of information. Nowhere is this more apparent than in journalists' fixation on conflictual reporting of Donald Trump. During the 2016 primary season, reporters across U.S. media outlets provided Trump significantly more coverage than other Democratic or Republican candidates, understanding that his perverse and incendiary comments would draw in shocked and outraged audiences. Trump was able to dominate the news because his brand of tabloid politics was profitable to media outlets. After his election, around-the-clock coverage of Trump's malicious, spiteful, and propagandistic attacks on critics, minority groups, and the press aided news outlets in cultivating viewers, thereby increasing advertising revenues and profits.

Support for the tabloidization of the news in pursuit of profits was best articulated by CBS President Les Moonves, who celebrated Trump's rise to national prominence. Moonves reflected about the primary season: "Man, who could have expected the ride we're all having right now . . . The money's rolling in and this is fun . . . I've never seen anything like this, and this is going to be a very good year for us. Sorry. It's a terrible thing to say, but bring it on,

Donald. Keep going . . . I'm just saying for us, economically, Donald Trump's place in this election is a good thing."[96] Tabloidization of politics is lamented by intellectuals who deplore the decline of American discourse, but incendiary, bigoted, and Jerry Springeresque rhetoric is deemed more profitable to media corporations' financial bottom line, and serves advertisers well.[97]

Trump's Attacks on the Media

The relationship between the press and the Trump administration deteriorated quickly after the 2016 election. Trump's former press secretary, Sean Spicer, actively berated journalists in his first press conference, refusing to take questions, and lambasting reporters for supposedly underestimating the size of the crowd attending Trump's inauguration on the National Mall.[98] Non-partisan fact checkers dismissed Spicer's claims as false due to photographic evidence that Trump's audience was smaller than Obama's 2009 inauguration crowd.[99] The manufactured inauguration controversy came to symbolize a Trump presidency that routinely provided false information to the press and the public. The administration quickly gained infamy, after White House counselor Kellyanne Conway asserted on NBC's *Meet the Press* with Chuck Todd that "alternative facts" were just as good as real ones, in response to the inauguration dispute.[100]

It is ironic that Trump, despite his contempt for facts, displayed such a concern with alleged journalistic dishonesty.[101] But what lesson did the battle between the press and Trump offer the nation regarding the nature of media-government relations? Did the fiasco demonstrate media independence from government? Did it suggest the media have a liberal bias? I answer both questions with a "no," elaborating below.

Reporters routinely challenged the Trump administration's political messages after he took office. *The New York Times* featured numerous stories suggesting the Trump administration lied, and that Trump offered "inaccurate" and "false" claims on various issues, while *CNN* and *The Washington Post*, made similar claims.[102] *The Washington Post* concluded that, in his first month in office, Trump "averaged four falsehoods or misleading statements a day." There wasn't "a single day of Trump's presidency in which he has said nothing false or misleading."[103]

The dispute between journalists and Trump centered on numerous issues. To name a few, reporters questioned Trump on inaugural crowd sizes, for making false claims about voter fraud in the 2016 election, for referring to numerous nonexistent terror attacks in Atlanta, Georgia, Bowling Green, Kentucky, and Sweden, for erroneously claiming the media invented the rift between his administration and intelligence agencies over Russia's alleged role in the 2016 election, for falsely stating the media do not report on violent terror attacks, for inaccurately asserting that the violent crime rate in 2017 reached a record high for the last half-century, and for erroneously claiming that Democratic legislation required him to break up undocumented children and parents when being detained and processed for deportation.[104]

Reporters' conflicts with Trump were real, but the emphasis on administrative-press infighting also misses a number of important points. First, Trump and his presidency were ultimately media creations. It is unlikely that the reality-TV star would have been as successful as he was in the primary if it were not for disproportionate attention directed toward his campaign from across the media.[105] Media corporations made the Trump political phenomenon possible by their pursuit of profits and in service of advertisers gravitating toward tabloid media content. Journalists did shift toward criticizing Trump's candidacy late in the 2016 election cycle, but they also played an integral role in his victory over competing Republican primary candidates. Second, opposition to Trump did not stem from a longstanding liberal bias on the part of reporters against Republicans. As previously discussed, there is little scholarly evidence of a liberal bias in the news across American presidencies. But Trump is seen as far outside the "mainstream" of American political culture. Political spin, deception, and lies have long been a part of official U.S. politics and governmental communication. But no president was ever so brazen or shameless in pushing obviously false claims as Trump.

Reporters clearly took issue with the Trump administration's clumsy propaganda efforts. Their desire to attract larger audiences and advertising profits ran directly contrary to reporters' concern with retaining credibility with news consumers. Without a consistent effort on the part of journalists to challenge Trump's misinformation, there would be little reason for news audiences to consume propaganda masquerading as news. To not challenge fictitious terror attacks, false statistics about crime rates, and bogus claims about voter fraud would be a serious risk to reporters' and various news outlets' reputations. To allow obvious falsehood after falsehood to go unchallenged meant reporters would be abandoning even a minimal commitment to accuracy in reporting. Trump's deceptions operated on a different level than previous official misinformation campaigns, the latter of which were difficult to spotlight without serious investigation. George W. Bush's claims about Iraqi WMDs were difficult for reporters to authoritatively debunk sitting in the White House press room. Democrats' promise that Obamacare would not interfere with preexisting insurance plans was difficult to challenge without watching the implementation of the bill play out in real time. In contrast, Trump's consistently false claims were much easier to identify. Citizens without any journalistic training could recognize them via simple Google searches or visits to non-partisan fact-checking websites. For reporters to uncritically disseminate these falsehoods would threaten what little trust remained between them and the general public.

Finally, the blatant condescension and contempt with which the Trump administration treated journalists meant that a combative relationship was inevitable. Routine insults directed at reporters had a polarizing effect, pushing reporters to do even more fact checking, and identifying an even larger number of administration falsehoods and lies. This conflicted relationship reached a fever pitch when Trump began blacklisting reporters from White House access for critical news coverage, as occurred with reporters from *CNN*, *The New York Times*, the *Los Angeles Times*, and *Politico* in the first month of Trump's presidency. *CNN* was prohibited from even asking Trump questions after they ran a report discussing claims that the Russian government held a dossier including compromising information about Trump. Within just weeks, *The New York Times*, *CNN*, the *Los Angeles Times*, and *Politico* reporters were also prohibited from attending White House press briefings, prompting a boycott of these meetings from the *Associated Press* and *Time* magazine.[106] Although media corporations were profiting in a big way from the tabloid-style coverage of the Trump administration's many falsehoods and shenanigans, the relationship between the press and the president had also become abusive, with journalists regularly exposed to daily attacks and diatribes by the president and his staff. The abuse reached new heights under administration spokespersons like Sarah Huckabee Sanders, who became infamous for her nasty personal attacks on reporters who asked her critical questions on the administration's immigration policies.[107]

Presidential-press relations worsened once Trump took office. But the growing conflict did not suggest that reporters were at war with the political establishment so much as with Trump himself. Journalists' longstanding embrace of bipartisan dominance of the news meant that an official source bias in the news was still in effect. Reporters merely came together to challenge a president who was widely seen by both parties (especially during the 2016 campaign) as a political embarrassment. Government officials have always relied on one-sided rhetoric and spin, but nothing as blatantly contemptuous as the positions expressed by Trump.

A Corporate Class Bias

Extensive evidence suggests that pro-corporate and pro-advertiser biases pervade the mass media. Ben Bagdikian, a former editor of the *Washington Post* and Dean at the University of California, Berkley, has long argued that the media exhibit pro-corporate biases, since most media are owned by for-profit corporations. In *The Media Monopoly*, Bagdikian wrote in the 1980s about how a few dozen corporations controlled most of what Americans read, heard, and saw. Updating the book in the 2000s, he found a half-dozen to a dozen corporations controlled most of the U.S. media.

Bagdikian's concern with corporate media bias is reinforced in other academic studies. One *Pew* survey finds that a third of journalists avoid stories they feel could damage advertisers.[108] Another study finds 80 percent of reporters feel pressure from advertisers is a growing problem; 45 percent are aware of instances when news content was "compromised" by advertisers.[109] The prevalence of censorship against views critical of advertisers threatens to deprive the public of vital information provided via investigative journalism. When corporations pressure journalists to ignore corporate illegality or wrongdoing, the public is kept in the dark, and discourse is hindered in the name of protecting the interests of the corporate class.

Political Pacification via Mass Consumption

Censorship of the news is a common problem. But a more encompassing form of pro-business bias is the quest to sell consumerism to the public as fundamental to their way of life. This bias pervades everything the media do. And this bias toward mass advertising has existed for a century. The rise of modern advertising is relevant to the discussion of politics and the media because of how consumerism increasingly diverts public attention from important political issues. A discussion of mass consumerism is not simply a sociological issue, but also a political one. In a fragmented media landscape, fewer Americans pay attention to the news, instead building their identities through consumer culture. A consumer identity is fundamentally different from alternative identities, such as defining oneself through interactions within one's community, or as related to non-consumer activities such as protests, community teach-ins and talks, and volunteering.

Most Americans reflexively accept mass consumerism. Over the years of my life, seldom have I heard family, friends, students, or acquaintances argue that mass consumerism is an abnormal or harmful phenomenon. But contrary to popular opinion, mass consumerism is quite unnatural. It never existed in the history of humanity before the last hundred years. Prior to the twentieth century, advertising existed in the U.S., but products were typically marketed for function, rather than social status. Items should be purchased, advertisers claimed, because they were durable and of high quality.[110] All of this changed by the early twentieth century, when mass consumerism emerged as a means of enriching the corporate class. This is when the idea of consumption as a symbol of personal status, lifestyle, and identity took root. Advertisers understood that most Americans did *not* view consumerism as a personal statement about their lifestyle, personality, or self-worth, as consumer identities were not naturally accepted by most citizens in the late nineteenth century.[111] To this day, advertisers understand mass consumerism is not inevitable or a naturally occurring phenomenon, as recognized by the fact that they spend hundreds of billions on advertising annually to create and sustain consumer demand for products.

Advertising is necessary to *create* wants and desires. Advertising is intended to normalize a worldview in which citizens define their well-being via consumption of products and services. Consumerism is based on the false notion that consumption empowers the masses. Citizens feel empowered in the short term after buying a new car, computer, home, clothing, or other items, because these items are signs of social status. But since consumer identities depend on the consumption process, citizens must *continue* to consume day after day to feel "empowered." In reality, this process creates *insecurity* and *disempowerment* since people must continue purchasing to feel fulfilled. The consumption process thrives by making Americans dependent on a corporate class that creates ads and mass-produces the products consumed. PR firms encourage the creation of consumer identities that emphasize self-centered, parochial, and private notions of citizenship running contrary to identities based on communal solidarity.

The classic documentary, *Century of the Self*, traces out the history of modern advertising and public relations, identifying Edward Bernays as a key figure in its development. Bernays, the father of modern public relations, helped solidify mass consumerism as a mainstream phenomenon in the post-World War I period. Public relations is central to the advertising industry, as it is vital in the branding of consumer products, in addition to selling products through manipulation of human needs and emotions. A psychologist and the nephew of Sigmund Freud, Bernays gained notoriety for his work in manipulating consumer emotions. He drew on his uncle's insights regarding how the subconscious mind and primitive human impulses influence human behavior. Bernays believed that, if basic human needs, impulses, and emotions could be effectively channeled, they could be used to construct consumer identities. By associating products with individual needs, people would believe they needed a product, even if they really only desired it. Bernays, with the help of countless others, succeeded in convincing Americans that impulse purchases and other forms of consumption fulfilled human needs, rather than wants. To this day, most consumption is driven by lifestyle concerns and efforts to project status. Few Americans wait until their car is no longer drivable before purchasing a new one. The same goes for clothes, computers, cell phones, and other electronics, which are replaced at far quicker rates than need be if such items existed purely for utility. Clothes, for example, are widely seen as a status symbol, "telling you something" about the personality and worth of the person wearing them.[112]

Bernays understood that selling mass consumerism was all about the corporate class manipulating Americans into buying things they otherwise would not purchase. In his book *Propaganda*, Bernays explained that selling goods was not simply about selling the item itself, but about selling an entire way of life.[113] Advertising and consumerism are sold from the top down, from advertisers and public relations executives to the public, and this requires manipulation. This much was clear from *Propaganda*, specifically Bernays's reference to the "invisible hand" in society of the political and business classes—those secretly working the public like a puppeteer manipulates a marionette.[114]

Manipulation of individuals' subconscious impulses, needs, and emotions, was vital to Bernays's project. Of note was Bernays's effort in the 1920s to sell cigarettes to young women, despite cigarette consumption being seen as a trashy, lower-class activity. Bernays understood that cigarettes could be sold to women by appealing subconsciously to basic needs such as sexuality, while also tying smoking to the woman's empowerment movement. Bernays paid attractive debutantes in the New York City Easter parade to smoke cigarettes, advertising them as their "torches of freedom."[115] Supposedly, if women smoked cigarettes, against established social convention, it demonstrated their commitment to independence and their desire to achieve equality with men. Bernays also pioneered an advertising campaign to convince women that cigarettes would make you sexually desirable by "keep[ing] you thin."[116] Women could reach for a cigarette, rather than candy or sweets, to stay slim and attract men.

The campaign to market cigarettes to women as a sign of their sexuality and independence was a classic example of manipulation. Women were encouraged to consume a cancerous substance, in the process making tobacco corporations fabulously wealthy. Other examples of manipulation of mass consciousness by the PR industry took root in later years, as seen in the effort to market diamonds to women as a sign of spousal love and commitment. This campaign was led by the De Beers Corporation, which held the dominant stake in the diamond industry from the late-nineteenth century onward. De Beers spent millions after World War II selling American women on the idea that their self-worth and their spouse's love were measured by the cost of their engagement rings. As *The Atlantic* magazine recounts: "De Beers proved to be the most successful cartel arrangement in the annals of modern commerce. While other commodities, such as gold, silver, copper, rubber, and grains, fluctuated wildly in response to economic conditions, diamonds have continued, with few exceptions, to advance upward in price every year since the Depression." The notion that diamonds symbolize love emerged in the 1940s, when the De Beers corporation hired the prominent advertising firm, N. W. Ayer, to market diamonds to women.[117]

N. W. Ayer was tasked with reversing the decline in diamond sales in the U.S. that occurred during the Great Depression. As *The Atlantic* notes, N. W. Ayer "stressed the need to strengthen the association in the public's mind between diamonds and romance. Since 'young men buy over 90 percent of all engagement rings,' it would be crucial to inculcate in them the idea that diamonds were a gift of love: the larger and finer the diamond, the greater the expression of love. Women had to be encouraged to view diamonds as an integral part of any romantic courtship."[118]

De Beers and N. W. Ayer constructed a consumer culture in which diamonds were tied to marriage and love. Ayer advertising campaigns and popular films convinced American women that "Diamonds are a girl's best friend," and that "Diamonds are forever" representative of a male's love toward his wife. Ayer's 1947 strategic planning document recognized: "we are dealing with a problem of mass psychology. We seek to . . . strengthen the tradition of the diamond engagement ring—to make it a psychological *necessity* capable of competing successfully at the retail level with utility goods and services."[119] Diamonds became a symbol of how "conspicuous consumption" had taken over American society. Diamonds are expensive, and represent a sign of economic status for the women wearing them. Women of all economic stripes come to believe that they can emulate upper-class living by wearing expensive diamonds. The association between diamonds and upper-class status was explicitly articulated by Ayer, which recommended future advertising to "promote the diamond as one material object which can reflect, in a very personal way, a man's . . . success in life."[120]

N. W. Ayer was increasingly successful in selling diamonds as a "necessity" by the early 1940s—the sale of diamonds increased by 55 percent from 1938 to 1941 alone. By the late 1950s, the norm of a diamond ring as a symbol of love had taken hold. As Ayer admitted: "Since 1939 an entirely new generation of young people has grown to marriageable age . . . To this new generation a diamond ring is considered a necessity to engagements by virtually everyone."[121]

The sale of diamonds is merely one of many ways advertisers manipulate emotions to sell products in service of Madison Avenue. Advertising and public relations campaigns sell products by associating them with subconscious human needs, impulses, and emotions. Large trucks are sold on football Sunday by marketing them as symbols of excitement, toughness, and masculinity, convincing many men that their sexual worth is tied to the size and horsepower of their vehicle. Fast food is sold by convincing Americans that the more meat they eat, the more masculine they are. This campaign is best personified in the notion that "real men" eat "man food," as captured in the *Wendy's* food ads marketing large cheeseburgers under the slogan "Are we not men?" Beer and fast food are also sold through sex. Large breasted women and scantily-clad models wrap themselves around each other while eating large sandwiches, as seen in *Arby's* ads, while sensually dripping sauce on each other. Shoes are sold by convincing Americans that certain brands are synonymous with being a real "athlete," best symbolized in the "Air Jordan" Nike shoe line. Bud Light is sold by convincing audiences that drinking this beer is a sign of refined taste and preference for "superior drinkability." In these instances, basic human emotions and needs are used to sell products. For cigarettes, the attempt was to appeal to the biological sexual needs to be attracted to others and feel attractive to others. For diamonds, the emotion is love, which speaks to the psychological need to feel connected to others, to sexual drive, and to human reproduction—all of which are tied to marriage. Food and beer ads speak to desires to appear masculine—hence sexually attractive. With regard to beer consumption, the perception that one is refined in their tastes speaks to the broader human need for recognition by peers, as group socialization and interactions are vital to human psychological and emotional development. Large trucks driving on rough terrains speak to a sense of excitement for audiences—excitement representing another basic human emotion and impulse.

Examples of commercial efforts to tie emotions to human needs are countless in America. The process through which these emotions are transferred to products is subconscious. No one I know consciously thinks buying Bud Light will guarantee women find them sexually desirable. Nor does buying a large truck or eating fast food guarantee women will find one a desirable sexual partner. Rather, the association between emotions and products is indirect. Basic emotions and primal human needs residing deep within the mind are subconsciously associated with products on store shelves—due to associations created in ads that draw positive feelings from consumers. This process is always occurring, even if most people are not aware of it.

As already mentioned, we live in an era in which Americans increasingly avoid politics, voting, and community engagement, preferring an existence in which self-worth is defined by consumerism. When citizens do interact in groups, it is typically through activities such as drinking, shopping, and other consumer behavior that fall within a capitalist economy. Noam Chomsky has long warned that consumerism effectively pacifies political thought and engagement.[122] But is there empirical evidence of this claim? Unfortunately, polling organizations rarely ask Americans about consumerism and politics within the same surveys. This makes it difficult to test Chomsky's thesis. Still, some evidence is available. For example, in the 2000s, *Pew* surveyed Americans about their consumer preferences alongside measurements of political interest. My analysis of *Pew's* survey finds a significant relationship between commitment to consumerism and political demobilization. As seen in figures 11.1 and 11.2, greater enjoyment of shopping and visiting "the mall" is significantly associated with decreased likelihood of voting, and declining interest in paying attention to political news.

The relationships between consumer sentiment, voting, and political attention are significant, after controlling for respondents' sex, age, education, race, income, political party, and ideology.

In chapter 4, I argued that power in America is exercised through "hegemonic" forces. "Hegemony," as Gramsci argued, refers to the process by which

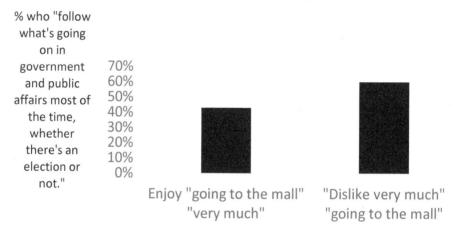

Figure 11.1. Politics, Consumerism, and the Public, 2003. Source: Pew Research Center, National Poll, July 14–August 5, 2003.

Figure 11.2. Voting, Consumerism, and the Public, 2003. Source: Pew Research Center, National Poll, July 14–August 5, 2003.

political officials and the corporate class guide public thought via socialization and propaganda. The inculcation of Americans with consumer identities is an important component of hegemonic control over the masses. This mechanism of control is effective against poorer Americans. Analyzing the 2003 *Pew* survey, we see that poverty and consumerism work jointly to suppress political consciousness. Poorer Americans—those from families earning less than $20,000 a year—are particularly vulnerable to being pacified by consumerism, compared to higher income individuals. As family poverty increases, and as commitment to consumerism increases, depoliticization also increases via a declining likelihood of voting or following political news.

The relationship between poverty and consumer diversion is not surprising at a time when low-cost entertainment products are widely available to the working class and poor. Electronic items such as televisions, cell phones, and video games are cheaper than they have ever been, making it easier for poor people to divert their attention away from the political and economic troubles of the nation, despite rising inequality and rapidly growing costs of essential items such as health care, healthy foods, and education.[123] And the relationship between poverty, consumerism, and political attention/participation is statistically significant, even after accounting for respondents' race, age, education, sex, political party, and ideology.

Directing public attention to consumerist trivialities serves the interests of the upper-class and corporate America. Fixation on consumption diverts Americans from problems in government, while deterring discussion of, and mobilization against a political process that largely serves the desires and agendas of the upper class. As long as Americans are preoccupied with the latest clothing fads and the newest iPhone, they are less likely to pay attention to or seek to change a political process dominated by the wealthy. Nearly half of Americans do not vote in presidential elections, and two-thirds do not vote in midterm elections. About half of Americans do not pay attention to the news. Large numbers of Americans gravitate toward fashionable consumption and consumer-driven identities, rather than political or community-based ones. These developments are of huge significance to democracy. For every intellectual lamenting the decline of political interest among the young, one answer to the question of "why" is that citizens are increasingly socialized to hold individualized, consumer-based, apolitical priorities. Understanding the causes of citizen apathy is necessary if we are to instill in the young a greater commitment to community and civic engagement.

Chapter 12

Public Opinion and Ideology

The Rise of Right-Wing Politics and Mass Resistance

In early 2018, Americans were surveyed about their opinions of government. The findings could be seen as somewhat contradictory. On the one hand, less than 40 percent of Americans approved of Trump's performance in office, while less than 20 percent held favorable views of Congress.[1] Similarly, less than 40 percent indicated they were satisfied with the federal government. On the other hand, support for actual government agencies was far higher, as captured in figure 12.1.[2] The findings from national surveys could be interpreted as demonstrating that the American public was deeply confused about matters related to politics and

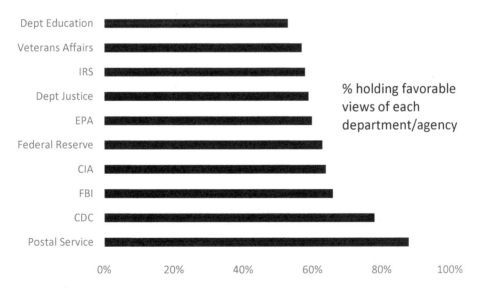

Figure 12.1. Public Opinion of Government Services, 2018. Sources: Pew Research Center, "Majorities Express Favorable Opinions of Several Federal Agencies, Including the FBI," *Pew Research Center*, February 14, 2018, http://www.people-press.org/2018/02/14/majorities-express-favorable-opinions-of-several-federal-agencies-including-the-fbi/.

government. Strong distrust and displeasure with government, after all, appears to contradict the strong support Americans express for the actual services that the government provides.

Nevertheless, one might argue that citizens were expressing rational opinions in that while they appreciate and support the services government provides them, these services are increasingly under assault in a neoliberal era in which both parties increasingly prioritize cuts in government services for the masses. As the above example suggests, Americans' level of political competence is an important matter, at least when it comes to assessing whether citizens are informed enough to pose a significant challenge to the rise of neoliberalism and upper-class dominance of government. This chapter is devoted in part to assessing competing claims about the public's competence, or lack thereof. The debate between these competing viewpoints is longstanding among political scientists.

Generalizing About Ideology and the Public

Is the American public more moderate, conservative, or liberal in their politics? There is some confusion on this topic, since surveys provide competing answers. On the one hand, and as seen in figure 12.2, polls show most Americans consistently self-identify as moderate-to-conservative. In 2016, *Gallup* found that 72

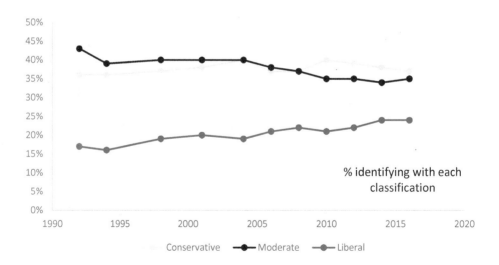

Figure 12.2. Self-Designated Ideology, 1992–2015. Source: Lydia Saad, "Conservatives Hang on to Ideology Lead by a Thread," *Gallup*, January 11, 2016, https://news.gallup.com/poll/188129/conservatives-hang-ideology-lead-thread.aspx.

percent of the public identified as either conservative or moderate.[3] In 2015, 57 percent said the federal government "is almost always wasteful and inefficient," and 53 percent of Americans said they wanted a "smaller government" with "fewer services."[4] In 2016, 57 percent of Americans said the "amount of federal income tax" they paid was "too high."[5] Fifty-one percent stated in the same year that "government regulation of business usually does more harm than good."[6] These findings can be interpreted to suggest Americans are center-right politically, with conservatives and moderates outnumbering liberals.

There is little hope of a progressive uprising in which citizens openly challenge the neoliberal, pro-business turn in politics, if the public is as conservative as they claim. But is America really center-right? Americans are notorious for contradicting themselves in surveys, suggesting that a more detailed analysis is necessary. Contrary to what most claim, a review of public attitudes on many issues suggests Americans are liberal-to-left in their beliefs, even if they do not admit it. On social and moral issues, Americans are split, often expressing conservative and liberal beliefs. But on economics and foreign policy, Americans are liberal.

Social-Moral Issues

The United States is a strongly religious country, more religious than other wealthy countries.[7] And high religiosity is associated with conservative thought. *Pew* survey data suggest that, of those attending church at least once a week, 46 percent are Republican, compared to 37 percent who are Democratic. Fifty percent of heavy church attenders are conservative, while just 15 percent are liberal.[8] The high religiosity of Americans translates into conservative leanings on many social-moral issues, although Americans are quite liberal on other issues. Consider the following beliefs, as shown in recent surveys.

- 61 percent support introducing daily prayer into public schools.[9]

- 71 percent embrace either creationism or god-guided evolution, and 55 percent support teaching creationism alongside evolution in public schools.[10]

- 61 percent favor the death penalty.[11]

On abortion, Americans appear to be strongly split in their attitudes. In 2016, 47 percent of Americans were pro-choice, compared to 46 percent who were pro-life.[12] But on other issues, Americans are strongly liberal. Recent surveys suggest:

- About two-thirds believe same-sex marriages should be legally recognized.[13]

- Three-quarters believe the U.S. should provide a path to legal status for unauthorized immigrants.[14]

- More than half favor making gun control laws stricter.[15]

These findings suggest that Americans are divided on social issues. On issues like the death penalty and public prayer, Americans have remained consistently conservative over time. On same-sex marriage and gun control, the public is more liberal.

Journalist Thomas Frank believes that working-class Americans are diverted from recognizing the class war fought by the upper-class and corporate America against working people, with Republican officials directing the masses toward hot-button social issues such as abortion and immigration. Working-class Americans, Frank argues, vote for Republicans based on social issues, while the party pursues economic policies that harm the masses and benefit the wealthy, corporations, and upper class.[16] No doubt there are some Americans that fit Frank's profile. But his argument has been largely debunked in social scientific research, which finds that lower-income and working-class Americans are more likely to vote Democratic and hold progressive-left political attitudes, not conservative ones.[17] Much of the support for the Republican Party comes from middle- and middle-upper-class Americans, more than from the working-class and disadvantaged.

Economic Issues

Americans claim to be moderate-to-conservative on economic issues.[18] Most support "free market" capitalism.[19] A majority blame the national deficit on "wasteful" government spending, while a plurality feel government regulates business too much.[20] Most feel taxes are too high. And a plurality of Americans blame poverty on government welfare programs, which allegedly enable individual laziness.[21] Americans see themselves as "conservative egalitarians," claiming to be conservative, but also strongly supporting government social welfare spending, greater taxes on the wealthy, and redistribution of economic resources from the rich to the middle class and poor.[22] Most Americans support welfare programs, and want spending levels maintained or increased.[23] Most oppose cuts to welfare programs benefitting the masses and poor.[24] Across numerous issues, one sees a leftist streak in public thought:

- Just 10 percent want cuts to Social Security, and only 15 percent support Medicare cuts.[25]

- 71 percent support increasing or keeping the same aid to the needy and poor.[26]

- 60 percent want greater federal funding for education.[27]

- 65 percent call for increasing or keeping the same spending on unemployment aid.[28]

- 74 percent believe corporations hold too much influence over American life, and most support greater regulations on Wall Street, in addition to greater regulations on various industries and consumer goods.[29]

- 60 percent support raising taxes on those earning more than $250,000 a year, while 54 percent want government to use the tax revenues to reduce inequality, by increasing spending on programs to benefit the poor.[30]

- During the 2009 debate over health care, 60 percent supported a public option, in which the government would pay for health insurance for the uninsured. In 2016, 58 percent of citizens favored replacing the Affordable Care Act with universal health care.[31]

All of these opinions suggest a strong liberal-left streak in American political thought. Contrary to claims that they prefer "less government," most Americans support an active government that helps the masses and the needy. These progressive attitudes could surely serve as the foundation for mass public pressure on government to prioritize welfare programs aiding the needy and poor, rather than continuing to pursue policies that benefit the wealthy and upper class.

Foreign Policy Issues

Americans are strongly to the left on foreign policy, and are more progressive than both the Republican and Democratic Parties.[32] Most Americans opposed the wars fought during the Bush and Obama years. Most want the U.S. to be active in world affairs, but prefer less militarist policies. They want the U.S. to cooperate with other countries whenever possible, rather than simply go to war. The "War on Terrorism" was popular for the first half of the 2000s, but public support for foreign wars quickly eroded under Bush's presidency. During the Obama years, military interventions received limited public support.

While most Americans initially supported the invasion of Iraq, a majority opposed the war by the late-2000s.[33] By late-2006, 61 percent of Americans opposed the war and an equal number wanted withdrawal of troops.[34] By 2011, nearly two-thirds of Americans thought the war in Afghanistan was not worth fighting, and three-quarters supported withdrawal.[35] In 2013, nearly 60 percent opposed Obama's proposed intervention in Syria against President Bashar Assad, following his reported use of chemical weapons against civilians. While 60 percent of Americans agreed in late-2014 with U.S. military strikes in Iraq and Syria against ISIS, most opposed use of ground troops, only supporting aerial bombing of alleged terrorist targets.[36]

Aside from opposition to military engagements, Americans express liberal-left preferences on other policy issues. Some examples include the following:

- 72 percent of Americans support a "standing U.N. peacekeeping force selected, trained, and commanded by the United Nations."[37]

- Nearly three-quarters of Americans believe the U.S. should work toward reducing its nuclear weapons.[38]

- 68 percent supported negotiations over war with Iran in 2015, in an effort to reach a broad nuclear agreement on prohibiting Iran from developing nuclear weapons.[39]

- At the height of the Iraq war, 74 percent of Americans felt "promoting democracy" was not a good enough reason for war. "War for democracy" was part of Bush's "freedom agenda," despite the strong rejection of that agenda by Americans.[40]

- In late-2015, 65 percent opposed sending Special Forces to Iraq or Syria to fight ISIS, and 76 percent opposed sending ground troops.[41]

- In 2017, 53 percent of Americans opposed a Trump foreign policy that banned those immigrating from Muslim-majority countries.[42]

In sum, Americans are strongly anti-war, oppose U.S. militarism, and prefer that their country work with other countries to promote global security. They also oppose policies that discriminate against Muslim-majority nations, and reject rhetoric framing Muslims as a blanket threat to national security and American values.[43] These values suggest that the public remains a major impediment to imperialist foreign policies, which have historically been embraced by both major parties. Declassified government documents reveal that U.S. presidents have long been motivated by aggressive, violent foreign policies aimed at strengthening capitalism, and asserting American business dominance throughout the world. But Americans oppose U.S. militarism, and resist long-term military occupations in the Middle East that are motivated by efforts to increase American corporations' access to, and control over foreign raw materials such as oil.

Ideology and Public Moods

The above data suggest that, on two of the three major issue areas—Americans are left in their politics. Other scholarship confirms that Americans are "symbolically conservative" but "operationally liberal" in their policy attitudes.[44] Reviewing hundreds of survey questions from the 1950s through the 2000s, some studies find the public goes through "mood" shifts over the decades, becoming more and less liberal over time.[45] Despite the swings, more than half of Americans have consistently held liberal-left beliefs over the last half-century.[46]

Ideological Polarization

Despite the general trend in which most Americans are liberal-left in their politics, scholarly research also highlights growing ideological polarization in America. Democratic Americans are becoming more liberal, while Republicans are becoming more conservative. *Pew* has surveyed Republican and Democratic Americans, finding that polarization increased by nearly 20 percentage points from 1987 to 2012, according to an analysis of 48 political questions. Another *Pew* study from 2014 also found significant polarization. While 30 percent of Democrats held "consistently liberal" or "mostly liberal" views in 1994, 56 percent held such views in 2014. Republicans' trajectory was somewhat different. They became *less* conservative from 1994 to 2004, but then more conservative from 2004 to 2014. Forty-five percent of Republicans held "mostly conservative" or "consistently conservative" views in 1994, while just 31 percent did so by 2004, although it rose to 53 percent by 2014.[47]

There is disagreement among scholars about whether polarization is occurring. It may be that membership in each party has changed so that Democratic Americans are more uniformly liberal, and Republicans are more conservative. So, the parties are better "sorted" ideologically, without an overall shift in the public toward conservative and liberal beliefs.[48] It seems clear, however, that polarization has indeed occurred. Looking at all Americans, one also sees polarization among independents, Republicans, and Democrats, as seen in figure 12.3. According to *Pew* surveys, the percent of Republicans holding conservative beliefs increased from 50 percent in the mid-1990s to 59 percent in 2015. Similarly, the percent of Democrats holding liberal beliefs increased from 30 percent in the mid-1990s to 62 percent in 2015. Finally, there was leftward shift among independents; although one in five held liberal beliefs in the mid-1990s, it had increased to a third by 2015.[49] At first, polarization may be seen as posing a roadblock to a progressive mass-uprising, aimed at limiting the rightward, pro-business, and upper-class bias in politics. If Americans are more divided than ever, how can they unite in fighting against big businesses' perversion of politics in favor of the wealthy? But concerns about polarization may be overblown. In 2017, 70 percent of Americans were either independents or Democrats. And with both groups moving to the left in their politics, there is already a potentially mass progressive faction that could transform the American political system if effectively mobilized.

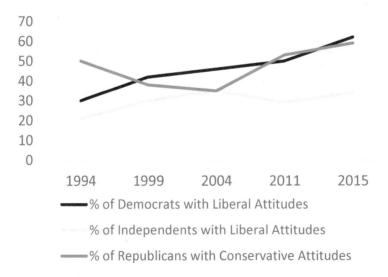

Figure 12.3. Polarization in America, 1994–2015. Source: Pew Research Center, "5 Facts About America's Political Independents," *Pew Research Center*, July 1, 2016, http://www.pewresearch.org/fact-tank/2016/07/05/5-facts-about-americas-political-independents/ft_16-07-01_independents_conservlib/.

Competing Theories of Public Opinion

Intellectuals disagree about how to describe the American public. Progressive-left intellectuals like Howard Zinn and Noam Chomsky long argued that Americans form rational opinions that should be taken seriously by government.[50] In line with these claims, "democratic theory" refers to a school of thought in which some intellectuals trust the ability of Americans to form stable, informed, and even wise opinions on political issues. This theory contrasts with "elite theory," which argues that Americans are incapable of developing informed opinions. Elite theorists, including figures like public relations founder Edward Bernays and intellectual Walter Lippmann, saw the public as apathetic, incompetent, and poorly informed. They held little faith in the average person. Bernays believed that political leaders and the business class should decide on important political matters, since the public was too ignorant to develop informed political opinions.[51] Both elite and democratic theory capture aspects of public opinion. There are many cases in which people develop informed opinions after paying close attention to politics. However, Americans also struggle regularly to form rational, informed opinions on topics with which they lack familiarity, especially when faced with misinformation campaigns coordinated by political elites, corporate media, and corporate interest groups.

Elite Theory

Some scholarship claims that Americans are so ignorant to politics that most hold "non-attitudes."[52] The masses are perceived to be as politically sophisticated as Homer Simpson, which is not encouraging when assessing prospects for democracy. Late-night comedy programs echo the "non-attitudes" position, airing segments in which the "person on the street" is revealed to hold few to no substantive opinions about politics. On Jimmy Kimmel's program, Americans are asked whether they prefer "Obamacare" or the "Affordable Care Act"; many are oblivious to the fact that they are the same, but are still quick to offer attacks on "Obamacare" as harmful.[53] The conclusion drawn from these anecdotes seems to be that, if many Americans have opinions, they are so superficial and misinformed that they are not very meaningful.

National surveys uncover troubling levels of public ignorance on politics. About two-thirds of Americans cannot name the three branches of government, and a third cannot name a single branch.[54] In 2014, only 38 percent of Americans knew that Republicans controlled the House of Representatives, and that Democrats controlled the Senate.[55] Two-thirds of Americans are unable to recall the name of their House representative.[56] Elite theorists argue that most Americans fail to form a consistent liberal or conservative ideology because of their inattention to politics.[57] Americans are seen as fickle and moody in their beliefs.[58] Recent surveys confirm that most Americans do not closely follow the news. Just one-in-five pays "very close" attention to foreign news stories, while only one-in-three indicates the same for national news stories.[59] In short, public political attentiveness leaves much to be desired.

The social scientific evidence for elite theory traces back to the 1960s, when political scientists concluded that people could be broken down into five groups, ranging from greater to lower levels of political sophistication. These include: 1. Ideologues; 2. Near-ideologues; 3. Those with a "group-oriented" identity; 4. Those voting based on the "nature of the times"; and 5. Those with "non-attitudes."[60] Only the first group was seen as forming politically sophisticated attitudes. Ideologues paid regular attention to politics, and had either a liberal or conservative ideology. Near-ideologues were somewhat similar to ideologues; they made reference to liberal and conservative ideologies, but did not put much stock in either as structuring their own beliefs.

Group-oriented individuals formed opinions largely independent of ideology. Today, one might be speaking of individuals who identified with Obama because they are African American, or supported Hillary Clinton because she is a woman and they are women, or voted for Trump because he is a businessman and they respect business owners. These forms of voting are superficial if they are based on identity politics alone, and divorced from the political positions the official adopts. "Nature of the times" voters select candidates based on changes in reality at specific points in time. Examples include those voting against Democrats because they were unhappy with the Korean War fought under Democratic President Harry Truman, or those who voted against Republicans during the 2008 economic crash because Republicans were associated with failing to help the average person in a time of crisis.

Finally, individuals with "no issue content" hold "no shred of policy significance whatever."[61] Some vote for or against candidates based on superficial, empty rhetoric. Or they vote based on the perceived physical attractiveness of a candidate. Whatever the reason, it is superficial and divorced from serious political assessments. Previous scholarship concluded that most American voters fit into the final three categories (no issue content, nature of the times, group-oriented), rather than the first two (ideologues and near-ideologues).[62] The findings are not encouraging when considering future prospects for a bottom-up democracy that effectively challenges and rolls back growing business and upper-class dominance of the political system.

Elite theory predicts that most Americans follow the lead of political elites, rather than independently forming opinions. As the argument goes, the average American fails to form sophisticated views about politics; only a relatively small number of Americans—those who are highly educated and who pay close attention to the news—are more likely to be "indoctrinated" to accept the positions of political elites.[63] For elite theorists, concerns with the public's lack of political knowledge validate their distrust of the masses and democracy.

There is significant evidence that highly-educated and higher-income Americans are different from other Americans politically. *Pew* polling from figure 12.4 finds highly-educated and higher-income Americans are more likely to pay attention to the news. About half of those with a high school education or less pay attention to news, while the numbers are about the same for those with "some college." However, almost 60 percent of those with bachelor's degrees pay attention to news, while the number is two-thirds for those with graduate degrees.[64] As shown in figure 12.5, less than half of Americans with incomes under $50,000 a year pay attention to the news, while the number is more than half for those earning from $50,000 to $150,000, but about two-thirds for those with incomes over $150,000.[65] Probably because they spend more time paying attention to and thinking about politics, more affluent Americans are more likely to have well-developed ideologies and to be more strongly committed to their ideological convictions. Speaking to this trend, highly-educated and higher-income Americans are far less likely to express favorable opinions of

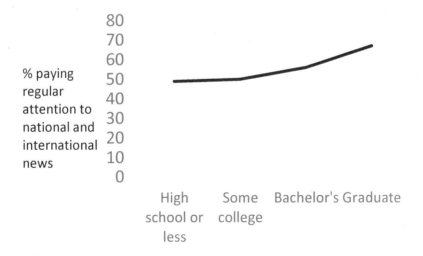

Figure 12.4. Attention to News by Education Level. Source: Pew Research Center, "Pew Media Survey," *Pew Research Center*, July 2007.

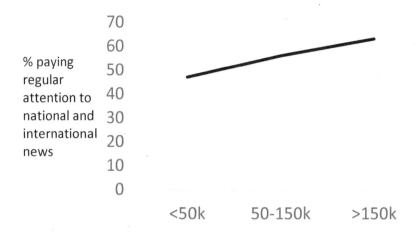

70
60
% paying
regular   50
attention to 40
national and 30
international 20
news
10
0

<50k   50-150k   >150k

Figure 12.5. Attention to News by Income. Source: Pew Research Center, "Pew Media Survey," *Pew Research Center*, July 2007.

socialism, and far more likely to support capitalism. In contrast, the difference between support for capitalism and socialism is negligible among less-educated and lower-income Americans.[66]

Finally, because many Americans are not paying attention to the news and politics, they are less likely to see the relevance of participating in politics. As a result, only about half of those in the poorest fifth of the income distribution voted in 2012, compared to two-thirds of those in the middle fifth, and more than 80 percent for those in the top fifth.[67]

Similarly, voter turnout averaged a third or less for those with a high school education or less in 2012, although turnout was between two-thirds to 80 percent for those with college undergraduate and graduate degrees.[68] Engagement in civic activities such as contacting a legislator or participating in a town hall meeting is significantly higher for those with college degrees and those with higher incomes (over $75,000 a year) than those without college degrees and with lower incomes (under $75,000 a year). Efforts to communicate with others about political issues are significantly higher for those with college degrees and higher incomes (over $75,000 a year) than those without college degrees and with lower incomes (under $75,000).[69] The above statistics suggest that, not only are more affluent and upper-class Americans more attentive and involved in politics, they are also in a better position to influence politics. If masses of poorer and less-educated citizens do not pay attention or vote, there is little chance of them rolling back the intensifying upper-class control over the political process.

Elite theory is not simply about highlighting differences between compet-ing classes of Americans. It also claims most Americans are simply incapable of democratic governance due to their ignorance. In the elections and voting chapter, ample evidence was presented that voters select between candidates for superficial reasons. Other surveys also suggest profound public ignorance and misinformation. For example, one can look to Sarah Palin's "death panels" controversy. In August 2009, the former Alaskan governor and Republican Vice-Presidential candidate nearly derailed Democratic heath care reform because of her conspiracy-mongering. On *Facebook*, Palin warned Americans of Obama's alleged plan to kill grandparents and children with disabilities:

> As more Americans delve into the disturbing details of the nationalized health care plan that the current administration is rushing through Congress, our collective jaw is dropping, and we're saying not just no, but hell no! . . . government health care will not reduce the cost [of health care]; it will simply refuse to pay the cost. And who will suffer the most when they ration care? The sick, the elderly, and the disabled, of course. The America I know and love is not one in which my parents or my baby with Down Syndrome will have to stand in front of Obama's 'death panel' so his bureaucrats can decide, based on a subjective judgment of their 'level of productivity in society,' whether they are worthy of health care. Such a system is downright evil.[70]

Palin's conspiracy was wholly inaccurate in describing health care reform. There were no "death panels" created, to be used against elderly and disabled Americans. The legislation contained a provision requiring doctors to consult terminally-ill patients about their end-of-life options. But this was a far cry from a "death panel" that denies life-saving care.

Despite the dubious nature of Palin's post, it received massive attention in the conservative and traditional media. By late-2009, 41 percent of Americans believed in the death panels myth, despite it receiving *Politifact*'s "lie of the year" award.[71] One could counter that this was just one case of misinformation. But there are many other cases from which to draw. In 2010, four in ten Republicans thought Obama was "doing many things Hitler did," while 25 percent of Republicans thought Obama was the "anti-Christ." Thirteen percent of all Americans agreed Obama was the anti-Christ, while another 13 percent just could not be sure, totaling one-quarter of Americans.[72] In 2010, 55 percent of voters thought Obama was a "socialist," and 67 percent of Republicans agreed.[73] This finding was troubling, considering Obama dedicated his tenure to bailing out troubled banks and auto corporations, and passing a market-based health care reform.

Public ignorance relates to scientific issues as well. Opposing government-mandated vaccinations, one-third of adults with children agreed in 2014 that vaccines cause autism, despite the complete lack of scientific evidence for this claim.[74] Another poll from 2015 found that while just 6 percent believed vaccines cause autism, 52 percent were "unsure" about the relationship.[75] Despite the vast majority of climate scientists concluding that global warming is occurring and that humans are primarily responsible, less than half of Americans in 2016 believed in "climate change due to human activity," while only 27 percent concurred that "almost all" climate scientists agreed global warming is "human caused."[76] Clearly, the public is susceptible to conservative rhetoric denying that manmade climate change is real. This rhetoric is articulated by personalities such as Donald Trump, who argues that global warming is fraudulent and made up by China to hurt the U.S. economy.[77]

In another example of conspiratorial thinking, 31 percent of Americans in 2007 believed the September 11 attacks were either a secret inside job by the Pentagon and the Bush administration, or that the government knowingly allowed the attacks to happen. Another 5 percent were not sure about whether the government planned the attacks, meaning more than a third of Americans fell into or potentially fell into the 9/11 conspiracy theory.[78] Despite the "9/11 truth" conspiracy, there has never been any credible evidence presented of federal involvement in the September 11 attacks.

Public misinformation is sometimes driven by racism. A case-in-point is the right-wing fantasy treating former President Obama as a foreign, exotic other. In 2011, almost half of Americans believed Obama was not born in the U.S. or were unsure if he was really an American.[79] This position gained steam when a group of extremists nicknamed the "birthers" began organizing at Congressional town hall meetings in 2009, claiming Obama was not a "real" American. Many claimed his birth certificate was forged, despite numerous non-partisan fact-checking groups and political officials having seen his birth certificate and debunking the conspiracy.[80] Furthermore, in 2010, 18 percent of Americans thought Obama is a Muslim, while another 43 percent were unsure, despite his Christian background.[81] The numbers grew by 2015, with 29 percent of all Americans believing he is a Muslim, and 43 percent of Republicans agreeing.[82] Considering the longstanding demonization of Muslims in America, the association of Obama with Islam was hardly flattering, and was intended to present him as a "fifth column" internal threat to American national security, democracy, and cultural values.

Civics literacy questions also suggest American understandings of the world are woefully inadequate. One 2006 survey found that two-thirds of Americans could not identify Iraq on a map, despite the U.S. occupying the country. Similarly, 43 percent of Americans in 2006 could not find the state of New York on a map. Perhaps most disturbing of all was a 2015 survey finding that one in four Americans was not aware that the Earth revolves around the sun. These findings should give Americans pause to wonder how much the average person can be trusted to develop wise opinions about the world. After all, informed mass consent is vital to democracy.

In the age of Trump, concerns with misinformation continue. In line with the president's false claims of widespread voter fraud, and despite a failure to find evidence of systematic abuse, 46 percent of voters claim that voter fraud happens "somewhat" or "very often."[83] Trump supporters are heavily susceptible to misinformation. Fifty-one percent agree the nonexistent terror attack on Bowling Green, Tennessee, (which the administration claims occurred) demonstrated that Trump's immigration ban on Muslim majority countries was necessary.[84] Trump supporters embrace false information if it works against the Democratic Party. Sixty-seven percent believe, falsely, that unemployment increased under Obama. Forty percent erroneously believe Trump won the popular vote, in line with the president's claims, while 60 percent falsely believe millions of illegal votes were cast for Clinton. Seventy-three percent embrace the myth that billionaire liberal investor George Soros pays protesters to demonstrate against Trump. Finally, almost 40 percent believe, inaccurately, that the stock market fell significantly during Obama's presidency, despite record profits posted by corporate America.[85]

Democratic Theory

Any mass rebellion against neoliberalism requires not only active, but informed citizens. Some believe this is possible, and that claims about American ignorance are exaggerated.[86] Democratic theorists argue that, while many Americans are uninformed or misinformed, there are enough well-informed Americans for public opinion to be taken seriously. For democratic theorists, the question is not whether Americans are politically competent, but whether a large enough number of Americans are competent *enough* that they are able to contribute to, and pressure for democratic governance.

Most Americans hold relatively stable opinions that do not change much over time, contrary to the claim that most hold "non-attitudes." To the extent that Americans change their opinions over time, shifting beliefs correspond to changing political realities in the world. In other words, changing attitudes are "rational" because they are a product of engagement in real-world developments. This point is documented in one study of public opinion, which examined hundreds of political issues in surveys from the 1950s onward, concluding that for the vast majority of issues, public opinion was remarkably stable over time. In less than 10 percent of survey questions did public opinion fluctuate significantly, and it was usually because an issue was salient in the news and in politics.[87]

Other evidence suggests most Americans do pay attention to real-world issues. As I discussed in the introduction, it is common to see half of Americans or more say they pay "very close" or "fairly close" attention to the news. Because so many are following the news, a majority are able to accurately answer political and civics questions. For example, in one survey from the late-2000s, 69 percent of Americans could name the Vice President; 66 percent knew the name of their state governor; 68 percent knew the U.S. maintains a trade deficit with other countries; 76 percent knew which party controlled the House of Representatives; 88 percent knew that tainted food and dangerous (lead-paint laden) toys the U.S. was dealing with at the time were coming from China; 74 percent knew the name of the House Speaker; 71 percent knew that Vladimir Putin was Russia's president; 67 percent knew the branches of Islam include the Sunni and Shia; and 56 percent were aware of how many U.S. soldiers were killed in Iraq. A survey from 2012 found that 67 percent of respondents were aware the Democratic Party supported raising taxes on high income earners; 66 percent knew Democrats supported expanding gay rights; 63 percent knew Democrats embraced a "path to citizenship" for illegal immigrants; and 58 percent knew Democrats wanted to cut military spending. Seventy-one percent knew the Republican Party was the more conservative of the two parties; 61 percent knew Republicans supported restricting abortion; 60 percent knew Republicans supported drilling in the National Arctic Wildlife Refuge; and 53 percent knew Republicans wanted to cut government spending. It is unlikely this many citizens would know these political facts if they were not paying attention to politics.[88]

Some scholars argue that Americans use information they find in the media to develop informed political opinions. Americans "tame the information tide," relying on audio-visual forms of news content.[89] The average voter retains "low information rationality."[90] They form rational opinions, even with relatively low amounts of information. In other words, they are rational *enough* in their thinking. Many have weak incentives to follow politics closely every day; they are busy with school, work, and family. But by using various short cuts, citizens gather information about the political process. Short cuts include scanning media headlines, catching segments of television or radio newscasts while preparing for work or school, or sharing information with friends or family during the day. In small group settings, although individuals often lack specific details about politics, when people share information within a group, they quickly form thoughtful, and even complex insights.[91]

Despite claims that politics and civic engagement are largely the province of the upper class, surveys suggest this is not the case. One 2009 survey, for example, found that in the 12 months before being contacted, two-thirds of Americans engaged in at least one political or community activity outside of voting. These included: signing a petition, contacting a political official, working with fellow community members to solve a problem, attending a political meeting, contributing money to a political campaign, joining an interest group to influence policy, attending a political speech or rally, sending a letter to a newspaper, volunteering for a political candidate, making a speech about a local issue, or attending a demonstration.[92]

What about the notion that Americans are ignorant to the identities of their political leaders? This finding, highly touted by some, is misleading. It is well known that most Americans cannot recall the names of their Congressional leaders. However, instant recall, which is required in any phone survey, is a high bar to cross for individuals surveyed about many political questions in a short period of time. Surveys show less than half of Americans are able to recall the names of incumbents running for reelection. However, *recognition* of officials from a list of names—a lower bar to clear—is higher. Nine in ten Americans recognize the names of their representative and senators.[93] So contempt for the public may be unfounded. Most Americans know the names of their representatives, participate in political activities outside of voting, and are knowledgeable about many political topics.

I undertake a case study below covering the Iraq war, to further explore claims that the public holds stable, rational opinions that change predictably over time. I look at the war period between 2003, when the U.S. invaded Iraq, through 2007, when the Iraqi civil war was in full swing and thousands of American soldiers and hundreds of thousands of Iraqi civilians were killed. First off, there was tremendous stability in public attitudes regarding Iraq. When Americans were asked if they thought the war was "worth fighting," if they supported Bush's handling of the war, if they supported withdrawing troops, and if they supported a full withdrawal, opinions fluctuated only modestly in polls from one month to the next.[94] Public attitudes were extraordinarily stable, suggesting Americans held real opinions on these issues, contrary to the claim that most hold "non-attitudes." Furthermore, public opinion surveys showed opposition to war increased incrementally from 2003 to 2007. Opposition to war, as measured in the four questions above, increased from between 30 to 40 percent of Americans in 2003, to as much as 60 to 70 percent by 2007.[95]

Why did opposition to war increase? Available evidence suggests opposition was related to various factors, including anger over growing U.S. casualties, concern with growing Iraqi casualties and civil war, increased feelings that the war was not morally defensible and that it was unwinnable, anger over the false reasons provided by the Bush administration for war, and suspicion that the war was fought to further the interests of capitalist elites in controlling Iraqi oil. In June 2005, most Americans—including those who were paying attention to the news and Iraq and those who were not—were aware that approximately 1,000 to 2,000 U.S. troops had been killed since 2003. In April 2006, a majority knew that 2,500 troops were killed since 2003. There is little reason to think that most Americans would be aware of casualty estimates if they were not paying attention to Iraq.[96] Not only did most citizens know the number of soldiers killed, but correct casualty assessments were associated with growing opposition to war and increased support for withdrawing from Iraq. For example, those providing accurate casualty assessments in June 2005 were nearly 20 percentage points more likely to support Iraq withdrawal than those providing inaccurate estimates.[97] In sum, growing war opposition was rational in that it was a product of people paying attention to events in Iraq regarding U.S. casualties. Most Americans were well informed on the human costs of war.

Other evidence also suggested Americans were forming rational opinions on the war. As depicted in figure 12.6, violence in Iraq—as measured in attacks per month—grew significantly from 2003 to 2007, as did Iraqi civilian casualties.[98] Fluctuations in reporting of violent incidents in Iraq from 2003 to 2007 corresponded with fluctuations in support for, and opposition to war. When news

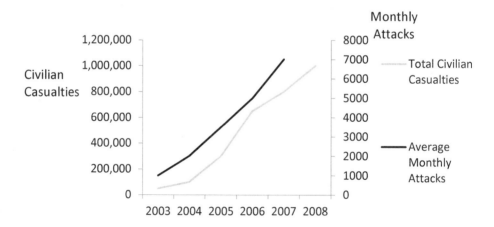

Figure 12.6. Iraq Violence and Civilian Casualties, 2003–2008. Sources: Anthony H. Cordesman, "Trends in Iraqi Violence, Casualties, and Impact of War: 2003–2015," *Center for Strategic and International Studies*, October 5, 2015, https://csis-prod.s3.amazonaws.com/s3fspublic/legacy_files/files/publication/150914_Trends_in_Iraqi_Violence_Casualties.pdf; Rob Stein, "100,000 Civilian Deaths Estimated in Iraq," *Washington Post*, October 29, 2004, http://www.washingtonpost.com/wp-dyn/articles/A7967-2004Oct28.html; Jomana Karadsheh, "Study: War Blamed for 655,000 Iraqi Deaths," *CNN.com*, October 11, 2006, http://www.cnn.com/2006/WORLD/meast/10/11/iraq.deaths/; Luke Baker, "Iraq Conflict Has Killed a Million Iraqis: Survey," *Reuters*, January 30, 2008, http://www.reuters.com/article/us-iraq-deaths-survey-idUSL3048857920080130.

coverage of violence increased, opposition to war grew. When coverage of violence fell, opposition fell.[99] Overall, as violence grew, the public became increasingly unhappy that the war was growing more chaotic, violent, and deadly over time.

By 2006, war opposition was also tied to concerns the U.S. was not doing enough to prevent an emerging civil war in Iraq. As figure 12.7 documents, those worried that the U.S. was not making progress in deterring a civil war were far more likely to support withdrawal.[100] This concern was rational in that the U.S. was not making progress in preventing a civil war; instead it was pursuing an unpopular occupation associated with growing violence.

Finally, opposition to war grew as most Americans expressed concerns that Bush lied to make the case for war, and worried that the war was motivated by corporate oil interests. As documented in figure 12.8, survey data from 2011 found those feeling the Bush administration misled the nation about WMDs were twice as likely to oppose the Iraq war, compared to those feeling Bush did not mislead the public.[101]

Concerns about manipulation were rational, in light of evidence that the administration knowingly ignored intelligence that raised questions about whether Iraq possessed WMDs.[102] The administration ignored this intelligence because it undermined the push for war, but a war fought on false pretenses is also one that Americans rejected once they became aware of the deception. Furthermore, more than three-quarters of Americans in the mid-2000s agreed that oil interests played a role in motivating the U.S. invasion of Iraq.[103] This conclusion was echoed by U.S. leaders' historical admissions that use of force in the Middle East is vital in order to control the region's oil.

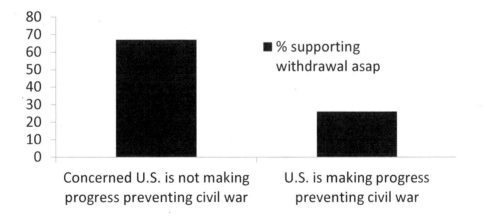

Figure 12.7. Concern with Civil War and War Attitudes, 2006. Source: Anthony DiMaggio, *Selling War, Selling Hope: Presidential Rhetoric, the News Media, and U.S. Foreign Policy Since 9/11* (Albany, NY: State University of New York Press, 2015).

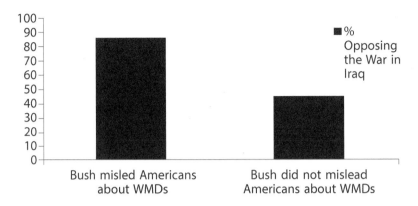

Figure 12.8. Concern about WMD-Deception and War Attitudes, 2011. Source: Anthony DiMaggio, *Selling War, Selling Hope: Presidential Rhetoric, the News Media, and U.S. Foreign Policy Since 9/11* (Albany, NY: State University of New York Press, 2015).

The Iraq war is significant because it suggests Americans do form rational opinions. While Americans may be manipulated in the short term, such as in the run-up to the Iraq war, it became difficult to maintain war support as official statements increasingly contradicted what people observed in the real world. Citizens demonstrated the ability to engage in rational thought regarding the war, as they became more aware of how developments on the ground in Iraq contradicted Bush's rhetoric. The administration claimed progress was being made on suppressing the Iraqi insurgency, protecting Iraqi civilians, and reducing violence. These claims were invalidated by the emerging civil war and growing death and destruction from 2003 through 2007. Americans increasingly recognized Bush's propaganda and tuned it out.

If the Iraq war was an isolated incident of public rationality, there would be little reason for optimism regarding prospects for democracy. But there are many examples of the public challenging misinformation, drawing on personal experiences and knowledge that run counter to official and business propaganda. These cases suggest Americans think rationally, basing their opinions on real world experiences and considerations. I explore some of these examples below.

1. Despite consistent efforts from Republican officials and the fossil fuel industry to confuse the public about the mounting threat of global warming, Americans increasingly rely on their own experiences to challenge this propaganda. Recognition that global warming is "causing a serious impact now" increased from 43 percent of Americans to 56 percent from 2010 to 2016.[104] This growing awareness occurred because of public experiences with increasingly

chaotic, extreme weather, which scientists conclude becomes more likely with climate change.[105] As one survey of the public from 2008 to 2011 found, most Americans cited weather changes, warmer temperatures, or glacier melt as the primary reasons for recognizing climate change.[106] Official and fossil-fuel industry efforts to deny climate change became less effective over time as the public drew on its own weather-related experiences in recognizing that warming was occurring.

2. Even though there was much controversy over Obamacare, Americans became increasingly resistant to repeal once many got insurance under the law, and benefitted from taxpayer insurance subsidies, the prohibition on denying people care due to preexisting conditions, and the Medicaid expansion. Despite Republican rhetoric demonizing the law, by early 2017, 54 percent of Americans approved of Obamacare, the highest level of support ever seen to that point. Even among the 43 percent who disapproved, 25 percent wanted the GOP to improve the law, not repeal it. In total, 79 percent of Americans approved the law or sought to improve upon it.[107] Public protests at town hall meetings across the country suggested that much of the public was anxious about the Republican repeal agenda, preferring instead to keep the law in effect.[108]

3. Decades of experience in benefitting from Medicare and Social Security mean that efforts to privatize these programs are met with stiff resistance. In 2005, President Bush pushed hard for privatizing Social Security, promoting a mix of benefit cuts and the creation of private accounts through which individuals would invest their retirement earnings in the stock market. The campaign was met with derision by the public, which opposed cutting benefits and eliminating a program that was already paying out guaranteed benefits to seniors.[109] Republican Congressman Paul Ryan proposed privatizing Medicare in 2011 in his "Path to Prosperity" budget proposal. As with Social Security, public opposition to Medicare privatization was strong. Seniors worried that being forced to buy insurance plans on the marketplace would result in increased costs, and they already benefitted from government covering their insurance.[110] In short, there was little incentive to support privatization. With both Social Security and Medicare, the public drew on its knowledge of, and experiences with these programs to question pro-business official agendas.

Why is Public Opinion so Often Misinformed?

Many intellectuals claim the public is ignorant to politics. But rarely do they discuss why. Noam Chomsky and Edward Herman argued in *Manufacturing Consent* that corporate, upper-class, and governmental interests seek to use the media and political propaganda to manipulate the public in favor of elite agendas. Recent research suggests that consumption of the news is often correlated with greater public ignorance. Political leaders and the corporate media misinform the masses in pursuit of their own agendas. One now infamous example is the "birthers," the group of conspiracy theorists who believed Obama was secretly not born in the U.S., and a citizen of either Kenya or Indonesia. The birther conspiracy was promoted by numerous media pundits and personalities, including Sean Hannity, Rush Limbaugh, and Donald Trump. Birtherism had no basis in reality, as non-partisan fact-checking groups verified Obama was born in the United States. This did not stop conservative politicians and corporate media pundits from pushing the conspiracy, which emerged in 2009 and gained popularity in 2010 and 2011. In 2011, 43 percent of Americans either believed Obama was not born in the U.S., or could not be sure if he was born here.[111] The birther conspiracy was heavily covered in the U.S. press, with nearly one in ten stories devoted to Obama's citizenship by mid-2011.[112]

The "birther" conspiracy is a prominent example of elite-driven misinformation. But it is far from the only example of elite propaganda. Recent research suggests that, for numerous issues, the closer citizens follow the news, the more confused or misinformed they become.[113] Polling on health care reform in mid-to-late 2009 found most Americans who paid close attention to the news on health care reform were more likely to be confused about the basic details of the Democratic Party's proposal.[114] Attention to the news should have produced less uncertainty and greater knowledge. Growing public confusion was a problem, however, due to sustained coverage of "death panels" in the news, amidst conservative attacks on Democrats for promoting "socialism" and a "government takeover" of health care.[115] Most Americans were worried Obama was a socialist, and many worried about mythic "death panels."

As discussed in the media chapter, public misinformation was also apparent among those paying attention to news on Iraq. Americans were more likely to believe Bush's claims that Iraq was developing WMDs, despite much evidence suggesting the contrary. A last example of elite manipulation is global warming. Although the public has slowly become better informed on climate change over time, polling data from 2009 suggested that those who had heard "a lot" about global warming in the news and elsewhere were more likely to disagree that: 1. Global warming is occurring, and 2. That government should take steps to limit

CO_2 emissions.[116] Many Americans were confused, believing that there was still significant disagreement among climatologists, likely due to claims from Republican political leaders, conservative corporate media, and the fossil-fuel industry claims that the science on climate change was unsettled.

Research on public opinion does not suggest the public is incapable of developing informed political views. Government and business elites struggle to influence mass attitudes for: 1. Issues with which Americans already have significant prior experience and knowledge of; and 2. Topics in which the public already holds strong prior views that cut against elite messages.[117] These findings suggest there is hope that the public may play a more active, informed role in politics, and that the masses—including middle-class and poorer Americans, may be able to fight back against growing corporate and upper-class control of the political system.

In an era of mass distrust of government, it is troubling to see Americans manipulated by corporate media, political leaders, and elite business interests. Misinformation on vital issues like global warming clearly benefits the fossil-fuel corporations, but greatly threatens sustainability on planet earth and human survival. When the masses embrace wars based on fraudulent claims made by elites, or fail to understand the basic details of major reforms due to elite-driven obfuscation, democracy becomes difficult, if not impossible. But Americans also demonstrate the ability to think rationally about politics, especially as they become more familiar with, and knowledgeable of individual political topics over time. Rational thought, exercised independently of the business class and neoliberal politicians, is greatly needed in the battle for a meaningful democracy that serves the interests of the people.

Chapter 13

Civil Liberties and the Quest for Corporate Personhood

Americans take pride in the United States as a bastion of freedom, a place where people can feel free to disagree, no matter how controversial their opinions. But this narrative is deeply flawed. Corporations are non-democratic entities, and employees of business establishments do not actually benefit from free speech protections, as the First Amendment freedom of speech and expression apply against government. In the workplace and increasingly outside of it, freedom of speech and expression apply to the owners of businesses and major corporations, but not to their workers. Furthermore, government has a long history of repressing controversial political views, contrary to basic First Amendment guarantees.

As *The Washington Post* reported in 2017, "corporations aren't just enforcing speech codes at the office. Increasingly, they are cracking down on their workers' expression outside of it." The newspaper cites numerous examples, including the story of a Philadelphia Eagles stadium employee who was fired after criticizing the team's player hiring via Facebook.[1] In another case, a nurse in a Florida retirement home was fired after posting requests for help on Facebook in the wake of Hurricane Erma. The employee grew increasingly distraught after the elderly residents had gone without air conditioning in the extreme heat for days, but the negative PR was not appreciated by her employer for portraying the company "in an unfavorable light."[2]

These stories are not unique. They are merely symptoms of a broader problem—the complete lack of free speech rights for American workers—who are monitored inside the workplace and out for "disagreeable" or "controversial" speech. This practice is a blatant violation of the spirit of freedom of speech and expression, even if it is not technically a violation of the First Amendment. In a country where corporate executives and management are empowered to determine who is allowed to speak, the U.S. has fallen into an authoritarian pattern of relations between employers and employees. Government may prioritize freedom of speech as it applies to government restrictions on expression, but it has little to say about authoritarianism, as practiced by the corporate class.

275

What are Civil Liberties?
And Why Do They Matter?

Civil liberties refer to rights that government must not take away. They are "negative" rights, established in the Bill of Rights. They include: freedom of speech, association, religion, and the press, the right to privacy, protection against cruel and unusual punishment, the right to life and liberty, and protection against denial of due process, a civil trial, and a trial of one's peers. The First Amendment protects free speech, expression, religion, association, and the press. It states: "Congress shall make no law respecting an establishment of religion, or prohibiting the free exercise thereof; or abridging the freedom of speech, or of the press; or the right to the people peaceably to assemble, and to petition the Government for redress of grievances." These rights apply against the entire government, not just Congress, since the courts have interpreted the Fourteenth Amendment's due process clause—protecting individual life, liberty, and property—as imposing limits on all parts of government.

Freedom of speech includes the spoken and written word, and symbolic speech. In *Cohen v. California*, the court ruled an individual could wear a shirt with the words "fuck the draft," without violating obscenity standards, as this reflected an individual's political position on the Vietnam War. In *Texas v. Johnson*, the court ruled flag burning was constitutionally permissible, contrary to a state law forbidding desecration of "venerable objects." These cases embody the principle that the nature of political content is irrelevant to its acceptability under the law.

There are also significant limits to individual expression. The Supreme Court declared in *Roth v. United States* (1957) and *Miller v. California* (1973) that obscene expressions are not protected by the First Amendment, although local communities must decide whether expressions are obscene. Obscenity trials often include sexual content, graphic violence, potentially profane language, and other expressions that may be "patently offensive" and lacking "serious literary, artistic, political, and scientific value" (*Miller v. California*). Defining obscenity, however, is difficult since what is obscene varies from person to person and from community to community.

A second limit on free expression relates to slander and libel—consciously lying in spoken or written form. Media outlets and individuals can be sued for defamation by engaging in slander or libel. This principle was expressed by the Supreme Court in *New York Times v. Sullivan* (1964), which required individuals to demonstrate a media entity knowingly lied and damaged one's reputation to receive monetary damages. This standard is difficult to meet, since one must demonstrate a media outlet knowingly lied.

The points above suggest that, at least in modern times, government has generally protected free-speech Americans against punishment from government, albeit with some exceptions. But the negative freedom of free speech is radically truncated when corporations and other employers are exempt from respecting it. These employers may be able to claim that they must police employees in the workplace because they require obedience in order to conduct business in a timely, efficient manner, or that they worry about controversial employee speech making a company "look bad." But by stepping into individuals' private lives and policing speech and expression, the corporate class has demonstrated that they are willing to engage in totalitarian, repressive tactics aimed at suppressing dissent that would make George Orwell blush. Few employees have a social media presence strong enough that a controversial statement from an employee is likely to negatively affect an employer on any noticeable level. And yet corporate employers have shamelessly taken to suppressing free speech outside the workplace, simply because they can, and because the law empowers them to do so.

The language in the Bill of Rights says nothing about freedom from discrimination for speech as related to employment with private corporations. Employers are prohibited from discriminating against individuals based on sex, sexual orientation, race, ethnicity, or age, but these practices are separate from free speech. Private sector employers enjoy almost "untrammeled power" to censor employee speech and expressions. Private corporations operate according to a system of "employment at will." Employers fire employees without establishing "just cause."[3] The empowerment of private employers over "free speech" was institutionalized by the Supreme Court in *Adair v. United States* (1908), in which an employee for a railroad company was fired for joining a labor organization. While firing employees for labor organizing is illegal under the National Labor Relations Act, *Adair* made it clear there is no constitutional right to express oneself in the private sector.

Qualified Free Speech, the First Amendment, and the Rise of Corporate Power

Another area subject to restrictions is free speech in educational institutions. Faculty and students within these venues have seen their freedom of speech increasingly restricted, despite a broader societal trend in favor of empowering corporations and the corporate class with nearly unlimited free speech. Since the late 1980s, the national courts have increasingly sided with administrators and against students, imposing limits on acceptable speech. Administrators restrict faculty's freedom of speech in the name of protecting schools from controversial ideas. For example, Ward Churchill, a professor at the University of Colorado, was fired in 2007 after a firestorm of criticism from outside the university at places like *Fox News*, in response to an essay he wrote after the 2001 terrorist attacks. Churchill argued that those working at the World Trade Center were part of an imperialistic system against which radical groups like al Qaeda were rebelling. Churchill's claims were widely deemed insensitive toward the victims of 9/11, and the essay motivated the University of Colorado Board of Regents to terminate Churchill's employment, despite his having tenure. While most Americans would reject the ideological thrust of Churchill's essay, his firing was troubling for those committed to freedom of speech in educational institutions.

In 2014, newly hired professor Steven Salaita was also terminated, from the University of Illinois, in retaliation for *Twitter* comments on the Israeli-Palestinian conflict. Salaita condemned Israel for killing children in its attacks on Palestinian lands, and for engaging in racism against Palestinians. The University of Illinois' Chancellor Phyllis Wise explained the school denied his employment because of his demeanor in expressing criticisms, citing his "personal and disrespectful words or actions that demean and abuse either viewpoints themselves or those who express them." Wise's justification for firing Salaita was a lack of civility, but the firing also revealed contempt for free speech.

Churchill and Salaita's firings suggest free speech is far from absolute in higher education, particularly in cases when administrators disagree with the ideological thrust of the position in question. Educational institutions claim to be committed to academic freedom, but this is not at all clear in the case of controversial speech. On the one hand, the Supreme Court has ruled in several cases that academics benefit from free speech under the First Amendment. In *Sweezy v. New Hampshire* (1957), the court ruled that being a Marxist is constitutionally protected under freedom of speech, and that states cannot legally investigate and punish socialists without violating the First Amendment. In that case, Justice Felix Frankfurter spoke of "the four essential freedoms of the university—to determine for itself on academic grounds who may teach, what may be taught, how it shall be taught, and who may be admitted to study." Similarly, in *Keyishian v. Board of Regents* (1967), the Supreme Court declared states cannot punish or prohibit employees for joining the Communist Party. The court's majority declared, "the university is a traditional sphere of free expression" and that academic freedom is "fundamental to the function of society." Justice William Brennan explained: "our nation is deeply committed to safeguarding academic freedom, which is of transcendent value to all of us and not merely to the teachers concerned. That freedom is therefore a special concern of the First Amendment." The classroom was deemed a "marketplace of ideas," for students and faculty to explore.

Despite the above cases, other rulings raise questions about academic freedom. In *Hong v. Grant* (2010), the Ninth Circuit Court of Appeals found professors can be denied raises if they are critical of university hiring practices. In *Garcetti v. Ceballos* (2006), the Supreme Court ruled: "when public employees make statements pursuant to their official duties, the employees are not speaking as citizens for First Amendment purposes, and the Constitution does not insulate their communications from employer discipline." Finally, in *Urofsky v. Gilmore* (2000), the Fourth Circuit Court of Appeals declared faculty do not share First Amendment protections regarding sexually explicit materials. The case addressed whether faculty can use university property to research the history of Internet pornography. The court ruled: "to the extent the Constitution recognizes any right of academic freedom, the right inheres in the university, not in individual professors." The phrase was notable in suggesting that administrators, who traditionally speak for universities, hold First Amendment protections, but not faculty.

Even if the law protects faculty speech made independent of the running of a college or university, the cost of destroying free speech is cheap for university administrators. The University of Illinois paid out an $875,000 settlement for firing Salaita, in violation of his free speech rights.[4] But this is a small price to pay for destroying free speech and tenure protections on college campuses. With firings like those of Salaita and Churchill, a chilling effect is created within institutions of higher learning. Faculty are forced to watch what they say, for fear of being terminated. A settlement like Salaita's in the hundreds of thousands may initially seem like a lot of money, but it is far from enough to sustain an academic throughout their career, especially if they are blacklisted from new academic jobs by college administrators because of their "controversial" speech.

If faculty free speech protections are not on firm ground, students benefit even less from protected speech. Several court cases suggest students do not benefit from "free" speech at all, short of administrators recognizing that "right." Such limits trace back to *Hazelwood v. Kuhlmeier* (1988), in which the Supreme Court ruled that faculty advisors, rather than high school student journalists, held authority over reporting sensitive issues like teenage pregnancy and divorce. Students were only able to exercise "free" speech without censorship if administrators designated newspapers or areas of schools as "publicly designated forums." The significance of this ruling was that it suggested students do *not* hold free speech rights, since rights cannot be granted or taken away by government based on the political preferences of government officials.

The limits of student free speech intensified in 2007 via *Morse v. Frederick*. In that case, high school students were suspended by school administration for carrying a poster reading "Bong Hits 4 Jesus" during the 2002 Olympic torch relay event. The event was supervised by the students' high school. One student was subsequently punished for advocating illegal drug use. Ruling in favor of suppressing free speech, Supreme Court Chief Justice John Roberts declared that schools can punish students for advocating drug use due to an "important—indeed, perhaps compelling interest" in discouraging drug use. In this case, the promised social good of keeping students off drugs trumped free speech rights.

While faculty and students are increasingly restricted in what they are allowed to say, government has quietly been empowering the corporate class under broad free speech protections. With no sense of irony, *Morse v. Frederick* was issued the same week the Supreme Court eliminated restrictions on free speech for the wealthy. In *FED v. Wisconsin Right to Life* (2007), the court struck down campaign finance rules prohibiting PACs from funding political ads in the months before general and primary elections. The case involved an anti-abortion group that ran ads related to a judicial election. The ads, the Supreme Court argued, did not constitute advocacy for or against a candidate (prohibited under election law), meaning they could not be banned. In defending the court's ruling, Justice Roberts argued "the First Amendment requires us to err on the side of protecting political speech rather than suppressing it," and that "we give the benefit of the doubt to speech, not censorship." But the ruling stood in contrast to *Morse v. Frederick*. These two rulings were controversial because they moved toward limiting free speech for actual persons (high school students), while enhancing free speech for artificial corporate "persons." In the *Morse* and *Wisconsin* cases, the Supreme Court demonstrated a clear class-bias in favor of corporations and the upper class, while limiting free speech for the mass public.

The trend toward strengthening free speech "rights" for the corporate class was intensified in 2010 via *Citizens United v. Federal Election Commission*, when the Supreme Court removed spending restrictions on issue ads for primary and general elections—this time eliminating the prohibition on advocacy for or against political candidates. As figure 13.1 depicts, the ruling was highly unpopular across party lines, with most Americans rejecting its legitimacy.

The trend of limiting the rights of people was also intensified, with the *Hosty v. Carter* (2005) case, in which the Seventh Circuit Court of Appeals applied the limits previously imposed on high school students (*Hazelwood v. Kuhlmeier*) to college settings. The case involved a student newspaper at Governor's State University in Illinois, which was subject to "prior restraint" censorship by administrators declaring their intent to review all newspaper content before it was published, after the paper criticized the administration for firing a faculty member. The Seventh Circuit ruled college students cannot express themselves unless the comments are disseminated through a publicly designated forum, classified as such by administration. Such forums could include a student newspaper

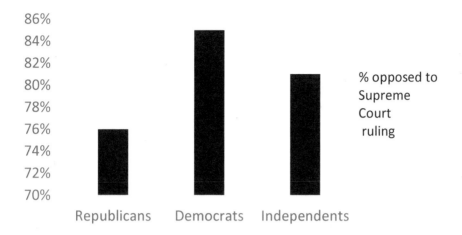

Figure 13.1. Public Opposition to Citizens United, 2010. Source: Dan Eggen, "Poll: Large Majority Opposes Supreme Court's Decision on Campaign Financing," *Washington Post*, February 17, 2010, http://www.washingtonpost.com/wp-dyn/content/article/2010/02/17/AR2010021701151.html.

or an area on campus, referred to as a "free speech zone." The implications of this ruling were much the same as the *Hazelwood* ruling: students do not have free speech unless administrators choose to grant them that "right." And if the right has to be granted, it is not a right, but a privilege. The Supreme Court approved of *Hosty v. Carter* when it refused to hear the case on appeal in 2006.

Freedom of Religion, the First Amendment, and the Rise of "Religious" Corporations

Freedom of religion is a second protection in the First Amendment, although it has also been appropriated in recent years in favor of empowering corporate "persons." It includes two components: the Establishment Clause and Free Exercise Clause. Both are captured in this passage: "Congress shall make no law respecting an *establishment* of religion, or prohibiting the *free exercise* thereof." The First Amendment requires government play an agnostic role regarding religion—neither favoring nor opposing it. The Constitution does not state there must be a "wall of Separation" between church and state; this phrase originated from Thomas Jefferson's writings. But the Supreme Court has ruled that separating church and state is required under the Free Exercise and Establishment clauses. The separation plays out in different ways, depending on the cases appearing before the courts. For example, *Everson v. Board of Education* (1947) explored the use of taxpayer funds (related to transportation) for children attending private religious schools. The Supreme Court ruled the Establishment Clause applies against the actions of states, and not merely to Congress, because of the Due Process Clause of the Fourteenth Amendment. The Due Process Clause says no state shall "deprive any person of life, liberty, or property"—with liberty requiring the protection of religious freedom. In the *Everson* case, all students, attending public or private schools, were equally guaranteed a right to school transportation. Furthermore, the court found that private school travel reimbursements were paid to families, not religious organizations, thereby avoiding a violation of the Establishment Clause. In *Engel v. Vitale* (1962), the Supreme Court reinforced the principle of separating church and state by prohibiting officially-sanctioned prayer within public schools. Finally, *Abington Township v. Schempp* (1963) declared public school bible readings were unconstitutional.

The Supreme Court developed a test to determine if government interactions with private religious organizations and religious individuals violate the separation of church and state. It is called the "Lemon Test," based on the 1971 case, *Lemon v. Kurtzman*. In that case, the court ruled public school resources could not be used to aid private religious schools. But the case went beyond school supplies. The Supreme Court decided that, for an interaction between government and a religious institution or individuals to be legal, a government act must meet a three-pronged test. First, the action must have a secular intent; second, it must neither inhibit nor advance religion (it must be agnostic); third, there must be no excessive government-religious entanglement. While the three-pronged test might at first seem unclear, its application demonstrates how the criteria relate to government actions.

One example of a government action that passed the three-pronged Lemon test is school vouchers. In *Zelman v. Simmons-Harris* (2000), the Supreme Court determined taxpayer-funded vouchers for private schools were constitutional. Use of these funds did not violate the lemon test because the primary purpose of vouchers was educational, rather than religious. Also, government neither directly promoted nor impeded religion, as parents chose to send their children to religious schools. Finally, there was no excessive government-religious entanglement, so long as students had religious and non-religious school options.

If school vouchers pass the Lemon test, creationism does not. Creationism, as promoted in science classes, was deemed unconstitutional by the Supreme Court in *Edwards v. Aguillard* (1987). Creationism violated the Lemon test because: 1. it had a religious purpose—teaching religious values in the classroom; 2. teaching religious values advanced religion in a public institution; and 3. there was an excessive religious-government entanglement since public school students were forced to learn religious values. Years after Creationism was deemed unconstitutional, supporters at the conservative *Discovery Institute* repackaged it with a new name: "Intelligent Design."[5] Internal documents from the organization demonstrated this was done to re-introduce Creationism under a new name.[6] Looking at the main tenets of "Intelligent Design," one can see why critics called it creationism repackaged. The theory argues the origin of life is best explained through a process where organisms are created by an intelligent designer, rather than developing through evolution and natural selection. Forms of life do not evolve over time, but are spontaneously created by some unnamed higher power.

Intelligent design, the *Discovery Institute* admitted privately, was simply a rehash of Creationism. But by remaining silent on what power is responsible for this "Intelligent Design," supporters obscured the theory's overlap with creationism. The courts reject notions that the two are separate, however, as reflected in *Kitzmiller v. Dover Area School District* (2005). In that case, a federal district court threw out a curriculum in the Pennsylvania Dover school district including Intelligent Design, taught alongside evolution in biology courses. The court ruled "Intelligent Design" violated the Establishment Clause, since the theory was "nothing less than the progeny of creationism."[7]

Despite longstanding protections for individuals' freedom of religion, the Supreme Court appears increasingly concerned with establishing religious "rights" for corporations. This was made apparent in the *Burwell v. Hobby Lobby* case (2014), in which the court ruled that "closely held" corporations—those with ownership that shares similar religious values—have the "right" not to offer reproductive services in their health care plans, as previously required under Obamacare. In this case, *Hobby Lobby* claimed that paying for reproductive, contraceptive, or abortion services violated its owners' religious values. And the Supreme Court agreed, reaffirming the language of the Religious Freedom Restoration Act (1993), which protected individuals from government in cases where individuals feel their religious freedoms are violated.

The *Hobby Lobby* case is a seminal decision in that it exhibited a blatant bias in favor of the "rights" of corporations and the corporate class, while restricting the rights of employees. Businesses have a "right" not to pay for contraceptive services for religious reasons. But workers have no right to employer-provided contraceptive benefits, despite the Supreme Court's previous ruling in *Roe v. Wade* that women hold a right to decide for themselves whether to seek an abortion. Individuals are likely to argue for or against the *Hobby Lobby* ruling based on their personal views of abortion and contraception, but there is no arguing that this case represented a significant expansion of corporate power over employees.

With the election of Donald Trump, America's commitment to freedom of religion came under increasing assault. This time, Muslims were designated as part of a legal underclass, to be discriminated against when it came to immigration and travel. Trump consistently engaged in campaign rhetoric that demonized Muslim minorities, portraying them as a serious national security threat.[8] After assuming office, Trump imposed a travel ban against seven Muslim-majority nations. Although he claimed the ban was not religiously motivated, this was contradicted by his counsel, Rudy Giuliani, who admitted the ban was intended to target Muslims.[9] Various federal courts struck down Trump's initial ban in early 2017, but Trump reissued the ban via executive order, the second time exempting Iraq, in addition to allowing re-entry to permanent residents and visa holders from banned countries after travelling internationally.[10] The ban was temporary—90 days for travelers and 120 days for refugees.[11] The ban was again challenged, however, by a federal district judge who ruled that it was a form of religious discrimination against Muslims.[12] This ruling was fueled by the Department of Homeland Security's own conclusion the seven nations banned posed no demonstrable security threat to the U.S.[13]

Class divisions are not always about economics. In this case, Muslims were discriminated against by the Justice Department, and relegated to a secondary legal and social status, based purely on their religious beliefs. Trump's attempts to demonize Islam reflected a deep contempt for basic First Amendment religious freedoms for minorities. Support for his ban from a sizable minority of Americans—47 percent according to one poll—suggested that many Americans were willing to throw out religious freedoms if the target was a small, non-Christian minority.[14] But the demonization of Muslims is also relevant in that it speaks to the corporatization of rights. At a time when businesses like Hobby Lobby were conferred religious "rights," the Trump administration openly embraced attacks on the rights of actual humans—in this case Muslim migrants.

Despite the Islamophobia exhibited by many Americans, the public was divided in its perceptions of Muslims. Trump struggled to vilify Muslims throughout the mid-2010s. Polling data over time suggested that, despite Trump's claims about the need to take action against Muslims, Americans became increasingly supportive of this minority group. While 53 percent of Americans held favorable views of Muslims in November 2015, the number rose to 70 percent by October 2016. Similarly, while just 37 percent of Americans held favorable views of Islam in November 2015, 49 percent did by October 2016.[15] The dramatic increase in public sympathy was likely provoked by Trump's blanket attacks on Islam, which were apparently viewed as alarmist, especially by Democrats and independent Americans, even if not by Republicans.[16]

The Fourth Amendment:
Individual and Corporate Rights to Privacy?

The Supreme Court's commitment to the First Amendment is limited by its restrictions on free speech. The court has also chipped away at citizen privacy rights under the Fourth Amendment. The Fourth Amendment states individuals have the right "to be secure in their persons, houses, papers, and effects, against unreasonable searches and seizures"; this right "shall not be violated, and no Warrants shall issue, but upon probable cause, supported by Oath or affirmation, and particularly describing the place to be searched, and the persons to be seized." The Supreme Court has reaffirmed this right in *Mapp v. Ohio* (1961) and *Wolf v Colorado* (1949), which state that evidence seized without probable cause is to be excluded in a court of law. Furthermore, once arrested, citizens have a right to remain silent (*Miranda v. Arizona*, 1966) and a right to counsel (*Miranda v. Arizona* and *Gideon v. Wainwright*, 1962). But privacy rights are increasingly under assault by the Supreme Court, as related to law enforcement searches pursued in the "War on Drugs." The court has also deferred to the executive branch's assault on privacy rights, seen in growing government spying powers in the "War on Terror."

Concerning search and seizure, the Supreme Court stated in several cases that privacy rights should be traded in the name of fighting drugs. In *Illinois v. Caballes* (2005), the court ruled it was not a violation of privacy to walk dogs around cars searching for drugs within the normal amount of time of a traffic stop, even without probable cause of drug possession. Privacy rights were further limited in *Kentucky v. King* (2011), when the Supreme Court declared police can legally break into the wrong person's home when pursing a drug suspect, and if drugs are found in this person's home, they can be prosecuted, despite a lack of probable cause or warrant. In *Florence v. Board of Chosen Freeholders* (2012), the court ruled police can strip search or inner cavity search arrested individuals for drugs, under the suspicion they may be criminals, even without probable cause or reasonable suspicion that a crime was committed.

Privacy was also limited by the government following September 11 in the name of fighting terrorism. In 2005, President Bush was exposed by *The New York Times* for illegally ordering the National Security Agency (NSA) to spy on phone calls going in and out of the U.S. without warrants, as required under the 1978 Foreign Intelligence Surveillance Act and the Wiretap Act. Rather than punishing the president for violating privacy rights, Congress changed the law to relax spying restrictions via the Foreign Intelligence Surveillance Act Amendments of 2008, which allowed warrantless spying on international phone calls that are allegedly related to terror investigations. Domestic spying expanded under Obama.

Leaked information from NSA whistleblower Edward Snowden revealed the Obama administration created a massive NSA-run international surveillance system for collecting large amounts of data on American and foreign citizens. Obama's "metadata" collection continued through both of his terms, with phone records collected for over 120 million Verizon subscribers.[17] The revelation caused great controversy among civil liberties advocates and critics of the imperial presidency.

While the government's commitment to free speech is inconsistent at best, its record is worse regarding Fourth Amendment protections, as applied to national security and corporate power. The right to privacy was abandoned under the Bush and Obama presidencies, under the assumption that Americans needed security more than privacy. Neither president intended on Americans discovering their spying programs, and both were greatly angered when whistleblowers exposed their actions. Despite promises to keep Americans safe via expanded spying, neither administration presented evidence that their surveillance prohibited a single terror attack. To the contrary, some evidence emerged after September 11 suggesting that surveillance prior to the terror attacks was associated with greater insecurity. President Bush ordered the NSA to spy on international calls prior to September 11, and the agency actually intercepted communications between the September 11 hijackers prior to the attacks.[18] But because it collected such a large volume of data, the NSA was unable to analyze the records in time to prevent the attacks.[19]

Outside "national security" issues, the Supreme Court has begun to push the claim that corporations have Fourth Amendment rights to privacy. For example, in *Los Angeles v. Patel* (2015), two citizens and hotel owners challenged a Los Angeles city law requiring that hotels keep long-term records of customers' names, addresses, vehicle information, and billing information, arguing that it represented a violation of patron's right to privacy. The Supreme Court ruled that city police's efforts to search these records without a warrant were unconstitutional, but the case may be remembered most for its broader significance, in that the claimants were a mix of individuals and "business associations."[20] The relevance is in the latter—business groups—being included within a ruling claiming a right to privacy under the Fourth Amendment. This ruling, if further developed by the courts in future precedents, means the potential for institutionalization of Constitutional corporate "rights" to privacy. This development would be perverse, in light of the Supreme Court's chipping away of privacy rights for actual persons in the "War on Terror" and the "War on Drugs."

A History of Government Suppression of Dissent

The federal government has a history of repressing civil liberties against dissidents in the name of promoting social order, and in the quest to promote corporate capitalism. Americans like to think that the U.S. is unusual in its strong commitment to free speech. But the government holds a poor record of protecting free speech during times of social turmoil and war. One early example is the Alien and Seditions Acts of 1798, which criminalized dissent during the U.S. war with France. The acts were intended to intimidate critics of the Federalist Party and President John Adams, and violated free speech rights. The courts did nothing to oppose Adams's attack on the Constitution, although the anti-Federalists later rescinded much of the legislation when Thomas Jefferson took office.

During the Civil War, Abraham Lincoln suspended habeas corpus, arresting those who criticized the war. Lincoln violated Article 1, Section 9 of the Constitution, which stated that "The privilege of the writ of habeas corpus shall not be suspended, unless when in cases of rebellion or invasion the public safety may require it." Lincoln claimed that public safety was being served by punishing those undermining the war, particularly those obstructing the movement of union troops in Baltimore en route to Washington, DC. But Lincoln also arrested those who simply criticized the war. Secretary of War Edwin Stanton ordered the arrest of all "engaged, by act, speech, or writing, in discouraging volunteer enlistments, or in any way giving aid and comfort to the enemy, or in any other disloyal practice against the United States" subjecting them to trials "before a military commission."[21] Between 10,000 and 15,000 Americans were detained without a civil trial.[22] These actions violated citizens' First Amendment rights.

The government increasingly sided with corporate capitalist elites, against citizen challenges to this system of power, in the early-to-mid twentieth century. The government's war on socialism spanned decades—another example of contempt for free speech. During World War I, the Wilson administration passed the Espionage and Sedition Acts of 1917 and 1918, arresting socialists and other war critics. The Supreme Court validated the arrests in *Schenck v. United States* (1919). Approximately 1,500 people were arrested on charges that they endangered national security.[23] For many socialists, the war was a dangerous imperial adventure fought to further American capitalism, with the U.S. seeking to assert its power on an international stage. Union leader and socialist Eugene Debs condemned a "war waged for conquest and plunder," with "the working class . . . freely shed[ing] their blood and furnish[ing] the corpses," despite not holding "a voice in either declaring war or making peace."[24] Looking back, it is clear that Debs and other protesters were denied their basic freedom of speech rights under the First Amendment.

Between 1919 and 1920, the government's war on socialism continued with the Palmer Raids. Attorney General Alexander Mitchell Palmer ordered the ransacking of prominent socialist and union leaders' offices in dozens of cities, arresting thousands and deporting hundreds of foreign citizens.[25] These acts blatantly violated the rights to free speech and privacy. The attack on leftists continued into the 1950s, to the delight of the corporate class. During the "Red Scare," government again declared war on socialism and communism. The Smith Act of 1940, for example, made it illegal to advocate the overthrow of government. Socialists and communists were punished accordingly. Anti-communist hysteria reached new heights in the 1950s with the rise of "McCarthyism." Named after Wisconsin Senator Joe McCarthy, this period saw an emerging consensus among political officials and business elites that a secret communist menace threatened the country. McCarthy claimed, without evidence, that more than 200 "card-carrying" communists had infiltrated the federal government.[26] His campaign was aided by the House of Representatives' "House on Un-American Activities Committee." Hundreds of artists were blacklisted from their jobs in Hollywood under suspicion of being communists, and after being called to testify before Congress.[27] Thousands were accused of being communists, including government employees, teachers, and union activists, and were fired from their jobs.[28] McCarthyism is now widely seen as one of the most shameful, heinous, and anti-democratic moments in American history.

Despite the end of McCarthyism by the mid-1950s, attacks on dissidents continued in subsequent years. During the Vietnam War, the FBI secretly spied on and sought to undermine the anti-war movement, viewing it as anti-American, communist-infiltrated, and a threat to national security. The FBI's COINTELPRO (Counter-Intelligence Program) spied on and disrupted protest groups during the late 1960s and early 1970s. Targets included socialists, communists, civil rights activists, and anti-war activists, which were all deemed subversive communist threats. The FBI illegally spied on civil rights leaders Martin Luther King Jr. and Malcolm X, infiltrated anti-war groups, and harassed anti-war activists by collecting false evidence and committing perjury to achieve court convictions, while committing violent acts against dissidents, including home break-ins, vandalism, burglary, beatings, and assassinations.[29] Investigating the COINTELPRO program, a Congressional committee chaired by Senator Frank Church concluded it was "indisputably degrading to a free society":

> The legal questions involved in [COINTELPRO] intelligence programs were often not considered. On other occasions, they were intentionally disregarded in the belief that because the programs served the 'national security' the law did not apply. While intelligence officers on occasion failed to disclose to their superiors programs which were illegal or of questionable legality, the Committee finds that the most serious breaches of duty were those of senior officials, who were responsible for controlling intelligence activities and generally failed to assure compliance with the law. Many of the techniques used would

> be intolerable in a democratic society even if all of the targets had been involved in violent activity, but COINTELPRO went far beyond that . . . the Bureau conducted a sophisticated vigilante operation aimed squarely at preventing the exercise of First Amendment rights of speech and association. . . .[30]

Denial of civil liberties also extends to minority groups during periods of war. During World War II, Japanese Americans were interned under the assumption that those of Japanese ancestry were a security threat. More than 100,000 people were interned in concentration camps, even second-generation Japanese Americans who did not speak Japanese.[31] They were denied due process rights, in a racist and shameful moment in U.S. history. The general responsible for the detainment—John Dewitt—infamously defended the program by declaring: "A Jap's a Jap—it makes no difference whether he is an American citizen or not."[32] On a smaller, but still significant scale, 762 Muslims were also detained without due process, mainly for visa-related violations, in the months after September 11, 2001. They were held for months, denied contact with their families or with legal representation, under the fear that they *might* be a security threat. Most were deported following detainment.[33] The denial of due process was illegal under the Fifth Amendment and Habeas Corpus rights; and the detainments were racially and religiously motivated, in violation of the First Amendment. Journalist Steven Brill recounts:

> In the days after the attacks, Attorney General Ashcroft told FBI Director Robert Mueller that any male from eighteen to forty years old from Middle Eastern or North African countries who the FBI simply learned about was to be questioned and questioned hard. And anyone from those countries whose immigration papers were out of order—anyone—was to be turned over to the Immigration and Naturalization Services.[34]

Detainment without due process or issuance of a writ of Habeas Corpus is unconstitutional. But it was not surprising after September 11, 2001, considering the significant anti-Muslim bigotry in the U.S. Despite the vast majority of Muslims rejecting violent acts of extremism and terrorism, many Americans simply assume this group is a national security threat, and few Americans after 9/11 protested the treatment of Muslims, cementing their social status as part of a "deviant" underclass.[35]

To summarize, this chapter reviewed the state of civil liberties in America. It argued that, despite the importance of the Bill of Rights, the U.S. government has a checkered history in protecting those rights. Ironically, individual civil liberties such as free speech, religious rights, and privacy rights are increasingly limited, while the Supreme Court enhances corporations' "rights" through judicial fiat. This development is a threat to democratic government, with legal protections increasingly reserved for corporate interests over actual people.

Chapter 14

Civil Rights and the Fight for Equality

In September 2017, President Donald Trump moved to end the Deferred Action for Childhood Arrivals program (DACA), which was implemented under former President Barack Obama. The program allowed minors who had entered the U.S. illegally to receive a deferred deportation, and granted them eligibility for a work permit. Eight-hundred-thousand people were referred to as "the Dreamers" in reference to The Dream Act, which would formally protect the work permit initiative for unauthorized immigrants, but which had not passed Congress by late-2017.[1] Trump's reasoning for terminating DACA was that it represented an "amnesty-first approach," while Attorney General Jeff Sessions argued that the initiative had "denied jobs to hundreds of thousands of Americans by allowing those same illegal aliens to take those jobs."[2]

Numerous news reports undermined the notion that DACA cost jobs, citing a lack of factual evidence for this claim.[3] But the "they take our jobs" position was too well entrenched on the American right, with xenophobia being a hallmark of the Trump campaign and administration's rhetoric. The attacks on immigrants, documented and undocumented, meant the relegation of Mexican and Hispanic immigrants to a secondary, underclass status in American politics and society. This discrimination represented a significant rollback of the protections that had been gained by nearly a million "Dreamers" under Obama. The attacks on immigrants also represent a significant civil rights issue, as I discuss in this chapter.

What are Civil Rights?

Whereas civil liberties refer to citizen protections that government must not suppress, civil rights are protections created to benefit disadvantaged groups. Civil rights include laws guaranteeing the right to vote regardless of skin color (the Voting Rights Act of 1965), freedom from discrimination (the Civil Rights

Act of 1964), protections for the disabled (The American Disabilities Act of 1990), and the right to marriage regardless of sexual orientation (via Supreme Court ruling). Many groups, including women, black Americans, Hispanics, gays and lesbians, transgendered peoples, and the disabled, are covered under civil rights laws.

Despite much progress in establishing and protecting civil rights for the disadvantaged, massive inequality remains between more and less affluent socio-economic groups, and it is growing. In the neoliberal political era, inequality manifests itself across many dimensions, including gender, race, ethnicity, sexual orientation, and economics. In other words, class divisions are not only about incomes or wealth, but also about how Americans are treated differently based on sexual orientation, gender identity, race, and ethnicity. This chapter is devoted to exploring how inequality has manifested itself in different ways, with individuals and societal institutions discriminating against a variety of historically marginalized groups.

Immigration Reform

Immigration reform is a contentious issue in American politics. Conservatives and Republicans have followed Trump's lead, supporting a wall between the U.S. and Mexico—based on calls to "get tough" on illegal immigration. "Xenophobia" refers to intense feelings of distrust, fear, or hatred against "foreigners," and Trump's blanket attacks on Mexican immigrants as "rapists" and "drug dealers" clearly fit this description. Such rhetoric fits within a broader history of discrimination against Latino/a immigrants, which has contributed to the marginalization and relegation of many to a lower-class status. Democrats have been somewhat less conservative, although hardly liberal, on immigration policy. Former President Barack Obama called for a "path to citizenship" for unauthorized immigrants, but he was also responsible for even more deportations than occurred under President George W. Bush.[4]

During his time in office, Obama developed a reputation as a conservative on immigration. *Politifact* reports Obama deported an average of 32,886 people per month in his first six years in office, compared to Bush, who deported 20,964 per month.[5] In 2014, Obama issued an executive order granting amnesty to some unauthorized immigrants. As many as four million undocumented immigrants who were in the U.S. for at least five years could apply for amnesty from deportation and be allowed to legally work in the U.S.[6] Nearly another million were shielded from deportation via expansion of the "Dreamers" program, in which young immigrants entering the U.S. as children were protected from deportation.[7]

Under Obama, a dispute between the parties emerged over Central American children seeking to enter the U.S. (in mid-to-late 2014). The key issue was whether refugees would be granted asylum from persecution. Tens of thousands of children from Honduras, El Salvador, and Guatemala had fled growing drug and gang violence, for fear of being murdered if they did not join street gangs.[8] The children began the long trek from their home countries to the border, hoping the U.S. would protect them from growing violence and instability in Central America. When they reached the U.S., these child refugees fell headfirst into a national debate over whether they would remain in the U.S. once detained, or be forcibly returned to their countries of origin. Republicans called for speedy deportation; Democrats favored granting some refugee status.[9] Obama announced a plan in which child refugees could join relatives in the U.S. after being granted a visa. Republicans lambasted the president for giving the refugees a "free pass," prompting condemnations of the party as callous to the suffering of children fleeing violence.[10]

The controversy over Central American child refugees elicited strong feelings from a public in which many, including President Trump, embrace xenophobic discrimination against "foreigners." About a quarter of Americans viewed the children as "illegal immigrants" who should be deported, while two-thirds saw them as refugees who should be shielded from violence.[11] But in the heavily demobilized, apathetic world of American politics, there was little public pressure on government to accept the refugees in mass. Because of this lack of pressure, the Obama administration moved forward with plans to deport the vast majority of the 60,000 children who reached the border by mid-2014 (only 4,000 of them would be granted visas).[12] Despite Obama's opposition to aiding most child refugees, Republicans continued their attack on the president. Republican Senator Jeff Sessions argued Obama was "incentivizing" refugees to travel to the U.S. by promising "citizenship for anyone in the world who arrives illegally in the country by a certain age."[13] This claim was wrong, as Obama sought to deport the vast majority of refugees. The administration continued its reactionary policy toward child refugees through 2016. As the *New York Times* reported, the Department of Homeland Security stepped up deportations "to send a tough enforcement message to Central America and to try to head off a seasonal swell of illegal crossings of the southwest border."[14]

Republican opposition to immigration dominated the 2016 election. Republican presidential candidate Ted Cruz called for eliminating *all* immigration to the U.S. "as long as American unemployment remains unacceptably high."[15] Trump proclaimed: "When Mexico sends its people, they're not sending their best. They're sending people that have a lot of problems, and they're bringing those problems with them. They're bringing drugs. They're bringing crime. They're rapists." Trump promised to build a wall between the U.S. and Mexico to deal with the "problem" of immigration, and promised Mexico would pay for it.[16] This promise is broken upon taking office, as he declared a "national emergency" in early 2019 to draw on taxpayer treasury funds to build a wall that had not been authorized by Congress.

Trump's xenophobic claims about immigrant dangers bore little resemblance to reality. First-generation immigrants commit fewer crimes than second-generation or "native born" Americans.[17] Furthermore, Trump's attack on Mexicans for stealing American jobs was contradicted by public opinion polling suggesting the vast majority of Americans feel that illegal immigrants take jobs that most Americans do not want, and that undocumented immigrants are "as honest and hard-working" as U.S. citizens.[18] Still, a sizable contingent of Americans, and a majority of Trump voters, were sympathetic to his rhetoric, and expressed anxiety over immigration.[19]

Finally, there was little evidence of an illegal immigration crisis. Data from the Department of Homeland Security revealed that unauthorized border crossings between the U.S. and Mexico fell to a 46-year low by 2017.[20] Furthermore, as one can see from figure 14.1, illegal entries from Mexico have been steadily declining since the 1980s, as measured by annual border detainment figures.

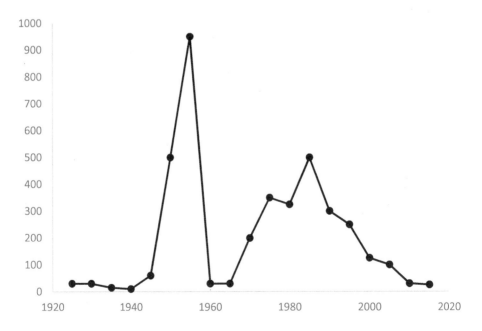

Figure 14.1. Annual Border Apprehensions, 1925–2017 (Per Border Patrol Agent). Source: David Bier, "With Border Crossings at a Trickle, Why Build a Mexico Wall?" *Newsweek*, February 1, 2018, http://www.newsweek.com/border-crossings-trickle-why-build-mexico-wall-797287.

These findings speak to the fabricated nature of the immigration "crisis" under Trump, contrary to the president's alarmist and propagandistic rhetoric.

Trump's rhetoric on immigration was notoriously draconian, as his fixation on undocumented immigrants lent comfort to "alt-right" white nationalists seeking to define the U.S. as a white ethno-state. Despite this reactionary tone, fewer unauthorized immigrants were deported in Trump's first year in office (about 225,000) than in Obama's last year in office (about 240,000).[21] But Trump's tough talk on cracking down on illegal immigration occurred in other ways. For example, his administration was widely vilified for separating parents and children in undocumented families that were detained by federal authorities. The practice became highly contentious after a tense session between White House reporters and Press Secretary Sarah Huckabee Sanders, in which the latter, echoing comments from Attorney General Jeff Sessions, argued that the family separations were part of the Trump administration's efforts to implement "biblical" law.[22] These comments were alarming to citizens who supported the separation of church and state and who saw the practice as anti-family.[23]

Trump's scapegoating of immigrants drew attention away from the dominant societal business interests that have long taken advantage of low-wage labor from undocumented immigrants. The primary target of his anger were those of Mexican descent, who were depicted as threatening America's economic greatness, jobs, and security. Although most Americans are not prejudiced against immigrants, Trump's election meant the empowerment of a sizable minority of Americans who embrace xenophobic stereotypes.

Women's Rights: The Elusive Struggle

Ask Americans if they support equal rights between men and women and they will say yes. In a 2010 *Pew Research Center* survey, 97 percent said "women should have equal rights with men," and 97 percent said "women should be able to work outside the home."[24] If support for equal rights is universal, why is there still significant economic inequality between men and women? As documented in figure 14.2, gender-based pay inequality has declined for decades, although in 2014 women still earned just 79 percent of what men earned.[25] Why has gender inequality persisted? Is it due simply to differences in life choices? Or due to a broader system of sexism and discrimination? The answer is complicated, involving multiple factors.

One of the highest profile events related to ongoing gender inequality was the 2016 election. Americans wondered whether history would be made with the election of a female president. But Hillary Clinton did not become president, and the election spoke to Americans' continued problems with sexism and misogyny. Trump gained infamy during the election for his numerous sexist comments

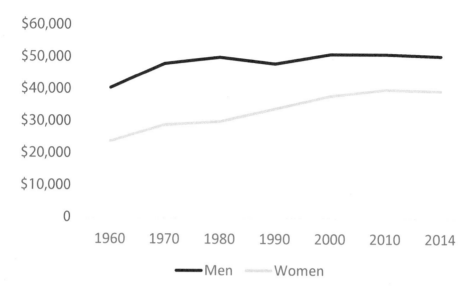

Figure 14.2. Decreasing Inequality in Male-Female Earnings, 1960–2014. Source: Carolyn B. Maloney, "Gender Pay Inequality: Consequences for Women, Families, and the Economy," *Senate Joint Economic Committee, U.S. Congress*, April 2016, https://www.jec.senate.gov/public/_cache/files/0779dc2f-4a4e-4386-b847-9ae919735acc/gender-pay-inequality----us-congress-joint-economic-committee.pdf.

toward woman. These included references to women as worthy or inferior based on perceived sexual attractiveness; his attempts to denigrate women (particularly female reporters) because their bodies undergo menstruation; his bragging about engaging in sexual assault, and sexist attacks on Clinton herself as "such as nasty woman" after her criticisms of Trump's efforts to avoid paying taxes.[26]

Not every person who voted for Trump is strongly preoccupied with gender-based issues in America. Still, Trump's electoral success suggests several things about American political culture: 1. Some Americans, even if they do not openly express sexist views, are willing to tolerate and normalize sexism from political leaders; and 2. Many American voters are disinterested in broader societal efforts to combat sexism. The latter point was clear in the *Pew Research Center*'s exit polling, which found that just seven percent of Trump supporters saw "sexism" as a "very big problem" in the country today.[27] The 2016 election will be remembered as a milestone moment, not only because of the defeat of the country's first female presidential candidate, but due to the ascendance of the most openly sexist president in modern American history.

Many Americans are reluctant to admit they hold sexist attitudes, but election surveys exposed voters' gender stereotypes, particularly in the 2016 presidential primary. For Trump, the top reasons voters cited for supporting him included the following: he is not a "career politician"; he is a "good business-man"; he "speaks his mind" and is "outspoken"; he is "strong"; and he has a strong stance on immigration.[28] These justifications were heavily gendered; they spoke to support for a male candidate that conformed to traditional stereotypes of men as powerful, economically successful, and assertive. In contrast, Clinton supporters cited reasons linked to matriarchal stereotypes. While she was seen as "capable" and "qualified," other top reasons cited by supporters included claims that she was "experienced" after serving as First Lady under Bill Clinton and as Secretary of State under Obama; she was "caring" and "connected" to the people's "needs"; she is a woman, and many supported having a woman president; and because people thought she had a "good platform."[29] Three of the top five reasons provided by Clinton supporters were based on gendered feelings that she was capable of playing a nurturing, caring role in serving the people.

Most Americans claim to support gender equality, but many also embrace gendered stereotypes. Despite 97 percent of Americans agreeing men and women should be equal, 25 percent agree that "a woman's place is in the home."[30] These findings suggest many individuals hold contradictory and misogynistic ideas about gender and family relations in America.

Misogynistic gender norms are widespread in American culture. Women are pressured into homemaker roles in families, and experience discrimination in the workplace. Consider for example the class action lawsuit filed by more than 1.5 million women against Wal-Mart for sex discrimination. Complaints against the company included: male managers holding meetings at strip-clubs and at Hooters; systematic denial of female promotions; and reluctance to hire women into management positions.[31] Furthermore, Wal-Mart's sales force is 72 percent female, despite women holding only a third of management positions—half as many as Target and Sears.[32] This evidence suggests sexism remains a problem in American corporate culture. The Supreme Court's dismissal of the Wal-Mart class action lawsuit suggests that the federal government is content to downplay the lower-class status imposed on many women by corporate America.

Many women accept patriarchal gender norms because of pressure from parents, spouses, and friends. When I was growing up in the 1980s, my mother and the mothers of my friends accepted the notion that a women's place was at home caring for children. Most did not seek out job opportunities outside the home, and when they did the jobs were part-time and lower-pay. I still know families where husbands and wives believe the woman's "proper" place is in the home. I know husbands in these households who believe they are the "spiritual leaders" of the family (a patriarchal notion if there ever was one), and that they hold a "special" relationship with God. The "role" of the woman, in these set-tings, is to listen to and embrace the husband's "superior" and "godly" wisdom. Some of these patriarchs even try to dictate how their wives vote.

Gender-based wage inequality is driven in large part by career paths. Women are more likely than men to work in lower-pay jobs as secretaries, administrative assistants, cashiers, retail sales associates, maids, receptionists, and office clerks. Historically, women were less likely to attend college programs and seek high-paying, high-skilled, professional jobs. The *American Bar Association* reported that, out of 86,590 students entering law school in 2009, the number of men exceeded women by 2,950.[33] This is a seven-percentage point discrepancy favoring men. The *American Medical Association of Colleges* estimated in 2013 that 53 percent of students enrolling in medical schools were men, and 47 percent were women, and the *Wall Street Journal* reported in 2012 that women only made up one-third of doctors and lawyers in the U.S.[34] The *National Science Foundation* estimates men are twice as likely to major in computer science than women, and four times more likely to enroll in engineering.[35] In 2011, the Census Bureau reported women comprised one-quarter of all workers in occupations related to math, science, engineering, and technology.[36] Business positions see similar trends. According to the Executive MBA Council Program, in 2015 just 27 percent of MBA business students were women.[37] Women represent just five percent of CEOs for Fortune 1,000 companies, and in 2014 just 11 of the 200 highest paid CEOs in the U.S. were women.[38] The above disparities were not likely the result of systematic discrimination in the college acceptance process. Many graduate programs go out of their way to encourage applications from under-represented groups, including women and minorities. Rather, the differential attendance rates appear to a large degree to reflect inequalities in application rates between men and women.

Some will attribute gender inequalities to differences in life and educational choices. But "life choices" are also the product of gendered stereotypes and sexist norms. A 2000 University of Michigan study on the gender-gap between male and female applicants to business schools found several reasons why women applied to graduate programs less often. These included: a lack of female role models to inspire female applicants; an erroneous assumption that women's math skills are inferior; lack of employer encouragement for women to apply to graduate programs; and a perceived incongruence between earning a graduate degree and having a family.[39]

Career trajectories are influenced by our responses to gender norms. Men and women are susceptible to gendered conceptions of which jobs are "appropriate" for them, based on fitting into masculine and feminine identities. And some research concludes that "Tendencies toward traditional gender-stereotypical preferences become even stronger after college, when some women's aspirations to establish a family encourage a shift toward more traditional feminine occupational fields."[40] The predisposition toward choosing one field over another—in anticipation of, or after having a family—suggests the persistence of cultural values pressuring women to accept patriarchal occupational norms. This widely observed trend is dangerous for women at a time when 50 percent of marriages end in divorce, and women "choose" to forego career opportunities, raises, and promotions, sacrificing occupational earnings for their families.

Differences in pay are tied to gender norms, driven by acceptance of "appropriate" roles of men and women in the home and workplace. Differences have nothing to do with men and women's intellectual capabilities. Department of Education statistics suggest women earn more bachelor's degrees than men, more quickly than men, and with better grades.[41] Furthermore, the Bureau of Labor Statistics finds that women who avoid marriage and children, thereby removing "homemaker" pressures—earn comparable salaries to men.[42]

How is gender inequality relevant to politics? The answer: government, through civil rights legislation and programs assisting women, can help alleviate inequalities between the sexes, and fight the relegation of millions of women to poverty and a lower-class status. Civil rights law in the 1960s created a legal climate to protect women against discrimination in the workplace and elsewhere, and the country's commitment to equal rights could be strengthened by passage of a Constitutional Equal Rights Amendment prohibiting gender-based discrimination.

Government can become more active in combating gender inequality. Government could prioritize greater welfare spending, to reduce the number of women in poverty. If women are left behind due to foregoing educational opportunities in the push to be "homemakers," government could fund free tuition for all students to help mothers who choose to enter/re-enter educational institutions and in pursuit of new occupational training. More generous child tax credits would aid single-parent families, especially those run by women. Taxpayer subsidies to assist families in paying for childcare and other needs will also help single mothers succeed. Both Trump and Clinton announced child care assistance plans in the 2016 election, suggesting that the issue resonates with the public. Greater subsidies of various kinds will help economically vulnerable, female-led households. These families are at great risk in an era of growing inequality.

Gay and Lesbian Rights: An Ascendant Movement

The gay and lesbian rights movement has experienced great success. In the 1980s and 1990s, gay and lesbian individuals were overwhelmingly "in the closet," refusing to openly identify themselves for fear of persecution. But this changed in the first two decades of the twentieth century. The gay and lesbian rights movement became increasingly accepted in mainstream culture. In 2016, 68 percent of Americans agreed consensual sex between gay and lesbian individuals should not be illegal.[43] Seventy percent supported allowing gays and lesbians to openly serve in the military.[44] Fifty-two percent supported a law banning discrimination against gays and lesbians in the workplace.[45] Eighty-one percent felt it was unacceptable for businesses to discriminate against gays and lesbians. And 60 percent agreed it should be illegal for business establishments to discriminate against gay and lesbian patrons.[46] As figure 14.3 documents, support for same-sex marriage has grown significantly, from less than a third of Americans in the mid-1990s to a majority by the mid-2010s, with 67 percent in favor in 2018.[47] In a sign of the wide-ranging appeal of the gay and lesbian rights movement, one sees that support for same-sex marriage increased across all the generational cohorts in figure 14.4.[48] Support grew most quickly among millennials, but the across-the-board gains suggest that, with enough effort, social movements can promote their agendas even among their opponents.

The courts responded positively to the rise of the gay and lesbian rights movement, striking down laws that discriminated based on sexual orientation. In *Lawrence v. Texas* (2003), the Supreme Court found that anti-sodomy laws violated the equal protection rights of gay and lesbian individuals to engage in consensual sex. In *Obergefell v. Hodges* (2015), the court mandated every state recognize same-sex marriage. All Americans, regardless of sexual orientation, must be treated equally under the law, according to the Fourteenth Amendment. This justification was used by numerous federal courts, including the Supreme Court, in *United States v. Windsor* (2013), which struck down the Defense of Marriage Act (1996) as unconstitutional. Due to the growing popularity of the

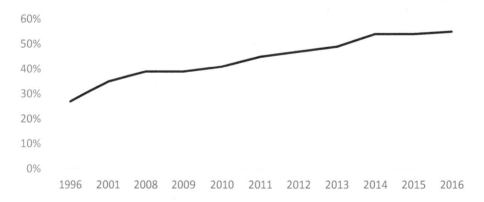

Figure 14.3. Support for Same-Sex Marriage, 1996–2016. Sources: Polling Report, "Pew Research Center," *Pollingreport.com*, June 1996–March 2016, http://www.pollingreport. com/lgbt2.htm; Polling Report, "Gallup Poll," *Pollingreport.com*, May 1–10, 2018, http:// www.pollingreport.com/lgbt.htm.

Figure 14.4. Changing Opinions of Same-Sex Marriage by Generation, 2005–2015. Source: Hunter Schwarz, "How Gay Marriage Became a Major Issue for a Generation Uninterested in Marriage," *Washington Post*, June 23, 2015, https://www.washingtonpost.com/news/the-fix/wp/2015/06/23/how-gay-marriage-became-a-major-issue-for-a-generation-uninterested-in-marriage/?utm_term=.8bfd2c60cacd.

gay and lesbian rights movement, Republican officials increasingly downplay their opposition to same-sex marriage, for fear of appearing backwards and "on the wrong side of history."[49]

There is clearly an oppressive class dimension in America related to sexual orientation. Gay and lesbian Americans are more likely to be discriminated against in hiring, firing, and in their wages. Recent data suggest that gay and bisexual men earn between 10 percent and 32 percent less than heterosexual men, even when holding job qualifications constant. Furthermore, the mean household income for same-sex couples is 20 percent less than that of heterosexual couples.[50] While it is illegal to pay individuals less or discriminate in hiring because of one's sexual orientation, it remains a fact of life as of 2019. However, ongoing discrimination in hiring could certainly be addressed via affirmative action initiatives in the public and private sector.[51]

Civil Rights and Racial Inequality: An Enduring Legacy

Racial inequality has been pervasive throughout the entirety of American history. Black Americans were not even deemed "lower-class" in early history—particularly slaves—since they held no legal rights. After slavery ended, "Jim Crow" segregation and rampant racism ensured that blacks were systematically denied employment, ensuring their placement in an "underclass" marked by mass poverty.[52] But significant progress has been made in fighting racism in America in modern times. In the 1960s, half of black Americans lived in neighborhoods that were more than 80 percent black. By the 2010s, just 20 percent were living in such neighborhoods.[53] Claims that the U.S. became "post-racial" were common after Obama's presidential victory in 2008.[54] But this claim is astonishingly naïve considering that racial segregation is still a major feature of American life.

Obama's election in 2008 was certainly historic. When I was in high school in the mid-1990s, my history teacher assured us Americans would never elect a black president, since black Americans are 13 percent of the population, and masses of whites would never vote for a minority candidate. Much had changed by 2008, with 43 percent of white voters choosing Obama.[55]

Despite talk of a post-racial era, racial inequality persists. In 2014, the median black and Hispanic families in the U.S. earned 59 percent and 71 percent, respectively, of the median white family.[56] In 2015, 2.7 times as many black Americans were poor compared to whites, while Hispanic poverty was 2.3 times higher than for whites.[57] While 12 percent of children from white and Asian families were poor in 2014, 31.9 percent and 36 percent of Hispanic and black children were poor.[58]

Incarceration rates also vary by race. Black Americans and Hispanics are incarcerated at five times and 1.4 times the rate of whites.[59] In 2010, black Americans were 40 percent of all prisoners in the U.S., despite being just 13 percent of the population.[60] Some might dismiss this finding, claiming that blacks commit crimes at higher rates than whites. But the numbers cited by conservatives greatly exaggerate black crime. Federal crime data shows that while blacks are 13 percent of the population, they commit about a fifth of violent crimes, but comprise 40 percent of those who are incarcerated.[61] Furthermore, race is not a significant predictor of drug possession or use, despite black men being much more likely to be incarcerated for drug possession.[62] Legal discrimination against minorities plays into ongoing class divisions, with people of color disproportionately designated unhireable because of felony convictions—convictions which whites are more likely to avoid.[63]

Unemployment is a third dimension of racial inequality. Black unemployment is twice that of whites, with 8.8 percent of black Americans unemployed in 2016, compared to 4.3 percent of whites.[64] As the *Pew Research Center* reflects, "Much has changed for African-Americans since the 1963 March on Washington (which, recall, was a march for 'Jobs and Freedom'), but one thing hasn't: The unemployment rate among blacks is double that among whites, as it has been for most of the past six decades."[65] The Bureau of Labor Statistics estimates Hispanic unemployment stood at 6.6 percent in 2016, compared to 4.3 percent white unemployment.[66] Heightened unemployment feeds into a racially-driven class divide. It is all but impossible to pull oneself out of poverty without decent job prospects.

A final dimension of inequality is in education. *Inside Higher Education* reports that, in 2012, SAT scores were 23 percentage points higher for whites than black students, and 18 percentage points higher compared to Hispanic students. The high school graduation rate for whites is 86 percent, but 69 percent for black Americans, and 73 percent for Hispanics.[67] In 2011, whites were six percentage points more likely than blacks to be enrolled in two-year colleges; blacks were 22 percentage points less likely than whites to have graduated college in four years.[68] Lower college completion rates for people of color mean lower earning potential in careers, which is an important point when discussing ongoing American class divisions.

Racial Inequality: Competing Explanations

Various explanations are offered for why racial inequality persists. One is that inequalities in life outcomes are exacerbated by interpersonal and systemic racism. A competing explanation is that a "culture of poverty" and "laziness" has taken hold of minorities because of overly-generous government welfare.

Claims about interpersonal racism are validated by recent historical events. Following Trump's electoral victory, racism is alive and well. Tens of millions of Americans voted for Trump, despite his bigoted comments against Hispanic immigrants, Muslims, and black Americans. Nearly half of Trump supporters agree that blacks are more "violent" and "criminal" than whites, while 40 percent describe blacks as lazier than whites.[69] Clearly, racist stereotypes persisted as a central political issue moving into the Trump presidency.

Most Americans recognize the ongoing problem of racism. In 2011, only 48 percent agreed "the U.S. has fulfilled the vision Martin Luther King outlined" in his "I Have a Dream Speech," with whites and blacks walking hand-in-hand, rejecting segregation and racism.[70] In 2016, only 37 percent of Americans agreed that "our country has made the changes needed to give blacks equal rights with whites."[71] And in 2018, 64 percent agreed that racism remained a major problem in America.[72]

Many conservatives, however, claim that an overly-generous welfare state enables laziness and poverty among people of color.[73] Historically speaking, since minorities were more likely to be poor, they are more likely to rely on welfare. The "welfare causes laziness" argument is popular among many Americans who view poverty to be a function of personal defects. In 2014, 63 percent of Americans felt that "blacks who can't get ahead in this country are mostly responsible for their own condition."

There is little evidence to justify the patronizing view that minorities are poor because they are lazy. There is no significant difference between whites, Hispanics, and blacks in their commitment to work and hours worked.[74] Furthermore, only a small number of minorities—8.8 percent of blacks and 6.6 percent of Hispanics—are unemployed, despite black and Hispanic poverty rates standing at 24 percent and 21 percent.[75] These findings suggest poverty among minorities cannot primarily be attributed to individuals who are unwilling to work.

A second problem with the "welfare causes laziness" thesis is that a large majority of welfare beneficiaries do not fit the common stereotype of able-bodied individuals who *choose* not to work. Most welfare benefits go to families with working parents.[76] Ninety-one percent of welfare beneficiaries in the 2010s were elderly, disabled, or employed.[77] Most elderly Americans are on limited, fixed incomes, and rely on welfare to help make ends. Furthermore, that disabled Americans require special assistance from taxpayers should be no surprise. Finally, it is strange to denigrate Americans working at poverty-level wages for not wanting to work. Of course, there are some individuals on welfare who are lazy, and some may rely on it as an unnecessary crutch. But there are broader social forces that explain why most individuals rely on welfare, and they have little to do with laziness among whites, blacks, or Hispanic Americans.

Contrary to conservative claims, academics have long focused on structural forces that perpetuate inequality and relegate many people of color to a poorer or lower-class status. These structural barriers are residential, educational, occupational, legal, and cultural in nature.

1. RESIDENTIAL SEGREGATION

Many Americans may oppose racism, but live in segregated communities. Most towns and cities are racially segregated, although less severely than a half-century ago. As depicted in figure 14.5, the 2010 Census found the average black American lived in a neighborhood that was 45 percent black and 36 percent white, despite blacks being 13 percent of the population.[78] Hispanic segregation rates were comparable to those in black communities. In contrast, the average non-Hispanic white person in the U.S. lived in a neighborhood that was 80 percent white, despite whites representing about two-thirds of the population.[79]

Modern segregation has its roots in American history. Racial slums were created via openly-practiced discrimination by whites during the nineteenth and twentieth centuries. Until the 1948 Supreme Court ruling of *Shelley v Kraemer*,

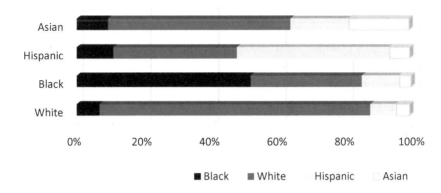

Figure 14.5. Segregation in Modern America, 2010 (Percent of each racial group residing in a neighborhood for the typical White, Black, Hispanic, or Asian American). Source: John Logan, "Separate and Unequal: The Neighborhood Gap for Blacks, Hispanics, and Asians in Metropolitan America," *Brown University*, July 2011, https://s4.ad.brown.edu/Projects/Diversity/Data/Report/report0727.pdf.

it was legal to prohibit black and Hispanic families from buying homes in white neighborhoods. Other forms of social control included white-on-black violence to discourage minorities from moving into white neighborhoods, redlining, and suburban white flight. Redlining refers to a practice by private banks in which lenders quietly drew lines around minority neighborhoods and refused to grant loans to people of color living in these areas. This practice was legal before the Civil Rights Act of 1965. Since minority applicants could not secure loans, it was difficult for them to move into white neighborhoods. "White flight," a term commonly used by historians, refers to how whites resisted desegregation via suburbanization. As black and Hispanic families began to move into formerly all-white neighborhoods during the 1960s and 1970s onward, white families left in mass, forming exclusive, largely white suburban enclaves. A common reason provided for opposition to desegregation was concern about rising crime rates during "times of change," but those fears were inextricably tied to racist stereotypes linking "black" and "Hispanic" with "criminal."[80]

Studies for decades documented racial discrimination in home loans.[81] Looking even at blacks with comparable incomes to whites, minority applicants are still more likely to be denied home loans.[82] In the 1990s, the Clinton administration pressured banks to grant more loans to minority applicants, although the problem of discrimination then trended in the opposite direction. Banks became more likely to target minority applicants for predatory lending. Black applicants were more likely to be pushed into low-quality loans with adjustable mortgage rates that could increase quickly in short periods of time.[83] These practices suggest the banking and housing industries have played a significant role in reinforcing societal racism.

The legacy of white flight and housing discrimination is evident in enduring patterns of residential segregation in the U.S. Compared to entire metropolitan populations, cities are overpopulated by minorities, and white affluent suburbs are underpopulated by minorities. The most segregated American cities include: Chicago, Atlanta, Milwaukee, Philadelphia, St. Louis, Washington DC, Baltimore, Cleveland, Baton Rouge, and New Orleans.[84]

2. EDUCATIONAL DISCRIMINATION

Residential segregation contributes to the perpetuation of poverty and lower-class status among people of color, since it limits educational and career opportunities. Most Americans attend schools within their communities. Thus, most American schools, like most towns and cities, are segregated. For example, 80 percent of Chicago metropolitan school districts were segregated in the 2010s. "Segregation" in this case includes any school district with a black or Hispanic population that is at least 75 to 80 percent higher than the metropolitan average, and that retains few minorities—typically less than 10 to 15 percent of all students attending.[85] These trends are the norm across the country. On average, a white student in the U.S. attends a school that is 73 percent white, 8 percent black, 12 percent Hispanic, and 4 percent Asian-American. However, the average black student attends a school that is 49 percent black, 17 percent Hispanic, 4 percent Asian-American, and 28 percent white.[86] So the average black student attends a school with nearly four times as many black students as should be the case.

Like black students, the average Hispanic student attends a school that is segregated—57 percent Hispanic, 11 percent black, 5 percent Asian-American, and just 25 percent white. So the average Hispanic student attends a school with more than three times as many Hispanic students as should be the case. Furthermore, school segregation is growing.[87] As depicted in figure 14.6, while the percent of black students attending majority white schools reached more than 40 percent in 1985, the number fell to nearly 20 percent by 2008.[88] In 2011, more than 40 percent of black students went to schools that were 90 percent minority or greater, compared to 35 percent of black students who went to schools with a 90 percent minority or greater concentration in 1991.[89]

Growing school segregation was likely a consequence of the growth of private and charter schooling. As affluent families self-select out of public schools, the pool of whites in those schools decreases.[90] Resegregation means an increased likelihood that poor students of color will be relegated to the margins, consigned to poverty and a lower-class status because of their diminished educational opportunities.

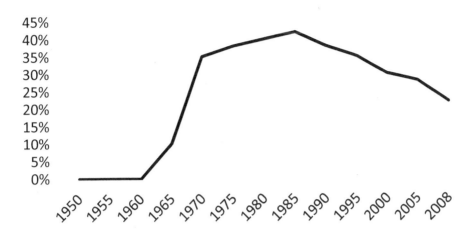

Figure 14.6. Desegregation and Resegregation of American Schools, 1950–2008 (% of Black Students Attending Majority White Schools). Source: Ian Milhiser, "American Schools are More Segregated Now Than They Were in 1968, and the Supreme Court Doesn't Care," *Think Progress*, August 13, 2015, https://thinkprogress.org/american-schools-are-more-segregated-now-than-they-were-in-1968-and-the-supreme-court-doesnt-care-cc7abbf6651c#.fjsaj52zs.

Segregation in schools matters because of funding inequality between whiter, more affluent schools, and poorer, heavily-minority schools. Poor minority communities struggle with funding compared to wealthier middle- and upper-class ones. Schools rely heavily on property tax funding, and school districts with more affluent neighborhoods raise more educational revenues. Local property taxes accounted for about 45 percent of all K-12 educational revenues across the 50 states.[91] And on average, educational funding in America's poorest school districts is 16 percent lower than in the wealthiest districts.[92]

Educational spending is statistically associated with academic performance.[93] While many studies find overall school spending is not correlated with student achievement, the relationship between funding and performance appears to be subtler.[94] Some research finds that factors such as teacher salary and educational level influence student outcomes.[95] Additionally, schools with more resources can hire more teachers. Schools with better student-teacher ratios commit greater time to instruction per student, improving academic performance.[96] In sum, money matters because it provides schools with more resources and students with better opportunities.

A second monetary factor associated with student performance is community wealth/poverty. Wealthier communities see higher academic performance in comparison to poor ones. In Illinois, a state I lived in for decades and closely researched, there is a significant relationship between community wealth and performance. Schools with higher percentages of poor students perform more poorly on standardized tests, and poorer academic results mean that students are less likely to be college-ready after high school graduation, less likely to attend college, and more likely to perform poorly when they do attend college. Figure 14.7 documents the relationship in Illinois between community poverty and academic performance, measured by college readiness.

Higher poverty schools—with at least three-quarters of students who are poor—consistently receive low academic marks, compared to wealthier schools— with poverty rates under 20 percent. On average, two-thirds of students in high-poverty schools graduate from high school, compared to the 90 to 100 percent graduation rate for wealthier schools. Only 10 percent of students in high-poverty schools are "college ready," compared to two-thirds of students at low poverty schools. Just 55 percent of students in high-poverty schools are enrolled in college twelve months after graduating high school, compared to three-quarters of students in low-poverty schools.[97] And academic performance is impacted by past experiences, with students from high-poverty high schools less likely to perform well in introductory-level college courses.[98]

Poverty and race were highly correlated in my research on Illinois school performance, with poor schools being more heavily minority-populated. For schools with low minority populations—less than 10 percent of students—academic performance was much higher than for minority-heavy schools—with more than 40

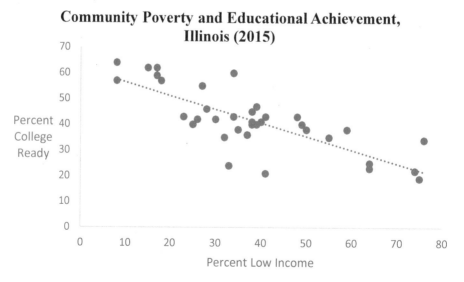

Figure 14.7. Community Poverty and Educational Achievement, Illinois, 2015. Source: Author's Survey, 2015, Illinois State Board of Education 2015 Report Card.

percent minority students. Whereas 55 percent of students in low-minority schools were deemed "college-ready" by the state, it was just 20 percent in high-minority schools. College enrollment twelve months after graduation was at 70 percent for low-minority schools, compared to 60 percent for high-minority schools. Graduation rates averaged 90 percent in low-minority schools, compared to 70 percent in high-minority schools. And race was a significant predictor of performance in entry-level college courses, with minority students performing more poorly, on average, than white students. National studies of the relationship between race, community wealth, and academic performance also demonstrate a significant relationship between these variables.[99]

While race is a significant predictor of academic outcomes, there is no evidence that students are academically inferior or superior because of race. In academic studies, race serves as a proxy for measuring poverty and wealth—schools that are overwhelmingly minority also tend to be poorer, compared to schools that are heavily white, which tend to be wealthier. But why does community wealth (or lack thereof) matter so much to educational performance? The answers are potentially many. Children from wealthier, middle- and upper-class families are more likely to benefit from various advantages. Greater family wealth or income means one parent can stay home to watch children and assist them educationally, whereas poorer families are less likely to enjoy this benefit. If parents from wealthier families are at home more often, they are likely to be more involved in their kid's academic affairs. They have more time to recognize child learning disabilities at an earlier age, and have more money to afford expensive therapies to help their children. Greater wealth means more resources for purchasing books in the home, and more time spent reading those books to children. Greater wealth means greater opportunities and time for extra-curricular learning activities, such as taking children to libraries and museums. Many wealthier and upper-class parents may be able to afford professional tutors if their children are not performing well academically. And wealthier, highly educated parents are better versed in various academic exercises, so they are better able to assist their children. Parents who spend more time with their children may also be better able to protect them from making destructive mistakes, such as using drugs. Wealth does not mean just one type of advantage for affluent families; it means potentially many.

3. Occupational Discrimination

When Americans think of occupational discrimination, they may imagine being denied a job because of skin color. This certainly occurs. Minority candidates are less likely to receive interviews for positions, compared to whites, even when educational qualifications between candidates is comparable. One academic study, "Jamal and Lakisha v. Greg and Ellen," found applicants with "black sounding" names received fewer call-backs for interviews than "white sounding" names, even when applicants had the same resumes.[100] But discrimination also occurs on a system-wide level. If one is denied adequate educational opportunities early in life, this impacts later educational opportunities at the collegiate level. Individuals with sub-par elementary and secondary education, and limited college opportunities suffer dwindling career prospects. Structurally speaking, lower earnings in poor black and Hispanic families is a function of unequal educational experiences. A well-established relationship exists between education and income, so the conclusion that education matters to earnings is hardly radical.[101]

Segregation and poverty within inner-cities also means fewer job opportunities. Urban white flight from cities to suburbs meant many well-paying jobs migrated to suburbs, following white residential relocation. Residential white flight produced occupational white flight.[102] The sociologist William Julius Wilson documented in the 1990s the rise of "jobless inner cities," due to urban decline and decay, and linked it to the rise of a black "under-class." If one travels through depressed slums of major cities like Chicago or St. Louis, it is blindingly obvious that these regions are unable to sustain middle-class lifestyles, considering the dearth of well-paying jobs. And the lack of opportunities within cities is structural—there simply are not enough well-paying jobs in depressed areas for those who want them.

Urban poverty remains pronounced, especially in minority communities. Black unemployment in the U.S. is twice the national average, and much of it is concentrated in inner-cities and older "inner-ring" suburbs. Furthermore, one sees meaningful differences in the ability to find jobs based on race. For example, just 16 percent of black Americans say "there are plenty of jobs available in my community," compared to 35 percent of whites.[103] In short, race is a meaningful divider in the occupational world.

4. LEGAL DISCRIMINATION

Racial discrimination is rampant in law enforcement. Deep distrust exists within minority communities against law enforcement.[104] The widespread perception is that people of color are discriminated against and harassed by police, whereas whites are treated far more favorably.

Racial differences in perceptions of the criminal justice system exist because individuals *are* treated differently based on race. For example, inequality is apparent in traffic stops. Blacks are three times more likely to be subject to police violence than whites, and the disparity persists, even after controlling for variation in crime rates among whites and blacks.[105] Across numerous measures, blacks are more likely to be subject to violence, even in cases when they do not resist arrest.[106] And the Department of Justice has released numerous reports criticizing police forces in Chicago, Baltimore, and Ferguson (Missouri) for systematically harassing and profiling people of color.[107]

Racial disparity is pronounced in the "War on Drugs." The number of incarcerated Americans increased from the 1980s through the 2010s from about 500,000 to 2.3 million, with those imprisoned being disproportionately minority and poor.[108] By the late-2000s, the U.S. had only five percent of the world's population, but 25 percent of all prisoners. Growing incarceration occurred at a time when violent crime was stagnant to declining.[109] Furthermore, most of the new offenses for which minorities were incarcerated were for nonviolent drug possession.[110]

Enforcement of the "War on Drugs" is largely concentrated in poorer minority communities. Inequality in enforcement of the drug war is even more controversial considering that whites use drugs such as hallucinogens, marijuana, pain killers, methamphetamine, and cocaine at higher rates than do minorities.[111] But minorities are targeted more often for drug offenses than whites. Thirty-five percent of drug arrests and 55 percent of drug convictions are against black Americans, and 74 percent of those imprisoned are black, although blacks are just 13 percent of drug users.[112] Blacks represent one million of the total 2.3 million incarcerated, a population-to-imprisonment imbalance of three-to-one.[113] Black and Hispanic individuals comprise 58 percent of all those incarcerated, but are only 31 percent of the population.[114]

Discrimination against minorities in the "War on Drugs" occurs in numerous stages of the criminal justice process. Within communities, racial profiling remains a problem, while the trial process is biased based on race and income against poorer and lower-class citizens. Law enforcement discriminate far more heavily against drug users in poorer minority communities regarding drug searches and arrests. This discrimination is justified by claiming that more crime occurs in poorer neighborhoods.[115] But this argument is self-serving. As previously noted, the claim that violent crime rates are higher among minorities is deeply exaggerated. Additionally, law enforcement artificially *create* higher crime rates in minority communities via racial profiling and aggressive drug searches. Higher arrest rates are inevitable when police stereotype blacks and Hispanics as more likely than whites to be criminals and drug users.

Racial profiling still occurs even when the "some communities have higher crimes rates" argument is removed from the equation. Highway studies in Illinois, Florida, Maryland, and New Jersey find minorities are more likely to be stopped and searched by police than whites, despite drug arrests being more common among whites stopped.[116] There is a simple explanation for the higher searches of minorities, coupled with the higher arrest rates for whites who are searched: police officers operate under the stereotype that minorities are drug users, and search their cars more often. In contrast, white drivers, who are not blanketly stereotyped as drug users, are less likely to get pulled over, unless they display some sign of intoxication. In those cases, police pull whites over, and are more likely to find drugs.

In the trial process, the number of convictions against minorities is already likely to be higher, since the number of charges against minorities is elevated due to racial profiling. And poorer people of color are less able to protect themselves against drug charges. Poorer minority defendants are more likely to rely on court-appointed attorneys, compared to more affluent whites, who can afford a private attorney. There are significantly lower incarceration rates for those securing private lawyers.[117] Court-appointed attorneys are often less experienced and over-worked compared to private attorneys, who can afford to charge more and take fewer cases.

Racial discrimination also persists in death penalty cases. Blacks and Hispanics are more likely to be convicted of the death penalty in murder cases, whereas whites charged with murder are more likely to receive life sentences. This discrimination was so blatant that it led the Supreme Court to outlaw the death penalty in *Furman v. Georgia* (1972). Following that case, evidence emerged that, after controlling for various factors, minorities were 1.7 times more likely to receive a death sentence compared to whites. Death sentences were 4.3 times more likely when the victim was white.[118] Since the 1970s, other evidence has surfaced of discrimination in death penalty cases. One study of North Carolina found the odds of receiving a death sentence were 3.5 times higher if the victim was white.[119] Furthermore, racial discrimination in death penalty cases still commonly occurs across the country.[120]

In other words, racial animosity is woven into the sentencing process, with white murders seen as more heinous than black or Hispanic murders, and with minority perpetrators treated more perniciously than white ones. These findings speak to the legal system's culpability in artificially creating a minority-based underclass.

Legal discrimination against minorities plays into occupational discrimination. If minorities are disproportionately targeted for felony drug convictions, the number of minorities with felony records will be greater than for whites. In the pre-civil rights era, blacks were denied jobs simply because of their skin color. Today, minorities are denied jobs because employers do not want to hire ex-felons.[121] Avoiding ex-felon hires does not make an employer racist, but it reinforces a racist legal system that discriminates against people of color.

5. Cultural Discrimination

Cultural discrimination is the process by which people of color are criminalized, enabling white Americans to force them into a lower-class status. Cultural discrimination is endemic in the media, which traffic in racist stereotypes, dehumanizing minorities and reinforcing white privilege. These practices are not explicit; journalists do not blatantly announce they are attacking minorities. Rather, implicit racial stereotypes dominate news and entertainment programs. Entertainment programs regularly traffic in racial stereotypes, and crime news coverage is disproportionately linked to minorities.

Media consumers often embrace stereotypes of minorities as lazy, deviant, and dangerous. Reporters over-represent blacks as criminals, compared to the actual number of blacks committing crimes. White people are over-represented as victims of crime, compared to the actual number of whites who are victims.[122] Whites exhibit "a super-humanization bias" when forming "perceptions of blacks." They are more likely to associate certain words with blacks over whites, including "ghost," "paranormal," "spirit," "wizard," "supernatural," "magic," and "mystical." Some cultural examples of "superhuman" qualities attributed to black athletes in the media include "Magic" Johnson and Michael "Air Jordan," and cinematic portrayals of blacks as supernatural figures, such as Morgan Freeman as "God" (*Bruce Almighty*).[123] One example of the superhuman bias was expressed by right-wing pundit Rush Limbaugh, who referred to the president as "Barack the Magic Negro" in a radio segment that spoke of whites voting for Obama to compensate for historic guilt over racism ("he makes guilty whites feel good") and because he did not conform to black stereotypes ("cause he's not from the hood").[124]

The superhuman portrayal of blacks reemerged during the testimony of Ferguson police officer Darren Wilson, regarding his grand jury trial for the shooting of Michael Brown. Eyewitness testimony was mixed regarding whether Wilson was guilty of excessive force or murder. However, Wilson's testimony was noteworthy in that he described Brown as a "demon" when recounting their altercation. This characterization fits within the broader cultural framework attributing superhuman powers to blacks. This kind of discourse makes it more difficult for Americans to challenge racial stereotypes. Negative depictions of blacks as super-human criminals create an "aggressor-victim" mindset, where blacks are deemed criminals and whites the victims of black violence.

Social science research finds that subtle racist news messages activate racist attitudes in audiences. Americans are subconsciously "primed" to embrace racial stereotypes, thereby supporting more intense punishments against blacks for violent crimes.[125] In one experiment, participants were separated into three groups, all of which viewed a five-minute crime news video. All groups saw the same video, with one exception—the image of the person depicted in the story. One group saw a black perpetrator. The second group saw a white perpetrator. The third group saw no image, serving as a "control" by being exposed to no racial content. Viewing the crime video with a black offender image produced greater support for "get tough on crime" policies than did viewership of the white image. The effect was noteworthy for white participants, while minority viewers were unaffected. Also revealing were the results from the "control group." Most participants in this group (60 percent) falsely recalled seeing an image. Of that 60 percent, most (70 percent) thought the image was of a black male. This finding suggests individuals came into the experiment with racial baggage, embracing stereotypes associating "black" with "criminal." This implicit baggage meant that the news can activate preexisting biases already in people's minds after years of being exposed to racial stereotyping in the media.

Other evidence relates racist stereotyping back to elections. Some research shows that candidates utilize the media to perpetuate racist images, in pursuit of their political goals.[126] Dozens of studies find that whites' political beliefs are influenced by media coverage characterizing black Americans as lazy, welfare dependent, violent, or demanding special favors."[127] The negative images in many Americans' minds linking people of color to poverty are fueled by media stereotypes. Recent research finds that news stories on poverty are heavily racialized, over-representing minorities as poor and on welfare, compared to the actual minority poverty rate. And opposition to welfare grows during periods when media increasingly link welfare to minorities.[128] Exposure to stories linking poverty and welfare to blacks increases the likelihood of attributing poverty to laziness, and fosters less support for welfare spending.[129] In short, media-induced stereotypes reinforce racially charged attacks on the welfare state.

Most whites do not recognize structural barriers in minority poor communities. The refusal to recognize structural barriers plays into racial stereotyping. If no barriers to racial equality exist outside of "bad behavior" and "laziness," then why support welfare programs benefitting poorer, lower-class people of color? Most black Americans in surveys agree that some people of color engage in bad behavior in their communities. In fact, black respondents are *more* likely to cite bad behavior as an explanation for problems in black communities. But most blacks also agree, unlike most whites, that structural barriers impede poverty reduction and limit individual opportunity. Opinions spotlighting alleged personality defects, which both whites and blacks agree are "big problem[s]" for minority communities include the following statements: "Too many teenage girls having children" (78 percent of blacks; 61 percent of whites agree); "Crime in their [black] neighborhoods" (60 percent of blacks and whites); "People depend too much on welfare" (63 percent of blacks, 53 percent of whites); "People not following moral and religious values" (63 percent of blacks, 50 percent of whites); "Drugs and alcoholism" (66 percent of blacks, 50 percent of whites); and "Too many parents never getting married" (51 percent of blacks, 49 percent of whites).[130] Assertions about structural problems in black communities, however, are recognized by most blacks, but not whites, including the following: "Not enough jobs paying decent wages" (68 percent of blacks, 48 percent of whites agree); "Public schools not providing a good education" (54 percent of blacks, 42 percent of whites); "Racism in society in general" (56 percent of blacks, 31 percent of whites); "The government not spending enough on social programs" (52 percent of blacks, 24 percent of whites); and "Racism in the workplace" (46 percent of blacks, 25 percent of whites agree).[131] One 2016 survey finds that whites are less likely than blacks to agree that blacks "have a harder time getting ahead than whites" because of "racial discrimination," "lower quality schools," and a "lack of jobs." Just 19 percent of whites agree "discrimination [is] built into laws and institutions."[132] These problems are well documented, even if most whites refuse to recognize structural barriers to racial equality.

Moving Forward

Institutions of racism have persisted for centuries, perpetuating racial inequality from generation to generation. This is not to suggest that those from poor, lower-class backgrounds cannot improve their position in life. But by ignoring the structural barriers to success, we do little to develop solutions for how to reduce racial inequality. With the rise of upper-class and business dominance of politics, poor minority communities are increasingly at risk of being left behind. Black activists recognize this problem, and are mobilizing in opposition to system-supported racial and economic inequality. With an eye toward spotlighting structural racism, Black Lives Matter protesters place police brutality, racial profiling, and societal racism at the forefront of the national discussion. Protests of police shootings (Michael Brown in Ferguson, Alton Sterling in Baton Rouge, and others), vigilante violence (Trayvon Martin's death in Miami Gardens), and police brutality (Eric Garner in New York City) dominated the news during the 2010s, and became symbols of a movement that has pushed to realize Martin Luther King Jr.'s dream of ending racism in America. This movement has succeeded in drawing attention to the problem of racial inequality. In 2013, 57 percent of Americans believed "race relations in the United States" were "generally good" in August 2013, but that number fell to just 26 percent by July 2016, following wave after wave of Black Lives Matter protests in city after city. This significant decline in such a short period—30 percentage points in just three years—suggests a serious change in the way Americans look at race. Still, the findings from this chapter suggest much more work must be done before the structures of racism are dismantled. With Donald Trump's emergence as the leader of the Republican Party, the negative backlash against civil rights activists grew, as seen in U.S. Attorney General Jeff Sessions's announcement that the Department of Justice was no longer interested in investigating charges of racism and police brutality by local police forces.[133]

Chapter 15

Economic Policy

Growing Inequality and Business Power in Politics

In 2017, *The Washington Post* reported that U.S. health outcomes were among the worst for poor people in the world. For those making less than $22,500 a year, nearly 40 percent reported being in "poor or fair health," when surveyed from 2011 to 2013, nearly three times worse than those making more than $47,700 a year, in which only 12 percent reported poor or fair health. Of 32 wealthy and middle-income countries, the only countries with wider inequality in health outcomes were Chile and Portugal.[1]

The differences between the U.S. and other countries were not an accident. In a for-profit health care system, little attention is given to how the poor can afford increasingly expensive health care treatments and insurance. While Obamacare made some progress in increasing the number of the insured, and in providing financial subsidies and aid to working-class Americans and the poor, 28 million Americans remained uninsured at the beginning of 2017.[2] In a system in which government has little interest in regulating health care costs, the ever-increasing cost of health care is unaffordable for many in the working class. The U.S. welfare state is stingy, not only with regard to health care, but across most programs, as I discuss in this chapter. With so little interest in combating inequality and poverty, poorer and lower-class Americans are subject to the discipline of the marketplace, struggling to afford basic needs such as health care.

This chapter spotlights the increasingly elitist nature of American public policy in the neoliberal era. More and more, government exists to serve upper-class and corporate interests, with declining interest in representing the wants and needs of the masses of middle-class and poorer Americans. The preference for the wealthy and neglect of the masses manifests itself in a variety of ways: in an anemic and declining welfare state that is under assault due to the growing fixation on wave-after-wave of tax cuts for the rich; in the growing attacks on the poor and the welfare state in the corporate media; and via increasingly popular neoliberal policies that privilege corporate elites over the working class and the poor.

U.S. Budgeting and Taxation: Correcting Myths and Misconceptions

In the neoliberal era, propaganda abounds, with politicians and media pundits conveying the false impressions that budgets and taxes are a crushing burden on middle-America and the wealthy, and that government confers undeserved benefits on the poor. I debunk these myths in detail in this chapter.

Government Taxation and Spending

Americans are not taxed as much, and government does not spend as much as is commonly believed. More than half of Americans believed in 2014 that federal taxes were too high.[3] But what is the reference point? As of 2016, taxes in the U.S. equaled 25 percent of Gross Domestic Product (GDP).[4] Compared to the size of the economy, a 25 percent taxation-to-GDP rate was relatively low compared to other wealthy countries. Austria, Finland, France, Norway, Italy, Belgium, Sweden, and Denmark all taxed their citizens at more than 40 percent of GDP. Other countries did not tax that much, but taxed much higher than the U.S. Those taxing at greater than 30 percent of GDP, but less than 40 percent included: The Netherlands, Luxembourg, Germany, Iceland, U.K., Spain, Israel, New Zealand, and Canada. Switzerland, Ireland, Japan, South Korea, and Australia taxed at under 30 percent of GDP, but at a rate greater than the U.S.[5] Overall, the U.S. taxed citizens *the least* compared to all other wealthy countries.

In 2016, the U.S. was also near the bottom of the list of wealthy countries in government spending. Some countries maintained government spending that was at or exceeded 50 percent of GDP, including: Belgium, Denmark, France, Finland, and the Netherlands. All these countries spent more than the U.S., which spent at 39 percent of GDP. Japan's and Canada's spending were 42 and 41 percent of GDP, respectively, while Norway and Germany were both at 44 percent of GDP. Australia, in contrast, spent at 36 percent of GDP—less than the U.S. The only first-world countries spending less than the U.S. were South Africa, South Korea, Australia, and Switzerland.[6] Contrary to the "big government" myth, the U.S. is one of the most conservative governments in the first world when it comes to taxing and spending.

Welfare Myths

Many Americans believe the federal government redistributes wealth from the upper class to the poor via overly-generous welfare programs. More than half of

Americans in 2015 wanted "smaller government," while 44 percent said "government aid to the poor does more harm than good by making people too dependent on government assistance."[7] But the U.S. government is no Robin Hood; it is the least committed of all first-world countries to redistributing economic resources from the wealthy to the middle class and poor.[8]

Welfare recipients are depicted in anti-government rhetoric as exploiting programs. They are "lazy," "good-for-nothings," who prefer "free benefits," "drug use," and "having lots of babies" over work. The image of the Cadillac-driving, steak-and-lobster eating welfare-cheat was popularized by the Reagan administration in the 1980s, and is now common, feeding the view that the poor are secretly well off, while the victimized upper class suffers under high taxes that fund the extravagance of the undeserving poor.[9]

But these depictions are not grounded in reality. Ninety-one percent of welfare recipients in the 2010s were either employed, disabled, or seniors, and most welfare went to families with working parents.[10] Welfare beneficiaries are far less likely to own a car compared to non-beneficiaries—let alone a fancy car or a Cadillac—and are more likely to report troubles holding a job due to transportation problems.[11] Just one-quarter of those on welfare own a home, compared to three-quarters of non-welfare beneficiaries.[12] The average family size in the U.S. does not vary based on whether one receives welfare, laying waste to the claim that welfare recipients have "lots of babies" to avoid work.[13] And the vast majority of individuals on welfare do not use drugs, contrary to popular depictions.[14] State monitoring programs find drug use is less common by welfare recipients than non-recipients; less than one percent of beneficiaries test positive for drugs in states where testing occurs.[15]

U.S. welfare spending is quite meager.[16] The average American family (of 3) in the poorest 20 percent of the income distribution receives just $9,000 in social welfare benefits per year. This includes funding from Temporary Assistance to Needy Families, Medicaid, housing subsidies, and food stamps, among other benefits. This translates into $3,000 a year for each family member, or just $250 a month per person a month. These benefits are stingy, contrary to conservative claims that the poor are abusing the system.

The federal food stamp program is hardly lavish. The average family in the bottom fifth of income earners gets $1,600 in food stamp benefits a year. That means $133.33 per month. For a family of three, that translates into $3.33 per day, or $1.11 per person a day. Contrary to claims that beneficiaries are long-term moochers, most food stamps recipients are on the program temporarily, with two-thirds receiving benefits for one to three years.[17] Despite widespread complaints about abuse, documented fraud constitutes just 1.5 percent of program spending.[18]

Claims that food stamp beneficiaries are wasteful in their purchases are not accurate. The U.S. Department of Agriculture's study of the food stamp program concludes beneficiaries are no more likely to spend money on junk food or sugary drinks than non-beneficiary households. There are "no major differences in the expenditure patterns of beneficiary and non-beneficiary households, no matter how the data are categorized." These households are virtually identical for consumption of "meats, fruits, vegetables, milk, eggs, and bread," for purchases of "cereal, prepared foods, dairy products, rice, and beans," and consumption of "sweetened beverages, desserts, salty snacks, candy, and sugar."[19]

Temporary Assistance for Needy Families (TANF) is another program criticized for abuse. But the average TANF benefit for a family of three averaged from $303 to $521 a month depending on the state, or just $101 to $174 a month per person.[20] And at least half of TANF beneficiaries in each state, and at least 90 percent of two-parent family beneficiaries must hold jobs to benefit from the program.[21] This makes it hard to "game" the system by receiving benefits without working. TANF benefits are temporary, with a five-year lifetime limit, so there is no way beneficiaries can stay on the program long-term. Finally, two-thirds of TANF recipients rely on the program temporarily, receiving benefits, on average, for less than a year.[22] In other words, the program works as a temporary aid, not as an alternative to work.

Compared to welfare for the rich, social welfare spending is low. Consider estimates for the cost in 2014 of various welfare programs for the needy, working-class, and poor: $55 billion for the Earned Income Tax Credit; $21 billion for TANF; $75 billion for food stamps; $18 billion for housing vouchers, $228 billion for Medicaid, and $43.7 billion for disability benefits, totaling $441 billion a year.[23] Projected over a decade—at 2014 levels—this amounts to $4.4 trillion. This is a significant amount of money, but it pales in comparison to corporate welfare subsidies. One recent estimate, counting various benefits such as pharmaceutical industry monopoly patents granted by government, various tax loopholes and other corporate tax subsidies, export-import bank subsidies, and other welfare programs that benefit wealthy Americans, finds $1.54 trillion in corporate welfare benefits per year.[24] Over ten years, that totals $15.4 trillion, a subsidy 3.5 times larger than the benefits going to the poor. One could add to this President Trump's tax cuts, with one estimate suggesting a cost of as much as $5.9 trillion, of which nearly half would go to the top one percent of income earners.[25] The grand total of corporate welfare is estimated at over $20 trillion—more than the U.S. owed for its entire national debt in 2016.

The U.S. does not spend large amounts of money on welfare programs for the poor relative to the rich. And what is spent on the poor has not grown in recent years. The costs of TANF and cash subsidies have fallen dramatically since the 1990s.[26] Medicaid and food stamp costs, while growing in the late-2000s and early-2010s due to the rise in national poverty after the 2008 economic crash, both fell by the mid-to-late 2010s.[27] Public housing and housing voucher subsidies also fell from the early-to-mid 2010s.[28] The only welfare programs that saw growing costs during the 2010s were Medicare and Social Security, due to the baby boomer generation increasingly entering retirement.[29] But Medicare and Social Security are seldom attacked by political officials, and are often depicted as programs that benefit "deserving" middle- and upper-class Americans. They are not generally referred to as "welfare," but as "entitlements."

With the modest and declining costs of welfare for the poor, and the large disparities between welfare for the upper and lower classes, why are poor Americans the subject of so much anger from political officialdom and the public? A simple answer is that American political elites have long been committed to fighting a class war against the poor, and to the benefit of the upper-class and wealthy. By scapegoating the poor and framing the wealthy as the victims of the poor, officials add fuel to the fire in pushing for government deregulation of corporations, additional tax cuts for the upper class, and maintaining other forms of corporate welfare.

Wasteful Spending?

Americans fixate on "wasteful" government spending, but most of the budget goes to popular programs. A budgetary breakdown of major programs for 2016 included: "defense," military spending, and veteran's benefits (19 percent of the budget); Social Security, unemployment insurance, and government labor costs (36 percent); Medicare, Medicaid, and Child Health Insurance Program (28 percent); discretionary spending, including food stamps, TANF, disability benefits, unemployment benefits, working-class tax credits, transportation spending, scientific research, and other programs (11 percent); and interest on the debt (6 percent). National surveys find that most Americans oppose cutting spending in nearly all of these areas. The public does seem to be open to significant reductions in military spending.[30] But few political officials support this option, preferring to target welfare instead.

The American Tax Structure

A common myth is that the wealthy are soaked in taxes.[31] To the contrary, corporate tax rates were near historic lows in the late-2010s, compared to previous rates in the post-World War II era. While the U.S. technically has the third highest marginal corporate income tax rate in the world, this tells us little about corporate taxes because of all the business loopholes. *Citizens for Tax Justice's* study of major U.S. corporations estimates the actual corporate tax rate is 19.4 percent, far lower than the marginal corporate income tax rate of 39 percent.[32] In comparison, the *Tax Foundation* estimates the global average marginal corporate tax rate is 22.9 percent, meaning U.S. corporate taxes come in below the world average.[33] Furthermore, tax rates for high-income earners were near all-time lows in early 2017. Overall, taxes on the wealthy and the upper class were between moderately progressive to flat, depending on how one interprets available data. Wealthier Americans pay more into the federal income tax, which is progressive (the more one earns, the larger percent of taxes one pays). However, the progressivity of the federal income tax has fallen dramatically since the 1940s and 1950s, when the top income tax bracket was taxed at 91 percent of earnings, compared to the last two decades, when the top income tax bracket ranged between 28 to 40 percent.

What is lost by fixating on federal income tax rates is that this is merely one tax. Other taxes are less biased against the wealthy, and some are regressive, with the poor paying a larger percent than the wealthy. The payroll tax, for example, falls on American workers. State and local taxes in the U.S. are also regressive, relying heavily on sales taxes. Sales taxes are applied to much of the earnings of working-class and poor Americans, as these groups spend much of their incomes on basic needs. In contrast, upper-class, higher-income Americans often hold income in reserve after paying their bills; this income is untouched by the sales tax.

According to the *Institute on Taxation and Economic Policy*, and as seen in table 15.1, after accounting for the federal income tax, payroll tax, corporate taxes, and state and local taxes, the U.S. tax system ranges from moderately progressive to flat. Looking at "total taxes" from table 15.1 upper-class individuals in the top 20 percent of income earners paid 30.1 percent of their income into taxes in 2018, compared to the second highest 20 percent of earners, who paid 29 percent, the middle 20 percent of the income distribution, which paid 25.4 percent, the second poorest 20 percent, who paid 25.4 percent, and the poorest 20 percent, which paid 15.9 percent. But these figures tell only part of the story. An alternative examination of the tax system and table 15.1 would focus on what percent of all taxes each income group pays, compared to their share of all income earned. Using this benchmark, one sees a flat tax rate. The poorest 20 percent of Americans earned just 3.5 percent of all income in 2018, and paid just 1.9 percent of all taxes; the middle 20 percent of earners paid 18.8

Table 15.1. Incomes and Federal, State, and Local Taxes, 2018

Income Earners	Total Share of all Income	Total Share of all Taxes	Total Taxes as a % of Income
Lowest 20%	3.5%	1.9%	15.9%
Second Lowest 20%	7.1%	5.0%	20.8%
Middle 20%	11.3%	9.8%	25.4%
Second Highest 20%	18.8%	18.8%	29.0%
Next 15%	24.6%	26.2%	30.5%
Next 4%	14.4%	15.1%	29.5%
Top 1%	22.9%	20.3%	30.4%

Source: Institute on Taxation and Economic Policy, "Who Pays Taxes in America in 2018?" *Institute on Taxation and Economic Policy*, April 2018, https://itep.org/wp-content/uploads/WPTIA2018.pdf

percent of all taxes, and earned 18.8 percent of all income. Members of the upper-class—the top 20 percent of income earners—paid 64.2 percent of all taxes, but earned 61.9 percent of all income. In sum, each income group paid a flat tax in that there was parity between their shares of income earned and taxes paid.

While upper-class individuals pay a larger percent of their incomes into taxes, they also control a disproportionate share of all income. Taxing the wealthiest 20 percent at a higher rate may anger higher-income Americans who feel they pay more than their fair share, but the reality is that there simply are not enough tax revenues to go around among the poor to fund a four-trillion-dollar budget, especially when the poorest 40 percent earn just 10.6 percent of all national income, and the poorest 20 percent earn just 3.5 percent of all income.

Responsible Republicans, Spend-Thrift Democrats?

A final economic myth is the claim that the Republican Party supports "responsible" government spending, while the Democrats spend recklessly. This claim is contradicted by the history of federal spending in recent decades. From 1945 to 1979, both parties consistently spent less than the federal government took in from tax revenues. And since 1980, both parties have contributed to deficit spending. Contrary to right-wing rhetoric, the largest growth in national debt since 1980 occurred under both parties' watch, via Republican President George W. Bush and Democratic President Barack Obama. Much of this deficit increase during the Bush years was due to tax cuts for upper-class income earners and increased military spending, the latter of which largely benefitted one segment of the upper-class—military contractors. The Clinton Administration briefly balanced the budget by 2000, although Obama presided over deficit spending almost as large as that seen under George W. Bush.[35] Part of the reason for these deficits was increased social welfare obligations, amidst declining tax revenues, after the 2008 economic crash. A second reason was high military spending, coupled with the loss of revenues from the Bush tax cuts, both of which continued through much of Obama's presidency. Neither party has balanced the budget in modern times, but Republicans have performed even worse due to their tax cuts for the wealthy.

The Bush tax cuts were a huge gift to the upper class, with 75 percent of the cuts directed to the top 20 percent of income earners.[36] The Bush Administration and its supporters promised the cuts would produce strong economic growth that would benefit all.[37] Although the tax cuts added trillions to the national debt, they did little to promote growth. The economic recovery following the "dot-com" crash, from 2001 to 2007, was the weakest recovery (up to that point) from a recession in post-World War II history, with the U.S. averaging 2.7 percent annual growth. Compare this to previous recoveries from recessions: the 1991–2001 recovery (3.4 percent annual growth); 1982–1990 (4.2 percent growth); 1980–1981 (4.4 percent growth); 1975–1980 (4.3 percent growth); 1970–1973 (5.2 percent growth); 1961–1969 (4.8 percent growth); 1958–1960 (5.7 percent growth); 1954–1957 (3.9 percent growth); and 1949–1953 (7.5 percent growth).[38]

The Bush era saw some of the weakest job growth in the post-World War II era. During Bush's presidency, 150,877 jobs were created on average per month. Only the Kennedy and George H. W. Bush administrations averaged less growth (at 126,667 and 129,412 jobs per month). All other presidents from Roosevelt through Obama had greater monthly job creation.[39] Furthermore, the Bush years were associated with a large increase in inequality. From 1948 to 1979, the bottom 90 percent of income earners captured 67 percent of all income growth, whereas the top 10 percent captured about a third. In contrast, from 2000 to 2007, the bottom 90 percent of income earners saw zero gains, with all income growth captured by the top 10 percent, and with the top one percent capturing 75 percent of gains.[40] Income inequality escalated under the Trump Administration, following its large tax cuts for the rich.

Neoliberalism and the Rise of Inequality

Neoliberalism envisions government not as a tool for empowering and representing the masses of middle-class and poorer Americans, but as a weapon to be wielded by the wealthy against the many. I discuss six features of neoliberalism that have emerged in modern times. These include: 1. The push for government deregulation; 2. A growing commitment to the belief that workers are disposable and have few rights; 3. The decline of U.S. manufacturing jobs via outsourcing; 4. "Drift," or the idea that, as cost of living rises and pay for the masses stagnates to declines, the federal government shoulders no responsibility for addressing these developments; 5. Efforts to cut social welfare programs; and 6. The strengthening of corporate welfare, with taxpayers becoming responsible for protecting corporate profits.

Deregulation

Deregulation has occurred in various industries, including the airlines, the media, the finance sector, in the beef and drug industries, and with labor law. With the Airline Deregulation Act of 1978, the federal government removed restrictions on fare rates, flight routes, and market entry for new airline corporations, significantly increasing the profitability of existing airlines. Media deregulation occurred in the 1990s, when Congress eased ownership rules that allowed for the consolidation of media ownership, with a small number of media corporations able to buy up large numbers of media outlets, and with consolidation particularly pronounced in the radio and cable industries.[41] Financial sector deregulation occurred in the 1990s and 2000s via the removal of regulations on commodities futures and the elimination of rules requiring a legal separation between ownership of traditional banks and firms engaging in risky speculative investments. The bureaucracy chapter documented the decline of government regulation over the meat and drug industries—which have endangered public health. Finally, U.S. labor has entered a period of prolonged decline. Businesses pay a lower minimum wage every year, so long as Congress refuses to raise it to keep pace with inflation. The federal government fails to enforce labor laws against large corporations, which illegally fire workers for union organizing.

The above changes dramatically increase the power of major corporations, while harming the public. Consumers have much to fear from contaminated meat and pharmaceutical drugs. Airline and media deregulation were followed by a flurry of consolidations, as fewer and fewer companies bought up competing firms. Media and airline consolidation allowed for rising cable, phone, and airline rates, with just four corporations controlling 75 percent of air travel in the 2010s.[42] Deregulation of finance and banking interests encouraged reckless investing and home loans resulting in the collapse of the housing market and home values, and a massive loss of median household wealth. Declining labor protections have depressed working-class incomes.

Disposable Workers

The rise of disposable workers is another major development of neoliberalism. Increasingly, employers present working Americans with a choice between bad jobs and no jobs. One can have a job at low pay, with an ever-declining value of the minimum wage, or no job at all, as employers threatening to fire workers if the minimum wage is raised, or when employees seek to unionize. "Employment at will" often means employment with low pay and few benefits. Complaining about poor work conditions can lead to being fired for "insubordination." Such abuses are endured by workers when they have no collective, democratic means of negotiating with employers for better treatment and pay.

The job climate was not always so harsh. Academics and historians documented the rise of the "Fordist" workplace in the mid-twentieth century. One scholar defines Fordism as a "manufacturing system designed to spew out standardized, low cost goods and afford its workers decent enough wages to buy them."[43] The idea is that employers retain a social responsibility to provide workers a higher standard of living, providing decent pay and benefits. Fordism as a practice was personified in the actions of auto manufacturer Henry Ford, who in 1914 raised assembly line employee wages from $2 to $5 a day, thereby enabling his workers to purchase Ford cars.[44] But most corporations opposed raising wages during the early-twentieth century, and labor unions were widely despised by business leaders, as was establishing a minimum wage. In the 1930s, however, the federal government outlawed child labor, imposed a 40-hour work week, established a minimum wage, and allowed workers to unionize to collectively bargain for pay and benefits. These changes were significant. Government was committed to regular increases in the minimum wage throughout the 1950s and 1960s—increases that translated into increases in worker pay that outpaced inflation.[45]

The driving force behind Fordism was the belief that if government forced employers to treat their employers well, this would benefit workers and the economy. By corporations "spreading the wealth" of their profits, it meant healthy income growth for the typical worker, continued profits for businesses, and strong economic growth via a strong middle class. Unionization contributed greatly to the growth of the middle class. Between the 1940s and 1970s, the nation saw growing pay for the average worker, coupled with steady corporate profits and strong economic growth. By the 1980s onward, however, the U.S. moved toward a post-Fordist, neoliberal model, one that I refer to as "the Wal-Mart model."

The Wal-Mart model is very different from Fordism. There are still well-paying, largely service-based occupations today—at least for those who are well-educated and highly-skilled. But with the decline of manufacturing jobs, the number of low-skill, low-paying jobs, is rising. The Wal-Mart model rejects the belief that employees deserve decent pay and benefits. This mindset is clear in the employment methods of Wal-Mart, Target, McDonalds, and other service-based businesses. Employees are paid low wages; many are denied health insurance. Worker contributions for health care also tend to be higher at corporations characterized by lower levels of pay.[46] Employees are intimidated into obedience, since those who try to organize are fired. These practices are common today. The federal government endorses the Wal-Mart model by keeping the minimum wage low and allowing corporations to fire workers for organizing.

The assault on labor has profound consequences. While the number of Americans in unions was nearly one-third by the mid-twentieth century, just one in ten were in a union by the mid-2010s.[47] Union decline meant a corresponding decline in pay. There was a 1:1 ratio between the decline in unionization from the 1960s through the 2000s, and the middle-classes' share of national income.[48] Unsurprisingly, if corporations pay workers less, as they have been for male workers, this results in greater profits for businesses. The decline in unionization and middle-class incomes means a significant increase in the share of income going to the upper class, specifically to the top one percent of income-earners.[49]

Labor's decline was caused in large part by outsourcing of union jobs to other countries. Corporations pay sweatshop workers a fraction of the U.S. minimum wage, and avoid expensive environmental regulations. Outsourcing began in the 1970s and 1980s, as U.S. businesses faced increased competition from firms abroad. To "remain competitive" while boosting profits, U.S. corporations eliminated union jobs in favor of sweatshop labor abroad. Manufacturing jobs as a percent of U.S. employment declined. As documented in figure 15.1, that share was 25 percent in 1960, but just 15 percent by 1990, and less than 10 percent by 2011.[50] During these decades, the U.S. transitioned from a manufacturing to a service economy. Occupations were increasingly divided between high-skilled, high-pay jobs demanding extensive education, and low-skilled, low-pay jobs.

The federal government played a significant role in this process. Officials did little to criticize corporations for outsourcing, and never threatened to revoke corporate charters or ban these businesses from selling their products and services in the U.S. By the 1990s, the U.S. government was *promoting* outsourcing. The NAFTA agreement, passed under President Bill Clinton, escalated the shift of manufacturing jobs to Mexico. Americans who previously earned a middle-class income assembling automobiles were left to seek employment at a fraction of their previous pay. The federal government's reluctance to punish corporations for firing workers for union organizing ensured that newly created service-based jobs in the U.S. paid low wages compared to previous union jobs. While President Trump promised to return factory jobs to the U.S., his proposed tax on goods from Mexico was unlikely to reverse a trend in outsourcing that had been

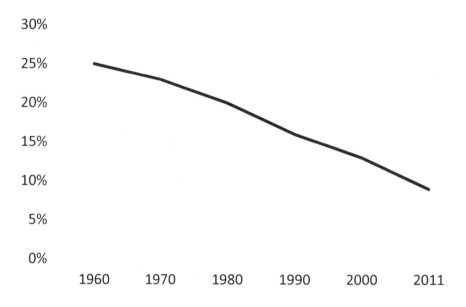

Figure 15.1. U.S. Deindustrialization, 1960–2011 (Manufacturing as a % of all Employment). Source: Martin Neil Baily and Barry P. Bosworth, "U.S. Manufacturing: Understanding its Past and its Potential Future," *Brookings Institution*, February 5, 2014, https://www.brookings.edu/research/u-s-manufacturing-understanding-its-past-and-its-potential-future/.

occurring for decades, especially when the cost could simply be shifted to the public via increased prices for goods.

The declining minimum wage had repercussions for the working poor. During the Fordist era, the federal government regularly increased the minimum wage so its value grew beyond inflation. The minimum wage was raised by a total of $10.07 in value (in 2014 dollars) between 1950 and 1969—over 20 years. That wage reached a high value (in 2014 dollars) of $10.94 an hour in the late 1960s.[51] The 1970s onward, however, saw serious decline in the minimum wage. In the 20 years from 1970 to 1989 the minimum wage was raised a total of just $6.51 in value in 2014 dollars. Similarly, the wage was raised a total of only $5.31 in 2014 dollars in the 20 years from 1990 to 2009.[52] As of 2016, the minimum wage had fallen to just $7.25 an hour compared to its value of $10.94 in 1969—a 34 percent decline. Republicans lambasted Obama after calling for a $10.10 minimum wage in 2014, but that was still a reduction of 8 percent from the wage's 1969 value.

Estimates suggest the minimum wage should have been $22 an hour in the early-2010s if its value had kept pace with growing worker productivity from the late-1960s onward.[53] The failure of the minimum wage to gain or hold its value meant employers shifted the cost of inflation to workers. In an age of growing profits and productivity, the fruits of American labor were captured by those in the upper class who owned businesses, not those who worked for them. The stagnation of household earnings and the decline of male earnings suggest "free market" promises that corporations will provide their workers "just rewards" as the economy and profits grow is a myth. To the contrary, businesses pressure employees to work harder for *less*.

An elaborate ideological system defends businesses for paying low wages. An army of media pundits and politicians claim that raising the minimum wage harms workers, since employers will supposedly offset the cost by firing workers or raising the price of goods and services. If the cost of goods and services goes up (inflation), workers could lose ground even with higher pay.

There is little evidence to validate these claims. Recent research—synthesizing many scholarly studies—finds little evidence of negative effects of raising the minimum wage on unemployment. Most studies find no negative effect, or such a very small effect as to be negligible.[54] My own research on state minimum wage increases in the 2000s found that states raising the minimum wage meant higher wages for fast-food workers, without a negative impact on employment or inflation. This finding is noteworthy because it suggests the "the minimum wage causes inflation" claim is not valid. To the contrary, I found that workers who did *not* receive a minimum wage increase were hurt by inflation, while those in states raising wages saw income growth that outpaced inflation. The positive effect of the minimum wage on earnings, after adjusting for inflation, is also apparent in national data, as frequent raises in the minimum wage in the 1950s and 1960s significantly increased its value after accounting for inflation.

There is no meaningful link between minimum wage increases and inflation. As depicted in figure 15.2, changes in the inflation rate from the late-1940s through the early-2010s were not statistically associated with changes in the minimum wage's value.[55] And a Chicago Federal Reserve study concludes that a higher minimum wage actually stimulates economic activity by increasing incomes and consumer spending.[56] As *Forbes* summarized the study: "increasing the minimum wage to $9 would increase consumer spending by $28 billion. When spending increases, manufacturers and other purveyors of goods and services can actually charge less or at least avoid increasing their prices, because they're increasing overall revenue."[57]

Why do conservative pundits and politicians oppose the minimum wage if it has no meaningful effect on unemployment and inflation, and if it helps workers? The simple answer is that they are interested in enhancing corporate profits, not worker pay. Seeking ever-increasing profits, businesses have an economic incentive to push employees to work more hours, more productively, for less. This means greater profits for corporations and greater wealth for upper-class business elites.

Figure 15.2. Minimum Wage and Inflation, 1945–2014. Sources: Department of Labor, "Wage and Hour Division," 2017; Bureau of Labor Statistics, "CPI: All Urban Consumers," *U.S. Department of Labor*, 2017, https://data.bls.gov/timeseries/CUUR0000SA0L1E? output_view=pct_12mths; and: Jamie Hopkins, "How to Mitigate Inflation Risk in A Retirement Income Plan," *Fortune*, March 30, 2014, https://www.forbes.com/sites/jamie hopkins/2014/03/30/how-to-mitigate-inflation-risk-in-a-retirement-income-plan/#77f13b 7940c3.

Drift

Political scientists speak of the concept of "drift."[58] It refers to how, in the neoliberal era, citizens are increasingly left to drift along, without government assistance, despite growing cost of living and declining wages. Drift also applies to the rising costs of higher education, health care, housing, and consumer goods. *The New York Times* estimates prices for all consumer items increased by 200 percent from the mid-1980s to the early-2010s. However, costs of other expenses increased more quickly, including gasoline (300 percent increase), medical care (more than 350 percent), and higher education (nearly 600 percent).[59] Higher education has seen runaway growth in costs. In 1980, a worker earning the minimum wage could work 6.5 weeks to cover annual tuition costs at a state university. But by 2010, someone working at the minimum wage had to work 23 weeks to cover tuition.[60] These cost-of-living changes outpace pay increases for nearly all Americans. From the late-1970s through the late-2000s, the take-home pay for the bottom 20 percent of income earners grew by just 16 percent, and the second poorest 20 percent by 12 percent. The middle 20 percent of income earners saw a 25 percent increase, and the top 20 percent saw a 95 percent increase. It was only the top one percent and .01 percent that saw their incomes increase to match or surpass cost of living increases, with 300 percent and nearly 800 percent growth, respectively.[61]

Some consumer products and services have gotten cheaper in recent years. Prices for cell-phone service plans, televisions, computers, vehicles, toys, and clothing fell between 20 to 100 percent from 2005 to 2014. But the cost of other major items such as food, vehicle maintenance, health care, child care, and education increased.[62] Many of the items that decreased in cost were non-essential consumer items—televisions, computers, cell-phone plans, and toys. Many items that increased in cost—food, health care, and child care—are necessities. Higher education is not a necessity, but is increasingly necessary *if* one wants to avoid a low-income career.

Under neoliberalism, government does not prioritize assisting middle-class and poor Americans in regulating cost of living for necessities, despite individual and family incomes stagnating to declining. These costs are pushed onto Americans, who conservatives insist must be "personally responsible." Claiming individual responsibility for covering human needs is puzzling considering upper-class business elites' receipt of trillions in corporate welfare subsidies. What is the moral or ethical defense for subsidizing business interests, while disciplining the masses? Many conservatives claim the rich deserve their position in the economic hierarchy because they work hard, but most Americans work hard in their jobs.[63]

The Assault on Social Welfare

Over the last four decades, both parties called for and implemented cuts in social welfare programs for the poor and needy. In the 1980s, Reagan cut federal aid to the poor for urban transit and public housing, Medicaid, and food stamps.[64] The rhetoric of "personal responsibility" became prominent, despite wealthier, upper-class citizens receiving tax cuts, protectionist trade policies such as tariffs on foreign imports, and increased military spending benefitting military contractors.[65] The push to cut welfare continued under Clinton with the elimination of Aid to Families with Dependent Children (AFDC), which provided cash subsidies to the poor.[66] The push to transform welfare programs to benefit corporate America has also begun, with Republicans' seeking to privatize Social Security and Medicare, forcing workers to invest retirement earnings in the stock market, and requiring seniors to purchase for-profit health insurance.[67] Obama continued the neoliberal push by calling for cuts to Social Security and Medicare.[68] And Trump supported trillions in tax cuts for the wealthy, spending cuts for the EPA, legal aid to the poor, and food stamps for immigrants.[69]

The Effects of Neoliberalism

Government efforts to empower corporate and upper-class interests, at the expense of the masses, have increased inequality. From the 1940s to the 1970s, the U.S. was characterized by strong unions, a stronger minimum wage, an ascendant welfare system under the Great Society, and higher taxes on the wealthy to pay for those benefits. Inequality was far lower than in later decades. But from the 1980s onward, unions were weakened, the minimum wage declined, the welfare system was under assault, and tax cuts for the wealthy became the norm. The declining value of the minimum wage, and declining pay for male workers, meant declining opportunities for upward mobility.[70] From the 1940s through the 1970s the country experienced what *The New York Times* calls the "Great Prosperity," because of the widespread opportunities and high pay for workers. In contrast, the *Times* deemed the 1980s onward the "Great Regression." [71]

During the "Great Prosperity," worker productivity increased by 119 percent, and average hourly worker compensation and pay increased 100 percent and 72 percent, respectively.[72] As corporate profits increased, a rising tide really did lift all boats, improving the lives of the working poor and middle class, so long as the federal government protected unions and maintained a higher minimum wage. In contrast, from 1979 to 2009, worker productivity increased by 80 percent, but average hourly compensation and pay increased just 8 and 7 percent, respectively.[73] Businesses increasingly opposed compensating workers for increasing productivity, and the decline of unions and the minimum wage meant workers' life prospects were increasingly precarious. Growing inequality meant that corporate profits never "trickled down" to the masses. Between 1979 and 2007, the top one percent to .01 percent of income earners, making between $450,000 and $40 million a year, saw their incomes grow by 300 percent and nearly 800 percent, respectively, after inflation.[74] The top 20 percent saw their incomes grow by about 95 percent. By comparison, the rest of America saw little increase in their incomes, with the middle 20 and poorest 20 percent's incomes largely stagnating.[75]

Growing income inequality intensified under Obama. From 2009 to 2012, incomes for the top one percent increased 31 percent, and 95 percent of all income gains went to the top one percent of earners.[76] These statistics suggest the economy was broken, no longer functioning for the benefit of the middle class and poor, despite corporations and the wealthiest segment of the upper class getting back to pre-recession profits by 2010.[77] This point might have been lost on many Americans in the flurry of warnings from corporate America that workers must "tighten their belts" during "tough" economic times. Many workers probably accepted these claims considering the appearance of a precarious economy, with economic growth averaging just 2.1 percent a year from 2010 to 2015, far lower than the average growth in previous economic recoveries.[78] Furthermore, unemployment levels remained relatively high during this period, ranging from a high in 2010 of 10 percent, to a low of more than 5 percent in 2015.[79] Much was made of the low unemployment rate and sustained economic growth in the early years of Trump's presidency. But these developments did nothing to roll back long-term trends that harmed American workers, including stagnating pay, growing costs of living, and increasing inequality.

Despite a weak economy, corporations posted record profits from 2010 onward. Corporate profits after taxes reached 10 percent of GDP annually by 2014, compared to profits that ranged between six and eight percent from the 1960s through the 2000s.[80] Profits remained near record levels in 2016, despite the rising public anger over middle- and lower-class Americans being cut out of the "recovery."[81] The median net worth of households, in contrast, fell by 40 percent from 2007 to 2013, and there was an 18 percent decline in net worth from 2005 to 2011.[82] The median household income also declined by 7 percent from 2007 to 2014, despite growing labor productivity and record corporate profits.[83]

How have working Americans' incomes stagnated-to-declined, despite record profits? The simple answer is cannibalism. Businesses have various tools to squeeze greater profits out of workers. These techniques include: pushing early retirements on higher-salaried employees and replacing them with lower-pay, temporary workers; forcing employees to work longer hours for no pay raise; and downsizing employees out of positions, forcing the remaining workforce to compensate for lost productivity. Worker insecurity is now the defining feature of the economy, with 94 percent of new jobs created from 2005 to 2015 being temporary, contract-based, part-time, on-call, or some other form of contingent labor.[84]

Growing corporate profits, coupled with increased labor productivity and stagnating household incomes, are trends that date back decades. As seen in figure 15.3, while labor productivity nearly doubled from 1979 to 2013, median household earners saw just a 13 percent increase in income, while the minimum wage fell by 22 percent.[85] The income of the average working male declined by 28 percent from the early-1970s through the early-2010s.[86] Incomes earned by the top .01 percent increased by almost 800 percent, while CEO pay increased by over 900 percent within this period.[87] With such stark differences, it makes

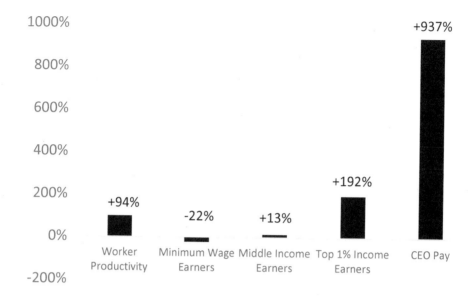

Figure 15.3. Worker Productivity, Earnings, and the Wealthy, 1979–2013. Sources: Russell Sage Foundation, "Chartbook of Social Inequality," *Russell Sage Foundation*, 2012, http://www.russellsage.org/sites/all/files/chartbook/Income%20and%20Earnings.pdf. For increasing CEO Pay, see: Rebecca Hiscott, "CEO Pay Has Increased by 937 Percent Since 1978," *Huffington Post*, June 12, 2014, http://www.huffingtonpost.com/2014/06/12/ceo-pay-report_n_5484622.html; For rising pay of the top one percent of income earners, see: Chad Stone, Danilo Trisi, Arloc Sherman, and Emily Horton, "A Guide to Statistics on Historical Trends in Income Inequality," *Center on Budget and Policy Priorities*, November 7, 2016, http://www.cbpp.org/research/poverty-and-inequality/a-guide-to-statistics-on-historical-trends-in-income-inequality; For the declining value of the minimum wage, see: Annalyn Kurtz and Tal Yellin, "Minimum Wage Since 1938," *CNN Money*, 2015, http://money.cnn.com/interactive/economy/minimum-wage-since-1938/; For the rise in labor productivity over time, see: Bureau of Labor Statistics, "Productivity Change in Nonfarm Business Sector, 1946-2016," *U.S. Department of Labor*, 2017, https://www.bls.gov/lpc/prodybar.htm.

little sense to speak of neoliberalism as benefitting the masses. Rather, the upper echelon of the upper class monopolized growing profits at the expense of the many.

Although males have lost income in the last four decades, women have found new employment opportunities, supplementing dwindling male incomes. From 1975 to 2009, the average number of hours worked by a family in the U.S. increased by nearly 25 percent for two-parent families.[88] Much of this increase came from women entering the workforce. In 1975, 47 percent of women with children under 18 worked, compared to 71 percent in 2008.[89] The average family worked harder despite stagnating pay and growing cost of living. Furthermore, growing household debt increased the strain on families. Between 1980 and 2007, average household debt increased by 120 percent, compared to a 26 percent increase from 1947 to 1980.[90] It is easy to dismiss growing debt as families "living beyond their means," but most bankruptcies are due to health care costs.[91] And in a broken health care system, health care costs are the most commonly cited financial problem with which families struggle.[92]

By the 2010s, the U.S. economic divide reached record levels. The poverty rate was 13.5 percent in 2015, or more than 43 million Americans.[93] The "near-poverty" rate—those making 150 percent of the official poverty rate—was one-third of the public.[94] A family of four in near-poverty earned just $36,900 in 2016. Most Americans would likely agree that families earning this income will find it difficult to "make it," in terms of affording adequate health care, food, housing, transportation, clothing, education, and saving for retirement.

Income and wealth inequality are stark. In the 2010s, members of the upper class, including the top one percent of income-earners, took home more than the bottom 80 percent.[95] By mid-decade, the top one percent earned 21.6 percent of all national income, while the top 20 percent earned 60 percent.[96] Wealth inequality was more extreme. In 2012, the top one percent owned 35 percent of all wealth, and the top 10 percent held 77 percent of all national wealth.[97] The bottom 40 percent were have-nots, in the sense that they held no wealth, while the bottom 50 percent had just 1.1 percent of wealth.[98] The second wealthiest 20 percent and the middle 20 percent of Americans held just 11 percent of wealth.[99]

What about recognition of growing, record levels of inequality? On a general level, most Americans recognize inequality exists, and are unhappy about it. In 2016, 78 percent of Americans agreed "the rich are getting richer and the poor are getting poorer."[100] In 2012, 77 percent agreed "there is too much power in the hands of a few rich people and large corporations in the United States."[101] In 2015, 63 percent said the societal "distribution of money and wealth should be more evenly distributed."[102]

Despite these findings, awareness of inequality and class divisions is underdeveloped. A 2011 national survey found the "average" American believed the wealthiest 20 percent of citizens held 59 percent of all wealth, when the real figure was 84 percent. Differences were more extreme when comparing what Americans wanted the wealth distribution to look like and what it actually looked like. Respondents said the "ideal" wealth breakdown would mean the richest 20 percent hold 32 percent of all wealth, compared to the actual level, at 84 percent.[103] Despite half of the country holding no financial wealth, in 2015, 54 percent of Americans denied the country was "divided into two groups, the haves and the have-nots."[104]

Much of the reason for failing to recognize a divide between haves and have-nots comes from the public's excessive optimism. Despite stagnating wages for 80 percent of Americans over the last four decades, a 2016 survey found 61 percent of Americans agreed "most people can get ahead with hard work."[105] As figure 15.4 shows, acceptance of the notion that hard work ensures one can "get ahead" is statistically linked to a refusal to recognize the economic divide between haves and have-nots.[106] Furthermore, Americans are notoriously reluctant to recognize classes outside of the "middle class," preferring to avoid terms like "lower class," and "upper class," despite the U.S. having the highest inequality in the first world, and half of Americans holding no wealth.[107] Just 2 percent of Americans identify as upper class in the richest country in history, and only 11 percent call themselves lower class, despite a third of Americans being poor or near-poor.[108] Those in the upper class consistently downplay their elite status, while poor Americans overestimate their class position.[109] Although the bottom 20 percent of income earners take home less than $20,000 a year, only 40 percent of those from households earning less than this amount classify themselves as "lower class." Those earning over $150,000 a year fall in the top 20 percent of income-earners, but just 18 percent of them acknowledge they are "upper-class."[110]

The naïve view that hard work will "get you ahead" is contradicted by the reality of growing inequality and stagnating-to-declining wages over the last four decades. Americans *have* been working harder, via growing labor productivity and increased family work hours, with nearly all income-gains going to the top

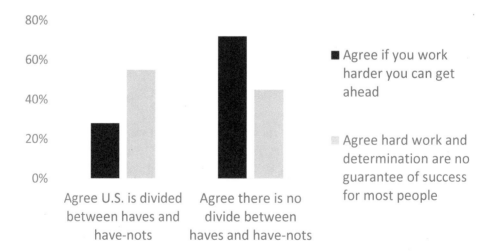

Figure 15.4. Attitudes about Economic Mobility and Class Consciousness, 2011. Source: Pew Research Center, December 2011 Monthly Poll, *Pew Research Center*, December 7–11, 2011.

one percent of earners in the last decade. The failure to acknowledge the divide between haves and have-nots speaks to a longstanding individualistic culture, in which the life outcomes of the poor are rationalized as "deserved" due to laziness, and wealth is celebrated as the product of "hard work," intelligence, and virtue.

Recognition of record inequality and the class divide is made more difficult by denials in the media. *Fox News* and the *Heritage Foundation* claim poverty is not as bad as some think. In a 2011 study, *Heritage* concluded: "most of the persons whom the government defines as 'in poverty' are not poor in any ordinary sense of the term. The overwhelming majority of the poor have air conditioning, cable TV, and a host of other modern amenities. They are well housed, have an adequate and reasonably steady supply of food, and have met their other basic needs, including medical care."[111] Right-wing pundit Bill O'Reilly said: "82 percent of poor families have a microwave. Seventy-eight percent have air conditioning. More than one television, 65 percent. Cable or satellite TV, 64 percent . . . Cell phones, 55 percent. Personal computer, 39 percent . . . So how can you be so poor and have all this stuff?"[112]

By drawing on notions of poverty as a third-world phenomenon, marked by homelessness and starvation, the *Heritage* study sought to redefine what it *really* means to be poor. Poverty in the U.S. is accompanied by access to consumer and technological conveniences that would be unthinkable in poor countries or in the U.S. 50 to 100 years ago. However, poverty is about more than simply technological conveniences. One must also examine inequality in quality of life measurements.

Numerous quality of life indicators were missing from the *Heritage* study. It did not look at access to quality health care, healthy food, educational opportunities, legal services, or quality housing. The poor are less likely to benefit from basic legal representation. Graduation rates are lower in poor neighborhoods, and affording higher education costs is a struggle for poor Americans. Individuals in poorer communities are more likely to report chronic and severe illnesses and to lack access to healthy foods, while suffering from higher obesity rates. Finally, poor families are more likely to face evictions due to inability to pay rent.[113]

A comprehensive understanding of poverty must look at inequality between the poor and other income groups along many dimensions. While the poor have access to cheap electronic and other goods, what good is a television if one is unable to afford quality health care or healthy food? What good is a cell phone if one cannot afford to send their children to college or secure decent educational opportunities? Poorer Americans purchase cheap consumer items as a form of diversionary entertainment, but they are no substitute for basic needs.

It appears that many Americans are pacified by cheap electronics and consumer goods. Many divert their attention from politics, focusing on consumerism and entertainment. Neil Postman made this claim in his classic book, *Amusing Ourselves to Death*. He maintained that individuals are lobotomized into blissful ignorance via entertainment programs, which diverts attention from important political, economic, and social issues. Postman warned: "When a population becomes distracted by trivia, when cultural life is redefined as a perpetual round of entertainments, when serious public conversation becomes a form of baby-talk, when, in short, a people become an audience and their public business a vaudeville act, then a nation finds itself at risk; culture-death is a clear possibility."[114] These warnings seem apropos considering the rise of mass non-voting, and the decline of political and media attentiveness, as Americans fixate on technological trinkets such as cell phones, video games, and TV. With consumer goods cheaper than ever, the threats of mass apathy and de-politicization are pronounced.

What can government do to reduce inequality? Some claim individuals must "work harder" to get ahead. This advice ignores the larger structural changes in the U.S. that are beyond individual control. Long-term decline in worker pay and union protections, growing education and health care costs, and a rising work burden, are problems that will not be "dealt with" by "rolling up your sleeves and working harder." These are structural problems, requiring structural solutions.

High inequality is not inevitable. The U.S. is the most unequal country in the first world, and unequal outcomes are driven by government policy. The U.S. has seen the rise of neoliberal policies in recent decades, but other countries have done a better job of resisting these trends, at least more so than the U.S. Looking to other countries, we see more progressive taxes, more generous welfare spending, and stronger labor protections. These countries are more committed to a government that aids the many, not just the wealthy. As a result, other first-world countries rank lower on inequality measures than the U.S.[115]

There is much the U.S. government has done to reduce poverty and inequality in the past. From the 1930s onward, New Deal protections for the poor and working Americans resulted in a significant reduction in inequality.[116] More broadly, first-world governments' efforts to expand welfare spending from the 1960s through 1990s resulted in significant declines in poverty rates, often falling by half or more.[117] In the U.S., poverty reduction coincided with the "War on Poverty" and Johnson's "Great Society" initiatives.

There are various policies that would likely reduce poverty and inequality today. These include: raising the minimum wage; passing an "Employee Free Choice Act," making it easier for workers to form unions through a secret ballot vote; instituting student loan forgiveness; introducing a universal health care system to provide affordable care to all; and increased spending on education, to aid underperforming schools. Such initiatives will do much to reverse the declining living standards of millions.

Chapter 16

Imperialism and U.S. Foreign Policy

Protecting Business Interests Abroad

In the run-up to the 2016 election, President-to-be Donald Trump had some controversial things to say about U.S. foreign policy. He promised not only to "bomb the shit" out of the Islamic State in Iraq and Syria (ISIS), but to steal Iraqi oil for U.S. oil corporations in the process.[1] Trump outlined a plan to "take the oil" in Iraqi areas controlled by ISIS, presumably involving a long-term re-occupation of Iraq. Speaking with disdain over the previous U.S. occupation of Iraq, he stated: "We go in, we spend $3 trillion, we lose thousands and thousands of lives . . . what happens is we get nothing. You know, it used to be to the victor belong the spoils." But if Trump were to order a re-occupation of Iraq, U.S. extraction, he argued, would not amount to theft in light of the costs the U.S. has paid to fight wars in Iraq: "You're not stealing anything. We're reimbursing ourselves . . . at a minimum, and I say more. We're taking back $1.5 trillion to reimburse ourselves."[2]

Whether Trump realized it or not, he was advocating for a criminal foreign policy agenda that was openly embraced by historical colonial powers. Resource extraction, to the benefit of an occupying country, was the crux of colonial policy during the age of European colonialism. Many critics of U.S. foreign policy portray the U.S. as a neocolonial power, seeking to dominate other countries' politics and to exploit their economic resources, to the benefit of American corporations and the wealthy. Trump's plan fit well within this neocolonial framework.

International Relations and Theories of Power

Global politics is defined by competing theories seeking to explain how countries behave in the international arena. Two major theories of international relations are realism and idealism. Realism dates back hundreds of years to thinkers such as Niccolo Machiavelli, an Italian politician who penned the classic work, *The Prince*. Machiavelli's work was a tactical manual for how to seize political power and preserve it through cunning, manipulation, intimidation, and violence. *The Prince* depicted politics between states as driven by conflict over power.[3]

Other realists such as Hans Morgenthau, Kenneth Waltz, and John Mearsheimer have further developed realist theory.[4] Realists stress various themes. First, global politics is characterized by anarchy between states.[5] No single overarching authority structure exerts formal control over countries. Strong states informally dominate the international arena, but organizations like the United Nations lack the power to consistently enforce international law. Second, despite official claims that they seek to promote democracy and human rights abroad, powerful countries are really interested in maximizing their power and security.[6] Countries are self-interested and seek to expand their power through coercion and violence, in contradiction to their noble rhetoric. Third, states are unified, rational actors.[7] A country's concern with maximizing self-interest transcends any political party or official. States are rational actors insofar as they seek to enhance their power and security on a global stage. When possible, states use violence as their primary dispute resolution mechanism since violence is more likely to produce material gains than compromise. In short, powerful states do what they want, dominating other countries, while weaker states do what they must—suffering under coercion and violence imposed on them.

It is possible to adopt a "realist" analysis, while also incorporating a leftist perspective that sees U.S. foreign policy as primarily interested in enhancing corporate capitalist and upper-class interests. International Relations scholar Ronald Osborn refers to this approach as "left realism," in reference to the perspectives of anti-imperialists such as Noam Chomsky, among other intellectuals.[8] Traditionally, realism has not given a lot of explicit attention to domestic economic interests as the primary driver of U.S. foreign policy. Broader references to national interests in security, influence, and power can be interpreted without explicit reference to corporate power and business interests, although "left realism" suggests that realism is also compatible with an anti-imperialist critique of U.S. foreign policy goals and actions.

While realism is popular among many scholars, competing theories include idealism and democratic peace theory. Rather than depicting the U.S. and other powerful countries as dominating others by force, idealism sees democratic countries as concerned with promoting human rights, democracy, development, and the raising of living standards across the globe. Idealism is popular—in fact it is the dominant approach to framing U.S. foreign policy among political officials. U.S. leaders routinely claim their actions are motivated by concerns for the poor, disadvantaged, and repressed, and that they seek to protect these groups against war, human rights abuses, and dictatorial coercion and violence.

Idealism has its roots in the history of the U.S. presidency of Woodrow Wilson. The term "Wilsonian idealism" reflected the president's stated support—

as indicated in his "Fourteen Points" speech—for promoting peace, democracy, free trade, and national self-determination.[9] Wilson justified U.S. entrance into World War I under claims that the German military was committing human rights atrocities throughout Europe, and that the country was a threat to Western civilization. He claimed the U.S. had a moral obligation to end the threat.

Democratic peace theory, an outgrowth of idealism, has its roots in the ideas of enlightenment philosopher Immanuel Kant. Democratic peace theory claims that democracies do not go to war with each other. The theory assumes democratic countries are special; since they democratically represent their people, this respect for democracy and the rule of law means they will seek to promote these principles throughout the world. The roots of democratic peace theory trace back to Kant's 1795 essay, "Perpetual Peace," where he argued Republican governments are less likely than authoritarian ones to engage in aggression against others.[10] This claim was further developed to argue that democratic governments are more likely to behave peacefully toward other democracies.[11] Democratic peace theory and idealism frame western political leaders as committed to human rights, democracy, the rule of law, and freedom.

Problems with Idealism and Democratic Peace Theory

Democratic peace theory and idealism provide comfort to Americans that their political leaders are selflessly committed to aiding the poor and repressed around the world. But major problems beset both theories. One problem is that U.S. politics is not very democratic, as I document in this book, so to argue that a strong tradition of democracy at home ensures democracy-promotion abroad rests on a very shaky foundation. Furthermore, U.S. foreign policy is not very benevolent. The U.S. directs much of its foreign aid to repressive regimes that hold contempt for democracy and human rights.

In 2017, the top recipients of U.S. foreign and military aid were Israel, Egypt, Afghanistan, Pakistan, and Jordan.[12] A closer look at these aid recipients reveals the anti-democratic company the U.S. keeps. The government of Afghanistan is one of the most corrupt in the world; many of its officials are known to traffic in heroine and the poppy trade.[13] The government nominally presides over a failed state ruled by warlords.[14] Women are widely repressed, and denied basic rights such as political equality and education.[15] The Afghan government is also accused by human rights monitors of engaging in torture against prison detainees.[16] Egypt and Pakistan are widely condemned for their dictatorial politics. Egypt's military dictatorship stifles freedom of speech and religion, engages in torture, mass detainment without due process, and resists democratic elections.[17] The Egyptian military overthrew the democratically-elected government of Mohamed Morsi in 2013, following a democratic uprising in 2011 that removed previous dictator Hosni Mubarak.[18] In 2017, Egypt was described by *Human Rights Watch* as a "human rights crisis . . . Authorities have banned protests, imprisoned tens of thousands—often after unfair trials—and outlawed the country's largest opposition group, the Muslim Brotherhood . . . National Security officers commit torture and enforced disappearances, and many detainees have died in custody from mistreatment."[19]

Pakistan, while technically run by a democratically elected government, suffers from instability due to fundamentalist insurgency. Radical groups control large segments of the country, have successfully assassinated government officials in the past, and are allied with Pakistan's secret intelligence, the ISI, which has a long history of tolerating and supporting extremist groups such as the Taliban.[20] The Pakistani military is condemned for lacking civilian oversight, while the national courts operate without transparency, relying on secret tribunals that issue death sentences against the accused.[21]

Jordan is a dictatorship, run by a king who has no interest in democracy. In 2016, King Abdullah dissolved Jordan's lower house of Parliament, in complete contempt for any notion of checks and balances in government.[22] The Jordanian government criminalizes dissent voiced against the King and the monarchy, or any speech deemed to be critical of Islam.[23]

Israel is also known for its human rights abuses against Palestinians. Israel is the last remaining colonial country, as it has illegally engaged in a military occupation and colonization of Palestinian lands for a half-century. The Israeli military has engaged in abuse and torture against Palestinian detainees designated as terrorist suspects.[24] Israel is generally recognized as a democracy in terms of respecting elections within its borders. But it holds a poor human rights reputation with regard to Palestinians, and is widely criticized as a result throughout the world.[25]

The overlap between human rights violations and increased U.S. aid raises a question: what is to be gained by funding human rights violators? Some possible reasons include the following. First, U.S. leaders support repressive foreign leaders because they are more likely to side with U.S. business and economic interests than leftist political leaders who question capitalism. The U.S. preference for business-friendly, repressive foreign leaders has been articulated in declassified U.S. government documents from years past. Second, countries that repress their or neighboring citizens are strategic assets. U.S. leaders historically framed Israel's aggressive policies against its neighbors as valuable to the U.S. Nixon, for example, referred to Israel as one of the America's "cops on the beat" in the Middle East, while the Reagan administration acknowledged the need to "develop a more mature *strategic* relationship with the government of Israel."[26] During the Cold War, pro-U.S. allies were seen as assets in the conflict with the Soviet Union and communism. In modern times, Middle Eastern U.S. allies are often oil-rich dictatorships—including Saudi Arabia, Kuwait, the United Arab

Emirates, Qatar, and Bahrain—that feed a steady, cheap supply of petroleum to the U.S. and its allies.

Finally, military aid to repressive countries props up the "military industrial complex," which President Dwight Eisenhower warned about in his farewell address.[27] Eisenhower spoke against a large segment of the economy—military industries—which retain a major interest in profiting from destruction and instability throughout the world. Eisenhower's military industrial complex included lobbyists employed by military contractors granting large campaign contributions to Congress, thereby pressuring legislators to seek increased military spending.

Imperialism and U.S. Foreign Policy

U.S. foreign policy contradicts many of the assumptions driving idealism and democratic peace theory. There is a long record of government policy documents suggesting American officials seek to maximize political, economic, and military power across the globe, at the expense of democracy, poverty-reduction, and human rights. In 2014, the U.S. accounted for 34 percent of all world military spending, far more than any other country. At $610 billion, that spending exceeded the combined allocations of the next seven largest countries combined, including China, Russia, Saudi Arabia, France, the United Kingdom, India, and Germany.[28] Figure 16.1 documents U.S. spending in 2015, in comparison to the

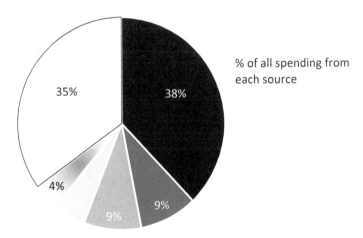

Figure 16.1. World Military Spending, 2015. Source: Adam Taylor and Laris Karklis, "This Remarkable Chart Show How U.S. Defense Spending Dwarfs the Rest of the World," *Washington Post*, February 9, 2016, https://www.washingtonpost.com/news/worldviews/wp/2016/02/09/this-remarkable-chart-shows-how-u-s-defense-spending-dwarfs-the-rest-of-the-world/?utm_term=.062c5c4bde4e.

next 14 biggest spenders, and compared to all other countries.[29] Clearly, the U.S. has no equal regarding military spending. This spending is used to strengthen capitalism and U.S. military power abroad.

A discussion of imperialism should be central to any analysis of U.S. foreign policy. I define imperialism as the process through which a country's power is expanded via coercion and military force, and in pursuit of its own economic interests. Despite a substantial record of government documents exposing U.S. foreign policy as driven by selfish interests, recognition of U.S. imperialism is not common among U.S. intellectuals. Examining U.S. material and imperialistic motives is necessary, however, to understanding foreign policy decision making.

Traditional colonial powers brazenly claimed to be helping poor people of color across the globe. They spoke of a "White Man's Burden" to civilize the subjects in their colonies. Formal colonialism is all but dead today with virtually every country in the world disavowing colonial occupations of other countries. Most U.S. political leaders do not openly declare imperialist aspirations; rather, these goals are quietly acknowledged in classified government documents. Realist claims are consistently declared in these communications, although they are also obscured by rhetoric proclaiming support for human rights and democracy.

Imperial policy planning transcends historical periods, and is evident during the Cold War and after. George Kennan, the "father" of anti-communist "containment" policy at the U.S. State Department, spoke in his policy planning studies about U.S. imperialism. Writing under the alias of author "X," Kennan discussed in the journal *Foreign Policy* the need for the U.S. to protect itself from Soviet aggression, and the importance of a "patient but firm and vigilant containment of Russian expansive tendencies."[30] Kennan's Policy Planning Study 23, however, cast global politics in blunter terms. Regarding Africa, Kennan advocated:

> A union of Western European nations would undertake jointly the economic development and exploitation of the colonial and dependent areas of the African Continent [following World War II] . . . The African Continent is little exposed to communist pressures; and most of it is not today a subject of great power rivalries. It lies easily accessible to the maritime nations of Western Europe, and politically they control or influence most of it. Its resources are still relatively undeveloped.[31]

Kennan's writings revealed contempt for democracy and human rights, and a fixation on increasing U.S. power and control over material resources. As he argued in Policy Planning Study 23, following the collapse of the old European colonial powers:

We [the U.S.] have about 50% of the world's wealth but only 6.3% of its population. In this situation, we cannot fail to be the object of envy and resentment. Our real task in the coming period is to devise a pattern of relationships which will permit us to maintain this position of disparity. To do so, we will have to dispense with all sentimentality and day-dreaming . . . we need not deceive ourselves that we can afford today the luxury of altruism and world-benefaction . . . We should cease to talk about vague and unreal objectives such as human rights, the raising of the living standards, and democratization. The day is not far off when we are going to have to deal in straight power concepts. The less we are then hampered by idealistic slogans, the better.[32]

Kennan described the Middle East as vital to U.S. national security, considering its tremendous oil resources. The State Department described Saudi Arabian oil as "a stupendous source of strategic power," and "probably the richest economic prize in the world in the field of foreign investment."[33] Saudi oil must "remain under American control for the dual purposes of supplementing and replacing our dwindling reserves, and of preventing this power potential from falling into unfriendly hands."[34]

Kennan and the State Department's frank admissions were *not* publicly advertised, but cloaked in classified documents. During the Cold War, U.S. leaders regularly referred to foreign policy as motivated by "self-defense" against the aggressive and imperialist Soviet Union, and as concerned with human rights, freedom, and democracy. Democratic President Harry Truman stated about U.S. involvement in the Korean War: "In my generation, this was not the first occasion when the strong had attacked the weak . . . Communism was acting in Korea just as Hitler, Mussolini, and the Japanese had acted ten, fifteen, and twenty years earlier. I felt certain that if South Korea was allowed to fall, Communist leaders would be emboldened to override nations closer to our own shores."[35] Similarly, Republican President Dwight Eisenhower stated about U.S. goals in the Cold War:

We seek peace, knowing that peace is the climate of freedom. And now, as in no other age, we seek it because we have been warned, by the power of modern weapons, that peace may be the only climate possible for human life itself . . . The only answer to a [Soviet] regime that wages total cold war is to wage total peace . . . Military power serves the cause of security by making prohibitive the cost of any aggressive attack. It serves the cause of peace by holding up a shield behind which the patient constructive work of peace can go on.[36]

Eisenhower promised U.S. motives were pure:

> To remain secure and prosperous themselves, wealthy nations must extend the kind of cooperation to the less fortunate members that will inspire hope, confidence and progress. A rich nation can for a time, without noticeable damage to itself, pursue a course of self-indulgence, making its single goal the material ease and comfort of its own citizens—thus repudiating its own spiritual and material stake in a peaceful and prosperous society of nations. But the enmities it will incur, the isolation into which it will descend, and the internal moral and physical softness that will be engendered, will, in the long term, bring it to disaster.[37]

Official policy during the Cold War stressed that the U.S. was defending itself from Soviet aggression. The U.S. sought to block a "domino effect," in which one country falling to communism would lead to many others falling. These warnings were used to defend wars in Korea and Vietnam. Direct confrontation between the U.S. and Soviet Union was suicidal, since both countries possessed nuclear weapons. The concern about nuclear Armageddon led U.S. policymakers and pundits to warn of "mutually assured destruction" (or "MAD"), acknowledging the futility of nuclear war.

Serious concern with MAD did not lead U.S. leaders to behave less confrontationally toward the Soviet Union. U.S. policy planners such as Paul Nitze of the National Security Council described four options for the U.S. in National Security Report (NSC) 68: 1. continuation of previous policy, in which the U.S., according to some planners, seemed to be losing its competitive edge when compared to growing Soviet influence in the world; 2. a move toward isolation; 3. war against the Soviets; or 4. A policy of containment aimed at "foster[ing] the seeds of decay" from within the Soviet Union. Nitze opted for the fourth option, recommending the U.S. enter a military arms race to bankrupt the Soviets. NSC 68 advocated "a substantial increase in expenditures for military purposes" and "for the United States, in cooperation with other free countries, to launch a build-up of strength which will support a firm policy directed to the frustration of the Kremlin design."[38]

U.S. motives were quite different from the rhetoric that was fed to the public. U.S. officials quietly acknowledged their goal was to prevent Soviet or indigenous dominance of national oil reserves in developing countries, which if allowed, would threaten U.S. businesses' interest in dominating those resources. Oil-rich dictatorships selling petroleum to the U.S. at low prices received American support. Truman told Saudi leaders: "no threat to your kingdom could occur which would not be a matter of immediate concern to the United States."[39] Testifying before Congress in 1951, Eisenhower said "there is no more strategically important area in the world."[40] In National Security Council memorandum 5432/1, the Eisenhower administration wrote of "radical and nationalistic regimes" in poorer countries, which were responsible to public pressure for "the immediate improvement in the low living standards of the masses."[41] Seeking "a political and economic climate conducive to private investment," Eisenhower attacked governments that pushed for a more equal distribution of their natural resources. Concerning Middle East oil, Eisenhower's government wrote: "if we choose to combat radical Arab nationalism and to hold Persian Gulf oil by force if necessary, a logical corollary would be to support Israel as the only strong pro-West power left in the Near East."[42] Eisenhower linked the Cold War to concern with raw materials, warning that Indochina's fall to communism meant a loss of the "tin and tungsten that we so greatly value from that area."[43]

Like Eisenhower, President Jimmy Carter was willing to use force to control Middle East oil. Carter's National Security Advisor Zbigniew Brzezinski admitted: "Not only does America benefit economically from the relatively low costs of Middle Eastern oil, but America's security role in the region gives it indirect but politically critical leverage on the European and Asian economies that are also dependent on energy exports from the region."[44] Kennan advocated keeping "power over what Japan imports in the way of oil and other things" to reserve "veto power over what she does."[45] Nixon's Secretary of State Henry Kissinger called "cheap and plentiful oil" the "basic premise" upon which post-war Western capitalism was constructed.[46] Kissinger remarked that "the only feasible countervailing power to OPEC's control of oil is power itself: military power."[47] To combat OPEC "extortion" and high oil prices, Kissinger claimed, the U.S. should foster stronger relations with Iran and Saudi Arabia.[48] Nixon's Secretary of Defense Melvin Laird explained that Middle Eastern allies Israel, Saudi Arabia, and Iran would serve as local "cops on the beat" promoting American strategic interests.[49]

Despite his rhetorical support for human rights, Carter sought U.S. dominance over Middle Eastern oil. Authoring *National Security Directive 63*, his administration responded to the 1979 Soviet invasion of Afghanistan, stating that any "attempt by any outside force to gain control of the Persian Gulf region will be regarded as an assault on the vital interests of the United States. It will be repelled by the use of any means necessary, including military force."[50]

Carter established a Rapid Development Task Force to deter perceived threats to U.S. strategic interests in the Middle East. The task force served as the U.S. military command structure (later renamed Centcom) for the region. It empowered the U.S. to act quickly against powers hostile to U.S. interests. The "Carter Doctrine," established in Carter's 1980 State of the Union address, spoke of containing the Soviet Union and the "grave threat" it posed "to the free movement of Middle East oil."[51] Reagan prioritized aiding the Saudi dictatorship. In *National Security Directive 35* (1982), the administration depicted "inefficient economies"—those leaning toward socialism or communism—and "the growing scarcity of resources, such as oil" as creating "opportunities for Soviet expansion." To deal with this threat: "The U.S. shall maintain a global posture and shall strive to increase its influence worldwide through the maintenance and improvement of forward deployed forces and rapidly deployable U.S.-based forces, together with periodic exercises, security assistance, and special operations."[52]

The end of the Cold War was a pivotal moment in world history, but the goals of U.S. policy did not change. The George H. W. Bush administration announced a "New World Order," "where diverse nations are drawn together in common cause to achieve universal aspirations of mankind—peace and security, freedom, and the rule of law."[53] But despite this rhetoric, imperial aspirations remained. Bush's *1991 National Security Strategy* (NSS) addressed "threats to the oil supplies that flow through the Persian Gulf" following the collapse of the Soviet Union. The U.S. was preoccupied with threats to its dominance that existed, not merely in oil-rich nations, but in adjacent countries. U.S. military initiatives in Lebanon (1983–1984) and Libya (1986) were central to projecting military power. As Bush's *NSS* elaborated: the U.S. would focus on "threats to United States interests that could not be laid at the Kremlin's door. Therefore, we will maintain a naval presence . . . in the Persian Gulf . . . We will conduct periodic exercises and pursue improved host nation support and prepositioning of equipment throughout the region."[54]

The fixation on Middle Eastern oil was also expressed in the Bush administration's *Defense Policy Guidance* report (1992). The report was authored by Under-Secretary of Defense Paul Wolfowitz, who served as one of the main planners of the 2003 U.S. invasion of Iraq. In the document, Wolfowitz wrote: "the number one objective of American post-Cold war political and military strategy should be preventing the emergence of a rival superpower . . . In the Middle East, our overall objective is to remain the predominant outside power in the region and preserve U.S. and Western access to the region's oil." The U.S. would deter "any hostile power from dominating a region [the Middle East] whose resources would, under consolidated control, be sufficient to generate global power."[55]

Material interests run contrary to human rights concerns. This much was clear in the 1991 Gulf conflict, in which the U.S. went to war with Iraq after its invasion of neighboring Kuwait. The Bush Administration clearly elevated oil interests over human rights. Despite the President calling attention to Iraq's previous human rights atrocities under dictator Saddam Hussein, Bush refused to condemn those human rights atrocities in the late-1980s, at the height of

Hussein's criminal attacks on the Iraq's Kurdish population. The U.S. sought to strengthen ties with Hussein, at least before he invaded Kuwait, a U.S. ally. National Security Directive 26 (October 2, 1989), elaborated upon the administration's thinking. Titled "United States Policy Toward the Persian Gulf," it was authored before the 1990 invasion of Kuwait, and explained:

> Access to Persian Gulf oil and the security of key friendly states in the area are vital to United States national security. The United States remains committed to its vital interests in the region, if necessary and appropriate through the use of military force, against the Soviet Union or any other force with interests inimical to our own . . . The United States will continue to sell United States military equipment to help friendly regional states meet their legitimate self-defense requirements . . . Normal relations between the United States and Iraq would serve our longer term interests and promote stability in both the Gulf and the Middle East. The United States should propose political and economic incentives for Iraq to moderate its behavior and to increase our influence with Iraq . . . We should pursue, and seek to facilitate, opportunities for United States firms to participate in the reconstruction of the Iraqi economy, particularly in the energy area.[56]

U.S. policy shifted quickly after Iraq invaded Kuwait. In National Security Directive 54, titled "Responding to Iraqi Aggression in the Gulf," the administration again depicted Iraqi oil as vital to U.S. national security. The document reiterated the U.S. commitment to using force to control Iraqi oil. It reversed course, however, by labeling Hussein an enemy of state: "by virtue of its unprovoked invasion of Kuwait . . . and its subsequent brutal occupation" Iraq became "a power with interests inimical to our own."[57] Shortly after, the U.S. went to war with Iraq, punishing it for its attack on an oil-rich neighbor.

After the Gulf War, the Clinton administration reaffirmed U.S. strategic and business interests in Middle Eastern oil. Clinton's *National Security Strategy* (1996) emphasized the dangers of terrorism and weapons of mass destruction developed by dictatorial governments. It called for keeping "U.S. forces forward developed," even during "peacetime," and for the "use of our armed forces" to preserve "our economic well-being." Clinton's *NSS* referenced the 1991 Gulf War as affirming the U.S. commitment to its oil interests. It stressed the "free flow of oil," which was a "vital interest." And it emphasized the need for maintaining "combat equipment," "naval vessels," "aviation bases," and "ground forces" within the "Persian Gulf" region.[58]

The preoccupation with oil persisted after the September 11 terror attacks. Vice President Dick Cheney's Energy Task Force wrote of the need to "open up areas of their [Middle East countries] energy sectors to foreign investment."[59] After the invasion, and as Iraq spiraled into civil war, Bush and Cheney warned that withdrawal of troops would empower al Qaeda to gain control of Iraq and "use oil as a weapon" against the U.S.[60]

In its 2002 *National Security Strategy*, the Bush administration formally acknowledged its material and capitalist foreign policy interests. The document established plans to "further strengthen market incentives and market institutions" while concentrating on "emerging markets and the developing world." The Bush administration was committed to "preemptive" strikes to fight terrorism, and sought to "strengthen our own energy security," while "expand[ing] the sources and types of global energy supplied" to the U.S. America would "dissuade future military competition" from abroad.[61] Senior aides to Bush stated after the 2003 Iraq invasion that the conflict represented a "first step . . . a first test, but not the last," in showcasing the U.S. commitment to 1. Democracy-promotion; 2. Delivering a "clear warning . . . that support for terror will not be tolerated"; and 3. Serving as a "demonstration effect," that the U.S. would "never allow American military supremacy to be challenged in the way it was during the Cold War." The blatant contradiction between promoting democracy and exerting military supremacy over other countries was lost on the administration, even if it was apparent to much of the world, which strongly opposed the U.S. war with Iraq.

During the 2010s, little changed in terms of U.S. foreign policy interests. The Obama administration carefully avoided recognizing strategic oil interests in its 2010 and 2015 *National Security Strategies*, instead announcing support for ecologically sustainable economic development, democracy, human rights, and global security.[62] But the administration's contempt for democracy was still apparent. For example, in 2011, the Obama administration announced that U.S. foreign policy encouraged "regime alteration" over "regime change," regarding U.S. support for authoritarian regimes in the Middle East. As the *Wall Street Journal* reported, the goal was to "help keep longtime allies who are willing to reform in power, even if it means the full democratic demands of their newly emboldened citizens might have to wait."[63] The reference to emboldened citizens was in response to the "Arab Spring," in which dictatorial U.S. allies such as Saudi Arabia, Egypt, Qatar, and others engaged in bloody repressions against their own citizens, seeking to suppress demands for revolutionary change and democratic representation. Support for regimes in the midst of intensifying repression against their own people laid waste to Obama's claim that these regimes would "alter" their repressive behavior.

The Trump presidency represented a return to the blunt imperialist language of the George W. Bush administration, and even an intensification of that language. During his presidential campaign, Trump sought to bully Mexico to pay for a wall between the countries, based on blanket racist and xenophobic stereotypes framing Mexican immigrants as rapists and drug dealers. Trump's appointees desired confrontation with U.S. "enemies" such as China, with the explicit goal of projecting military power. Trump's Secretary of State Rex Tillerson spoke of imposing a military blockade against China in the South China Sea to block efforts to build airfields and radar facilities on the Spratley and Paracel islands.[64] Support for the blockade meant the U.S. could risk nuclear war with China, in the pursuit of imperial hubris. This hubris was well-personified by Trump's former Chief Strategist Steve Bannon, who warned in March 2016: "we're going to war in the South China Sea in five to 10 years . . . there's no doubt about that. They're taking their sandbars and making basically stationary aircraft carriers and putting missiles on those. They come here to the United States in front of our face—and you understand how important face is—and say it's an ancient territorial sea."[65] The reference to saving "face" by threatening nuclear war was a brazen indication of imperial aggression. Finally, in a gift to the fossil fuel industry, Trump withdrew from the Paris Agreement, which sought to curb global CO_2 emissions, and was supported by nearly every country on the globe. Despite being one of the largest carbon polluters on the planet, Trump abandoned any sort of U.S. commitment to combat climate change, announcing a plan for the "reassertion of American sovereignty."[66] This approach left little room for claims that Trump was concerned with promoting an idealistic foreign policy based on mutual understanding and international cooperation.

Imperialism: The Basics

This chapter described U.S. policy goals as driven by capitalist and imperialist interests. But how are the stated goals above translated into action? American imperialism seeks to enhance the wealth and power of the corporate class via actions largely hidden from the public. Unless one undertakes a close analysis of U.S. history, they are unlikely to identify the techniques used in the pursuit of imperialism. Five ways the U.S. exercises imperialism are explored here.

First, the U.S. has long sought to overthrow governments refusing to comply with the interests of the American investor class. Socialistic governments that nationalize natural resources, even those that are democratically elected, are historically the target of secret overthrow campaigns orchestrated by the Central Intelligence Agency (CIA). The U.S. has long sought to overthrow or disrupt "enemy" governments refusing to conform to U.S. capitalist and business class interests, and challenging western materialist values, including North Korea, Iran, Cuba, and various socialist republics throughout Latin America. Attempted overthrows were pursued by the CIA and via wars against democratically elected governments, socialist countries, or other countries seeking to remain independent of the U.S. These countries included Iran (1953), Guatemala (1952), Venezuela (2002), Indonesia (1965), Syria (1956–1957), Cambodia (1970), Congo (1961), Brazil (1964), Greece (1967), the Dominican Republic, Cuba (1961), Nicaragua (1980s), Haiti (2004), Honduras (2009), and Syria (2012), among others.[67]

In modern times, many wars have been fought against countries with economic and strategic agendas running contrary to the U.S. capitalist class. These include: World War II (1939–1945), the Korean War (1950–1953), the Vietnam War (1955–1975), the invasion of Grenada (1983), the invasion of Panama (1989), the Afghanistan war (2001–present), the Iraq wars (1991, 2003–2011), and the war with Libya (2011). Since 1945, the U.S. government attempted to overthrow more than four dozen foreign governments, and pursued numerous wars despite widespread destruction to infrastructure and civilian casualties.[68] Many U.S. wars were fought in blatant disregard for international law, which outlaws use of force except in cases of U.N. Security Council authorization or self-defense against an ongoing military attack.

Second, the U.S. maintains a direct military presence in most countries throughout the world via advisers and bases. During the 2000s, the U.S. had a military presence in about 90 percent of the countries in the world, and maintained 725 military bases.[69] This global presence is vital to projecting U.S. military power and dominance. While U.S. expansion via foreign military bases is seen by American leaders as natural, the attempts of other countries to expand their power, as seen in Russia's annexation of Crimea, and China's incursion into the South China Sea, are reflexively viewed as unacceptable threats to U.S. interests and to world order.

Third, the subversion of democracy throughout the world occurs via American efforts to funnel money into other country's elections in favor of preferred candidates. The U.S. intervened in dozens of elections in the post-World War II era.[70] While interventions by foreign countries are illegal in U.S. elections, the U.S. interferes in other countries' elections with impunity.

Finally, the U.S. grants foreign aid to repressive allies, thereby solidifying their hold over power. We provide direct aid to severe human rights violators—regimes that are also more likely to side with U.S. economic, strategic, and military interests. U.S. aid is funneled to corrupt and repressive foreign leaders indirectly via financial institutions such as the International Monetary Fund and World Bank. These organizations lend billions to leaders who confiscate much of the "aid" and direct it to allies of the regime, political cronies, family, and friends. This debt, borrowed in countries such as Indonesia, Egypt, and Nigeria, is "odious debt," meaning the poor are made to pay it back, despite not benefitting from it.[71]

The U.S. Image Abroad

As a result of its policies, the U.S. is not very popular abroad. Presidents who openly articulate belligerent foreign policies tend to be the least popular. For example, George W. Bush was far less popular than Barack Obama.[72] Polls of the Middle East find the U.S. has long been distrusted, with most feeling the U.S. supports repressive foreign governments for selfish, material reasons.[73] Rather than hating American freedom or democracy, most in the Muslim world are angry at U.S. policies, such as U.S. support for Israel's occupation of Palestine and U.S. wars in the Middle East. A 2011 multi-national poll found relations "between Muslims and westerners" were seen as "bad" by most respondents particularly those from Britain, Spain, Germany, France, the Palestinian territories, Turkey, Lebanon, Egypt, Jordan, Pakistan, and Indonesia. When asked what accounts for the "lack of prosperity in Muslim nations," the most common answer among respondents from Muslim-majority countries was "U.S. and Western policies," with other common reasons being "government corruption" in U.S.-backed regimes and a "lack of democracy."[74] This poor relationship with the U.S. arises from injustices suffered at the hands of American empire. In a 2009 survey, majorities in eight of nine Muslim-majority countries felt the U.S. "abuses its greater power to make us do what the U.S. wants"; most rejected claims that the U.S. "treats [them] fairly." A majority or plurality in each country said the U.S. "consider[s] [their] country's interests" either "not much" or "not at all," while most felt the U.S. "use[s] the threat of military force to gain advantages" over them.[75]

The U.S. is seen as a rogue state because of its militaristic policies. Strong majorities in five Muslim-majority countries surveyed in 2007 felt the U.S. "provokes more conflict than it prevents," while polling from 2011 found most in six Muslim-majority countries were concerned "the U.S. could become a military threat to [their] country someday."[76] Most surveyed in Muslim-majority countries agree "democracy is not a real U.S. objective in the Middle East"; only small minorities agree the main U.S. motivation is to "protect itself from terrorist attacks."[77] Most Muslims feel the U.S. seeks "to expand the geographic borders of Israel" and "maintain control over Middle East oil resources."[78] Most in Muslim-majority countries think "America pretends to be helpful to Muslim countries, but in fact everything it does is part of a scheme to take advantage of people in the Middle East and steal their oil."[79] Most feel the U.S. should "remove its bases and military forces from all Islamic countries."[80]

Muslim fears of the U.S. were shared by much of the rest of the world during Bush's time in office. After the Iraq invasion, the U.S. was widely viewed as threatening world peace. One 2003 poll found that across 11 countries surveyed, most thought the U.S. was more dangerous than Iran, Syria, North Korea, or China. Only al Qaeda was seen as a bigger threat, revealing what company the U.S. kept in the court of international opinion.[81] Later multi-national polling from 2006 produced similar results.[82]

Polling from the Obama years revealed mixed results, including general favorability toward the U.S., but continued distrust of U.S. policy, despite the president's idealistic rhetoric about democracy, development, and human rights. On the one hand, polling in 2015 found majorities in most countries surveyed in Europe, Asia, Africa, and Latin America (although not the Middle East) held favorable views of the U.S. Majorities in Europe, Asia, and Africa had confidence in Obama to "do the right thing in world affairs," although majority support was not evident in most countries surveyed in Latin America and the Middle East. Majorities in countries surveyed in Europe, the Middle East, and Asia supported U.S. military actions against ISIS, although such support was lacking in countries surveyed in Latin America and Africa.[83]

On the other hand, the 2015 survey from above found little support for U.S. interrogation tactics after 9/11, which were widely condemned as relying on torture.[84] Other polls also documented distrust. One global poll in 2009 found majorities or pluralities in 19 of 22 countries thought the U.S. "abuses its greater power to make us do what the U.S. wants," rather than the U.S. "more often treat[ing] us fairly."[85] U.S. policy was least popular in the area of the world—the Middle East—where the U.S. is the most active militarily. Clearly, the people of the region recognized the harmful impact that U.S. foreign policy has had on them.

Global support for the U.S. presidency was significantly higher in the Obama years than during Bush, likely because of Obama's drawing down of the Iraq war, coupled with his rhetoric stressing the need to promote human rights, freedom, and democracy. But such confidence evaporated with the political rise of Trump. Polling during the 2016 election found low support levels for Donald Trump across most countries, and once entering office, many world leaders quickly soured on his abrasive, abusive approach toward dealing with other countries.[86]

Idealism in U.S. Foreign Policy?

If the U.S. is not driven by concerns with democracy and human rights, why do so many politicians, academics, and media pundits traffic in idealistic rhetoric?

A simple answer is that U.S. leaders and many Americans seek to rationalize questionable acts. Most individuals do not want to believe their actions or those of their government are harming others. No one wants to see themselves as a militarist or ogre, or think their actions are driven by selfishness. It is a common human trait to rationalize one's behavior, assuming that what is good for oneself is good for others too, or at least not harmful. The policy documents discussed in this chapter are damning in that they expose selfish, imperialist interests of U.S. officials and the corporate-capitalist class. But those same documents also include valiant rationalizations of U.S. foreign policy as driven by noble principles. For example, Eisenhower's National Security Council memorandum (5432/1) spoke of the raising of living standards in Latin America as a danger to U.S. economic dominance of, and investments in the region. But it also articulated a need for "economic development" in Latin America, the preservation of "the free world," "collective defense" against Soviet aggression, the promotion of "economic stability," moving toward a hemispheric "self-governing status," and "safeguarding of the hemisphere." In short, selfish motives are often justified through noble rhetoric.

Rationalization of imperialism was also evident in the 2003 Iraq war. While U.S. intervention in Iraq has long been driven by oil interests, humanitarian and democratic rhetoric was commonly cited by the Bush administration to justify war. But the administration regularly acted in ways to undermine Iraqi popular opinion. It violently occupied a country in which most wanted a U.S. withdrawal.[87] Iraqis also opposed U.S. efforts to impose a "caucus" election system, in which the U.S. would select local notables to choose Iraq's parliamentary leaders.[88] This form of "democracy" was anything but, and revealed paternalistic contempt for the public.

How did the U.S. defend its unpopular actions? A revealing answer is seen in the writings of Larry Diamond, a Stanford University scholar appointed as an advisor to the Bush administration, and who provided recommendations for how to promote "democracy" in Iraq. Diamond laid out a tortured rationalization for the illegal U.S. occupation. He claimed the U.S. failed in its supposedly noble efforts to promote democracy. Diamond provided an account of how the U.S. military in mid-2003 forcibly ended the local democratic elections taking place in Iraq. He claimed the Iraqis simply were not ready for elections, despite the fact that they were already taking place. Rather than allow the elections to play out, Diamond preferred the caucus system described above.[89] This preference revealed blatant contempt for self-determination, considering how unpopular the U.S. imposition of leaders was with most Iraqis. The plan was a "democratic" façade, masking U.S. contempt for Iraqi independence.

Justifying the shutdown of elections in the name of democracy suggests a willful blindness to the repressive effects of one's actions. Coercion is the antithesis of democracy. Democracy must be embraced by the people, not imposed from above or outside. U.S. officials have long articulated selfish motives, and embraced unpopular policies throughout the world that serve the interests of the U.S. corporate class, not the citizens of other countries. Global suspicion of American leaders is unsurprising, considering the negative effects of U.S. imperialism.

Conclusion

Where Do We Go from Here?

The concern with a growing business and upper-class bias in politics discussed throughout this book raises questions about the quality of American democracy. But the political situation is not hopeless. Progressive change is possible, if citizens are willing to fight for it. Mass social movements need to be built, and are the only way that the political system will be pressured to represent the interests and needs of the people.

The ground work is already being laid for progressive change. The post-2008 period has seen a level of citizen activism and movement building that is unusually high compared to the last few decades. The rise of Black Lives Matter suggests that anger over racial profiling and police brutality has reached a boiling point, and that poor people of color will no longer tolerate these repressive acts. Occupy Wall Street's emergence suggested growing anxiety over inequality and the political power of financial sector elites. The "Fight for $15" labor movement demonstrates that low-wage workers are unwilling to accept their "fate" as disposable people. The protests of Trump show that much of America is fed up with the status quo of white, upper-class male dominance of the political process.

Modern social movements are a start in terms of pushing for change. But public mobilization will have to intensify and reach a critical mass in coming years for the political system to be forced into taking progressive reforms seriously. Working-class Americans, the poor, the young, and people of color need to become more active in street protests, and more involved in electoral activism, in order to develop the foundation for a sustainable coalition that will consistently pressure the political system for democratic representation. Without this mass uprising, government will continue its shift toward serving business and upper-class elites, while marginalizing the middle- and lower-classes.

If citizens become more active in the political process and in movement building, many possibilities emerge. And it helps to have thought through what specifically it is that people want from government. I lay out some possible reforms here that I believe should be pursued, with an eye toward fleshing out what progressive governance might look like in the real world of politics. Significant institutional and legal reform will be required in order to reduce inequality and combat upper-class dominance of politics. A Constitutional Convention would greatly help in codifying these reforms into law. Positive reforms include:

- Introducing an economic bill of rights, guaranteeing access to food, shelter, clean air and water, education (elementary, secondary, and collegiate), a stable retirement income, a living wage that allows individuals to provide for basic needs, the right to form a union, access to affordable child care and universal health insurance, and guaranteed access to quality news and information, paid for through taxpayer funded public media.

- Restructuring of elections to maximize turnout, with elections occurring once every four years for all political offices, including for President and all members of Congress.

- Opening up political offices to traditionally marginalized groups, via the elimination of age restrictions on who can run for President or Congress (anyone 18 and older), and allowing any citizens, even if not born in the U.S., to run for President.

- Congressional term limits to correspond with Presidential term limits, perhaps a 4-year or 8-year limit for the House and Senate.

- The introduction of elections for members of the federal courts, so as to provide democratic accountability in this branch of government. And if elections are not feasible because of concerns with the perverting power of money in campaigns, term-limits (4 or 8 years) should be introduced, so as to allow for the eventual removal of judges who become increasingly out of touch with the interests and needs of the mass public.

- The complete removal of money from campaigns and the election process in terms of campaign-ad or issue-ad spending. All candidates for various offices, regardless of their party affiliation, should be guaranteed time slots on television and radio, and this requirement should be mandated as part of the Federal Communication Commission's stipulations for corporations being granted public broadcasting licenses.

- Corresponding with the elimination of money from politics, a declaration should be included in the Constitution that corporations are not, in fact, people, and that they are not entitled to personhood or "free speech," contrary to Supreme Court claims.

- Inclusion of citizen empowerment initiatives at the national level, including the initiative (citizen-proposed laws) and recall (removal) of members of Congress or Presidents who have lost the public faith.

There are plenty of reforms Congress should also consider in terms of improving the quality of American democracy. Congress should return to the old pre-1975 filibuster rules, which made it much harder for a minority of Senators to block voting on important political issues. Additionally, Congress should outlaw discriminatory state efforts that marginalize poor people of color and third parties. This would require the elimination of state ballot access laws that favor major parties, and the granting of automatic ballot access in all states to all parties that wish to run candidates in elections. Congress should also pass a blanket ban on voter I.D. laws that discriminate against the poor, to be replaced with a federal responsibility to automatically register all American citizens to vote. Congress should revisit immigration policy, granting automatic amnesty to all unauthorized immigrants who are in the U.S., but unable to participate in politics. Furthermore, individuals who live in the U.S. long-term but who are not citizens should be made eligible for citizenship more quickly, after a year of residency, assuming they fulfill the responsibilities of citizens such as paying taxes and respecting the law.

Congress also needs to institute a major series of reforms if the Constitution is to include an economic bill of rights. Such initiatives would include, first and foremost, a return to strongly progressive taxation, similar to that seen in other wealthy countries. These tax revenues are needed to cover funding for universal health care, child care services, a living wage (indexed to inflation), additional protections for workers seeking to unionize, universal access to education (including higher education), and other social welfare guarantees mentioned above. To stave off the worst predicted consequences of climate change, Congress also needs to recommit the U.S. to the Paris Agreement, and work toward significant cuts in CO_2 emissions via greater regulations on automobiles and coal-burning power plants, and an infusion of funding into a massive green jobs initiative to assist the country in shifting from non-renewable to renewable energy consumption.

For Congress to lead with these reform efforts, a genuinely progressive party is needed, rather than a two-party system that largely serves upper-class and business interests, while throwing scraps to the masses, middle class, and poor. Whether this progressive party ends up being the Democrats or a third party is yet to be determined, but there will need to be a viable institutional mechanism to translate progressive ideas into actual policies. The Bernie Sanders "revolution," and the large support for it among younger Americans, suggests that there is some potential for the Democratic Party to become a genuinely progressive party. But such a party will not emerge in the U.S.—not until the masses of disadvantaged and marginalized people of this country join together to push for and demand electoral transformation.

Other reforms are also needed. The executive branch should reinstate its investigations, through the Department of Justice, of local polices forces accused of discriminatory behavior against poor people of color. While the Trump administration abandoned this commitment, any significant reform of police departments, and any effective effort to tackle structural racism will need the resources of the federal government to succeed. Furthermore, Americans also need to be more vigilant in terms of limiting the growing powers of the imperial presidency. If members of Congress are unwilling to exercise their power of impeachment against Presidents who violate the law and the Constitution, citizens must take to the streets and demand impeachment, or the introduction of a mechanism, such as recall, that allows citizens to remove a sitting President who has lost the public faith.

Finally, a renewed anti-war movement is necessary to keep presidents in check in their pursuit of unpopular, imperialist foreign wars. Any military activities that put American forces in harm's way should require a popular referendum vote, in which a majority of Americans must sign off on using force before a president is authorized to go to war. Coupled with the War Powers act, such a requirement would still provide the president with the power to temporarily use force in emergencies in order to preserve national security. But something as significant as war should require serious consideration on the part of the public. Going to war is no laughing matter, and governments should not be allowed to do it without citizens having thoroughly reflected on the destructive costs that wars wreak on the U.S. and other countries.

A reinvigoration of the anti-war movement will require better education of the masses, away from the parochialism that dominates our political culture. Americans pay little attention to world affairs until a crisis emerges, and by then it is too late to educate oneself about how the U.S. should engage with the rest of the world. Congress can aid in the fight against our overly-parochial education system by requiring history and global politics coursework in middle school, high school, and college, so that Americans gain a more cosmopolitan perspective in understanding how they fit in with the rest of the world. A public media system will be vital for refocusing Americans' attention on political matters.

While Americans have become increasingly angry in modern times with the failure of government to provide for citizens' wants and needs, and there has been a growth in citizen activism and movement building as of late, a much greater mobilization is needed to sustain a wave of political reforms akin to the New Deal of the 1930s or the Great Society of the 1960s. But we should not kid ourselves either. Mass political mobilization will require years, perhaps decades of public vigilance and action, to succeed. Still, there is nothing inevitable about the rise of corporate and upper-class control over American politics that has taken hold in recent decades. Politics of, by, and for the wealthy can be rolled back with a serious, vigilant, and sustained commitment from the mass public.

I have argued throughout this book that American government is seriously failing the people, as it exhibits elitist tendencies in favor of the rich over the people. I have done my best in this conclusion to lay out some possible ways in which the U.S. political system can be transformed to improve American democracy. But ultimately it will be up to the American people to determine what kind of country they want to live in, and what kind of changes they expect from government. The key questions moving forward are simple: how do you want American government to change? And where do we go from here?

Notes

Introduction

1. Aaron Sharockman, "The Truth (So Far) Behind the 2016 Campaign," *Politifact*, June 29, 2016, http://www.politifact.com/truth-o-meter/article/2016/jun/29/fact-checking-2016-clinton-trump/; *Politifact*, "Bernie Sander's File," Politifact, 2016, http://www.politifact.com/personalities/bernie-s/

2. Sharockman, "The Truth (So Far) Behind the 2016 Campaign," 2016.

3. Politifact, "Ted Cruz's File," *Politifact*, 2016, http://www.politifact.com/personalities/ted-cruz/; Politifact, "John Kasich's File," *Politifact*, 2016, http://www.politifact.com/personalities/john-kasich/; Politifact, "Ben Carson's File," *Politifact*, 2016, http://www.politifact.com/personalities/ben-carson/; Politifact, "Jeb Bush's File," *Politifact*, 2016, http://www.politifact.com/personalities/jeb-bush/; Politifact, "Marco Rubio's File," *Politifact*, 2016, http://www.politifact.com/personalities/marco-rubio/; Politifact, "Carly Fiorina's File," *Politifact*, 2016, http://www.politifact.com/personalities/carly-fiorina/

4. Ben Carson was deemed the most deceptive candidate of all, with 82 percent of his statements being false.

5. Chris Cilizza, "Donald Trump Just Keeps Lying," *CNN.com*, August 3, 2017, http://www.cnn.com/2017/08/03/politics/donald-trump-mexico-boy-scouts-lies/index.html

6. Michael Parenti, *Democracy for the Few* 9th Edition (Belmont, CA: Wadsworth Publishing, 2010).

7. C. Wright Mills, *The Power Elite* (Oxford: Oxford University Press, 2000).

8. G. William Domhoff, *Who Rules America? Power and Politics* (New York: McGraw Hill, 2006).

9. David Lowery and Holly Brasher, *Organized Interests and American Government* (Long Grove, IL: Waveland, 2011).

10. Matt Egan, "Record Inequality: The Top 1% Controls 38.6% of America's Wealth," *CNN.com*, September 27, 2017, http://money.cnn.com/2017/09/27/news/economy/inequality-record-top-1-percent-wealth/index.html

11. Harold D. Lasswell, *Politics: Who Gets What, When, How* (Gloucester, MA: Peter Smith Publishing, 1990).

12. Martin P. Wattenberg, *Is Voting for Young People?* (New York: Routledge, 2015).

13. Markus Prior, *Post-Broadcast Democracy: How Media Choice Increases Inequality in Political Involvement and Polarizes Elections* (Cambridge: Cambridge University Press, 2007).

14. Martin Gilens and Benjamin I. Page, "Testing Theories of American Politics," *Perspectives on Politics*, 12, no. 3 (2014): 564–81.

15. Jim Tankersley and Ana Swanson, "Donald Trump is Assembling the Richest Administration in Modern American History," *Washington Post*, November 30, 2016, https://www.washingtonpost.com/news/wonk/wp/2016/11/30/donald-trump-is-assembling-the-richest-administration-in-modern-american-history/?utm_term=.b12ef627a416

16. Pew Research Center, "Beyond Distrust: How Americans View Their Government," *Pew Research Center*, November 23, 2015, http://www.people-press.org/2015/11/23/2-general-opinions-about-the-federal-government/

17. For longstanding concerns about business power, see: C. Wright Mills, *The Power Elite* (Oxford: Oxford University Press, 2000); and G. William Domhoff, *Who Rules America? The Triumph of the Corporate Rich* (New York: McGraw Hill, 2013). For growing public concern with elite rule, see: American National Election Study, "Is the Government Run for the Benefit of All, 1964–2012," 2012, *Electionstudies.org*, http://www.electionstudies.org/nesguide/toptable/tab5a_2.htm

18. John Zaller, "Elite Leadership of Mass Opinion: New Evidence From the Gulf War," in *Taken By Storm: The Media, Public Opinion, and U.S. Foreign Policy in the Gulf War*, eds. W. Lance Bennett and David Paletz (Chicago: University of Chicago Press, 1994): 186–209; Scott L. Althaus, *Collective Preferences in Democratic Politics: Opinion Surveys and the Will of the People* (Cambridge: Cambridge University Press, 2003); Philip E. Converse, "The Nature of Belief Systems in Mass Publics," in *Ideology and Discontent*, ed. David Apter (New York: Free Press, 1964).

19. Annenberg Public Policy Center, "Americans Know Surprisingly Little About Their Government, Survey Finds," *Annenberg Public Policy Center*, September 17, 2014, http://www.annenbergpublicpolicycenter.org/americans-know-surprisingly-little-about-their-government-survey-finds/

20. Emeralde Jensen-Roberts, "How Many People Know Their Senators?" *Boston Globe*, March 29, 2015, https://www.bostonglobe.com/magazine/2015/03/28/how-many-people-know-their-senators/yfgXyHR96X7YGhesaNQbnM/story.html

21. Michael X. Delli Carpini and Scott Keeter, *What Americans Know About Politics and Why it Matters* (New Haven, CT: Yale University Press, 1997).

22. Kendall Breitman, "Poll: Majority of Millennials Can't Name a Senator From Their Home State," *Politico*, February 3, 2015, http://www.politico.com/story/2015/02/poll-millennials-state-senators-114867; Chris Cilizza, "Ameicans Know Literally Nothing About the Constitution," *CNN.com*, September 13, 2017, http://www.cnn.com/2017/09/13/politics/poll-constitution/index.html; Haven Insights, "Just 37 Percent of Americans Can Name Their Representative," *Haven Insights*, 2017, http://www.haveninsights.com/just-37-percent-name-representative/

23. Joanna Weiss, "Millennials Don't Believe in Voting," *Boston Globe*, August 21, 2015, https://www.bostonglobe.com/opinion/2015/08/20/millennials-don-believe-voting/cGb7sx5ZvkmDCsNd3shTDO/story.html

24. Thom File, "Young-Adult Voting: An Analysis of Presidential Elections, 1964–2012," *U.S. Census Bureau*, April 2014, https://www.census.gov/prod/2014pubs/p20-573.pdf

25. Wattenberg, *Is Voting for Young People?* 2015.

26. American Press Institute, "Social and Demographic Differences in News Habits and Attitudes," *American Press Institute*, March 17, 2014, https://www.americanpressinstitute.org/publications/reports/survey-research/social-demographic-differences-news-habits-attitudes/

27. Jon Huang, Samuel Jacoby, Michael Strickland, and K. K. Rebecca Lai, "Election 2016: Exit Polls," *The New York Times*, November 8, 2016, https://www.nytimes.com/interactive/2016/11/08/us/politics/election-exit-polls.html?_r=0/ Anthony DiMaggio, *Rebellion in America: Citizen Uprisings, the News Media, and the Politics of Plutocracy* (New York: Routledge, 2019).

28. Gallup, "Trust in Government," *Gallup*, 2016, http://www.gallup.com/poll/5392/trust-government.aspx

29. Pew Research Center, "Beyond Distrust: How Americans View their Government," *Pew Research Center*, November 23, 2015, http://www.people-press.org/2015/11/23/1-trust-in-government-1958-2015/

30. Pew Research Center, "Beyond Distrust," 2015.

31. Greg Sargent, "The Reason Reasons Americans Distrust Government," *Washington Post*, November 2, 2011, https://www.washingtonpost.com/blogs/plum-line/post/the-real-reasons-americans-distrust-government/2011/11/08/gIQA3mB30M_blog.html

32. Pew, "Beyond Distrust," 2015.

33. Harold Meyerson, "Americans See a Government of, by and for the Rich," *Washington Post*, November 18, 2015, https://www.washingtonpost.com/opinions/americans-see-a-government-of-by-and-for-the-rich/2015/11/18/8c8e001a-8e19-11e5-acff-673ae92ddd2b_story.html?utm_term=.3bb586ac7352

34. Pew Research Center, "Most See Inequality Growing, but Partisans Differ Over Solutions," *Pew Research Center*, January 23, 2014, http://www.people-press.org/2014/01/23/most-see-inequality-growing-but-partisans-differ-over-solutions/

35. Russell Dalton, *The Good Citizen: How a Younger Generation is Reshaping American Politics* (Washington DC: CQ Press, 2008).

36. Dalton, *The Good Citizen*, 2008.

37. Aaron Smith, "Civic Engagement in the Digital Age," *Pew Research Center*, April 25, 2013, http://www.pewinternet.org/2013/04/25/civic-engagement-in-the-digital-age/

38. Anthony DiMaggio, "Youth in Revolt: Why Millennials are the Key to Future Social Transformation," *Truthout*, September 16, 2017, http://www.truth-out.org/opinion/item/41951-youth-in-revolt-why-millennials-are-the-key-to-future-social-transformation

39. Michael McDonald, "Voter Turnout," *United States Election Project*, 2016, http://www.electproject.org/home/voter-turnout/voter-turnout-data

40. Drew Desilver, "U.S. Voter Turnout Trails Most Developed Countries," *Pew Research Center*, August 2, 2016, http://www.pewresearch.org/fact-tank/2016/08/02/u-s-voter-turnout-trails-most-developed-countries/

Chapter 1

1. Frank Monaghan, *John Jay: Defender of Liberty* (New York: Bobbs-Merrill Company, 1935), 323.

2. Walter Stahr, *John Jay: Founding Father* (New York: Bloomsbury, 2006), 224.

3. Michael J. Klaman, *The Framers' Coup: The Making of the U.S. Constitution* (New York: Oxford University Press, 2016): X.

4. Charles A. Beard, *An Economic Interpretation of the Constitution of the United States* (New York: Dover Publications, 2004): 12, 149–51.

5. Margaret Jacob, *The Enlightenment: A Brief History with Documents* (New York: St. Martin's Press, 2000).

6. John Locke, "Second Treatise of Government," in *Modern Political Thought: Readings from Machiavelli to Nietzsche*, ed. David Wootton (Cambridge, MA: Hackett, 1996): 310–96.

7. Locke, "Second Treatise of Government," 1996.

8. Locke, "Second Treatise of Government," 1996.

9. Allen Jayne, *Jefferson's Declaration of Independence: Origins, Philosophy, and Theology* (Lexington, KY: University Press of Kentucky, 1998).

10. Klaman, *The Framer's Coup*, 2016.

11. Alan Gibson, *Interpreting the Founding: Guide to the Enduring Debates over the Origins and Foundations of the American Republic* (Lawrence, KS: University Press of Kansas, 2010).

12. Karen O'Connor and Larry Sabato, *American Government: Roots and Reform* (New York: Allyn and Bacon, 1996).

13. Steffen W. Schmidt, II, Mack C. Shelley, and Barbara A. Bardes, *American Government and Politics Today*, 2003–2004 Edition (Stamford, CT: Thomson Wadworth 2004).

14. Burns, et al., *Government by the People*, 2000.

15. Gibson, *Interpreting the Founding*, 2010.

16. Gibson, *Interpreting the Founding*, 2010.

17. Michael Thompson, *The Politics of Inequality: A Political History of the Idea of Economic Inequality in America* (New York: Columbia University Press, 2012); Clement Fatovic, *America's Founding and the Struggle over Economic Inequality* (Lawrence, KS: University Press of Kansas, 2015).

18. Gary B. Nash, "Poverty and Poor Relief in Pre-Revolutionary Philadelphia," *The William and Mary Quarterly* 33, no. 1 (1976): 3–30; Gary B. Nash, "Urban Wealth and Poverty in Pre-Revolutionary America," *Journal of Interdisciplinary History* 6, no. 4 (1976): 545–84; Jeffrey G. Williamson and Peter H. Lindert, "Long Term Trends in American Wealth Inequality," *National Bureau of Economic Research* 1980, http://www.nber.org/chapters/c7443.pdf

19. Howard Zinn, *A People's History of the United States* (New York: Harper Collins, 1999).

20. Zinn, *A People's History of the United States*, 1999.

21. Zinn, *A People's History of the United States*, 1999.

22. Ronald Takaki, *A Different Mirror: A History of Multicultural America* (New York: Back Bay Books, 2002).

23. Takaki, *A Different Mirror*, 2002.

24. Zinn, *A People's History of the United States*, 1999.

25. Zinn, *A People's History of the United States*, 1999.

26. Takaki, *A Different Mirror*, 2002.

27. Takaki, *A Different Mirror*, 2002.

28. Kevin Roberts, "Demographics," *Encyclopedia of African American History, 1619–1895: From the Colonial Period to the Age of Frederick Douglass*, ed. Paul Finkelman (Oxford: Oxford University Press, 2006): 376.

29. Roberts, "Demographics," 2006: 384.

30. Eric Foner, *Give Me Liberty! An American History* (New York: W. W. Norton, 2012).

31. Takaki, *A Different Mirror*, 2002.

32. Takaki, *A Different Mirror*, 2002.

33. Alexander Keyssar, *The Right to Vote: The Contested History of Democracy in the United States* (New York: Basic Books, 2009).

34. Keyssar, *The Right to Vote*, 2009.

35. Sean Willentz, *The Rise of American Democracy: Jefferson to Lincoln* (New York: W. W. Norton, 2006).

36. Keyssar, *The Right to Vote*, 2009.

37. Steven Mintz, "Winning the Vote: A History of Voting Rights," *The Gilder Lehrman Institute of American History*, 2017, https://www.gilderlehrman.org/history-by-era/government-and-civics/essays/winning-vote-history-voting-rights

38. Forrest McDonald, *Novus Ordo Seclorum* (Lawrence, KS: University Press of Kansas, 1985); Zinn, *A People's History of the United States*, 1999; Richard K. Matthews, "James Madison's Political Theory: Hostage to Democratic Fortune," *The Review of Politics*, 67, no. 1 (2005).

39. Kathy Matson, "The Revolution, the Constitution, and the New Nation," in *The Cambridge Economic History of the United States, Volume 1*, eds. Stanley L. Engerman and Robert E. Gallman (Cambridge: Cambridge University Press, 1996): 363–402.

40. Samuel Kernell, Gary C Jacobson, and Thad Kousser, *The Logic of American Politics* (Washington DC: CQ Press, 2011).

41. Kernell, Jacobson, and Kousser, *The Logic of American Politics*, 2011.

42. Kernell, et al., *The Logic of American Politics*, 2011; Woody Holton, *Unruly Americans and the Origins of the Constitution* (New York: Hill and Wang, 2008); David Szatmary, *Shays' Rebellion: The Making of an Agrarian Insurrection* (Amherst, MA: University of Massachusetts Press, 1984).

43. Holton, *Unruly Americans*, 2008.

44. Holton, *Unruly Americans*, 2008.

45. Holton, *Unruly Americans*, 2008.

46. Holton, *Unruly Americans*, 2008.

47. Holton, *Unruly Americans*, 2008.

48. Holton, *Unruly Americans*, 2008.

49. Holton, *Unruly Americans*, 2008.

50. Holton, *Unruly Americans*, 2008.

51. Holton, *Unruly Americans*, 2008.

52. Holton, *Unruly Americans*, 2008.

53. Holton, *Unruly Americans*, 2008; Klaman, *The Framers' Coup*, 2016.

54. Holton, *Unruly Americans*, 2008.

55. Szatmary, *Shays' Rebellion*, 1984.

56. Zinn, *A People's History of the United States*, 1999.

57. R. J. Cutler, "Shays' Rebellion: 10 Days that Unexpectedly Changed America," *The History Channel*, 2006.

58. Szatmary, *Shays' Rebellion*, 1984.

59. Szatmary, *Shays' Rebellion*, 1984.

60. Cutler, "Shays' Rebellion," 2006.

61. Szatmary, *Shays' Rebellion*, 1984.

62. Cutler, "Shays' Rebellion," 2006.

63. Szatmary, *Shays' Rebellion*, 1984.

64. Kernell, et al., *The Logic of American Politics*, 2011.

65. Zinn, *A People's History of the United States*, 1999.

66. Cutler, "Shays' Rebellion," 2006.

67. Szatmary, *Shays' Rebellion*, 1984.

68. Holton, *Unruly Americans*, 2008.

69. Holton, *Unruly Americans*, 2008.

70. Holton, *Unruly Americans*, 2008.

71. Szatmary, *Shays' Rebellion*, 1984.

72. Zinn, *A People's History of the United States*, 1999.

73. Forrest McDonald, *Alexander Hamilton: A Biography* (New York: W. W. Norton, 1979).

74. David Robertson, *The Original Compromise: What the Constitution's Framers Were Really Thinking* (Oxford: Oxford University Press, 2013).

75. Willard Sterne Randall, *George Washington: A Life* (New York: Owl Books, 1997).

76. Noble E. Cunningham Jr., *Jefferson v. Madison: Confrontations that Shaped a Nation* (New York: St. Martin's Press, 2000).

77. Michael P. Federici, *The Political Philosophy of Alexander Hamilton* (Baltimore, MD: The Johns Hopkins University Press, 2012); Alexander Hamilton, "The Federalist No. 9," *Yale University Law School*, 2008, http://avalon.law.yale.edu/18th_century/fed09.asp

78. Robert Dahl, *How Democratic is the American Constitution?* (New Haven, CT: Yale University Press, 2003).

79. James Madison, "The Federalist #10," *The Federalist Papers*, 1787.

80. Jason Frank and Isaac Kramnick, "What 'Hamilton' Forgets About Hamilton," *The New York Times*, June 10, 2016, https://www.nytimes.com/2016/06/11/opinion/what-hamilton-forgets-about-alexander-hamilton.html?_r=0

81. John E. Hill, *Democracy, Equality, and Justice: John Adams, Adam Smith, and Political Economy* (Lanham, MD: Lexington Books, 2007); Alan Taylor, *American Revolutions: A Continental History, 1750–1804* (New York: W. W. Norton, 2016).

82. Gordon S. Wood, "How Democratic is the Constitution," *The New York Review of Books*, February 23, 2006, http://www.nybooks.com/articles/2006/02/23/how-democratic-is-the-constitution/

83. Akhil Reed Amar, *America's Constitution: A Biography* (New York: Random House, 2006).

84. Alexander Hamilton, "The Federalist No. 72," *The Federalist Papers*, 1788.

85. Matthews, "James Madison's Political Theory," 2005.

86. Matthews, "James Madison's Political Theory," 2005.

87. Zinn, *A People's History of the United States*, 1999.

88. Schmidt, et al., *American Government and Politics Today*, 2004.

89. Charles A. Beard, *An Economic Interpretation of the Constitution of the United States* (Mineola, NY: Dover Publications, 2004).

90. Beard, *An Economic Interpretation of the Constitution of the United States*, 2004.

91. Gibson, *Interpreting the Founding*, 2010.

92. Robert McGuire, *To Form a More Perfect Union: A New Economic Interpretation of the United States Constitution* (Oxford: Oxford University Press, 2003).

93. James Madison, "The Federalist No. 10," *The Federalist Papers*, 1787.

94. James Madison, "The Federalist No. 51," *The Federalist Papers*, 1788.

95. Madison, "The Federalist No. 51," 1788.

96. Madison, "The Federalist No. 51," 1788.

97. Michael P. McDonald, "National General Election VEP Turnout Rates, 1789–Present," *United States Election Project*, June 11, 2014, http://www.electproject.org/national-1789-present

98. Madison, "The Federalist #10, 1787.

99. David Waldstreicher, *Slavery's Constitution: From Revolution to Ratification* (New York: Hill and Wang, 2010).

100. Michael Martin and Eric Foner, "End of Slave Trade Meant New Normal for America," *National Public Radio*, January 10, 2008, http://www.npr.org/templates/story/story.php?storyId=17988106

101. George William Van Cleve, *A Slaveholders' Union: Slavery, Politics, and the Constitution in the Early American Republic* (Chicago: University of Chicago, 2010).

102. Van Cleve, *A Slaveholder's Union*, 2010.

103. Waldstreicher, *Slavery's Constitution*, 2010.

104. Van Cleve, *A Slaveholder's Union*, 2010.

105. PBS, "Growth and Entrenchment of Slavery," *Corporation for Public Broadcasting*, 2016, http://www.pbs.org/wgbh/aia/part3/3narr6.html; PBS, "Slavery and the Making of America: A Nation Divided," *Corporation for Public Broadcasting*, 2016, http://www.pbs.org/wnet/slavery/timeline/1860.html

106. Luke Mayville, *John Adams and the Fear of American Oligarchy* (Princeton, NJ: Princeton University Press, 2016).

107. Luke Mayville, "Fear of the Few: John Adams and the Power Elite," *Polity*, 47, no. 1 (2015), 5–32.

108. Madison, "The Federalist #51," 1788.

109. I. Bernard Cohen, *Science and the Founding Fathers: Science in the Political Thought of Thomas Jefferson, Benjamin Franklin, John Adams, and James Madison* (New York: W. W. Norton, 1997); Jonathan A. Glickstein, *American Exceptionalism, American Anxiety: Wages, Competition, and Degraded Labor in the Antebellum United States* (Charlottesville, VA: University of Virginia Press, 2002).

110. Fatovic, *America's Founding and the Struggle over Economic Inequality*, 2015.

111. Fatovic, *America's Founding and the Struggle over Economic Inequality*, 2015.

112. Madison, "The Federalist #10," 1787.

113. Fatovic, *America's Founding and the Struggle over Economic Inequality*, 2015.

114. James Madison, "Letter to James K. Paulding," *National Archives: Founders Online*, March 10, 1827, https://founders.archives.gov/documents/Madison/99-02-02-0936

115. "Madison's Constitutional Vision: The Legacy of Enumerated Powers," in *James Madison and the Future of Limited Government*, John Curtis Samples, ed. (Washington DC: CATO Institute, 2002): 25–41.

116. Thompson, *The Politics of Inequality*, 2012.

117. James Madison, "Detached Memoranda, ca. 31 January 1820," *National Archives: Founders Online*, January 31, 1820, https://founders.archives.gov/documents/Madison/04-01-02-0549

118. Thomas Jefferson, "Thomas Jefferson to George Logan, 12 November 1816," *National Archives: Founders Online*, November 12, 1816, https://founders.archives.gov/documents/Jefferson/03-10-02-0390

119. John C. Rives, *Abridgement of the Debates of Congress, from 1789 to 1856* (New York: D. Appleton and Company, 1860).

120. Theodore Roosevelt, "Platform of the Progressive Party," *PBS.org*, August 6, 1912, http://www.pbs.org/wgbh/americanexperience/features/primary-resources/tr-progressive/?flavour=mobile

121. Franklin Roosevelt "Address at Madison Square Garden, New York City," *The American Presidency Project*, October 31, 1936, http://www.presidency.ucsb.edu/ws/?pid=15219

Chapter 2

1. Anthony DiMaggio, "From Bad to Worse: Forecasting the Effects of Republican Health Care Reform," *Counterpunch*, May 12, 2017, https://www.counterpunch.org/2017/05/12/from-bad-to-worse-forecasting-the-effects-of-republican-health-care-reform/

2. Anthony DiMaggio, "A Better Deal: Dissecting the Democrats' Populist Turn in Rhetoric and Relaity," *Counterpunch*, July 28, 2017, https://www.counterpunch.org/2017/07/28/a-better-deal-dissecting-the-democrats-populist-turn-in-rhetoric-and-reality/

3. DiMaggio, "From Bad to Worse," 2017.

4. Ciara Torres-Spelliscy, "The History of Corporate Personhood," *The Brennan Center for Justice*, April 7, 2014, https://www.brennancenter.org/blog/hobby-lobby-argument

5. Torres-Spelliscy, "The History of Corporate Personhood," 2014.

6. Nina Totenberg, "When Did Companies Become People? Excavating the Legal Evolution," *National Public Radio*, July 28, 2014, http://www.npr.org/2014/07/28/335288388/when-did-companies-become-people-excavating-the-legal-evolution

7. Robert A. Carp, Ronald Stidham, Kenneth L. Manning, and Lisa M. Holmes, *Judicial Process in America* (Washington DC: CQ Press, 2016); Alen Rappaport, "Making it Rain: Members of Congress are Mostly Millionaires," *The New York Times*, January

12, 2015, https://www.nytimes.com/politics/first-draft/2015/01/12/making-it-rain-members-of-congress-are-mostly-millionaires/; Agustino Fontevecchia, "Forbe's 2016 Presidential Candidate Wealth List," *Forbes*, September 29, 2015, https://www.forbes.com/sites/afontevecchia/2015/09/29/forbes-2016-presidential-candidate-net-worth-list/#2d332e6e2871

8. Carp, et al., *Judicial Process in America*, 2016; Rappaport, "Making it Rain," 2015; Fontevecchia, "Forbe's 2016 Presidential Candidate Wealth List," 2015.

9. Todd Donovan, Daniel A. Smith, Tracy Osborn, and Christopher Z. Mooney, *State and Local Politics*: Institutions and Reform (Stamford, CT: Cengage, 2015).

10. Donovan, et al., *State and Local Politics*, 2015.

11. Adam Liptak, "'We the People' Loses Appeal with People Around the World," *The New York Times*, February 6, 2012, http://www.nytimes.com/2012/02/07/us/we-the-people-loses-appeal-with-people-around-the-world.html

12. Liptak, "'We the People' Loses Appeal with People Around the World," 2012.

13. Liptak, "'We the People' Loses Appeal with People Around the World," 2012.

14. Chris Cillizza, "People Hate Congress: But Most Incumbents Get Re-Elected. What Gives?" *Washington Post*, May 9, 2013, https://www.washingtonpost.com/news/the-fix/wp/2013/05/09/people-hate-congress-but-most-incumbents-get-re-elected-what-gives/?utm_term=.6042fa4afa62

15. Sarah Binder, "How We Count Senate Filibusters and Why it Matters," *Washington Post*, May 15, 2014, https://www.washingtonpost.com/news/monkey-cage/wp/2014/05/15/how-we-count-senate-filibusters-and-why-it-matters/?utm_term=.d2d8841d55f9

16. Martin Gilens, *Affluence and Influence: Economic Inequality and Political Power in America* (Princeton, NJ: Princeton University Press, 2014).

17. Pew Research Center, "Super PACs Having Negative Impact, Say Voters Aware of 'Citizens United' Ruling," *Pew Research Center*, January 17, 2012, http://www.people-press.org/2012/01/17/super-pacs-having-negative-impact-say-voters-aware-of-citizens-united-ruling/

18. Drew DeSilver, "Global Inequality: How the U.S. Compares," *Pew Research Center*, December 19, 2013, http://www.pewresearch.org/fact-tank/2013/12/19/global-inequality-how-the-u-s-compares/

19. Laurie Kellman and Emily Swanson, "AP-NORC Poll: Thre-Quarters in U.S. Say They Lack Influence," *U.S. News and World Report*, July 13, 2017, https://www.usnews.com/news/politics/articles/2017-07-13/ap-norc-poll-three-quarters-in-us-say-they-lack-influence

20. Donald S. Lutz, *Principles of Constitutional Design* (Cambridge: Cambridge University Press, 2008).

21. Frank Newport, "Americans Support Proposal to Eliminate Electoral College System," *Gallup*, January 5, 2001, http://www.gallup.com/poll/2140/americans-support-proposal-eliminate-electoral-college-system.aspx

22. Art Swift, "Americans' Support for Electoral College Rises Sharply," *Gallup*, December 2, 2016, http://www.gallup.com/poll/198917/americans-support-electoral-college-rises-sharply.aspx

23. Tami Luhby, "Bush Tax Cuts, Stock Market Widen Income Gap," *CNN Money*, January 4, 2012, http://money.cnn.com/2012/01/03/news/economy/income_inequality/index.

htm; Jeanne Sahadi and Tami Luhby, "How the GOP Health Care Bills Help the Rich," *CNN Money*, June 23, 2017, http://money.cnn.com/2017/06/23/news/economy/tax-cuts-obamacare-repeal-senate-bill/index.html

24. Levinson, *Our Undemocratic Constitution*, 2008.

Chapter 3

1. David Weigel, "Sanders Introduces Universal Health Care, Backed by 15 Democrats," *Washington Post*, September 13, 2017, https://www.washingtonpost.com/powerpost/sanders-will-introduce-universal-health-care-backed-by-15-democrats/2017/09/12/d590ef26-97b7-11e7-87fc-c3f7ee4035c9_story.html

2. Robert Pear, "Medicare for All or State Control: Health Care Plans Go to Extremes," *The New York Times*, September 12, 2017, https://www.nytimes.com/2017/09/13/us/politics/health-care-obamacare-single-payer-graham-cassidy.html

3. Danielle Kurtzleben, "Here's What's in Bernie Sanders' 'Medicare For All' Bill," *National Public Radio*, September 14, 2017, http://www.npr.org/2017/09/14/550768280/heres-whats-in-bernie-sanders-medicare-for-all-bill

4. Thomas Anton, *American Federalism and Public Policy: How the System Works* (New York: Random House, 1989).

5. Eric Rauchway, *The Great Depression and the New Deal: A Very Short Introduction* (New York: Oxford University Press, 2008); Linda Levine, "The Labor Market During the Great Depression and the Current Recession," *Congressional Research Service*, June 19, 2009, https://digital.library.unt.edu/ark:/67531/metadc26169/m1/1/high_res_d/R40655_2009Jun19.pdf

6. Ester R. Fuchs, *Mayors and Money: Fiscal Policy in New York and Chicago* (Chicago: University of Chicago Press, 1992).

7. David E. Hamilton, "Herbert Hoover: Domestic Affairs," *University of Virginia Miller Center*, 2017, https://millercenter.org/president/hoover/domestic-affairs

8. Pew Research Center, "State Governments Viewed Favorably as Federal Rating Hits New Low," *Pew Research Center*, April 15, 2013, http://www.people-press.org/2013/04/15/state-govermnents-viewed-favorably-as-federal-rating-hits-new-low/; Lydia Saad, "In U.S., Local and State Governments Retain Positive Ratings," *Gallup*, October 3, 2011, http://www.gallup.com/poll/149888/local-state-governments-retain-positive-ratings.aspx; Gallup, "Government," *Gallup.com*, 2017, http://www.gallup.com/poll/27286/government.aspx

9. Gallup, "Government," 2017.

10. Pew Research Center, "Deficit: More Concern, Less Optimism," *Pew Research Center*, April 26, 2011, http://www.people-press.org/2011/04/26/deficit-more-concern-less-optimism/

11. Eric McClam, "Many Americans Blame 'Government Welfare' for Persistent Poverty, Poll Finds," *NBC News*, June 6, 2013, https://www.nbcnews.com/feature/in-plain-sight/many-americans-blame-government-welfare-persistent-poverty-poll-finds-v18802216

12. Kevin Arceneaux, "Does Federalism Weaken Democratic Representation in the United States? *Publius*, 35, no. 2 (2005): 297–311.

13. Saundra K. Schneider, William G. Jacoby, and Daniel C. Lewis, "Public Opinion Toward Intergovernmental Policy Responsibilities," *Publius*, 41, no. 1 (2011): 1–30.

14. Schneider, et al., "Public Opinion Toward Intergovernmental Policy Responsibilities," 2011.

15. Pew Research Center, "Ratings of Federal Agencies, Congress, and the Supreme Court," *Pew Research Center*, November 23, 2015, http://www.people-press.org/2015/11/23/4-ratings-of-federal-agencies-congress-and-the-supreme-court/

16. Pew Research Center, "Beyond Distrust: How Americans View Their Government," *Pew Research Center*, November 23, 2015, http://www.people-press.org/2015/11/23/beyond-distrust-how-americans-view-their-government/

17. Pew Research Center, "As Sequester Deadline Looms, Little Support for Cutting Most Programs," *Pew Research Center*, February 22, 2013, http://www.people-press.org/2013/02/22/as-sequester-deadline-looms-little-support-for-cutting-most-programs/

18. Richard L. Cole, John Kincaid, and Andrew Parkin, "Public Opinion on Federalism in the United States and Canada in 2002," *Publius*, 32, no. 4 (2002): 123–48.

19. David Brunori, "Where is the Outrage Over Corporate Wefare?" *Forbes*, March 14, 2014, https://www.forbes.com/sites/taxanalysts/2014/03/14/where-is-the-outrage-over-corporate-welfare/#2c711c0827dd

20. Jacob S. Hacker and Paul Pierson, *American Amnesia: How the War on Government Led us to Forget What Made America Prosper* (New York: Simon and Schuster, 2017).

21. Cole C. Kingseed, *The American Civil War* (Westport, CT: Greenwood Press, 2004).

22. Christopher J. Olsen, *Roots of Secession: Slavery and Politics in Antebellum Virginia* (Chapel Hill, NC: University of North Carolina Press, 2003); Charles B. Dew, "Apostles of Disunion: Southern Secession Commissioners and the Causes of the Civil War" (Charlottesville, VA: University of Virginia Press, 2002).

23. Howard Jones, *Abraham Lincoln and a New Birth of Freedom: The Union and Slavery in the Diplomacy of the Civil War* (Lincoln, NE: University of Nebraska Press, 1999).

24. Margaret E. Keck and Kathryn Sikkink, *Activists Beyond Borders: Advocacy Networks in International Politics* (Ithaca, NY: Cornell University Press, 1998).

25. Approximately 8.4 million people lived in the seceding slave states, according to the 1860 U.S. census. This represents about a quarter of the total U.S. population at the time. See the United States Census Bureau data page at: https://www.census.gov/prod/www/decennial.html. With regard to the claim that the majority of Americans supported the abolitionist cause, unfortunately, modern public opinion polls were not available in the mid-nineteenth century. However, electoral measures are available for measuring the public will. The most obvious evidence of support for abolition would be Lincoln's electoral victories in the 1860 and 1864 elections. Lincoln was vocally opposed to expanding slavery prior to his first election, and issued the Emancipation Proclamation in 1863, the year before the 1864 election. Lincoln's victory in the 1864 election suggests a clear majority mandate existed not merely for preventing the spread of slavery, but for abolishing it entirely.

26. James L. Huston, *Calculating the Value of the Union: Slavery, Property Rights, and the Economic Origins of the Civil War* (Chapel Hill, NC: University of North Carolina

Press, 2016); Roger L. Ransom, *Conflict and Compromise: The Political Economy of Slavery, Emancipation, and the American Civil War* (Cambridge: Cambridge University Press, 1989).

27. Keck and Sikkink, *Activists Beyond Borders: Advocacy Networks in International Politics* (Ithaca, NY: Cornell University Press, 1998); Harold Holzer and Norton Garfinkle, *A Just and Generous Nation: Abraham Lincoln and the Fight for American Opportunity* (New York: Basic Books, 2015).

28. Francis Fox Piven and Richard Cloward, *Poor People's Movements: Why They Succeed, How They Fail* (New York: Vintage Books, 1978).

29. Franklin D. Roosevelt, "Address Accepting the Presidential Nomination at the Democratic National Convention in Chicago," *The American Presidency Project*, July 2, 1932, http://www.presidency.ucsb.edu/ws/?pid=75174

30. Roosevelt, "Address Accepting the Presidential Nomination at the Democratic National Convention in Chicago," 1932.

31. Kim Phillips-Fein, *Invisible Hands: The Businessmen's Crusade Against the New Deal* (New York: W. W. Norton, 2010).

32. Adam Cohen, "Public Works: When 'Big Government' Plays its Role," *The New York Times*, November 13, 2007, http://www.nytimes.com/2007/11/13/opinion/13tues4.html

33. James S. Olson, *Historical Dictionary of the Great Depression, 1929–1940* (Westport, CT: Greenwood Press, 2001).

34. Jason Scott Smith, *Building New Deal Liberalism: The Political Economy of Public Works, 1933–1956* (Cambridge: Cambridge University Press, 2006); Timothy J. Bartik, *Jobs for the Poor: Can Labor Demand Policies Help?* (New York: Sage, 2001). The Bureau of Labor Statistics estimated that national unemployment stood at 10.4 million people in 1938, so 3.3 million people were put to work under the WPA, representing 32 percent of all unemployed Americans. The BLS counted those employed under public works as unemployed, even though they were receiving paychecks. For more on this practice, see: Jeremy Holden, "Fox News' Wallace Falsely Claimed 'Unemployment in 1937, 1938 was Higher than it was in 1933,' " *Media Matters for America*, January 31, 2009, http://media matters.org/research/2009/01/21/fox-news-wallace-falsely-claimed-unemployment-i/146907. For the data on the unemployment rate in 1938, see: Bureau of Labor Statistics, "Labor Force, Employment, and Unemployment, 1929–1939: Estimating Methods," *Bureau of Labor Statistics*, October 1, 2014, https://www.bls.gov/opub/mlr/1948/article/pdf/labor-force-employment-and-unemployment-1929-39-estimating-methods.pdf

35. Lyndon B. Johnson, "Remarks at the University of Michigan," *The American Presidency Project*, May 22, 1964, http://www.presidency.ucsb.edu/ws/?pid=26262%20

36. Megan Stanley, Ife Floyd, and Misha Hill, "TANF Cash Benefits Have Fallen by More than 20 Percent in Most States and Continue to Erode," *Center on Budget and Policy Priorities*, October 17, 2016, http://www.cbpp.org/research/many-states-cutting-tanf-benefits-harshly-despite-high-unemployment-and-unprecedented-need; Ife Floyd and Liz Schott, "TANF Benefits Fell Further in 2011 and are Worth Much Less than in 1996 in Most States," *Center on Budget and Policy Priorities*, November 21, 2011, http://www.cbpp.org/research/tanf-benefits-fell-further-in-2011-and-are-worth-much-less-than-in-1996-in-most-states

37. Ronald Reagan, "Inaugural Address," *The American Presidency Project*, January 20, 1981, http://www.presidency.ucsb.edu/ws/?pid=43130

38. Alana Samuels, "The End of Welfare as We Know it," *The Atlantic*, April 1, 2016, https://www.theatlantic.com/business/archive/2016/04/the-end-of-welfare-as-we-know-it/476322/; William J. Clinton, "Address Before a Joint Session of the Congress on the State of the Union," *The American Presidency Project*, January 23, 1996, http://www.presidency.ucsb.edu/ws/?pid=53091

39. Zac Auter, "U.S. Uninsured Rate Holds at Low of 10.9% in Fourth Quarter," *Gallup*, January 9, 2017, http://www.gallup.com/poll/201641/uninsured-rate-holds-low-fourth-quarter.aspx; Jenna Levy, "In U.S., Uninsured Rate Dips to 11.9% in the First Quarter," *Gallup*, April 13, 2015, http://www.gallup.com/poll/182348/uninsured-rate-dips-first-quarter.aspx

Chapter 4

1. Tessa Berenson, "Reminder: The House Voted to Repeal Obamacare More Than 50 Times," *Time*, March 24, 2017, http://time.com/4712725/ahca-house-repeal-votes-obamacare/

2. Lori Robertson, "The 24 Million Talking Point," *Factcheck.org*, May 9, 2017, http://www.factcheck.org/2017/05/24-million-talking-point/; Nathaniel Weixel, "CBO: 22 Million Would Lose Coverage Under Senate ObamaCare Replacement," *The Hill*, July 20, 2017, http://thehill.com/policy/healthcare/342941-cbo-22-million-would-lose-coverage-under-senate-obamacare-replacement

3. Jennifer Steinhauer and Robert Pear, "G.O.P. Support of Senate Health Repeal Erodes During Break," *The New York Times*, July 7, 2017, https://www.nytimes.com/2017/07/07/us/politics/republicans-health-care-bill.html?mcubz=3

4. Leeron Hoory, "GOP Reps Return Home to Angry Constituents in Health Care Town Halls," *AOL News*, May 9, 2017, https://www.aol.com/article/news/2017/05/09/gop-reps-return-home-to-angry-constituents-in-health-care-town-h/22078406/; Diamond Naga Siu, "Republican Senators Hit by Calls From Voters Worried About Obamacare Repeal Bill," *Politico*, June 27, 2017, http://www.politico.com/story/2017/06/27/republican-health-care-bill-voter-response-239981; Tim Stelloh, "Protesters Rail Against GOP's Latest Obamacare Repeal Effort," *NBC News*, June 27, 2017, https://www.nbcnews.com/politics/congress/protesters-rail-against-gop-s-latest-obamacare-repeal-effort-n777026

5. Alicia Parlapiano, Wilson Andrews, Jasmine C. Lee, and Rachel Shorey, "How Each Senator Voted on Obamacare Repeal Proposals," *The New York Times*, July 28, 2017, https://www.nytimes.com/interactive/2017/07/25/us/politics/senate-votes-repeal-obamacare.html?mcubz=3

6. Ashley Killough, "Republicans Opposing GOP Health Care Plan Hear From Voters During Recess," *CNN.com*, July 5, 2017, http://www.cnn.com/2017/07/05/politics/republicans-health-care-plan-july-4-holiday/index.html; Charlotte Alter, "How Women Helped Save Obamacare," *Time*, July 29, 2017, http://time.com/4878724/donald-trump-

gop-health-care-women/; Eric Bradner, "Nevada's Heller Dogged by Summer of Reversals on Health Care," *CNN.com*, September 21, 2017, http://www.cnn.com/2017/09/21/politics/dean-heller-nevada-health-care/index.html

7. M. J. Lee, Phil Mattingly, and Ted Barrett, "Latest Health Care Bill Collapses Following Moran, Lee Defections," *CNN.com*, July 18, 2017, http://www.cnn.com/2017/07/17/politics/health-care-motion-to-proceed-jerry-moran-mike-lee/index.html

8. John Bresnahan, Burgess Everett, Jennifer Haberkorn, and Seung Min Kim, "Senate Rejects Obamacare Repeal," *Politico*, July 28, 2017, http://www.politico.com/story/2017/07/27/obamacare-repeal-republicans-status-241025

9. Jacob Kauffman, "Update: Senator Cotton Backs Healthcare Repeal Without Replacement, Governor Disagrees," *KASU.org*, July 19, 2017, http://kasu.org/post/update-senator-cotton-backs-healthcare-repeal-without-replacement-governor-disagrees

10. Ed Kilgore, "GOP Senators Begin to Question Health-Care Bill's Tax Cuts for the Rich," *New York Magazine*, July 28, 2017, http://nymag.com/daily/intelligencer/2017/06/gop-senators-question-health-bills-tax-cuts-for-the-rich.html

11. United States Senate, "Vote Summary: On Passage of the Bill (H.R. 3762)," *United States Senate*, December 3, 2015, https://www.senate.gov/legislative/LIS/roll_call_lists/roll_call_vote_cfm.cfm?congress=114&session=1&vote=00329

12. Pew Research Center, "For the First Time, 2010 Health Care Law Draws Majority Approval," *Pew Research Center*, February 23, 2017, http://www.pewresearch.org/fact-tank/2017/02/23/support-for-2010-health-care-law-reaches-new-high/ft_17-02-23_healthcare_approval/

13. Peter Sullivan, "Final GOP Tax Bill Repeals Obamacare Mandate," *The Hill*, December 15, 2017, http://thehill.com/policy/healthcare/365185-final-gop-tax-bill-repeals-obamacare-mandate

14. Anthony DiMaggio, "Health Care Repeal Fallout: On the Front Lines of the Campaign for Universal Health Care," *Counterpunch*, July 11, 2017, https://www.counterpunch.org/2017/07/11/health-care-repeal-fallout-on-the-front-lines-of-the-campaign-for-universal-health-care/

15. Jack L. Walker, Jr., *Mobilizing Interest Groups in America: Patrons, Professions, and Social Movements* (Ann Arbor, MI: University of Michigan Press, 1991).

16. Duncan Campbell, "New Enron Scandal Link to Bush," *Guardian*, February 1, 2002, https://www.theguardian.com/business/2002/feb/02/enron.usnews

17. Robert Scheer, "The Enron Story Everyone is Missing: The Bush-Ken Lay Connection," *Truthdig*, May 26, 2006, http://www.truthdig.com/report/item/20060526_enron_bush_lay

18. John Nichols, "Enron: What Dick Cheney Knew," *The Nation*, April 15, 2002, https://www.thenation.com/article/enron-what-dick-cheney-knew/

19. Michael Abramowitz and Steven Mufson, "Papers Detail Industry's Role in Cheney's Energy Report," *The Washington Post*, July 18, 2007, http://www.washingtonpost.com/wp-dyn/content/article/2007/07/17/AR2007071701987.html; *The Washington Post*, "Energy Task Force Meetings Participants, *The Washington Post*, 2016, http://www.washingtonpost.com/wp-srv/politics/documents/cheney_energy_task_force.html

20. Lloyd Vries, "Bush Disses Global Warming Report," *CBS News*, June 3, 2002, http://www.cbsnews.com/news/bush-disses-global-warming-report/; Andrew C. Revkin, "Bush Climate Plan Says Adapt to Inevitable/Cutting Gas Emissions Not Recommended," *San Francisco Chronicle*, June 3, 2002, http://www.sfgate.com/green/article/Bush-climate-plan-says-adapt-to-inevitable-2831358.php

21. Robert Yoon, "Goldman Sachs was Top Obama Donor," *CNN.com*, April 20, 2010, http://www.cnn.com/2010/POLITICS/04/20/obama.goldman.donations/

22. Theodore Lowi, *The End of Liberalism: The Second Republic of the United States* (New York: W. W. Norton, 2009).

23. Megan Leonhardt, "The Lasting Effects of Occupy Wall Street—Five Years Later," *Time*, September 16, 2016, http://time.com/money/4495707/occupy-wall-street-anniversary-effects/

24. Naomi Oreskes and Erik M. Conway, *Merchants of Doubt: How a Handful of Scientists Obscured the Truth on Issues from Tobacco Smoke to Global Warming* (London: Bloomsbury, 2011).

25. Bill Adair and Angie Drobnic Holan, "Politifact's Lie of the Year: 'A Government Takeover of Health Care,'" *Politifact*, December 16, 2010, http://www.politifact.com/truth-o-meter/article/2010/dec/16/lie-year-government-takeover-health-care/

26. Anthony DiMaggio, *Rebellion in America: Citizen Uprisings, the News Media, and the Politics of Plutocracy* (New York: Routledge, 2019).

27. Tanja Babich, "Minimum Wage Protesters Demand $15 an Hour at McDonald's Headquarters," *ABC 7 Chicago*, May 21, 2015, http://abc7chicago.com/news/minimum-wage-protesters-demand-$15-an-hour/733797/; Heesun Wee, "Fight for $15: McDonald's Workers Protest to Raise Minimum Wage," *CNBC*, April 15, 2015, http://www.cnbc.com/2015/04/15/fight-for-15-mcdonalds-workers-protest-to-raise-minimum-wage.html

28. Michael Winter, Jeff Ayres, and Bill Laitner, "Protesters Nationwide Call for $15 Minimum Wage," *USA Today*, December 4, 2014, http://www.usatoday.com/story/news/nation/2014/12/04/minimum-wage-fast-food-protests/19908011/

29. Ryan Rifai, "U.S. Sees Largest Protests Calling for $15 Minimum Wage," *Al Jazeera*, November 29, 2016, http://www.aljazeera.com/news/2016/11/sees-largest-protests-calling-15-minimum-wage-161129164539058.html

30. Bob Chiarito, "Hundreds Protest Over Minimum Wage at McDonald's Stockholder Meeting," *Reuters*, May 24, 2017, https://www.reuters.com/article/us-usa-wages-protest/hundreds-protest-over-minimum-wage-at-mcdonalds-stockholder-meeting-idUSKBN18K2EB; Matthew Kazin, "Fast Food Workers Set to Protest in Push for $15," *Fox News*, February 11, 2018, http://www.foxnews.com/us/2018/02/11/fast-food-workers-set-to-protest-in-push-for-15-minimum-wage.html

31. Aimee Picchi, "How Low-Wage Employers Cost Taxpayers $153B a Year," *CBS News*, April 13, 2015, http://www.cbsnews.com/news/how-low-wage-employers-cost-taxpayers-153-billion-a-year/

32. Barry Ritholtz, "How McDonalds and Wal-Mart Became Welfare Queens," *Bloomberg News*, November 13, 2013, https://www.bloomberg.com/view/articles/2013-11-13/how-mcdonald-s-and-wal-mart-became-welfare-queens

33. Jillian Rayfield, "McDonald's to Employees: Get a Second Job!" *Salon. com*, July 17, 2003, http://www.salon.com/2013/07/17/mcdonalds_suggested_budget_for_ employees_recommends_a_second_job/

34. Bruce Drake, "Polls Show Strong Support for Minimum Wage Hike," *Pew Research Center*, March 4, 2014, http://www.pewresearch.org/fact-tank/2014/03/04/polls-show-strong-support-for-minimum-wage-hike/; Ariel Edwards-Levy, "Raising the Minimum Wage is a Really, Really Popular Idea," *Huffington Post*, April 13, 2016, http://www.huffingtonpost. com/entry/minimum-wage-poll_us_570ead92e4b08a2d32b8e671

35. Anthony R. DiMaggio, *Citizens in Rebellion: Citizen Uprisings, the News Media, and the Politics of Plutocracy* (New York: Routledge, 2019).

36. Jeff Guo, "Income Inequality Today May be Higher Today Than in Any Other Era," *The Washington Post*, July 1, 2016, https://www.washingtonpost.com/news/wonk/ wp/2016/07/01/income-inequality-today-may-be-the-highest-since-the-nations-founding/ ?utm_term=.ff1cd67bf89c; Drew Desilver, "For Most Workers, Real Wages Have Barely Budged for Decades," *Pew Research Center*, October 9, 2014, http://www.pewresearch.org/ fact-tank/2014/10/09/for-most-workers-real-wages-have-barely-budged-for-decades/

37. Alyssa Davis and Lawrence Mishel, "CEO Pay Continues to Rise as Typical Workers are Paid Less," *Economic Policy Institute*, June 12, 2014, http://www.epi.org/ publication/ceo-pay-continues-to-rise/; Shawn Sprague, "What Can Labor Productivity Tell Us About the U.S. Economy," *Bureau of Labor Statistics*, 3, no. 12 (2014), https://www. bls.gov/opub/btn/volume-3/what-can-labor-productivity-tell-us-about-the-us-economy.htm

38. Jared Bernstein, "The Rise in Family Work Hours Leads Many Americans to Struggle to Balance Work and Family," *Economic Policy Institute*, July 7, 2004, http://www. epi.org/publication/webfeatures_snapshots_07072004/

39. National Conference of State Legislatures, "State Minimum Wages," Ncsl.org, January 5, 2017, http://www.ncsl.org/research/labor-and-employment/state-minimum-wage-chart.aspx

40. David Cooper, "20 States Raise Their Minimum Wages While the Federal Minimum Continues to Erode," *Economic Policy Institute*, December 18, 2014, http:// www.epi.org/blog/20-states-raise-their-minimum-wages-while-the-federal-minimum-continues-to-erode/; Sarah Whitten, "16 States to Raise Minimum Wage in 2016," *CNBC*, December 24, 2015, http://www.cnbc.com/2015/12/24/13-states-to-raise-minimum-wage-in-2016.html; Ann Robertson and Bill Leumer, "The Necessity for, and Obstacles to, Transforming the Unions into a Fighting Force for Workers," *Counterpunch*, March 10, 2017, http://www.counterpunch.org/2017/03/10/the-necessity-for-and-obstacles-to-transforming-the-unions-into-a-fighting-force-for-workers/

41. Anthony DiMaggio, "An American Uprising: Assessing Opportunities for Progressive Political Change," *Counterpunch*, April 20, 2017, https://www.counterpunch.org/2017/04/20/ an-american-uprising-assessing-opportunities-for-progressive-political-change/

42. Justin Worland, "Global CO_2 Concentration Passes Threshold of 400 ppm— And That's Bad for the Climate," *Time*, October 24, 2016, http://time.com/4542889/ carbon-dioxide-400-ppm-global-warming/

43. Suzanne Goldenberg, Lauren Gambino, Damian Carrington, James Randerson, Karl Mathiesen, and Oliver Milman, "Climate Change Marches: Kerry Cites Fight Against

Ebola and ISIS as Thousands Join Protests," *Guardian*, September 22, 2014, https://www.theguardian.com/environment/2014/sep/21/-sp-climate-change-protest-melbourne-london-new-york-protest

44. Damian Carrington, "Planet Likely to Warm by 4C by 2100, Scientists Warn," *The Guardian*, December 31, 2013, https://www.theguardian.com/environment/2013/dec/31/planet-will-warm-4c-2100-climate

45. Reuters, "UN: Cut Carbon Emissions by 2100 to Save the World from Climate Change," *CNBC.com*, November 2, 2014, http://www.cnbc.com/2014/11/02/un-cut-carbon-emissions-by-2100-to-save-the-world-from-climate-change.html

46. Clare Foran, "Donald Trump and the Triumph of Climate-Change Denial," *The Atlantic*, December 25, 2016, https://www.theatlantic.com/politics/archive/2016/12/donald-trump-climate-change-skeptic-denial/510359/

47. Benjamin I. Page, Larry M. Bartels, and Jason Seawright, "Democracy and the Policy Preferences of Wealthy Americans," *Perspectives on Politics* 11, no. 1 (2013): 51–73.

48. Dana Nuccitelli, "Survey Finds 97% of Climate Science Papers Agree Warming is Man-Made," *The Guardian*, May 16, 2013, https://www.theguardian.com/environment/climate-consensus-97-per-cent/2013/may/16/climate-change-scienceofclimatechange

49. Eli Rosenberg, Jennifer Medina, and John Eligon, "Protesters Take Anti-Trump Message to His Doorstep and Plan Next Steps," *The New York Times*, November 12, 2016, https://www.google.com/amp/s/mobile.nytimes.com/2016/11/13/us/trump-protest-rallies.amp.html

50. CBS/Associated Press, "Anti-Trump Protests Not Letting Up for Sixth Week Straight Day After Election," *CBS News*, November 14, 2016, http://www.cbsnews.com/news/anti-trump-protests-not-letting-up-for-sixth-straight-day-after-presidential-election/; Madison Park, Ralph Ellis, Khushbu Shah, and Azadeh Ansari, "Anti-Trump Protests Move through Fifth Day," *CNN.com*, November 14, 2016, http://www.cnn.com/2016/11/13/us/protests-elections-trump/

51. Heidi M. Przybyla and Fredreka Schouten, "At 2.6 Million Strong, Women's Marches Crush Expectations," *USA Today*, January 21, 2017, http://www.usatoday.com/story/news/politics/2017/01/21/womens-march-aims-start-movement-trump-inauguration/96864158/

52. *The Guardian*, "Thousands Protest Against Trump Travel Ban in Cities and Airports Nationwide," *The Guardian*, January 29, 2017, https://www.theguardian.com/us-news/2017/jan/29/protest-trump-travel-ban-muslims-airports; Tammy Webber, " 'We Do Care': Tax Day Protesters Call on Trump to Release Tax Returns in Rallies Across U.S.," *Associated Press*, April 15, 2017, http://www.chicagotribune.com/news/nationworld/ct-donald-trump-tax-day-march-20170415-story.html; The Hill, "Live Coverage: March for Science Rally is Underway," *The Hill*, April 22, 2017, http://thehill.com/policy/energy-environment/330037-live-coverage-march-for-science-seeks-to-send-message-to-trump; Ai Rogin and David Caplan, "Protesters Opposing GOP Health Care Bill Descend on Lawmakers, Some Arrested," *ABC News*, July 7, 2017, http://abcnews.go.com/Politics/protesters-opposing-gop-health-care-bill-descend-lawmakers/story?id=48491443

53. Amy B Wang, "Trump Asked for a 'Muslim Ban,' Giuliani Says—and Ordered a Commission to do it 'Legally,' " *The Washington Post*, January 29, 2017, https://www.

washingtonpost.com/news/the-fix/wp/2017/01/29/trump-asked-for-a-muslim-ban-giuliani-says-and-ordered-a-commission-to-do-it-legally/?utm_term=.57a9ef424824

54. Ariane de Vogue, Eli Watkins, and Alanne Orjoux, "Judges Temporarily Block Part of Trump's Immigration Order, WH Stands by it," *CNN.com*, January 29, 2017, http://www.cnn.com/2017/01/28/politics/2-iraqis-file-lawsuit-after-being-detained-in-ny-due-to-travel-ban/; Adam Liptak, "Court Refuses to Reinstate Travel Ban, Dealing Trump Another Legal Loss," *The New York Times*, February 9, 2017, https://www.nytimes.com/2017/02/09/us/politics/appeals-court-trump-travel-ban.html

55. Adam Liptak and Michael D. Shear, "Supreme Court Upholds Trump's Travel Ban, Delivering Endorsement of Presidential Power," *The New York Times*, June 26, 2018, https://www.nytimes.com/2018/06/26/us/politics/supreme-court-trump-travel-ban.html?hp&action=click&pgtype=Homepage&clickSource=story-heading&module=a-lede-package-region&region=top-news&WT.nav=top-newsf

56. *Gallup*, "Gallup Daily: Trump Job Approval," *Gallup*, 2017, http://www.gallup.com/poll/201617/gallup-daily-trump-job-approval.aspx

57. John Dewey, *Democracy and Education* (New York: New Press, 1916).

58. G. William Domhoff, "Theories of Power: Alternative Theoretical Views," *University of California Santa Cruz*, April 2005, http://www2.ucsc.edu/whorulesamerica/theory/alternative_theories.html

59. Domhoff, "Theories of Power," 2005.

60. Arthur F. Bentley, *The Process of Government: A Study of Social Pressures* (Piscataway, NJ: Transaction Publishers, 1995); David B. Truman, *The Governmental Process: Political Interests and Public Opinion* (Westport, CT: Praeger, 1981).

61. Truman, *The Governmental Process*, 1981.

62. Sincere T. Kirabo, "Noam Chomsky: America is a Plutocracy Masquerading as a Democracy," *Salon*, October 6, 2015, https://www.salon.com/2015/10/06/noam_chomsky_america_is_a_plutocracy_masquerading_as_a_democracy_partner/

63. C. Wright Mills, *The Power Elite* (Oxford: Oxford University Press, 2000).

64. Lowi, *The End of Liberalism*, 1999.

65. Lowi, *The End of Liberalism*, 1999.

66. For academic analysis discussing "iron triangles," see: A. G. Jordan, *Iron Triangles, Wooly Corporatism, and Elastic Nets: Images of the Policy Process* (Cambridge: Cambridge University Press, 1981); Thomas L. Gais, *Interest Groups, Iron Triangles, and Representative Institutions in American National Government* (Westport, CT: Praeger, 1991); Gordon Adams, *The Iron Triangle: The Politics of Defense Contracting* (Piscataway, NJ: Transaction Publishers, 1981); Raymond Vernon, Debora L. Spar, and Glenn Tobin, *Iron Triangles and Revolving Doors: Cases in U.S. Foreign Economic Policymaking* (Westport, CT: Praeger, 1991). For textbooks discussing iron triangles, see: Bardes, Shelley, Schmidt, *American Government and Politics Today*, 2008; and Thomas A. Birkland, *An Introduction to the Policy Process: Theories, Concepts, and Models of Public Policy Making* (Armonk, NY: M. E. Sharpe, 2010).

67. Anthony DiMaggio, "'Boons' for Business: The Real Victors Behind Market-Driven Health Care Reform," *Monthly Review Online*, March 25, 2010, https://mronline.org/2010/03/25/boons-for-business-the-real-victors-behind-market-driven-health-care-reform/

68. Mancur Olson, *The Logic of Collective Action: Public Goods and the Theory of Groups* (Cambridge, MA: Harvard University Press, 1971).

69. Robert S. Erikson, Gerald C. Wright, and John P. McIver, *Statehouse Democracy: Public Opinion and Policy in the American States* (Cambridge: Cambridge University Press, 1993); Benjamin I. Page and Robert Y. Shapiro, "The Effects of Public Opinion on Policy," *American Political Science Review*, 77, no. 1 (1983): 175–90; James A. Stimson and Michael B. MacKuen, and Robert S. Erikson, "Dynamic Representation," *American Political Science Review*, 89, no. 3 (1995): 543–65; Robert S. Erikson, Michael B. MacKuen, and James A. Stimson, *The Macro Polity* (Cambridge: Cambridge University Press, 2002).

70. Doug McAdam, *Political Process and the Development of Black Insurgency, 1930–1970* (Chicago: University of Chicago Press, 1999); Todd Gitlin, *The Whole World is Watching: Mass Media in the Making and Unmaking of the New Left* (Berkley: University of California Press, 1981); Christopher Bosso, *Environment Inc.: From Grassroots to Beltway* (Lawrence, KS: University Press of Kansas, 2005); Laurel Weldon, *When Protest Makes Policy: How Social Movements Represent Disadvantaged Groups* (Ann Arbor, MI: University of Michigan Press, 2012); Theda Skocpol and Vanessa Williamson, *The Tea Party and the Remaking of American Conservatism* (Oxford: Oxford University Press, 2013); Rhonda F. Levine, *Class Struggle and the New Deal: Industrial Labor, Industrial Capital, and the State* (Lawrence, KS: University Press of Kansas, 1988); Corrine M. McConnaughy, *The Woman Suffrage Movement in America: A Reassessment* (Cambridge: Cambridge University Press, 2015); Kerry Eleveld, *Don't Tell Me to Wait: How the Fight for Gay Rights Changed America and Transformed Obama's Presidency* (New York: Basic Books, 2015); Sam Pizzigati, *The Rich Don't Always Win: The Forgotten Triumph over Plutocracy that Created the American Middle Class, 1900–1970* (New York: Seven Stories Press, 2012); Piven and Cloward, *Poor People's Movements*, 1978; Keck and Sikking, *Activists Beyond Borders*, 1998).

71. Walker, Jr., *Mobilizing Interest Groups in America*, 1991.

72. Walker, Jr., *Mobilizing Interest Groups in America*, 1991; Jeffrey M. Berry, *The Interest Group Society* (New York: Longman, 1997).

73. Walker, Jr., *Mobilizing Interest Groups in America*, 1991.

74. Thomas Ferguson, *Golden Rule: The Investment Theory of Party Competition and the Logic of Money-Driven Political Systems* (Chicago: University of Chicago Press, 1995); Levine, *Class Struggle and the New Deal*, 1988.

75. Doug McAdam, *Political process and the Development of Black Insurgency, 1930–1970* (Chicago: University of Chicago Press, 1999); Daniel Q. Gillion, *The Political Power of Protest: Minority Activism and Shifts in Public Policy* (Cambridge: Cambridge University Press, 2013).

76. For a review of these studies, see: Frank R. Baumgartner and Beth L. Leech, *Basic Interests: The Importance of Groups in Politics and in Political Science* (Princeton, NJ: Princeton University Press, 1998).

77. Frank R. Baumgartner, Jeffrey M. Berry, Marie Hojnacki, David C. Kimball, and Beth L. Leech, *Lobbying and Policy Change: Who Wins, Who Loses, and Why* (Chicago: University of Chicago Press, 2009).

78. This finding is referred to as "punctuated equilibrium," in which most of the time, there are few changes in policies or in funding for major agencies or programs, although such consistency is occasionally interrupted. See: Frank R. Baumgartner and Bryan D. Jones, *Agendas and Instability in American Politics* (Chicago: University of Chicago Press, 2009); Bryan D. Jones and Frank R. Baumgartner, *The Politics of Attention: How Government Prioritizes Problems* (Chicago: University of Chicago Press, 2005).

79. Jeanne Sahadi, "A world with No IRS? Really?" *CNNmoney*, November 4, 2015, http://money.cnn.com/2015/11/04/pf/taxes/abolish-the-irs/

80. Marie Hojnacki and David C. Kimball, "Organized Interests and the Decision of Whom to Lobby in Congress," *American Political Science Review*, 92, no. 4 (1998): 775–90.

81. Berry, *The Interest Group Society*, 1997.

82. Martha A. Derthick, *Up in Smoke: From Legislation to Litigation in Tobacco Politics* (Washington DC: CQ Press, 2011).

83. Gallup, "Tobacco Smoking," *Gallup*, 2017, http://www.gallup.com/poll/1717/tobacco-smoking.aspx

84. Constance A. Nathanson, "Social Movements as Catalysts for Policy Change," *Journal of Health Politics*, 24, no. 3 (1999): http://irasilver.org/wp-content/uploads/2011/08/Reading-SMs-against-smoking-guns-Nathanson.pdf; Derthick, *Up in Smoke*, 2001.

85. Mike Wallace and Lowell Bergman, "Wigand: 60 Minutes' Most Famous Whistleblower," *CBS News*, August 28, 2011, http://www.cbsnews.com/news/wigand-60-minutes-most-famous-whistleblower/

86. Derthick, *Up in Smoke*, 2011.

87. Derthick, *Up in Smoke*, 2011.

88. Derthick, *Up in Smoke*, 2011.

89. Gallup, "Tobacco Smoking," 2017.

90. Kaiser Family Foundation, "Percent of Adults Who Smoke," *Kaiser Family Foundation*, 2015, http://kff.org/other/state-indicator/smoking-adults/?currentTimeframe=0

91. Gallup, "Tobacco Smoking," 2017.

92. *U.S. News and World Report*, "Poll: U.S. Adults Support Smoking Ban in Cars with Kids," *U.S. News and World Report*, July 23, 2013, http://health.usnews.com/health-news/news/articles/2013/07/23/poll-us-adults-support-smoking-ban-in-cars-with-kids

93. Matt Grossmann, *The Not-so-Special Interests: Interest Groups, Public Representation, and American Governance* (Palo Alto, CA: Stanford University Press, 2012); A. Trevor Thrall, "The Myth of the Outside Strategy: Mass Media News Coverage of Interest Groups," *Political Communication*, 23, no. 4 (2006): 407–20.

94. Gillion, *The Political Power of Protest*, 2013; Paul Burstein and William Freudenburg, "The Impact of Public Opinion, Antiwar Demonstrations, and War Costs on Senate Voting on Vietnam War Motions," *American Journal of Sociology*, 84, no. 1 (1978): 99–122; Nayda Terkildsen and Frauke Schnell, "How Media Frames Move Public Opinion: An Analysis of the Women's Movement," *Political Research Quarterly*, 50, no. 4 (1997): 879–900.

95. Baumgartner, et al., *Lobbying and Policy Change*, 2009.

96. Deniz Igan and Prachi Mishra, "Making Friends," *International Monetary Fund*, June 2001, https://www.imf.org/external/pubs/ft/fandd/2011/06/pdf/igan.pdf

97. Bob Biersack, "The Big Spender Always Wins?" *Center for Responsive Politics*, January 11, 2012, http://www.opensecrets.org/news/2012/01/big-spender-always-wins/

98. Wesley Lowery, "91% of the Time the Better-Financed Candidate Wins. Don't Act Surprised," *The Washington Post*, April 4, 2014, https://www.washingtonpost.com/news/the-fix/wp/2014/04/04/think-money-doesnt-matter-in-elections-this-chart-says-youre-wrong/

99. Jorg L. Spenkuch and David Toniatti, "Political Advertising and Election Outcomes," *Working Paper*, April 2016, http://www.kellogg.northwestern.edu/faculty/spenkuch/research/advertising.pdf

100. Eric Lipton and Steve Eder, "Trump Nominees' Filings Threaten to Overwhelm Federal Ethics Office," *The New York Times*, January 6, 2017, https://www.nytimes.com/2017/01/06/us/politics/trump-nominees-federal-ethics-office.html?_r=0

101. Eric Strauss, "The Average Salary of First Term Congressmen," *Houston Chronicle*, 2012, http://work.chron.com/average-salary-first-term-congressmen-8529.html

102. Tom Gerencer, "The Net Worth of Congress," *Money Nation*, November 12, 2015, http://moneynation.com/the-net-worth-of-congress/; Russ Choma, "Millionaire's Club: For First Time, Most Lawmakers are Worth $1 Million-Plus," *Center for Responsive Politics*, January 9, 2014, https://www.opensecrets.org/news/2014/01/millionaires-club-for-first-time-most-lawmakers-are-worth-1-million-plus/

103. Gerencer, "The Net Worth of Congress," 2015.

104. For evidence of lobbyists allying with members of Congress with which they already agree, see: Hojnacki and Kimball, "Organized Interests and the Decision of Whom to Lobby in Congress," 1998. For evidence that wealthy Americans are significantly more likely to hold conservative views, especially on issues of business power, see: Benjamin I. Page, Larry M. Bartels, and Jason Seawright, "Democracy and the Policy Preferences of Wealthy Americans," *Perspectives on Politics*, 11, no. 1 (2013): 51–73. For evidence that Congress is significantly more likely to represent the interests of the top 20 percent over the median income American or the bottom 80 percent, see: Martin Gilens, *Affluence and Influence: Economic Inequality and Political Power in America* (Princeton, NJ: Princeton University Press, 2014); and Martin Gilens and Benjamin I. Page, "Testing Theories of American Politics," *Perspectives on Politics*, 12, no. 3 (2014): 564–81. Finally, for evidence on how growing affluence of members of Congress—measured by blue-collar versus white-collar professions—impacts the likelihood of taking conservative, pro-business policy positions, see: Nicholas Carnes, *White Collar Government: The Hidden Role of Class in Economi Policy Making* (Chicago: University of Chicago Press, 2013).

105. Domhoff, *Who Rules America?* 2013.

106. Jennifer Wang, "Donald Trump's Fortune Falls $800 Million to $3.7 Billion," *Fortune*, September 28, 2016, http://www.forbes.com/sites/jenniferwang/2016/09/28/the-definitive-look-at-donald-trumps-wealth-new/#7cdf8bf37e2d

107. Michael Gavis, "Barack Obama's Net Worth on his 55th Birthday," *Time*, August 4, 2016, http://time.com/money/4439729/barack-obama-net-worth-55th-birthday/

108. Daniel Gross, "How Hillary and Bill Clinton Parlayed Decades of Public Service into Vast Wealth," *Fortune*, February 15, 2016, http://fortune.com/2016/02/15/hillary-clinton-net-worth-finances/

109. Stephanie Condon, "Why is Congress a Millionaire's Club?" *CBN News*, Marcy 27, 2012, http://www.cbsnews.com/news/why-is-congress-a-millionaires-club/

110. Open Secrets, "George W. Bush: Net Worth Over Time," *Center for Responsive Politics*, 2008, https://www.opensecrets.org/pfds/summary.php?cid=N00008072%20&year=2008

111. Edwin Durgy, "What Mitt Romney is Really Worth: An Exclusive Analysis of his Latest Finances," *Fortune*, May 16, 2012, http://www.forbes.com/sites/edwindurgy/2012/05/16/what-mitt-romney-is-really-worth/#66f3608d2927

112. Augustino Fontevecchia, "Forbes' 2016 Presidential Candidate Wealth List," *Forbes*, September 29, 2015, http://www.forbes.com/sites/afontevecchia/2015/09/29/forbes-2016-presidential-candidate-net-worth-list/#533920f0435d

113. The "Revolving Door" between those serving between government offices and in the private sector is commonly studied by groups like *The Center for Responsive Politics*.

114. Stuart Silverstein, "This is Why Your Drug Prescriptions Cost so Damn Much," *Mother Jones*, October 21, 2016, http://www.motherjones.com/politics/2016/10/drug-industry-pharmaceutical-lobbyists-medicare-part-d-prices

115. Bruce Bartlett, "Medicare Part D: Republican Budget Busting," *The New York Times*, November 19, 2013, https://economix.blogs.nytimes.com/2013/11/19/medicare-part-d-republican-budget-busting/?_r=0

116. Bartlett, "Medicare Part D," 2013.

117. P. J. Huffstutter and Martha Graybow, "Special Report: Did Diane Sawyer Smear 'Pink Slime,'" *Reuters*, March 4, 2013, http://www.reuters.com/article/us-usa-media-abc-bpi-idUSBRE92313R20130304

118. Arr Oh, "Pink Slime, Deconstructed," *Scientific American*, March 27, 2012, https://blogs.scientificamerican.com/guest-blog/pink-slime-deconstructed/

119. Josh Sanburn, "One Year Later, The Makers of 'Pink Slime' are Hanging on, and Fighting Back," *Time*, March 6, 2013, http://time.com/5978/one-year-later-the-makers-of-pink-slime-are-hanging-on-and-fighting-back/

120. Jim Avila, "Beef Products Inc. Comeback: "It's Not 'Pink Slime,'; It's Safe, Nutritious and 'It's Beef,'" *ABC News*, March 27, 2012, http://abcnews.go.com/Business/beef-products-comeback-pink-slime-safe-nutritious-beef/story?id=16014232

121. Open Secrets, "Former Members: Number of Former Members: 432," *Center for Responsive Politics*, 2017, https://www.opensecrets.org/revolving../top.php?display=Z

122. Elizabeth Brown, "More Than 2,000 Spin Through Revolving Door," *Center for Public Integrity*, April 7, 2005, https://www.publicintegrity.org/2005/04/07/6570/more-2000-spin-through-revolving-door

123. Cristina Marcos, "A Lifetime Ban on Lobbying for Lawmakers," *The Hill*, June 3, 2014, http://thehill.com/blogs/floor-action/house/208104-bill-would-bar-lawmakers-from-becoming-lobbyists-for-life

124. Lee Drutman, "About Half of Retiring Senators and a Third of Retiring House Members Register as Lobbyists," *Vox*, January 15, 2016, http://www.vox.com/2016/1/15/10775788/revolving-door-lobbying

125. Daniel Butler, *Representing the Advantaged: How Politicians Reinforce Inequality* (Cambridge: Cambridge University Press, 2014).

126. Gilens, *Affluence and Influence*, 2014.

127. Carnes, *White Collar Government*, 2013.

128. Lyle Scruggs and Thomas J. Hayes, "The Influence of Inequality on Welfare Generosity," *Politics and Society* 45 (1) 2017, 35–66.

129. Edward S. Herman and Noam Chomsky, *Manufacturing Consent: The Political Economy of the Mass Media* (New York: Pantheon, 2002).

130. David Forgacs, ed. *The Antonio Gramsci Reader: Selected Writings, 1916–1935* (New York: New York University Press, 2000).

131. Andrew Fieldhouse and Ethan Pollack, "Tenth Anniversary of the Bush-Era Tax Cuts," *Economic Policy Institute*, June 1, 2011, http://www.epi.org/publication/tenth_anniversary_of_the_bush-era_tax_cuts/

132. Zachary A. Goldfarb, "The Legacy of the Bush Tax Cuts, in Four Charts," *The Washington Post*, January 2, 2013, https://www.washingtonpost.com/news/wonk/wp/2013/01/02/the-legacy-of-the-bush-tax-cuts-in-four-charts/?utm_term=.54d305aba925

133. DiMaggio, *The Politics of Persuasion*, 2017.

134. DiMaggio, *The Politics of Persuasion*, 2017.

135. Annie Augustine, "Poll: Americans Side with Democrats on Bush Tax Cuts," *The Atlantic*, Dec 3, 2010, https://www.theatlantic.com/politics/archive/2010/12/poll-americans-side-with-democrats-on-bush-tax-cuts/67455/

136. Anthony R. DiMaggio, *Selling War, Selling Hope: Presidential Rhetoric, the News Media, and U.S. Foreign Policy After 9/11* (Albany, NY: State University of New York Press, 2015).

137. Anthony R. DiMaggio, "The Propaganda Model and Manufacturing Consent: U.S. Public Compliance and Resistance," in *Cambridge Companion to Chomsky*, ed. James McGilvray (Cambridge: Cambridge University Press, 2017): 275–94.

138. Jacob S. Hacker and Paul Pierson, *Off Center: The Republican Revolution and the Erosion of American Democracy* (New Haven, CT: Yale University Press, 2005); Jacob S. Hacker and Paul Pierson, *Winner-Take-All Politics: How Washington Made the Rich Richer—and Turned its Back on the Middle Class* (New York: Simon and Schuster, 2011); Marc Hetherington, *Why Trust Matters: Declining Political Trust and the Demise of American Liberalism* (Princeton, NJ: Princeton University Press, 2006).

139. Anthony R. DiMaggio, *The Politics of Persuasion: Media Bias and Economic Policy in the Modern Era* (Albany, NY: State University of New York Press, 2017).

140. DiMaggio, *The Politics of Persuasion*, 2017.

141. DiMaggio, *The Politics of Persuasion*, 2017.

142. Gilens and Page, "Testing Theories of American Politics," 2014. Andrew S. McFarland, *Neopluralism: The Evolution of Political Process Theory* (Lawrence, KS: University

Press of Kansas, 2004); David Lowery and Holly Brasher, *Organized Interests and American Government* (Long Grove, IL: Waveland Press, 2004).

Chapter 5

1. Pew Research Center for the People & the Press Poll, "April, 2017 Monthly Poll," *Pew Research Center*, April 2017.

2. Pew Research Center, "Public Dissatisfaction with Washington Weighs on the GOP," *Pew Research Center*, April 17, 2017, http://www.people-press.org/2017/04/17/3-views-of-congress/

3. Hannah Fingerhut, "Support for 2010 Health Care Law Reaches New High," *Pew Research Center*, February 23, 2017, http://www.pewresearch.org/fact-tank/2017/02/23/support-for-2010-health-care-law-reaches-new-high/

4. Aldrich, *Why Parties*, 2011.

5. Cox and McCubbins, *Legislative Leviathan*, 1993.

6. Cox and McCubbins, *Legislative Leviathan*, 1993.

7. Gary W. Cox and Matthew D. McCubbins, *Setting the Agenda: Responsible Party Government in the U.S. House of Representatives* (Cambridge: Cambridge University Press, 2005).

8. Chris Van Hollen, "Congressional Record–House: H6556," *Congressional Record*, October 12, 2013, https://www.gpo.gov/fdsys/pkg/CREC-2013-10-12/pdf/CREC-2013-10-12-pt1-PgH6556-3.pdf

9. GovTrack, "H.R. 3590 (111th): Patient Protection and Affordable Care Act," *GovTrack*, 2017, https://www.govtrack.us/congress/votes/111-2010/h165; *GovTrack*, "H.R. 3590 (111th): Patient Protection and Affordable Care Act," *GovTrack*, 2017, https://www.govtrack.us/congress/votes/111-2009/s396

10. Krehbiel, *Information and Legislative Organization*, 1992.

11. Krehbiel, *Information and Legislative Organization*, 1992.

12. Teresa Welsh, "Blog Buzz: Right and Left Slam Ryan's Budget," *U.S. News*, March 12, 2013, https://www.usnews.com/opinion/articles/2013/03/12/right-and-left-slams-paul-ryans-path-to-prosperity-budget

13. John R. Parkinson, "House Passes Paul Ryan Budget Proposal in Partisan Vote," *ABC News*, April 15, 2011, http://abcnews.go.com/Politics/paul-ryans-budget-proposal-passes-house-democrats-medicare/story?id=13384520

14. Lori Montgomery and Philip Rucker, "Republicans Embrace Rep. Ryan's Government Budget Plan for 2012," *The Washington Post*, April 5, 2011, https://www.washingtonpost.com/business/economy/republicans-embrace-rep-ryans-government-budget-plan-for-2012/2011/04/05/AFla6ulC_story.html; Speaker Ryan's Press Office, "Speaker Boehner Calls on House to Pass GOP's 'Path to Prosperity' Budget," *Speaker.gov*, March 29, 2012, http://www.speaker.gov/speech/speaker-boehner-calls-house-pass-gops-path-prosperity-budget

15. Among others, both Republican Senator John McCain and Democratic President Barack Obama have publicly criticized "pork barrel" spending. David Jackson,

John Fritze and *USA Today*, "Obama Vows to Reduce Pork Barrel Spending," *ABC News*, 2017, http://abcnews.go.com/Politics/story?id=7058542; Shawn Zeller, "McCain's Got Obama Over a Pork Barrel," *Politifact*, September 16, 2008, http://www.politifact.com/truth-o-meter/statements/2008/sep/16/john-mccain/mccains-got-obama-over-a-pork-barrel/

16. Robert M. Stein and Kenneth N. Bickers, *Perpetuating the Pork Barrel: Policy Subsystems and American Democracy* (Cambridge: Cambridge University Press, 1997).

17. Diana Evans, *Greasing the Wheels: Using Pork Barrel Projects to Build Majority Coalitions in Congress* (Cambridge: Cambridge University Press, 2004).

18. Evans, *Greasing the Wheels*, 2004; Jonathan Weisman and Jim VandeHei, "Road Bill Reflects The Power of Pork," *The Washington Post*, August 11, 2005, http://www.washingtonpost.com/wp-dyn/content/article/2005/08/10/AR2005081000223.html

19. Weisman and Jim VandeHei, "Road Bill Reflects The Power of Pork," 2005, http://www.washingtonpost.com/wp-dyn/content/article/2005/08/10/AR2005081000223.html

20. Ken Silverstein and Jeff Moag, "The Pentagon's 300-Billion-Dollar Bomb," *Mother Jones*, January/February 2000, http://www.motherjones.com/politics/2000/01/pentagons-300-billion-dollar-bomb

21. Silverstein and Moag "The Pentagon's 300-Billion-Dollar Bomb," 2000, http://www.motherjones.com/politics/2000/01/pentagons-300-billion-dollar-bomb

22. *Why We Fight*, directed by Eugene Jarecki (2006. New York: Sony Picture Classics, 2006), DVD.

23. Rebecca U. Thorpe, *The American Warfare State: The Domestic Politics of Military Spending* (Chicago: University of Chicago Press, 2014).

24. Niv Sultan, "Defense Sector Contributions Locked in on Committee Members," *The Huffington Post*, March 6, 2017, http://www.huffingtonpost.com/entry/defense-sector-contributions-locked-in-on-committee_us_58b84bf8e4b051155b4f8c81

25. Thorpe, *The American Warfare State*, 2014.

26. Kristina C. Miler, *Constituency Representation in Congress: The View From Capitol Hill* (Cambridge: Cambridge University Press, 2010).

27. Patrick O'Connor, "House GOP Bans Earmarks," *The Wall Street Journal*, November 18, 2010, http://blogs.wsj.com/washwire/2010/11/18/house-gop-bans-earmarks/

28. Austin Wright and Jeremy Herb, "The Rise of the 'Zombie' Earmark," *Politico*, October 20, 2015, http://www.politico.com/story/2015/10/zombie-earmarks-defense-spending-pet-projects-214938

29. Carnes, *White Collar Government*, 2013.

30. Will Tucker, "Personal Wealth: A Nation of Extremes, and a Congress Too," *Opensecrets.org*, November 17, 2015, https://www.opensecrets.org/news/2015/11/personal-wealth-a-nation-of-extremes-and-a-congress-too/

31. Tim Worstall, "Six Waltons Have More Wealth Than the Bottom 30% of Americans," *Forbes*, December 14, 2011, https://www.forbes.com/sites/timworstall/2011/12/14/six-waltons-have-more-wealth-than-the-bottom-30-of-americans/#3487d84e62f5

32. Tucker, "Personal Wealth," 2015.

33. Tucker, "Personal Wealth," 2015.

34. Gabrielle Levy, "The 115th Congress by Party, Race, Gender, and Religion," *U.S. News and World Report*, January 5, 2017, https://www.usnews.com/news/politics/slideshows/the-115th-congress-by-party-race-gender-and-religion

35. Philip Bump, "Nearly Everyone in Congress has a College Degree. Most Americans Don't," *The Washington Post*, February 2, 2017, https://www.washingtonpost.com/news/politics/wp/2017/02/02/nearly-everyone-in-congress-has-a-college-degree-most-americans-dont/?utm_term=.6ef6e8f2ddfc

36. Central Intelligence Agency, "The World Factbook," *Central Intelligence* Agency, 2017, https://www.cia.gov/library/publications/the-world-factbook/fields/2177.html; Jennifer E. Manning, "Members of the 115th Congress: A Profile," *Congressional Research Service*, March 13, 2017, https://fas.org/sgp/crs/misc/R44762.pdf

37. Russ Choma, "One Member of Congress = 18 American Households: Lawmakers' Personal Finances Far From Average," *Opensecrets.org*, January 12, 2015, https://www.opensecrets.org/news/2015/01/one-member-of-congress-18-american-households-lawmakers-personal-finances-far-from-average/

38. David Weigel, "Ted Cruz: 'I Had More Legislation Pass the Senate Than All But a Handful of Republicans,'" *Bloomberg*, March 25, 2015, http://www.bloomberg.com/politics/articles/2015-03-25/ted-cruz-i-had-more-legislation-pass-the-senate-than-all-but-a-handful-of-republicans-; Azmat Khan, "The Republicans' Plan for the New President," *PBS Frontline*, January 15, 2013, http://www.pbs.org/wgbh/frontline/article/the-republicans-plan-for-the-new-president/; Greg Sargent, "Biden: McConnell Decided to Deny Us Cooperation Before We Took Office," August 10, 2012, https://www.washingtonpost.com/blogs/plumline/post/biden-mcconnell-decided-to-withhold-all-cooperation-even-before-we-took-office/2012/08/10/64e9a138-e302-11e1-98e7-89d659f9c106_blog.html?utm_term=.03d7aeba77ec; Michael Grunwald, "The Party of No: New Details on the GOP Plot to Obstruct Obama," *Time*, August 23, 2012, http://swampland.time.com/2012/08/23/the-party-of-no-new-details-on-the-gop-plot-to-obstruct-obama/

39. James Fallows, "How the Modern Faux-Filibuster Came to Be," *The Atlantic*, April 2, 2012, https://www.theatlantic.com/politics/archive/2012/04/how-the-modern-faux-filibuster-came-to-be/255374/

40. Shane Ferro, "Why the Democrats Voted to Change the Filibuster Rules," *Reuters*, November 22, 2013, http://blogs.reuters.com/data-dive/2013/11/22/why-the-democrats-voted-change-filibuster-rules/

41. United States Senate, "Cloture Motions," *Senate.gov*, 2017, https://www.senate.gov/pagelayout/reference/cloture_motions/clotureCounts.htm

42. United States Senate, "Cloture Motions: Motions Filed," 2017, http://www.senate.gov/reference/clotureCounts.htm; Kathleen Alvarez Tritak, "Calendar of Business," *Senate of the United States*, 2017, https://www.gpo.gov/fdsys/pkg/CCAL-113scal-2014-12-16/pdf/CCAL-113scal-2014-12-16-pt0.pdf#5; Paige Lavender, "House Reduces Workdays On 2014 Calendar After Working So Hard In 2013," *The Huffington Post*, October 31, 2013, http://www.huffingtonpost.com/2013/10/31/house-calendar-2014_n_4181969.html

43. Mark Murray, "113th Congress Not the Least Productive in Modern History," *NBC News*, December 29, 2014, http://www.nbcnews.com/politics/first-read/113th-congress-not-least-productive-modern-history-n276216

44. Philip Bump, "Here's Yet Another Way of Looking at How Unproductive Congress Is," *The Washington Post*, May 17, 2014, https://www.washingtonpost.com/news/the-fix/wp/2014/05/17/heres-yet-another-way-of-looking-at-how-unproductive-congress-is/

45. GovTrack, "Statistics and Historical Comparison: Bills by Final Status," *GovTrack*, 2017, https://www.govtrack.us/congress/bills/statistics

46. Murray, "113th Congress Not the Least Productive in Modern History," 2014, http://www.nbcnews.com/politics/first-read/113th-congress-not-least-productive-modern-history-n276216

47. Louis Jacobson, "Harry Reid says 82 Presidential Nominees Have Been Blocked Under President Barack Obama, 86 Blocked Under All Other Presidents," *Politifact*, November 22, 2013, http://www.politifact.com/truth-o-meter/statements/2013/nov/22/harry-reid/harry-reid-says-82-presidential-nominees-have-been/

48. William Saletan, "The Chutzpah of 'Compromise,'" *Slate*, September 30, 2013, http://www.slate.com/articles/news_and_politics/frame_game/2013/09/obamacare_shutdown_compromise_how_republicans_invented_a_fake_middle_ground.html

49. Saletan, "The Chutzpah of 'Compromise,'" 2013, http://www.slate.com/articles/news_and_politics/frame_game/2013/09/obamacare_shutdown_compromise_how_republicans_invented_a_fake_middle_ground.html

50. Lori Robertson, "GOP's 'Job-Killing' Whopper, Again," *FactCheck.org*, February 21, 2012, http://www.factcheck.org/2012/02/gops-job-killing-whopper-again-2/

51. Igor Volsky, "Blow By Blow: A Comprehensive Timeline of the GOP's 4-Year Battle To Kill Obamacare," *ThinkProgress*, March 23, 2014, https://thinkprogress.org/blow-by-blow-a-comprehensive-timeline-of-the-gops-4-year-battle-to-kill-obamacare-5dd069a5518a#.865qgmjnb

52. Global Wire Services, "Obama Drives US toward Socialism, GOP Says," *Boston Globe*, February 28, 2009, http://archive.boston.com/news/nation/washington/articles/2009/02/28/obama_drives_us_toward_socialism_gop_says/; *The Huffington Post*, "Michele Bachmann Vows To 'Dismantle' Obama's 'System Of Socialism,'" *The Huffington Post*, December 28, 2011, http://www.huffingtonpost.com/2011/12/28/michele-bachmann-socialism-obama_n_1172472.html; Liz Halloran, "Top Republicans: Yeah, We're Calling Obama Socialist," *NPR*, March 5, 2010, http://www.npr.org/templates/story/story.php?storyId=124359632

53. Richard Rubin, "57% of Americans Say Their Income Taxes Are Too High. Only 55.5% Pay Income Tax. What?" The *Wall Street Journal*, April 18, 2016, http://blogs.wsj.com/economics/2016/04/18/57-of-americans-say-their-income-taxes-are-too-high-only-55-5-pay-income-tax-what/

54. Avik Roy, "Can Republicans Repeal Obamacare Without Disrupting Coverage for Tens of Millions?" *Forbes*, September 27, 2014, https://www.forbes.com/forbes/welcome/?toURL=https://www.forbes.com/sites/theapothecary/2014/09/27/can-republicans-

repeal-obamacare-without-disrupting-coverage-for-tens-of-millions/&refURL=https://www.
google.com/&referrer=https://www.google.com/

55. Don Seymour, "Boehner on NBC Nightly News: 'ObamaCare is the Biggest Job-Killer We Have in America Today,'" *Speaker.gov*, January 6, 2011, http://www.speaker.gov/general/boehner-nbc-nightly-news-%E2%80%9Cobamacare-biggest-job-killer-we-have-america-today%E2%80%9D

56. Robert Pear, "Justice Department Says Crucial Provisions of Obamacare are Unconstitutional," *The New York Times*, June 7, 2018, https://www.nytimes.com/2018/06/07/us/politics/trump-affordable-care-act.html

57. Sarah Ferris, "Showdown Scars: How the $4 Trillion 'Grand Bargain' Collapsed," *The Hill*, February 10, 2016, http://thehill.com/policy/finance/268857-showdown-scars-how-the-4-trillion-grand-bargain-collapsed

58. Matt Bai, "Obama vs. Boehner: Who Killed the Debt Deal?" *The New York Times Magazine*, March 28, 2012, http://www.nytimes.com/2012/04/01/magazine/obama-vs-boehner-who-killed-the-debt-deal.html

59. Erik Wasson and Russell Berman, "Boehner: 'We Are Not Close' to Reaching a Debt Deal with Obama," *The Hill*, July 22, 2011, http://thehill.com/homenews/house/172985-boehner-we-are-not-close-to-a-debt-ceiling-deal

60. Bai, "Obama vs. Boehner: Who Killed the Debt Deal?" 2012, http://www.nytimes.com/2012/04/01/magazine/obama-vs-boehner-who-killed-the-debt-deal.html; Russell Berman, "Boehner Backing Away from Grand Compromise on Debt, Tax Reform," *The Hill*, July 10, 2011, http://thehill.com/blogs/blog-briefing-room/news/170551-boehner-backing-away-from-grand-compromise-on-debt

61. Louis Woodhill, "$10 in Spending Cuts For $1 in Tax Increases? No Thanks.," *Forbes*, August 17, 2011, https://www.forbes.com/forbes/welcome/?toURL=https://www.forbes.com/sites/louiswoodhill/2011/08/17/10-in-spending-cuts-for-1-in-tax-increases-no-thanks/&refURL=https://www.google.com/&referrer=https://www.google.com/

62. Lori Montgomery, "In Debt Talks, Obama Offers Social Security Cuts," *The Washington Post*, July 6, 2011, https://www.washingtonpost.com/business/economy/in-debt-talks-obama-offers-social-security-cuts/2011/07/06/gIQA2sFO1H_story.html?utm_term=.71c1644bffa0; Janet Novack, "Obama Wants $1.5 Trillion in Tax Hikes, Mostly on Rich," *Forbes*, September 19, 2011, https://www.forbes.com/sites/janetnovack/2011/09/19/obama-wants-1-5-trillion-in-tax-hikes-mostly-on-rich/

63. Michael Grunwald, "The Party of No: New Details on the GOP Plot to Obstruct Obama," *Time*, August 23, 2012, http://swampland.time.com/2012/08/23/the-party-of-no-new-details-on-the-gop-plot-to-obstruct-obama/

64. Robert Draper, *Do Not Ask What Good We Do: Inside the U.S. House of Representatives* (Florence, MA: Free Press, 2012).

65. Greg Sargent, "Biden: McConnell Decided to Deny Us Cooperation Before We Took Office," *The Washington Post*, August 10, 2012, https://www.washingtonpost.com/blogs/plum-line/post/biden-mcconnell-decided-to-withhold-all-cooperation-even-before-we-took-office/2012/08/10/64e9a138-e302-11e1-98e7-89d659f9c106_blog.html?utm_term=.3f935cf65d6d

66. Sargent, "Biden: McConnell Decided to Deny Us Cooperation Before We Took Office," 2012, https://www.washingtonpost.com/blogs/plum-line/post/biden-mcconnell-decided-to-withhold-all-cooperation-even-before-we-took-office/2012/08/10/64e9a138-e3 02-11e1-98e7-89d659f9c106_blog.html?utm_term=.3222c7989270

67. Sargent, "Biden: McConnell Decided to Deny Us Cooperation Before We Took Office," 2012, https://www.washingtonpost.com/blogs/plum-line/post/biden-mcconnell-decided-to-withhold-all-cooperation-even-before-we-took-office/2012/08/10/64e9a138-e3 02-11e1-98e7-89d659f9c106_blog.html?utm_term=.809c1f1b43cf

68. Grunwald, "The Party of No: New Details on the GOP Plot to Obstruct Obama," 2012.

69. Konstantin Kilibarda and Daria Roithmayr, "The Myth of the Rust Belt Revolt," *Slate*, December 1, 2016, http://www.slate.com/articles/news_and_politics/politics/2016/12/the_myth_of_the_rust_belt_revolt.html

70. Hacker and Pierson, *Winner-Take-All Politics*, 2011.

71. Ariel Edwards-Levy, "Most People Think Congress Is Great at Representing Wealthy, But Not the Less Well-Off," *The Huffington Post*, January 15, 2015, http://www.huffingtonpost.com/2015/01/15/congress-wealthy-poll_n_6482050.html

72. Kilibarda and Roithmayr, "The Myth of the Rust Belt Revolt," 2016.

73. Polling Report, "Quinnipiac University Poll," *Pollingreport.com*, May 31–June 5, 2018, http://www.pollingreport.com/CongJob.htm; Polling Report, "Quinnipiac University Polls, October 29–November 2, 2015 through January 19–23, 2018, *Pollingreport.com*, http://www.pollingreport.com/cong_rep.htm

74. John R. Hibbing, Elizabeth Theiss-Morse, *Congress as Public Enemy: Public Attitudes toward American Political Institutions* (Cambridge: Cambridge University Press, 1995).

75. Frank Newport, "Americans See Congress as Ineffective, Self-Serving, Entrenched," *Gallup*, June 23, 2010, http://www.gallup.com/poll/141008/americans-congress-ineffective-self-serving-entrenched.aspx

76. Tom Jensen, "Congress Less Popular than Cockroaches, Traffic Jams," *Public Policy Polling*, January 8, 2013, http://www.publicpolicypolling.com/main/2013/01/congress-less-popular-than-cockroaches-traffic-jams.html

77. Gallup Poll, "Congress and the Public," *Gallup*, 2017, http://www.gallup.com/poll/1600/congress-public.aspx

78. For evidence on representing constituents, see: Richard Fenno Jr., *Home Style: House Members in Their Districts* (New York: Longman Publishers, 2002). Also see: Bruce Cain, John Ferejohn, and Morris Fiorina, *The Personal Vote: Constituency Service and Electoral Independence* (Chicago: University of Chicago Press, 1990). For a discussion of growing public polarization, and polarization as a reason for declining electoral competitiveness in Congressional races in favor of incumbents, see: Alan I. Abramowitz, Brad Alexander, Matthew Gunning, "Incumbency, Redistricting, and the Decline of Competition in U.S. House Elections," *The Journal of Politics* 68, no. 1 (2006): 75–88.

79. Gallup Poll, "Congress and the Public," *Gallup*, 2017, http://www.gallup.com/poll/1600/congress-public.aspx

80. Lisa Desjardins, "CNN Analysis: Congress in D.C. Far Less than it Used to Be," *CNN News*, August 1, 2013, http://www.cnn.com/2013/08/01/politics/congress-work-time/

Chapter 6

1. Phillip Bump, "What was Trump Talking About with a $12 a Year Health Insurance," *The Washington Post*, July 20, 2017, https://www.washingtonpost.com/news/politics/wp/2017/07/20/what-was-trump-talking-about-with-12-a-year-health-insurance/?utm_term=.20d84cc9bf5a

2. DiMaggio, *The Politics of Persuasion*, 2017.

3. DiMaggio, *The Politics of Persuasion*, 2017.

4. Charles Cameron, *Veto Bargaining: Presidents and the Politics of Negative Power* (Cambridge: Cambridge University Press, 2000).

5. CQ Poll, "CQ Roll Call's Vote Studies—2013 in Review," 2014, http://media.cq.com/votestudies/

6. DiMaggio, *Selling War, Selling Hope*, 2015.

7. Andrew Pincus, "The Solicitor General's Report Card," *SCOTUS Blog*, July 2, 2014, http://www.scotusblog.com/2014/07/the-solicitor-generals-report-card/

8. Walter Pincus, "The Solicitor General's Report Card," 2014, http://www.scotusblog.com/2014/07/the-solicitor-generals-report-card/; Adam Liptak, "Why Obama Struggled at Court and Trump May Strain to Do Better," *The New York Times*, January 23, 2017, https://www.nytimes.com/2017/01/23/us/politics/obama-supreme-court-win-rate-trump.html

9. Margaret Meriwether Cordray and Richard Cordray, "The Solicitor General's Changing Role in Supreme Court Litigation," *Boston College Law Review*, 51 (2010): 1323–382. https://www.bc.edu/content/dam/files/schools/law/bclawreview/pdf/51_5/01_cordray.pdf

10. Jeffrey A. Segal and Harold J. Spaeth, *The Supreme Court and the Attitudinal Model Revisited* (Cambridge: Cambridge University Press, 2002).; Cass R. Sunstein and David Schkade, "A Bench Tilting Right," *The Washington Post*, October 30, 2004, http://www.washingtonpost.com/wp-dyn/articles/A10799-2004Oct29.html

11. Ryan C. Black and Ryan J. Owens, 2009. "Solicitor General Influence and the United States Supreme Court," Southern Political Science Association. Harvard University, January 7–10, http://www.vanderbilt.edu/csdi/archived/working%20papers/Ryan%20Owens.pdf

12. Black and Owens, 2009. "Solicitor General Influence and the United States Supreme Court," http://www.vanderbilt.edu/csdi/archived/working%20papers/Ryan%20Owens.pdf

13. Jack Knight and Lee Epstein, *The Choices Justices Make* (Washington DC: CQ Press, 1997); Timothy R. Johnson, "The Supreme Court, the Solicitor General, and the Separation of Powers," *American Politics Research*, 31, no. 4 (2003): 426–51. http://users.polisci.umn.edu/~tjohnson/MyPapers/APR2003.pdf

14. Stephen Skowronek, *Presidential Leadership in Political Time: Reprise and Reappraisal* (Lawrence, KS: University Press of Kansas, 2011); Curt Nichols and Adam S.

Myers, "Exploring the Opportunity for Reconstructive Leadership: Presidential Responses to Enervated Political Regimes," *American Politics Research*, 38, no. 5 (2010): 806–41.

15. 24/7 Wall St. "The Net Worth of Every American President, from Washington to Obama: 24/7 Wall Street," *The Huffington Post*, February 21, 2011, http://www.huffingtonpost.com/2011/02/21/the-net-worth-of-the-amer_n_825939.html

16. Agustino Fontevecchia, "Forbes' 2016 Presidential Candidate Wealth List," *Forbes*, October 19, 2015, http://www.forbes.com/sites/afontevecchia/2015/09/29/forbes-2016-presidential-candidate-net-worth-list/3/#16183fed64db

17. Eric Lipton and Steve Eder, "Trump Nominees' Filings Threaten to Overwhelm Federal Ethics Office," *The New York Times*, January 6, 2017, https://www.nytimes.com/2017/01/06/us/politics/trump-nominees-federal-ethics-office.html?_r=0

18. Tax Foundation, "U.S. Federal Individual Income Tax Rates History, 1862–2013," *Tax Foundation*, October 17, 2013, https://taxfoundation.org/us-federal-individual-income-tax-rates-history-1913-2013-nominal-and-inflation-adjusted-brackets/

19. Andrew Fieldhouse and Ethan Pollack, "Tenth Anniversary of the Bush-Era Tax Cuts," *Economic Policy Institute*, June 1, 2011, http://www.epi.org/publication/tenth_anniversary_of_the_bush-era_tax_cuts/; Andrew Fieldhouse, "The Bush Tax Cuts Disproportionately Benefitted the Wealthy," *Economic Policy Institute*, June 4, 2011, http://www.epi.org/publication/the_bush_tax_cuts_disproportionately_benefitted_the_wealthy/

20. Janet Novack, "Trump Plan Delivers Massive Tax Cuts to the 1% and Sharp Kick to the Upper Middle Class," *CNBC*, September 29. 2017, https://www.forbes.com/sites/janetnovack/2017/09/29/trump-plan-delivers-massive-tax-cuts-to-the-1-and-sharp-kick-to-upper-middle-class/#7d7fb65f1099; Associated Press, "$5 Trillion Question for Trump Tax Plan: How to Pay for it?" *CNBC*, September 28, 2017, https://www.cnbc.com/2017/09/28/5-trillion-question-for-trump-tax-plan-how-to-pay-for-it.html

21. Matt O'Brien, "The Trump Tax Cuts Would be the Most Insane Giveaway to the Rich Ever," *The Washington Post*, October 3, 2017, https://www.washingtonpost.com/news/wonk/wp/2017/10/03/the-trump-tax-cuts-would-be-the-most-insane-giveaway-to-the-rich-ever/?utm_term=.bd55628a1ed0

22. Tami Luhby, "Bush Tax Cuts, Stock Market Widen Income Gap," *CNN Money*, January 4, 2012, http://money.cnn.com/2012/01/03/news/economy/income_inequality/index.htm

23. Clara Jeffery and Monika Bauerlein, "The Job Killers," *Mother Jones*, November/December 2011, http://www.motherjones.com/politics/2011/10/republicans-job-creation-kill/

24. Bruce Bartlett, "Tax Cuts and 'Starving the Beast,'" *Forbes*, May 7, 2010, https://www.forbes.com/2010/05/06/tax-cuts-republicans-starve-the-beast-columnists-bruce-bartlett.html

25. Ben Mathis-Lilley, "Trump Was Recorded in 2005 Bragging about Grabbing Women 'by the Pussy,'" *Slate*, October 7, 2016, http://www.slate.com/blogs/the_slatest/2016/10/07/donald_trump_2005_tape_i_grab_women_by_the_pussy.html

26. Stop and frisk and its unconstitutionality due to racial discrimination: Michelle Ye Hee Lee, "Trump's False Claim that Stop and Frisk in NYC Wasn't Ruled Unconstitutional," *The Washington Post*, September 28, 2016, https://www.washingtonpost.com/

news/fact-checker/wp/2016/09/28/trumps-false-claim-that-stop-and-frisk-was-not-ruled-unconstitutional/?utm_term=.27ee295a879e; DOJ investigations of racism in police departments: Eric Lichtblau, "Sessions Indicates Justice Department Will Stop Monitoring Troubled Police Agencies," *The New York Times*, February 28, 2017, https://www.nytimes.com/2017/02/28/us/politics/jeff-sessions-crime.html; For more on his racially insensitive comments, see: Liam Stack, "Ben Carson Refers to Slaves as 'Immigrants' in First Remarks to HUD Staff," *The New York Times*, March 6, 2017, https://www.nytimes.com/2017/03/06/us/politics/ben-carson-refers-to-slaves-as-immigrants-in-first-remarks-to-hud-staff.html; Philip Bump, "'They Friends of Yours?': Trump Asks Black Reporter to set up Meeting with Black Caucus," *The Washington Post*, February 16, 2017, https://www.washingtonpost.com/news/politics/wp/2017/02/16/trump-asks-a-black-reporter-to-set-up-a-meeting-with-black-members-of-congress/?utm_term=.9e87c684d4d9; Yamiche Alcindor, "After Backlash, DeVos Backpedals on Remarks on Historically Black Colleges," *The New York Times*, February 28, 2017, https://www.nytimes.com/2017/02/28/us/politics/betsy-devos-historically-black-colleges-statement.html

27. Michele L. Swers, *The Difference Women Make: The Policy Impact of Women in Congress* (Chicago: University of Chicago Press, 2002).

28. Andy Baker and Corey Cook, "Representing Black Interests and Promoting Black Culture: The Importance of African American Descriptive Representation in the U.S. House," *Du Bois Review* 2, no. 2 (2005): 227–46.

29. Carnes, *White Collar Government*, 2013.

30. Gilens, *Affluence and Influence*, 2014; Gilens and Page, "Testing Theories in American Politics," 2014; Butler, *Representing the Advantaged*, 2014.

31. Neil Sheehan and Herick Smith, *The Pentagon Papers: The Secret History of the Vietnam War* (New York: Bantam, 1971).

32. Jesse Nunes, "Pentagon Report Debunks Prewar Iraq-Al Qaeda Connection, *The Christian Science Monitor*, April 6, 2007, http://www.csmonitor.com/2007/0406/p99s01-duts.html; MSCNC Staff and News Service Reports, "9/11 Panel Sees No Link Between Iraw, Al-Qaida," *NBC News*, June 16, 2004, http://www.nbcnews.com/id/5223932/ns/us_news-security/t/panel-sees-no-link-between-iraq-al-qaida/

33. John Walcott, "What Donald Rumsfeld Knew We Didn't Know About Iraq," *Politico*, January 24, 2016, http://www.politico.com/magazine/story/2016/01/iraq-war-wmds-donald-rumsfeld-new-report-213530

34. Marjorie Cohn, "FISA Revised: A Blank Check for Domestic Spying," *The Huffington Post*, August 9, 2007, http://www.huffingtonpost.com/marjorie-cohn/fisa-revised-a-blank-chec_b_59884.html

35. Dominic Rushe, Ewen MacAskill, Ian Cobain, Alan Yuhas and Oliver Laughland, "Rectal Rehydration and Waterboarding: The CIA Torture Report's Grisliest Findings," *The Guardian*, December 11, 2014, https://www.theguardian.com/us-news/2014/dec/09/cia-torture-report-worst-findings-waterboard-rectal

36. Louis Jacobson, "Ron Paul Says Torture is Banned Under U.S., International Law," *PolitiFact*, November 15, 2011, http://www.politifact.com/truth-o-meter/statements/2011/nov/15/ron-paul/ron-paul-says-torture-banned-under-us-internationa/

37. Adam Hudson, "Bush's Fourth Term Continues": Guantanamo, Torture, Secret Renditions; Indefinite Detention," *Truthout*, May 30, 2014, http://www.truth-out.org/news/item/24030-bushs-fourth-term-continues-guantanamo-torture-secret-renditions-indefinite-detention; Brian Ross and Maddy Sauer, "1,245 Secret CIA Flights Revealed by European Parliament," *ABC News*, November 30, 2006, http://blogs.abcnews.com/the blotter/2006/11/1245_secret_cia.html

38. "Torture by Proxy," *The New York Times*, March 8, 2005, http://www.nytimes.com/2005/03/08/opinion/torture-by-proxy.html; Human Rights Watch, "US/Jordan: Stop Renditions to Torture," *Human Rights Watch*, April 7, 2008, https://www.hrw.org/news/2008/04/07/us/jordan-stop-renditions-torture

39. Stephen E. Atkins, "Guantanamo Bay Detainment Camp," in *The War on Terror Encyclopedia: From the Rise of Al-Qaeda to 9/11 and Beyond*, ed. Jan Goldman (Santa Barbara, CA: ABC-CLIO, 2014): 161.

40. Oliver Burkeman, "White House 'Knew of Abuse' at Guantanamo," *The Guardian*, September 17, 2004, https://www.theguardian.com/world/2004/sep/17/warcrimes.oliverburkeman

41. Tom Lasseter, "Day 1: America's Prison for Terrorists Often Held the Wrong Men," *McClatchy*, June 15, 2008, http://www.mcclatchydc.com/news/special-reports/article24484918.html

42. Lasseter, "Day 1: America's Prison for Terrorists Often Held the Wrong Men," 2008, http://www.mcclatchydc.com/news/special-reports/article24484918.html

43. Human Rights Watch, "Background Paper on Geneva Conventions and Persons Held by U.S. Forces," *Human Rights Watch*, January 29, 2002, https://www.hrw.org/legacy/backgrounder/usa/pow-bck.htm

44. Alex McBride, "Supreme Court History: The Future of the Court," *PBS.org*, 2005, http://www.pbs.org/wnet/supremecourt/future/landmark_hamdan.html

45. Charlie Savage, "Cole Attack Trial Will Test Tribunal System," *The New York Times*, November 30, 2009, http://www.nytimes.com/2009/12/01/us/01cole.html

46. Edward J. Klaris, "Justice Can't Be Done in Secret," *The Nation*, May 23, 2002, https://www.thenation.com/article/justice-cant-be-done-secret/

47. Paul R. Rice and Benjamin Parlin Saul, "Is the War on Terrorism a War on Attorney-Client Privilege?" *Criminal Justice Magazine*, 17, no. 2 (2002) http://www.americanbar.org/publications/criminal_justice_magazine_home/crimjust_cjmag_17_2_privilege.html

48. David Greenberg, "Uncivil Courts," *Slate*, December 5, 2001, http://www.slate.com/articles/news_and_politics/history_lesson/2001/12/uncivil_courts.html

49. Charlie Savage, "Obama Drops Veto Threat Over Military Authorization Bill After Revisions," *The New York Times*, December 14, 2011, http://www.nytimes.com/2011/12/15/us/politics/obama-wont-veto-military-authorization-bill.html

50. Greg Miller, "Obama Preserves Renditions as Counter-Terrorism Tool," *Los Angeles Times*, February 1, 2009, http://articles.latimes.com/2009/feb/01/nation/na-rendition1

51. Bonnie Kristian, "George W. Bush Launched 50 Drone Strikes. Obama Has Launched 500," *This Week*, September 9, 2015, http://theweek.com/speedreads/576283/george-w-bush-launched-50-drone-strikes-obama-launched-500

52. Paul Lewis, Spencer Ackerman and Nicholas Watt, "US Surveillance has 'Expanded' Under Obama, says Bush's NSA Director," *The Guardian*, June 9, 2013, https://www.theguardian.com/world/2013/jun/09/us-surveillance-expanded-obama-hayden

53. Charlie Savage and Mark Landler, "White House Defends Continuing U.S. Role in Libya Operation," *The New York Times*, June 15, 2011, https://www.nytimes.com/2011/06/16/us/politics/16powers.html

54. The Avalon Project, "War Powers Resolution," *Yale Law School*, 2018, http://avalon.law.yale.edu/20th_century/warpower.asp

55. Ayesha Rascoe, "U.S. Military Probing More Possible Civilian Deaths in Yemen Raid," *Reuters*, February 2, 2017, http://www.reuters.com/article/us-usa-trump-commando-idUSKBN15G5RX

56. Charlie Savage, "U.S. Says Troops Can Stay in Syria Without New Authorization," *The New York Times*, February 22, 2018, https://www.nytimes.com/2018/02/22/us/politics/isis-syria-american-troops.html; Thomas Gibbons-Neff, Jeremy White, and David Botti, "The U.S. Has Troops in Syria. So Do the Russians and Iranians. Here's Where," *The New York Times*, April 11, 2018, https://www.nytimes.com/interactive/2018/04/11/world/middleeast/syria-military-us-russia-iran.html

57. Dan Roberts and Tom McCarthy, "Obama Orders US Special Forces to 'Assist' Fight Against Isis in Syria," *Guardian*, October 30, 2015, https://www.theguardian.com/world/2015/oct/30/syria-us-deployment-troops-obama-special-operations

58. Charlie Savage and Jonathan Weisman, "N.S.A. Collection of Bulk Call Data is Ruled Illegal," *The New York Times*, May 7, 2015, http://www.nytimes.com/2015/05/08/us/nsa-phone-records-collection-ruled-illegal-by-appeals-court.html?_r=0

59. Peter Baker, "Bush Says U.S. Pullout Would Let Iraq Radicals Use Oil as a Weapon," *The Washington Post*, November 5, 2006, http://www.washingtonpost.com/wp-dyn/content/article/2006/11/04/AR2006110401025.html

60. Ledyard King, "Democrats Vent but Can't Stop Trump from Leaving Paris Climate Agreement," *USA Today*, May 31, 2017, https://www.usatoday.com/story/news/politics/2017/05/31/democrats-vent-but-cant-stop-trump-leaving-paris-climate-agreement/102343042/

61. Ben Protess and Julie Hirschfeld Davis, "Trump Moves to Roll Back Obama-Era Financial Regulations," *The New York Times*, February 3, 2017, https://www.nytimes.com/2017/02/03/business/dealbook/trump-congress-financial-regulations.html

62. Avalon Zoppo and Amanda Proneca Santos, "Here's the Full List of Donald Trump's Executive Orders," *NBC News*, July 24, 2017, https://www.nbcnews.com/politics/white-house/here-s-full-list-donald-trump-s-executive-orders-n720796

63. Zoppo and Santos, "Here's the Full List of Donald Trump's Executive Orders," 2017.

64. Jason Le Miere, "Trump, the Hypocritical Imperial President, is on Pace to Double Obama's Number of Executive Orders," *Newsweek*, October 13, 2017, http://www.newsweek.com/trump-obama-executive-order-president-684368

65. Michele Gorman, "Poll Finds Majority Disapprove of President Trump's Executive Orders," *Newsweek*, February 2, 2017, www.newsweek.com/trump-executive-orders-majority-disapproval-poll-551873

66. Glenn Kessler and Michael Ye Hee Lee, "Trump's Claim that 'the President Can't Have a Conflict of Interest," *The Washington Post*, November 23, 2016, https://www.washingtonpost.com/news/fact-checker/wp/2016/11/23/trumps-claim-that-the-president-cant-have-a-conflict-of-interest/

67. Kessler and Lee, "Trump's Claim that 'the President Can't Have a Conflict of Interest," 2016; Michael S. Schmidt, Maggie Haberman, Charlie Savage, and Matt Apuzzo, "Trump's Lawyers, in Confidential Memo, Argue to Head Off a Historic Subpoena," *The New York Times*, June 2, 2018, https://www.nytimes.com/2018/06/02/us/politics/trump-lawyers-memo-mueller-subpoena.html?hp&action=click&pgtype=Homepage&clickSource=story-heading&module=first-column-region&region=top-news&WT.nav=top-news

68. David Frost and Richard M. Nixon, "'I Have Impeached Myself,'" *Guardian*, May 1977, https://www.theguardian.com/theguardian/2007/sep/07/greatinterviews1

69. DiMaggio, *Selling War, Selling Hope*, 2015.; Brigitte L. Nacos, Yaeli Bloch-Elkon, and Robert Y. Shapiro, *Selling Fear*, 2011.; Bonn, *Mass Deception*, 2010.

70. DiMaggio, *Selling War, Selling Hope*, 2015; DiMaggio, *The Politics of Persuasion*, 2017; Nacos et al., *Selling Fear*, 2011; Bonn, *Mass Deception*, 2010; Stephen J. Farnsworth, *Spinner in Chief: How Presidents Sell Their Policies and Themselves* (New York: Routledge, 2015); Ben Fritz, Bryan Keefer, and Brendan Nyhan, *All the President's Spin: George W. Bush, the Media, and the Truth* (New York: Touchstone Books, 2004).

71. Nacos, *Selling Fear*, 2011.

72. Herman and Chomsky, *Manufacturing Consent*, 2002.

73. George W. Bush, "Text of President Bush's 2003 State of the Union Address, *The Washington Post*, January 28, 2003, http://www.washingtonpost.com/wp-srv/onpolitics/transcripts/bushtext_012803.html

74. "Transcript of Obama's 2016 State of the Union Address," *The New York Times*, January 12, 2016, https://www.nytimes.com/2016/01/13/us/politics/obama-2016-sotu-transcript.html?mtrref=www.google.com&gwh=9849BFDA1E200D21CB83C690482EA52C&gwt=pay

75. "Donald Trump's Congress Speech (Full Text)," *CNN*, March 1, 2017, http://www.cnn.com/2017/02/28/politics/donald-trump-speech-transcript-full-text/

76. "Van Jones: The Moment Trump Became President," *CNN*, 2017, http://www.cnn.com/videos/politics/2017/03/01/donald-trump-congress-address-navy-seal-widow-van-jones-bts.cnn; "Wallace: 'Tonight Donald Trump Became the President of the United States,'" *Fox News*, February 28, 2017, http://insider.foxnews.com/2017/02/28/chris-wallace-praises-trump-address-congress-says-he-became-president

77. Anthony Salvanto, Sarah Dutton, Jennifer De Pinto, Fred Backus and Kabir Khanna, "Viewers Strongly Approve of Trump's Speech to Congress," *CBS News*, March 1, 2017, http://www.cbsnews.com/news/cbs-news-poll-viewers-strongly-approve-president-trump-speech-call-it-unifying-presidential/

78. George W. Bush, "Address to the Nation on Iraq," *The American Presidency Project*, March 17, 2003, http://www.presidency.ucsb.edu/ws/index.php?pid=63713&st=Address+to+the+Nation+on+Iraq&st1=

79. George W. Bush, "Address Before a Joint Session of the Congress on the State of the Union," *The American Presidency Project*, January 29, 2002, http://www.presidency.ucsb.edu/ws/index.php?pid=29644&st=state+of+the+union&st1=

80. George W. Bush, "Address to the United Nations General Assembly in New York City," *The American Presidency Project*, September 12, 2002 http://www.presidency. ucsb.edu/ws/index.php?pid=64069&st=Address+to+the+United+Nations+General+ Assembly+in+New+York+City&st1=

81. George W. Bush, "Address Before a Joint Session of the Congress on the State of the Union," *The American Presidency Project*, January 28, 2003, http://www.presidency. ucsb.edu/ws/index.php?pid=29645&st=state+of+the+union&st1=

82. Dick Cheney, "Eyes on Iraq: In Cheney's Words: The Administration Case for Removing Saddam Hussein," *The New York Times*, August 27, 2002, http://www.nytimes. com/2002/08/27/world/eyes-iraq-cheney-s-words-administration-case-for-removing-saddam-hussein.html

83. George W. Bush, "Address to the Nation on Iraq from Cincinnati, Ohio," *The American Presidency Project*, October 7, 2002, http://www.presidency.ucsb.edu/ws/?pid=73139

84. Bush, Address to the Nation on Iraq from Cincinnati, Ohio, http://www. presidency.ucsb.edu/ws/?pid=73139

85. George W. Bush, "Address to the United Nations General Assembly in New York City," *The American Presidency Project*, September 12, 2002, http://www.presidency. ucsb.edu/ws/?pid=64069

86. George W. Bush, "The President's Radio Address," *The American Presidency Project*, March 15, 2003, http://www.presidency.ucsb.edu/ws/index.php?pid=25128

87. John Walcott, "What Donald Rumsfeld Knew We Didn't Know About Iraq," *Politico*, January 24, 2016, http://www.politico.com/magazine/story/2016/01/iraq-war-wmds-donald-rumsfeld-new-report-213530

88. Joseph C. Wilson, "What I Didn't Find in Africa," *The New York Times*, July 6, 2003, http://www.nytimes.com/2003/07/06/opinion/what-i-didn-t-find-in-africa.html

89. Wilson, "What I Didn't Find in Africa," http://www.nytimes.com/2003/07/06/opinion/what-i-didn-t-find-in-africa.html

90. CNN, "Transcript of ElBaradei's U.N. Presentation," *CNN.com*, March 7, 2003, http://www.cnn.com/2003/US/03/07/sprj.irq.un.transcript.elbaradei/

91. William Rivers Pitt and Scott Ritter, *War on Iraq: What Team Bush Doesn't Want You to Know* (New York City: Context Books, 2002).

92. DiMaggio, *Selling War, Selling Hope*, 2015.

93. "Hans Blix Warned Tony Blair Iraq Might Not Have WMD," *The Telegraph*, January 22, 2010, http://www.telegraph.co.uk/news/worldnews/middleeast/iraq/7051059/Hans-Blix-warned-Tony-Blair-Iraq-might-not-have-WMD.html

94. Rebecca Leung, "Clarke's Take on Terror," *CBS News*, March 19, 2004, http://www.cbsnews.com/news/clarkes-take-on-terror/

95. Norman Solomon, "Rumsfeld's Handshake Deal with Saddam," *Counterpunch*, December 8, 2005, http://www.counterpunch.org/2005/12/08/rumsfeld-s-handshake-deal-with-saddam/

96. Peter Baker, "Bush Says U.S. Pullout Would Let Iraq Radicals Use Oil as a Weapon," *The Washington Post*, November 5, 2006, http://www.washingtonpost.com/wp-dyn/content/article/2006/11/04/AR2006110401025.html

97. PBS, "Excerpts from 1992 Draft 'Defense Planning Guidance,'" *PBS Frontline*, 2005, http://www.pbs.org/wgbh/pages/frontline/shows/iraq/etc/wolf.html

98. David E. Sander and Steven R. Weisman, "A Nation at War: Iraq's Neighbors; Bush's Aides Envision New Influence in Region," *The New York Times*, April 10, 2003, http://www.nytimes.com/2003/04/10/us/a-nation-at-war-iraq-s-neighbors-bush-s-aides-envision-new-influence-in-region.html

99. Anthony DiMaggio, *Mass Media, Mass Propaganda: Examining American News in the War on Terror* (Lanham, MD: Lexington Books, 2008); Scott A. Bonn, *Mass Deception: Moral Panic and the U.S. War on Iraq* (New Brunswick, NJ: Rutgers University Press, 2010); Anthony DiMaggio, *Selling War, Selling Hope: Presidential Rhetoric, the News Media, and U.S. Foreign Policy Since 9/11* (Albany, NY: State University of New York Press, 2015).

Chapter 7

1. Jim Avila, "Is Pink Slime in the Beef at Your Grocery Store?" *ABC News*, March 8, 2012, http://abcnews.go.com/blogs/headlines/2012/03/is-pink-slime-in-the-beef-at-your-grocery-store/

2. Avila, "Is Pink Slime in the Beef at Your Grocery Store?" 2012, http://abcnews.go.com/blogs/headlines/2012/03/is-pink-slime-in-the-beef-at-your-grocery-store/

3. Josh Sanburn, "The Surprising Reason 'Pink Slime' Meat is Back," *Time*, August 26, 2014, http://time.com/3176714/pink-slime-meat-prices-bpi-beef/

4. Benjamin I. Page, Larry M. Bartels, and Jason Seawright, "Democracy and the Policy Preferences of Wealthy Americans," *Perspectives on Politics*, 11, no. 1 (2013): 51–73.

5. Page, Bartels, and Seawright, "Democracy and the Policy Preferences of Wealthy Americans," 2013.

6. Page, Bartels, and Seawright, "Democracy and the Policy Preferences of Wealthy Americans," 2013.

7. This definition of government bureaucracy, from the sociologist Max Weber, is cited in: George C. Edwards, Martin P. Wattenberg, and Robert L. Lineberry, *Government in America: People, Politics, and Policy: Brief Version* (New York: Longman Publishers, 2003): 407.

8. Page, Bartels, and Seawright, "Democracy and the Policy Preferences of Wealthy Americans," 2013.

9. U.S. Census Bureau, "State Government Employment and Payroll Data: March 2015: 2015 Annual Survey of Public Employment and Payroll," *U.S. Census Bureau*, 2015, https://factfinder.census.gov/faces/tableservices/jsf/pages/productview.xhtml?src=bkmk; U.S. Census Bureau, "Local Government Employment and Payroll Data: March 2015: 2015 Annual Survey of Public Employment and Payroll" *U.S. Census Bureau*, 2015, https://factfinder.census.gov/faces/tableservices/jsf/pages/productview.xhtml?src=bkmk; Governing, "Federal Employees by State," *Governing.com*, 2016, http://www.governing.com/gov-data/federal-employees-workforce-numbers-by-state.html

10. Max Sier, "Five Myths About Federal Workers," *The Washington Post*, December 5, 2010, http://www.washingtonpost.com/wp-dyn/content/article/2010/12/03/AR2010120303160.html; Lauren Carroll, "Sean Spicer's Claim of a 'Dramatic Expansion in the Federal Workforce' is Exaggerated," *Politifact*, January 24, 2017, http://www.politifact.com/truth-o-meter/statements/2017/jan/24/sean-spicer/sean-spicers-claim-federal-workforce-has-expanded-/

11. Christopher Ingraham, "The Trump Administration Just Told a Whopper About the Size of the Federal Workforce," *The Washington Post*, January 23, 2017, https://www.washingtonpost.com/news/wonk/wp/2017/01/23/the-trump-administration-just-told-a-whopper-about-the-size-of-the-federal-workforce/?utm_term=.29baf15922fb

12. Paul Fain, "Next Phase for Gates's Completion Agenda," *Inside Higher Ed*, March 11, 2015, https://www.insidehighered.com/news/2015/03/11/gates-foundation-announces-four-priority-policy-areas-college-completion-data-system; Nick Anderson, "Gates Foundation Playing Pivotal Role in Changes for Education System," *The Washington Post*, July 12, 2010, http://www.washingtonpost.com/wp-dyn/content/article/2010/07/11/AR2010071103628.html?sid=ST2010071201582; Motoko Rich, "Grants Back Public-Charter Cooperation," *The New York Times*, December 5, 2012, http://www.nytimes.com/2012/12/05/education/gates-foundation-gives-25-million-to-charter-school-collaboration.html

13. *The Week* Staff, "Rush Limbaugh vs. Sandra Fluke: A Timeline," *The Week*, March 9, 2012, http://theweek.com/articles/477570/rush-limbaugh-vs-sandra-fluke-timeline; Tom Sightings, "Retirees Aim to Avoid Public School Taxes," *U.S. News*, September 17, 2013, http://money.usnews.com/money/blogs/on-retirement/2013/09/17/retirees-aim-to-avoid-public-school-taxes

14. Emma Brown, "Five Myths About Charter Schools," *The Washington Post*, October 14, 2016, https://www.washingtonpost.com/opinions/five-myths-about-charter-schools/2016/10/14/150b5b70-914f-11e6-9c85-ac42097b8cc0_story.html?utm_term=.c009c6e60be2; Dylan Matthews, "Does Teacher Merit Pay Work? A New Study Says Yes." *The Washington Post*, July 23, 2012, https://www.washingtonpost.com/news/wonk/wp/2012/07/23/does-teacher-merit-pay-work-a-new-study-says-yes/; Valerie Strauss, "Why Dangling Rewards in Front of Students and Teachers is Counterproductive," *The Washington Post*, October 10, 2016, https://www.washingtonpost.com/news/answer-sheet/wp/2016/10/05/why-dangling-rewards-in-front-of-students-and-teachers-is-counterproductive/

15. Benjamin Radcliff, *The Political Economy of Human Happiness: How Voters' Choices Determine the Quality of Life* (Cambridge: Cambridge University Press, 2013).

16. Geoff Williams, "Can I Afford to Send My Child to Private School?" *U.S. News*, February 3, 2015, http://money.usnews.com/money/personal-finance/articles/2015/02/03/can-i-afford-to-send-my-child-to-private-school

17. Shannon Hall, "Exxon Knew About Climate Change Almost 40 Years Ago," *Scientific American*, October 26, 2015, https://www.scientificamerican.com/article/exxon-knew-about-climate-change-almost-40-years-ago/

18. *Who Killed the Electric Car?* directed by Chris Paine (Los Angeles, CA: Electric Entertainment, 2006), DVD.

19. Nicola Jones, "How the World Passed a Carbon Threshold and Why it Matters," *Yale Environment 360*, January 26, 2017, https://e360.yale.edu/features/how-the-world-passed-a-carbon-threshold-400ppm-and-why-it-matters

20. Earth Observatory, "How is Today's Warming Different from the Past?" *NASA*, 2017, https://earthobservatory.nasa.gov/Features/GlobalWarming/page3.php

21. Ian Johnston, "Climate Change May Be Escalating So Fast It Could Be 'Game Over,' Scientists Warn," *Independent*, November 9, 2016, http://www.independent.co.uk/news/science/climate-change-game-over-global-warming-climate-sensitivity-seven-degrees-a7407881.html; Amy Lieberman and Susanne Rust, "Big Oil Braced for Global Warming While It Fought Regulations," *Los Angeles Times*, December 31, 2015, http://graphics.latimes.com/oil-operations/

22. Sean Gorman, "Don Beyer Says 97 Percent of Scientists Believe Humans Contribute to Global Warming," *Politifact*, April 4, 2016, http://www.politifact.com/virginia/statements/2016/apr/04/don-beyer/don-beyer-says-97-percent-scientists-believe-human/

23. Amy Jeter and Craig Palosky, "An Estimated 52 Million Adults Have Pre-Existing Conditions That Would Make Them Uninsurable Pre-Obamacare," *Kaiser Family Foundation*, December 12, 2016, http://kff.org/health-reform/press-release/an-estimated-52-million-adults-have-pre-existing-conditions-that-would-make-them-uninsurable-pre-obamacare/

24. Dan Mangan, "Obamacare Pushes Nation's Health Uninsured Rate to Record Low 8.6 Percent," *CNBC*, September 7, 2016, http://www.cnbc.com/2016/09/07/obamacare-pushes-nations-health-uninsured-rate-to-record-low.html

25. Dan Munro, "Annual Healthcare Cost for Family of Four Now at $25,826," *Forbes*, May 24, 2016, http://www.forbes.com/sites/danmunro/2016/05/24/annual-healthcare-cost-for-family-of-four-now-at-25826/#ca9726652261

26. "World Health Organization Assesses the World's Health Systems," *World Health Organization*, June 21, 2000, http://www.who.int/whr/2000/media_centre/press_release/en/

27. Andrew Villegas and Phil Galewitz, "Uninsured Rate Soars, 50+ Million Americans Without Coverage," *Kaiser Health News*, September 16, 2010, http://khn.org/news/census-uninsured-rate-soars/

28. David Squires and Chloe Anderson, "U.S. Health Care from a Global Perspective," *The Commonwealth Fund*, October 8, 2015, http://www.commonwealthfund.org/publications/issue-briefs/2015/oct/us-health-care-from-a-global-perspective

29. Dan Mangan, "US Health-Care Spending is High. Results Are . . . Not So Good," *CNBC*, October 8, 2015, http://www.cnbc.com/2015/10/08/us-health-care-spending-is-high-results-arenot-so-good.html

30. David U. Himmelstein, Steffie Woolhandler, Ida Hellander, and Sidney M. Wolfe, "Quality of Care in Investor-Owned vs Not-for-Profit HMOS," *Journal of the American Medical Association*, 282, no. 2 (1999): 159–63.

31. "Health Care Costs and Election 2008," *Kaiser Family Foundation*, October 14, 2008, http://kff.org/health-costs/issue-brief/health-care-costs-and-election-2008/

32. Munro, "Annual Healthcare Cost for Family of Four Now at $25,826," https://www.forbes.com/sites/danmunro/2016/05/24/annual-healthcare-cost-for-family-of-four-now-at-25826/#7f3afb751f52

33. Dan Mangan, "Wealthy Spending More on Health Care than Poor and Middle Class, Reversing Trend," *CNBC*, July 6, 2016, http://www.cnbc.com/2016/07/06/wealthy-spending-more-on-health-care-than-poor-and-middle-class-reversing-trend.html

34. Louis Jacobson, "Pascrell Says 53 Percent of Americans Cut Back on Health Care Due to Costs," *Politifact*, July 30, 2009, http://www.politifact.com/truth-o-meter/statements/2009/jul/30/bill-pascrell/pascrell-says-53-percent-americans-cut-back-health/

35. Madison Park, "45,000 American Deaths Associated with Lack of Insurance," *CNN*, September 18, 2009, http://www.cnn.com/2009/HEALTH/09/18/deaths.health.insurance/; David Morgan, "Over 26,000 Annual Deaths for Uninsured: Report," *Reuters*, June 20, 2012, http://www.reuters.com/article/us-usa-healthcare-deaths-idUSBRE85J15720120620

36. Nick Baumann, "Tea Party Frontrunner: Abolish Public Schools," *Mother Jones*, October 13, 2010, http://www.motherjones.com/politics/2010/10/david-harmer-abolish-public-schools

37. Steven Rosenfeld, "Netflix Billionaire Reed Hastings' Crusade to Replace Public School Teachers With Computers," *Alternet*, March 3, 2016, http://www.alternet.org/education/netflix-billionaire-reed-hastings-crusade-replace-public-school-teachers-computers; Media Matters Staff, "Fox's Kennedy: 'There Really Shouldn't Be Public Schools,'" *Media Matters*, February 19, 2015, http://mediamatters.org/video/2015/02/19/foxs-kennedy-there-really-shouldnt-be-public-sc/202571; Lyndsey Leyton, "GOP-led States Increasingly Taking Control from Local School Boards," *The Washington Post*, February 1, 2016, https://www.washingtonpost.com/local/education/gop-led-states-increasingly-taking-control-from-local-school-boards/2016/02/01/c01a8e4e-bad3-11e5-b682-4bb4dd403c7d_story.html; Valerie Strauss, "Trump's Perplexing Comments About Education." *The Washington Post*, August 19, 2016, https://www.washingtonpost.com/news/answer-sheet/wp/2016/08/19/trumps-perplexing-comments-about-education/

38. Valerie Strauss, "Study: Private School Vouchers Favored By DeVos Don't Offer Real Advantage Over Public Schools," *The Washington Post*, February 27, 2017, https://www.washingtonpost.com/news/answer-sheet/wp/2017/02/27/devos-favors-private-school-vouchers-but-new-study-says-they-dont-offer-real-edge-over-public-schools/?utm_term=.6bd72eeb33ba; Christopher Lubienski and Sarah Theule Lubienski, *The Public School Advantage: Why Public Schools Outperform Private Schools* (Chicago: University of Chicago Press, 2013).

39. Anthony DiMaggio, "The ITT Fraud: For-Profit Education and the Crisis of the Commons," *Counterpunch*, September 5, 2016, http://www.counterpunch.org/2016/09/05/the-itt-fraud-for-profit-education-and-the-crisis-of-the-commons/

40. DiMaggio, "The ITT Fraud: For-Profit Education and the Crisis of the Commons," 2016, http://www.counterpunch.org/2016/09/05/the-itt-fraud-for-profit-education-and-the-crisis-of-the-commons/

41. Consumer Finance Protection Bureau, "CFPB Sues For-Profit College Chain ITT For Predatory Lending," *Consumer Financial Protection Bureau*, February 26, 2014, http://www.consumerfinance.gov/about-us/newsroom/cfpb-sues-for-profit-college-chain-itt-for-predatory-lending/

42. Katie Lobosco, "Students are Graduating with $30,000 in Loans," *CNN*, October 18, 2016, http://money.cnn.com/2016/10/18/pf/college/average-student-loan-debt/

43. Libby A. Nelson, "'Hall of Shame,' Again," *Inside Higher Ed*, June 28, 2013, https://www.insidehighered.com/news/2013/06/28/education-department-releases-annual-tuition-pricing-lists

44. Travis Mitchell, "Chart: See 20 Years of Tuition Growth at National Universities," *U.S. News*, July 29, 2015, http://www.usnews.com/education/best-colleges/paying-for-college/articles/2015/07/29/chart-see-20-years-of-tuition-growth-at-national-universities

45. Floyd Norris, "Consumer Debt Suggests Growing Confidence," *The New York Times*, May 16, 2014, https://www.nytimes.com/2014/05/17/business/economy/rise-in-consumer-debt-suggests-growing-confidence.html

46. Josh Mitchell, "More Than 40% of Student Borrowers Aren't Making Payments," *The Wall Street Journal*, April 7, 2016, http://www.wsj.com/articles/more-than-40-of-student-borrowers-arent-making-payments-1459971348

47. Zack Friedman, "Student Loan Debt in 2017: A $1.3 Trillion Crisis," *Forbes*, February 21, 2017, https://www.forbes.com/sites/zackfriedman/2017/02/21/student-loan-debt-statistics-2017/#5ded10655dab

48. Maggie Severns, "The Student Loan Debt Crisis in 9 Charts," *Mother Jones*, June 5, 2013, http://www.motherjones.com/politics/2013/06/student-loan-debt-charts/

49. Michael Stratford, "Obama Expands IBR, Pushes Refinancing," *Inside Higher Ed*, June 10, 2014, https://www.insidehighered.com/news/2014/06/10/obama-expands-income-based-repayment-older-borrowers-pushes-democrats%E2%80%99-student-loan

50. Dina ElBoghdady. "Student Debt May Hurt Housing Recovery by Hampering First-Time Buyers," *The Washington Post*, February 17, 2014, https://www.washingtonpost.com/business/economy/student-debt-may-hurt-housing-recovery-by-hampering-first-time-buyers/2014/02/17/d90c7c1e-94bf-11e3-83b9-1f024193bb84_story.html

51. Aimee Picchi, "Young Adults Living With their Parents Hits a 75-Year High," *CBS News*, December 21, 2016, http://www.cbsnews.com/news/percentage-of-young-americans-living-with-their-parents-is-40-percent-a-75-year-high/

52. Michael Mitchell, Michael Leachman, and Kathleen Masterson, "Funding Down, Tuition Up," *Center on Budget and Policy Priorities*, August 15, 2016, http://www.cbpp.org/research/state-budget-and-tax/funding-down-tuition-up

53. Walt Bogdanich, "F.D.A. Is Unable to Ensure Drugs Are Safe, Panel is Told," *The New York Times*, November 2, 2007, http://www.nytimes.com/2007/11/02/washington/02FDA.html

54. Bogdanich, "F.D.A. Is Unable to Ensure Drugs Are Safe, Panel is Told," 2007, http://www.nytimes.com/2007/11/02/washington/02FDA.html

55. Bogdanich, "F.D.A. Is Unable to Ensure Drugs Are Safe, Panel is Told," 2007, http://www.nytimes.com/2007/11/02/washington/02FDA.html

56. Gardiner Harris, "Heparin Contamination May Have Been Deliberate, F.D.A. Says," *The New York Times*, April 30, 2008, http://www.nytimes.com/2008/04/30/health/policy/30heparin.html

57. Gardiner Harris, "U.S. Identifies Tainted Heparin in 11 Countries," *The New York Times*, April 22, 2008, http://www.nytimes.com/2008/04/22/health/policy/22fda.html

58. U.S. Food & Drug Administration, "What Does FDA Require Drug Manufacturers to do to Prevent Contaminated Drugs? If Contamination Occurs, How Must They Correct the Problem?" *U.S. Food & Drug Administration*, April 25, 2017, https://www.fda.gov/AboutFDA/Transparency/Basics/ucm207016.htm

59. Gardiner Harris, "Deal Would Bring Inspections of Overseas Drug Suppliers," *The New York Times*, August 13, 2011, http://www.nytimes.com/2011/08/13/science/13drug.html

60. Government Accountability Office, "Drug Safety: FDA has Improved its Foreign Drug Inspection Program, but Needs to Assess the Effectiveness and Staffing of its Foreign Offices," *Government Accountability Office*, December 2016, http://www.gao.gov/assets/690/681689.pdf

61. I base this claim on my many years of experience talking about the decline of regulatory standards in the beef industry among my students. Most are horrified to hear about problems with E. coli in restaurant and grocery store beef.

62. Centers for Disease Control and Prevention, "Burden of Foodborne Illness: Findings," *Centers for Disease Control and Prevention*, July 15, 2016, https://www.cdc.gov/foodborneburden/2011-foodborne-estimates.html; CNN Library, "E. Coli Outbreaks Fast Facts," *CNN*, March 13, 2017, http://www.cnn.com/2013/06/28/health/e-coli-outbreaks-fast-facts/

63. Eric Schlosser, *Fast Food Nation: The Dark Side of the All-American Meal* (Boston: Mariner Books, 2012); Jeff Flock, "Oprah Accused of Whipping Up Anti-Beef 'Lynch Mob,'" *CNN*, January 21, 1998, http://www.cnn.com/US/9801/21/oprah.beef/

64. The New York Times, "Random Testing for E. Coli Is Set for Meatpacking Sites," *The New York Times*, September 26, 2002, http://www.nytimes.com/2002/09/26/us/random-testing-for-e-coli-is-set-for-meatpacking-sites.html

65. Government Accountability Office, "Food Safety: USDA and FDA Need to Better Ensure Prompt and Complete Recalls of Potentially Unsafe Food," *Government Accountability Office*, October 2004, http://www.gao.gov/new.items/d0551.pdf

66. David Brown, "USDA Orders Largest Meat Recall in U.S. History," *The Washington Post*, February 18, 2008, http://www.washingtonpost.com/wp-dyn/content/article/2008/02/17/AR2008021701530.html

67. Susan K. Urahn and Allan Coukell, "Emerging Pathogens in Meat and Poultry," *Pew Charitable Trusts*, September 2016, http://www.pewtrusts.org/~/media/assets/2016/09/emergingpathogensinmeatandpoultry.pdf

68. Government Accountability Office, "Food Safety: USDA and FDA Need to Better Ensure Prompt and Complete Recalls of Potentially Unsafe Food," 2004.

69. Lyndsey Layton, "House Republicans Vote to Cut Funds to Implement Food Safety Law," *The Washington Post*, June 16, 2011, https://www.washingtonpost.com/politics/house-republicans-vote-to-cut-funds-to-implement-food-safety-law/2011/06/16/AGMS82XH_story.html?utm_term=.60fd2ef20c8b

70. Suzy Khimm, "These GOP Budget Cuts Might Make You Puke (or Worse)," *Mother Jones*, March 9, 2011, http://www.motherjones.com/politics/2011/03/gop-budget-cuts-food-safety

71. Jen Christensen, "What Government Tests Found in Your Meat," *CNN*, April 16, 2013, http://www.cnn.com/2013/04/15/health/meat-drugs/

72. Reuters, "Meat Plants Face Shutdown Due to Impending Sequester, USDA Says," *The Huffington Post*, February 26, 2013, http://www.huffingtonpost.com/2013/02/26/meat-plant-shutdown-sequester_n_2769367.html

73. Jim Avila, "USDA to Let Industry Self-Inspect Chicken," *ABC News*, April 18, 2012, http://abcnews.go.com/blogs/headlines/2012/04/usda-to-let-industry-self-inspect-chicken/

74. Avila, "USDA to Let Industry Self-Inspect Chicken," 2012, http://abcnews.go.com/blogs/headlines/2012/04/usda-to-let-industry-self-inspect-chicken/

75. Dina Fine Maron, "Trump Administration Restricts News from Federal Scientists at USDA, EPA," *Scientific American*, January 24, 2017, https://www.scientificamerican.com/article/trump-administration-restricts-news-from-federal-scientists-at-usda-epa/

76. Doina Chiacu and Valerie Volcovici, "EPA Chief Pruitt Refuses to Link CO2 and Global Warming," *Scientific American*, 2017, https://www.scientificamerican.com/article/epa-chief-pruitt-refuses-to-link-co2-and-global-warming/

77. Taylor Tepper, "President Trump Wants to Kill These 17 Federal Agencies and Programs. Here's What They Actually Cost (and Do)," *Time*, January 24, 2017, http://time.com/money/4639544/trump-nea-sesame-street-budget-cut/

Chapter 8

1. Drew Desilver and Patrick Van Kessel, "As More Money Flows into Campaigns, Americans Worry about its Influence," *Pew Research Center*, December 7, 2015, http://www.pewresearch.org/fact-tank/2015/12/07/as-more-money-flows-into-campaigns-americans-worry-about-its-influence/; Pew Research Center, "Super PACs Having Negative Impact, Say Voters Aware of 'Citizens United' Ruling," *Pew Research Center*, January 17, 2012, http://www.people-press.org/2012/01/17/super-pacs-having-negative-impact-say-voters-aware-of-citizens-united-ruling/

2. Dave Gilson, "It's Not the 1 Percent Controlling Politics. It's the .01 Percent," *Mother Jones*, April 23, 2015, http://www.motherjones.com/kevin-drum/2015/04/one-percent-campaign-giving; Ben Piven, "After Citizens United, Wealthy Donors' Campaign Spending Skyrocketed," *Al Jazeera America*, January 1, 2015, http://america.aljazeera.com/articles/2015/1/15/aftercitizensunitedwealthydonorscampaignspendingskyrocketed.html

3. Cecilie Gaziano, "Relationship Between Public Opinion and Supreme Court Decisions: Was Mr. Dooley Right?" *Communication Research*, 5, no. 2 (1978): 131–49; Jeffrey R. Lax and Justin H. Phillips, "Public Opinion and Policy Responsiveness," *American Political Science Review*, 103, no. 3 (2009): 367–86; Christopher J. Casillas, Peter K. Enns, and Patrick C. Wohlfarth, "How Public Opinion Constrains the U.S. Supreme Court," *American Journal of Political Science*, 55, no. 1 (2011): 74–88; Matthew E. K. Hall, "The Semiconstrained Court: Public Opinion, the Separation of Powers, and the U.S. Supreme Court's Fear of Nonimplementation," *American Journal of Political Science*, 58, no. 2 (2014): 352–66.

4. Justin McCarthy, "Americans' Support for Gay Marriage Remains High, at 61%," *Gallup*, May 18, 2016, http://www.gallup.com/poll/191645/americans-support-gay-marriage-remains-high.aspx

5. Herman and Chomsky, *Manufacturing Consent*, 2002; DiMaggio, *Selling War, Selling Hope*, 2015; DiMaggio, *The Politics of Persuasion*, 2017; Bonn, *Mass Deception*, 2010; Nacos, et al., *Selling Fear*, 2011; Bernays, *Propaganda*, 2004; Anthony R. DiMaggio, "The Propaganda Model and Manufacturing Consent: U.S. Public Compliance and Resistance," in *Cambridge Companion to Chomsky*, ed. James McGilvray (Cambridge: Cambridge University Press, 2017): 275–94.

6. Gilens and Page, "Testing Theories of American Politics," 2014; Benjamin I. Page and Robert Y. Shapiro, "Effects of Public Opinion on Policy," *American Political Science Review*, 77, no. 1 (1983): 175–90.

7. Jeffrey A. Segal and Harold J. Spaeth, *The Supreme Court and the Attitudinal Model* (Cambridge: Cambridge University Press, 2002).

8. Kevin Lyles, *The Gatekeepers: Federal District Courts in the Political Process* (Westport, CT: Praeger, 1997).

9. Segal and Spaeth, *The Supreme Court and the Attitudinal Model*, 2002.

10. Hannah Fairfield and Adam Liptak, "A More Nuanced Breakdown of the Supreme Court," *The New York Times*, June 26, 2014, https://www.nytimes.com/2014/06/27/upshot/a-more-nuanced-breakdown-of-the-supreme-court.html

11. Segal and Spaeth, *The Supreme Court and the Attitudinal Model*, 2002.

12. David Cole, "Obamacare Upheld: How and Why Did Justice Roberts Do It?" *The Nation*, June 28, 2012, https://www.thenation.com/article/obamacare-upheld-how-and-why-did-justice-roberts-do-it/

13. Ralph A. Rossum and G. Alan Tarr, *American Constitutional Law: The Structure of Government, Volume 1* (Boulder, CO: Westview Press, 2013).

14. National Federation of Independent Business et al. v. Sebelius, Secretary of State of Health and Human Services," 11 U.S. 1 (2012), https://www.supremecourt.gov/opinions/11pdf/11-393c3a2.pdf

15. National Federation of Independent Business et al. v. Sebelius, Secretary of State of Human and Health Services, 2012.

16. National Federation of Independent Business et al. v. Sebelius, Secretary of State of Human and Health Services, 2012.

17. National Federation of Independent Business et al. v. Sebelius, Secretary of State of Human and Health Services, 2012.

18. Lucas A. Powe Jr., *The Supreme Court and the American Elite, 1789–2008* (Cambridge, MA: Harvard University Press, 2011).

19. Robert A. Carp, Ronald Stidham, and Kenneth L. Manning, *Judicial Process in America* (Washington DC: CQ Press, 2013).

20. Carp, et al., *Judicial Process in America*, 2011.

21. See the cases *Citizens United v. FEC* (2010) and *Buckley v Valeo* (1976).

22. Michael Parenti, *Democracy for the Few* (Boston, MA: Cengage Learning, 2010).

23. Adam Liptak, "Justices Rule for Wal-Mart in Class-Action Bias Case," *The New York Times*, June 20, 2011, http://www.nytimes.com/2011/06/21/business/21bizcourt.html

24. Wal-Mart, "Walmart Company Statement Related to Order Denying Class Certification in Dukes, et al., v. Wal-Mart Stores Inc." *Walmart*, August 2, 2013, http://corporate.walmart.com/_news_/news-archive/2013/08/02/walmart-company-statement-related-to-order-denying-class-certification-in-dukes-et-al-v-wal-mart-stores-inc

25. Bruce Barry, *Speechless: The Erosion of Free Expression in the American Workplace* (Oakland, CA: Berrett Koehler, 2007); Chris Isidore, "Free Speech on the Job, and What That Means," *CNN.com*, August 8, 2017, http://money.cnn.com/2017/08/08/technology/google-workplace-free-speech/index.html

26. United States Supreme Court, "Janus v. American Federation of State, County, and Muncipal Employees, Council 31, et al.," *United States Supreme Court*, June 27, 2018, https://www.supremecourt.gov/opinions/17pdf/16-1466_2b3j.pdf

27. Gillion, *The Political Power of Protest*, 2013; Gerald N. Rosenberg, *The Hollow Hope: Can Courts Bring About Social Change?* (Chicago: University of Chicago Press, 2008).

Chapter 9

1. David Smith, "Most Americans Do Not Feel Represented by Democrats or Republicans—Survey," *The Guardian*, October 25, 2016, https://www.theguardian.com/us-news/2016/oct/25/american-political-parties-democrats-republicans-representation-survey

2. John H. Aldrich, *Why Parties? A Second Look* (Chicago: University of Chicago Press, 2011); Paul M. Sniderman and Edward H. Stiglitz, *The Reputational Premium: A Theory of Party Identification and Policy Reasoning* (Princeton, NJ: Princeton University Press, 2012).

3. Open Secrets, "Democratic Party: Top Industries, 2016 Cycle," *Center for Responsive Politics*, 2016, https://www.opensecrets.org/parties/indus.php?cycle=2016&cmte=DPC

4. Open Secrets, "Republican Party: Top Industries, 2016 Cycle," *Center for Responsive Politics*, 2016, https://www.opensecrets.org/parties/indus.php?cycle=2016&cmte=RPC

5. Wesley Lowery, "91% of the Time the Better-Financed Candidate Wins. Don't Act Surprised," *The Washington Post*, April 4, 2014, https://www.washingtonpost.com/news/the-fix/wp/2014/04/04/think-money-doesnt-matter-in-elections-this-chart-says-youre-wrong/?utm_term=.a5226406134b

6. Doug Palmer, "POLITICO-Harvard poll: Americans say 'TPP who?'" *Politico*, September 23, 2016, http://www.politico.com/story/2016/09/americans-say-tpp-who-228598

7. Editorial, "Gates Foundation Failures Show Philanthropists Shouldn't Be Setting America's Public School Agenda," *Los Angeles Times*, June 1, 2016, http://www.latimes.com/opinion/editorials/la-ed-gates-education-20160601-snap-story.html

8. *USA Today*, "Obama Backs Teacher Merit Pay," *USA Today*, March 10, 2009, http://usatoday30.usatoday.com/news/education/2009-03-10-obama-teachers_N.htm; Valerie Strauss, "Obama's Real Education Legacy: Common Core, Testing, Charter

Schools," *The Washington Post*, October 21, 2016, https://www.washingtonpost.com/news/answer-sheet/wp/2016/10/21/obamas-real-education-legacy-common-core-testing-charter-schools/?utm_term=.d1e981ee4473; Chris Staiti, "Teacher Tenure Is a 'Broken Status Quo,' Secretary Duncan Says," *Bloomberg*, June 16, 2014, https://www.bloomberg.com/news/articles/2014-06-16/teacher-tenure-is-a-broken-status-quo-secretary-duncan-says

9. Kevin Carey, "Dismal Voucher Results Surprise Researchers as DeVos Era Begins," *The New York Times*, February 23, 2017, https://www.nytimes.com/2017/02/23/upshot/dismal-results-from-vouchers-surprise-researchers-as-devos-era-begins.html?_r=0

10. Annalyn Kurtz and Tal Yellin, "Minimum Wage Since 1938," *CNN Money*, November 3, 2015, http://money.cnn.com/interactive/economy/minimum-wage-since-1938/

11. Lawrence F. Katz and Alan B. Krueger, "The Rise and Nature of Alternative Work Arrangements in the United States, 1995–2015," March 29, 2016, https://krueger.princeton.edu/sites/default/files/akrueger/files/katz_krueger_cws_-_march_29_20165.pdf

12. Jean Edward Smith, *Eisenhower in War and Peace* (New York: Random House Trade Paperbacks, 2013).

13. Miller Center, "Dwight D. Eisenhower: Domestic Affairs," *University of Virginia*, 2017, http://millercenter.org/president/biography/eisenhower-domestic-affairs

14. Miller Center, "Richard Nixon: Domestic Affairs," *University of Virginia*, 2017, http://millercenter.org/president/biography/nixon-domestic-affairs

15. CBS, "Study: Privatized Medicare Would Cost Patients More," *CBS News*, October 15, 2012, http://www.cbsnews.com/news/study-privatized-medicare-would-cost-patients-more/

16. Alicia Budich, "Paul Ryan's 2015 Budget Plan Includes Major Spending Cuts," *CBS News*, April 1, 2014, http://www.cbsnews.com/news/paul-ryans-2015-budget-plan-includes-major-spending-cuts/

17. Joshua Gillin, "Income Tax Rates Were 90 Percent Under Eisenhower, Sanders Says," *Politifact*, November 15, 2015, http://www.politifact.com/truth-o-meter/statements/2015/nov/15/bernie-s/income-tax-rates-were-90-percent-under-eisenhower-/

18. Devin Henry, "Climate Change: Where the GOP Field Stands," *The Hill*, January 23, 2016, http://thehill.com/policy/energy-environment/266716-climate-change-where-the-gop-field-stands

19. Pew Research Center, "Section 2: Perception of the Candidates," *Pew Research Center*, September 16, 2004, http://www.people-press.org/2004/09/16/section-2-perception-of-the-candidates/

20. Pew Research Center, "Section 1: Barack Obama's Performance and Image," *Pew Research Center*, January 19, 2012, http://www.people-press.org/2012/01/19/section-1-barack-obamas-performance-and-image/

21. Pew Research Center, "As Fiscal Cliff Nears, Democrats Have Public Opinion on Their Side," *Pew Research Center*, December 13, 2012, http://www.people-press.org/2012/12/13/section-1-views-of-obama-congress-the-parties/

22. Pew Research Center, "October 2014 Monthly Poll," *Pew Research Center*, October 2014.

23. Pew Research Center, "January 2017 Monthly Poll," *Pew Research Center*, January 2017.

24. Larry M. Bartels, *Unequal Democracy: The Political Economy of the New Gilded Age* (Princeton, NJ: Princeton University Press, 2010).

25. Hacker and Pierson, *Winner-Take-All Politics*, 2011.

26. Open Secrets, "Cost of Election," *Center for Responsive Politics*, 2017, https://www.opensecrets.org/overview/cost.php?display=T&infl=Y

27. Dave Gilson, "The Crazy Cost of Becoming President, From Lincoln to Obama," *Mother Jones*, February 20, 2012, http://www.motherjones.com/mojo/2012/02/historic-price-cost-presidential-elections

28. Jon Greenberg, "MSNBC's Melber: Congressional Wealth Climbed While Median American Saw No Change," *PunditFact*, February 11, 2014, http://www.politifact.com/punditfact/statements/2014/feb/11/ari-melber/msnbcs-melber-congressional-wealth-climbed-while-m/

29. Russ Choma, "Millionaires' Club: For First Time, Most Lawmakers are Worth $1 Million-Plus," *Center for Responsive Politics*, January 9, 2014, https://www.opensecrets.org/news/2014/01/millionaires-club-for-first-time-most-lawmakers-are-worth-1-million-plus/

30. Jeff Sommer, "Retirees Face Up to the 'Million-Dollar Illusion,'" *CNBC*, June 10, 2013, https://www.cnbc.com/id/100803102

31. Carnes, *White Collar Government*, 2013.

32. Quoctrung Bui, "50 Years of Shrinking Union Membership, in One Map," *NPR*, February 23, 2015, http://www.npr.org/sections/money/2015/02/23/385843576/50-years-of-shrinking-union-membership-in-one-map

33. Anthony DiMaggio and Paul Street, "Paranoia & Fantasy on the Right," *Counter-Punch*, July 27, 2012, http://www.counterpunch.org/2012/07/27/paranoia-fantasy-on-the-right/; Kim Moody, "Who Put Trump in the White House?" *Jacobin*, January 11, 2017, https://www.jacobinmag.com/2017/01/trump-election-democrats-gop-clinton-whites-workers-rust-belt/

34. Jake Rosenfeld, *What Unions No Longer Do* (Cambridge, MA: Harvard University Press, 2014).

35. Bureau of Labor Statistics, "Union Members Summary," *United States Department of Labor*, January 26, 2017, https://www.bls.gov/news.release/union2.nr0.htm

36. Ruy Teixeira and Joel Rogers, *America's Forgotten Majority: Why the White Working Class Still Matters* (New York: Basic Books, 2001).

37. Pew Research Center, "Immigrants and Their Descendants Accounted for 72 Million in U.S. Population Growth from 1965 to 2015; Projected to Account for 103 Million More by 2065," *Pew Research Center*, September 23, 2015, http://www.pewhispanic.org/2015/09/28/modern-immigration-wave-brings-59-million-to-u-s-driving-population-growth-and-change-through-2065/ph_2015-09-28_immigration-through-2065-02/

38. Congressional Budget Office, "A Description of the Immigrant Population—2013 Update," *U.S. Congress*, May 8, 2013, https://www.cbo.gov/publication/44134

39. CAP Immigration Team, "The Facts on Immigration Today," *Center for American Progress*, October 23, 2014, https://www.americanprogress.org/issues/immigration/reports/2014/10/23/59040/the-facts-on-immigration-today-3/

40. Natalie Jomini Stroud, *Niche News: The Politics of News Choice* (Oxford: Oxford University Press, 2011).

41. Jeffrey M. Berry and Sarah Sobieraj, *The Outrage Industry: Political Opinion Media and the New Incivility* (Oxford: Oxford University Press, 2014); Stroud, *Niche News*, 2011; Kathleen Hall Jamieson, *Echo Chamber; Rush Limbaugh and the Conservative Media* (Oxford: Oxford University Press, 2010); Matthew Levendusky, *How Partisan Media Polarize America* (Chicago: University of Chicago Press, 2013); David Barker, *Rushed to Judgment? Talk Radio, Persuasion, and American Political Behavior* (New York: Columbia University Press, 2002).

42. Pew Research Center, "In Changing News Landscape, Even Television is Vulnerable," *Pew Research Center*, September 27, 2012, http://www.people-press.org/2012/09/27/in-changing-news-landscape-even-television-is-vulnerable/; Ethan Epstein, "Is Rush Limbaugh in Trouble?" *Politico Magazine*, May 24, 2016, http://www.politico.com/magazine/story/2016/05/is-rush-limbaugh-in-trouble-talk-radio-213914

43. Ian Chipman, "Ali Yurukoglu: How Biased News Impacts Your Vote," *Stanford Business*, October 30, 2014, https://www.gsb.stanford.edu/insights/ali-yurukoglu-how-biased-news-impacts-your-vote; Stefano DellaVigna and Ethan Kaplan, "The Fox News Effect: Media Bias and Voting*," *Quarterly Journal of Economics* 122, no. 3 (2007): 1187–234, https://doi.org/10.1162/qjec.122.3.1187

44. Michael W. Clune, "When Neoliberalism Exploded," *Salon*, March 9, 2013, https://www.salon.com/2013/03/09/the_world_according_to_milton_friedman_partner/; David Harvey, "Neoliberalism is a Political Project," *Jacobin*, July 23, 2016, https://www.jacobinmag.com/2016/07/david-harvey-neoliberalism-capitalism-labor-crisis-resistance/

45. American National Election Study, "The ANES Guide to Public Opinion and Election Behavior," *Election Studies*, 2017, http://www.electionstudies.org/nesguide/toptable/tab5a_2.htm

46. iPoll, "ORC Public Opinion Index," *iPoll*, August 1965; iPoll, "Harris Survey," *iPoll*, December 1965.

47. iPoll, "Harris Survey," *iPoll*, October 1965.

48. iPoll, "Harris Survey," *iPoll*, April 1966.

49. Tom LoBianco, "Report: Aide Says Nixon's War on Drugs Targeted Blacks, Hippies," *CNN.com*, March 24, 2016, http://www.cnn.com/2016/03/23/politics/john-ehrlichman-richard-nixon-drug-war-blacks-hippie/index.html

50. iPoll, "Confidence and Concern: Citizens View American Government Survey," *iPoll*, September 1973.

51. iPoll, "ORC Public Opinion Index," *iPoll*, January 1975.

52. iPoll, "Harris Survey," *iPoll*, September 1975.

53. American National Election Study, "The ANES Guide to Public Opinion and Election Behavior," *Election Studies*, 2017, http://www.electionstudies.org/nesguide/toptable/tab5a_2.htm

54. American National Election Study, "The ANES Guide to Public Opinion and Election Behavior," *Election Studies*, 2017, http://www.electionstudies.org/nesguide/toptable/tab5b_3.htm

55. iPoll, "Harris Survey," *iPoll*, April 1973.

56. iPoll, "Amalgam Survey," *iPoll*, December 1973.

57. Martin P. Wattenberg, *The Decline of American Political Parties, 1952–1996* (Cambridge, MA: Harvard University Press, 1998).

58. John Sides, "Three Myths about Political Independents," *The Monkey Cage,* December 17, 2009, http://themonkeycage.org/2009/12/three_myths_about_political_in/

59. Sides, "Three Myths about Political Independents," 2009; Gallup, "Party Affiliation," 2016.

60. Sides, "Three Myths about Political Independents," 2009; Gallup, "Party Affiliation," 2016.

61. Sides, "Three Myths about Political Independents," 2009; Gallup, "Party Affiliation," 2016.

62. Sides, "Three Myths about Political Independents,"2009; Gallup, "Party Affiliation," *Gallup,* 2016, http://www.gallup.com/poll/15370/party-affiliation.aspx

63. Pew Research Center, "Millennials in Adulthood," *Pew Research Center,* March 7, 2014, http://www.pewsocialtrends.org/2014/03/07/millennials-in-adulthood/

64. Pew Research Center, "The Generation Gap and the 2012 Election," *Pew Research Center,* November 3, 2011, http://www.people-press.org/2011/11/03/section-2-generations-and-the-2012-election/

65. Charlotte Alter, "Nearly a Quarter of GOP Millennials Have Defected from the Party of Trump, Study Says," *Time,* May 19, 2017, http://time.com/4786694/donald-trump-republican-party-switch-poll/

66. Hannah Hartig, John Lapinski, and Stephanie Perry, "Millennial Poll: Democrats Can't Take Their Vote for Granted," *NBC News,* September 27, 2017, https://www.nbcnews.com/politics/politics-news/poll-democrats-can-t-take-millennial-vote-granted-n804836

67. Paul Taylor and Mark Hugo Lopez, "Six Take-Aways from the Census Bureau's Voting Report," *Pew Research Center,* May 8, 2013, http://www.pewresearch.org/fact-tank/2013/05/08/six-take-aways-from-the-census-bureaus-voting-report/

68. Joanna Weiss, "Millennials Don't Believe in Voting," *Boston Globe,* August 21, 2015, https://www.bostonglobe.com/opinion/2015/08/20/millennials-don-believe-voting/cGb7sx5ZvkmDCsNd3shTDO/story.html

69. Circle, "An Estimated 24 Million Young People Voted in 2016 Election," *The Center for Information and Research on Civic Learning and Engagement,* November 9, 2016, http://civicyouth.org/an-estimated-24-million-young-people-vote-in-2016-election/

70. Thom File, "Young Adult Voting: An Analysis of Presidential elections, 1964–2012: Population Characteristics," *U.S. Census Bureau,* April 2014, https://www.census.gov/prod/2014pubs/p20-573.pdf

71. Wattenberg, *Is Voting for Young People?,* 2015.

72. Pew Research Center, "Trends in News Consumption: 1991–2012," *Pew Research Center,* September 27, 2012, http://www.people-press.org/files/legacy-pdf/2012%20News%20Consumption%20Report.pdf

73. Pew Research Center, "Americans Spending More Time Following the News," *Pew Research Center,* September 12, 2010, http://www.people-press.org/2010/09/12/section-1-watching-reading-and-listening-to-the-news/

74. Center on Budget and Policy Priorities, "Policy Basics: Where Do Our Federal Tax Dollars Go?" *Center on Budget and Policy Priorities*, March 4, 2016, http://www.cbpp.org/research/federal-budget/policy-basics-where-do-our-federal-tax-dollars-go

75. David Brunori, "Where is the Outrage Over Corporate Welfare?" *Forbes*, March 14, 2014, https://www.forbes.com/sites/taxanalysts/2014/03/14/where-is-the-outrage-over-corporate-welfare/#182b81e827dd; Glenn Kessler, "Revisiting the Cost of the Bush Tax Cuts," *The Washington Post*, May 10, 2011, https://www.washingtonpost.com/blogs/fact-checker/post/revisiting-the-cost-of-the-bush-tax-cuts/2011/05/09/AFxTFtbG_blog.html?utm_term=.e7cb73692094

76. Aaron Blake, "More Young People Voted for Bernie Sanders than Trump and Clinton Combined—by a Lot," *The Washington Post*, June 20, 2016, https://www.washingtonpost.com/news/the-fix/wp/2016/06/20/more-young-people-voted-for-bernie-sanders-than-trump-and-clinton-combined-by-a-lot/?utm_term=.bf550a3db635

77. Anthony DiMaggio, *Rebellion in America: Citizen Uprisings, the News Media, and the Politics of Plutocracy* (New York: Routledge, 2019).

78. Lydia Saad, "Aversion to Other Candidate Key Factor in 2016 Vote Choice," *Gallup*, October 6, 2016, http://www.gallup.com/poll/196172/aversion-candidate-key-factor-2016-vote-choice.aspx

79. CNN Politics, "Exit Polls," 2016.

80. Konstantin Kilibarda and Daria Roithmayr, "The Myth of the Rust Belt Revolt," *Slate*, December 1, 2016, http://www.slate.com/articles/news_and_politics/politics/2016/12/the_myth_of_the_rust_belt_revolt.html

81. Louis Jacobson, "Yes, Donald Trump Did Call Climate Change a Chinese Hoax," *Politifact*, June 3, 2016, http://www.politifact.com/truth-o-meter/statements/2016/jun/03/hillary-clinton/yes-donald-trump-did-call-climate-change-chinese-h/

82. Samuel Chamberlain, "Trump Tells Congressional Leaders 3–5 Million 'Illegals' Cost Him Popular Vote," *Foxnews.com*, January 24, 2017, http://www.foxnews.com/politics/2017/01/24/trump-tells-congressional-leaders-3-5-million-illegals-cost-him-popular-vote.html; Bill Chappell, "Bogus 'Bowling Green Massacre' Claim Snarls Trump Adviser Conway," *National Public Radio*, February 3, 2017, http://www.npr.org/sections/thetwo-way/2017/02/03/513222852/bogus-bowling-green-massacre-claim-snarls-trump-adviser-conway; Lindsey Pulse, "Spicer Cites Terror Attack in Atlanta that Didn't Happen," *Aol.com*, February 9, 2017, https://www.aol.com/article/news/2017/02/09/spicer-cites-attack-by-foreign-nationals-that-didnt-happen/21710593/; Eric Bradner, "Trump's Sweden Comment Raises Questions," *CNN.com*, February 19, 2017, http://www.cnn.com/2017/02/19/politics/trump-rally-sweden/index.html

83. Nicholas Carnes and Noam Lupu, "It's Time to Bust the Myth: Most Trump Voters Were Not Working Class," *The Washington Post*, June 5, 2017, https://www.washingtonpost.com/news/monkey-cage/wp/2017/06/05/its-time-to-bust-the-myth-most-trump-voters-were-not-working-class/?utm_term=.18b467788afb; Anthony DiMaggio, "Election Con 2016: New Evidence Demolishes the Myth of Trump's 'Blue-Collar' Populism," *Counterpunch*, June 16, 2017, https://www.counterpunch.org/2017/06/16/93450/; Anthony DiMaggio, "Donald Trump and the Myth of Economic Populism: Demolishing a False Narrative," *Counterpunch*,

August 16, 2016, https://www.counterpunch.org/2016/08/16/donald-trump-and-the-myth-of-economic-populism-demolishing-a-false-narrative/; Anthony DiMaggio, "White Supremacist America: Trump and the 'Return' of Right-Wing Hate Culture," *Counterpunch*, September 16, 2016, https://www.counterpunch.org/2016/09/16/white-supremacist-america-trump-and-the-return-of-right-wing-hate-culture/; Eric Draitser, "Donald Trump and the Triumph of White Identity Politics," *Counterpunch*, March 24, 2017, https://www.counterpunch.org/2017/03/24/donald-trump-and-the-triumph-of-white-identity-politics/

84. A regression analysis of the August 2016 national Pew Research Center electoral survey finds that Trump voters, statistically speaking, were more likely to be male, white, middle-to-upper income, older, less educated, conservative, and Republican. All of these variables were significant predictors of Trump support.

85. A regression analysis of the August 2016 national Pew Research Center electoral survey finds that reactionary social issues were significant drivers of support for Trump. Significant predictors of support for Trump among the general public included feelings of antagonism toward Muslims, concern with terrorism (itself related to antagonism toward Muslims as a "foreign threat,") opposition to regulating guns, and support for strengthening "border security" between the U.S. and Mexico. In this survey, opinions about the minimum wage, concern with government helping the needy, and concern that free trade had hurt individuals and their families, were not significant predictors of Trump support, but instead were irrelevant to his rise to political prominence. Trump voters were also significantly more likely to say they were not concerned with the gap between the rich and poor, suggesting an elitist mindset in line with upper-class values.

86. Ronald Brownstein, "The Billionaire Candidate and His Blue-Collar Following," *The Atlantic*, September 11, 2015, https://www.theatlantic.com/politics/archive/2015/09/the-billionaire-candidate-and-his-blue-collar-following/432783/; Claire Cain Miller, "What Donald Trump Might Do for Working-Class Families," *The New York Times*, November 29, 2016, https://www.nytimes.com/2016/11/29/upshot/what-donald-trump-might-do-for-working-class-families.html?_r=0; Damian Paletta and David Nakamura, "Rallying Blue-Collar Workers in Cincinnati, Trump Blames Democrats for Obstructing his Agenda," *The Washington Post*, June 7, 2017, https://www.washingtonpost.com/politics/rallying-blue-collar-workers-in-cincinnati-trump-blames-democrats-for-obstructing-his-agenda/2017/06/07/af92c186-4baa-11e7-bc1b-fddbd8359dee_story.html?utm_term=.739eae87e37f

87. Ron Elving, "Poll: 1 in 5 Americans Trusts the Government," *National Public Radio*, November 23, 2015, http://www.npr.org/2015/11/23/457063796/poll-only-1-in-5-americans-say-they-trust-the-government

88. Justin McCarthy, "Majority in U.S. Maintain Need for Third Major Party," *Gallup*, September 25, 2015, http://www.gallup.com/poll/185891/majority-maintain-need-third-major-party.aspx; Byron Tau, "More Americans Consider Third-Party Options," *Wall Street Journal*, May 24, 2016, http://blogs.wsj.com/washwire/2016/05/24/more-americans-consider-third-party-options/

89. Drew Desilver, "U.S. Voter Turnout Trails Most Developed Countries," *Pew Research Center*, August 2, 2016, http://www.pewresearch.org/fact-tank/2015/05/06/u-s-voter-turnout-trails-most-developed-countries/; Lyn Ragsdale and Gerhard Peters, "Voter

Turnout in Presidential Elections: 1828–2012," *The American Presidency Project*, 2017, http://www.presidency.ucsb.edu/data/turnout.php

90. Jeffrey M. Jones, "In U.S., Perceived Need for Third Party Reaches New High," *Gallup*, October 11, 2013, http://www.gallup.com/poll/165392/perceived-need-third-party-reaches-new-high.aspx

91. Joseph G. Rayback, *Free Soil: The Election of 1848* (Lexington, KY: University Press of Kentucky, 1970).

92. Sid Milkis and Carah Ong, "Transforming American Democracy: TR and the Bull Moose Campaign of 1912," *Miller Center*, June 20, 2012, http://millercenter.org/ridingthetiger/bull-moose-campaign-1912

93. Pew Research Center, "Most Americans Say Government Doesn't Do Enough to Help Middle Class," *Pew Research Center*, February 4, 21016, http://www.pewsocialtrends.org/2016/02/04/most-americans-say-government-doesnt-do-enough-to-help-middle-class/

94. Jeffrey M. Jones, "Little Support for Third-Party Candidates in 2012 Election," *Gallup*, July 6, 2012, http://www.gallup.com/poll/155537/little-support-third-party-candidates-2012-election.aspx; Mona Chalabi, "Did Third-Party Candidates Jill Stein and Gary Johnson Lose Clinton the Election?" *Guardian*, November 10, 2016, https://www.theguardian.com/us-news/2016/nov/10/third-party-candidate-gary-johnson-jill-stein-clinton-loss; Elen L. Weintraub, "Federal Elections 2012," *Federal Election Commission*, July 2013, http://www.fec.gov/pubrec/fe2012/federalelections2012.pdf

95. John F. Bibby and L Sandy Maisel, *Two Parties—or More? The American Party System* (Boulder, CO: Westview Press, 2002).

96. Steven J. Rosenstone, Roy L. Behr, and Edward H. Lazarus, *Third Parties in America* (Princeton, NJ: Princeton University Press, 1996).

97. Anthony R DiMaggio, "Bigotry for Profit and 'Fun': Traversing the Wasteland of U.S. Elections," *Counterpunch*, October 10, 2016, http://www.counterpunch.org/2016/10/10/87468/

98. Open Secrets, "Money Wins Presidency and 9 of 10 Congressional Races in Priciest U.S. Election Ever," *Center for Responsive Politics*, November 5, 2008, http://www.opensecrets.org/news/2008/11/money-wins-white-house-and/

99. Bob Biersack, "The Big Spender Always Wins?" *Center for Responsive Politics*, January 11, 2012, https://www.opensecrets.org/news/2012/01/big-spender-always-wins/

100. George Farah, *No Debate: How the Presidential and Democratic Parties Secretly Control the Presidential Debates* (New York: Seven Stories Press, 2004).

101. Farah, *No Debate*, 2004.

102. Jonathan Easley and Ben Kamisar, "Third-Party Candidates Face Uphill Climb to Get Place on Presidential Debate Stage," *The Hill*, May 12, 2016, http://thehill.com/homenews/campaign/279624-third-party-candidates-face-uphill-climb-to-get-place-on-presidential

103. NCSL.org, "Getting on the Ballot: What it Takes," *National Conference of State Legislatures*, February 2012, http://www.ncsl.org/documents/legismgt/elect/Canvass_Feb_2012_No_27.pdf

104. G. Bingham Powell, Jr., *Elections as Instruments of Democracy* (New Haven, CT: Yale University Press, 2000); Richard G. Niemi and Herbert F. Weisberg, "Why is Voter

Turnout Low (And Why is it Declining?)" in *Controversies in Voting Behavior*, Richard G. Niemi and Herbert F. Weisberg, eds. (Washington DC: CQ Press, 2001): 22–37.

Chapter 10

1. Drew Desilver, "Turnout was High in the 2016 Primary Season, but Just Short of 2008 Record," *Pew Research Center*, June 10, 2016, http://www.pewresearch.org/fact-tank/2016/06/10/turnout-was-high-in-the-2016-primary-season-but-just-short-of-2008-record/

2. Pew Research Center, "Who Votes, Who Doesn't, and Why," *Pew Research Center*, October 18, 2006, http://www.people-press.org/2006/10/18/who-votes-who-doesnt-and-why/

3. Michael P. McDonald, "National General Election VEP Turnout Rates, 1789–Present," *United States Elections Project*, June 11, 2014, http://www.electproject.org/national-1789-present

4. Michael P. McDonald, "2014 November General Election Turnout Rates," *United States General Elections Project*, December 30, 2015, http://www.electproject.org/2014g; Michael P. McDonald, "2012 November General Election Turnout Rates," *United States General Elections Project*, September 3, 2014, http://www.electproject.org/2012g; Michael P. McDonald, "2016 November General Election Turnout Rates," *United States Election Project*, 2017, http://www.electproject.org/2016g

5. Konstantin Kilibarda and Daria Roithmayr, "The Myth of the Rust Belt Revolt," *Slate*, December 1, 2016, http://www.slate.com/articles/news_and_politics/politics/2016/12/the_myth_of_the_rust_belt_revolt.html

6. Julianna Goldman, "Donald Trump's Cabinet Richest in U.S. History, Historians Say," *CBS News*, December 20, 2016, https://www.cbsnews.com/news/donald-trump-cabinet-richest-in-us-history-historians-say/

7. McDonald, "2016 November General Election Turnout Rates," 2017.

8. Drew Desilver, "U.S. Voter Turnout Trails Most Developed Countries," *Pew Research Center*, August 2, 2016, http://www.pewresearch.org/fact-tank/2016/08/02/u-s-voter-turnout-trails-most-developed-countries/

9. Robert W. McChesney and John Nichols, *People Get Ready: The Fight Against a Jobless Economy and a Citizenless Democracy* (New York: Nation Books, 2016).

10. Michael P. McDonald, "The Competitive Problem of Voter Turnout," *The Washington Post*, October 31, 2006, http://www.washingtonpost.com/wp-dyn/content/article/2006/10/30/AR2006103000712.html; Drew Desilver, "For Most Voters, Congressional Elections Offer Little Drama," *Pew Research Center*, November 3, 2014, http://www.pewresearch.org/fact-tank/2014/11/03/for-most-voters-congressional-elections-offer-little-drama/; Steven L. Taylor, "Why so Many House Races (Nearly All) are Noncompetitive," *Christian Science Monitor*, October 14, 2014, http://www.csmonitor.com/USA/Politics/Politics-Voices/2014/1014/Why-so-many-House-races-nearly-all-are-noncompetitive

11. Open Secrets, "Money Wins Presidency and 9 of 10 Congressional Races in Priciest U.S. Election Ever," 2008.

12. Drew Desilver, "Only 1 in 7 House Districts Were Competitive in 2012," *Pew Research Center*, November 5, 2013, http://www.pewresearch.org/fact-tank/2013/11/05/only-1-in-7-house-districts-were-competitive-in-2012/; Taylor, "Why so Many House Races (Nearly All) are Noncompetitive," 2014.

13. Michael D. Regan, "Why is Voter Turnout so Low in the U.S.? *PBS*, November 6, 2016, http://www.pbs.org/newshour/updates/voter-turnout-united-states/

14. Gary C. Jacobson, "Measuring Campaign Spending Effects in U.S. House Elections," in *Capturing Campaign Effects*, Henry E. Brady and Richard Johnson, eds. (Ann Arbor, MI: University of Michigan Press, 2006): 199–220.

15. Spenkuch and Toniatti, "Political Advertising and Election Outcomes," 2016.

16. Adam Bonica, "Working Paper: Why are There so Many Lawyers in Congress?" *Midwest Political Science Association Conference*, April 2017.

17. Nicholas Confessore, Sarah Cohen, and Karen Yourish, "Small Pool of Rich Donors Dominates Election Giving," *The New York Times*, August 1, 2015, https://www.nytimes.com/2015/08/02/us/small-pool-of-rich-donors-dominates-election-giving.html?mcubz=3

18. Scott Clement, "Why Don't Americans Vote? We're Too Busy," *The Washington Post*, July 17, 2015, https://www.washingtonpost.com/news/the-fix/wp/2015/07/17/why-dont-americans-vote-were-too-busy/?utm_term=.9b38b61f228c

19. Pew Research Center, "In Deadlocked Race, Neither Side has Ground Game Advantage," *Pew Research Center*, October 31, 2012, http://www.people-press.org/2012/10/31/in-deadlocked-race-neither-side-has-ground-game-advantage/; Pew Research Center, "Democrats Now More Positive on Campaign 2012," *Pew Research Center*, September 12, 2012, http://www.people-press.org/2012/09/12/democrats-now-more-positive-on-campaign-2012/

20. Seth Motel, "For Many Americans, a "Meh' Midterm," *Pew Research Center*, October 8, 2014, http://www.pewresearch.org/fact-tank/2014/10/08/for-many-americans-a-meh-midterm/

21. Wattenberg, *Is Voting for Young People?* 2015; Markus Prior, *Post-Broadcast Democracy: How Media Choice Increases Inequality in Political Involvement and Polarizes Elections* (Cambridge: Cambridge University Press, 2007).

22. Niemi and Weisburg, "Why Voter Turnout is Low (And Why is it Declining)? 2001; Steven J. Rosenstone and John Mark Hansen, "Solving the Puzzle of Participation in Electoral Politics," in *Controversies in Voting Behavior*, Richard G. Niemi and Herbert F. Weisberg, eds. (Washington DC: CQ Press, 2001): 69–82; Mark N. Franklin, "Electoral Participation," in *Controversies in Voting Behavior*, Richard G. Niemi and Herbert F. Weisberg, eds. (Washington DC: CQ Press, 2001): 83–99.

23. Robert D. Putnam, *Bowling Alone: The Collapse and Revival of American Community* (New York: Touchstone, 2000).

24. Prior, *Post-Broadcast Democracy*, 2007.

25. Pew Research Center, "Who Votes, Who Doesn't, and Why," *Pew Research Center*, October 18, 2016, http://www.people-press.org/2006/10/18/who-votes-who-doesnt-and-why/

26. Pew Research Center, "Beyond Distrust: How Americans View Their Government," 2015.

27. Lydia Saad, "Voters, Especially Independents, Lack Interest in Election," *Gallup*, November 4, 2014, http://news.gallup.com/poll/179147/voters-especially-independents-lack-interest-election.aspx; Pew Research Center, "Independent Oppose Party in Power . . . Again," *Pew Research Center*, September 23, 2010, http://www.people-press.org/2010/09/23/independents-oppose-party-in-power-again/

28. Jeffrey M. Jones, "Trust in Federal Gov't on International Issues at New Low," *Gallup*, September 10, 2014, http://www.gallup.com/poll/175697/trust-federal-gov-international-issues-new-low.aspx

29. National Conference of State Legislatures, "Felon Rights," *NCSL.org*, September 29, 2016, http://www.ncsl.org/research/elections-and-campaigns/felon-voting-rights.aspx

30. Pew Research Center, "Who Votes, Who Doesn't, and Why," 2016; McDonald, "2016 November General Election Turnout Rates," 2017.

31. Bradley Jones, "Americans' Views of Immigrants Marked by Widening Partisan, Generational Divides," *Pew Research Center*, April 15, 2016, http://www.pewresearch.org/fact-tank/2016/04/15/americans-views-of-immigrants-marked-by-widening-partisan-generational-divides/

32. Nadwa Mossaad, U.S. Lawful Permanent Residents: 2014," *U.S. Department of Homeland Security*, April 2016, https://www.dhs.gov/sites/default/files/publications/Lawful_Permanent_Residents_2014.pdf

33. American Community Survey Reports, "The Foreign-Born Population in the United States: 2010," *U.S. Census Bureau*, May 2012, https://www.census.gov/prod/2012pubs/acs-19.pdf

34. Reid Wilson, "GOP Platform Calls for Tough Voter ID Laws," *The Hill*, July 19, 2016, http://thehill.com/blogs/ballot-box/288302-gop-platform-calls-for-tough-voter-id-laws

35. Philip Bump, "There Have Been Just Four Documented Cases of Voter Fraud in the 2016 Election," *The Washington Post*, December 1, 2016, https://www.washingtonpost.com/news/the-fix/wp/2016/12/01/0-000002-percent-of-all-the-ballots-cast-in-the-2016-election-were-fraudulent/?utm_term=.e6dfc75625ec; Lorraine C. Minnite, "The Politics of Voter Fraud," *Project Vote*, March 2007, http://www.projectvote.org/wp-content/uploads/2007/03/Politics_of_Voter_Fraud_Final.pdf; Justin Levitt, "A Comprehensive Investigation of Voter Impersonation Finds 31 Credible Incidents Out of One Billion Ballots Cast," *The Washington Post*, August 6, 2014, https://www.washingtonpost.com/news/wonk/wp/2014/08/06/a-comprehensive-investigation-of-voter-impersonation-finds-31-credible-incidents-out-of-one-billion-ballots-cast/?utm_term=.f30067ac7c92

36. Simon Malroy, "Wisconsin's Voter ID Sham: Republican Rep Admits the Law Targets Democrats," *Salon*, April 6, 2016, http://www.salon.com/2016/04/06/wisconsins_voter_id_sham_republican_rep_admits_the_law_targets_democrats_its_time_for_the_rest_of_the_gop_to_say_it_too/; Jamelle Bouie, "Republicans Admit Voter-ID Laws are Aimed at Democratic Voters," *Daily Beast*, August 28, 2013, http://www.thedailybeast.com/articles/2013/08/28/republicans-admit-voter-id-laws-are-aimed-at-democratic-voters.html; Editorial, "Republicans and Voter Suppression," *The New York Times*, April 5, 2016, http://www.nytimes.com/2016/04/05/opinion/republicans-and-voter-suppression.html?_r=0

37. Over 90 million voting eligible Americans did not vote in 2016. *The Washington Post* reports that 2 percent of non-voters are not able to vote due to registration problems. So in total, nearly two million people appear to be disenfranchised due to registration problems. For more on these statistics, see: Clement, "Why Don't Americans Vote? We're 'Too Busy,'" 2015, and: McDonald, "2016 November General Election Turnout Rates," 2017.

38. Clement, "Why Don't Americans Vote? We're 'Too Busy,'" 2015.

39. Data is available on voting over time for Australia and Chile via country profiles at the International Institute for Democracy and Electoral Assistance, at: http://www.idea.int/data-tools/data/voter-turnout

40. IDEA, "Chile," *International Institute for Democracy and Electoral Assistance,* 2017, http://www.idea.int/data-tools/question-view/521

41. Laura Santhanam, "22 Countries Where Voting is Mandatory," *PBS Newshour,* November 3, 2014, http://www.pbs.org/newshour/rundown/22-countries-voting-mandatory/

42. IDEA, "Germany," *International Institute for Democracy and Electoral Assistance,* 2017, http://www.idea.int/data-tools/question-view/521

43. Franklin, "Electoral Participation," in *Controversies in Voting Behavior,* 2001.

44. Stephen Ansolabehere and Shanto Iyengar, *Going Negative: How Political Advertisements Shrink and Polarize the Electorate* (New York: Free Press, 1997).

45. Donovan Slack, "RIP Positive Ads in 2012," *Politico,* November 4, 2012 http://www.politico.com/story/2012/11/rip-positive-ads-in-2012-083262; University of Wisconsin Advertising Project, "Political Advertising in 2008," March 17, 2010, http://wiscadproject.wisc.edu/wiscads_report_031710.pdf

46. Richard G. Niemi and Herbert F. Weisberg, "Why is Voter Turnout Low (And Why is it Declining?)" in *Controversies in Voting Behavior,* Richard G. Niemi and Herbert F. Weisberg, eds. (Washington DC: CQ Press, 2001): 22–37; Ansolabehere and Iyengar, *Going Negative,* 1997.

47. Kim L. Fridkin and Patrick J. Kenney, "Variability in Citizens' Reactions to Different Types of Negative Campaigns," *American Journal of Political Science,* 55, no. 2 (2011): 307–25.

48. Jake Rosenfeld, "Economic Determinants of Voting in an Era of Union Decline," *Social Science Quarterly,* 91, no. 2 (2010), 379–96; Jan E. Leighley and Jonathan Nagler, "Unions, Voter Turnout, and Class Bias in the U.S. Electorate, 1964–2004," *Journal of Politics,* 69, no. 2 (2007): 430–41; John T. Delaney, Marick F. Masters, and Susan Schwochau, "Unionism and Voter Turnout," *Journal of Labor Research,* 9, no. 3 (1988): 221–36.

49. Leighley and Nagler, "Unions, Voter Turnout, and Class Bias in the U.S. Electorate," 2007.

50. Bryce Covert, "Fewer Labor Unions Means More Income Inequality," *Think Progress,* February 27, 2015, https://thinkprogress.org/fewer-labor-unions-means-more-income-inequality-26ba1ea919fd#.f4gsppeum; Zaid Jilani, "Chart: How Income Inequality Skyrocketed and the 1 Percent Profited from the Decline of Unions," *Think Progress,*

October 21, 2011, https://thinkprogress.org/chart-how-income-inequality-skyrocketed-and-the-1-percent-profited-from-the-decline-of-unions-f098379015df#.on4imyh64

51. Lila Shapiro, "Union-Busting Tactics More Pervasive than Previously Thought: Study," *Huffington Post*, June 28, 2011, http://www.huffingtonpost.com/2011/06/28/union-busting-tactics_n_886203.html

52. Steven Greenhouse, "Democrats Drop Key Part of Bill to Assist Unions," *The New York Times*, July 16, 2009, http://www.nytimes.com/2009/07/17/business/17union.html?mcubz=3

53. Drew Desilver, "Global Inequality: How the U.S. Compares," *Pew Research Center*, December 19, 2013, http://www.pewresearch.org/fact-tank/2013/12/19/global-inequality-how-the-u-s-compares/

54. Frederick Solt, "Does Economic Inequality Depress Electoral Participation? Testing the Schattschneider Hypothesis," *Political Behavior*, 32, no. 2 (2010): 285–301; Frederick Solt, "Economic Inequality and Democratic Political Engagement," *American Journal of Political Science*, 52, no. 1 (2008): 48–60.

55. Anthony DiMaggio, Working Book Manuscript: *Class Politics: Class Consciousness, False Consciousness, and Political Attitudes in Modern America*, 2018.

56. Sean Mcelwee, "The Rich Aren't Just Megadonors. They're Also Dominating the Voting Booth," *Politico*, January 7, 2015, http://www.politico.com/magazine/story/2015/01/income-gap-at-the-polls-113997

57. Pew Research Center, "Nonvoters: Who They Are, What They Think," *Pew Research Center*, November 1, 2012, http://www.people-press.org/2012/11/01/nonvoters-who-they-are-what-they-think/

58. Linda Lyons, "Teens Stay True to Parents' Political Perspectives," *Gallup*, January 4, 2005, http://www.gallup.com/poll/14515/teens-stay-true-parents-political-perspectives.aspx

59. Larry M. Bartels, *Unequal Democracy: The Political Economy of the New Gilded Age* (Princeton, NJ: Princeton University Press, 2010); Andrew Gelman, *Red State, Blue State, Rich State, Poor State: Why Americans Vote the Way They Do* (Princeton, NJ: Princeton University Press, 2009); Jan Leighley and Jonathan Nagler, *Who Votes Now? Demographics, Issues, Inequality, and Turnout in the United States* (Princeton, NJ: Princeton University Press, 2013).

60. Michael S. Lewis Beck, William J. Jacoby, Helmut Norpoth, and Herbert F. Weisberg, *The American Voter Revisited* (Ann Arbor, MI: University of Michigan Press, 2008).

61. Lewis Beck, et al., *The American Voter Revisited*, 2008.

62. Lewis Beck, et al., *The American Voter Revisited*, 2008.

63. Anthony R. DiMaggio, *The Rise of the Tea Party: Corporate Media and Political Discontent in the Age of Obama* (New York: Monthly Review Press, 2011).

64. Sides, "Three Myths about Political Independents," 2009.

65. Enten, "Americans Aren't Becoming More Politically Independent, They Just Like Saying They Are," 2015.

66. CNN Politics, "Exit Polls," 2016.

67. Cheryl Boudreau and Scott A. MacKenzie, "Informing the Electorate? How Party Cues and Policy Information Affect Public Opinion About Initiatives," *American Journal of Political Science*, 58, no. 1 (2014): 48–62; Paul Goren, Christopher M. Federico, and Miki Caul Killilson, "Source Cues, Partisan Identities, and Political Value Expression," *American Journal of Political Science*, 53, no. 4 (2009): 805–20; Marty Cohen, David Karol, Hans Noel, and John Zaller, *The Party Decides: Presidential Nominations Before and After Reform* (Chicago: University of Chicago Press, 2008); John Zaller, *The Nature and Origins of Mass Opinion* (Cambridge: Cambridge University Press, 1992); Russell J. Dalton, *Citizen Politics: Public Opinion and Political Parties in Advanced Industrial Democracies* (Washington DC: CQ Press, 2013): Adam J. Berinsky, *In Time of War: Understanding American Public Opinion from World War II to Iraq* (Chicago: University of Chicago Press, 2009).

68. David Dayen, "Donald Trump is Right: Deficits Don't Matter," *New Republic*, May 11, 2016, https://newrepublic.com/article/133431/donald-trump-right-deficits-dont-matter

69. Pew Research Center, "Deficit Reduction Declines as Policy Priority," *Pew Research Center*, January 24, 2014, http://www.people-press.org/2014/01/27/deficit-reduction-declines-as-policy-priority/1-25-2014_02/

70. Bob Cesca, "The GOP's Entire Identity is Based on a Lie: How the Obama Presidency Exposed Republican Deficit Delusions," *Salon*, October 16, 2015, http://www.salon.com/2015/10/16/the_gops_entire_identity_is_based_on_a_lie_how_the_obama_presidency_exposed_republican_deficit_delusions/

71. Pew Research Center, "Majority Views NSA Phone Tracking as Acceptable Anti-Terror Tactic," *Pew Research Center*, June 10, 2013, http://www.people-press.org/2013/06/10/majority-views-nsa-phone-tracking-as-acceptable-anti-terror-tactic/

72. Federal Reserve Bank of St. Louis, "Federal Surplus or Deficit [-] as Percent of Gross Domestic Product," *Federal Reserve Bank of St. Louis*, January 27, 2017, https://fred.stlouisfed.org/series/FYFSGDA188S

73. Janet Novack, "Trump Plan Delivers Massive Tax Cuts to the 1% and Sharp Kick to the Upper Middle Class," *Forbes*, September 29, 2017, https://www.forbes.com/sites/janetnovack/2017/09/29/trump-plan-delivers-massive-tax-cuts-to-the-1-and-sharp-kick-to-upper-middle-class/#1ed8883b1099

74. Emily Guskin and Carolyn Y. Johnson, "Half of Americans Think President Trump's Tax Plan Will Favor the Wealthy," *The Washington Post*, September 26, 2017, https://www.washingtonpost.com/news/wonk/wp/2017/09/26/half-of-americans-think-president-trumps-tax-plan-will-favor-the-wealthy/?utm_term=.90327f74b4ee

75. Andrew Flowers, "The Democratic Base is Shifting, But the Party's Position on Trade Isn't," *FiveThirtyEight*, May 4, 2015, https://fivethirtyeight.com/features/the-democratic-base-is-shifting-but-the-partys-position-on-trade-isnt/

76. David Nakamura, "Obama Defends Free Trade Push to Supporters: This Isn't NAFTA," *The Washington Post*, April 23, 2015, https://www.washingtonpost.com/news/post-politics/wp/2015/04/23/obama-defends-free-trade-push-to-supporters-this-isnt-nafta/?utm_term=.55bee001abc6; David E. Bonior, "Obama's Free-Trade Conundrum," *The New York Times*, January 29, 2014, https://www.nytimes.com/2014/01/30/opinion/obamas-free-trade-conundrum.html?mcubz=3

77. Robert E. Scott and Elizabeth Glass, "Trans-Pacific Partnership, Currency Manipulation, Trade, and Jobs," *Economic Policy Institute*, March 3, 2016, http://www.epi.org/publication/trans-pacific-partnership-currency-manipulation-trade-and-jobs/

78. Anthony Downs, *An Economic Theory of Democracy* (New York: Harper and Row, 1957).

79. Stephen A. Jessee, *Ideology and Spatial Voting in American Elections* (Cambridge: Cambridge University Press, 2012).

80. Richard G. Niemi and Herbert F. Weisberg, "What Determines the Vote? in *Controversies in Voting Behavior*, Richard G. Niemi and Herbert F. Weisberg, eds. (Washington DC: CQ Press, 2001): 93–106.

81. David E. Repass, "Issue Salience and Party Choice," *American Political Science Review*, 65, no. 2 (1971): 389–400.

82. Gerald M. Pomper, "From Confusion to Clarity: Issues and American Voters, 1956–1968," *American Political Science Review*, 66, no. 2 (1972): 415–28; Norman H. Nie, Sydney Verba, and John R. Petrocik, *The Changing American Voter* (Cambridge, MA: Harvard University Press, 1976).

83. Pew Research Center, "What the Public Knows About Political Parties," *Pew Research Center*, April 11, 2012, http://www.people-press.org/2012/04/11/what-the-public-knows-about-the-political-parties/

84. Stephen Ansolabehere, Jonathan Rodden, and James M. Snyder Jr., "The Strength of Issues; Using Multiple Measures to Gauge Preference Stability, Ideological Constraint, and Issue Voting," *American Political Science Review*, 102, no. 2 (2008): 215–32.

85. Pew Research Center, "With Voters Focused on Economy, Obama Lead Narrows," *Pew Research Center*, April 17, 2012, http://www.people-press.org/2012/04/17/section-2-issues-of-the-2012-campaign/

86. Pew Research Center, "What Voters Know About Campaign," *Pew Research Center*, August 10, 2012, http://www.people-press.org/2012/08/10/what-voters-know-about-campaign-2012/

87. Pew Research Center, "2016 Campaign: Strong Interest, Widespread Dissatisfaction," *Pew Research Center*, July 7, 2016, http://www.people-press.org/2016/07/07/5-candidate-traits-and-perceptions/

88. Pew Research Center, "Top Voting Issues in 2016 Election," *Pew Research Center*, July 7, 2016, http://www.people-press.org/2016/07/07/4-top-voting-issues-in-2016-election/

89. Global opposition to, and suspicion of U.S. policy is explored at length in the foreign policy chapter of this book.

90. The Atlantic, "The Wright Post 9/11 Sermon," *The Atlantic*, March 22, 2008, https://www.theatlantic.com/daily-dish/archive/2008/03/the-wright-post-9-11-sermon/218678/

91. Kate Kenski, Bruce W. Hardy, and Kathleen Hall Jamieson, *The Obama Victory: How Media Money, and Message Shaped the 2008 Election* (Oxford: Oxford University Press, 2010).

92. Jim Rutenberg and Jeff Zeleny, "Bain Attacks Make Inroads for President," *The New York Times*, June 30, 2012, http://www.nytimes.com/2012/07/01/us/politics/bain-attacks-make-inroads-for-president.html?_r=0

93. Rutenberg and Zeleny, "Bain Attacks Make Inroads for President," 2012.

94. Nate Silver, "The Bottom Could Fall Out for Trump," *FiveThirtyEight*, October 8, 2016, https://fivethirtyeight.com/features/the-bottom-could-fall-out-for-trump/

95. Edward Tufte, "Determinants of the Outcomes of Midterm Congressional Elections," *American Political Science Review*, 69, no. 3 (1975): 812–26; Morris P. Fiorina, "Economic Retrospective Voting in American National Elections: A Micro-Analysis," *American Journal of Political Science*, 22, no. 2 (1978): 426–43; Morris P. Fiorina, *Retrospective Voting in American National Elections* (New Haven, CT: Yale University Press, 1981); Michael S. Lewis-Beck, *Economics and Elections* (Ann Arbor, MI: University of Michigan Press, 1988); D. Roderick Kiewiet, *Macroeconomics and Micropolitics: The Electoral Effects of Economic Issues* (Chicago: University of Chicago Press, 1983); Gary C. Jacobson and Samuel Kernell, *Jacobson and Kernell: Strategy and Choice in Congressional Elections* (New Haven, CT: Yale University Press, 1981).

96. Christopher H. Achen and Larry M. Bartels, "Musical Chairs: Pocketbook Voting and the Limits of Democratic Accountability," *American Political Science Association Conference Presentation*, September 8, 2004, https://my.vanderbilt.edu/larrybartels/files/2011/12/musical-chairs.pdf

97. James E. Campbell, Bryan J. Dettrey, and Hongxing Yin, "The Theory of Conditional Retrospective Voting: Does the Presidential Record Matter Less in Open-Seat Elections?" *Journal of Politics*, 72, no. 4 (2010): 1083–095; David J. Lanoue, "Retrospective and Prospective Voting in Presidential-Year Elections, *Political Research Quarterly*, 47, no. 1 (1994): 193–205; Richard Nadeau and Michael S. Lewis-Beck, "National Economic Voting in U.S. Presidential Elections," *Journal of Politics*, 63, no. 1 (2001): 159–81.

98. Paul L. Street and Anthony R. DiMaggio, *Crashing the Tea Party: Mass Media, Republican Politics, and the Campaign to Remake American Politics* (New York: Routledge, 2011).

99. Richard Nadeau and Michael S. Lewis-Beck, "National Economic Voting in U.S. Presidential Elections," in *Controversies in Voting Behavior*, eds. Richard G. Niemi and Herbert F. Weisberg (Washington DC: CQ Press, 2001): 200–20.

100. Campbell, et al., "The Theory of Conditional Retrospective Voting," 2010).

101. Campbell, et al., "The Theory of Conditional Retrospective Voting," 2010).

102. Lynn Vavreck, *The Message Matters: The Economy and Presidential Campaigns* (Princeton, NJ: Princeton University Press, 2009).

103. Jeffrey M. Jones, "Obama's Character Edge Offsets Romney's Economic Advantage," *Gallup*, July 24, 2012, http://www.gallup.com/poll/156134/obama-character-edge-offsets-romney-economic-advantage.aspx

104. Mark Blumenthal, "Will Obama's Post-Convention Bounce Fade Like McCain's in 2008?" *Huffington Post*, September 13, 2012, http://www.huffingtonpost.com/2012/09/13/obamas-post-convention-bounce-polls-2012_n_1880520.html

105. John Nichols, "Young Voter Turnout Fell 60% From 2008 to 2010; Dems Won't Win in 2012 if the Trend Continues," *The Nation*, November 16, 2010, https://www.thenation.com/article/young-voter-turnout-fell-60-2008-2010-dems-wont-win-2012-if-trend-continues/

106. Paul L. Street and Anthony R. DiMaggio, *Crashing the Tea Party: Mass Media, Republican Politics, and the Campaign to Remake American Politics* (New York: Routledge, 2011).

107. I surveyed 250 Introduction to American government students in the spring of 2016, at a community college in the Midwest. The goal of the survey was to ask students not only what candidate they supported, but why—something that national polls had largely failed to shed light on. The most common reasons that students supported Sanders included statements that he cared about the poor and needy, and was seeking to help students and others when it comes to providing for affordable college and better health care benefits.

108. Aaron Blake, "74-Year-Old Bernie Sanders's Remarkable Dominance Among Young Voters, in 1 Chart," *Los Angeles Times*, March 17, 2016, https://www.washingtonpost.com/news/the-fix/wp/2016/03/17/74-year-old-bernie-sanderss-amazing-dominance-among-young-voters-in-1-chart/?utm_term=.00789b6157e2; Cathleen Decker, "Why Young Voters are Flocking to Sanders and Older Ones to Clinton," *Los Angeles Times*, April 19, 2016, http://www.latimes.com/politics/la-na-clinton-sanders-age-20160419-story.html

109. *Rebellion in America: Citizen Uprisings, the News Media, and the Politics of Plutocracy* (New York: Routledge, 2019).

110. Murray Edelman, *Symbolic Uses of Politics* (Champaign, IL: University of Illinois Press, 1985).

111. Amy Goodman and Juan Gonzalez, "Chomsky: The Assault on Democracy," *Alternet*, April 9, 2006, http://www.alternet.org/story/34600/chomsky%3A_the_assault_on_democracy

112. Kayla Webley, "How the Nixon-Kennedy Debate Changed the World," *Time*, September 23, 2010, http://content.time.com/time/nation/article/0,8599,2021078,00.html

113. Webley, "How the Nixon-Kennedy Debate Changed the World," 2010.

114. Tom Rosentiel, Mark Jurkowitz, and Tricia Sartor, "How the Media Covered the 2012 Primary Campaign," *Pew Research Center: Journalism and Media*, April 23, 2012, http://www.journalism.org/2012/04/23/frames-campaign-coverage/

115. Pew Research Center, "Winning the Media Campaign," *Pew Research Center: Journalism and Media*, October 22, 2008, http://www.journalism.org/2008/10/22/top-storylines/; Pew Research Center, "Winning the Media Campaign 2012," *Pew Research Center: Journalism and Media*, http://www.journalism.org/2012/11/01/frame-which-aspects-race-got-attention-and-which-ones-didnt/

116. Thomas E. Patterson, "News Coverage of the 2016 Presidential Primaries: Horse Race Reporting has Consquences," *Shorenstein Center on Media, Politics, and Public Policy*, July 11, 2016, https://shorensteincenter.org/news-coverage-2016-presidential-primaries/

117. Gabriel S. Lenz and Chappell Lawson, "Looking the Part: Television Leads Less Informed Citizens to Vote Based on Candidates' Appearance," *American Journal of Political Science*, 55, no. 3 (2011): 574–89.

118. Alexander Todorov, Anesu Mandisodza, Amir Goren, and Crystal C. Hall, "Inferences of Competence from faces Predict Election Outcomes," *Science*, 308, no. 5728 (2005): 1623–626; Christopher Y. Olivola and Alexander Todorov, "Elected in

100 Milliseconds: Appearance-Based Trait Inferences and Voting," *Journal of Nonverbal Behavior*, 34, no. 2 (2010): 83–110; Daniel J. Benjamin and Jesse M. Shapiro, "Thin-Slice Forecasts of Gubernatorial Elections," The Review of Economics and Statistics, 91, no. 3 (2009): 523–36; Charles C. Ballew II and Alexander Todorov, "Predicting Political Elections from Rapid and Unreflective Face Judgments," *Proceedings of the National Academy of Sciences of the United States of America*, 104, no. 46 (2007): 17498–7953.

119. Emily Greenhouse, "There's a Science of Snap Political Judgments—and Trump and Clinton are Winning," *Bloomberg News*, February 25, 2016, https://www.bloomberg.com/politics/articles/2016-02-25/trump-clinton-win-in-the-science-of-snap-political-judgments

120. Susan A. Banducci, Jeffrey A. Karp, Michael Thrasher, and Colin Rallings, "Ballot Photographs as Cues in LowInformation Elections," *Political Psychology*, 29, no. 6 (2008): 903–17.

121. Richard G. Niemi and Herbert F. Weisberg, "What Determine the Vote?" in *Classics in Voting Behavior*, eds. Richard G. Niemi and Herbert F. Weisberg (Washington DC: CQ Press, 1993): 93–106; Warren E. Miller and J. Merrill Shanks, "Multiple-Stage Explanation of Political Preferences," in *Controversies in Voting Behavior*, eds. Richard G. Niemi and Herbert F. Weisberg (Washington DC: CQ Press, 2001): 221–39.

122. Gabriel S. Lenz, *Follow the Leader? How Voters Respond to Politicians' Policies and Performance* (Chicago: University of Chicago Press, 2012).

123. Miller and Shanks, "Multiple-Stage Explanation of Political Preferences," 2001.

124. Associated Press, "What it Means if Trump Names China a Currency Manipulator," *CNBC*, December 29, 2016, http://www.cnbc.com/2016/12/29/what-it-means-if-trump-names-china-a-currency-manipulator.html

125. Justin McCarthy, "Clinton Preferred for Experience; Sanders, for Care," *Gallup*, March 31, 2016, http://www.gallup.com/poll/190397/clinton-preferred-experience-sanders-care.aspx

126. Frank Newport and Lydia Saad, "Trump Support Built on Outsider Status, Business Experience," *Gallup*, March 4, 2016, http://www.gallup.com/poll/189773/trump-support-built-outsider-status-business-experience.aspx

127. Newport and Saad, "Trump Support Built on Outsider Status, Business Experience," 2016.

128. McCarthy, "Clinton Preferred for Experience; Sanders, for Care," 2016.

129. Pew Research Center, "2016 Campaign Strong Interest, Widespread Dissatisfaction," *Pew Research Center*, July 7, 2016, http://www.people-press.org/2016/07/07/2016-campaign-strong-interest-widespread-dissatisfaction/

130. Lydia Saad, "Aversion to Other Candidate Key Factor in 2016 Vote Choice," *Gallup*, October 6, 2016, http://www.gallup.com/poll/196172/aversion-candidate-key-factor-2016-vote-choice.aspx; Pew Research Center, "In Their Own Words: Why Voters Support and Have Concerns About Clinton and Trump," *Pew Research Center*, September 21, 2016, http://www.people-press.org/2016/09/21/in-their-own-words-why-voters-support-and-have-concerns-about-clinton-and-trump/

131. Saad, "Aversion to Other Candidate Key Factor in 2016 Vote Choice," 2016; Pew, "In Their Own Words: Why Voters Support and Have Concerns About Clinton and Trump," 2016.

132. George Stephanopoulos, "ABC This Week with George Stephanopoulos," *ABC News*, August 16, 2015, http://abcnews.go.com/Politics/week-transcript-donald-trump/story?id=33086722

133. Goodman and Gonzalez, "Chomsky: The Assault on Democracy," 2006.

134. Goodman and Gonzalez, "Chomsky: The Assault on Democracy," 2006.

135. Open Secrets, "Total Cost of Election: 1998–2016," *Center for Responsive Politics*, 2017, https://www.opensecrets.org/overview/cost.php

Chapter 11

1. Anthony DiMaggio, "Class Sub-Conscious: Hegemony, False Consciousness, and the Development of Political and Economic Policy Attitudes," *Critical Sociology* 4, no. 13 (2015): 493–516.

2. My analysis of inequality draws on the *Nexis Uni* database, and examines stories in various media that focus on U.S. politics, from the 2006 to 2011 period.

3. Anthony DiMaggio, "The Propaganda Model and Manufacturing Consent: U.S. Public Compliance and Resistance," in *The Cambridge Companion to Chomsky*, ed. James McGilvray (Cambridge: Cambridge University Press, 2017): 275–94.

4. Maxwell McCombs, *Setting the Agenda: Mass Media and Public Opinion* (Cambridge: Polity, 2014); James W. Dearing and Everett M. Rogers, *Agenda Setting* (Thousand Oaks, CA: Sage, 1996).

5. For media priming, see: Shanto Iyengar, *Is Anyone Responsible? How Television Frames Political Issues* (Chicago: University of Chicago Press, 1994); for framing effects, see: Anthony R. DiMaggio, *The Politics of Persuasion: Media Bias and Economic Policy in the Modern Era* (Albany, NY: State University of New York Press, 2017); Anthony R. DiMaggio, *Selling War, Selling Hope: Presidential Rhetoric, the News Media, and U.S. Foreign Policy Since 9/11* (Albany, NY: State University of New York Press); Scott Bonn, *Mass Deception: Moral Panic and the U.S. War in Iraq* (New Brunswick, NJ: Rutgers University Press, 2010).

6. Timothy E. Cook, *Governing with the News: The News Media as a Political Institution* (Chicago: University of Chicago Press, 2005).

7. Robert W. McChesney, *The Problem of the Media: U.S. Communication Politics in the Twenty-First Century* (New York: Monthly Review Press, 2004).

8. Robert W. McChesney and John Nichols, "The Rise of Professional Journalism," *In These Times*, December 7, 2005, http://inthesetimes.com/article/2427/

9. William R. Leach, *Land of Desire: Merchants, Power, and the Rise of a New American Culture* (New York: Vintage Books, 1994).

10. Gerald J. Baldasty, *The Commercialization of News in the Nineteenth Century* (Madison, WI: University of Wisconsin Press, 1992).

11. Michael Schudson, *Discovering the News: A Social History of American Newspapers* (New York: Basic Books, 1981).

12. Dan Schiller, *Objectivity and the News: The Public and the Rise of Commercial Journalism* (Philadelphia, PA: University of Pennsylvania Press, 1981).

13. Robert W. McChesney, "Journalism, Democracy . . . and Class Struggle," *Monthly Review*, 52, no. 6 (2000), https://monthlyreview.org/2000/11/01/journalism-democracy-and-class-struggle/

14. McChesney, "Journalism, Democracy . . . and Class Struggle," 2000.

15. McChesney, "Journalism, Democracy . . . and Class Struggle," 2000.

16. Melissa Bell, "Richard Nixon and Roger Ailes 1970s Plan to Put the GOP on TV," *The Washington Post*, July 1, 2001, https://www.washingtonpost.com/blogs/blogpost/post/richard-nixon-and-roger-ailes-1970s-plan-to-put-the-gop-on-tv/2011/07/01/AG1W7XtH_blog.html?utm_term=.7246963ae1e3

17. Brian Todd and Dugald McConnell, "Ailes and Nixon," *CNN.com*, July 1, 2011, http://politicalticker.blogs.cnn.com/2011/07/01/ailes-and-nixon/

18. Tim Dickinson, "How Roger Ailes Built the Fox News Fear Factory," *Rolling Stone*, May 25, 2011, http://www.rollingstone.com/politics/news/how-roger-ailes-built-the-fox-news-fear-factory-20110525; Gabriel Sherman, *The Loudest Voice in the Room: How the Brilliant, Bombastic Roger Ailes Built Fox News—and Divided a Country* (New York: Random House, 2017).

19. Pew Research Center, "In Changing News Landscape, Even Television is Vulnerable," *Pew Research Center*, September 27, 2012, http://www.people-press.org/2012/09/27/in-changing-news-landscape-even-television-is-vulnerable/

20. Pew Research Center, "Cable TV: Primetime Viewership," *Pew Research Center*, 2015, http://www.journalism.org/media-indicators/cable-tv-prime-time-viewership/; Pew Research Center, "Cable TV: Daytime Viewership," 2015, http://www.journalism.org/media-indicators/cable-tv-daytime-viewership/

21. Amy Mitchell, Jeffrey Gottfried, and Michael Barthel, "Trump, Clinton Voters Divided in Their Main Source for Election News," *Pew Research Center*, January 18, 2017, http://www.journalism.org/2017/01/18/trump-clinton-voters-divided-in-their-main-source-for-election-news/

22. Pew, "In Changing News Landscape, Even Television is Vulnerable," 2012.

23. Mitchell, et al., "Trump, Clinton Voters Divided in Their Main Source for Election News," 2017.

24. Hannah Karp, "Talk Radio's Advertising Problem," *Wall Street Journal*, February 3, 2015, https://www.wsj.com/articles/talk-radios-advertising-problem-1423011395

25. Hayley C. Cuccinello, "Trevor Noah's 'Daily Show' Reaches 100th Episode, But Noah is Still Struggling," *Forbes*, April 28, 2016, https://www.forbes.com/sites/hayleycuccinello/2016/04/28/trevor-noahs-daily-show-reaches-100th-episode-but-noah-is-still-struggling/#3d99ea992c24

26. Ben Lindbergh, "A Statistical Analysis of Stephen Colbert's First 100 Episodes of 'The Late Show,'" *538.com*, February 26, 2016, https://fivethirtyeight.com/features/a-statistical-analysis-of-stephen-colberts-first-100-episodes-of-the-late-show/; Michael O'Connell, "John Oliver's Talk Show Ratings Edging Out HBO Colleague Bill Maher," *Hollywood Reporter*, September 25, 2014, http://www.hollywoodreporter.com/news/john-olivers-talk-show-ratings-735187; Rick Kissell, "Ratings: CBS' 'Late show with Stephen

Colbert' Has Best Week Since February," *Variety*, May 12, 2016, http://variety.com/2016/tv/news/ratings-cbs-late-show-with-stephen-colbert-best-week-since-february-1201772646/

27. Pew, "In Changing Media Landscape, Even Television is Vulnerable," 2012.

28. Anthony DiMaggio, "Youth in Revolt: Why Millennials are the Key to Future Social Transformation," *Truthout*, September 16, 2017, http://www.truth-out.org/opinion/item/41951-youth-in-revolt-why-millennials-are-the-key-to-future-social-transformation

29. For example, Colbert gained notoriety for skewering Bill O'Reilly during his time at Comedy Central. Stewart had a reoccurring segment on his Daily Show program referring to Fox News as "bullshit mountain." Noah pokes fun at cable news anchors like Wolf Blitzer for using puns in poor taste to refer to foreign leaders such as North Korea's Kim Jong Un. During the 2000s, John Stewart gained notoriety for appearing on the CNN program "Crossfire," criticizing the Republican and Democratic-allied hosts of the show for engaging in "partisan hackery."

30. Matthew A. Baum, *Soft News Goes to War: Public Opinion and American Foreign Policy in the New Media Age* (Princeton, NJ: Princeton University Press, 2011).

31. Anthony DiMaggio, "You are What You Watch," Working Paper, 2016.

32. Pew, "In Changing Media Landscape, Even Television is Vulnerable," 2012.

33. Amy Mitchell, Jeffrey Gottfried, Jocelyn Kiley, and Katerina Eva Matsa, "Political Polarization and Media Habits," *Pew Research Center*, October 21, 2014, http://www.journalism.org/2014/10/21/political-polarization-media-habits/; Kathleen Hall Jamieson, *Echo Chamber; Rush Limbaugh and the Conservative Media* (Oxford: Oxford University Press, 2010); Matthew Levendusky, *How Partisan Media Polarize America* (Chicago: University of Chicago Press, 2013); Natalie J. Stroud, *Niche News: The Politics of News Choice* (Oxford: Oxford University Press, 2011).

34. Steven Kull, "Misperceptions, the Media, and the Iraq War," *Program on International Policy Attitudes*, October 2, 2003, http://www.pipa.org/OnlineReports/Iraq/IraqMedia_Oct03/IraqMedia_Oct03_rpt.pdf

35. Matt Corley, "Fox News Viewers Overwhelmingly Misinformed About Health Care Reform Proposals," *Think Progress*, August 19, 2009, https://thinkprogress.org/fox-news-viewers-overwhelmingly-misinformed-about-health-care-reform-proposals-b0843b3c1b0b#.j9sebo46o

36. Jon A. Krosnick and Bo MacInnis, "Frequent Viewers of Fox News are Less Likely to Accept Scientists' Views of Global Warming," *Stanford University*, December 2010, https://woods.stanford.edu/sites/default/files/files/Global-Warming-Fox-News.pdf

37. Clay Ramsay, Steven Kull, Ethan Lewis, and Stefan Subias, "Misinformation and the 2010 Election," *Worldpublicopinion.org*, December 10, 2010, http://drum.lib.umd.edu/bitstream/handle/1903/11375/Misinformation_Dec10_rpt.pdf

38. In the March 2011 *Pew* media consumption survey, there is no statistically significant relationship between watching John Stewart and whether individuals are registered to vote or not. In the June 2012 *Pew* media consumption survey, there is no statistically significant relationship between watching John Stewart or Stephen Colbert and whether individuals are registered to vote or not.

39. Pew, "In Changing Media Landscape, Even Television is Vulnerable," 2012.

40. Pew, "In Changing Media Landscape, Even Television is Vulnerable," 2012.

41. I examined the March 2011 *Pew Research Center* political survey, which covered consumption of entertainment based "soft news" programs. Employing a simple bivariate, ordered logistic regression, I examined whether John Stewart viewers were more or less likely to watch other types of political programs, including *The New York Times*, local newspapers, broadcast news, and cable news.

42. Markus Prior, *Post-Broadcast Democracy: How Media Choice Increases Inequality in Political Involvement and Polarizes Elections* (Cambridge: Cambridge University Press, 2007).

43. Pew, "In Changing Media Landscape, Even Television is Vulnerable," 2012.

44. Pew, "In Changing Media Landscape, Even Television is Vulnerable," 2012.

45. Katerina Eva Matsa, "Network News: Fact Sheet," *Pew Research Center*, June 15, 2016, http://www.journalism.org/2016/06/15/network-news-fact-sheet/

46. Pew, "In Changing Media Landscape, Even Television is Vulnerable," 2012.

47. Michael Barthel, "Newspaper Circulation Falls in 2014," *Pew Research Center*, April 28, 2015, http://www.journalism.org/chart/newspaper-circulation-falls-in-2014/

48. Amy Mitchell, "State of the News Media 2015," *Pew Research Center*, April 29, 2015, http://www.journalism.org/files/2015/04/FINAL-STATE-OF-THE-NEWS-MEDIA.pdf

49. Pew, "In Changing Media Landscape, Even Television is Vulnerable," 2012.

50. Jesse Holcomb, Amy Mitchell, and Tom Rosentiel, "Cable: Audience vs. Economics," *Project for Excellence in Journalism*, 2011, http://www.stateofthemedia.org/2011/cable-essay/

51. Pew, "Cable TV: Primetime Viewership," 2015.

52. Prior, *Post-Broadcast Democracy*, 2007.

53. Wattenberg, *Is Voting for Young People?* 2015.

54. Pew, "In Changing Media Landscape, Even Television is Vulnerable," 2012.

55. Valerie Strauss, "Question for the Ages: What Books When?" *The Washington Post*, March 24, 2008, http://www.washingtonpost.com/wp-dyn/content/article/2008/03/23/AR2008032301756.html

56. Robert W. McChesney and John Nichols, *The Death and Life of American Journalism: The Media Revolution That Will Begin the World Again* (New York: Nation Books, 2011); Kyle Heim, "Framing the 2008 Iowa Democratic Caucuses: Political Blogs and Second Level Intermedia Agenda Setting," *Journalism & Mass Communication Quarterly*, 90, no. 3 (2013): 500–519.

57. Joseph Lichterman, "The State of the News Media 2015," *Nieman Lab*, April 29, 2015, http://www.niemanlab.org/2015/04/the-state-of-the-news-media-2015-newspapers-%E2%86%93-smartphones-%E2%86%91/

58. Lichterman, "The State of the News Media 2015," 2015.

59. Margaret Sullivan, "The Search for Local Investigative Reporting's Future," *The New York Times*, December 5, 2015, http://www.nytimes.com/2015/12/06/public-editor/margaret-sullivan-new-york-times-public-editor.html

60. Jodi Enda, "Retreating from the World," *American Journalism Review*, December/January 2011, http://ajrarchive.org/article.asp?id=4985

61. Mary Walton, "Investigative Shortfall," *American Journalism Review*, September 2010, http://ajrarchive.org/Article.asp?id=4904

62. McChesney and Nichols, *The Death and Life of American Journalism*, 2011.

63. Art Swift, "Americans' Trust in Mass Media Sinks to New Low," *Gallup*, September 14, 2016, http://www.gallup.com/poll/195542/americans-trust-mass-media-sinks-new-low.aspx

64. Pew Research Center, "Press Widely Criticized, But Trusted More than Other Information Sources," *Pew Research Center*, September 22, 2011, http://www.people-press.org/2011/09/22/press-widely-criticized-but-trusted-more-than-other-institutions/#overview

65. Pew, "Press Widely Criticized, But Trusted More than Other Information Sources," 2011; Amy Mitchell, Jeffrey Gottfried, Michael Barthel, and Elisa Shearer, "The Modern News Consumer," *Pew Research Center*, July 7, 2016, http://www.journalism.org/2016/07/07/trust-and-accuracy/

66. Bernard Goldberg, *Bias: A CBS Insider Exposes How the Media Distorts the News* (Washington, DC: Regnery Publishing, 2001); Tim Groseclose, *Left Turn: How Liberal Media Bias Distorts the American Mind* (New York: St. Martin's Press, 2012).

67. S. Robert Lichter, Stanley Rothman, and Linda S. Lichter, *The Media Elite: America's New Powerbrokers* (Winter Park, FL: Hastings House, 1990); David H. Weaver and G. Cleveland Wilhoit, *The American Journalist in the 1990s: U.S. News People at the End of an Era* (New York: Routledge, 1996); Media Research Center, "The Liberal Media: Every Poll Shows Journalists are More Liberal than the American Public—And the Public Knows it," *Media Research Center*, 2017, http://www.mrc.org/special-reports/liberal-mediaevery-poll-shows-journalists-are-more-liberal-american-public-%E2%80%94-and

68. David Croteau, "Examining the 'Liberal Media' Claim," *Fairness and Accuracy in Reporting*, June 1, 1998, http://fair.org/press-release/examining-the-quotliberal-media quot-claim/

69. Dave D'Alesio and Mike Allen, "Media Bias in Presidential Elections: A Meta-Analysis," *Journal of Communication*, 50, no. 4 (2000): 133–56.

70. Political communication is my primary field of scholarly inquiry. In my two decades of studying the media, I have seen very few academic studies that allege a liberal bias in the media. Instead, numerous studies claim that the media share a broader bias in favor of news that undermines government in general. Other studies claim a pro-business bias in the news, or a pro-government bias. But the field is very far from a consensus that the media are liberally biased. Most studies simply do not support this claim.

71. Halpin, et al., "The Structural Imbalance of Political Talk Radio," 2007.

72. Justin McCarthy, "Trust in Mass Media Returns to All-Time Low," *Gallup*, September 17, 2014, http://www.gallup.com/poll/176042/trust-mass-media-returns-time-low.aspx

73. Anthony DiMaggio, "Bias in the Eye of the Beholder," *Counterpunch*, October 11, 2011. http://www.counterpunch.org/2011/10/11/bias-in-the-eye-of-the-beholder/

74. Paul A. Beck, "Voters 'Intermediation Environments in the 1988 Presidential Contest," *Public Opinion Quarterly* 55, no. 3 (1991): 371–94; Russell J. Dalton, Paul A. beck, and Robert Huckfeldt, "Partisan Cues and the Media: Information Flows in the 1992 Presidential Election," *American Political Science Review*, 92, no. 1 (1998): 111–26.

75. Glenn J. Hansen and Hyunjung Kim, "Is the Media Biased Against Me? A Meta-Analysis of the Hostile Media Effect Research," *Communication Research Reports*, 28, no. 2 (2011): 169–79; Daniel Quackenbush, "Public Perceptions of Media Bias: A Meta-Analysis of American Media Outlets During the 2012 Presidential Election," *Elon University*, 2013, http://www.elon.edu/docs/e-web/academics/communications/research/vol4no2/05danielquackenbushejfall13.pdf

76. Limbaugh routinely refers to the media as the "drive-by media" in their alleged opposition to conservatives. For more on Hannity's claims of a liberal media, see: Sean Hannity, *Let Freedom Ring: Winning the War of Liberty over Liberalism* (New York: William Morrow, 2004); Media Matters Staff, "Sean Hannity: Why Should Mainstream Journalists 'Have a Seat in the White House Press Room,'" *Media Matters for America*, November 22, 2016, http://mediamatters.org/video/2016/11/22/sean-hannity-why-should-mainstream-journalists-have-seat-white-house-press-room/214608; Sean Hannity, "Left-Wing Media Stunned that Trump Hits Back, *Foxnews.com*, January 13, 2017, http://www.foxnews.com/opinion/2017/01/13/sean-hannity-left-wing-media-stunned-that-trump-hits-back.html

77. Jonathan M. Ladd, *Why Americans Hate the Media and How it Matters* (Princeton, NJ: Princeton University Press, 2011).

78. Thomas E. Patterson, "Pre-Primary News Coverage of the 2016 Presidential Race: Trump's Rise, Sander's Emergence, Clinton's Struggle," *Shorenstein Center on Media, Politics, and Public Policy*, June 13, 2016, https://shorensteincenter.org/pre-primary-news-coverage-2016-trump-clinton-sanders/

79. Eliza Collins, "Les Moonves: Trump's Run is 'Damn Good for CBS,'" *Politico*, February 29, 2016, http://www.politico.com/blogs/on-media/2016/02/les-moonves-trump-cbs-220001

80. Vappu Tyska, *Youth and Society: The Long and Winding Road* (Toronto: Canadian Scholars Press, 2008).

81. Katherine A. Beckett and Theodore Sasson, *The Politics of Injustice: Crime and Punishment in America* (Thousand Oaks, CA: Sage, 2003).

82. Mark Jurkowitz, Paul Hitlin, Amy Mitchell, Laura Santhanam, Steve Adams, Monica Anderson, and Nancy Vogt, "The Changing TV News Landscape," *Project for Excellence in Journalism*, 2013, http://www.stateofthethemedia.org/2013/special-reports-landing-page/the-changing-tv-news-landscape/

83. Scott Stossel, "The Man who Counts the Killings," *The Atlantic*, May 1997, https://www.theatlantic.com/magazine/archive/1997/05/the-man-who-counts-the-killings/376850/

84. James Shanahan and Michael Morgan, *Television and its Viewers: Cultivation Theory and Research* (Cambridge: Cambridge University Press, 1999).

85. Beckett and Sasson, *The Politics of Injustice*, 2003.

86. Larry J. Sabato and Mark Stencel, *Peepshow: Media and Politics in an Age of Scandal* (Lanham, MD: Rowman and Littlefield, 2000).

87. CNN, "Poll: Too Much Lewinsky Coverage," *CNN.com*, January 29, 1998, http://edition.cnn.com/ALLPOLITICS/1998/01/29/poll/

88. Jonathan Mermin, *Debating War and Peace: Media Coverage of U.S. Intervention in the Post-Vietnam Era* (Princeton, NJ: Princeton University Press, 1999); W. Lance

Bennett, Regina G. Lawrence, and Steven Livingston, *When the Press Fails: Political Power and the News Media from Iraq to Katrina* (Chicago: University of Chicago Press, 2007); DiMaggio, *The Politics of Persuasion*, 2017; Bonn, *Mass Deception*, 2010; Mark Major, *The Unilateral Presidency and the News Media: The Politics of Framing Executive Power* (New York: Palgrave, 2014).

89. Herman and Chomsky, *Manufacturing Consent*, 1988.

90. Anthony R. DiMaggio, *Mass Media, Mass Propaganda: Examining American News in the "War on Terror"* (Lanham, MD: Lexington Books, 2008).

91. Leon V. Sigal, *Reporters and Officials: The Organization and Politics of Newsmaking* (Lexington, MA: DC Heath & Co., 1973); Steve Rendall and Tara Broughel, "Amplifying Officials, Squelching Dissent," *Fairness and Accuracy in Reporting*, May 1, 2003, http://fair.org/extra/amplifying-officials-squelching-dissent/; DiMaggio, *The Politics of Persuasion*, 2017.

92. DiMaggio, *Mass Media, Mass Propaganda*, 2008.

93. Mike Mount, "Hussein's Iraq and al Qaeda Not Linked, Pentagon Says," *CNN.com*, March 13, 2008, http://www.cnn.com/2008/US/03/13/alqaeda.saddam/; Julian Borger, "There Were No Weapons of Mass Destruction in Iraq," *Guardian*, October 7, 2004, https://www.theguardian.com/world/2004/oct/07/usa.iraq1

94. DiMaggio, *Selling War, Selling Hope*, 2015.

95. Bartholomew H. Sparrow, Uncertain Guardians: *The News Media as a Political Institution* (Baltimore, MD: Johns Hopkins University Press, 1999).

96. Anthony DiMaggio, "Bigotry for Profit and 'Fun': Traversing the Wasteland of U.S. Election News," *Counterpunch*, October 10, 2016, http://www.counterpunch.org/2016/10/10/87468/

97. Neil Postman, *Amusing Ourselves to Death: Public Discourse in the Age of Showbusiness* (New York: Penguin, 2005).

98. Chris Cilliza, "Sean Spicer Held a Press Conference. He Didn't Take Questions. Or Tell the Whole Truth," *The Washington Post*, January 21, 2017, https://www.washingtonpost.com/news/the-fix/wp/2017/01/21/sean-spicer-held-a-press-conference-he-didnt-take-questions-or-tell-the-whole-truth/?utm_term=.57de1fc14718

99. Cillizza, "Sean Spicer Held a Press Conference," 2017; Lori Rorbertson and Robert Farley, "Fact Check: The Controversy Over Trump's Inauguration Crowd Size," *USA Today*, January 24, 2017, http://www.usatoday.com/story/news/politics/2017/01/24/fact-check-inauguration-crowd-size/96984496/

100. Eric Bradner, "Conway: Trump White House Offered 'Alternative Facts' on Crowd Size," *CNN.com*, January 23, 2017, http://www.cnn.com/2017/01/22/politics/kellyanne-conway-alternative-facts/

101. Linda Qiu, "Fact Check: Trump Blasts 'Fake News' and Repeats Inaccurate Claims at CPAC," *The New York Times*, February 24, 2017, https://www.nytimes.com/2017/02/24/us/politics/fact-check-trump-blasts-fake-news-and-repeats-inaccurate-claims-at-cpac.html; Rebecca Savransky, "Trump Berates CNN Reporter: 'You are Fake News,'" *The Hill*, January 11, 2017, http://thehill.com/homenews/administration/313777-trump-berates-cnn-reporter-for-fake-news

102. Michael Shear and Emmarie Huetteman, "Trump Repeats Lie About Popular Vote in Meeting with Lawmakers," *The New York Times*, January 23, 2017, https://www.nytimes.com/2017/01/23/us/politics/donald-trump-congress-democrats.html; Julie Hirschfeld Davis and Matthew Rosenberg, "With False Claims, Trump Attacks Media on Turnout and Intelligence Rift," *The New York Times*, January 21, 2017, https://www.nytimes.com/2017/01/21/us/politics/trump-white-house-briefing-inauguration-crowd-size.html; Linda Qiu, "Fact Check: What Trump Got Wrong at His Rally," *The New York Times*, February 18, 2017, https://www.nytimes.com/2017/02/18/us/politics/fact-check-trump-florida-rally.html; Qiu, "Fact Check: Trump Blasts 'Fake News' and Repeats Inaccurate Claims at CPAC," 2017; Dan Barry, "In a Swirl of 'Untruths' and 'Falsehoods,' Calling a Lie a Lie," *The New York Times*, January 25, 2017, https://www.nytimes.com/2017/01/25/business/media/donald-trump-lie-media.html; Chris Cillizza, "Donald Trump's Streak of Falsehoods Now Stands at 33 Days," *The Washington Post*, February 21, 2017, https://www.washingtonpost.com/news/the-fix/wp/2017/02/21/donald-trumps-unbroken-streak-of-falsehoods-now-stands-at-33-days/?utm_term=.da21a3d87b4b; Eli Watkins, "Jake Tapper Spars with Kellyanne Conway over WH Falsehoods," *CNN.com*, February 8, 2017, http://www.cnn.com/2017/02/07/politics/kellyanne-conway-jake-tapper-interview-cnntv/

103. Cillizza, "Donald Trump's Streak of Falsehoods Now Stands at 33 Days," 2017.

104. Betsy Klein, "Comparing Donald Trump and Barack Obama's Inaugural Crowd Sizes," *CNN.com*, January 21, 2017, http://www.cnn.com/2017/01/20/politics/donald-trump-barack-obama-inauguration-crowd-size/; Camila Domonoske, "Trump Adviser Repeats Baseless Claims of Voter Fraud in New Hampshire," *National Public Radio*, February 12, 2017, http://www.npr.org/sections/thetwo-way/2017/02/12/514837432/trump-adviser-repeats-baseless-claims-of-voter-fraud-in-new-hampshire; AJ Willingham, "Here's What Actually Happened in Bowling Green," *CNN.com*, February 3, 2017, http://www.cnn.com/2017/02/03/politics/bowling-green-not-massacre-terrorists-trnd/; Fox News, "Spicer Takes Heat for Citing 'Atlanta' Terror Attack, Says he Meant Orlando," *Foxnews.com*, February 9, 2017, http://www.foxnews.com/politics/2017/02/09/spicer-takes-heat-for-citing-atlanta-terror-attack-says-meant-orlando.html; Johan Ahlander, "Sweden Hits Back at Trump, Defends Generous Immigration Policies," *Reuters*, February 23, 2017, http://www.reuters.com/article/us-usa-trump-sweden-idUSKBN1622KH; J. Weston Phippen, "Trump Blames his Rift with the CIA on the Media," *The Atlantic*, January 21, 2017, https://www.theatlantic.com/politics/archive/2017/01/trump-speaks-with-cia/514052/; Philip Bump, "President Trump is Now Speculating that the Media is Covering up Terrorist Attacks," *The Washington Post*, February 6, 2017, https://www.washingtonpost.com/news/politics/wp/2017/02/06/president-trump-is-now-speculating-that-the-media-is-covering-up-terrorist-attacks/?utm_term=.965396e6b291; Jeremy Diamond, "Trump Falsely Claims U.S. Murder Rate is 'Highest' in 47 Years," *CNN.com*, February 7, 2017, http://www.cnn.com/2017/02/07/politics/donald-trump-murder-rate-fact-check/; Tal Kopan, Lauren Fox, and Phil Mattingly, "Trump Again Falsely Blames the Democrats for his Administration's Family Separations," *CNN.com*, June 16, 2018, https://www.cnn.com/2018/06/15/politics/family-separation-democrats-trump/index.html

105. Thomas E. Patterson, "Pre-Primary News Coverage of the 2016 Presidential Race: Trump's Rise, Sanders' Emergence, Clinton's Struggle," *Shorenstein Center on Media, Politics, and Policy*, June 13, 2006, http://shorensteincenter.org/pre-primary-news-coverage-2016-trump-clinton-sanders/

106. Callum Borchers, "White House Blocks CNN, New York Times from Press Briefing Hours after Trump Slams Media," *The Washington Post*, February 24, 2017, https://www.washingtonpost.com/news/the-fix/wp/2017/02/24/white-house-blocks-cnn-new-york-times-from-press-briefing-hours-after-trump-slams-media/?utm_term=.10d29ccca307; Max Greenwood, "AP, Time Skip WH Briefing After Other News Outlets Excluded," *The Hill*, February 24, 2017, http://thehill.com/homenews/administration/321057-ap-time-magazine-boycott-spicer-press-gaggle-after-other-news-outlets

107. Elizabeth Zwirz, "Sarah Sanders Slams CNN Star Jim Acosta in Tense Briefing: 'It's Hard for You to Understand Even Short Sentences,'" *Foxnews.com*, June 15, 2017, http://www.foxnews.com/politics/2018/06/14/sarah-sanders-slams-cnn-star-jim-acosta-in-tense-briefing-its-hard-for-to-understand-even-short-sentences.html

108. Columbia Journalism Review, "Censorship: How Often and Why," *Pew Research Center*, April 30, 2000, http://www.people-press.org/2000/04/30/self-censorship-how-often-and-why/

109. Lawrence Soley, "'The Power of the Press has a Price,'" *Fairness and Accuracy in Reporting*, July 1, 1997, http://fair.org/extra/the-power-of-the-press-has-a-price/

110. Adam Curtis, Century of the Self, *BBC 2*, 2002.

111. Leach, *Land of Desire*, 1994.

112. Curtis, "Century of the Self," 2002.

113. Edward Bernays, *Propaganda* (New York: Ig Publishing, 2004).

114. Bernays, *Propaganda*, 2004.

115. Curtis, "Century of the Self," 2002; Joshua Zeitz, *Flapper: A Madcap Story of Sex, Style, Celebrity, and the Women Who Made America Modern* (New York: Broadway Books, 2007); Larry Tye, *The Father of Spin: Edward L. Bernays and the Birth of Public Relations* (London: Picador, 2002); Stuart Ewen, *PR! A Social History of Spin* (New York: Basic Books, 1996).

116. John Stauber and Sheldon Rampton, *Toxic Sludge is Good for You: Lies, Damn Lies, and the Public Relations Industry* (Monroe, ME: Common Courage Press, 2002).

117. Edward Jay Epstein, "Have You Ever Tried to Sell a Diamond?" *The Atlantic*, February 1982, https://www.theatlantic.com/magazine/archive/1982/02/have-you-ever-tried-to-sell-a-diamond/304575/

118. Epstein, "Have You Ever Tried to Sell a Diamond?" 1982.

119. Epstein, "Have You Ever Tried to Sell a Diamond?" 1982.

120. Epstein, "Have You Ever Tried to Sell a Diamond?" 1982.

121. Epstein, "Have You Ever Tried to Sell a Diamond?" 1982.

122. Mark Achbar, "Manufacturing Consent: Noam Chomsky and the Media," *Zeitgeist Films*, 1993.

123. Annie Lowrey, "Changed Life of the Poor: Better Off, But Far Behind," *The New York Times*, April 30, 2014, https://www.nytimes.com/2014/05/01/business/economy/changed-life-of-the-poor-squeak-by-and-buy-a-lot.html?_r=0

Chapter 12

1. Gallup, "Trump Job Approval (Weekly)," *Gallup*, 2018, http://news.gallup.com/poll/203207/trump-job-approval-weekly.aspx; Polling Report, "Quinnipiac Poll: Congress Job Rating," *Pollingreport.com*, February 2–5, 2018, http://www.pollingreport.com/CongJob.htm

2. Pew Research Center, "Majorities Express Favorable Opinions of Several Federal Agencies, Including the FBI," *Pew Research Center*, February 14, 2018, http://www.people-press.org/2018/02/14/majorities-express-favorable-opinions-of-several-federal-agencies-including-the-fbi/

3. Lydia Saad, "Conservatives Hang on to Ideology Lead by a Thread," *Gallup*, January 11, 2016, https://news.gallup.com/poll/188129/conservatives-hang-ideology-lead-thread.aspx

4. Pew, "Beyond Distrust," 2015.

5. Polling Report, "Gallup Poll, April 6–10, 2016," *Pollingreport.com*, April 2016, http://www.pollingreport.com/budget.htm

6. Pew Research Center, "Monthly Poll, August 2016," *Pew Research Center*.

7. Angelina E. Theodorou, "Americans are in the Middle of the Pack Globally When it Comes to Importance of Religion," *Pew Research Center*, December 23, 2015, http://www.pewresearch.org/fact-tank/2015/12/23/americans-are-in-the-middle-of-the-pack-globally-when-it-comes-to-importance-of-religion/

8. Pew Research Center, "Attendance at Religious Services," *Pew Research Center*, 2017, http://www.pewforum.org/religious-landscape-study/attendance-at-religious-services/

9. Rebecca Riffkin, "In U.S., Support for Daily Prayer in Schools Dips Slightly," *Gallup*, September 25, 2014, http://www.gallup.com/poll/177401/support-daily-prayer-schools-dips-slightly.aspx

10. Gallup, "Evolution, Creationism, Intelligent Design," *Gallup*, 2017, http://www.gallup.com/poll/21814/evolution-creationism-intelligent-design.aspx; William Saletan, "God's Work?" *Slate*, December 4, 2014, http://www.slate.com/articles/health_and_science/human_nature/2014/12/creationism_poll_how_many_americans_believe_the_bible_is_literal_inerrant.html

11. Andrew Dugan, "Solid Majority Continue to Support Death Penalty," *Gallup*, October 15, 2015, http://www.gallup.com/poll/186218/solid-majority-continue-support-death-penalty.aspx

12. Gallup, "Abortion," *Gallup*, 2017, http://www.gallup.com/poll/1576/abortion.aspx

13. Gallup, "Marriage," *Gallup*, 2017, http://www.gallup.com/poll/117328/marriage.aspx

14. Sara Kehaulani Goo, "What Americans Want to do About Illegal Immigration," *Pew Research Center*, August 24, 2015, http://www.pewresearch.org/fact-tank/2015/08/24/what-americans-want-to-do-about-illegal-immigration/

15. CNN/ORC, "CNN/ORC International Poll," *CNN/ORC*, June 20, 2016, http://i2.cdn.turner.com/cnn/2016/images/06/20/cnn_orc_poll_june_20.pdf

16. Thomas Frank, *What's the Matter with Kansas? How Conservatives Won the Heart of America* (New York: Holt, 2005).

17. Andrew Gelman, *Red State, Blue State, Rich State, Poor State: Why Americans Vote the Way They Do* (Princeton, NJ: Princeton University Press, 2009); Bartels, *Unequal Democracy*, 2010; Anthony DiMaggio, "Capitalism in Crisis: Getting Ready for Change in the Age of Trump," *Counterpunch*, March 13, 2017, https://www.counterpunch.org/2017/03/13/capitalism-in-crisis-getting-ready-for-change-in-the-age-of-trump/; DiMaggio, "Election Con 2016," 2017.

18. Jeffrey M. Jones, "On Social Ideology, the Left Catches Up to the Right," *Gallup*, May 22, 2015, http://www.gallup.com/poll/183386/social-ideology-left-catches-right.aspx

19. GlobeScan, "Sharp Drop in American Enthusiasm for Free Market, Poll Shows," *Common Dreams*, April 6, 2011, http://www.commondreams.org/news/2011/04/06/sharp-drop-american-enthusiasm-free-market-poll-shows

20. Andrew Dugan, "In U.S., Half Still Say Gov't Regulates Business Too Much," *Gallup*, September 18, 2015, http://www.gallup.com/poll/185609/half-say-gov-regulates-business.aspx

21. Gallup, "Taxes," *Gallup*, 2017, http://www.gallup.com/poll/1714/taxes.aspx; Jim Norman, "Most Americans in 15 Years Say Their Bill Is Too High," *Gallup*, April 14, 2016, http://www.gallup.com/poll/190778/americans-years-say-tax-bill-high.aspx; Erin McClam, "Many Americans Blame 'Government Welfare' for Persistent Poverty, Poll Finds," *NBC News*, June 6, 2013, http://www.nbcnews.com/feature/in-plain-sight/many-americans-blame-government-welfare-persistent-poverty-poll-finds-v18802216

22. Benjamin I. Page and Lawrence R. Jacobs, *Class War? What Americans Really Think about Economic Inequality* (Chicago: University of Chicago Press, 2009).

23. Pew Research Center, "In Deficit Debate, Public Resists Cuts in Entitlements and Aid to Poor" *Pew Research Center*, December 19, 2013, http://www.people-press.org/2013/12/19/in-deficit-debate-public-resists-cuts-in-entitlements-and-aid-to-poor/

Pew Research Center, "Fewer Want Spending to Grow, But Most Cuts Remain Unpopular," *Pew Research Center*, February 10, 2011, http://www.people-press.org/2011/02/10/fewer-want-spending-to-grow-but-most-cuts-remain-unpopular/

24. Pew Research Center, "As Sequester Deadline Looms, Little Support for Cutting Most Programs," *Pew Research Center*, February 22, 2013, http://www.people-press.org/2013/02/22/as-sequester-deadline-looms-little-support-for-cutting-most-programs/

25. Pew, "As Sequester Deadline Looms, Little Support for Cutting Most Programs," 2013.

26. Pew, "As Sequester Deadline Looms, Little Support for Cutting Most Programs," 2013.

27. Pew, "As Sequester Deadline Looms, Little Support for Cutting Most Programs," 2013.

28. Pew, "As Sequester Deadline Looms, Little Support for Cutting Most Programs," 2013.

29. CBS News & New York Times, "CBS News/New York Times Poll," *Polling Report*, May 28–31, 2015, http://www.pollingreport.com/business.htm; CNN & Opinion Research Corporation, "CNN/Opinion Research Corporation Poll," *Polling Report*, July 16–21, 2010, http://www.pollingreport.com/business.htm; Pew Research Center, "Section

2: Views of Government Regulation," *Pew Research Center*, February 23, 2012, http://www.people-press.org/2012/02/23/section-2-views-of-government-regulation/

30. Max Ehrenfreund, "It Looks Like the GOP is Being Abandoned by its Own Voters on a Crucial Issue," *The Washington Post,* June 30, 2016, https://www.washingtonpost.com/news/wonk/wp/2016/06/30/even-most-republicans-now-support-higher-taxes-for-the-rich/; Pew Research Center, "Most See Inequality Growing, but Partisans Differ Over Solutions," *Pew Research Center*, January 23, 2014, http://www.people-press.org/2014/01/23/most-see-inequality-growing-but-partisans-differ-over-solutions/

31. Maggie Fox, "Most in U.S. Want Public Health Option," *Reuters*, December 3, 2009, http://www.reuters.com/article/us-healthcare-usa-poll-idUSTRE5B20OL20091203; Frank Newport, "Majority in U.S. Support Idea of Fed-Funded Healthcare System, *Gallup*, May 16, 2016, http://www.gallup.com/poll/191504/majority-support-idea-fed-funded-healthcare-system.aspx

32. Benjamin I. Page and Marshall M. Bouton, *The Foreign Policy Disconnect: What Americans Want from Our Leaders But Don't Get* (Chicago: University of Chicago Press, 2006).

33. DiMaggio, *Selling War, Selling Hope*, 2015.

34. CNN, "Poll: Opposition to Iraq War at All-Time High," *CNN.com*, September 25, 2006, http://www.cnn.com/2006/POLITICS/08/21/iraq.poll/; CNN, "Poll: 60 Percent of Americans Oppose Iraq War," *CNN.com,* August 9, 2006, http://www.cnn.com/2006/US/08/09/iraq.poll/

35. Scott Wilson and Jon Cohen, "Poll: Nearly Two-Thirds of Americans Say Afghan War Isn't Worth Fighting," *The Washington Post*, March 15, 2011, https://www.washingtonpost.com/world/poll-nearly-two-thirds-of-americans-say-afghan-war-isnt-worth-fighting/2011/03/14/ABRbeEW_story.html

36. Jeffrey M. Jones and Frank Newport, "Slightly Fewer Back ISIS Military Action vs. Past Actions," *Gallup*, September 23, 2014, http://www.gallup.com/poll/177263/slightly-fewer-back-isis-military-action-past-actions.aspx

37. World Public Opinion, "World Publics Favor New Powers for the U.N.," *Worldpublicopinion.net*, May 9, 2007, http://worldpublicopinion.net/world-publics-favor-new-powers-for-the-un/

38. Steven Kull, "Americans on WMD Proliferation," *The Program on International Policy Attitudes*, April 15, 2004, http://www.pipa.org/OnlineReports/WMDProliferation/WMD_Prolif_Apr04/WMDProlif_Apr04_rpt.pdf

39. Jennifer Agiesta, "Poll: Iran Negotiations Popular," *CNN*, March 17, 2015, http://www.cnn.com/2015/03/17/politics/iran-negotiations-gop-letter-poll/

40. Chicago Council on Foreign Relations/Program for International Policy Attitudes (PIPA), "Americans on Promoting Democracy," *PIPA.org*, September 29, 2005, http://www.pipa.org/OnlineReports/AmRole_World/Democratization_Sep05/Democratization_Sep09_rpt_revised.pdf

41. Kristina Wong, "Poll: Americans Want More Action Against ISIS, but Oppose Ground Troops," *The Hill*, November, 16, 2015, http://thehill.com/policy/defense/260313-poll-americans-want-more-action-against-isis-but-oppose-ground-troops

42. CNN/ORC, "CNN/ORC International Poll," *CNN/ORC*, February 3, 2017, http://i2.cdn.turner.com/cnn/2017/images/02/03/rel2a.-.trump.pdf

43. Clearly, Trump sought during the campaign to cultivate American bigotry against Muslims, to build support for a policy that discriminated against Muslim-majority nations. This effort failed, as public support for Muslims grew significantly between 2015 and 2016, to the point where 70 percent of Americans held favorable opinions of Muslims by October 2016, a growth of 17 percentage points from November 2015. For more on changing public opinion, see: Shibley Telhami, "How Trump Changed Americans' View of Islam—for the Better," *The Washington Post*, January 25, 2017, https://www.washingtonpost.com/news/monkey-cage/wp/2017/01/25/americans-dont-support-trumps-ban-on-muslim-immigration/?utm_term=.408dce92ef2b

44. Christopher Ellis and James A. Stimson, *Ideology in America* (Cambridge: Cambridge University Press, 2012).

45. Ellis and Stimson, *Ideology in America*, 2012; James Stimson, *Tides of Consent: How Public Opinion Shapes American Politics* (Cambridge: Cambridge University Press, 2015).

46. Ellis and Stimson, *Ideology in America*, 2012.

47. Pew Research Center, "Political Polarization in the American Public," *Pew Research Center*, June 12, 2014, http://www.people-press.org/2014/06/12/political-polarization-in-the-american-public/

48. Morris Fiorina, "Americans Have Not Become More Politically Polarized," *The Washington Post*, June 23, 2014, https://www.washingtonpost.com/news/monkey-cage/wp/2014/06/23/americans-have-not-become-more-politically-polarized/?utm_term=.1267ad0447ef; Morris Fiorina and Samuel Abrams, *Culture War? The Myth of a Polarized America* (New York: Longman, 2010); Matthew Levendusky, *The Partisan Sort: How Liberals Became Democrats and Conservatives Became Republicans* (Chicago: University of Chicago Press, 2009); Alan I. Abramowitz, *The Disappearing Center: Engaged Citizens, Polarization, and American Democracy* (New Haven, CT: Yale University Press, 2011).

49. Pew Research Center, "5 Facts About America's Political Independents," *Pew Research Center*, July 1, 2016, http://www.pewresearch.org/fact-tank/2016/07/05/5-facts-about-americas-political-independents/ft_16-07-01_independents_conservlib/

50. Howard Zinn, *A People's History of the United States* (New York: Harper Perennial, 2005).; Bill Moyers, "Meaningful Democracy," in *A World of Ideas: Conversations with Thoughtful Men and Women about American Life Today and the Ideas Shaping Our Future* (New York: Doubleday, 1989), 38–58, https://chomsky.info/1988____/

51. Edward Bernays, *Propaganda* (New York: Ig Publishing, 2004); Edward Bernays, *Crystallizing Public Opinion* (New York: Ig Publishing, 2011).

52. Philip E. Converse, "The Nature of Belief Systems in Mass Publics" in *Ideology and Discontent*, ed. David Apter (New York: Collier-Macmillan, 1964).

53. Megan McCluskey, "Watch Jimmy Kimmel Prove People Still Think Obamacare and the Affordable Care Act Are Different Things," *Time*, January 18, 2017, http://time.com/4637918/jimmy-kimmel-obamacare-vs-affordable-care-act/

54. Reid Wilson, "Only 36 Percent of Americans Can Name the Three Branches of Government," *The Washington Post*, September 18, 2014, https://www.washingtonpost.com/

blogs/govbeat/wp/2014/09/18/only-36-percent-of-americans-can-name-the-three-branches-of-government/?utm_term=.b7507c8a8378

55. Wilson, "Only 36 Percent of Americans Can Name the Three Branches of Government," 2014.

56. Elizabeth Mendes, "Americans Down on Congress, OK with Own Representative," *Gallup*, May 9, 2013, http://www.gallup.com/poll/162362/americans-down-congress-own-representative.aspx

57. Converse, "The Nature of Belief Systems in Mass Publics," 1964.

58. George F. Kennan, *American Diplomacy: Sixtieth-Anniversary Expanded Edition* (Chicago: University Of Chicago Press, 2012); Converse, "The Nature of Belief Systems in Mass Publics," 1964.

59. Pew Research Center, "American Trends Panel Poll," *Pew Research Center*, January 2016.

60. Converse, "The Nature of Belief Systems in Mass Publics," 1964.

61. Converse, "The Nature of Belief Systems in Mass Publics," 1964.

62. Converse, "The Nature of Belief Systems in Mass Publics," 1964.

63. John R. Zaller, "Elite Leadership of Mass Opinion: New Evidence from the Gulf War," in *Taken By Storm: The Media, Public Opinion, and U.S. Foreign Policy in the Gulf War*, ed. David L. Paletz (Chicago: University Of Chicago Press, 1994), 186–209.

64. Pew Research Center, "Pew Media Survey," *Pew Research Center*, July 2007.

65. Pew Research Center, "Pew Media Survey," *Pew Research Center*, July 2007.

66. DiMaggio, *The Rise of the Tea Party*, 2011.

67. Demos, "Registering Millions: Celebrating the Success and Potential of the National Voter Registration Act at 20," *Demos.org*, 2017, http://www.demos.org/registering-millions-success-and-potential-national-voter-registration-act-20

68. Michael P. McDonald, "Voter Turnout Demographics," *United States Elections Project*, 2017, http://www.electproject.org/home/voter-turnout/demographics

69. Aaron Smith, "Civic Engagement in the Digital Age," *Pew Research Center*, April 25, 2013, http://www.pewinternet.org/2013/04/25/civic-engagement-in-the-digital-age/

70. Dan Farber, "Palin Weighs in on Health Care Reform," *CBS News*, August 8, 2009, https://www.cbsnews.com/news/palin-weighs-in-on-health-care-reform/

71. Angie Drobnic Holan, "PolitiFact's Lie of the Year: 'Death Panels,'" *Politifact*, December 18, 2009, http://www.politifact.com/truth-o-meter/article/2009/dec/18/politifact-lie-year-death-panels/; Glenn Thrush, "Poll: 41 Percent Believe in Death Panels," *Politico*, September 14, 2009, http://www.politico.com/blogs/on-congress/2009/09/poll-41-percent-believe-in-death-panels-021365

72. Robert Schlesinger, "Party of Nuts: Poll Shows GOP Thinks Obama is Muslim, Socialist," *U.S. News*, March 24, 2010, https://www.usnews.com/opinion/blogs/robert-schlesinger/2010/03/24/party-of-nuts-poll-shows-gop-thinks-obama-is-muslim-socialist

73. Schlesinger, "Party of Nuts: Poll Shows GOP Thinks Obama is Muslim, Socialist," 2010.

74. Sally Greenberg, "State of Confusion: One-Third of American Parents Continue to Link Vaccines and Autism," *The Huffington Post*, April 28, 2014, http://www.huffingtonpost.com/sally-greenberg/vaccines_b_5169266.html

75. Frank Newport, "In U.S., Percentage Saying Vaccines Are Vital Dips Slightly," *Gallup*, March 6, 2015, http://www.gallup.com/poll/181844/percentage-saying-vaccines-vital-dips-slightly.aspx

76. Pew Research Center, "1. Public Views on Climate Change and Climate Scientists," *Pew Research Center*, October 4, 2016, http://www.pewinternet.org/2016/10/04/public-views-on-climate-change-and-climate-scientists/

77. Louis Jacobson, "Yes, Donald Trump Did Call Climate Change a Chinese Hoax," *Politifact*, June 3, 2016, http://www.politifact.com/truth-o-meter/statements/2016/jun/03/hillary-clinton/yes-donald-trump-did-call-climate-change-chinese-h/

78. Zogby, "Zogby America Likely Voters," *Zogby*, August 23–27, 2007, http://www.911truth.org/images/ZogbyPoll2007.pdf

79. Stephanie Condon, "Poll: One in Four Americans Think Obama Was Not Born in U.S.," *CBS News*, April 21, 2011, http://www.cbsnews.com/news/poll-one-in-four-americans-think-obama-was-not-born-in-us/

80. Jess Henig, "Born in the U.S.A.," *Fact Check*, August 21, 2008, http://www.factcheck.org/2008/08/born-in-the-usa/; Robert Farley, "Trump on Birtherism: Wrong, and Wrong," *Fact Check*, September 16, 2016, http://www.factcheck.org/2016/09/trump-on-birtherism-wrong-and-wrong/

81. Pew Reseach Center, "Growing Number of Americans Say Obama is a Muslim," *Pew Reseach Center*, August 18, 2010, http://www.pewforum.org/2010/08/18/growing-number-of-americans-say-obama-is-a-muslim/

82. Sarah Pullam Bailey, "A Startling Number of Americans Believe President Obama is a Muslim," *The Washington Post*, September 14, 2015, https://www.washingtonpost.com/news/acts-of-faith/wp/2015/09/14/a-startling-number-of-americans-still-believe-president-obama-is-a-muslim/?utm_term=.2cec8ca31ee6

83. Emily Guskin and Scott Clement, "Poll: Nearly Half of Americans Say Voter Fraud Occurs Often," *The Washington Post*, September 15, 2016, https://www.washington-post.com/news/the-fix/wp/2016/09/15/poll-nearly-half-of-americans-say-voter-fraud-occurs-often/?utm_term=.b44471394da9

84. Taylor Link, "Poll: Trump Voters Are OK with Using Bowling Green Massacre to Justify Immigration Ban," *Salon*, February 10, 2017, http://www.salon.com/2017/02/10/poll-trump-voters-are-ok-with-using-bowling-green-massacre-to-justify-immigration-ban/

85. Steve Benen, "Trump, His Supporters, and the Persistence of the 'Reality Gap,'" *MSNBC News*, December 9, 2016, http://www.msnbc.com/rachel-maddow-show/trump-his-supporters-and-the-persistence-the-reality-gap

86. Noam Chomsky, "On Democracy," *Chomskyinfo.org*, summer 1996, https://chomsky.info/1996summer/

87. Benjamin I. Page and Robert Y. Shapiro, *The Rational Public: Fifty Years of Trends in Americans' Policy Preferences* (Chicago: University of Chicago Press, 1992).

88. Pew Research Center, "Public Knowledge of Current Affairs Little Changed by News and Information Revolutions," *Pew Research Center*, April 15, 2007, http://www.people-press.org/2007/04/15/public-knowledge-of-current-affairs-little-changed-by-news-and-information-revolutions/

89. Doris A. Graber, *Processing Politics: Learning from Television in the Internet Age* (Chicago: University of Chicago Press, 2001).

90. Samuel Popkin, *The Reasoning Voter: Communication and Persuasion in Presidential Campaigns* (Chicago: University of Chicago Press, 1994).

91. William A. Gamson, *Talking Politics* (Cambridge: Cambridge University Press, 1992).

92. Aaron Smith, Kay Lehman Schlozman, Sidney Verba, and Henry Brady, "The Current State of Civic Engagement in America," *Pew Research Center*, September 1, 2009, http://www.pewinternet.org/2009/09/01/the-current-state-of-civic-engagement-in-america/

93. Gary Jacobson, *The Politics of Congressional Elections* (London: Pearson, 2012).

94. Anthony R. DiMaggio, *When Media Goes to War: Hegemonic Discourse, Public Opinion, and the Limits of Dissent* (New York: Monthly Review Press, 2010).

95. DiMaggio, *When Media Goes to War*, 2010.

96. DiMaggio, *When Media Goes to War*, 2010.

97. DiMaggio, *Selling War, Selling Hope*, 2015.

98. Anthony H. Cordesman, "Trends in Iraqi Violence, Casualties, and Impact of War: 2003–2015," *Center for Strategic and International Studies*, October 5, 2015, https://csis-prod.s3.amazonaws.com/s3fs-public/legacy_files/files/publication/150914_Trends_in_Iraqi_Violence_Casualties.pdf; Rob Stein, "100,000 Civilian Deaths Estimated in Iraq," *The Washington Post*, October 29, 2004, http://www.washingtonpost.com/wp-dyn/articles/A7967-2004Oct28.html; Jomana Karadsheh, "Study: War Blamed for 655,000 Iraqi Deaths," *CNN.com*, October 11, 2006, http://www.cnn.com/2006/WORLD/meast/10/11/iraq.deaths/; Luke Baker, "Iraq Conflict Has Killed a Million Iraqis: Survey," *Reuters*, January 30, 2008, http://www.reuters.com/article/us-iraq-deaths-survey-idUSL3048857920080130

99. DiMaggio, *When Media Goes to War*, 2010.

100. DiMaggio, *Selling War, Selling Hope*, 2015.

101. DiMaggio, *Selling War, Selling Hope*, 2015.

102. DiMaggio, *Selling War, Selling Hope*, 2015.

103. Roper Center, "American Voters and Security Survey," *iPoll*, December 2004.

104. Polling Report, "CBS News Poll, Dec. 9–13, 2016," *Pollingreport.com*, April 2017, http://www.pollingreport.com/enviro.htm

105. Graham Readfearn, "Was That Climate Change? Scientists Are Getting Faster at Linking Extreme Weather to Warming," *The Guardian*, September 14, 2016, https://www.theguardian.com/environment/planet-oz/2016/sep/15/was-that-climate-change-scientists-are-getting-faster-at-linking-extreme-weather-to-warming.

106. Christopher Borick and Barry Rabe, "Fall 2011 National Survey of American Public Opinion on Climate Change," *Issues in Governance Studies*, February 2012, https://www.brookings.edu/wp-content/uploads/2016/06/02_climate_change_rabe_borick.pdf

107. David Wright, "Polls: Support for Obamacare at All-Time High," *CNN*, February 24, 2017, http://www.cnn.com/2017/02/24/politics/pew-survey-obamacare-support-record-high/

108. Victoria Colliver, "Republicans Face Anger Over Obamacare Repeal During Town Halls," *Politico*, February 4, 2017, http://www.politico.com/story/2017/02/republicans-obamacare-repeal-town-halls-234651

109. DiMaggio, *The Politics of Persuasion*, 2017.

110. DiMaggio, *The Politics of Persuasion*, 2017.

111. Lymari Morales, "Obama's Birth Certificate Convinces Some, But Not All, Skeptics," *Gallup*, May 13, 2011, http://www.gallup.com/poll/147530/obama-birth-certificate-convinces-not-skeptics.aspx

112. David Folkenflik, "Obama Chides Media for Role in 'Birther' Conroversy," *NPR*, April 27, 2011, http://www.npr.org/2011/04/27/135778712/role-of-media-in-the-birther-controversy; Pew Research Center, "Too Much Coverage: Birth Certificate, Royal Wedding," *Pew Research Center*, May 3, 2011, http://www.people-press.org/2011/05/03/too-much-coverage-birth-certificate-royal-wedding/

113. Anthony DiMaggio, "Mediated Ignorance," *CounterPunch*, June 24, 2011, http://www.counterpunch.org/2011/06/24/mediated-ignorance/

114. DiMaggio, *The Rise of the Tea Party*, 2011.

115. DiMaggio, *The Rise of the Tea Party*, 2011.

116. Anthony DiMaggio, " 'Conspiracy' Science: Mass Media and the Conservative Backlash on Global Warming," *MR Online*, March 10, 2010, https://mronline.org/2010/03/10/conspiracy-science-mass-media-and-the-conservative-backlash-on-global-warming/

117. DiMaggio, *The Politics of Persuasion*, 2017.

Chapter 13

1. Frederick deBoer, "Corporations are Cracking Down on Free Speech Inside the Office—and Out," *The Washington Post*, August 10, 2017, https://www.washingtonpost.com/outlook/corporations-are-cracking-down-on-free-speech-inside-the-office--and-out/2017/08/10/6a98809a-7baf-11e7-a669-b400c5c7e1cc_story.html?utm_term=.61960dd1497d

2. Joe Capozzi, "After Irma, Nursing Home Worker Fired After Seeking Help on Facebook," *Palm Beach Post*, September 22, 2017, http://www.palmbeachpost.com/news/after-irma-nursing-home-worker-fired-after-seeking-help-facebook/J2llNH5ljV4EeV2BdEiqPM/

3. Bruce Barry, *Speechless: The Erosion of Free Expression in the American Workplace* (Oakland, CA: Berrett-Koehler Publishers, 2007).

4. Jodi S. Cohen, "University of Illinois Oks $875,000 Settlement to End Steven Salaita Dispute," *Chicago Tribune*, November 12, 2015, http://www.chicagotribune.com/news/local/breaking/ct-steven-salaita-settlement-met-20151112-story.html

5. Karl Giberson, "Discovery Institute Still Undermining Science," *Huffington Post*, November 5, 2016, http://www.huffingtonpost.com/karl-giberson-phd/discovery-institute-still_b_8479280.html

6. NOVA, "Intelligent Design on Trial," *PBS*, November 13, 2007, http://www.pbs.org/wgbh/nova/evolution/intelligent-design-trial.html

7. Laurie Goodstein, "Judge Bars 'Intelligent Design' From Pa. Classes," *The New York Times*, December 20, 2005, http://www.nytimes.com/2005/12/20/science/sciencespecial2/judge-bars-intelligent-design-from-pa-classes.html

8. Mark Hensch and Jesse Byrnes, "Trump: 'Frankly, We're Having Problems with the Muslims,'" *The Hill*, March 22, 2016, http://thehill.com/blogs/ballot-box/presidential-races/273857-trump-frankly-were-having-problems-with-the-muslims; Dean Obeidallah, "Donald Trump's Horrifying Word About Muslims," *CNN.com*, November 21, 2015, http://www.cnn.com/2015/11/20/opinions/obeidallah-trump-anti-muslim/; Jenna Johnson and David Weigel, "Donald Trump Calls for 'Total' Ban on Muslims Entering United States," *The Washington Post*, December 8, 2015, https://www.washingtonpost.com/politics/2015/12/07/e56266f6-9d2b-11e5-8728-1af6af208198_story.html?utm_term=.b1cfead5fba4

9. Rebecca Savransky, "Guiliani: Trump Asked Me How to Do a Muslim Ban 'Legally,'" *The Hill*, January 29, 2017, http://thehill.com/homenews/administration/316726-giuliani-trump-asked-me-how-to-do-a-muslim-ban-legally

10. Glenn Thrush, "Trump's New Travel Ban Blocks Migrants from Six Nations, Sparing Iraq," *The New York Times*, March 6, 2017, https://www.nytimes.com/2017/03/06/us/politics/travel-ban-muslim-trump.html

11. Thrush, "Trump's New Travel Ban Blocks Migrants from Six Nations, Sparing Iraq," 2017.

12. Laura Jarrett, "Trump Admin to Appeal Travel Ban Rulings 'Soon,'" *CNN.com*, March 16, 2017, http://www.cnn.com/2017/03/15/politics/travel-ban-blocked/

13. Vivian Salama and Alicia A. Caldwell, "DHS Intelligence Report Disputes Threat Posed by 7 Travel Ban Nations," *Associated Press*, February 14, 2017, http://www.chicagotribune.com/news/nationworld/ct-dhs-report-travel-ban-nations-20170224-story.html

14. Jennifer Agiesta, "CNN/ORC Poll: Majority Oppose Trump's Travel Ban," *CNN.com*, February 3, 2017, http://www.cnn.com/2017/02/03/politics/donald-trump-travel-ban-poll/

15. Shibley Telhami, "How Trump Changed Americans' View of Islam—for the Better," *The Washington Post*, January 25, 2017, https://www.washingtonpost.com/news/monkey-cage/wp/2017/01/25/americans-dont-support-trumps-ban-on-muslim-immigration/?utm_term=.5fbb0c80728d

16. Telhami, "How Trump Changed Americans' View of Islam—for the Better," 2017.

17. Glenn Greenwald, "NSA Collecting Phone Records of Millions of Verizon Customers Daily," *Guardian*, June 6, 2013, https://www.theguardian.com/world/2013/jun/06/nsa-phone-records-verizon-court-order

18. Jason Leopold, "Bush Authorized Domestic Spying Before 9/11," *Truthout*, January 13, 2006, http://truth-out.org/archive/component/k2/item/59967:jason-leopold--bush-authorized-domestic-spying-before-911

19. Jonathan Stein and Tim Dickinson, "Lie by Lie: A Timeline of How We Got into Iraq," *Mother Jones*, September/October 2006, http://www.motherjones.com/politics/2011/12/leadup-iraq-war-timeline; Francie Grace, "9/10 Message: 'Tomorrow is Zero Hour,'" *CBS News*, June 21, 2002, http://www.cbsnews.com/news/9-10-message-tomorrow-is-zero-hour/

20. Kent Greenfield and Adam Winkler, "The U.S. Supreme Court's Cultivation of Corporate Personhood," *The Atlantic*, June 24, 2015, https://www.theatlantic.com/politics/archive/2015/06/raisins-hotels-corporate-personhood-supreme-court/396773/

21. Mark E. Neely, Jr., *The Fate of Liberty: Abraham Lincoln and Civil Liberties* (Oxford: Oxford University Press, 1992).

22. David Greenberg, "Lincoln's Crackdown," *Slate*, November 30, 2011, http://www.slate.com/articles/news_and_politics/history_lesson/2001/11/lincolns_crackdown.html

23. Miller Center, "Woodrow Wilson: Domestic Affairs," *University of Virginia*, 2017, https://millercenter.org/president/wilson/domestic-affairs

24. Jay Feldman, *Manufacturing Hysteria: A History of Scapegoating, Surveillance, and Secrecy in Modern America* (New York: Anchor Books, 2011).

25. Gregory Dehler, "Palmer Raids: United States History," *Encyclopedia Britannica*, 2017, https://www.britannica.com/topic/Palmer-Raids

26. Joseph McCarthy, "Telegram from Senator Joseph McCarthy to President Harry S. Truman," *National Archives*, 2017, https://www.archives.gov/education/lessons/mccarthy-telegram

27. American Masters, "Arthur Miller, Elia Kazan, and the Blacklist: None Without Sin," *PBS*, August 23, 2006, http://www.pbs.org/wnet/americanmasters/arthur-miller-mccarthyism/484/

28. Arthur Herman, *Joseph McCarthy: Reexamining the Life and Legacy of America's Most Hated Senator* (New York: Free Press, 1999).

29. Ward Churchill and Jim Vander Wall, *The COINTELPRO Papers: Documents from the FBI's Secret Wars Against Dissent in the United States* (Boston, MA: South End Press, 1990).

30. Churchill and Vander Wall, *The COINTELPRO Papers*, 1990.

31. Peter Irons, *Justice at War: The Story of the Japanese-American Internment Cases* (Berkley, CA: University of California Press, 1993).

32. Irons, *Justice at War*, 1993.

33. Associated Press, "Lawsuit Brought by Muslims Rounded up after 9/11 Gets Go-Ahead from Court," *Guardian*, June 21, 2015, https://www.theguardian.com/us-news/2015/jun/21/lawsuit-muslims-september-11-roundup-abuse

34. Steven Brill, *After: How America Confronted the September 12 Era* (New York: Simon and Schuster, 2003).

35. Pew Research Center, "Muslim Americans: No Signs of Growth in Alienation or Support for Extremism," *Pew Research Center*, August 30, 2011, http://www.people-press.org/2011/08/30/muslim-americans-no-signs-of-growth-in-alienation-or-support-for-extremism/; Shibley Telhami, "What Americans Really Think About Muslims and Islam," *Brookings Institute*, December 9, 2015, https://www.brookings.edu/blog/markaz/2015/12/09/what-americans-really-think-about-muslims-and-islam/

Chapter 14

1. Michael D. Shear and Julie Hirschfeld Davis, "Trump Moves to End DACA and Calls on Congress to Act," *The New York Times*, September 5, 2017, https://www.nytimes.com/2017/09/05/us/politics/trump-daca-dreamers-immigration.html

2. Shear and Davis, "Trump Moves to End DACA and Calls on Congress to Act," 2017.

3. Danielle Kurtzleben, "Fact Check: Are DACA Recipients Stealing Jobs Away from Other Americans?" *National Public Radio*, September 6, 2017, http://www.npr.org/2017/09/06/548882071/fact-check-are-daca-recipients-stealing-jobs-away-from-other-americans; Elliot Spagat and Chris Rugaber, "Fact Check: What the Trump Administration Said About DACA," *Chicago Tribune*, September 5, 2017, http://www.chicagotribune.com/news/nationworld/politics/factcheck/ct-fact-check-daca-20170905-story.html

4. Serena Marshall, "Obama has Deported More People Than Any Other President," *ABC News*, August 29, 2016, http://abcnews.go.com/Politics/obamas-deportation-policy-numbers/story?id=41715661

5. Louis Jacobson, "Has Barack Obama Deported More People Than any Other President in U.S. History?" *Politifact*, August 10, 2012, http://www.politifact.com/truth-o-meter/statements/2012/aug/10/american-principles-action/has-barack-obama-deported-more-people-any-other-pr/

6. Michael D. Shear and Robert Pear, "Obama's Immigration Plan Could Shield Five Million People," *The New York Times*, November 19, 2014, https://www.nytimes.com/2014/11/20/us/politics/obamacare-unlikely-for-undocumented-immigrants.html

7. Lauren Etter, "Young 'Dreamers' See Peril as Trump Plans for Deportations," *Bloomberg News*, November 14, 2016, https://www.bloomberg.com/politics/articles/2016-11-14/young-dreamers-see-peril-as-trump-plans-for-mass-deportations

8. P. J. Tobia, "No Country for Lost Kids," *PBS Newshour*, June 20, 2014, http://www.pbs.org/newshour/updates/country-lost-kids/

9. Halimah Abdullah, "Immigrants or Refugees? A Difference with Political Consequences," *CNN.com*, July 17, 2014, http://www.cnn.com/2014/07/17/politics/immigration-border-crisis-refugee-politics/

10. Esther Yu Hsi Lee, "No, Obama Didn't Create the Migrant Children Crisis," *Think Progress*, June 20, 2014, https://thinkprogress.org/no-obama-didnt-create-the-migrant-children-crisis-bb94da37ec86#.g5nmaqxa4; Albor Ruiz, "Turning Away Children at the U.S. Border Who Are Fleeing Poverty and Violence in Central America is Cruel," *New York Daily News*, July 6, 2014, http://www.nydailynews.com/new-york/turning-fleeing-central-american-children-u-s-border-cruel-article-1.1854642; E. J. Dionne, "Bordering on Heartless," *The Washington Post*, July 13, 2014, https://www.washingtonpost.com/opinions/ej-dionne-republicans-are-bordering-on-heartless/2014/07/13/cc152306-092e-11e4-8a6a-19355c7e870a_story.html?utm_term=.822772f07749

11. Cathy Lynn Grossman, "Survey: Most Americans See Migrant Central American Children as Refugees," *The Washington Post*, August 1, 2014, https://www.washingtonpost.com/local/survey-most-americans-see-migrant-central-american-children-as-refugees/2014/08/01/eb7682c6-1806-11e4-9e3b-7f2f110c6265_story.html?utm_term=.8042d819883b

12. Esther Yu Hsi Lee, "Obama Plans to Allow Some Central American Kids to Apply for Refugee Status from Home," *Think Progress*, October 1, 2014, https://thinkprogress.org/obama-plans-to-allow-some-central-american-kids-to-apply-for-refugee-status-from-home-d5034e5f8908#.ruvsdphlp

13. Lee, "No, Obama Didn't Create the Migrant Children Crisis," 2014.

14. Preston, "U.S. Will Step up Deportations, Focusing on Central Americans," 2016.

15. Ted Cruz, "Cruz Immigration Plan," *Tedcruz.org*, 2017, https://www.tedcruz.org/cruz-immigration-plan/

16. Daily Mail, "We Will Build a Great Wall and Mexico Will Pay: Trump in August," *Daily Mail*, 2017, http://www.dailymail.co.uk/video/news/video-1325329/Trump-build-great-wall-Mexico-pay.html

17. Philip Bump, "Surprise! Donald Trump is Wrong About Immigrants and Crime," *The Washington Post*, July 2, 2015, https://www.washingtonpost.com/news/the-fix/wp/2015/07/02/surprise-donald-trump-is-wrong-about-immigrants-and-crime/?utm_term=.15d80b8d0df8

18. Alexander Bolton, "Poll: Most Americans Have Positive View of Illegal Immigrants," *The Hill*, August 28, 2016, http://thehill.com/blogs/blog-briefing-room/293608-poll-67-percent-think-illegal-immigrants-more-likely-to-commit

19. Anthony DiMaggio, "White Supremacist America: Trump and the 'Return' of Right-Wing Hate Culture," *Counterpunch Magazine*, September 16, 2016, http://www.counterpunch.org/2016/09/16/white-supremacist-america-trump-and-the-return-of-right-wing-hate-culture/; DiMaggio, "The Anti-Trump Uprising," 2016.

20. John Burnett, "Arrests for Illegal Border Crossings Hit 46-Year Low," *National Public Radio*, December 5, 2017, https://www.npr.org/2017/12/05/568546381/arrests-for-illegal-border-crossings-hit-46-year-low

21. Miriam Valverde, "Have Deportations Increased Under Donald Trump? Here's What the Data Shows," *Politifact*, December 19, 2017, http://www.politifact.com/truth-o-meter/article/2017/dec/19/have-deportations-increased-under-donald-trump-her/

22. Sebastian Murdock, "Sarah Huckabee Sanders Cites Bible as Reason to Detain Immigrant Children," *Huffington Post*, June 14, 2018, https://www.huffingtonpost.com/entry/sarah-huckabee-sanders-cites-bible-as-reason-to-detain-immigrant-children_us_5b22c277e4b0d4fc01fc9b1d

23. Julia Jacobs, "Session's Use of Bible Passage to Defend Immigration Policy Draws Fire," *The New York Times*, June 15, 2018, https://www.nytimes.com/2018/06/15/us/sessions-bible-verse-romans.html; Sarah Ruiz-Grossman, "Hundreds Protest in Cities Across U.S. Against Trump's Immigrant Family Separations," *Huffington Post*, June 14, 2018, https://www.huffingtonpost.com/entry/protests-trump-immigrant-family-separations_us_5b22bb70e4b0d4fc01fc9218

24. Pew Research Center, "Gender Equality Universally Embraced, But Inequalities Acknowledged," *Pew Research Center*, July 1, 2010, http://www.pewglobal.org/2010/07/01/gender-equality/

25. Carolyn B. Maloney, "Gender Pay Inequality: Consequences for Women, Families, and the Economy," *Senate Joint Economic Committee, U.S. Congress*, April 2016, https://www.jec.senate.gov/public/_cache/files/0779dc2f-4a4e-4386-b847-9ae919735acc/gender-pay-inequality----us-congress-joint-economic-committee.pdf

26. Jessica Estepa, "Donald Trump on Carly Fiorina: 'Look at that Face!'" *USA Today*, September 10, 2015, http://www.usatoday.com/story/news/nation-now/2015/09/10/

trump-fiorina-look-face/71992454/; Philip Rucker, "Trump Says Fox's Megyn Kelly Had 'Blood Coming Out of Her Wherever,'" *The Washington Post*, August 8, 2015, https://www.washingtonpost.com/news/post-politics/wp/2015/08/07/trump-says-foxs-megyn-kelly-had-blood-coming-out-of-her-wherever/?utm_term=.cdab2d1fdd09; Ben Mathis Liley, "Trump was Recorded in 2005 Bragging About Grabbing Women 'by the Pussy,'" *Slate*, October 7, 2016, http://www.slate.com/blogs/the_slatest/2016/10/07/donald_trump_2005_tape_i_grab_women_by_the_pussy.html; Daniella Diaz, "Trump Calls Clinton 'A Nasty Woman,'" *CNN.com*, October 20, 2016, http://www.cnn.com/2016/10/19/politics/donald-trump-hillary-clinton-nasty-woman/

27. Pew Research Center, "A Divided and Pessimistic Electorate," 2016.

28. Newport and Saad, "Trump Support Built on Outsider Status, Business Experience," 2016.

29. McCarthy, "Clinton Preferred for Experience; Sanders, for Care," 2016.

30. Reuters, "Is a Woman's Place in the Home? 1 in 4 Say Yes-Poll," *Reuters*, March 8, 2010, http://uk.reuters.com/article/women-poll-idUKLNE62704620100308

31. Associated Press, "Female Wal-Mart Workers; Meetings Held at Strip Clubs," *USA Today*, April 29, 2003, usatoday30.usatoday.com/money/.../2003-04-29-walmart-discrimination-suit_x.htm; Al Norman, "Sex Discrimination Wal-Mart: The 'Bitches' Story That Won't Go Away," *Huffington Post*, July 20, 2016, http://www.huffingtonpost.com/entry/sex-discrimination-t-wal-mart-dthe-biktches-story_us_578bbafae4b0b107a24147d3

32. Jami Floyd, "Women Accuse Wal-Mart of Bias," *ABC News*, June 19, 2003, http://abcnews.go.com/Business/story?id=88057&page=1

33. Ann Farmer, "Are Young Women Turning Their Backs on Law School?" *Perspectives*, 18, no. 4 (2010). http://www.americanbar.org/content/dam/aba/publishing/perspectives_magazine/women_perspectives_spring10_turning_backs_law_school.authcheckdam.pdf

34. Association of American Medical Colleges, "Medical School Applicants, Enrollment Reach All-Time Highs," *Association of American Medical Colleges*, October 24, 2013, https://www.aamc.org/newsroom/newsreleases/358410/20131024.html; Josh Mitchell, "Women Notch Progress: Females Now Constitute One-Third of Nation's Ranks of Doctors and Lawyers," *Wall Street Journal*, December 4, 2012, https://www.wsj.com/articles/SB10001424127887323717004578159433220839020

35. Jenny Marder, "Why Engineering, Science Gender Gap Persists," *PBS Newshour*, April 25, 2012, http://www.pbs.org/newshour/rundown/science-engineering-and-the-gender-gap/

36. Liana Christin Landivar, "Disparities in STEM Employment by Sex, Race, and Hispanic Origin," *American Community Survey Reports*, September 2013, https://www.census.gov/prod/2013pubs/acs-24.pdf

37. Executive MBA Council, "Industry Insights," *Executive MBA Council*, 2017, http://www.embac.org/research-in-context.html

38. Claire Cain Miller, "An Elusive Jackpot: Richest Come to Women as CEOs, but Few Get There," *The New York Times*, June 7, 2014, https://www.nytimes.com/2014/06/08/business/riches-come-to-women-as-ceos-but-few-get-there.html?_r=0

39. Nancy Rivera Brooks, "Women Face More Obstacles in Getting MBA, Survey Finds," *Los Angeles Times*, May 13, 2000, http://articles.latimes.com/2000/may/13/business/fi-29528

40. Reuma Gadassi and Itamar Gati, "The Effect of Gender Stereotypes on Explicit and Implicit Career Preferences," *Counseling Psychologist*, 37, no. 5 (2009): 902–22.

41. Mark Perry and Andrew Biggs, "The '77 Cents on the Dollar' Myth About Women's Pay," *Wall Street Journal*, April 7, 2014, https://www.wsj.com/articles/mark-j-perry-and-andrew-g-biggs-the-77-cents-on-the-dollar-myth-about-womens-pay-1396905943

42. Bureau of Labor Statistics, "Median Weekly Earnings by Sex, Marital Status, and Presence and Age of Own Children Under 18 in 2012," *U.S. Department of Labor*, December 3, 2013, https://www.bls.gov/opub/ted/2013/ted_20131203.htm

43. Gallup, "Gay and Lesbian Rights," *Gallup*, 2016, http://www.gallup.com/poll/1651/gay-lesbian-rights.aspx

44. Gallup, "Gay and Lesbian Rights," 2016.

45. Emily Swanson, "Workplace Discrimination Poll Finds Most Favor Law Protecting Gays, Lesbians," *The Huffington Post*, June 22, 2013, http://www.huffingtonpost.com/2013/06/22/workplace-discrimination-poll_n_3480243.html

46. Harris, "Majority of Americans Agree: Businesses and Government Officials Should Not Discriminate Against LGBT People," *Harris Polls*, October 6, 2015, http://www.theharrispoll.com/politics/Businesses-Govt-Should-Not-Discriminate-against-LGBT.html

47. Polling Report, "Pew Research Center," *Pollingreport.com*, June 1996–March 2016 http://www.pollingreport.com/lgbt2.htm; Polling Report, "Gallup Poll," *Pollingreport.com*, May 1–10, 2018, http://www.pollingreport.com/lgbt.htm

48. Hunter Schwarz, "How Gay Marriage Became a Major Issue for a Generation Uninterested in Marriage," *Washington Post*, June 23, 2015, https://www.washingtonpost.com/news/the-fix/wp/2015/06/23/how-gay-marriage-became-a-major-issue-for-a-generation-uninterested-in-marriage/?utm_term=.8bfd2c60cacd

49. Jeremy W. Peters and Jonathan Martin, "Gay Marriage Case Offers GOP Political Cover," *The New York Times*, January 18, 2015, https://www.nytimes.com/2015/01/19/us/politics/marriage-case-offers-gop-political-cover.html

50. Crosby Burns, "The Gay and Transgender Wage Gap," *Center for American Progress*, April 16, 2012, https://www.americanprogress.org/issues/lgbt/news/2012/04/16/11494/the-gay-and-transgender-wage-gap/

51. Chris Matthews, "Firing for Sexual Orientation is Illegal, Says EEOC," *Fortune*, July 17, 2015, http://fortune.com/2015/07/17/gay-discrimination-illegal-workplace/

52. William Julius Wilson, *The Truly Disadvantaged: The Inner City, the Underclass, and Public Policy* (Chicago: University of Chicago Press, 2012).

53. Dennis Judd and Todd Swanstrom, *City Politics* (New York: Routledge, 2014).

54. Anthony DiMaggio, "Transcending Race?" *Counterpunch*, November 14, 2008, http://www.counterpunch.org/2008/11/14/transcending-race/

55. David Paul Kuhn, "Exit Polls: How Obama Won," *Politico*, November 5, 2008, http://www.politico.com/story/2008/11/exit-polls-how-obama-won-015297

56. Valerie Wilson, "New Census Data Show No Progress in Closing Stubborn Racial Income Gaps," *Economic Policy Institute*, September 16, 2015, http://www.epi.org/blog/new-census-data-show-no-progress-in-closing-stubborn-racial-income-gaps/

57. Kaiser Family Foundation, "Poverty Rate by Race/Ethnicity," *Kaiser Family Foundation*, 2015, http://kff.org/other/state-indicator/poverty-rate-by-raceethnicity/?currentTimeframe=0

58. National Poverty Center, "Poverty in the United States," *University of Michigan*, 2015, http://www.npc.umich.edu/poverty/

59. Ashley Nellis, "The Color of Justice: Racial and Ethnic Diversity in State Prisons," *The Sentencing Project*, June 14, 2016, http://www.sentencingproject.org/publications/color-of-justice-racial-and-ethnic-disparity-in-state-prisons/

60. Leah Sakala, "Breaking Down Mass Incarceration in the 2010 Census: State-by-State Incarceration Rates by Race/Ethnicity," *Prison Policy Initiative*, May 28, 2014, https://www.prisonpolicy.org/reports/rates.html; Karen R. Humes, Nicholas A. Jones, and Roberto R. Ramirez, "Overview of Race and Hispanic Origin: 2010," *U.S. Census Bureau*, March 2011, http://www.census.gov/prod/cen2010/briefs/c2010br-02.pdf

61. For overestimates of black crime, see the following: Heather MacDonald, *The War on Cops: How the New Attack on Law and Order Makes Everyone Less Safe* (New York: Encounter Books, 2016); Jon Greenberg, "Trump's Pants on Fire Tweet that Blacks Killed 81% of White Homicide Victims," *Politifact*, November 23, 2015, http://www.politifact.com/truth-o-meter/statements/2015/nov/23/donald-trump/trump-tweet-blacks-white-homicide-victims/. For actual violent crime committed by blacks, see Ana Swanson, "Whites Greatly Overestimate the Share of Crimes Committed by Black People," *The Washington Post*, December 1, 2014, https://www.washingtonpost.com/news/wonk/wp/2014/12/01/whites-greatly-overestimate-the-share-of-crimes-committed-by-black-people/?utm_term=.bf28467cd80c

62. NAACP, "Criminal Justice Fact Sheet," *NAACP*, 2017, http://www.naacp.org/criminal-justice-fact-sheet/

63. Michele Alexander, *The New Jim Crow: Mass Incarceration in the Age of Colorblindness* (New York: New Press, 2012).

64. Sonari Glinton, "Unemployment May Be Dropping, But It's Still Twice as High for Blacks," *National Public Radio*, February 5, 2016, http://www.npr.org/2016/02/05/465748249/african-americans-face-uncertain-reality-despite-low-unemployment-rate

65. Drew Desilver, "Black Unemployment Rate is Consistently Twice That of Whites," *Pew Research Center*, August 21, 2013, http://www.pewresearch.org/fact-tank/2013/08/21/through-good-times-and-bad-black-unemployment-is-consistently-double-that-of-whites/

66. Bureau of Labor Statistics, "Unemployment Rates for Hispanics or Latinos by State in 2015," *U.S. Department of Labor*, March 10, 2016, https://www.bls.gov/opub/ted/2016/unemployment-rates-for-hispanics-or-latinos-by-state-in-2015.htm

67. Governing, "State High School Graduation Rates by Race, Ethnicity," *Governing*, 2011–2012, http://www.governing.com/gov-data/education-data/state-high-school-graduation-rates-by-race-ethnicity.html

68. Ben Casselman, "Race Gap Narrows in College Enrollment, But Not in Graduation," *Fivethirtyeight.com*, https://fivethirtyeight.com/features/race-gap-narrows-in-college-enrollment-but-not-in-graduation/

69. Emily Flitter and Chris Kahn, "Exclusive: Trump Supporters More Likely to View Blacks Negatively—Reuters/Ipsos Poll," *Reuters*, June 28, 2016, htttp://www.reuters.com/article/us-usa-election-race-idUSKCN0ZE2SW

70. Paul Steinhauser, "CNN Poll: Americans Split on MLK Vision," *CNN*, January 17, 2011, http://politicalticker.blogs.cnn.com/2011/01/17/cnn-poll-americans-split-on-mlk-vision/

71. Pew Research Center, "Press Political Survey: November 2016," *Pew Research Center*, November 30–December 6, 2016, http://www.people-press.org/question-search/?qid=1889676&pid=51&ccid=51#top

72. Andrew Arenge, Stephanie Perry, and Dartunorro Clark, "Poll: 64 Percent of Americans Say Racism Remains a Major Problem," *NBCnews.com*, May 29, 2018, https://www.nbcnews.com/politics/politics-news/poll-64-percent-americans-say-racism-remains-major-problem-n877536

73. John Perazzo, "How the Liberal Welfare State Destroyed Black America," *Front Page Magazine*, May 5, 2016, http://www.frontpagemag.com/fpm/262726/how-liberal-welfare-state-destroyed-black-america-john-perazzo; Peter Morici, "African-Americans Should Start Voting for Republicans, Again," *Fox News*, June 22, 2016, http://www.foxnews.com/opinion/2016/06/22/african-americans-should-start-voting-for-republicans-again.html

74. Martin Gilens, *Why Americans Hate Welfare: Race, Media, and the Politics of Antipoverty Policy* (Chicago: University of Chicago Press, 2000).

75. Kaiser, "Poverty Rate by Race/Ethnicity," 2015.

76. Eric Morath, "Get a Job? Most Welfare Recipients Already Have One," *Wall Street Journal*, April 13, 2015, http://blogs.wsj.com/economics/2015/04/13/get-a-job-most-welfare-recipients-already-have-one/

77. Arloc Sherman, Robert Greenstein, and Kathy Ruffing, "Contrary to 'Entitlement Society' Rhetoric, Over Nine-Tenths of Entitlement Benefits Go to Elderly, Disabled, or Working Households," *Center for Budget and Policy Priorities*, February 11, 2012, http://www.cbpp.org/research/contrary-to-entitlement-society-rhetoric-over-nine-tenths-of-entitlement-benefits-go-to

78. John Logan, "Separate and Unequal: The Neighborhood Gap for Blacks, Hispanics, and Asians in Metropolitan America," *Brown University*, July 2011, https://s4.ad.brown.edu/Projects/Diversity/Data/Report/report0727.pdf

79. Logan, "Separate and Unequal," 2011.

80. I recall this excuse being cited numerous times by my parents and their friends during the 1980s, when they described to me why it was that suburbs and cities were so different from each other, racially speaking, and in terms of explaining why minorities were so over-concentrated in urban slums.

81. James H. Carr and Isaac F. Megbolugbe, "The Federal Reserve Bank of Boston Study on Mortgage Lending Revisited," *Journal of Housing Research*, 4, no. 2 (1993):

277–313; Raphael W. Bostic, "The Role of Race in Mortgage Lending: Revisiting the Boston Fed Study," *Federal Reserve Board of Governors*, December 1996, https://www.federalreserve.gov/pubs/feds/1997/199702/199702pap.pdf

82. Jay Fitzgerald, "Black, Latino Mortgage Rejection Rates Still High," *Boston Globe*, December 22, 2015, https://www.bostonglobe.com/business/2015/12/21/blacks-latinos-still-rejected-for-mortgages-higher-rates/kng3Kuc4v3uIK1pmDqBSjO/story.html

83. Nick Carey, "Racial Predatory Loans Fueled U.S. Housing Crisis: Study," *Reuters*, October 4, 2010, http://www.reuters.com/article/us-usa-foreclosures-race-id USTRE6930K520101004

84. Nate Silver, "The Most Diverse Cities are Often the Most Segregated," *Fivethirtyeight.com*, May 1, 2015, https://fivethirtyeight.com/features/the-most-diverse-cities-are-often-the-most-segregated/

85. I base these calculations on my examination of the racial demographic background of high schools across the Chicago metropolitan region, as based on the Illinois State Board of Education's "Report Card" data during the early 2010s.

86. Jamelle Bouie, "Still Separate and Unequal," *Slate*, May 15, 2014, http://www.slate.com/articles/news_and_politics/politics/2014/05/brown_v_board_of_education_60th_anniversary_america_s_schools_are_segregating.html

87. Bouie, "Still Separate and Unequal," 2014.

88. Ian Milhiser, "American Schools are More Segregated Now Than They Were in 1968, and the Supreme Court Doesn't Care," *Think Progress*, August 13, 2015, https://thinkprogress.org/american-schools-are-more-segregated-now-than-they-were-in-1968-and-the-supreme-court-doesnt-care-cc7abbf6651c#.fjsaj52zs

89. Bouie, "Still Separate and Unequal," 2014.

90. Valerie Strauss, "Study: Private School Vouchers Favored by Devos Don't Offer Real Advantage over Public Schools," *The Washington Post*, February 27, 2017, https://www.washingtonpost.com/news/answer-sheet/wp/2017/02/27/devos-favors-private-school-vouchers-but-new-study-says-they-dont-offer-real-edge-over-public-schools/?utm_term=.f0f3283f3c43

91. Corey Turner, "Why America's Schools Have a Money Problem," *National Public Radio*, April 18, 2016, http://www.npr.org/2016/04/18/474256366/why-americas-schools-have-a-money-problem

92. Emma Brown, "In 23 States, Richer School Districts Get More Local Funding than Poorer Schools," *The Washington Post*, March 12, 2015, https://www.washingtonpost.com/news/local/wp/2015/03/12/in-23-states-richer-school-districts-get-more-local-funding-than-poorer-districts/?utm_term=.efe8c8165c04

93. Rob Greenwald, Larry V. Hedges, and Richard D. Laine, "The Effect of School Resources on Student Achievement," *Center on Budget and Policy Priorities*, November 5, 2002, http://www.cbpp.org/archives/11-7-02sfp3.htm

94. CBS, "Study: No Link Between School Spending, Student Achievement," *CBSnews.com*, April 7, 2014, http://washington.cbslocal.com/2014/04/07/study-no-link-between-school-spending-student-achievement/; Dan Lips and Shanea Watkins, "Does Spending More on Education Improve Academic Achievement?" *The Heritage Foundation*,

September 8, 2008, http://www.heritage.org/research/reports/2008/09/does-spending-more-on-education-improve-academic-achievement; Eric A. Hanushek, "The Impact of Differential Expenditures on School Performance," *Educational Researcher*, 18, no. 4 (1989): 45–62.

95. Greenwald, et al., "The Effect of School Resources on Student Achievement," 2002; Linda Darling-Hammond, "Teacher Quality and Student Achievement: A Review of State Policy Evidence," *University of Washington Center for the Study of Teaching and Policy*, 1999, http://epaa.asu.edu/ojs/article/view/392; Ronald Ferguson, "Paying for Public Education: New Evidence on How and Why Money Matters," *Harvard Journal on Legislation* (1991): 465–98.

96. Grover J. Whitehurst and Matthew M. Chingos, "Class Size: What Research Says and What it Means for State Policy," *Brookings Institution*, May 11, 2011, https://www.brookings.edu/research/class-size-what-research-says-and-what-it-means-for-state-policy/; Nicole Anderson, "Per Pupil Spending: How Much Difference Does a Dollar Make?" *Utah State University*, May 2011, http://digitalcommons.usu.edu/cgi/viewcontent.cgi?article=1020&context=gradreports; John Mackenzie, "Public School Funding and Performance," *University of Delaware*, 2017, https://www1.udel.edu/johnmack/research/school_funding.pdf

97. In my analysis, I analyzed schools throughout the central Illinois, Springfield metropolitan region. I surveyed a few dozen public schools, including schools in Springfield and in surrounding communities. The Illinois State Board of Education compiles data for these schools, covering percentage of poverty within each school, and as related to various academic performance metrics. I find that school poverty is highly statistically significant, after controlling for other school factors including student-teacher ratio, racial composition of schools, number of teachers with master's degrees, teacher salaries, and instructional spending per pupil.

98. My analysis of academic performance assessed student midterm and final grades in my Introduction to American Politics course. Poverty rates in students' former high schools were highly statistically significant in predicting academic performance, after controlling for other student factors, including attendance rates, percent homework completed, writing ability (whether a student was designated special needs or not), hours spent studying for midterm and final exams, hours spent on reading and studying for the course overall, reliance on financial aid, employment status, hours worked, race, sex, age, residential status (living with parents or not), interest in politics, attendance (or non-attendance) of exam review sessions, and number of classes taken.

99. Sabrina Tavernise, "Income Gap Grows Between Rich and Poor, Studies Say," *The New York Times*, February 9, 2012, http://www.nytimes.com/2012/02/10/education/education-gap-grows-between-rich-and-poor-studies-show.html; With regard to race, I described in detail the racial gap in academic performance earlier in this chapter.

100. Marianne Bertrand and Sendhil Mullainathan, "Are Emily and Greg More Employable than Lakisha and Jamal? A Field Experiment on Labor Market Discrimination," *The American Economic Review*, 94, no. 4 (2004): 991–1013.

101. Tiffany Hsu, "College Graduates Earn 84% More Than High School Grads, Study Says," *Los Angeles Times*, August 5, 2011, http://latimesblogs.latimes.com/money_co/2011/08/college-gradutates-pay.html

102. Peter Dreier and John Mollenkopf, *Place Matters: Metropolitics for the Twenty-First Century* (Lawrence, KS: University Press of Kansas, 2014).

103. Pew Research Center, "News Interest Index Poll: January 2006," *Pew Research Center*, 2006.

104. Mark Peffley and Jon Hurwitz, *Justice in America: The Separate Realities of Blacks and Whites* (Cambridge: Cambridge University Press, 2010).

105. Timothy Williams, "Study Supports Suspicion that Police are More Likely to Use Force on Blacks," *The New York Times*, July 7, 2016, https://www.nytimes.com/2016/07/08/us/study-supports-suspicion-that-police-use-of-force-is-more-likely-for-blacks.html?_r=0

106. Quoctrung Bui and Amanda Cox, "Surprising New Evidence Shows Bias in Police Use of Force but Not in Shootings," *The New York Times*, July 11, 2016, https://www.nytimes.com/2016/07/12/upshot/surprising-new-evidence-shows-bias-in-police-use-of-force-but-not-in-shootings.html

107. Julie Bosman and Mitch Smith, "Chicago Police Routinely Trampled on Civils Rights, Justice Dept. Says," *The New York Times*, January 13, 2017, https://www.nytimes.com/2017/01/13/us/chicago-police-justice-department-report.html?_r=0; Matt Apuzzo and John Eligon, "Ferguson Police Tainted by Bias, Justice Department Says," *The New York Times*, March 4, 2015, https://www.nytimes.com/2015/03/05/us/us-calls-on-ferguson-to-overhaul-criminal-justice-system.html; Richard A. Oppel Jr., Sheryl Gay Stolberg, and Matt Apuzzo, "Justice Department to Release Blistering Report of Racial Bias by Baltimore Police," *The New York Times*, August 9, 2016, https://www.nytimes.com/2016/08/10/us/justice-department-to-release-blistering-report-of-racial-bias-by-baltimore-police.html

108. Katie Sanders, "Is the U.S. Prison Population as Big as Russia, China and North Korea Combined?" *Politifact*, December 16, 2014, http://www.politifact.com/punditfact/statements/2014/dec/16/matthew-cooke/us-prison-population-big-russia-china-and-north-ko/; NAACP, "Criminal Justice Fact Sheet," 2017.

109. Lydia Saad, "Most Americans Believe Crime in U.S. is Worsening," *Gallup*, October 31, 2011, http://www.gallup.com/poll/150464/americans-believe-crime-worsening.aspx

110. Christopher Ingraham, "Police Arrest More People for Marijuana Use than for All Violence Crimes—Combined," *The Washington Post*, October 12, 2016, https://www.washingtonpost.com/news/wonk/wp/2016/10/12/police-arrest-more-people-for-marijuana-use-than-for-all-violent-crimes-combined/?utm_term=.880527a46d17; Nicole Flatow, "Police Made More Arrests for Drug Violations than Anything Else in 2012," *Think Progress*, September 17, 2013, http://thinkprogress.org/justice/2013/09/17/2627601/people-arrested-drug-abuse-violations-2012/

111. Substance Abuse and Mental Health Services Administration, "National Survey on Drug Use and Health," *U.S. Department of Health and Human Services*, 2011, https://www.samhsa.gov/data/sites/default/files/2011MHFDT/2k11MHFR/Web/NSDUHmhfr2011.htm

112. Daniel Burton-Rose, *The Ceiling of America: An Inside Look at the U.S. Prison Industry* (Monroe, ME: Common Courage Press, 2002).

113. NAACP, "Criminal Justice Fact Sheet," 2017.

114. NAACP, "Criminal Justice Fact Sheet," 2017.

115. Bill O'Reilly, "The O'Reilly Factor," *Fox News*, July 19, 2014, 8:20 PM ET.

116. Michele Alexander, *The New Jim Crow: Mass Incarceration in the Age of Colorblindness* (New York: New Press, 2012); Sharon LaFraniere and Andrew Lehren, "The Disproportionate Risks of Driving While Black," *The New York Times*, October 24, 2015, http://www.nytimes.com/2015/10/25/us/racial-disparity-traffic-stops-driving-black.html; Kent Willis, "Fear of the Truth Drives Dodge of Racial Profiling Study," *American Civil Liberties Union*, August 23, 2000, https://acluva.org/387/fear-of-the-truth-drives-dodge-of-racial-profiling-study/

117. Malcolm D. Holmes, Harmon M. Hosch, Howard C. Daudistel, Dolores A. Perez, and Joseph B. Graves, "Ethnicity, Legal Resources, and Felony Dispositions in Two Southwestern Jurisdictions," *Justice Quarterly*, 13, no. 1 (1996): 11–30.

118. Matt Ford, "Racism and the Execution Chamber," *The Atlantic*, June 23, 2014, https://www.theatlantic.com/politics/archive/2014/06/race-and-the-death-penalty/373081/; David R. Dow, "The Death Penalty, Still Racist and Arbitrary," *The New York Times*, July 8, 2011, http://www.nytimes.com/2011/07/09/opinion/09dow.html

119. Dow, "Death Penalty, Still Racist and Arbitrary," 2011.

120. Dow, "Death Penalty, Still Racist and Arbitrary," 2011.

121. Alexander, *The New Jim Crow*, 2012.

122. Robert Entman and Andrew Rojecki: *The Black Image in the White Mind: Media and Race in America* (Chicago: University of Chicago Press, 2001).

123. Matthew Hutson, "Whites See Blacks as Superhuman: And That's Not Exactly a Compliment," *Slate*, November 14, 2014, http://www.slate.com/articles/health_and_science/science/2014/11/whites_see_blacks_as_superhuman_strength_speed_pain_tolerance_and_the_magical.html

124. Adam Serwer, "Latching onto L.A. Times Op-Ed, Limbaugh Sings 'Barack, the Magic Negro,'" *Media Matters for America*, March 20, 2007, https://mediamatters.org/video/2007/03/20/latching-onto-la-times-op-ed-limbaugh-sings-bar/138345

125. Franklin D. Gilliam Jr., and Shanto Iyengar, "Prime Suspects: The Influence of Local Television News on the Viewing Public," *American Journal of Political Science*, 44, no. 3 (2000): 560–573.

126. Tali Mendelberg, *The Race Card: Campaign Strategy, Implicit Messages, and the Norm of Equality* (Princeton, NJ: Princeton University Press, 2001).

127. Tali Mendelberg, "Racial Priming Revived," *Perspectives on Politics*, 6, no. 1 (2008): 109–23.

128. Gilens, *Why Americans Hate Welfare*, 2000.

129. Franklin D. Gilliam Jr., "The 'Welfare Queen' Experiment: How Viewers React to Images of African-American Mothers in Welfare," *Nieman Reports*, 1999, http://niemanreports.org/articles/the-welfare-queen-experiment/; James D. Johnson, Nelgy Olivo, Nathan Gibson, William Reed, and Leslie Ashburn-Nardo, "Priming Media Stereotypes Reduces Support for Social Welfare Policies," *Personality and Social Psychology Bulletin*, 35, no. 4 (2009): 463–76.

130. Polling Report, "Newsweek Poll: April 16–19, 1999," *Pollingreport.com*, 1999, http://www.pollingreport.com/race2.htm

131. Polling Report, "Newsweek Poll," 1999.

132. Pew Research Center, "On Views of Race and Inequality, Blacks and Whites are Worlds Apart," *Pew Research Center*, June 27, 2016, http://www.pewsocialtrends.org/2016/06/27/on-views-of-race-and-inequality-blacks-and-whites-are-worlds-apart/

133. Jonathan Smith, "Sessions Doesn't Want to Investigate Police: Here's Why We Need to," *The Washington Post*, March 10, 2017, https://www.washingtonpost.com/posteverything/wp/2017/03/10/sessions-doesnt-want-to-investigate-police-heres-why-we-need-to/?utm_term=.07ac1115d1e8

Chapter 15

1. Carolyn Y. Johnson, "America is a World Leader in Health Inequality," *The Washington Post*, June 5, 2017, https://www.washingtonpost.com/news/wonk/wp/2017/06/05/america-is-a-world-leader-in-health-inequality/?utm_term=.350987f809df

2. Kaiser Family Foundation, "Key Facts About the Uninsured Population," *Kaiser Family Foundation*, September 19, 2017, https://www.kff.org/uninsured/fact-sheet/key-facts-about-the-uninsured-population/

3. Bruce Drake, "On Tax Day, Americans' Views of Taxes and the IRS," *Pew Research Center*, April 15, 2014, http://www.pewresearch.org/fact-tank/2014/04/15/on-tax-day-americans-views-of-taxes-and-the-irs/

4. Heritage Foundation, "2017 Index of Economic Freedom: United States," *The Heritage Foundation*, 2017, http://www.heritage.org/index/country/unitedstates#limited-government

5. All of these numbers are drawn from the Heritage Foundation's "Index of Economic Freedom."

6. All of these numbers are drawn from the Heritage Foundation's "Index of Economic Freedom."

7. Pew Research Center, "Beyond Distrust: How Americans View Their Government," *Pew Research Center*, November 23, 2015, http://www.people-press.org/2015/11/23/2-general-opinions-about-the-federal-government/; Pew Research Center, "Most Say Government Policies Since Recession Have Done Little to Help Middle Class, Poor," *Pew Research Center*, March 4, 2015, http://www.people-press.org/2015/03/04/most-say-government-policies-since-recession-have-done-little-to-help-middle-class-poor/

8. Elise Gould and Hilary Wething, "Issue Brief 339: U.S. Poverty Rates Higher, Safety Net Weaker than in Peer Countries," *Economic Policy Institute*, July 24, 2012, http://www.epi.org/publication/ib339-us-poverty-higher-safety-net-weaker/

9. Arthur Delaney, "GOP Bill Aims to Ban Food Stamps for Steak and Lobster in New York: The Battle Over Poor People's Diets Isn't Going Away," *Huffington Post*, February 19, 2016, http://www.huffingtonpost.com/entry/food-stamps-steak-new-york_us_56c74299e4b0928f5a6b9ac8

10. UC Berkley Labor Center, "The High Public Cost of Low Wages," *University of California, Berkley*, 2011, http://laborcenter.berkeley.edu/the-high-public-cost-of-low-wages/; Arloc Sherman, Robert Greenstein, and Kathy Ruffing, "Contrary to 'Entitlement Society'

Rhetoric, Over Nine-Tenths of Entitlement Benefits Go to Elderly, Disabled or Working Households," *Center on Budget and Policy Priorities*, February 11, 2012, http://www.cbpp.org/research/contrary-to-entitlement-society-rhetoric-over-nine-tenths-of-entitlement-benefits-go-to

11. Heidi Goldberg, "State and County Supported Car Ownership Programs Can Help Low-Income Families Secure and Keep Jobs," *Center on Budget and Policy Priorities*, November 28, 2001, http://www.cbpp.org/archives/11-8-01wel.htm

12. Bryce Covert, "Your Assumptions About Welfare Recipients Are Wrong," *Think Progress*, December 18, 2013, https://thinkprogress.org/your-assumptions-about-welfare-recipients-are-wrong-22c03293de62#.7juz0hzdh

13. Covert, "Your Assumptions About Welfare Recipients Are Wrong," 2013.

14. Covert, "Your Assumptions About Welfare Recipients Are Wrong," 2013.

15. Darlena Cunha, "Why Drug Testing Welfare Recipients is a Waste of Taxpayer Money," *Time* Magazine, August 15, 2014, http://time.com/3117361/welfare-recipients-drug-testing/; Bryce Covert and Josh Israel, "What 7 States Discovered After Spending More Than $1 Million Drug Testing Welfare Recipients," *Think Progress*, February 26, 2015, http://thinkprogress.org/economy/2015/02/26/3624447/tanf-drug-testing-states/

16. Congressional Budget Office, "Growth in Means-Tested Programs and Tax Credits for Low-Income Households," *Congressional Budget Office*, February 11, 2013, https://www.cbo.gov/publication/43934; CBO, "Growth in Means Tested Programs and Tax Credits for Low Income Households"

17. Arthur Delaney, "How Long Do People Stay on Public Benefits?" *Huffington Post*, May 29, 2015, http://www.huffingtonpost.com/2015/05/29/public-benefits-safety-net_n_7470060.html

18. Kim Severson, "Food Stamp Fraud, Rare but Troubling," *The New York Times*, December 18, 2013, http://www.nytimes.com/2013/12/19/us/food-stamp-fraud-in-the-underground-economy.html

19. Food and Nutrition Service Office of Policy Support, "Foods Typically Purchased by Supplemental Nutrition Assistance Program (SNAP) Households," *United States Department of Agriculture*, November 2016, https://www.fns.usda.gov/sites/default/files/ops/SNAPFoodsTypicallyPurchased.pdf

20. Megan Stanley, Ife Floyd, and Misha Hill, "TANF Cash Benefits Have Fallen by More Than 20 Percent in Most States and Continue to Erode," *Center on Budget and Policy Priorities*, October 17, 2016, http://www.cbpp.org/research/family-income-support/tanf-cash-benefits-have-fallen-by-more-than-20-percent-in-most-states

21. Center on Budget and Policy Priorities, "Policy Basics: An Introduction to TANF," *Center on Budget and Policy Priorities*, June 15, 2015, http://www.cbpp.org/research/policy-basics-an-introduction-to-tanf

22. Arthur Delaney, "How Long Do People Stay on Public Benefits?" *Huffington Post*, May 29, 2015, http://www.huffingtonpost.com/2015/05/29/public-benefits-safety-net_n_7470060.html

23. Mike Konczal, "No, We Don't Spend $1 Trillion on Welfare Each Year," *The Washington Post*, January 12, 2014, https://www.washingtonpost.com/news/wonk/wp/2014/01/12/no-we-dont-spend-1-trillion-on-welfare-each-year/?utm_term=.ad24e66a2569

24. US Uncut, "10 Corporate Welfare Programs That Will Make Your Blood Boil," *US Uncut*, 2017, http://usuncut.com/class-war/10-corporate-welfare-programs-that-will-make-your-blood-boil/

25. Jeanne Sahadi, "Trump's Latest Tax Plan is Cheaper, But Still Costs a Lot," *CNN Money*, September 19, 2016, http://money.cnn.com/2016/09/19/news/economy/trump-tax-plan-cost/; Janet Novack, "Trump Tax Plan Gives 47% of Cuts to Richest 1%, New Analysis Finds," *Forbes*, October 11, 2016, http://www.forbes.com/sites/janet novack/2016/10/11/trump-tax-plan-gives-47-of-cuts-to-richest-1-new-analysis-finds/#3f96aee 259fc; Robert Greenstein, Chye-Ching Huang, and Isaac Shapiro, "Revised Trump Tax Plan Heavily Tilted Toward Wealthiest Tax Policy Center, Analysis Shows," *Center on Budget and Policy Priorities*, October 11, 2016, http://www.cbpp.org/research/federal-tax/revised-trump-tax-plan-heavily-tilted-toward-wealthiest-tax-policy-center

26. Tami Luhby, "Welfare Spending Cut in Half Since Reform," *CNN Money*, August 9, 2012, http://money.cnn.com/2012/08/09/news/economy/welfare-reform/

27. Sarah Cliff, "The State of Medicaid (In Charts!)," *The Washington Post*, July 17, 2012, https://www.washingtonpost.com/news/wonk/wp/2012/07/17/the-state-of-medicaid-in-charts/?utm_term=.b5b1742023c4; Dottie Rosenbaum, "SNAP is Effective and Efficient," *Center on Budget and Policy Priorities*, March 11, 2013, http://www.cbpp.org/research/snap-is-effective-and-efficient

28. Center on Budget and Policy Priorities, "Chart Book: Cuts in Federal Assistance Have Exacerbated Families' Struggles to Afford Housing," *Center on Budget and Policy Priorities*, April 12, 2016, http://www.cbpp.org/research/housing/chart-book-cuts-in-federal-assistance-have-exacerbated-families-struggles-to-afford

29. Juliette Cubanski and Tricia Neuman, "The Facts on Medicare Spending and Financing," *Kaiser Family Foundation*, July 20, 2016, http://kff.org/medicare/issue-brief/the-facts-on-medicare-spending-and-financing/; Congressional Budget Office, "The Budget and Economic Outlook: 2015–2025," *Congressional Budget Office*, January 2015, https://www.cbo.gov/sites/default/files/114th-congress-2015-2016/reports/49892-Outlook2015.pdf

30. Justin McCarthy, "Americans Split on Defense Spending," *Gallup*, February 20, 2015, http://www.gallup.com/poll/181628/americans-split-defense-spending.aspx

31. Robert J. Samuelson, "Both Sander's and Clinton's Tax Plans Will Soak the Rich," *The Washington Post*, March 13, 2016, https://www.washingtonpost.com/opinions/soaking-the-rich-a-primer/2016/03/13/5471df74-e7b2-11e5-b0fd-073d5930a7b7_story.html?utm_term=.f52cbdb074d7; Glenn Beck, "Soaking the Rich Never Works," *Fox News*, February 9, 2010, http://www.foxnews.com/story/2010/02/09/soaking-rich-never-works.html; Stephen Moore, "Sorry, Mr. Obama: Here's Why Raising Taxes on the Rich Won't Work," *Fox News*, February 25, 2015, http://www.foxnews.com/opinion/2015/02/25/sorry-mr-obama-here-why-raising-taxes-on-rich-wont-work.html

32. Citizens for Tax Justice, "The Sorry State of Corporate Taxes," *Citizens for Tax Justice*, March 2017, http://www.ctj.org/corporatetaxdodgers/sorrystateofcorptaxes.php

33. Kyle Pomerleau, "Corporate Income Tax Rates Around the World," *The Tax Foundation*, October 1, 2015, https://taxfoundation.org/corporate-income-tax-rates-around-world-2015/

34. Institute on Taxation and Economic Policy, "Who Pays Taxes in America in 2017?" *Institute on Taxation and Economic Policy*, April 2017, https://itep.org/wp-content/uploads/taxday2017.pdf

35. Philip Bump, "The Story Behind Obama and the National Debt, in 7 Charts," *The Washington Post*, January 7, 2015, https://www.washingtonpost.com/news/the-fix/wp/2015/01/07/the-story-behind-obama-and-the-national-debt-in-7-charts/?utm_term=.e9bd8ada76c5

36. Zachary A. Goldfarb, "The Legacy of the Bush Tax Cuts, in Four Charts," *The Washington Post*, January 2, 2013, https://www.washingtonpost.com/news/wonk/wp/2013/01/02/the-legacy-of-the-bush-tax-cuts-in-four-charts/?utm_term=.54d305aba925

37. George W. Bush, "Tax Cut Speech," *C-Span*, February 2001, https://www.c-span.org/video/?c3943678/george-bush-tax-cut-speech-february-2001; Mark Wilson and William Beach, "The Economic Impact of President Bush's Tax Relief Plan," *The Heritage Foundation*, April 27, 2001, http://www.heritage.org/research/reports/2001/04/the-economic-impact-of-president-bushs-tax-relief-plan

38. Josh Bivens and John Irons, "A Feeble Recovery: The Fundamental Economic Weakness of the 2001–2007 Expansion," *Economic Policy Institute*, December 9, 2008, http://epi.3cdn.net/ff1869e11dfc0ef295_xxm6b9cj9.pdf

39. Mike Patton, "The Real Story of Job Creation," *Forbes*, November 2, 2012, https://www.forbes.com/sites/mikepatton/2012/11/02/the-real-story-of-job-creation/#68caf5a61b3f

40. Andrea Orr, "Income Inequality: It Wasn't Always This Way," *Economic Policy Institute*, February 9, 2011, http://www.epi.org/publication/income_inequality_it_wasnt_always_this_way/

41. Michael Corcoran, "Democracy in Peril: Twenty Years of Media Consolidation Under the Telecommunications Act," *Truthout*, February 11, 2016, http://www.truth-out.org/news/item/34789-democracy-in-peril-twenty-years-of-media-consolidation-under-the-telecommunications-act; Common Cause, "The Fallout from the Telecommunications Act of 1996," *Common Cause*, May 9, 2005, http://www.commoncause.org/research-reports/National_050905_Fallout_From_The_Telecommunications_Act_2.pdf

42. David Lazarus, "The Myth of Deregulation's Consumer Benefits," *Los Angeles Times*, February 14, 2013, http://articles.latimes.com/2013/feb/14/business/la-fi-lazarus-20130215; Cyrus Sanati, "Delta Proves That Consolidation Drives up Ticket Fares," *Fortune*, October 23, 2013, http://fortune.com/2013/10/23/delta-proves-that-consolidation-drives-up-ticket-fares/; Stephen Labaton, "Cable Rates Rising as Industry Nears End of Regulation," *The New York Times*, March 8, 1999, http://www.nytimes.com/1999/03/08/business/cable-rates-rising-as-industry-nears-end-of-regulation.html; Marc Lifsher, "PUC Says Phone Rates Can Rise 30%," *Los Angeles Times*, September 19, 2008, http://articles.latimes.com/2008/sep/19/business/fi-phones19

43. Victoria De Grazia, *Irresistible Empire: America's Advance through Twentieth-Century Europe* (Cambridge, MA: Belknap Press, 2006).

44. Charles E. Sorenson and Samuel T. Williams, *My Forty Years with Ford* (Detroit, MI: Wayne State University Press, 2006).

45. Annalyn Kurtz and Tal Yellin, "Minimum Wage Since 1938," *CNN Money*, 2017 http://money.cnn.com/interactive/economy/minimum-wage-since-1938/

46. Shelly Banjo, "Wal-Mart to End Health Insurance for Some Part-Time Employees," *Wall Street Journal*, October 7, 2014, https://www.wsj.com/articles/wal-mart-to-end-health-insurance-for-some-part-time-employees-1412694790

47. Dave Jamieson, "Union Membership Rate for U.S. Workers Tumbles to New Low," *Huffington Post*, January 23, 2013, http://www.huffingtonpost.com/2013/01/23/union-membership-rate_n_2535063.html

48. Zaid Jilani, "Chart: How Income Inequality Skyrocketed and the 1 Percent Profited from the Decline of Unions," *Think Progress*, October 21, 2011, https://thinkprogress.org/chart-how-income-inequality-skyrocketed-and-the-1-percent-profited-from-the-decline-of-unions-f098379015df#.n0hgla8bt

49. Jilani, "Chart: How Income Inequality Skyrocketed and the 1 Percent Profited from the Decline of Unions," 2011.

50. Martin Neil Baily and Barry P. Bosworth, "U.S. Manufacturing: Understanding its Past and its Potential Future," *Brookings Institution*, February 5, 2014, https://www.brookings.edu/research/u-s-manufacturing-understanding-its-past-and-its-potential-future/

51. I draw on the historical values of the minimum wage through the Department of Labor's website at: U.S. Department of Labor, "Wage and Hour Division (WHD)" *U.S. Department of Labor*, 2017, https://www.dol.gov/whd/minwage/chart.htm. Using an inflation calculator, I adjusted the value of the minimum wage for each year in the post-World War II era to 2014 dollars.

52. Department of Labor, "Wage and Hour Division," 2017.

53. John Schmitt, "The Minimum Wage is Too Damn Low," *Center for Economic and Policy Research*, March 2012, http://cepr.net/documents/publications/min-wage1-2012-03.pdf

54. David Card and Alan B. Krueger, *Myth and Measurement: The New Economics of the Minimum Wage* (Princeton, NJ: Princeton University Press, 1994); Hristos Doucouliagos and T. D. Stanley, "Publication Selection Bias in Minimum-Wage Research? A Meta-Regression Analysis," *British Journal of Industrial Relations*, 47, no. 2 (2009): 406–28.

55. For a history of minimum wage rates, see: Department of Labor, "Wage and Hour Division," 2017. For measures of inflation over time, see: Bureau of Labor Statistics, "CPI: All Urban Consumers," *U.S. Department of Labor*, 2017, https://data.bls.gov/timeseries/CUUR0000SA0L1E?output_view=pct_12mths; and: Jamie Hopkins, "How to Mitigate Inflation Risk in A Retirement Income Plan," *Fortune*, March 30, 2014, https://www.forbes.com/sites/jamiehopkins/2014/03/30/how-to-mitigate-inflation-risk-in-a-retirement-income-plan/#77f13b7940c3. Reviewing the above data, I find that there is no statistically significant relationship between the changing purchasing power of the minimum wage and the overall inflation rate. If the growing value of the minimum wage was causing inflation, one would expect that inflation would increase during years when the minimum wage's purchasing power was increasing, particularly during the 1940s, 1950s, and 1960s. But such a relationship is not observed.

56. Cameron Davis, "Study: A Minimum Wage Hike Would Stimulate the Economy," *Think Progress*, July 8, 2013, https://thinkprogress.org/study-a-minimum-wage-hike-would-stimulate-the-economy-f02ca75732fc

57. Tim Worstall, "The 7 Most Dangerous Myths About a $15 Minimum Wage," *Forbes*, August 4, 2015, http://www.forbes.com/sites/timworstall/2015/08/04/the-7-most-dangerous-myths-about-a-15-minimum-wage/#7777b6952c57

58. Hacker and Pierson, *Winner Take All Politics*, 2011.

59. Catherine Rampell, "Why Tuition has Skyrocketed at State Schools," *The New York Times Economix*, March 2, 2012, https://economix.blogs.nytimes.com/2012/03/02/why-tuition-has-skyrocketed-at-state-schools/?_r=0

60. John Schmitt and Marie-Eve Augier, "Affording Health Care and Education on the Minimum Wage," *Center for Economic and Policy Research*, March 2012, http://cepr.net/documents/publications/min-wage2-2012-03.pdf

61. Derek Thompson, "How You, I, and Everyone Got the Top 1 Percent All Wrong," *The Atlantic*, March 30, 2014, https://www.theatlantic.com/business/archive/2014/03/how-you-i-and-everyone-got-the-top-1-percent-all-wrong/359862/

62. Annie Lowrey, "Changed Life of the Poor: Better Off, but Far Behind," *The New York Times*, April 30, 2014, https://www.nytimes.com/2014/05/01/business/economy/changed-life-of-the-poor-squeak-by-and-buy-a-lot.html

63. Dean Schabner, "Americans Work More Than Anyone," *ABC News*, May 1, 2014, http://abcnews.go.com/US/story?id=93364

64. Robert Pear, "Reagan Seeks Cut of 40% in Funds for Mass Transit," *The New York Times*, January 5, 1986, http://www.nytimes.com/1986/01/05/us/reagan-seeks-cut-of-40-in-funds-for-mass-transit.html; Steven V. Roberts, "Food Stamps Program: How it Grew and How Reagan Wants To Cut it Back," *The New York Times*, April 4, 1981, http://www.nytimes.com/1981/04/04/us/food-stamps-program-it-grew-reagan-wants-cut-it-back-budget-targets.html?pagewanted=all; Spencer Rich, "Reagan Budget Means Drastic Cuts in Medicare and Medicaid Programs," *The Washington Post*, August 21, 1981, https://www.washingtonpost.com/archive/politics/1981/08/21/reagan-budget-means-drastic-cuts-in-medicare-and-medicaid-programs/5c74d19a-dfdc-4c57-924f-feb27dc78f9c/?utm_term=.dec16af608e2; Peter Dreier, "Reagan's Real Legacy," *The Nation*, February 4, 2011, https://www.thenation.com/article/reagans-real-legacy/

65. Sheldon L. Richman, "The Reagan Record on Trade: Rhetoric vs. Reality," *Cato Institute*, May 30, 1988, https://object.cato.org/pubs/pas/pa107.pdf; Jeanne Sahadi, "Taxes: What People Forget about Reagan," *CNN Money*, September 12, 2010, http://money.cnn.com/2010/09/08/news/economy/reagan_years_taxes/; Greg Schneider and Renae Merle, "Reagan's Defense Buildup Bridged Military Eras," *The Washington Post*, June 9, 2004, http://www.washingtonpost.com/wp-dyn/articles/A26273-2004Jun8.html

66. Alana Semuels, "The End of Welfare as We Know it," *The Atlantic*, April 1, 2016, https://www.theatlantic.com/business/archive/2016/04/the-end-of-welfare-as-we-know-it/476322/

67. Alison Kodjak, "Paul Ryan's Plan to Change Medicare Looks a Lot Like Obamacare," *National Public Radio*, November 26, 2016, http://www.npr.org/sections/health-shots/2016/11/26/503158039/paul-ryans-plan-to-change-medicare-looks-a-lot-like-obamacare; William A. Galston, "Why the 2005 Social Security Initiative Failed, and What it Means for the Future," *Brookings Institution*, September 21, 2007, https://www.brookings.edu/research/why-the-2005-social-security-initiative-failed-and-what-it-means-for-the-future/

68. Lori Montgomery, "In Debt Talks, Obama Offers Social Security Cuts," *The Washington Post*, July 6, 2011, https://www.washingtonpost.com/business/economy/in-debt-talks-obama-offers-social-security-cuts/2011/07/06/gIQA2sFO1H_story.html?utm_term=.ecb445665f0d

69. Bourree Lam, "Trump's 'Two-for-One' Regulation Executive Order," *The Atlantic*, January 30, 2017, https://www.theatlantic.com/business/archive/2017/01/trumps-regulation-eo/515007/; Howard Gleckman, "Memo to Steven Mnuchin: Trump's Tax Plan Would Add $7 Trillion to the Debt over 10 Years," *Forbes*, January 19, 2017, https://www.forbes.com/sites/beltway/2017/01/19/memo-to-steven-mnuchin-trumps-tax-plan-would-add-7-trillion-to-the-debt-over-10-years/#115f30406554; Jeanne Sahadi, "Trump Wants to Cut the Smallest Part of the Federal Budget," *CNN Money*, March 16, 2017, http://money.cnn.com/2017/03/15/news/economy/trump-budget-spending-cuts/; Caitlin Dewey, "Trump's Draft Plan to Cut Off Food Stamps for Immigrants Could Cause Some U.S. Citizens to Go Hungry," *The Washington Post*, February 3, 2017, https://www.washingtonpost.com/news/wonk/wp/2017/02/03/trumps-draft-plan-to-cut-off-food-stamps-for-immigrants-could-cause-some-u-s-citizens-to-go-hungry/?utm_term=.1ba441a537f5

70. Michael Greenstone and Adam Looney, "Trends: Reduced Earnings for Men in America," *Brookings Institution*, July 27, 2011, https://www.brookings.edu/research/trends-reduced-earnings-for-men-in-america/

71. Bill Marsh and Robert R. Reich, "The State of Working America," *The New York Times*, September 4, 2011, http://www.nytimes.com/imagepages/2011/09/04/opinion/04reich-graphic.html

72. Marsh and Reich, "The State of Working America," 2011.

73. Marsh and Reich, "The State of Working America," 2011.

74. Thompson, "How You, I, and Everyone Got the Top 1 Percent All Wrong," 2014.

75. Chad Stone and Arloc Sherman, "Income Gaps Between Very Rich and Everyone Else More Than Tripled in Last Three Decades, New Data Show," *Center on Budget and Policy Priorities*, June 25, 2010, http://www.cbpp.org/research/income-gaps-between-very-rich-and-everyone-else-more-than-tripled-in-last-three-decades-new

76. Louis Jacobson, "Ian Bremmer Compares Big Gains for Top 1 Percent to Stagnation for Bottom 99 Percent," *Politifact*, January 7, 2014, http://www.politifact.com/punditfact/statements/2014/jan/07/ian-bremmer/ian-bremmer-says-top-1-percent-saw-incomes-go-34-p/; Steven Rattner, "The Rich Get Even Richer," *The New York Times*, March 25, 2012, http://www.nytimes.com/2012/03/26/opinion/the-rich-get-even-richer.html

77. Catherine Rampell, "Corporate Profits Were the Highest on Record Last Quarter," *The New York Times*, November 23, 2010, http://www.nytimes.com/2010/11/24/business/economy/24econ.html

78. Federal Reserve Economic Data, "Real Gross Domestic Product," *Federal Reserve Bank of St. Louis*, 2017, https://fred.stlouisfed.org/series/A191RL1Q225SBEA

79. Bureau of Labor Statistics, "Labor Force Statistics from the Current Population Survey," *U.S. Department of Labor*, 2017, https://data.bls.gov/timeseries/LNS14000000

80. Floyd Norris, "Corporate Profits Grow and Wages Slide," *The New York Times*, April 4, 2014, https://www.nytimes.com/2014/04/05/business/economy/corporate-profits-grow-ever-

larger-as-slice-of-economy-as-wages-slide.html; Jamie McGeever, "Why are U.S. Corporate Profits so High? Because Wages are so Low," *Reuters*, January 24, 2014, http://blogs.reuters.com/macroscope/2014/01/24/why-are-us-corporate-profits-so-high-because-wages-are-so-low/.

81. Lawrence H. Summers, "Corporate Profits are Near Record Highs: Here's Why That's a Problem," *The Washington Post*, March 30, 2016, https://www.washingtonpost.com/news/wonk/wp/2016/03/30/larry-summers-corporate-profits-are-near-record-highs-heres-why-thats-a-problem/?utm_term=.6add646d4361

82. Rakesh Kochhar and Richard Fry, "Wealth Inequality has Widened Along Racial, Ethnic Lines Since End of Great Recession," *Pew Research Center*, December 12, 2014, http://www.pewresearch.org/fact-tank/2014/12/12/racial-wealth-gaps-great-recession/; U.S. Census Bureau, "Wealthy and Asset Ownership," *U.S. Census Bureau*, 2017, https://www.census.gov/people/wealth/files/Wealth%20Highlights%202011%20Revised%207-3-14.pdf

83. Carmen DeNavas-Walt and Bernadette D. Proctor, "Income and Poverty in the United States: 2014 Current Population Reports," *U.S. Census Bureau*, September 2015, https://www.census.gov/content/dam/Census/library/publications/2015/demo/p60-252.pdf

84. Katz and Krueger, "The Rise and Nature of Alternative Work Arrangements in the United States, 1995–2015," 2016.

85. For growing income inequality, see: Russell Sage Foundation, "Chartbook of Social Inequality," *Russell Sage Foundation*, 2012, http://www.russellsage.org/sites/all/files/chartbook/Income%20and%20Earnings.pdf. For increasing CEO Pay, see: Rebecca Hiscott, "CEO Pay Has Increased by 937 Percent Since 1978," *Huffington Post*, June 12, 2014, http://www.huffingtonpost.com/2014/06/12/ceo-pay-report_n_5484622.html. For rising pay of the top one percent of income earners, see: Chad Stone, Danilo Trisi, Arloc Sherman, and Emily Horton, "A Guide to Statistics on Historical Trends in Income Inequality," *Center on Budget and Policy Priorities*, November 7, 2016, http://www.cbpp.org/research/poverty-and-inequality/a-guide-to-statistics-on-historical-trends-in-income-inequality. For the declining value of the minimum wage, see: Annalyn Kurtz and Tal Yellin, "Minimum Wage Since 1938," *CNN Money*, 2015, http://money.cnn.com/interactive/economy/minimum-wage-since-1938/. For the rise in labor productivity over time, see: Bureau of Labor Statistics, "Productivity Change in Nonfarm Business Sector, 1946–2016," *U.S. Department of Labor*, 2017, https://www.bls.gov/lpc/prodybar.htm

86. Michael Greenstone and Adam Looney, "Trends: Reduced Earnings for Men in America," *Brookings Institution*, July 27, 2011, https://www.brookings.edu/research/trends-reduced-earnings-for-men-in-america/

87. Hiscott, "CEO Pay Has Increased By 937 Percent Since 1978," 2014; Thompson, "How You, I, and Everyone Got the Top 1 Percent All Wrong," 2014.

88. Hamilton Project, "Median Earnings and Annual Hours Worked for Two-Parent Families," *Brookings Institution*, July 8, 2011, http://www.hamiltonproject.org/charts/median_earnings_and_annual_hours_worked_for_two-parent_families

89. Marsh and Reich, "The State of Working America," 2011.

90. Marsh and Reich, "The State of Working America," 2011.

91. Dan Mangan, "Medical Bills are the Biggest Cause of U.S. Bankruptcies: Study," *CNBC*, June 25, 2013, http://www.cnbc.com/id/100840148; Alison Kodjak,

"Medical Bills Still Take a Big Toll, Even With Insurance," *National Public Radio*, March 8, 2016, http://www.npr.org/sections/health-shots/2016/03/08/468892489/medical-bills-still-take-a-big-toll-even-with-insurance

92. Zac Auter, "Healthcare Costs Top U.S. Families' Financial Concerns," *Gallup*, April 27, 2016, http://www.gallup.com/poll/191126/healthcare-costs-top-families-financial-concerns.aspx

93. Bernadette D. Proctor, Jessica L. Semega, and Melissa A. Kollar, "Income and Poverty in the United States: 2015," *U.S. Census Bureau*, September 13, 2016, http://www.census.gov/library/publications/2016/demo/p60-256.html; Center for Poverty Research, "What is the Current Poverty Rate in the United States?" *University of California, Davis*, 2017, http://poverty.ucdavis.edu/faq/what-current-poverty-rate-united-states

94. Jason DeParle, Robert Gebeloff, and Sabrina Tavernise, "Near Poor, Not Quite in Poverty, But Still Struggling," *The New York Times*, November 18, 2011, http://www.nytimes.com/2011/11/19/us/census-measures-those-not-quite-in-poverty-but-struggling.html

95. Citizens for Tax Justice, "Who Pays Taxes in America in 2016?" 2016.

96. Citizens for Tax Justice, "Who Pays Taxes in America in 2016?" 2016.

97. Christopher Ingraham, "If You Thought Income Inequality Was Bad, Get a Load of Wealth Inequality," *The Washington Post*, May 21, 2015, https://www.washingtonpost.com/news/wonk/wp/2015/05/21/the-top-10-of-americans-own-76-of-the-stuff-and-its-dragging-our-economy-down/?utm_term=.c6872b6ca68d

98. Ingraham, "If You Thought Income Inequality Was Bad, Get a Load of Wealth Inequality," 2015; Travis Waldron, "Report: Bottom Half of American Households Have Just 1 Percent of Nation's Wealth," *Think Progress*, July 19, 2012, https://thinkprogress.org/report-bottom-half-of-american-households-have-just-1-percent-of-nations-wealth-15a258fa083d#.jdv3hmzbq

99. Ingraham, "If You Thought Income Inequality Was Bad, Get a Load of Wealth Inequality," 2015.

100. Harris, "Americans' Sense of Alienation Remains at Record High," *Harris Polls*, July 28, 2016, http://www.theharrispoll.com/politics/Americans-Alienation-Remains-Record-High.html

101. Russell Heimlich, "Public Acceptance of Intermarriage Grows," *Pew Research Center*, February 21, 2012, http://www.pewresearch.org/daily-number/public-views-of-inequality-fairness-and-wall-street/

102. Frank Newport, "Americans Continue to Say U.S. Wealth Distribution is Unfair," *Gallup*, May 4, 2015, http://www.gallup.com/poll/182987/americans-continue-say-wealth-distribution-unfair.aspx

103. Jordan Weissmann, "Americans Have No Idea How Bad Inequality Really is," *Slate*, September 26, 2014, http://www.slate.com/articles/business/moneybox/2014/09/americans_have_no_idea_how_bad_inequality_is_new_harvard_business_school.html

104. Jennifer Agiesta, "CNN/ORC Poll: Economic Optimism Hits New Peak under Obama," *CNN.com*, April 21, 2015, http://www.cnn.com/2015/04/21/politics/cnn-poll-obama-economy-congress/

105. Pew Research Center, "Campaign Exposes Fissures over Issues, Values, and How Life has Changed in the U.S.," *Pew Research Center*, March 31, 2016, http://www.people-press.org/2016/03/31/3-views-on-economy-government-services-trade/

106. The relationship between opinions about working hard and getting ahead on the one hand, and opinions about the economic divide on the other, is statistically significant at the 1 percent level, after controlling for other variables, including respondents' sex, age, education, race, political party, class status (as a self-designated "have" or "have-not"), religious affiliation (Born-Again Christian or not), and ideology.

107. Drew Desilver, "Global Inequality: How the U.S. Compares," *Pew Research Center*, December 19, 2013, http://www.pewresearch.org/fact-tank/2013/12/19/global-inequality-how-the-u-s-compares/

108. Pew Research Center, "Racial Attitudes in America Survey," *Pew Research Center*, February 2016, http://www.people-press.org/question-search/?qid=1881795&pid=51&ccid=51#top

109. Sosnaud B., Brady D., and Frenk S., "Class in Name Only: Subjective Class Identity, Objective Class Position, and Vote Choice in American Presidential Elections," *Social Problems* 60, no. 1 (2013): 80–99.

110. Anthony DiMaggio, "The Anti-Trump Uprising: Class Delusions, Perverted Politics, and the Prospects for Real Change," *Counterpunch*, November 2016.

111. Rachel Sheffield and Robert Recto, "Air Conditioning, Cable TV, and an Xbox: What is Poverty in the United States Today?" *The Heritage Foundation*, July 19, 2011, http://www.heritage.org/research/reports/2011/07/what-is-poverty

112. David Shere, "Fox Cites Ownership of Appliances to Downplay Hardship of Poverty in America," *Media Matters for America*, July 22, 2011, http://mediamatters.org/research/2011/07/22/fox-cites-ownership-of-appliances-to-downplay-h/148574

113. Shere, "Fox Cites Ownership of Appliances to Downplay Hardship of Poverty in America," 2011.

114. Neil Postman, *Amusing Ourselves to Death: Public Discourse in the Age of Showbusiness* (New York: Penguin, 2005).

115. Desilver, "Global Inequality: How the U.S. Compares," 2013.

116. John Cassidy, "Piketty's Inequality Story in Six Charts," *The New Yorker*, March 26, 2014, http://www.newyorker.com/news/john-cassidy/pikettys-inequality-story-in-six-charts

117. Lane Kenworthy, "Do Social-Welfare Policies Reduce Poverty? A Cross-National Assessment," *Social Forces*, 77, no. 3 (1999): 1119–139; Stephanie Moller, Evelyne Huber, John D. Stephens, David Bradley, and Franois Nielsen, "Determinants of Relative Poverty in Advanced Capitalist Democracies," *American Sociological Review*, 68, no. 1 (2003): 22–51.

Chapter 16

1. Tim Lister, "Is Bombing the S*** Out of ISIS a Strategy?" *CNN*, November 15, 2016, http://www.cnn.com/2016/11/15/middleeast/donald-trump-isis-strategy/index.html

2. Julian Borger, "Trump's Plan to Seize Iraq's Oil: 'It's Not Stealing, We're Reimbursing Ourselves,'" *The Guardian*, September 21, 2016, https://www.theguardian.com/us-news/2016/sep/21/donald-trump-iraq-war-oil-strategy-seizure-isis

3. Niccolo Machiavelli, *The Prince* (New York: Penguin, 2009).

4. John J. Mearsheimer, *The Tragedy of Great Power Politics* (New York: W. W. Norton, 2014); Hans Morgenthau and Kenneth Thompson, *Politics Among Nations: The Struggle for Power and Peace* (New York: McGraw Hill, 1992); Kenneth N. Waltz, *Man, the State, and War: A Theoretical Analysis* (New York: Columbia University Press, 2001).

5. Kenneth Waltz, *Theory of International Politics* (Long Grove, IL: Waveland Press, 2010).

6. Mearsheimer, *The Tragedy of Great Power Politics*, 2014; Waltz, *Theory of International Politics*, 2010.

7. Jack Donnelly, *Realism and International Relations* (Cambridge: Cambridge University Press, 2000); Daniel A. Baldwin, *Neorealism and Neoliberalism: The Contemporary Debate* (New York: Columbia University Press, 1994).

8. Ronald Osborn, "Noam Chomsky and the Realist Tradition," *Review of International Studies* 35 (2009): 351–70.

9. Woodrow Wilson, "Address to a Joint Session of Congress on the Conditions of Peace," *American Presidency Project*, January 8, 1918, http://www.presidency.ucsb.edu/ws/?pid=65405

10. Immanuel Kant, *Perpetual Peace* (Indiana, IN: Hackett Publishers, 1983).

11. John R. Oneal and Bruce Russett, *Triangulating Peace: Democracy, Interdependence, and International Organizations* (New York: W. W. Norton, 2000).

12. Max Bearak and Lazaro Gamio, "The U.S. Foreign Aid Budget, Visualized," *The Washington Post*, October 18, 2016, https://www.washingtonpost.com/news/worldviews/wp/2016/09/26/the-u-s-foreign-aid-budget-visualized/?utm_term=.f52b73cd4846

13. Azam Ahmed, "Tasked with Combating Opium, Afghan Officials Profit from it," *The New York Times*, February 15, 2016, https://www.nytimes.com/2016/02/16/world/asia/afghanistan-opium-heroin-taliban-helmand.html?_r=0

14. Anup Kaphle, "The Warlords of Afghanistan," *The Washington Post*, April 1, 2015, https://www.washingtonpost.com/apps/g/page/world/the-warlords-of-afghanistan/967/

15. Monica Sarkar, "Women's Rights in Afghanistan: Are We Witnessing a Revolution?" *CNN.com*, April 8, 2015, http://www.cnn.com/2015/04/07/asia/afghanistan-amnesty-report/; Human Rights Watch, "Afghanistan: Events in 2015," *Human Rights Watch*, 2016, https://www.hrw.org/world-report/2016/country-chapters/afghanistan

16. Human Rights Watch, "Afghanistan: Events in 2015," 2016.

17. Human Rights Watch, "Egypt: Events in 2015," *Human Rights Watch*, 2016, https://www.hrw.org/world-report/2016/country-chapters/egypt

18. David D. Kirkpatrick, "Army Ousts Egypt's President; Morsi is Taken into Military Custody," *The New York Times*, July 3, 2013, http://www.nytimes.com/2013/07/04/world/middleeast/egypt.html

19. Human Rights Watch, "Egypt," *Human Rights Watch*, 2017, https://www.hrw.org/middle-east/n-africa/egypt

20. Mohsin Naqvi, "Benazir Bhutto Assassinated," *CNN.com*, December 27, 2007, http://www.cnn.com/2007/WORLD/asiapcf/12/27/pakistan.sharif/; Mubasher Bukhari, "Assassinated Pakistan Minister was on Watchlist for Retaliation," *Reuters*, August 17, 2015, http://www.reuters.com/article/us-pakistan-blast-idUSKCN0QM13L20150817; Quentin Sommerville, "Pakistan Helping Afghan Taliban," *BBC News*, February 1, 2012, http://www.bbc.com/news/world-asia-16821218

21. Human Rights Watch, "Pakistan: Events in 2016," *Human Rights Watch*, 2017, https://www.hrw.org/world-report/2017/country-chapters/pakistan

22. Suleiman AlpKhalidi, "Jordan's King Abdullah Dissolves Parliament, Names Caretaker PM," *Reuters*, May 29, 2016, http://www.reuters.com/article/us-jordan-politics-parliament-idUSKCN0YK08G

23. Human Rights Watch, "Jordan," *Human Rights Watch*, 2017, https://www.hrw.org/middle-east/n-africa/jordan

24. Amnesty International, "Israel and Occupied Palestinian Territories 2016/2017," *Amnesty International*, 2017, https://www.amnesty.org/en/countries/middle-east-and-north-africa/israel-and-occupied-palestinian-territories/report-israel-and-occupied-palestinian-territories/

25. United Nations, "SC/12657: Israel's Settlements Have No Legal Validity, Constitute Flagrant Violation of International Law, Security Council Reaffirms," *United Nations Security Council*, December 23, 2016, https://www.un.org/press/en/2016/sc12657.doc.htm; Jonathan Wachtel, "UN Resolution is One of Dozens of Rebukes Against Israel in 2016," *Foxnews.com*, December 27, 2016, http://www.foxnews.com/world/2016/12/27/un-resolution-is-one-dozens-rebukes-against-israel-in-2016.html

26. Ronald Reagan, "National Security Decision Directive 115: Visit of Prime Minister Shamir," *Ronald Reagan Presidential Library and Museum*, https://reaganlibrary.archives.gov/archives/reference/Scanned%20NSDDS/NSDD115.pdf; Noam Chomsky, *The Fateful Triangle: The United States, Israel, and the Palestinians* (Boston, MA: South End Press, 1999).

27. Dwight D. Eisenhower, "Farewell Radio and Television Address to the American People," *American Presidency Project*, January 17, 1961, http://www.presidency.ucsb.edu/ws/?pid=12086

28. Lauren Carroll, "Obama: U.S. Spends More on Military than Next 8 Nations Combined," *Politifact*, January 13, 2016, http://www.politifact.com/truth-o-meter/statements/2016/jan/13/barack-obama/obama-us-spends-more-military-next-8-nations-combi/

29. Adam Taylor and Laris Karklis, "This Remarkable Chart Show How U.S. Defense Spending Dwarfs the Rest of the World," *The Washington Post*, February 9, 2016, https://www.washingtonpost.com/news/worldviews/wp/2016/02/09/this-remarkable-chart-shows-how-u-s-defense-spending-dwarfs-the-rest-of-the-world/?utm_term=.062c5c4bde4e

30. Office of the Historian, "Kennan and Containment, 1947," *U.S. Department of State*, 2017, https://history.state.gov/milestones/1945-1952/kennan

31. George F. Kennan, "Report by the Policy Planning Staff: Policy Planning Study 23," *Office of the Historian: U.S. Department of State*, February 24, 1948, https://history.state.gov/historicaldocuments/frus1948v01p2/d4

32. Kennan, "Report by the Policy Planning Staff: Policy Planning Study 23," 1948.

33. Dean Acheson, "Memorandum by the Under Secretary of State (Acheson) to the Secretary of State," *Office of the Historian: U.S. Department of State*, October 9, 1945, https://history.state.gov/historicaldocuments/frus1945v08/d20

34. Michael T. Klare, *Blood and Oil: The Dangers and Consequences of America's Growing Dependency on Imported Petroleum* (New York: Holt Publishers, 2005).

35. Gary R. Hess, *Presidential Decisions for War: Korea, Vietnam, the Persian Gulf, and Iraq* (Baltimore, MD: Johns Hopkins University Press, 2009).

36. Dwight D. Eisenhower, "Second Inaugural Address," *American Presidency Project*, January 21, 1957, http://www.presidency.ucsb.edu/ws/?pid=10856; Dwight D. Eisenhower, "Annual Message to the Congress on the State of the Union," *American Presidency Project*, January 9, 1958, http://www.presidency.ucsb.edu/ws/?pid=11162

37. Dwight D. Eisenhower, "Annual Message to the Congress on the State of the Union," *American Presidency Project*, January 7, 1960, http://www.presidency.ucsb.edu/ws/?pid=12061

38. Harry S. Truman, "A Report to the National Security Council—NSC 68," *Harry S. Truman Library and Museum*, April 12, 1950, https://www.trumanlibrary.org/whistlestop/study_collections/coldwar/documents/pdf/10-1.pdf

39. Harry S. Truman, "President Truman to King Abdul Aziz Ibn Saud of Saudi Arabia," *Office of the Historian: U.S. Department of State*, October 31, 1950, https://history.state.gov/historicaldocuments/frus1950v05/d658

40. Isaac Alteras, *Eisenhower and Israel: U.S.-Israeli Relations, 1953–1960* (Gainesville, FL: University Press of Florida, 1993).

41. National Security Council, "Statement of Policy by the National Security Council: National Security Council 5432/1," *Office of the Historian: U.S. Department of State*, September 3, 1954, https://history.state.gov/historicaldocuments/frus1952-54v04/d12

42. National Security Council Planning Board, "Foreign Relations of the United States, 1958–1960: Paper Prepared by the National Security Council Planning Board," *Office of the Historian: U.S. Department of State*, July 29, 1958, https://history.state.gov/historicaldocuments/frus1958-60v12/d35

43. Dwight D. Eisenhower, "Remarks at the Governors' Conference, Seattle Washington," *The American Presidency Project*, August 4, 1953, http://www.presidency.ucsb.edu/ws/?pid=9663

44. Ahmed Mahdi, *Energy and U.S. Foreign Policy: The Quest for Resource Security After the Cold War* (New York: I. B. Tauris, 2012).

45. Michael Schaller, *Altered States: The United States and Japan Since the Occupation* (New York: Oxford University Press, 1997).

46. DiMaggio, *When Media Goes to War*, 2010.

47. Meg Jacobs, "Trump's Middle East Talk is Old GOP Policy," *CNN.com*, April 37, 2016, http://www.cnn.com/2016/04/27/opinions/trump-says-seize-the-oil-jacobs/

48. Henry Kissinger, *Henry Kissinger: The Complete Memoirs* (New York: Simon and Schuster, 2013).

49. V. G. Kiernan, *America: The New Imperialism: From White Settlement to World Hegemony* (London: Verso Press, 2005).

50. Jimmy Carter, "Presidential Directive: National Security Council 63," *Jimmy Carter Presidential Library and Museum*, January 15, 1981, https://www.jimmycarterlibrary.gov/documents/pddirectives/pd63.pdf

51. Jimmy Carter, "The State of the Union Address Delivered before a Joint Session of Congress," *American Presidency Project*, January 23, 1980, http://www.presidency.ucsb.edu/ws/?pid=33079

52. Ronald Reagan, "U.S. National Security Strategy: National Security Decision Directive 32," *Ronald Reagan Presidential Library and Museum*, May 20, 1982, https://reaganlibrary.archives.gov/archives/reference/Scanned%20NSDDS/NSDD32.pdf

53. George H. W. Bush, "Address before a Joint Session of the Congress on the State of the Union," *American Presidency Project*, January 29, 1991, http://www.presidency.ucsb.edu/ws/?pid=19253

54. George H. W. Bush, "National Security Strategy 1991," *National Security Strategy Archive*, August 1, 1991, http://nssarchive.us/national-security-strategy-1991/

55. Frontline, "Excerpts From 1992 Draft 'Defense Planning Guidance,'" *PBS.org*, 2017, http://www.pbs.org/wgbh/pages/frontline/shows/iraq/etc/wolf.html; Dale A. Vesser, "Defense Planning Guidance," *The National Security Archive: George Washington University*, February 18, 1992, http://nsarchive.gwu.edu/nukevault/ebb245/doc03_extract_nytedit.pdf

56. George H. W. Bush, "National Security Directive 26: U.S. Foreign Policy toward the Persian Gulf," *41 George Bush Presidential Library and Museum*, October 2, 1989, https://bush41library.tamu.edu/files/nsd/nsd26.pdf

57. George H. W. Bush, "National Security Directive 54: Responding to Iraqi Aggression in the Gulf," *41 George Bush Presidential Library and Museum*, January 15, 1991, https://bush41library.tamu.edu/files/nsd/nsd54.pdf

58. William J. Clinton, "A National Security Strategy of Engagement and Enlargement," *National Security Strategy Archive*, February 1996, http://nssarchive.us/NSSR/1996.pdf

59. Antonia Juhasz, "Whose Oil is it, Anyway?" *The New York Times*, March 13, 2007, http://www.nytimes.com/2007/03/13/opinion/13iht-edjuhasz.4893187.html

60. Peter Baker, "Bush Says U.S. Pullout Would Let Iraq Radicals Use Oil as a Weapon," *The Washington Post*, November 5, 2006, http://www.washingtonpost.com/wp-dyn/content/article/2006/11/04/AR2006110401025.html; Amanda Terkel, "Cheney Worried that Iraq Withdrawal Will 'Waste' the Sacrifice by U.S. Troops," *Think Progress*, June 29, 2009, https://thinkprogress.org/cheney-worried-that-iraq-withdrawal-will-waste-the-sacrifice-by-u-s-troops-eab4359334ed#.r2qik8sja

61. George W. Bush, "The National Security Strategy of the United States of America," *U.S. Department of State*, September 2002, https://www.state.gov/documents/organization/63562.pdf

62. Barack H. Obama, "Presidential Policy Directive 6," *The White House*, September 22, 2010, https://obamawhitehouse.archives.gov/the-press-office/2010/09/22/fact-sheet-us-global-development-policy; Barack H. Obama, "National Security Strategy 2010," *National*

Security Strategy Archive, May 27, 2010, http://nssarchive.us/national-security-strategy-2010/; Barack H. Obama, "National Security Strategy 2015," *National Security Strategy Archive*, February 6, 2015, http://nssarchive.us/national-security-strategy-2015/

63. Adam Entous and Julian E. Barnes, "U.S. Wavers on 'Regime Change,'" *Wall Street Journal*, March 5, 2011, https://www.wsj.com/articles/SB10001424052748703580004576180522653787198

64. David Brunnstrom and Matt Spetalnick, "Tillerson Says China Should be Barred from South China Sea Islands," *Reuters*, January 12, 2017, http://www.reuters.com/article/us-congress-tillerson-china-idUSKBN14V2KZ

65. Benjamin Haas, "We're Going to War in the South China Sea . . . No Doubt,'" *Guardian*, February 2, 2017, https://www.theguardian.com/us-news/2017/feb/02/steve-bannon-donald-trump-war-south-china-sea-no-doubt

66. Philip Rucker and Jenna Johnson, "Trump Announces U.S. Will Exit Paris Climate Deal, Sparking Criticism at Home and Abroad," *Washington Post*, June 1, 2017, https://www.washingtonpost.com/politics/trump-to-announce-us-will-exit-paris-climate-deal/2017/06/01/fbcb0196-46da-11e7-bcde-624ad94170ab_story.html?utm_term=.e2b75ebd4f5f

67. William Blum, *Rogue State: A Guide to the World's Only Superpower* (Monroe, ME: Common Courage Press, 2005); William Blum, *Killing Hope: U.S. Military and CIA Interventions Since World War II* (London: Zed Books, 2014); William Blum, "Overthrowing Other People's Governments: The Master List," *Williamblum.org*, February 2013, https://williamblum.org/essays/read/overthrowing-other-peoples-governments-the-master-list; Stephen Zunes, "The U.S. Role in the Honduras Coup and Subsequent Violence," *Common Dreams*, March 15, 2016, http://www.commondreams.org/views/2016/03/15/us-role-honduras-coup-and-subsequent-violence; Karen DeYoung and Louisa Loveluck, "Fearing Abandonment by Trump, CIA Backed Rebels in Syria Mull Alternatives," *The Washington Post*, December 3, 2016, https://www.washingtonpost.com/world/national-security/fearing-abandonment-by-trump-cia-backed-rebels-in-syria-mull-alternatives/2016/12/03/50419594-b8c1-11e6-a677-b608fbb3aaf6_story.html?utm_term=.f406064392ec

68. Blum, "Overthrowing Other People's Governments," 2013.

69. Chalmers Johnson, *The Sorrows of Empire: Militarism, Secrecy, and the End of the Republic* (New York: Metropolitan Books, 2005).

70. Blum, *Rogue State*, 2005.

71. John Pilger, *The New Rulers of the World* (London: Verso Books, 2003); Michael Kremer and Seema Jayachandran, "Odious Debt: When Dictators Borrow, Who Repays the Loan?" *Brookings Institution*, March 1, 2003, https://www.brookings.edu/articles/odious-debt-when-dictators-borrow-who-repays-the-loan/

72. DiMaggio, *Selling War, Selling Hope*, 2015.

73. Steven Kull, *Feeling Betrayed: The Roots of Muslim Anger at America* (Washington DC: Brookings Institution Press, 2011).

74. Pew Research Center, "Muslim-Western Tensions Persist," *Pew Research Center*, July 21, 2011, http://www.pewglobal.org/2011/07/21/muslim-western-tensions-persist/

75. Kull, *Feeling Betrayed*, 2011.

76. BBC: "Poll: World View of United States Role Goes from Bad to Worse," *BBC News*, January 23, 2007, http://www.bbc.co.uk/pressoffice/pressreleases/stories/2007/01_january/23/us.shtml; Pew Research Center, "Arab Spring Fails to Improve U.S. Image," *Pew Research Center*, May 17, 2011, http://www.pewglobal.org/2011/05/17/chapter-1-opinions-of-the-u-s-and-president-barack-obama/

77. BBC, "Muslim Public Opinion on U.S. Policy, Attacks on Civilians, and al Qaeda," *World Public Opinion*, January–February 2007, http://www.worldpublicopinion.org/pipa/pdf/feb07/BBC_IslamWest_Feb07_quaire.pdf; Kull, *Feeling Betrayed*, 2011.

78. BBC, "Muslim Public Opinion on U.S. Policy, Attacks on Civilians, and al Qaeda," 2007; Kull, *Feeling Betrayed*, 2011.

79. BBC, "Muslim Public Opinion on U.S. Policy, Attacks on Civilians, and al Qaeda," 2007; Kull, *Feeling Betrayed*, 2011.

80. BBC, "Muslim Public Opinion on U.S. Policy, Attacks on Civilians, and al Qaeda," 2007; Kull, *Feeling Betrayed*, 2011.

81. BBC, "Poll Suggests World Hostile to U.S.," *BBC News*, June 16, 2003, http://news.bbc.co.uk/2/hi/americas/2994924.stm

82. BBC, "U.S. 'Biggest Global Peace Threat,'" *BBC News*, June 14, 2006, http://news.bbc.co.uk/2/hi/5077984.stm

83. Richard Wike, Bruce Stokes, and Jacob Poushter, "America's Global Image," *Pew Research Center*, June 23, 2015, http://www.pewglobal.org/2015/06/23/1-americas-global-image/

84. Wike, Stokes, and Poushter, "America's Global Image," 2015.

85. World Public Opinion, "Thought Obama Viewed Positively, Still Much Criticism of U.S. Foreign Policy: Global Poll," *Worldpublicopinion.org*, July 7, 2009, http://worldpublicopinion.net/though-obama-viewed-positively-still-much-criticism-of-us-foreign-policy-global-poll/

86. Richard Wike, Jacob Poushter, and Hani Zainulbhai, "As Obama Years Draw to Close, President and U.S. Seen Favorably in Europe and Asia," *Pew Research Center*, June 29, 2016, http://www.pewglobal.org/2016/06/29/as-obama-years-draw-to-close-president-and-u-s-seen-favorably-in-europe-and-asia/; Gallup International, "WIN/Gallup International's Global Poll on the American Election," *Gallup International*, 2016, http://www.wingia.com/web/files/richeditor/filemanager/WINGIA_Global_Poll_on_US_Election_-_FINALIZED_Revised_Global_Press_Release.pdf

87. Yochi J. Dreazen, "U.S. Troops are Leaving Because Iraq Doesn't Want Them There," *Atlantic*, October 21, 2011, https://www.theatlantic.com/politics/archive/2011/10/us-troops-are-leaving-because-iraq-doesnt-want-them-there/247174/; Amit R. Paley, "Most Iraqis Favor Immediate U.S. Pullout, Polls Show," *The Washington Post*, September 27, 2006, http://www.washingtonpost.com/wp-dyn/content/article/2006/09/26/AR2006092601721.html

88. Jonathan Steele, "Why the U.S. is Running Scared of Elections in Iraq," *Guardian*, January 19, 2004, https://www.theguardian.com/world/2004/jan/19/usa.iraq

89. Larry Diamond, *Squandered Victory: The American Occupation and the Bungled Effort to Bring Democracy to Iraq* (New York: Henry Holt, 2006).

Index